GILES OF ROME'S *On Ecclesiastical Power*

THE RECORDS OF WESTERN CIVILIZATION

RECORDS OF WESTERN CIVILIZATION

GILES OF ROME'S
On Ecclesiastical Power

A MEDIEVAL THEORY
OF WORLD GOVERNMENT

A Critical Edition and Translation

R.W. DYSON

COLUMBIA UNIVERSITY PRESS / NEW YORK

COLUMBIA UNIVERSITY PRESS
Publishers Since 1893
New York Chichester, West Sussex
Copyright © 2004 Columbia University Press

Library of Congress Cataloging-in-Publication Data
Giles of Rome, Archbishop of Bourges, ca. 1243–1316.
[De ecclesiastica potestate. English]
Giles of Rome's On ecclesiastical power : a medieval theory of world
government / critical ed. and translation, R.W. Dyson.
p. cm.—(Records of Western civilization)
Includes bibliographical references and index.
ISBN 0–231–12802–9 (cloth : alk. paper)—ISBN 0–231–12803–7 (pbk. : alk. paper)
1. Popes—Temporal power—Early works to 1800. I. Dyson, R. W. II. Title.
III. Series.

BX1810.G5513 2004
262'.132—dc22

2004049364

Columbia University Press books are printed
on permanent and durable acid-free paper.

Printed in the United States of America
c 10 9 8 7 6 5 4 3 2 1
p 10 9 8 7 6 5 4 3 2 1

HT

magistro dilecto

Records of Western Civilization is a series published under the auspices of the Interdepartmental Committee on Medieval and Renaissance Studies of the Columbia University Graduate School. The Western Records are, in fact, a new incarnation of a venerable series, the Columbia Records of Civilization, which, for more than half a century, published sources and studies concerning great literary and historical landmarks. Many of the volumes of that series retain value, especially for their translations into English of primary sources, and the Medieval and Renaissance Studies Committee is pleased to cooperate with Columbia University Press in reissuing a selection of those works in paperback editions, especially suited for classroom use, and in limited cloth-bound editions.

Contents

Sigla and Abbreviations

C   MS Cremona, Biblioteca Governativa 81, ff. 1ʳ – 115ʳ.

F   Biblioteca Nazionale Centrale di Firenze, Codex Magliabechiano I.VII.12, ff. 1–104.

P   Paris, Bibliothèque Nationale, MS Lat. 4229, ff. 1–57.

V¹   Vatican, MS Lat. 5612, ff. 1–73ᵛ.

V²   Vatican, MS Lat. 4107.

CSEL   *Corpus scriptorum ecclesiasticorum Latinorum* (Vienna, 1866 *et seqq.*).

CCSL   *Corpus Christianorum, series Latina* (Turnhout: Brepols, 1954 *et seqq.*).

CIC   *Corpus iuris canonici,* ed. E. Friedberg (Leipzig, 1879).

MGH   *Monumenta Germaniae Historica.*

PG   *Patrologiae cursus completus, series Graeca,* ed. J.P. Migne (Paris, 1857 *et seqq.*).

PL   *Patrologiae cursus completus, series Latina,* ed. J.P. Migne (Paris, 1857 *et seqq.*).

Introduction

Giles of Rome — Aegidius or Egidius Romanus, surnamed Colonna (ca. 1247–1316) — combined several rôles in his distinguished career: senior ecclesiastic, prolific author and commentator, university teacher and political theorist.[1] It is under this last aspect that we are concerned with him. He produced two essays in political analysis: a treatise called *De regimine principum*, completed in about 1280, and the work here edited. The former is a fairly typical, though long, specimen of the class of works known as *specula regum* or *principis*: 'mirrors' meant to reflect an image of royal virtue for the emulation of kings and princes. It is a dissertation on the *Politics* and *Nicomachean Ethics* of Aristotle, possibly undertaken at the request of King Philip III of France for the instruction of his son, the future Philip IV, 'the Fair', to whom it is dedicated. It is remarkable among medieval treatises of its kind in containing no treatment of the place of the Church in the prince's realm, and no assertion of ecclesiastical rights and prerogatives.[2] *De ecclesiastica potestate*, some twenty years later in date than *De regimine principum*, is written from a theoretical perspective so different from the Aristotelianism and secularity of the earlier book that, considerations of style apart, it is often difficult to remember that the same author is responsible for both.[3] But this difference is easily accounted for. For all its didactic character,

1. In 1285 he became the first Augustinian regent-master at the University of Paris; he was Prior-General of the Augustinian Order of Hermits from 1291 to 1294 and Archbishop of Bourges from 1294 to 1316. Despite what is sometimes thought, he probably was not a member of the powerful Colonna family of Rome. The Colonna were sworn enemies of Boniface VIII and it is unlikely that one of their number would be so ardent a champion of him. According to T.S.R. Boase, who gives details of Boniface's relations with the Colonna, Giles's surname is 'almost certainly from a district of the city rather than from any connection with the family' (T.S.R. Boase, *Boniface VIII* (London: Constable, 1933), p. 175, n. 1). For biography and bibliography see F. Del Punta, S. Donati and C. Luna, 'Egidio Romano,' in *Dizionario Biografico degli Italiani*, 42 (Rome: Treccani, 1993), p. 319. See also the Introduction to G. Boffito and G.U. Oxilia, *Un trattato inedito di Egidio Colonna* (Florence: Successori Seeber, 1908); R. Scholz, *Die Publizistik zur Zeit Philipps des Schönen und Bonifaz VIII* (Stuttgart: Enke, 1903), p. 32.
2. The most recent edition of this work appeared in Rome in 1607 (repr., Aalen: Scientia, 1967). See also C.F. Briggs, *Giles of Rome's 'De regimine principum': Reading and Writing Politics at Court and University, c.1275–c.1525* (Cambridge: Cambridge University Press, 1999).
3. It has been suggested that Giles is not, in fact, the author of *De ecclesiastica potestate*, but on internal and other grounds the argument is unconvincing. It was developed by G. Vinay, 'Egidio Romano e la cosidetta "Questio in utramque partem",' *Bulletino dell' Istituto Storico Italiano per il medio evo e Archivo Muratoriano* 53 (1939), p. 43; see also R. Kuiters, 'Aegidius Romanus and the Authorship of "In utramque partem" and "De ecclesiastica potestate",' *Augustiniana* 8 (1958), p. 267; R.W. Dyson, *Three Royalist Tracts, 1296–1302* (Bristol: Thoemmes), p. xxix; R.W. and A.J. Carlyle, *A History of Medieval Political Theory in the West* (Edinburgh and

De regimine principum is a general survey of the principles of politics and related matters, composed with no particular cause or tendency in mind. In it,
Giles follows St. Thomas Aquinas (by whom he had probably been taught at the
University of Paris) in embracing the sort of humane and rational political doctrines which the thirteenth-century 'recovery' of Aristotle had made possible. By
contrast, *De ecclesiastica potestate* is a tract for the times: a defence of a highly
specific viewpoint, produced in the midst of a grave ecclesiastical emergency
and evidently called forth by loyalties and convictions of great intensity. In it,
Aristotelianism is by no means forgotten, but it is pressed with some ingenuity
into the service of the 'political Augustinianism' characteristic of an earlier generation.

(a) The Background

Between 1296 and 1303, Pope Boniface VIII and Philip the Fair were engaged in
two major episodes of strife, arising ostensibly from two perennial points of contention: the right of princes to tax the clergy in their realms (1296–1297) and the
issue of clerical immunity from secular jurisdiction (1301–1303). Each of these
controversies touched upon the most burning question of medieval political debate: that of how the relation between *regnum* and *sacerdotium*, the coercive
power of the prince and the spiritual authority of the Church, is to be conceived
and translated into practice. The story of these disputes is well known, but it will
be convenient to give a brief account of them here.[4]

    In 1296, Philip the Fair was at war with Edward I of England: a war made es-
pecially costly by the use of mercenary soldiers. Philip sought to defray his ex-
penses by imposing general, non-feudal taxes upon the clergy. Strictly speaking,
this was to act in breach of canon 46 of the fourth Lateran Council of 1215, which
had forbidden clerical taxation without papal permission.[5] Eighty years on, the
canon of 1215 was not quite a dead letter; but popes had been generally tolerant of
such taxation if the taxes could be shown to be financing a crusade against the
enemies of the Church. In this instance, the taxes were not only burdensome, but
were being levied for purposes of purely secular warfare. The French clergy appealed to Rome. On 24 February 1296 Boniface VIII responded by promulgating
the bull *Clericis laicos*.

London: Blackwood, repr. 1962), vol. 5, p. 405; R. Scholz, *Die Publizistik*, p. 40, 118; J.
Rivière, *Le problème de l'église et de l'état au temps de Philippe le Bel* (Paris: Champion,
1926), p. 226.

4. The major source of documentary evidence is P. Dupuy, *Histoire du différend d'entre le Pape
    Boniface VIIIe et Philippe le Bel Roy de France* (Paris, 1655). The following may be regarded
    as indispensable: T.S.R. Boase, *Boniface VIII*; G. Digard, *Philippe le Bel et le saint siège de
    1285 à 1303* (Paris: Sirey, 1936); H. Finke, *Aus den Tagen Bonifaz VIII* (Münster: Aschen-
    dorffschen Buchhandlung, 1902); J. Rivière, *Le problème de l'église et de l'état au temps de
    Philippe le Bel*; R. Scholz, *Die Publizistik*; J.R. Strayer, *The Reign of Philip the Fair* (Princeton,
    N.J.: Princeton University Press, 1980); C.T. Wood, *Philip the Fair and Boniface VIII* (New
    York: Krieger, 1967).
5. J.D. Mansi, *Collectio Conciliorum* (Lucca, 1728-1759), vol. 22, p. 953. H.J. Schroeder, *Disci-
    plinary Decrees of the General Councils* (St. Louis: Herder, 1937), p. 236.

Antiquity teaches that the laity have been exceedingly hostile to the clergy, and the experiences of the present time also show this clearly. For not content with their own boundaries, they strive for that which is forbidden, and loose the reins after unlawful things.[6]

This was a pugnacious enough beginning. Reaffirming the prohibition of 1215, the Bull forbade the clergy to pay, and laymen to collect, taxes on clerical property levied without papal consent. The penalty of excommunication incurred by those who disregarded this injunction was not to be lifted, save by special papal dispensation, until the moment of death, 'for it is our intention that so terrible an abuse of secular power shall not be carried on under any pretext whatsoever.'

Clericis laicos illustrates to perfection the self-defeating truculence which Boniface VIII was to exhibit throughout his encounters with Philip the Fair. The pope's apparently heedless and certainly damaging irascibility is a minor biographical mystery. Some attribute it to bouts of painful ill health; others to an over-anxious wish to stamp his authority on an office to which his title was in some quarters felt to be dubious.[7] Suitably emollient diplomacy could no doubt have eased matters. Scorning the possibility of negotiation, however, the pope chose to instruct the clergy and laity of France to disobey a royal command. He chose moreover to assert his own right to correct the 'terrible ... abuse of secular power' which he deemed that command to constitute. Put in these terms, the quarrel turned from the beginning upon a highly sensitive question: that of whether a king is or is not sovereign in his own realm.

Philip the Fair's immediate response to *Clericis laicos* was to forbid the export of 'horses, arms, money, and similar things' from the kingdom. On the face of it, this prohibition was made 'lest those things should chance to come into the hands of his enemies through the deceit of wicked men, to the prejudice of our lord the king and his kingdom.'[8] But this shrewd move had also the effect of depriving the papal treasury of the revenues of the Church in France: revenues so large that their loss threatened the entire Italian banking system.[9] Also, on 2 May 1297 Boniface became embroiled in an expensive and distracting quarrel with the Colonna family when, for reasons arising from ancient rivalries between the Colonna and the

6. *Les registres de Boniface VIII* (hereinafter *Reg.*), edited by G.A.L. Digard, M. Faucon and A. Thomas (Paris: Bibliothèque des Ecoles Françaises, 1884–1939), 1653.
7. His predecessor, the saintly hermit Celestine V, had abdicated – some said under pressure from Cardinal Gaetani, the future Boniface VIII. It was alleged also that Boniface VIII was responsible for the subsequent confinement and death of Celestine V. These events were a major scandal at the end of the thirteenth century. The question of whether papal abdication is lawful, and Boniface's succession therefore valid, was much discussed, especially by the pope's enemies. Giles of Rome wrote a treatise on the subject called *De renuntiatione papae* (1297), which has been edited and translated by J.R. Eastman (Lewiston, Queenston, Lampeter: Mellen, 1992). See also J.R. Eastman, *Papal Abdication in Later Medieval Thought* (Lewiston, Queenston, Lampeter: Mellen, 1990); 'La Renonciation de Célestin V et l'opinion théologique en France du vivant de Boniface VIII', *Revue d' histoire de l' église de France* 25 (1939), p. 183.
8. See *Antequam essent clerici* (ed. Dyson, *Three Royalist Tracts*, p. 3); Dupuy, *Histoire du différend*, p. 13; *Ordonnances des Rois de France* (Paris, 1723 *et seqq.*), vol. 11, p. 386.
9. See Boase, *Boniface VIII*, p. 139.

pope's family, the Gaetani, an armed band under Stefano Colonna made off with a large quantity of the pope's property.[10] Beset on all sides, the pope was forced to capitulate. In July 1297 he promulgated the Bull *Etsi de statu*, in which the provisions of *Clericis laicos* were formally withdrawn insofar as they related to France.[11] But the peace was to be a temporary one. Four years later, there occurred a further infraction of ecclesiastical liberties in France, and Boniface VIII returned to the fray with renewed enthusiasm.

In July 1295 Boniface had created the new See of Pamiers out of territories formerly lying within the large and ancient See of Toulouse. He named an old friend, Bernard de Saisset, Abbot of St Antonin, as its first Bishop. On 12 July 1301 in circumstances which are not wholly clear, Bishop de Saisset was arrested on charges of treason, blasphemy, and heresy. He was detained for some three months, tried before the king on 24 October, deprived of his See, and imprisoned. Philip sent an account of the proceedings to Boniface seeking the pope's approval of what had been done.[12] In so acting, the king was disregarding the established canonical principle that a delinquent bishop should be tried only by the pope. So flagrant was this disregard, indeed, that it is difficult to avoid the conclusion that the trial was an intentional act of provocation, aimed at bringing about a further contest with Rome which might free France finally from papal interference.

Boniface took the bait, if bait it was, immediately. Again with a signal lack of diplomatic sense, he threatened the king with excommunication, demanded the bishop's release, and revoked all the concessions made in *Etsi de statu* and related documents.[13] On 5 December 1301 he issued the bull *Ausculta fili*, setting out in minatory language and insulting detail his complaints as to Philip's conduct. He complained that the king was oppressing the nobles, clergy, and people of his realm; preventing the Roman See from exercising its rights with respect to vacant benefices; compelling clerics to appear in his courts to answer charges unrelated to their feudal tenures and obligations; not permitting ecclesiastical penalties to be carried out against those who molested the clergy; and not allowing ecclesiastical jurisdiction to be exercised in the monasteries of which he was guardian. All this was prefaced by the following unguarded words:

> We shall indeed explain more clearly, son, why, moved by urgent necessity and prompted by conscience, we are directing these complaints to you. For, though our merits are insufficient, God has placed us above kings and kingdoms, and He has imposed upon us the yoke of apostolic service: to uproot and destroy, to disperse and to scatter, to build and to plant, in His name and according to His teaching ... And so let no one persuade you, dearest son, that you have no superior and that you

10. For details of this episode and its consequences, see Boase, op. cit., and R.W. Dyson, *James of Viterbo on Christian Government* (Woodbridge: Boydell, 1995), p. viii.
11. *Reg.* 2354.
12 Bishop de Saisset was eventually allowed to go to Rome and in 1308 was restored to his See. For these events see J.M. Vidal, *Histoire des évêques de Pamiers*, vol. 1: *Bernard Saisset* (1232–1311) (Toulouse: Privat, 1926).
13. See *Salvator mundi*, 4 December 1301 (*Reg.* 4422); *Secundum divina*, 5 December (*Reg.* 4432).

are not subject to the head of the ecclesiastical hierarchy. For anyone who thinks this is a fool; and, if he obstinately affirms it, he is convicted as an unbeliever and is outside the fold of the Good Shepherd.[14]

It is said that when *Ausculta fili* was handed to the king on 10 February 1302, the Comte d'Artois seized it from his hand and cast it into the fire. The bull served to damage Boniface's standing in France still further. By the adroit manipulation of opinion, the king's energetic chief minister Pierre de Flotte was able to win over the French clergy. A misleading paraphrase of *Ausculta fili*, called *Deum time*, was put about. Its clear purpose was to create the impression that the pope had insulted the king and to persuade the clergy that the benefices which they held of the king were in jeopardy.[15] A strenuous reply, *Sciat tua maxima fatuitas*, was circulated in France, though probably never sent to Rome.[16] In February 1302, Philip summoned the nobles and clergy of France to advise him: the first convocation of what has become known as the 'Estates General' of France. The assembly was addressed by de Flotte. His chief complaint, evidently made on the strength of the spurious *Deum time*, was that Boniface had claimed to be lord of France *temporaliter*: had, in effect, asserted that the French kingdom was held of him as a papal fief.[17] The nobles and clergy of France dispatched incredulous and reproachful letters to the pope. Boniface sought to clarify his position, first in writing and then at a consistory held in Rome in the summer of 1302, where he and Cardinal Matthew of Aquasparta addressed an audience of French emissaries. This was a difficult occasion, with none of the bows and scrapes to which the pope was accustomed, and Boniface spoke in terms unlikely to soothe:

> We have been learned in the law for forty years, and we know very well that the powers established by God are two. How should or can anyone suppose that anything so foolish or stupid [as the contrary] is or has been in our head? We declare

14. *Reg.* 4424. The paraphrase of Jeremiah 1:10 — a passage much favoured by papal publicists — is undoubtedly made with St Bernard of Clairvaux's advice to Pope Eugenius III in mind. See *De consideratione*, ed. J. Leclerq et al., in *Opera sancti Bernardi* (Rome, Editiones Cistercienses, 1957), vol. 3, 2:6: 'Learn that you need a hoe and not a royal sceptre to do a prophet's work: that is, "to root up and pull down, to lay waste and destroy, to build and to plant;" for he to whom this was said, namely, Jeremiah, arises not to rule, but to uproot.' See also Innocent III's decretal *Novit*, quoted at n. 21, below.
15. 'Boniface, bishop, servant of the servants of God, to Philip, king of the French. Fear God and keep His commandments. We wish you to know that you are subject to us in spiritual and temporal matters alike. The collation of benefices and prebends does not belong to you in the least; and if you have custody of any vacant churches you are to keep their revenues for those who succeed to them. If you have conferred such benefices, we declare the collations null and void, and we revoke any that you have made in point of fact' (Dupuy, *Histoire du différend*, p. 44).
16. 'Philip, by the Grace of God king of the French, to Boniface, conducting himself as Supreme Pontiff, little greeting or none. Let Your Very Great Foolishness know that we are subject to no one in temporals; that the collation of vacant churches and prebends belongs to us as of royal right and that their revenues are ours; that the collations which we have made in the past and shall make in the future are valid; and that we shall manfully defend their holders against anyone. All who hold otherwise we deem to be fools and madmen' (Dupuy, *Histoire du différend*, p. 44).
17. Dupuy, *Histoire du Différend*, p. 63.

that we do not wish to usurp the jurisdiction of the king in any way ... But the king cannot deny that, like all the faithful, he is subject to us *ratione peccati* ... Our predecessors deposed three kings of France. They can read it in their chronicles and we in ours; one case is to be found also in the *Decretum*.[18] And although we are not worthy to walk in the footsteps of our predecessors, if the king committed the same crimes as those kings committed, or greater ones, we should, with grief and great sadness, dismiss him like a servant.[19]

This announcement was evidently intended to draw legitimacy from the hallowed words of Pope Gelasius I preserved in the Decretal *Duo sunt*[20] and from the precedent of Innocent III's decretal *Novit.*[21] But Boniface could hardly have cho-

18. C.15:6:3: *Alius item* (CIC I:756). This is the standard example of papal deposition: the alleged dismissal by Pope Zacharias of Childeric III in 749 in favour of Pepin III. See, e.g., R.W. Dyson, *Normative Theories of Society and Government in Five Medieval Thinkers* (Lewiston, Queenston, Lampeter: Mellen, 2003), Ch. 2; W. Ullmann, *The Growth of Papal Government in the Middle Ages* (London: Methuen, 1970), Ch. 2. It is not clear to what other cases the pope can be referring.
19. Dupuy, *Histoire du différend*, p. 77.
20. Dist. 96, c. 10 (CIC I:340): 'There are two orders, O August Emperor, by which this world is principally ruled: the consecrated authority of the pontiffs, and royal power. But the burden laid upon the priests in this matter is the heavier, for it is they who are to render an account at the Divine judgment even for the kings of men.' See esp. Dyson, *Normative Theories*, Ch. 2.
21. The expression *ratione peccati* — 'by reason of sin' — was coined by the decretalist commentators of the thirteenth century. The principle which it expresses was given its definitive, though certainly not its first, statement in Innocent III's decretal *Novit* of 1204. *Novit* is quintessentially a 'political' decretal, and furnished plentiful material for subsequent commentators and political theorists. It was written in defence of the pope's intervention in the quarrel between King John of England and Philip Augustus of France when Philip invaded John's great fief of Normandy as part of the imbroglio caused by John's marriage to Isabelle, daughter of Count Ademar of Angoulême. As Philip IV was to do, Philip Augustus successfully sought the support of the French clergy against the pope. Why, the bishops of France indignantly asked, should the pope intrude himself into a purely temporal dispute capable of being resolved in the king's own feudal courts? Innocent III replied:
> Let no one suppose that we wish to diminish or disturb the jurisdiction and power of the king ... When we are insufficient to exercise our own jurisdiction, why should we wish to usurp that of another? ... For we do not intend to judge concerning the fief, the judgment of which belongs to him, unless perhaps a special privilege or some custom to the contrary overrides the common law, but to decide concerning a sin, the judgment of which belongs to us beyond doubt, and we can and should exercise it against anyone ... There is no right-minded man who does not know that it belongs to our office to rebuke any Christian for any mortal sin and to coerce him with ecclesiastical penalties if he rejects our correction ... That we can and should rebuke is evident from the pages of both the Old and New Testaments ... That we can and should coerce is evident from what the Lord said to the prophet who was among the priests of Anathoth: 'Behold, I have set you over nations and over kingdoms, to root up and to pull down and to lay waste, and to destroy and to build and to plant.' No one doubts that all mortal sin must be rooted up and destroyed and pulled down. Moreover, when the Lord gave the keys of the kingdom of heaven to the blessed Peter He said [Matt. 16:19]: 'Whatever you shall bind on earth shall be bound in heaven, and whatever you shall release on earth shall be released in heaven.' ... Although we are empowered to proceed in this fashion against any criminal sin in order to recall the sinner from error to truth and from vice to virtue, this is especially true when the sin is against peace, which is the bond of love ... Finally, when a treaty of peace was made between the kings [of England and France] and confirmed on both sides by oaths which, however, were not kept for the agreed period, can we not take cognizance of

sen a less suitable moment to remind his opponents of the Gregorian principle that popes may depose kings.[22]

Simultaneously with the promulgation of *Ausculta fili*, the pope summoned the senior clergy of France to a council to be held in Rome in November 1302.[23] Philip was invited to send representatives. The king was told that the council would consider not only measures for strengthening the French Church, but also ways of securing 'your guidance and peace and salvation, and ... the good governance and prosperity of that kingdom.' Philip forbade the French bishops and abbots to attend. The majority elected to comply with his wishes. To be on the safe side, he posted guards on all roads out of France to prevent unauthorised departures. The proposed council fell completely flat. Less than half the French abbots and bishops were present, and no deliberations of any significance took place. The pope's sense of betrayal stung him into a final indiscretion. On 18 November 1302 he promulgated the celebrated Bull *Unam sanctam*.[24]

> Our faith urging us, we are bound to believe and hold, and we firmly believe and absolutely confess, that there is One, Holy, Catholic and Apostolic Church, outside whom there is neither salvation nor remission of sins ...
>
> We are taught by the words of the Gospel that within this Church and in her power there are two swords: that is, a spiritual and a temporal. For when the apostles said [Luke 22:38], 'Here are two swords' ... the Lord did not reply that this was too many, but enough. Certainly, he who denies that the temporal sword is in Peter's power has ill understood the Lord's words when He said, 'Put up *your* sword into its sheath' [Matt. 26:52]. Both, therefore, are in the power of the Church: that is, the spiritual sword and the material. But the latter is to be wielded on behalf of the Church and the former by the Church: the one by the priest, the other by the hands of kings and soldiers, though at the command and by the permission of the priest. And the one sword must be under the other, and temporal authority subject to the spiritual power ...[25]

> such a sworn oath, which certainly belongs to the judgment of the Church, in order to re-establish a broken treaty of peace?

So stated, the *ratione peccati* principle is impressive in its combination of simplicity and logic. The degree of temporal intervention which it can be used to justify, and which it was used to justify by the popes and canonists of the thirteenth century, is theoretically without limit.

22. See Gregory VII, *Dictatus papae*, item 12, and Gregory's letter of March 1081 to Bishop Hermann of Metz, both translated in Dyson, *Normative Theories*, App. II(a) and II(b).

23. *Reg.* 4432–4433.

24. *Reg.* 5382.

25. For the 'two swords' symbolism and its origins, see Dyson, *Normative Theories*, Ch. 3. Its *locus classicus*, paraphrased here and quoted and paraphrased in countless other places, is St. Bernard, *De consideratione* 4:3:

> Why should you again attempt to usurp the sword which you were once commanded to replace in its sheath? Nonetheless, those who deny that this sword belongs to you seem not to give sufficient attention to the words of the Lord when He said, speaking to Peter: 'Put up *your* sword into its sheath.' For it is here plainly implied that even the material sword is yours, to be drawn at your command even though not by your hand. Moreover, unless this sword also belonged to you in some sense, when the disciples said to Christ, 'Lord, behold, here are two swords,' He would not have answered as He did, 'It is enough,' but rather, 'it is too much.' We can therefore conclude that both swords, namely

Therefore, if the earthly power goes astray, it will be judged by the spiritual power; if a lesser spiritual power goes astray, [it will be judged] by its superior. But if the supreme [spiritual power goes astray,] it will be subject to judgment by God alone, not by man, as the Apostle attests: 'The spiritual man judges all things and is himself judged by no one' [I Cor. 2:15]. For although this authority was given to a man and is exercised by a man, it is not a human, but, rather, a divine power: given to Peter at God's mouth and established for him and his successors upon a Rock in Christ Himself, by Whom he was acknowledged when the Lord said to Peter, 'Whatever you shall bind,' and so on [Matt. 16:19]. Therefore, whoever resists this power so ordained of God resists the ordinance of God [cf. Rom. 13:2] ...

We therefore declare, state, define, and pronounce that it is entirely necessary to salvation for every human creature to be subject to the Roman Pontiff.

To Philip the Fair and his advisors, such a plain and official assertion of papal supremacy was the final straw. Addressing the Estates General in the spring of 1303, Philip the Fair's new chief minister Guillaume de Nogaret (de Flotte had fallen at the disastrous battle of Courtrai in the summer of 1302) urged that steps be taken for the pope's deposition. Theological experts at the University of Paris were set to work to find ways of justifying such a measure in terms of the pope's conduct and the doubtful and scandalous circumstances of his succession. During the ensuing months de Nogaret directed a concerted campaign of character assassination. In an extraordinary flow of propaganda, accusations of every kind of crime and sin were levelled at Boniface: accusations which revived and embellished similar ones made by the Colonna during the quarrel of 1297. The aged pontiff's unwholesome sexual proclivities were given due prominence, as was the charge that 'he has often said that he would ruin himself and the whole world and the whole Church to bring down the king of France.' In the heat of some moment or other, Boniface had said that he would rather be a dog than a Frenchman. This statement was solemnly repeated as proof that the pope was a heretic who believed that Frenchmen have no souls.[26]

During the summer of 1303 military preparations were put in hand. On 7 September the papal residence at Anagni was beseiged and entered by troops under de Nogaret and an old enemy of the pope, Sciarra Colonna — the same Sciarra Colonna who, twenty-five years later, was to place the imperial crown on the head of Ludwig of Bavaria. Their purpose, it seems, was to abduct the pope and have him deposed by a general council choreographed by the French king. An account has been left to us by an English eyewitness, William of Hundleby.[27] A pleasant though no doubt apocryphal story is that, as his persecutors burst in upon

the spiritual and the temporal, belong to the Church, and that though only the former is to be wielded by her own hand, both are to be employed in her service. It is for the priest to use the sword of the word, and to strike with the sword of steel belongs to the soldier, by the direct command of the emperor: but this must be by the authority and will of the priest.

26. Dupuy, *Histoire du différend*, p. 102.
27. Ed. and trans. H.G.J. Beck, *Catholic Historical Review* 32 (1947), p. 200. For other sources see Dyson, *James of Viterbo On Christian Government*, p. xv, n. 33.

him, the eighty-six year old pontiff confronted them in haughty silence, robed in full pontificals with a golden cross at his breast. As he watched looters carting away his possessions, he murmured to himself the words of Job 1:21: *Dominus dedit; Dominus abstulit. Sit nomen Domini benedictum*. Invited at swordpoint to relinquish the papal office and submit himself to judgment, the pope uncovered his throat. 'Here is my head, here is my neck. If I am betrayed as Christ was, I am ready to die as Christ's Vicar.' Only with difficulty was Sciarra Colonna restrained from striking him down there and then. The people of Anagni rallied to Boniface's side and the invaders were repulsed after a couple of days; but the pope's indomitable spirit was, apparently, broken at last. In much despondency he returned to Rome; in little more than a month he was dead.[28]

This sketch of events illustrates the amplitude of the papal claims which were made during the conflicts of 1296–1303 and the strength of reaction which those claims provoked. It is important to remember that Boniface VIII did not make any substantively new statements about the papacy's temporal authority. He was continuing a tradition of papal theorising going back some two and a half centuries and traceable in its outlines to foundations laid much earlier.[29] When we look at *Ausculta fili*, *Unam sanctam*, and the pope's statement at the consistory of 1302, we find no language or connotation which had not long been parts of the ecclesiastical arsenal. The 'two swords' imagery, the use of Jeremiah 1:10, and the assertion that 'the king is subject to us *ratione peccati*' — these are references back to the decretal *Novit* and to Bernard of Clairvaux's *De consideratione*, and in their general tenor the pope's statements add nothing to what had been said by his predecessors Gregory VII, Innocent III, and Innocent IV. However infuriating to the king of France, the claim that the pope or the Church can judge and depose kings had been made before. But the pope's forthright language, especially in *Unam sanctam*, was in the circumstances ill-advised. It is hardly to be doubted that Boniface's tactlessness and imprudence served the papacy's cause ill.

For all intents and purposes, Boniface's death and the events leading up to it mark the end of the medieval papacy's vision of its own world-wide political authority. The struggles of 1296–1303 were not so much a contest between Boniface VIII and Philip the Fair as a collision of two incompatible principles: the ideal of a universal papal monarchy transcending territorial boundaries and uniting the Christian world in the overarching community of Christendom; and the new conception, so rapidly supplanting older feudal loyalties, of the consolidated nation-state, brooking no interference from without and acknowledging no sovereign but its king. The conflict inflicted upon the vigour and credibility of the papacy a wound from which it never fully recovered and which was exacerbated by the calamities of the next hundred years: the 'Babylonish captivity' of the popes at Avignon from 1305 to 1377 and the 'Great Western Schism' of 1378 to 1417.

---

28. Sensational stories soon got about: that the pope had died raving mad; that he had been found dead in his room with his brains beaten out. But '[w]hen they opened his tomb in 1605, the body, well preserved, showed no signs of violence' (Boase, *Boniface VIII*, p. 351).
29. See Dyson, *Normative Theories*, passim.

One final struggle remained to be played out, between Ludwig of Bavaria and Pope John XXII after the disputed imperial election of 1314. For our purposes, it suffices to remark that this conflict served only to accelerate the political enfeeblement of the papacy and refine the arguments of its opponents. In the final analysis, it may be said that 'so far as any single event can mark the end of an era, the tragedy of Anagni symbolized the close of a period in papal history that had opened with an emperor standing barefoot before the gates of Canossa.'[30]

(b) De ecclesiastica potestate: The Argument

These are the turmoils which form the context and inspiration of Giles of Rome's *De ecclesiastica potestate*. The treatise cannot be dated with complete precision, but it was certainly composed at or near the climax of the pope's second conflict with Philip the Fair. (It is believed, incidentally, having regard to the similarities between passages in *De ecclesiastica potestate* and the Bull *Unam sanctam*, that Giles also had a hand in drafting the latter.[31]) The treatise appeared, probably in 1302, under a fulsome dedication to Boniface VIII.

The reader's immediate impression is likely to be that *De ecclesiastica potestate* is a derivative and reactionary piece of writing. As we remarked earlier, it embraces an inveterately old-fashioned 'political Augustinianism', and it cites no scriptural or other authority which had not been pressed into service often before.[32] But it is impossible not to be struck by the determination and ingenuity with which Giles carries well-worn arguments to the limits of their logical possibility. His work is the palmary example of papalist writing at its most ambitious, and it is in this fact, rather than in any originality of content or freshness of thought, that its interest to the political and ecclesiastical historian lies. Its aim is to set forth, at unprecedented length and with a degree of elaboration never previously attempted, the 'hierocratic' ideology of the medieval papacy: the doctrine that, even in temporal matters, the pope is the rightful judge and ruler of the whole world and that, at their true valuation, emperors and kings are no more than the sword-bearers of the Church.

De ecclesiastica potestate is not an easy read. Giles's style is formidably prolix, and we may suppose the work to have been written in haste and with little or no revision.[33] It is characterised by a degree of repetition and recapitulation for which even the author feels obliged to apologise. Its points are often

---

30. W.K. Ferguson, *Europe in Transition, 1300–1520* (London: Allen and Unwin, 1962), p. 291.
31. See A.P. Monahan, *Giles of Rome on Ecclesiastical Power* (Lewiston, Queenston, Lampeter: Mellen, 1990), Introduction.
32. As well as the Bible and Biblical glosses (over 235 citations), Giles cites the following: Aristotle (and Ps.-Aristotle) (42 times); St Augustine (41 times); canon law (32 times); Hugh of Saint Victor (16 times); Peter Comestor (9 times); Ps.-Dionysius (7 times); Bernard of Clairvaux (5 times); Averroes (twice); Hilary of Poitiers, Isidore of Seville, Peter Lombard, and Ptolemy (once each).
33. Richard Scholz, in *Aegidus Romanus De ecclesiastica potestate* (repr., Aalen: Scientia, 1961), p. xi, conjectures that it might have been written between February and August 1302, or possibly somewhat earlier.

made with a degree of obscurity which no amount of sympathy on the translator's part can entirely dispel. The book is markedly lacking in formal organisation. It is divided into three parts, but the same arguments and illustrations crop up, in varying states of development and various forms of expression, almost at random throughout the work and with few concessions to structural logic. The best advice that can be given to readers is that they read and re-read it several times, *longueurs* and all, and allow an increasingly complete impression to form in their minds. Side issues and ramifications apart, its contentions can be reduced to three general points, here stated in what I take to be a suitable logical order.

(a) There are two and only two ruling agencies in the world: the earthly power of kings and their representatives (the 'material sword') and the spiritual power of the Church (the 'spiritual sword'). Giles devotes his longest chapter (Pt. II, Ch. XIII) to this theme.

(b) The material sword is in all respects subordinate to the spiritual sword. All forms of temporal lordship (*dominium*) — a term which Giles uses to denote both the just ownership of temporal possessions and the rightful exercise of political power — owe their existence to the Church and are ultimately subject to the Church's judgment and control.

(c) No distinction can properly be drawn between the power of the Church and that of the pope. In effect, the Christian world is an absolute monarchy with the pope at its head, and everything that can be said about ecclesiastical or priestly power is also a statement about papal power.

Characteristically of authors of his kind, Giles adduces many more arguments in support of his points than are strictly necessary, in the evident hope that if some fail, others will succeed. The essence of what he has to say in expounding these three claims can be stated as follows.

(i) As his most consistent presupposition, Giles adopts an understanding of the world embodying three distinct but fairly well-integrated elements: the teleological science of Aristotle; a Neoplatonist metaphysic mediated through St. Augustine and the Pseudo-Dionysius; and certain assumptions founded upon feudal relations of service and allegiance. These elements compose a picture of the universe as an ordered hierarchy of subordinate and superordinate relations. Everything in the world is properly subject to something higher than itself, and everything answers to its purpose, and hence achieves its good, by serving and supporting that which is superior to it. The inanimate creation (water, earth) serves the plants, which, though non-sentient, are living things; the plants serve the beasts, which are sentient though non-intelligent; and the beasts serve men, who are alive, sentient and intelligent, and for whose bodily support all lesser material creatures are appointed.

Within these terms of reference, it goes without saying that spiritual power is by its nature superior to any material power: superior in dignity, in the scope of what it can accomplish, and hence in the degree of submission and service which

is its due. God governs all things; the angels direct the planets; the soul rules the body: 'the whole of corporeal nature is ordered towards the spiritual.'[34] Right order demands that that the whole material creation be subordinated to spiritual objectives. So far as human conduct is concerned, it requires that the use made of material possessions and temporal power should be regulated by constant reference to spiritual imperatives, for

> when a prince or any man possesses temporal things, those temporal possessions are not goods for him unless he orders them towards spiritual ends; for they lead not to salvation, but to the damnation of the soul.[35]

From this, Giles contends, it follows that secular princes must acknowledge God's spiritual representative on earth as their superior and guide in all respects. They must devote their power to purposes defined or approved by the Church and encounter her censure if they are negligent or delinquent. Thus, the *de iure* sovereignty of priestly power even in the temporal sphere — granted that this sovereignty is not always recognised *de facto* — is presented simply as an inference from the natural order itself.

(ii) Running alongside this naturalistic argument, we find three related assertions derived from scripture and from Hugh of Saint Victor's treatise *De sacramentis fidei Christianae*: that priestly power precedes royal or temporal power in time as well as in dignity and scope, that it brings royal power into being, and that the Church can in appropriate circumstances dethrone emperors and kings.[36] Giles's purpose in pursuing this line is to repulse the standard royalist contention — a contention which, by the late thirteenth century, had come to be supported by a reputable body of canonist commentary[37] — that 'both powers, the priestly and the royal or imperial alike, come immediately from God, and that the one ... is not appointed by the other,' and that kings are therefore answerable to God directly rather than to any spiritual superior on earth.[38] Scripture shows us, he says, that priesthood existed before kingship. It is not unlikely that, after the Fall, Adam offered sacrifices to God in recognition of his own servitude; it is certainly recorded that Abel and Noah offered such sacrifices, and to offer sacrifices to God is a work of priesthood. But the first king mentioned in scripture is Nimrod, 'who had descended from the stock of Noah through many generations after the

---

34. Pt. II, Ch. IV, p. 91.
35. Ibid.
36. E.g. Pt. I, Chaps. IV; VI; VIII; Pt. II, Ch. V.
37. The 'teachers' of canon law to whom he refers at Bk. II, Ch. XIV (p. 253) and elsewhere no doubt include the great glossator Huguccio of Pisa (see his commentary on Dist. 96, c. 6, ed. G. Catalano, *Impero, Regni e Sacerdozio nel Pensiero di Uguccio da Pisa* (Milan: Giuffrè, 1959), p. 64) and the anonymous author of *Summa 'Et est sciendum'*, on Dist. 22, c. 1: see A.M. Stickler, 'Imperator vicarius papae: Die Lehren der französisch-deutschen Dekretistenschule de 12. und beginnenden 13 Jahrhunderts über die Beziehungen zwischen Papst und Kaiser', *Mitteilungen des Instituts für Österreichische Geschichtsforschung* 62 (1954), p. 203. See also W. Ullmann, *Medieval Papalism: The Political Theories of the Medieval Canonists* (London: Methuen, 1949).
38. Pt. II, Ch. V, p. 101.

Flood.'[39] Among the Jews themselves, who were the forerunners of the Christian people, the distinction between secular and priestly power emerged when Moses delegated the adjudication of temporal disputes to judges; and the first actual king of the Jews, Saul, was appointed through Samuel the priest at the Lord's command. Therefore, 'since former things are the patterns and a mirror of later, all later kingships must be referred back to the first,'[40] all kings must acknowledge that their legitimacy comes from Saul's appointment by God through the priesthood (although, prudently, Giles does not try to elaborate the precise sense in which modern kings are the successors of Saul). The practical implication of this is that the priestly power, as God's agent in the appointment of temporal rulers, must supervise and judge the use made of secular power and can if necessary withdraw it from unworthy hands and transfer it to others.[41]

Thus, princes wield the material sword as trustees and delegates of God. In this sense it is certainly true that, in St. Paul's words, they are 'ordained of God.' But, in ordaining them, God has chosen to act through the agency of His Church. They are anointed by the Church and it is on her immediate behalf that they execute the 'judgment of blood' and administer secular business generally. The Church is therefore the sole earthly repository of both spiritual and secular authority. It is right and necessary that the material and spiritual swords should exercise distinct functions, but it should not be inferred from this that the Church cannot in principle intervene in criminal cases and other temporal matters. After all, long before kingship and priesthood had become distinct, the Lord said 'You shall not suffer a witch to live.'[42] Moreover, it is obvious that an inferior and derived power can do nothing which could not also be done by the superior power from which it is derived, even if the inferior can act in a different — that is, a lower — way.[43] Reasons of propriety and convenience alone make it necessary for the material sword to be entrusted to worldly ministers. The Church must not defile her hands with the blood of the guilty, and the clergy must have as large an area of freedom as possible from temporal anxieties so that they may attend without distraction to spiritual duties. As of right, however, the Church possesses both swords: the spiritual to use (*ad usum*) and the material to command (*ad nutum*).[44]

(iii) Much of part II (chaps. VII–XII) is devoted to the proposition that even the material possessions of the faithful are derived from the Church and revocable by her. This argument, if successful, would clearly be fatal to any royal claim to exercise independent or sovereign jurisdiction over ecclesiastical property. It is also a rebuttal of the common royalist assertion that kingdoms are somehow the inal-

---

39. Pt. I, Ch. VI, p. 35.
40. Pt. I, Ch. V, p. 25.
41. The standard illustration, to which Giles several times alludes, is the so-called *translatio imperii*: the translation of imperial authority from Byzantium to the west supposedly effected by Leo III's coronation of Charlemagne on Christmas Day, 800. For some account of this pivotal event see Dyson, *Normative Theories,* Ch. 2; Ullmann, *The Growth of Papal Government,* Ch. III.
42. Pt. I, Ch. III, p. 15.
43. E.g. Pt. II, Ch. X, pp. 165–171; Ch. XIII; Ch. XIV.
44. Pt. I, Ch. III; Ch. VII; Chaps. VIII–IX; Pt. II, Chaps. I–III; Pt. III, passim.

ienable 'property' of their kings. In an immediate and direct sense, Giles says, it is true that proprietors derive their property from their fathers by right of inheritance. But legal succession, though 'the beginning of justice'[45] — that is, though mere usurpation cannot be in any sense just — is insufficient of itself to establish a *dominium cum iustitia*: a lordship which is fully or completely just. Classically defined, justice is that virtue which renders to each his due. If a knight does not render due fealty to his lord, that which he holds of the lord in return for his fealty he holds unjustly, and it is just that he should be deprived of it. *A fortiori*, he who does not render due fealty to God is even more gravely unjust: witness the remark of St. Augustine at *De civitate Dei* 19:23 that there can be no true justice save in that commonwealth whose founder and ruler is Christ. It is therefore just by the same token that one who is not duly subject to God should be deprived of all that he holds of God — that is, of everything.

> For the difference between the Eternal King and a temporal king is so great that, if he who is not subject to a temporal king is justly liable to lose all that he holds of that king, it is manifestly clear that he who is not subject to God is still more liable to lose, and more unjust in possessing, that which he holds of God.[46]

Strictly speaking, such a one is already deprived *de iure* of all his lordship, by the mere fact of his estrangement from God. Even if it is not possible to remove it from him *de facto,* or if he is permitted to retain it by the indulgence of God or the Church, he nonetheless has no just title to what he has.

The individual's submission to God, therefore, is a precondition of all just lordship. This being so, what reason can anybody have for claiming to be a just lord of anything merely by right of inheritance? Every man comes into the world 'a child of wrath'[47] by reason of original sin. From the beginning of his life, each individual is turned away from God. Considered simply as the son of his father, no man is a rightful possessor. In addition to the stain of original sin contracted from Adam, every man is moreover a mortal sinner by his own acts, and for this reason also does not stand in a just relation to God. But the remedies for original and actual sin — the sacraments of baptism and penance — are available only within the Church and are validly conferred only in the Church's prescribed form. It is therefore not carnal generation, but spiritual regeneration, which is the foundation of all just lordship. All rightful property and all just power

> come rather from the Church and through the Church and because you are a son of the Church than from your carnal father and through him and because you are his son.[48]

It follows that unbelievers can have no rightful power or property at all. It follows also that, in principle even if not always in practice, the Church can take away the property of the believer who rejects the sacrament of penance or who is formally excluded from it by excommunication.

45. Pt. II, Ch. VII, pp. 131–133.
46. Pt. II, Ch. VIII, p. 147.
47. Eph. 2:3.
48. Pt. II, Ch. VII, p. 141.

In this connection, Giles furnishes two instances of the way in which excommunication annuls the legal conditions upon which temporal lordship depends. First: all agreements as to property ownership flow from communication or consensus of mind as between the parties. But, at least *de iure*, even if this principle is not always enforced in point of fact, no one may communicate with the excommunicate. Therefore, he cannot rightfully acquire new property; nor, Giles asserts — though with dubious logic — can he rightfully retain the property which he had acquired before his excommunication.[49] Second: in the initial and carnal sense, no inheritance can be transmitted other than through lawful matrimony. But matrimony is one of the Church's sacraments, and no one who is excluded from the Church by excommunication may receive any advantage from it. To all intents and purposes, the excommunicate becomes illegitimate and subject to all the legal disqualifications of bastardy.[50]

On these grounds, then, the Church is said to have a 'universal' lordship over temporal things as against the 'particular' or restricted lordship of lay persons:[51] a 'superior and primary' lordship as distinct from the 'inferior and secondary lordship' of the faithful.[52] The lordship vested in the Church is of such a kind and magnitude that it constitutes and controls, and includes the right to cancel or remove, that of the laity. No one has cause to resent these observations. It has not been denied that laymen may have temporal *dominium* of a sort. Rather, the proper extent and standing of their *dominium* relative to that of the Church has been examined and clarified. That which is Caesar's has been rendered to Caesar, and that which is God's to God.[53]

(iv) In intention if not always in practice, Giles uses the expressions 'Church' and 'Supreme Pontiff' or 'Supreme Priest' virtually as synonyms. The pope is the embodiment of the Church, and all lesser ecclesiastical judges are deputies of the pa-

---

49. Pt. II, Ch. XII, pp. 195–203.
50. Pt. II, Ch. XII, pp. 203–205.
51. Pt. II, Chaps. X–XI.
52. Pt. III, Ch. XI.
53. An apparent difficulty is presented to Giles's argument by two major historical documents to which, in other circumstances, the Church had been happy to appeal: the *Donatio Constantini* and the ninth-century confirmation of the *Donatio* by the emperor Louis I called the *Pactum Lodovicianum* — documents which appear to record a grant of lordship *to* the Church *by* temporal lords. Giles deals with this only briefly, as part of his discussion of Hugh of Saint Victor's statement that the Church has received property 'by the pious devotion of the faithful' (Pt. III, Ch. XI, p. 381; and see Pt. I, Ch. IV, p. 21). Anyone can transfer whatever interest in a piece of property he may have, but gifts to the Church confer upon her only an 'inferior and secondary' lordship in addition to the 'superior and primary' lordship which is always hers by right. The territories granted by the *Donatio* became the Church's property in the ordinary and everyday sense, but this does not alter the fact that she had an ultimate jurisdiction over them already. For another attempt to deal with the *Donatio Constantini* see James of Viterbo, *De regimine Christiano*, Pt. II, Ch. VIII (ed. Dyson, *James of Viterbo On Christian Government*, p. 119). See also Alanus Anglicus, Commentary on Dist. 96, c. 6, ed. A.M. Stickler, 'Alanus Anglicus als Verteidiger des monarchischen Papsttums', *Salesianum* 21 (1959), p. 361. On the *Donatio Constantini* see esp. W. Ullmann, *The Growth of Papal Government*, p. 74 and the many references there given. On the *Lodovicianum*, see the same author's 'The Origins of the Ottonianum', *Cambridge Historical Journal* 11 (1953), p. 114.

pal will. The pope's authority belongs to his office, not to his person. Even if an individual pope is incompetent or morally bad, this makes no difference to what he can do by virtue of his status (though it is unlikely, the ever-loyal Giles remarks, that one for whom the whole Church prays will be less than a saint).[54] It cannot, of course, be supposed that Christ has bestowed the whole of His power upon the Church. The Church cannot work miracles nor give effect to a sacrament other than in the form prescribed for her.[55] But all the power that Christ has given to the Church He has given to the pope to wield as a monarch. Though it is as impossible as it would be undesirable for the pope to superintend every detail of the Church's business in person, he has the authority to 'do without a secondary cause whatever he can do with a secondary cause.'[56] He can suspend any law, reverse the decision of any secular or ecclesiastical subordinate, and take personal charge of any case. He has this *plenitudo potestatis*, 'fullness of power', as the successor and heir of St. Peter, to whom Christ entrusted the feeding of His sheep and upon whom He conferred the keys of the kingdom of heaven. To the binding and releasing power granted to Peter at Matthew 16:18–19 there are no exceptions. Peter was charged with the feeding of every one of Christ's sheep, and there are no limits to what he can accomplish in the Church Militant. His power is comparable in scope to — and in an important sense is broader in scope than — that of the natural order itself: a power untrammelled by any earthly constraint, from which all lesser powers are derived like streams from a source.[57]

Having this monarchical supremacy and independence of all secondary agency, the pope is subject to the judgment of no man and can be bound by no law, civil or canon. He is 'a creature without halter and bridle.'[58] Just as God for the most part leaves the natural order to function according to its own laws, so, in the interests of peace and good order, the Supreme Pontiff should not ordinarily disturb the jurisdiction of secular princes: he ought not to make random and arbitrary exceptions to the 'common' law (that is, to the law which ordinarily applies to all in common). But his own deference to the 'common' law is free and uncoerced. He imposes halter and bridle upon himself, in imitation of the restraint of God, Whose vicar he is. And just as God sometimes disregards the laws of nature in order to perform a miracle, so also may the pope set aside the established human laws and act on his own *fiat* if circumstances so require.

(v) In part III, chapters I–VIII, Giles sets about forestalling objections to his theory of papal absolutism. Not the least awkward feature of this task is that the difficulties which he foresees mostly come from pronouncements of popes themselves. As often as not, of course, papal decretals were issued in response to a particular question or in the light of immediate circumstance, with no thought of laying down a hard and fast rule. Canon law therefore exhibits the drawback of all

54. Pt. I, Ch. II.
55. Pt. III, Ch. IX.
56. Pt. III, Ch. IX, p. 363.
57. Pt. II, Ch. IV; Pt. III, Chaps. II; X; XII.
58. Pt. III, Ch. VIII, p. 361.

precedent-based systems of law: that the 'precedents' established in the past do not always support the conclusions that it is desired to reach now, and ingenuity has to be expended on making them seem to do so. Giles finds himself wishing to claim for the papacy a more extensive power than, on the face of it, some of its occupants have. Responding to an enquiry from the Archbishop of Rheims, Pope Alexander III (*pont.* 1159–1181) had said in his decretal *Si duobus* that, save in matters involving the Church's own property, it is 'not according to the strictness of the law' that appeal may be made from a civil judge to the pope, though such a right of appeal might be established by custom.[59] Innocent III had declared in the decretal *Novit* that it was not his intention to judge a feudal dispute as such, and that judgment in such matters 'belongs to' the king. Also, in the decretal *Per venerabilem*, addressing the question of whether the pope may declare illegitimate sons legitimate for purely secular purposes, Innocent III had observed that 'not only in the patrimony of the Church, where we wield full power in temporal affairs, but in other regions also, on the examination of certain causes, we exercise a temporal jurisdiction occasionally.'[60] But this expression seems to mean that, outside the patrimony of the Church, the pope has only an occasional, not a usual or ordinary, jurisdiction in temporal matters. Assertions of similar purport occur in Alexander III's decretals *Lator* and *Causam*, in which, again answering routine enquiries and not evidently conscious of stating general principles, the pope had said clearly that it belongs not to the Church but to kings to adjudicate disputes over temporal possessions and inheritances.[61] In all these cases, popes appear to have acknowledged that their temporal jurisdic-

---

59. X. 2:28:7 (CIC II:412): 'You ask whether, if appeal is made to our court from a civil judge before or after judgment has been given, such appeal is valid. It certainly is valid in matters which are subject to our temporal jurisdiction. In other matters, though it may be valid according to the custom of a church, we believe that it is not valid according to the strictness of the law.'

60. X. 4:17:13 (CIC II:714). He goes on: 'But in Deuteronomy [17:8–9] this is contained: "If you shall perceive there to be a difficult and doubtful matter among you as between blood and blood, cause and cause, leprosy and leprosy, and if you shall see that the judgments within your gates are at variance, arise and go up to the place that the Lord your God shall choose. And you shall come to the priests of the tribe of Levi, and to whoever shall be judge at that time, and you shall ask of them, and they will judge you with true judgment." ... Three kinds of judgment are distinguished: the first between blood and blood, by which civil crimes are signified; the last between leper and leper, by which ecclesiastical crimes are signified; and an intermediate kind, between cause and cause, which refers to both civil and ecclesiastical cases. In these matters, whenever anything difficult or ambiguous has arisen, recourse is to be had to the Apostolic See, and if anyone disdains to obey its sentence out of pride, he shall ... be separated from the communion of the faithful ... by sentence of excommunication.'

61. X. 4:17:5: *Lator* (CIC II:711): 'The secular lord within whose jurisdiction the case of disputed inheritance is being argued is to be informed that the case is of such a kind, and he is to hear the case and give a decision upon the disputed inheritance'; X. 4:17:7: *Causam* (CIC II:712): 'Mindful that it pertains to the king and not to the Church to judge concerning such possession, and lest we seem to take away the rights of the King of England [Henry II], who has claimed that judgment of them pertains to him, we command you, our brethren [i.e. the bishops of London and Worcester] to take cognizance more fully of the principal cause [i.e. of legitimacy] while leaving judgment as to the possessions to the king.' See A. Morey, *Bartholomew of Exeter* (Cambridge: Cambridge University Press, 1937), p. 68.

tion is subject to restrictions of precisely the kind that Giles wishes to deny. What is to be made of this difficulty?

In dealing with this question, Giles is drawing upon a tradition of commentary already well established.[62] His treatment of it is lengthy, technical, and opaque. Part III of *De ecclesiastica potestate* discloses more stylistic blemishes than any previous part of the treatise. Possibly he was by now hurrying to finish it; but one's impression is that he feels himself to be on uncertain ground. Leaving aside his numerous and distracting recapitulations of earlier material, he sets forth two themes, one of which is a good deal more prominent than the other. His minor theme is the argument that none of the statements made by a particular pope can bind his successors. Because no pope has any more, or any less, authority than his successors will have, any pope can disregard or repeal the enactments of a predecessor if he so chooses.[63] Even if it were true, therefore, that Alexander III or Innocent III had chosen to impose limits on the Church's temporal jurisdiction during their own pontificates — though Giles does not accept that this is true — there would be no reason to regard their pronouncements as irrevocable.[64] This is, in fact, potentially a good argument, but Giles is reluctant to rely on it exclusively for fear, apparently, of seeming to show disrespect for papal authority: 'it is not fitting not to defer to the words of the Supreme Pontiff.'[65] His second theme is more minutely explored, and we shall devote correspondingly more attention to it.

Where the administration of her own private property is concerned — tithes and the other possessions which she has received 'by the pious gift of the faithful or other just title of acquisition'[66] — the Church has exactly the same kind of rights and jurisdiction as any other temporal lord. Giles is at pains to refute the dangerous suggestion made by 'certain persons' that the Church should not possess material things at all. We may take it that these 'certain persons' are the Franciscan Spirituals: the rigorist faction whose members had separated themselves from St. Francis's original foundation because they insisted, on the strength of Luke 10:4 and similar passages, that Christ had enjoined absolute literal poverty upon His disciples.[67] Boniface VIII was in dispute with this pertinacious group from the beginning of his pontificate, as John XXII was to be in the second decade of the fourteenth century. The first three chapters of Part II of *De ecclesiastica potestate* constitute a short essay in refutation of them. At Luke 10:4, Christ forbade His disciples to have possessions, but only, Giles insists, in the earliest part

62. See W. Ullmann, *Medieval Papalism*, passim; cf. also Henry of Cremona, *De potestate papae* (ed. R. Scholz, *Die Publizistik*, p. 459).

63. Pt. III, Chaps. I; IV.

64. See also the argument at Pt. III, Ch. IV, p. 315, that Alexander III's statement was of opinion only and therefore not to be taken as authoritative. This is because the pope had used the word *credimus*, 'we believe'.

65. Pt. III, Ch. I, p. 273.

66. Pt. III, Ch. I, p. 277.

67. See D. Douie, *The Nature and Effect of the Heresy of the Fraticelli* (Manchester: Manchester University Press, 1932); M.D. Lambert, *Franciscan Poverty: The Doctrine of the Absolute Poverty of Christ and the Apostles in the Franciscan Order* (London: SPCK, 1961).

of their ministry, when it was necessary for the Church to learn how to survive the rigours of this world and to impress sceptics with the moral power of the gospel. Subsequently, at Luke 22:25, the prohibition was withdrawn. In the modern world, where the Church's security and authority are not in doubt, it is lawful for her to have property of her own. She could hardly function without it, after all, and she would be held in low esteem by the laity if she were poor. The Church, then, can own property and may manage and dispose of her own property as she likes, although she will in practice delegate the administration of her practical affairs to laymen. In all other cases, the Church's jurisdiction in temporal matters is, Giles says, 'superior and primary,' but not normally 'immediate and executory.'[68]

This distinction between 'superior and primary' and 'immediate and executory' jurisdictions is, Giles argues, implicit in the decretals of Alexander III and Innocent III which seem to acknowledge that certain cases lie outside the Church's competence. Her jurisdiction is 'superior and primary' in the sense that, by virtue of the intrinsic superiority of the spiritual over the temporal, the Church's task is to oversee, and if necessary to correct, all aspects of the conduct of temporal princes. Nothing is exempt from the Church's jurisdiction in this sense. The pope has an ultimate or transcendent right to intervene in any temporal matter whatsoever. For two reasons, however, he does not usually avail himself of this right. First, it is proper that due order should be preserved among the powers: that the hierarchy of the universe should be preserved in its earthly aspect. It would not be conducive to this order if the immediate and executory jurisdiction of princes were disturbed by the indiscriminate permission of appeals to ecclesiastical courts. This is why it is not 'according to the strictness of the law' that appeal may be made from a civil judge to the pope: it is not according to the law as it applies in ordinary or unproblematical cases. Second, secular tribunals have been established precisely so that the Church's ministers shall not be distracted by worldly concerns. In the ordinary course of things, the pope gives his undivided attention to spiritual cases, which he never deputes to lay judges. But just as an ordinary builder's rule does not apply to irregularly-shaped stones, so does the rule prescribing that the Church should abstain from interference in temporal matters not apply in irregular or abnormal cases.[69] For good reason, the pope will indeed concern himself directly with temporal cases. He will allow the Church's 'superior and primary' jurisdiction to assume a more narrow and direct — an 'immediate and executory' — focus. This, Giles contends, is the true meaning of Innocent III's words in the decretal *Per venerabilem*: 'on the examination of certain causes, we exercise a temporal jurisdiction occasionally.' It may seem to some that this principle of occasionality restricts papal jurisdiction in temporals, but in fact the reverse is true. The 'certain causes' are precisely those which the pope considers too important or too difficult to be left to the tribunals of secular princes.

In what circumstances, then, will such 'occasional' jurisdiction come into play? Giles addresses this question in a group of chapters (part III, chaps. V–VIII)

68. Pt. III, Ch. V.
69. Pt. III, Ch. IV, p. 317.

which are, in effect, a commentary on the problematical decretals *Novit, Causam, Lator,* and *Per venerabilem.* He presents the following compendium of cases, here summarised in an order corresponding as nearly as possible to that in which he deals with them.

(a) The Church — that is, the pope or the ecclesiastical judges who act as his deputies — will take cognizance of all temporal questions which have a spiritual aspect because they are 'annexed to' (that is, because they are connected inseparably with) some matter which canon law places directly within the Church's competence. For instance, since it rests with her to judge questions of legitimacy, she is also competent to judge cases of disputed inheritance where the dispute arises out of an imputation of illegitimacy. By the same token, her ordinary jurisdiction in matrimonial causes also entitles her to judge disputes involving dowries.

(b) The Church will judge all temporal cases which are complicated by the fact that some element of sin or crime exists alongside or in association with the temporal issue and which therefore present a danger to the soul. This, of course, is the *ratione peccati* principle, and really constitutes the heart of the matter. Since, Giles says (paraphrasing *Novit*),

> all crimes and all mortal sins can be called spiritual in the sense that they slay our spirit and our soul, it follows that the spiritual power will be able to intervene in disputes involving any temporal questions whatsoever if those disputes are brought forward together with an allegation of crime. For it rests with the spiritual power to judge every mortal sin and to rebuke every Christian for it. For, otherwise, God would not have said in St Matthew's Gospel, 18[:15–17]: 'And if your brother should sin against you, go and rebuke him between yourself and him; and if he will not hear you, take one or two persons with you; and if he will not hear them, tell the Church.' He would not have said this if it did not rest with the Church to rebuke every Christian for every mortal sin. Therefore, it is clear that this condition by reason of which the Church can concern herself with temporal things, and by reason of which appeal can be made to the Church on temporal questions, is so broad and ample that it may embrace all temporal disputes whatsoever, since such a dispute can always involve an allegation of crime.[70]

(c) Since peace is so indispensable a prerequisite of the Church's work, she has an especially pressing responsibility to concern herself with any secular quarrel which endangers it. It is her task to act as arbiter between warring powers who are not subject to any common sovereign. Giles is ostensibly again commenting on the decretal *Novit,* but it seems reasonable to assume that he has the war between Edward I and Philip the Fair in mind.

(d) The Church will judge all temporal cases which involve 'ecclesiastical crimes': doctrinal or canonical offences such as perjury, heresy, usury, and sacrilege. Thus, for instance, it will be her duty to intervene when peace treaties which have been confirmed by oath are broken. Again, this comment on *Novit* is no doubt intended to have contemporary resonance also.

---

70. Pt. III, Ch. V, p. 327.

(e) She will exercise an appellate jurisdiction when recourse is had to her by injured parties who have no other means of redress. Such appeal will lie especially when the throne of the empire or of a kingdom is vacant and/or where the highest available civil judge is reasonably suspected of negligence or injustice. Giles's starting point here is Innocent III's permission of appeals from lay tribunals to the Bishop of Vercelli in the decretal *Licet*,[71] but he formulates this specific permission into a general principle: '[I]f the material sword is lacking, jurisdiction devolves upon the spiritual, to whom it belongs to be lord of all things.'[72]

(f) She will exercise such jurisdiction where a secular lord has allowed a right of appeal to an ecclesiastical judge to become customary. This is the principle which had been recognised in Alexander III's *Si duobus*. Such a customary right, once established, cannot be set aside by the lord or his successors. Anyone who attempted to do so would be acting 'beyond what is proper to his kind,' for no one can remove a right from a power higher than his own.[73]

(g) As a kind of *omnium gatherum*, Giles argues that the Church has an ordinary jurisdiction in all cases which, for one reason or another, cannot be resolved by the normal processes of secular judgment. The kind of cases which he has in mind are those which arise when the law is silent, or because a general law does not fit the particular circumstances, or because the dispute involves personages so great and powerful that the civil judges are hindered by fear from acting justly, or because the meaning of the law as it relates to the case at hand is not clear. In all such cases, recourse to the pope is permissible as a matter of course.

*

Despite the long and often weary way which *De ecclesiastica potestate* follows, its meaning could hardly be clearer. To Giles's mind, there is no case at all which is in principle exempt from papal cognizance on one or another of the grounds which he sets forth. If the pope refrains from intervening, this is not because he cannot or may not do so; rather, it is because he does not consider the case in question problematical or important enough to be worthy of his consideration. Moreover, Giles's assumption throughout is that the pope himself is the only judge of when he should receive an appeal or concern himself with temporal matters in some other way. To all intents and purposes, Giles's list of occasional

---

71. X. 2:2:10 (CIC II:250): 'If it happens that the laymen of Vercelli have obtained letters from the Apostolic See on matters pertaining to secular jurisdiction, we command that you judge them by our authority to be null and void, provided that the consuls and commune will do full justice to the plaintiffs in a secular trial. But if those who have taken their cases before the consuls feel themselves to be oppressed in any way, they are permitted to appeal to you for a hearing, as has been the custom, or to us if they prefer. This is especially so when the empire is vacant, so that those who are oppressed in the courts of their superiors cannot appeal to a secular judge. If there is reasonable cause of suspicion against the consuls, they shall be accused before arbitrators chosen by both parties, and the grounds of suspicion examined. If they prove just, recourse is to be be had to you for justice, or to us, as stated above.'

72. Pt. III, Ch. VII, p. 349.

73. Pt. III, Ch. IV, p. 315; Ch. VII, pp. 349–351.

or special cases excludes nothing. His general conclusion is that the pope may, at his own discretion and without regard to the jurisdiction of any other power, take any step whatsoever to secure the well-being, material as well as spiritual, of the flock whose shepherd he is. Like Boniface VIII, Giles is not saying anything new. He does, however, say old things in new ways. Above all, he says them with unexampled detail and rigour. *De ecclesiastica potestate* is without precedent in its defence not merely of ecclesiastical rights, but of the sovereign authority of the pope or, more strictly, of the papal office. The pope's temporal jurisdiction is to be exercised 'occasionally' and 'on the examination of certain causes.' But this does not mean that his temporal jurisdiction is inferior to the ordinary jurisdiction of kings and princes. On the contrary, in many instances, ecclesiastical jurisdiction will come into play precisely because the temporal case in question has some spiritual dimension or other important feature which places it beyond the circumscribed capacity of a merely secular court. In others, the pope will intervene in temporal disputes when recourse is had to him as the highest judge of appeal, whose function it is to correct the faults and repair the deficiencies of merely lay judgment. In effect, the pope is the *de iure* ruler of the entire world.

(c) *The Text*

Surprisingly enough, *De ecclesiastica potestate* did not become available in print until the first decade of the twentieth century. Before then, the chief resource at the disposal of students was a description and analysis furnished in 1862 by F.-X. Kraus.[74] The treatise was first printed in 1908 by G. Boffito and G.U. Oxilia (*Un trattato inedito di Egidio Colonna*); but this version, which has a long and valuable Introduction, is only a transcription — and a rather inaccurate one — of the unsatisfactory Florentine manuscript which we are here referring to as F. A critical edition was made subsequently by Richard Scholz of the University of Leipzig and published in 1929 (*Aegidius Romanus De ecclesiastica potestate*).

For all its undoubted virtues, a close study of Scholz's edition reveals shortcomings of a kind which have made a rehandling of the manuscript material seem desirable. It does not take account of our manuscript C (which Scholz appears not to have known). Its *apparatus criticus* is scanty, inconsistent and not seldom misleading. Moreover, Scholz allowed a number of readings to stand in his text which are clearly incorrect. It is a mistake to claim definitiveness, but it may be said at any rate that the present work is the most complete edition of *De ecclesiastica potestate* yet to appear. In order to try to recover Giles's text as fully as possible, I have used the five fourteenth-century manuscripts listed in the conspectus siglorum at the beginning of this volume.[75] There are two others in the Biblioteca An-

74. "Ägidius von Rom", *Österreichische Vierteljahrschrift für katholische Theologie* 1 (Vienna, 1862), p. 1.
75. For short descriptions of MSS P, F, V^1, and V^2 and the codices in which they appear, see Scholz, *Aegidius Romanus*, p. VI. For MS. C see G. Mazzatini and A. Sorbelli, *Inventari dei manoscritti della biblioteche d'Italia* 70 (Florence: Olschki, 1939), p. 60; G. Dotti, 'I codici Agostiniani della Biblioteca Statale di Cremona', *Augustiniana* 31 (1981), p. 371.

gelica, Rome: MS 130 (B. 4. 7), ff. 1–160ᵛ (incomplete and inaccurate, from the fifteenth century) and MS 367 (D. 1. 13), ff. 365–508 (inaccurate, from the seventeenth century), but these are without critical signifcance. In the same library there is a longish paraphrase (MS 181 (B. 7. 10), ff. 101ᵇ–106), also dating from the seventeenth century.

We have, of course, no way of knowing how many manuscripts of *De ecclesiastica potestate* may once have existed. The five here collated share several features which point to a lost common ancestor, *a*, which must have stood fairly close to the autograph. In the heading of part I, chapter V (pp. 2; 20) they all give *novem* instead of the obviously correct *nove*; again, *suple* [i.e. *suppleo* or *supplevi*] *quam potestas terrena* at the end of part I, chapter VI (p. 38) is evidently an early gloss which may be assumed not to have been present in the autograph. There are several other such instances, but these two examples may suffice. Manuscript C, though not the best overall, has some few readings better than anything found elsewhere: for example, *plano* at part I, chapter IX (p. 58) and *De Trinitate iv* at part I, chapter VII (p. 44) (all the other manuscripts give *palacio*, which, if not quite meaningless, is implausible in the context, and *De Trinitate ix*, which is erroneous). C also contains a number of short passages, some of which are confused or otherwise make poor sense, which the C scribe first copied and then on reflection struck out. These deleted passages do not appear in any of the other descendants of *a*, and suggest the existence of another, and presumably inferior, source, *b*, to which the C scribe had access but which he systematically disregarded in favour of *a*. Similarities exhibited by F, P, V¹, and V², taken together with their deviations from C, suggest that these four manuscripts share an ancestor, *c*, which is younger than *a*. F and V² clearly form a pair, as do P and V¹. F transmits numerous errors and unsatisfactory readings which, because C exhibits them as well, clearly go back to *a*. I am inclined to agree with Scholz that V² is a tidied-up copy of F, in which some, though by no means all, of these readings are removed; but because the scribe of V² reinstates a number of passages omitted by homoioteleuton from F, it is clear that he had access also to some source other than F: possibly P, but one cannot be sure. V² is a handsome and, on the whole, careful manuscript, though its scribe is himself rather prone to homoioteleuton. P and V¹ resemble each other closely, in ways tending to suggest that V¹ is a diligent copy of P. P itself is the work of an intelligent and alert scribe who has corrected most, though not all, of the unsatisfactory *a* readings which F preserves. His name, David Galensis ('David of Wales') appears at the foot of the last folio. Despite the importance attached to it by Boffito and Oxilia, F is by far the least reliable manuscript. It is the work of an inattentive copyist who made many small slips and who, judging from the manuscript's general character, worked in some haste. F and V² sometimes support a reading preferable to anything in the other manuscripts; but, for the most part, P and V¹ are our best witnesses. On some few occasions I have felt justified in adopting a conjectural reading not represented anywhere in the tradition. This has, of course, been done only where obviously necessary.

The following stemma accounts for the possible relations between the manu-scripts in what seems to be the most economical way. As always in these matters, the reality may have been a good deal more complex.

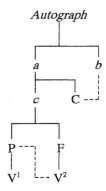

Autograph

Variant readings of any significance are recorded as far as is practicable in the critical notes. Trivial mistakes, scribal self-corrections and merely orthographical differences are for the most part not mentioned. In keeping with most current practice, medieval orthography has been preserved.

No one can translate Latin adequately except *à grand coups de dictionnaires,* and many Latin words do not pass so easily into English as might be supposed. I have revised and corrected the translation published by me in 1986,[76] which may now be regarded as superseded; but my aim, now as then, has been to produce a translation which is both accurate and readable. Where it was necessary to sacrifice the second desideratum to the first, however, I have invariably done so. I have in all cases thought it better to be inelegant than misleading. Where necessary, I have interpolated into the translation my own glosses in square brackets. I have taken minor liberties with the verbal tenses and moods of the original, and I have sometimes deviated more substantially from fidelity in the interests of intelligibil-ity. But, in all major respects, my translation is a literal one. At all events, I think it as literal a translation as could have been made.

For ease of use, all notes and references apart from critical notes appear at the foot of the English pages. For the same reason, Biblical references have been translated according to the conventions of the King James Version and its descen-dants: I Kings has become I Samuel, Paralipomenon has become Chronicles, and so on. A similar remark applies to the numbering of the Psalms.

76. *Giles of Rome on Ecclesiastical Power* (Woodbridge: Boydell).

GILES OF ROME'S *On Ecclesiastical Power*

Sanctissimo patri[1] ac domino suo, domino singulari, domino Bonifacio, divina providencia sacrosancte Romane ac universalis Ecclesie Summo Pontifici, Frater Egidius, eius humilis creatura, eadem miseracione Bituricensis Archiepiscopus, Aquitanie Primas, cum omni subieccione se ipsum ad pedum oscula beatorum, infrascriptam compilacionem de ecclesiastica potestate eisdem beatis pedibus humiliter offerentem.

[PRIMA PARS]

Incipiunt capitula prime partis presentis libri de ecclesiastica potestate, in qua tractatur de huiusmodi potestate[2] respectu materialis gladii et respectu potencie secularis.[3]

CAPITULUM I: In quo est prologus huius libri, declarans quod, ne ignoremur a Domino, non debemus Summi Pontificis potestatem[5] ignorare.

CAPITULUM II:[4] Quod Summus Pontifex est tante potencie quod est ille spiritualis homo qui iudicat omnia et ipse a nemine iudicatur.

CAPITULUM III: Quod Summus Pontifex est tante potencie quod ipse[6] est illa potestas sublimis[7] cui omnis anima debet esse subiecta.

CAPITULUM IV: Quod spiritualis potestas instituere habet terrenam potestatem et, si terrena potestas bona non fuerit, spiritualis potestas eam poterit iudicare.

CAPITULUM V: In quo adducuntur nove[8] raciones quod sacerdotalis potestas superior et dignior est omni regia potestate.

CAPITULUM VI: Quod sacerdotalis potestas non solum dignitate sed tempore prior est regia potestate.

CAPITULUM VII: Quod, sicut in homine est duplex substancia, corpus et spiritus, et sicut est dare duplicem cibum, corporalem et spiritualem, sic est ponere duplicem gladium, quorum unus alteri debet esse subiectus.

CAPITULUM VIII: Quomodo hii duo gladii in una et eadem persona, videlicet in Summo Pontifice, per quandam excellenciam reservantur.

CAPITULUM IX: Quod decet Ecclesiam habere[9] materialem gladium non ad usum, sed ad nutum; et quod sic habere huiusmodi gladium est maioris perfeccionis et excellencie pocioris.[10]

———————— ✳ ————————

1: patri] principi F   2: de huiusmodi potestate] huiusmodi de potestate summi pontificis P
3: Incipiunt ... secularis] *om.* V[1]   4: II] I F (*and so on, throughout the list*)   5: potestatem]
potenciam CP   6: ipse] *om.* PV[1]   7: sublimis] *om.* V[1]   8: nove] novem *mss*   9: Ecclesiam
habere] habere ecclesiam F   10: *In F, the lists of chapter headings which appear at the beginning
of each part are also collected into a single 'table of contents' at the front of the manuscript.*

To his Most Holy Father and Lord, the singular Lord, the Lord Boniface, by Divine Providence Supreme Pontiff of the Sacred Roman and Universal Church, Brother Giles, his humble creature, by the same Mercy Archbishop of Bourges and Primate of Aquitaine, presents himself with entire submission to kiss his blessed feet, humbly offering at those same blessed feet the following composition on ecclesiastical power.

[PART ONE]

Thus begin the chapters of the first part of the present book on ecclesiastical power, in which such power is treated with respect to the material sword and with respect to secular power.

CHAPTER I: In which is the prologue of this book, declaring that, lest we be ignored by the Lord, we must not be ignorant of the power of the Supreme Pontiff.

CHAPTER II: That the Supreme Pontiff is of such great power that he is that spiritual man who judges all things and is himself judged by no one.

CHAPTER III: That the Supreme Pontiff is of such great power that he himself is that sublime power to which every soul must be subject.

CHAPTER IV: That the spiritual power must institute the earthly power, and if the earthly power is not good, the spiritual power will be able to judge it.

CHAPTER V: In which new arguments are adduced showing that priestly power is superior to and greater in dignity than all royal power.

CHAPTER VI: That priestly power is prior to royal power not only in dignity, but also in time.

CHAPTER VII: That just as in man there is a twofold substance, body and spirit, and just as it is necessary to give a twofold food, bodily and spiritual, so is it necessary to posit two swords, one of which must be subject to the other.

CHAPTER VIII: How these two swords are reserved in one and the same person, namely, in the Supreme Pontiff, by reason of a certain excellence.

CHAPTER IX: That it is fitting for the Church to have the material sword not to use, but to command, and that to have such a sword in this way is a thing of greater perfection and more excellent power.

------------ ✳ ------------

CAPITULUM I: *In quo est prologus huius libri, declarans quod, ne ignoremur a Domino, non debemus Summi Pontificis potestatem ignorare.*[1]

Quoniam, ut Apostolus protestatur, 'Si quis autem[2] ignorat, ignorabitur,' id est, ut glossa exponit, a Deo in futuro reprobabitur et a Domino minime cognoscetur, velut in evangelio legitur, quod malis et ad sinistram stantibus[3] 'Nescio vos' Dominus est dicturus: ne ergo[4] in iudicio ignoremur a Domino, et ne reprobemur ab ipso, summo opere debemus[5] ignoranciam[6] fugere, et potissime illorum nescienciam,[7] ut glossa exponit, que fidem edificant atque mores.

Nam ad Summum Pontificem et ad eius plenitudinem potestatis spectat ordinare fidei simbolum et statuere que ad bonos mores spectare videntur. Quia, sive de fide sive de moribus questio oriretur, ad ipsum spectaret diffinitivam dare[8] sentenciam ac statuere nec non et firmiter ordinare quid Christiani sentire[9] deberent et in quam partem eorum unde sunt orta litigia esset a fidelibus declinandum, cuius causa et racio hec existit. Nam quia que[10] sunt fidei, et eciam[11] que[12] sunt morum, ab universali Ecclesia sunt tenenda, exinde igitur[13] et merito, unde dissenciones seu questiones oriri possent de moribus vel de fide, ad illum solum spectat huiusmodi lites dirimere et questiones exortas dissolvere qui est tocius Ecclesie apicem assecutus. Et quia solus Summus Pontifex noscitur esse talis, ad solum ipsum spectabit de exortis talibus et circumadiacentibus ordinare. Possunt itaque[14] doctores per viam doctrine de fide et[15] moribus tractatus[16] et libellos componere; sed quid sentencialiter sit tenendum, ubi posset[17] lis vel questio exoriri, ad solum Summum Pontificem pertinebit. Quare, si de pertinentibus ad fidem et mores, ut glosse diffiniunt magistrales, qui ignorat ignorabitur et[18] a Deo in finali iudicio reprobacionis sentenciam sorcietur, bene se habet de potestate Summi Sacerdocii iuxta modulum nostre sciencie tractatum componere, et per[19] dicta canonis sanctorum atque doctorum de prefata materia veritatem perquirere, ne per ignoranciam ignoremur et a Domino finaliter iudicemur.

Ubi non solum de eius spirituali potencia aliqua disserere[20] cogimur, sed et[21] de potestate ipsius super temporalia que dicenda sunt compellimur diffusius enarrare. Nam et hoc ad bonos mores pertinere dignoscitur, ut discant laici eciam in temporalibus, in quibus oppido[22] infesti sunt clericis, suis superioribus obedire. Igitur nimirum gracia veritatis, que pre aliis admittatur,[23] tractatum huiusmodi suscipientes pre manibus, ipsumque[24] per partes et capitula distinguemus prout rei congruencia postulabit. In quo tractatu rogamus quoscumque lectores ut nullam sentenciam proferant donec totum opus duxerint perlegendum.

1: CAPITULUM I ... *ignorare*] *om.* V[1]   2: autem] *del.* PV[1]   3: sinistram stantibus] sinistrantibus V[1]   4: ergo] *om.* V[1]   5: debemus] deberemus V[1]   6: ignoranciam] *marg., in a later hand*, P   7: nescenciam] nesciam F   8: diffinitivam dare] dare diffinitivam PV[1]   9: sentire] sentiri P   10: que] quecumque F   11: eciam] *om.* V[2]   12: que] quecumque F   13: igitur] sibi F   14: itaque] inquam V[1]   15: et] de *add.* FV[2]   16: tractatus] tractatum C   17: posset] possit F   18: et] id est PV[1]V[2]   19: per] *om.* V[2]   20: disserere] dirimere F diruere V[2]   21: et] *om.* P si V[1]   22: oppido] *om.* V[2]   23: admittatur] amicatur CF admicatur V[1] amictatur V[2]   24: ipsumque] ipsum quoque FV[1] ipsum et P

CHAPTER ·I: *In which is the prologue of this book, declaring that, lest we be ignored by the Lord, we must not be ignorant of the power of the Supreme Pontiff.*

For, as the Apostle attests, 'If any man be ignorant, he will be ignored,'[1] that is, as a gloss[2] explains, he will be condemned by God in the future and not in the least acknowledged by the Lord, as we read in the Gospel: that the Lord will say to the wicked and to those standing at His left hand, 'I know you not.'[3] Therefore, lest we be ignored by the Lord at the judgment, and lest we be condemned by Him, we must by supreme effort flee from ignorance, and especially, as the gloss explains, from lack of knowledge of those things which build up faith and morals.

Now it rests with the Supreme Pontiff and his fullness of power to ordain the articles of faith and to establish those things which seem to belong to good morals. For were a question to arise concerning either faith or morals, it would rest with him whose purpose and reason this is to give a definitive judgment and to establish and ordain most firmly what Christians should believe and towards which side the faithful should lean in the matters under dispute. But because those things which are of faith, and also those which are of morals, must be held by the universal Church, consequently, then, and properly, where dissensions or questions can arise over morals or faith, it rests only with one who has attained to the summit of the whole Church to bring such disputes to an end and to resolve the questions which emerge. And because only the Supreme Pontiff is known to be such a one, it will rest with him alone to set such questions and related issues in order when they arise. Thus, teachers can compose treatises and handbooks of faith and morals by way of instruction, but it will pertain to the Supreme Pontiff alone to declare what must be held as authoritative where dispute or question might arise. And so if, as the glosses of the masters indicate, he who is ignorant of matters pertaining to faith and morals will be ignored and will receive a sentence of condemnation from God at the Last Judgment, we do well to compose a treatise concerning the power of the Supreme Priest according to the small measure of our knowledge, and to seek out the truth from what is said on the foregoing subject in the works of saints and teachers lest, through ignorance, we be ignored and finally judged by the Lord.

But it is not only of his spiritual power that we are here constrained to say something. We are compelled also to state at greater length what must be said of his power over temporal things. For this too is to be distinguished as pertaining to good morals, so that the laity may learn to obey their superiors even in temporal matters, with respect to which they are very hostile to the clergy.[4] Thus, assuredly undertaking this treatise for the sake of truth, which is to be admitted before all else, we shall divide it into such parts and chapters as a proper treatment of the subject matter will require. And we ask all who read this treatise to offer no opinion until they have thoroughly studied the whole work.

1. I Cor. 14:38.
2. Peter Lombard, *Collectanea in omnes de Pauli apostoli epistolas*, PL 191:1672.
3. Matt. 25:41; Luke 13:25, 27.
4. A clear echo of the Bull *Clericis laicos*. See Introduction, p. xiii.

CAPITULUM II: *Quod Summus Pontifex est tante potencie quod est ille spiritualis homo qui iudicat omnia et ipse a nemine iudicatur.*

Duplicem esse perfeccionem, personalem et secundum statum, dicta sanctorum et doctorum communiter protestantur; que due perfecciones sic differre videntur: quod[1] perfeccio[2] personalis consistit in serenitate et in[3] mundicia consciencie, sed perfeccio status, et potissime status prelatorum et eorum omnium qui in die novissimo ante tribunal Christi astantes reddituri sunt de animabus fidelium racionem, consistit in iurisdiccione et in plenitudine potencie, ut ille sit[4] status perfeccior cui[5] potencia amplior et iurisdiccio plenior respondebit. Sensibiliter itaque, et per raciones exortas a sensibus, liquido ostendemus quod 'spiritualis homo iudicat omnia et ipse,' secundum quod huiusmodi, 'a nemine iudicatur.' Qui ergo est spiritualis secundum perfeccionem personalem, ille, secundum quod huiusmodi et secundum mensuram consciencie, non iudicatus ab aliis, poterit alia iudicare. Qui autem secundum statum est spiritualis et perfectus in summo secundum iurisdiccionem et plenitudinem potestatis, erit ille spiritualis homo qui omnia iudicabit et ipse a nemine poterit iudicari.

Dicemus autem, prout in alia sciencia habetur, quod rectum est iudex sui et obliqui. Sensibiliter[6] enim videmus in omnibus quod rectum singula iudicat recte, non rectum non recte; ut qui habent linguam rectam et non infectam, et[7] habent gustum sanum, de omnibus saporibus iudicabunt recte, ut dulcem saporem iudicabunt dulcem et amarum amarum: propter quod, habens gustum sanum, iudicabit omnia, id est[8] iudicabit omnes sapores, et ipse a nemine iudicabitur, id est a nemine reprehendetur, quia non errabit in iudicando de saporibus. Sic ergo iudicabit qui[9] non iudicabitur: id est, in suo iudicio non reprehendetur.[10] Sed habens linguam infectam et gustum non sanum, ut puta quia habet linguam repletam colera, nil[11] iudicabit recte, quia propter amaritudinem colere, qua ponitur lingua eius fore perfusa,[12] eciam dulce videbitur sibi amarum: iste sic infectus secundum gustum ab omnibus iudicabitur, id est ab omnibus reprehendetur, quia nullum iudicium dabit rectum.

Et quod dicimus de iudicio saporum veritatem habet de hiis que sunt morum et de omnibus aliis, ut homines mali secundum mores et habentes voluntatem infectam et affectam ad illicita ut plurimum iudicabunt perverse. Quia qualis unusquisque est,

1: quod] quia FV² 2: perfeccio] quidem *add.* CFV² 3: in] *del.* P 4: sit] sicut F 5: cui] in F 6: Sensibiliter] similiter V² 7: et] qui *add.* C 8: id est] *om.* FV² 9: iudicabit qui] iudicandum FV² 10: quia non ... reprehendetur] *om.* V¹ 11: nil] non FV¹V² 12: perfusa] perfusam F

CHAPTER II: *That the Supreme Pontiff is of such great power that he is that spiritual man who judges all things and is himself judged by no one.*[1]

The sayings of saints and teachers commonly attest that perfection is of two kinds: personal, and according to status. These two kinds of perfection seem to differ thus: personal perfection indeed consists in serenity and in purity of conscience, but perfection of status, and especially of the status of the prelates and of all those who, standing before the tribunal of Christ on the Last Day, must render an account of the souls of the faithful,[2] consists in jurisdiction and in fullness of power. And so [regardless of the personal qualities of its occupant] that status is the more perfect to which the more ample power and fuller jurisdiction will correspond. Thus, we shall show clearly, by reference to the senses and by arguments arising from the senses, that 'the spiritual man judges all things' and that, as such, he is himself 'judged by no one.' Therefore, he who is spiritual according to personal perfection is, as such and according to the measure of conscience, not judged by others and will be able to judge other things. But he who is spiritual according to status and supremely perfected according to jurisdiction and fullness of power will be that spiritual man who will judge all things [in the sense of exercising jurisdiction rather than moral discrimination], and [in this sense] he will himself be subject to the judgment of no one.

Also, we shall say that, as we gather from another science,[3] the 'right' [i.e. the 'norm'] is the judge [i.e. the standard] of both itself [i.e. of the 'normal'] and of what deviates from it. For we see by reference to the senses that, in all cases, what is right judges each thing rightly and what is not right does not judge rightly. For example, someone who has a tongue which is rightly disposed and not disordered, and who has a healthy sense of taste, will judge all tastes rightly: he will judge sweet tastes sweet and bitter ones bitter. And because he will judge all things, that is, he will judge all tastes, as having a healthy sense of taste, he will himself be judged by no one: that is, he will be condemned by no one, because he will not err in the judgment of tastes. So, therefore, will he judge who will not be judged: that is, who will not be condemned in his judgment. But he who has a disordered tongue and a sense of taste which is not healthy, perhaps because he has a tongue full of choler, will judge nothing rightly; for, because of the bitterness of the choler, anything placed on his tongue will be tainted, and that which is sweet will seem to him bitter. He whose sense of taste is thus disordered will be judged by all: that is, he will be condemned by all, because he will not give a right judgment of anything.

And what we say of the judgment of tastes holds true also of those things which belong to morals and of all other matters. Thus, men who are bad with respect to morals, having a will which is disordered and drawn towards forbidden things, will judge many things perversely; for, as each man is, so does his purpose

1. Cf. I Cor. 2:15; Dist. 40, c.6: *Si papa* (CIC I:146).
2. See Introduction, p. xvi and n. 20.
3. Aristotle, *De anima* 1:5 (411ª4); cf. *Ethics* 3:4f (1113ª15).

talis finis sibi videtur, et sic vivit et sic loquitur: ut gulosus semper loquitur de cibis, totam vitam suam ordinabit ad cibos, non comedet ut vivat, sed vivet ut comedat: huius deus venter erit. Et quia sic infectus est[1] secundum gulam et affectus ad cibos non bene iudicabit de usu cibariorum et ab omnibus iudicabitur, id est ab omnibus reprehendetur quia non dabit rectum iudicium de huiusmodi usu, ille ergo qui est infectus et non habet mentem sanam, nec est sanctus nec[2] spiritualis: ille est animalis homo et non sapit; id est, nullum saporem habet in hiis que Dei sunt. Qui ergo talis est quasi[3] nihil bene iudicat et ab omnibus[4] iudicatur. Sed habens mentem sanam et appetitum rectum, et qui est studiosus, id est bonus et sanctus et spiritualis, ille, quasi elevatus super omnia terrena, recte iudicabit de omnibus et a nullo poterit iudicari:[5] id est, reprehendi. Propter quod in tercio *Ethicorum* scribitur quod studiosus[6] 'singula iudicat recte[7] et in singulis ei verum apparet.' Simile est itaque de lingua et de mente, ut sicut habens infectam linguam non bene iudicat de saporibus, sic habens infectam mentem non bene iudicat de moribus. Spiritualis ergo et sanctus homo iudicat omnia et ipse a nemine iudicatur: id est, a nemine in suo iudicio reprehenditur.

Redeamus[8] ergo ad propositum et dicamus quod duplex est perfeccio, duplex sanctitas sive duplex spiritualitas. Una est personalis, alia[9] secundum statum, ut status clericorum est perfeccior statu laicorum et prelatorum quam subditorum. Sed si loquamur de perfeccione personali, multi sunt laici qui sunt sancciores et spiritualiores quam multi clerici, et multi subditi quam multi prelati. Semper tamen, secundum modum suum, veritatem habet quod Apostolus ait primo ad Corinthios II: quod 'spiritualis[10] iudicat omnia et ipse a nemine iudicatur.' Ut si accipiatur huiusmodi spiritualitas prout est[11] personalis et secundum mundiciam consciencie, qui talis est recte iudicabit de moribus et a nullo reprehendetur secundum mores. Tales autem spiritu Dei aguntur et filii Dei sunt. Tales quidem, licet nesciant cursus astrorum et proporciones geometricas et cavillaciones logicas,[12] sciunt tamen ea que sunt eis necessaria ad salutem, quia 'Unccio', id est Spiritus Sanctus, docet eos de omnibus partibus[13] et eis necessariis ad salutem. Sicut ergo iudex[14] qui[15] afficitur ad partes[16] numquam[17] bene iudicat de[18] partibus, sic qui afficitur ad illicitos mores[19] numquam bene iudicat de moribus.

1: est] *om.* FPV¹V²　　2: nec] est *add.* C　　3: quasi] quia V²　　4: omnibus] hominibus V¹　　5: poterit iudicari] iudicari poterit PV¹　　6: studiosus] *del.* P　*om.* V¹ enim *add.* FV²　　7: singula iudicat recte] recte iudicat singula PV¹'　　8: Redeamus] respondemus FV²　　9: alia] est *add.* V¹ 10: spiritualis] *del.* P. V¹ autem *add.* FV²　　11: prout est] *om.* PV¹　　12: logicas] loycas FV² 13: omnibus partibus] omnibus particularibus C partibus omnibus F　　14: iudex] radix FV² 15: qui] que F　　16: partes] illicitos mores FV²　　17: numquam] *add.* partes F　　18: partibus et … de] *om.* V²　　19: illicitos mores] mores illicitos C

seem to him, and so does he live and so does he speak. For example, the glutton is always speaking of food, and his whole life will be ordered towards food. He will not eat so that he may live; rather, he will live so that he may eat: his belly will be his god.[1] And because one who is thus disordered with respect to gluttony and drawn towards food will not judge well concerning the use of foods, and will be judged by all, that is, will be condemned by all because he will not give a correct judgment of such use, he who is disordered and who does not have a healthy mind, and who is neither holy nor spiritual, is a bestial man and not a man of taste: that is, he has no taste in those things which are of God. He who is such, therefore, judges almost nothing well, and is judged by all. But he who has a healthy mind and a rightly disposed appetite, and who is zealous, that is, good and holy and spiritual,[2] will judge all things rightly, being as it were elevated above all earthly considerations; and he will be subject to the judgment, that is, to the condemnation, of no one. For it is written at *Ethics* 3 that the zealous man 'judges each class of things rightly, and the truth appears to him in each.'[3] And so the tongue and the mind are similar in that, just as he who has a disordered tongue does not judge tastes well, so he who has a disordered mind does not judge well in matters of morals. Therefore, the spiritual and holy man judges all things and is himself judged by no one: that is, he is not condemned in his judgment by anyone.

Let us return to our proposition, therefore, and say that perfection or sanctity or spirituality is of two kinds: the one is personal, the other according to status. Thus, the status of the clergy is more perfect than the status of laymen, and that of rulers than that of subjects; but if we speak of personal perfection, there are many laymen who are holier and more spiritual than many clerics, and many subjects who are more so than many rulers. Nonetheless, what the Apostle says at I Corinthians 2 always has truth according to its own fashion: that the spiritual man judges all things and is himself judged by no one. For if such spirituality be considered insofar as it is personal and according to purity of conscience, then he who is such will judge rightly in moral matters and will be condemned by no one on moral grounds. For such persons are guided by the Spirit of God and are sons of God. No matter how ignorant they may be of the courses of the stars and the proportions of geometry and the niceties of logic, such persons will nonetheless understand those things which are necessary to them for salvation. For 'the anointing', that is, the Holy Spirit, teaches them of all things and [especially] in those things necessary to them for salvation.[4] Therefore, just as a judge who is favourably inclined towards one of the parties never judges between the parties well, so one who is favourably inclined towards those things which are morally forbidden never judges well in

1. Phil. 3:19; cf. Isidore of Seville, *Eymologiae* 2:21:13 (PL 82:136).
2. Cf. I Cor. 14:12.
3. *Ethics* 3:4 (1113ª29).
4. This sentence seems intended as gloss on I John 2:27, of which it is a somewhat awkward paraphrase.

Sic ergo censendum est de[1] perfeccione et de[2] spiritualitate personali,[3] quia consistit in mundicia consciencie.

Sed si loquamur de perfeccione et de[4] spiritualitate secundum statum, et potissime secundum statum prelatorum, qui consistit in iurisdiccione et in plenitudine potencie, sic qui est in[5] sancciori et alciori statu de pluribus iudicabit et non poterit a suis inferioribus iudicari; quia, ut ait Apostolus prima ad Corinthios IV: 'Qui autem iudicat me, Dominus est.' Ille itaque qui est in statu omnino supremo et omnino[6] sanctissimo, ille est homo spiritualis qui secundum suam potenciam et iurisdiccionem iudicat omnia, quia est dominus omnium, et ipse a nemine iudicatur, quia nemo mortalis sibi dominatur.

Videmus autem sensibiliter quod qui vult de aliis iudicare oportet quod sit eleva-tus super alia.[7] Qui autem est depressus et est in fovea, quasi nihil offertur oculis suis,[8] et ideo quasi de nihilo poterit iudicare. Sed qui est elevatus in[9] altum, cuius visus non habebit obstaculum, ille poterit de aliis iudicare. Iuxta[10] ergo duplicem perfeccionem et duplicem spiritualitatem[11] duplicem dicemus esse elevacionem, ut ille qui est spiritualis et perfectus personaliter est elevatus a mundo, et est elevatus super alios, secundum nitorem consciencie. Talis autem, quia est elevatus a mundo, poterit iudicare de mundo, id est de hominibus mundanis, asserens quod[12] eorum opera mala sunt. Talis quidem[13] benefaciens obmutescere faciet imprudenciam homi-num; propter quod non poterit ab aliis iudicari, id est non poterit[14] racionabiliter reprehendi. Sed qui est perfectus et sanctus et spiritualis secundum statum, et potis-sime secundum statum prelacionis, ille est elevatus secundum iurisdiccionem et secundum plenitudinem potencie. Ille omnia iudicabit, id est omnibus dominabitur, et non[15] poterit a nemine iudicari, id est nullus poterit sibi[16] dominari. Talis autem est Summus Pontifex, cuius status est sanctissimus et spiritualissimus. Ideo[17] omnes debent eum appellare Sanctissimum Patrem, et omnes debent se offerre ad eius oscula pedum[18] beatorum.

Que omnia[19] referendo ad statum habent veritatem necessariam, sed referendo ad personam habent veritatem secundum decenciam. Nam decens est quod qui est in statu sanctissimo et spiritualissimo, quod ipse[20] secundum perfeccionem personalem sit sanctissimus et spiritualissimus. Est eciam hoc racionabile et probabile, ut ille pro quo tota Ecclesia orat, quod sit spiritualis et sanctus. Ideo dicimus de illa[21] Sede quod vel sanctum recipit vel sanctum facit. Quare, si status Summi Pontificis est sanctissimus et spiritualissimus, et talis spiritualitas consistit in eminencia potencie, bene dictum est

---

1: de] *om.* C   2: de] *om.* C   3: personali] particulari F   4: de] *om.* V[1]   5: in] *om.* V[1]
6: omnino] *om.* V[1]   7: alia] omnia C   8: oculis suis] suis oculis F   9: in] oculis *add.* C
10: Iuxta] iure F   11: spiritualitatem] spiritualem F   12: quod] quia *mss*   13: quidem]
om. FV[2]   14: ab aliis ... poterit] *om.* F   15: non] *om.* V[1]   16: nullus poterit sibi] sibi
nullus poterit C   17: Ideo] *om.* F   18: oscula pedum] pedum oscula FV[2]   19: omnia] *om.* C
20: ipse] *del.* P est *add.* V[1]   21: illa] de *add.* V[1]

moral matters. In this way, therefore, must personal perfection and spirituality be understood, for it consists in purity of conscience.

But if we speak of perfection and spirituality according to status, and especially according to the status of the prelates, which consists in jurisdiction and in fullness of power, then he who occupies the holier and higher status will judge the more things and will not be able to be judged by his inferiors; for, as the Apostle says at I Corinthians 4, 'He who judges me is the Lord.'[1] Thus, he who occupies the status which is entirely supreme and entirely holy is that spiritual man who, according to his power and jurisdiction, judges all things, because he is lord of all things, and is himself judged by no one, because no mortal man is his lord.

Moreover, we see by reference to the senses that he who wishes to judge other things must be elevated above other things, but that he who is sunk down and in a pit has almost nothing presented to his eyes and so will be able to judge almost nothing. But he who is elevated on a height, whose vision will have no obstacle, will be able to judge other things. We shall say, therefore, that there are two kinds of elevation, answering to the two kinds of perfection and the two kinds of spirituality. Thus, he who is personally spiritual and perfected is elevated above the world, and is elevated over others, according to clearness of conscience; and such a man, because he is elevated above the world, will be able to judge the world: that is, worldly men, asserting that their works are evil. Indeed, by his good works such a one will strike the folly of men dumb; for it will not be possible for him to be judged by others: that is, it will not be possible to condemn him for any reason. But he who is perfected and holy and spiritual according to status, and especially according to the status of prelate, is elevated according to jurisdiction and according to fullness of power. He will judge all things, that is, he will be lord of all things; and he will not be subject to the judgment of anyone: that is, no one will be able to be his lord. And such a one is the Supreme Pontiff, whose status is the holiest and most spiritual of all. Thus, all men must call him Most Holy Father, and all must present themselves to kiss his blessed feet.

Insofar as they refer to status, all these things have necessary truth; but insofar as they refer to the person, they have truth only according to fitness.[2] It is fitting, however, that he who occupies the holiest and most spiritual status of all should himself be most holy and most spiritual according to personal perfection; and it is reasonable and probable that he for whom the whole Church prays is indeed spiritual and holy. And so we say of that See[3] that it either receives a saint or makes a saint.[4] If, therefore the status of the Supreme Pontiff is the holiest and most spiritual of all, and if such spirituality consists in eminence of power, then it is well said

1. I Cor. 4:4.
2. I.e. the 'perfection' which constitutes the jurisdiction of an office belongs to it regardless of whether its occupant is a good man or not; but personal perfection is attributed only contingently: not to the man *qua* man, but only to the good man. See also n. 1 on p. 193.
3. I.e. of the Apostolic See.
4. Cf. Ennodius of Pavia, *Libellus adversus eos qui contra synodum scribere praesumpserunt* (ed. W. Hartel, CCSL 6:295); Gregory VII, *Dictatus papae* 23: *Registrum* (ed. E. Caspar, MGH *Epist.* 2:1), p. 201.

quod Summus Pontifex, existens spiritualissimus[1] secundum statum et secundum eminenciam potencie, omnia iudicat, id est omnibus dominatur, et ipse a nemine poterit iudicari: id est, nemo poterit sibi[2] dominari nec eciam equari.[3]

CAPITULUM III: *Quod Summus Pontifex est tante potencie quod ipse est illa potestas sublimis cui omnis anima debet esse subiecta.*

Ut ait Apostolus in epistola ad Romanos: 'Omnis anima potestatibus sublimioribus subdita sit.' Ponitur enim[4] ibi 'anima'[5] pro toto homine; propter quod glossa, hoc[6] exponens, ait quod 'debemus esse ita perfecti in corpore Christi, ut omnis anima, id est omnis homo, subdita[7] sit, id est subiecta[8] sit, potestatibus sublimioribus.' Est enim homo compositus ex anima et carne, et cum hee sint due partes hominis, consuevit Scriptura Sacra[9] per utramque partem significare totum. Nam aliquando quidem in Scriptura Sacra per 'carnem'[10] significatur totus homo, iuxta illud quod scribitur in Iohanne: 'Verbum caro factum est,'[11] id est factus est homo, ut exponit Augustinus II *De Trinitate.* Sic[12] eciam, cum dicitur 'Et videbit omnis caro salutare Dei,' ibi eciam 'caro' ponitur pro toto homine, quia ut ibidem Augustinus ait: 'Caro sine mente vel sine anima non poterit videre salutare Dei.' Ponitur ergo ibi 'caro' pro toto homine: pro anima videlicet[13] et carne. Et sicut 'caro' ponitur pro toto homine,[14] ita et 'anima', que est altera pars compositi, poterit poni pro toto homine, sicut in loco preassignato, cum ait Apostolus quod 'omnis anima,' id est omnis homo, sit subditus potestatibus sublimioribus.

Nec vacat a misterio quod aliquando pro toto homine ponitur 'caro', aliquando 'anima'. Nam cum vellet Iohannes Evangelista tractare de Verbo sive de Dei Filio, quomodo[15] factus erat visibilis et quomodo[16] habitavit inter nos, maluit loqui de 'carne' quam de 'anima', eo quod est nobis magis visibilis et sensibilis[17] caro quam anima,[18] et pocius dicere voluit quod Verbum factum est caro quam Verbum factum est anima. Econverso autem in proposito,[19] Apostolus, volens tractare de obediencia et de[20] subieccione quam debent inferiores suis superioribus, quia huiusmodi obediencia debet fieri voluntarie et secundum mentem et secundum animam, ideo pocius[21] voluit[22] per 'animam' intelligere totum hominem quam per 'carnem'. Propter quod glossa, hoc exponens, ait quod omnis[23] anima subdita sit potestatibus sublimioribus quia 'non solum corpore, sed et voluntate,' ut ait, 'servire debemus.'

Huiusmodi itaque potestas sublimis[24] cui subdita debet esse omnis anima est uterque[25] gladius spiritualis et materialis. Nam regibus et principibus secularibus debemus esse subiecti, et eciam nostris[26] prelatis spiritualibus debemus humiliter

---

1: et talis ... spiritualissimus] *om.* V[1]   2: poterit sibi] sibi poterit CFV[2]   3: equari] equiparari F
4: Ponitur enim] videtur V[1]   5: ibi anima] anima ibi FV[2]   6: hoc] *om.* PV[1]   7: subdita] subditus F   8: subiecta] subiectus F   9: Sacra] *om.* F   10: per carnem] pro caro F   11: caro factum est] factum est caro PV[1]   12: Sic] sicut V[1]   13: videlicet] visibili P   14: pro anima ... homine] *om.* V[1]   15: quomodo] quando V[1]   16: quomodo] quando V[1]   17: sensibilis] stabilis F
18: eo quod ... anima] *om.* V[1]V[2]   19: in proposito] *om.* F   20: de] *om.* F   21: pocius] apostolus *add.* F   22: voluit] apostolus *add.* PV[1]V[2]   23: omnis] cum *mss*   24: potestas sublimis] potestatis sublimitati P   potestatis sublimitas V[1]   25: uterque] utique F   26: nostris] *del.* P   *om.* V[1]

that the Supreme Pontiff, being the most spiritual man according to status and according to eminence of power, judges all things, that is, is lord of all things, and will himself be subject to the judgment of no one: that is, no one will be able to be his lord or even his equal.

CHAPTER III: *That the Supreme Pontiff is of such great power that he himself is that sublime power to which every soul must be subject.*

As the Apostle says in the Epistle to the Romans, 'Let every soul be subject to the higher powers.'[1] Now 'soul' there stands for the whole man; and so, interpreting this, a gloss says that 'We must be so perfected in the Body of Christ that every soul, that is, every man, is subject to, that is, is set under, the higher powers.'[2] For a man is composed of soul and flesh; and, since there are these two parts of man, it is the custom of Sacred Scripture to signify the whole by one or other of the parts. For sometimes, indeed, the whole man is signified in Sacred Scripture by 'flesh', according to what is written in John: 'The Word was made flesh,'[3] that is, as Augustine explains at *De Trinitate* 2, was made man.[4] So also, when it is said, 'And all flesh shall see the salvation of God,'[5] 'flesh' there again stands for the whole man; for, as Augustine says in the same place: 'Flesh without mind or without soul will not be able to see the salvation of God.' Therefore, 'flesh' there stands for the whole man: that is, for soul and flesh. And just as 'flesh' stands for the whole man, so too 'soul', which is his other component part, will be able to stand for the whole man, as in the place already cited, when the Apostle says that 'every soul,' that is, every man, must be subject to the higher powers.

Nor is it without symbolic purpose that sometimes 'flesh' should stand for the whole man and sometimes 'soul'. For when John the Evangelist wished to treat of how the Word, or the Son of God, was made visible and of how He dwelt among us, he preferred to speak of 'flesh' rather than 'soul', since it is flesh rather than soul which is visible and perceptible to us; and so he chose to say that the Word was made flesh rather than that the Word was made soul. But, on the other side of the question, the Apostle wishes to treat of the obedience and submission which inferiors owe to their superiors; and so, since such obedience must be given willingly and with the mind and with the soul, he chose to designate the whole man by 'soul' rather than by 'flesh'. Hence, interpreting this, the gloss says that every soul must be subject to the higher powers because, as it says, 'we must serve not only in body, but also with the will.'[6]

Thus, that sublime power to which every soul must be subject is both a spiritual and a material sword. For we must be subject to kings and secular princes, yet we must also humbly obey our spiritual prelates. Hence also, the gloss

1. Rom. 13:1.
2. Peter Lombard, *Collectanea in omnes de Pauli apostoli epistolas*, PL 191:1504.
3. John 1:14.
4. *De Trinitate* 2:6 (CCSL 50:94).
5. Luke 3:6.
6. Peter Lombard, loc. cit.

obedire. Unde et glossa hoc exponit de potestatibus secularibus, dicens: 'Omnis ergo anima subdita sit potestatibus[1] secularibus, bonis vel malis regibus, principibus, tribunis, centurionibus et aliis huiusmodi'; et subdit quod: 'Si bonus fuerit[2] qui tibi preest, est tuus nutritor, si malus, est tuus temptator.' Sub utroque ergo, tam sub principante[3] bono quam sub malo, possumus proficere: sub bono quidem, quia per ipsum nutrimur et sic perficimur et proficimus;[4] sub malo vero quia per ipsum temptamur et per consequens probamur et purgamur.

Advertendum tamen quod glossa, in exponendo quod omnis anima sit[5] subdita potestatibus sublimioribus, potissime[6] descendit ad potestates seculares quia fideles non dubitabant quod[7] subditi esse deberent potestatibus spiritualibus. Dubitabant tantum utrum deberent subici potestatibus secularibus. Ideo glosse specialiter mencionem faciunt de secularibus potestatibus ut eciam talibus potestatibus fideles voluntarie serviant. Ipsa tamen verba textus secundum eorum sentenciam potissime competunt potestatibus spiritualibus. Nam cum ibi fiat[8] mencio de 'anima' ut[9] mente et voluntate[10] serviamus, hoc maxime faciendum[11] est circa spirituales potestates,[12] quibus mente et voluntate servire[13] debemus, quia potestates spirituales[14] non habent immediate et per se ipsas iudicium sanguinis, sed huiusmodi iudicium exercent per ministros alios et per potestates seculares.

Ergo potestates spirituales[15] requirunt quod mente et voluntate serviatur eis. Sed potestates seculares,[16] si non[17] servias eis voluntate et mente, cogent te per iudicium sanguinis et eciam per mortem, que est finis omnium terribilium, ut dicitur in *Ethicis*. Prelati quidem ecclesiastici per censuram ecclesiasticam et per excommunicacionem, numquam per iudicium sanguinis, hoc exercent. Immo, in Ecclesia talia exercentes iudicantur irregulares: non quod hoc agere sit peccatum, iubente[18] Domino, 'Non facieris maleficos vivere,' sed quia Ecclesia non debet habere maculam nec[19] rugam nec indecenciam aliquam. Quia quedam[20] indecencia esset quod[21] spiritualiter presidens[22] per se iudicium sanguinis exerceret. Ideo talia exercentur per seculares potestates.

Dicamus ergo quod si non obediatur potestatibus secularibus, racione iudicii sanguinis et quia habent materialem gladium qui potenciam habet in res corporales occidetur corpus; sed si non obediatur potestatibus spiritualibus, quia[23] huiusmodi potestates habent[24] spiritualem gladium qui pertingit usque ad animam et per inobedienciam potest eam separare a communione fidelium, ideo per talem gladium occiditur[25] anima. Nam sicut membrum amputatum a corpore de necessitate est

1: potestatibus] sublimioribus in voluntate serviat potestatibus *add.* C   2: fuerit] fuit F   3: principante] principe V[1]   4: perficimur et proficimus] perficimur C   proficimus et perficimur F   proficimus V[2]   5: sit] est C   6: potissime] *om.* F   7: quod] quin FPV[2]   8: ibi fiat] ibi fiat ideo PV[1] ideo ibi fiat FV[2]   9: ut] et F   10: voluntate] voluntarie F   11: faciendum] fiendum V[2]   12: spirituales potestates] potestates spirituales F   13: quibus mente ... servire] quibus mentem et voluntatem secundum ius F   14: potestates spirituales] spirituales potestates FV[2]   15: potestates spirituales] spirituales potestates FV[2]   16: potestates seculares] seculares potestates FV[2]   17: non] nisi V[2]   18: iubente] inhibente F   19: nec] neque V[1]   20: quedam] quidem F   21: quod] qua de F   22: presidens] residens FV[2]   23: quia] quum F   24: habent] habeat F   25: occiditur] occidetur F

interprets this [i.e. Romans 13:1] with reference to the secular powers, saying: 'Therefore let every soul be subject to the secular powers: to kings, princes, tribunes, rulers of hundreds and others such, whether good or bad.' And it adds that: 'If he who rules over you is good, he is your succour; if bad, he is your tempter.'[1] Under each, therefore, whether under a good ruler or under a bad, we are able to profit: under a good indeed, because we are sustained by him and so perfected and profited; and under a bad since, through him, we are tempted and consequently proved and purified.

It should be noted, however, that, in explaining that every soul should be subject to the higher powers, the gloss devotes special attention to the secular powers because the faithful did not doubt that they should be subject to the spiritual powers: they doubted only whether they should be subject to the secular powers. And so the glosses make special mention of the secular powers in order that the faithful might serve such powers willingly. Nonetheless, according to their sense the words of the text [of Romans 13:1] apply to the spiritual powers especially. For since mention is there made of 'soul' so that we should serve in mind and will, this service must above all be performed in relation to the spiritual powers, whom we must serve in mind and will because the spiritual powers do not have the judgment of blood immediately and in themselves, but execute such judgment through other ministers and through the secular powers.

The spiritual powers, therefore, require that the mind and will should serve them; but the secular powers, if you do not serve them in will and mind, compel you by the judgment of blood, and even by death, which, as is said in the *Ethics*, is the most terrible of all ends.[2] The prelates of the Church, however, accomplish this by means of ecclesiastical censure and through excommunication, never by the judgment of blood. Indeed, those within the Church who execute such judgments are deemed irregular:[3] not because it is a sin to do so — for the Lord has commanded, 'You shall not suffer a witch to live'[4] — but because the Church must have neither spot nor blemish nor any unseemliness.[5] For it would be a kind of unseemliness if, while ruling spiritually, she herself were also to execute the judgment of blood. Thus, such judgments are executed through the secular powers.

Let us say, therefore, that, if obedience is not given to the secular powers, the body will be slain by reason of the judgment of blood and because they have the material sword which holds sway in bodily matters. But if obedience is not given to the spiritual powers, then, because such powers have the spiritual sword, which strikes through to the soul and can separate it from the communion of the faithful for disobedience, the soul is slain by that sword. For just as a limb amputated from

---

1. Ibid.; cf. Exod. 18:25.
2. *Ethics* 3:6 (1115ª25).
3. That is, they incur canonical irregularity impeding them from the reception of tonsure and Holy Orders or preventing the exercise of orders already received. See Dist. 50, c. 4: *Miror* (CIC I:178); Cf. Aquinas, *Summa theologiae* IIaIIae 40:2.
4. Exod. 22:18.
5. Cf. Eph. 5:27.

membrum mortuum, quia ulterius non[1] potest cor in membrum sic abscissum[2] infundere[3] opera vite, sic anima non obediens potestatibus spiritualibus per censuram ecclesiasticam est spiritualiter mortua, quia spiritualis gracie influenciam sic[4] separata et[5] abscissa a communione fidelium participare non poterit.

Quare, si potestates seculares habent potenciam super totum hominem, quia eis non solum corpore sed eciam voluntate[6] servire debemus, huiusmodi tamen[7] potestas non competet eis nisi racione corporis seu racione rerum corporalium, quia materialis gladius, quem non sine causa portare dicuntur, per se et directe solas res corporales potest attingere. Sed spiritualis potestas, cuius instrumentum est spiritualis gladius qui ipsam animam attingit, potestatem habet in totum hominem racione anime. Et quia inter spirituales potestates potestas Summi Pontificis est omnino celsior et sublimior, bene dictum est quod potencia Summi Pontificis est[8] illa sublimis potestas cui omnis anima debet[9] esse subiecta; que, ut patet per habita, tanto excelsior[10] et nobilior est omni potestate terrena et seculari quanto anima est excellencior et nobilior corpore et quanto spiritualis vita excellencior[11] quam terrena.

CAPITULUM IV: *Quod spiritualis potestas instituere habet terrenam potestatem et, si terrena potestas bona non fuerit, spiritualis potestas eam poterit iudicare.*

Hugo de Sancto Victore, in libro *De sacramentis fidei Christiane* [libro secundo,] parte secunda, capitulo quarto, ait quod spiritualis potestas terrenam potestatem et instituere habet et iudicare[12] si bona non fuerit. Igitur[13] de Ecclesia et de potestate ecclesiastica verificatur illud vaticinium Ieremie: 'Ecce, constitui te hodie super gentes et regna, ut evellas et destruas et[14] disperdas et dissipes, edifices et plantes.' Illud[15] itaque vaticinium de ipso Ieremia[16] fuit impletum quando aliqua prophetavit de destruccione et edificacione aliquorum regnorum, propter quod per spiritum prophecie constitutus fuit super regna, ut ipsa edificaret[17] quantum ad regna de quibus prophetavit edificacionem; et constitutus est super ea, ut ipsa destrueret quantum ad regna de quibus prophetavit destruccionem. Istud tamen vaticinium[18] hodie de ipsa impletur Ecclesia, ut dicat Dominus[19] Ecclesie: 'Ecce, hodie,' id est a die qua formata[20] es, 'constitui te super gentes et regna, ut destruas et evellas ea de suo loco transferendo, edifices et plantes, ipsa quidem regna in loco alio edificando

1: ulterius non] non ulterius CFV² 2: abscissum] abrasum V² 3: infundere] influere FV²
4: sic] sit C 5: et] *om.* CPV¹V² 6: voluntate] voluntarie C 7: tamen] enim V¹ 8: omnino
celsior ... est] *om.* FV² 9: debet] dicitur F 10: excelsior] excellencior CFV² 11: excellencior] est *add.* FV² 12: habet et iudicare] *om.* F 13: Igitur] ergo F 14: et] *om.* C 15: Illud]
istud CFV² 16: Ieremia] Iesu F 17: edificaret] edificet CFV² 18: vaticinium] tamen *add.* V¹
19: Dominus] deus C 20: formata] fabricata PV¹

the body is of necessity a dead limb, because the heart can no longer infuse the force of life into a member thus cut off, so the soul which does not obey the spiritual powers is spiritually dead by reason of ecclesiastical censure, since that which is thus separated and cut off from the communion of the faithful will not be able to participate in the influx of spiritual grace.

And so, if the secular powers hold sway over the whole man, since we must serve them not only in body but also with the will, such power will nonetheless not belong to them except by reason of the body or by reason of bodily things, since the material sword which they are said to bear not without cause[1] can, of itself and directly, touch only bodily things. But the spiritual power, whose instrument is the spiritual sword which touches the soul itself, has power over the whole man by reason of the soul. And since, among spiritual powers, the power of the Supreme Pontiff is altogether higher and more sublime, it is well said that the power of the Supreme Pontiff is that sublime power to which every soul must be subject; which, as is clear from what has been said, is as much more exalted and noble than any earthly and secular power as the soul is more excellent and noble than the body and the spiritual life more excellent than the earthly.[2]

CHAPTER IV: *That the spiritual power must institute the earthly power, and if the earthly power is not good, the spiritual power will be able to judge it.*

Hugh of Saint Victor, in the book *De sacramentis fidei Christianae* 2:2:4,[3] says that the spiritual power must both institute the earthly power and judge it if it is not good. Thus, that prophecy of Jeremiah is shown to be true of the Church and of ecclesiastical power: 'Behold, I have today placed you above nations and kingdoms, to uproot and destroy and disperse and scatter, to build and to plant.'[4] This prophecy was brought to fulfilment in Jeremiah himself whenever he prophesied the destruction and building of any kingdoms. For, through the spirit of prophecy, he was placed above kingdoms: to build, as regards the kingdoms for which he prophesied building; and he was placed above them to destroy, as regards the kingdoms for which he prophesied destruction. Today, however, that prophecy is fulfilled in the Church herself, as though the Lord had said to the Church: 'Behold, today,' that is, from the day on which you were formed, 'I have placed you above nations and kingdoms, to destroy and uproot by transferring them from their place, and to build and to plant by building and planting those same kingdoms in

1. Rom. 13:4.
2. Cf. Hugh of Saint Victor, *De sacramentis* 2:2:4 (PL 176:417).
3. PL 176:418.
4. Jer. 1:10. This verse is frequently quoted or paraphrased by authors on both sides of the papalist debate: see, for example, the Bulls *Novit* and *Ausculta fili* as quoted at Introduction, pp. xiv and xvi. It appears also in the Bull *Unam sanctam.* See too the contemporary pamphlet *Rex pacificus* (ed. R.W. Dyson, *Quaestio de potestate papae (Rex pacificus)*, Lewiston, Queenston, Lampeter: Edwin Mellen, 1999), p. 95. St Bernard of Clairvaux, *De consideratione* 2:6, whom no doubt Giles has in mind, is the first author to apply it specifically to the pope. See Introduction, n. 14.

et plantando.' Quod et[1] alias factum est, quia Summus Pontifex transtulit imperium de oriente in occidentem,[2] ut in iuris sciencia est notatum.[3]

Concordant itaque rerum gesta cum auctoritate doctorum. Nam, ut patuit per Hugonem, spiritualis potestas habet potestatem terrenam instituere et habet de ea utrum bona sit iudicare; quod non esset nisi posset eam plantare et evellere. Plantare quidem eam potest, prout eam instituit; evellere vero, prout de ipsa iudicat an sit bona. In hoc itaque negocio non solum rerum gesta concordant auctoritati, quia Hugo hoc asserit et Ecclesia transferendo imperium non solum de iure sed de facto hoc fecit: sed et[4] prophetarum vaticinia sunt in hac materia conformia racioni, quia et Ieremias hoc prophetavit, quod potest exponi de Ecclesia, quod sit constituta super gentes et regna; et eciam hoc naturalis[5] racio persuadet.

Possumus enim ex ordine universi hoc liquido declarare, quod super gentes et regna sit Ecclesia constituta. Nam secundum Dionysium in *De angelica hierarchia*, lex divinitatis est infima in suprema per media reducere. Hoc ergo requirit ordo universi: ut infima in suprema per media reducantur. Si enim eque immediate infima reducerentur in suprema sicut et media, non esset universum recte ordinatum; quod est inconveniens dicere, et potissime in istis[6] potestatibus et auctoritatibus. Quod patet ex sentencia Apostoli ad Romanos XIII, qui, cum prius dixisset quod non est potestas nisi a Deo, postea immediate subiungit: 'Que autem sunt a Deo, ordinata sunt.' Si ergo duo sunt[7] gladii, unus spiritualis et alter temporalis, ut potest patere ex sentencia evangelii, 'Ecce gladii duo[8] hic,' ubi statim subiungit Dominus, 'Satis est,' quia[9] hii duo gladii sufficiunt in Ecclesia: oportet hos duos gladios, has duas auctoritates et potestates, a Deo esse; quia, ut dictum est, non est potestas nisi a Deo. Sic autem oportet hec ordinata esse, quia, ut tangebamus, que sunt a Deo oportet ordinata esse. Non essent autem ordinata nisi unus gladius reduceretur per alterum et nisi unus esset sub alio; quia, ut dictum est per Dionysium, hoc requirit lex divinitatis quam Deus dedit universis rebus creatis: id est, hoc requirit ordo universi, id est universarum creaturarum, ut non omnia eque immediate reducantur in suprema, sed infima per media et inferiora per superiora. Gladius ergo temporalis, tamquam inferior,[10] reducendus est per spiritualem tamquam per superiorem, et unus ordinandus[11] est sub alio tamquam inferior sub superiori.

1: et] *om.* F   2: occidentem] occidente FV²   3: notatum] vocatum F   4: et] est C
5: naturalis] universalis F   6: istis] ipsis CFV²   7: duo sunt] sunt duo CFV²   8: gladii duo]
duo gladii CF   9: quia] quod FV²   10: tamquam inferior] *om.* F   11: unus ordinandus]
materialis ordinatus F

another place.' For this has indeed been accomplished already, because the Supreme Pontiff has transferred the empire from the east to the west, as is recorded in the science of the law.[1]

Established facts, then, are in agreement with the authority of the learned. For, as is shown by Hugh, the spiritual power must institute the earthly power and must judge whether it be good, which would not be so unless it could plant and uproot it. It can indeed plant it inasmuch as it institutes it, and it certainly uproots it inasmuch as it judges whether it is good. In this matter, however, not only do established facts agree with authority (for Hugh asserts this, and the Church, by transferring the empire, has accomplished it not only *de iure* but also *de facto*): also, the utterances of the prophets on this subject are in conformity with reason. For Jeremiah himself has made this prophecy, which can be interpreted as applying to the Church: that she is placed above nations and kingdoms; and natural reason also confirms this.

For we can clearly show from the order of the universe that the Church is placed above nations and kingdoms. For according to Dionysius in *De angelica hierarchia*, it is the law of Divinity to lead the lowest back to the highest through the intermediate.[2] The order of the universe therefore requires this: that the lowest be led back to the highest through the intermediate. For if the lowest and the intermediate were both to be led back to the highest immediately and in the same fashion, the universe would not be rightly ordered. And that it is incorrect to say this, especially of the powers and authorities, is clear from what the Apostle says at Romans 13, who, when he had first said that there is no power except of God, immediately afterwards added: 'and the powers that be are ordained of God.'[3] If there are two swords, therefore, the one spiritual and the other temporal — as can be shown from what is said in the Gospel, 'Behold, here are two swords,' where the Lord at once added, 'It is enough';[4] for these two swords are sufficient in the Church — then these two swords, these two authorities and powers, must be of God; for, as has been said, there is no power except of God. And so they must be ordained [i.e. arranged in their proper order], since, as we have noted, those [powers] which are of God must be ordained. But they would not be ordained unless the one sword were led by the other and unless the one were under the other; for, as Dionysius has said, the law of Divinity which God has given to all created things requires this: that is, the order of the universe (that is, of all creatures) requires not that all things be led back to the highest immediately and in the same fashion, but that the lowest be led through the intermediate and the inferior through the superior. The temporal sword, therefore, as inferior, must be led by the spiritual as by a superior, and the one must be ordained under the other as inferior under superior.

1. See Introduction, n. 41. Given Giles's general interest in the decretals of Innocent III, the phrase *in iuris sciencia* may be intended as a reference to *Venerabilem* (X. 1:6:34: CIC II:79).
2. Ps.-Dionysius, *De angelica hierarchia* 10 (PG 175:1099).
3. Rom. 13:1.
4. Luke 22:38.

Sed[1] diceret aliquis quod reges et principes debent esse subiecti spiritualiter, non temporaliter, ut, secundum hoc, sit intelligendum quod dictum est[2] quod reges et principes spiritualiter, non temporaliter, subsint Ecclesie. Sed temporalia ipsa, diceret aliquis, Ecclesia recognoscit[3] ex dominio temporali, ut patuit[4] ex donacione et collacione quam fecit Ecclesie Constantinus. Sed sic dicentes vim argumenti[5] non capiunt. Nam si solum spiritualiter reges et principes subessent Ecclesie, non esset gladius sub gladio, non essent temporalia sub spiritualibus, non esset ordo in potestatibus, non reducerentur infima in suprema per media. Si igitur hec ordinata sunt, oportet gladium temporalem sub spirituali, oportet sub vicario Christi regna[6] existere; et de iure, licet aliqui de facto contrarie agant, oportet Christi vicarium super ipsis temporalibus habere dominium. Quia, etsi aliqua iura videntur dicere quod de facto, non de iure, a seculari curia ad Ecclesiam appellatur, exponenda sunt talia verba de iure consueto; vel possumus dicere quod simpliciter Ecclesia habet quoddam dominium super temporalibus. Sed quomodo[7] ex hoc appelletur[8] ad ipsam in ultima parte dicetur. Nam de iure, simpliciter dominans spiritualiter per quandam excellenciam, eciam super temporalibus habet dominium; quod si et aliqui timore secularium principum aliter notaverunt, non est eorum auctoritas admittenda. Potest autem Ecclesia animadvertere in seculares principes, cum temporalis gladius sit sub spirituali gladio constitutus.

CAPITULUM V:[9] *In quo adducuntur nove[10] raciones quibus sacerdotalis potestas superior[11] est et[12] dignior omni regia potestate.*

Quod sacerdotalis potestas dignitate et nobilitate precedat potestatem regiam et terrenam apud sapientes dubium esse non potest; quod possumus quadrupliciter declarare:[13] primo, ex decimarum dacione; secundo, ex benediccione et sanctificacione; tercio, ex ipsius potestatis accepcione;[14] quarto, ex ipsarum rerum gubernacione.

Prima via sic patet. Nam ex iure divino[15] et ex institucione divina omnes tenemur[16] ad dandum decimas, ita quod tota terrena potestas,[17] secundum quod terrena et[18] temporalis est, tenetur dare decimas[19] spirituali potestati. Dantur autem huiusmodi decime in recognicionem proprie servitutis, ut quilibet recognoscat[20] se servum Dei.

1: Sed] si PV[1]   2: aliquis quod ... dictum est] *om.* V[1]   3: recognoscit] recognoscat C
4: patuit] *om.* PV[1]   5: argumenti] arguendi C   6: regna] regnum V[2]F   7: quomodo]
quando V[1]   8: appelletur] appellaretur FV[1]   9: V] quartum C   10: *nove*] novem *mss*
11: *superior*] *om.* C   12: *et*] *om.* C   13: quadrupliciter declarare] declarare quadrupliciter FV[2]
14: accepcione] acceptacione V[1] institutione V[2]   15: ex iure divino] ex divino imperio FV[2]
16: tenemur] tenebantur FV[2]   17: potestas] que *add.* F   18: secundum quod ... et] *del.* F
19: dare decimas] decimas dare FV[2]   20: recognoscat] recognoscit PV[1]

But someone might say that kings and princes must be subject spiritually but not temporally, so that, according to this view, what has been said must be understood to mean that kings and princes are spiritually, but not temporally, subject to the Church.[1] Someone might also say that the Church has received temporal possessions themselves from a temporal lordship, as is clear from the donation and grant which Constantine made to the Church.[2] But those who speak in this way do not grasp the force of the argument. For if kings and princes were subject to the Church only spiritually, sword would not be under sword, temporal things would not be under spiritual, there would be no order among the powers, and the lowest would not be led back to the highest through the intermediate. If these things are ordained, then, the temporal sword must be under the spiritual, kingdoms must be under the Vicar of Christ, and, *de iure*, even though some may act contrary to this *de facto*, the Vicar of Christ must have lordship even over temporal things. For although certain laws say that appeal is made from a secular court to the Church only *de facto*, not *de iure*, such words must be interpreted as referring only to the normal application of the law.[3] Alternatively, we can say that the Church has a certain kind of lordship over temporal matters absolutely [even if not as a matter of day-to-day practice]. But the way in which appeal may be made to her on this ground will be discussed in the final part. For, *de iure,* simply as lord of spiritual things by reason of a certain excellence, she has lordship over temporal things also. And if any persons have written otherwise for fear of secular princes, their authority is not to be admitted. Rather, [it must be acknowledged that] the Church can act against secular princes because the temporal sword is placed under the spiritual sword.

CHAPTER V: *In which new arguments are adduced showing that priestly power is superior to and greater in dignity than all royal power.*

There can be no doubt among wise men that priestly power precedes royal and earthly power in dignity and nobility. We can show this in four ways: first, from the payment of tithes; second, from blessing and sanctification; third, from the inception of power itself; fourth, from the government of things themselves.

The first way proceeds thus. By divine law and by divine institution, we are all bound to pay tithes; and so every earthly power, inasmuch as it is earthly and temporal, is bound to pay tithes to the spiritual power.[4] And such tithes are paid in recognition of proper servitude, so that each man may acknowledge himself to be

---

1. For this view see, e.g., Huguccio of Pisa, *Summa Dist.* xxiii, c.6, as quoted by Walter Ullmann, *Medieval Papalism,* p. 142, n. 3.
2. See Introduction, n. 53, and Pt. III, Ch. XI.
3. Despite the expression 'certain laws,' it seems clear that Giles has in mind Alexander III's decretal *Si duobus* (X. 2:28:7: CIC II:412), to be discussed fully in Pt. III (see especially Pt. III, Ch. I). See also Introduction, pp. xxvi–xxxi.
4. E.g. Levit. 27:30–33; Num. 18:21, 24; 28:26–27; Deut. 14:22–29; see also X. 3:30:4: *Parochianos vero* (CIC II:561).

Sicut ergo[1] inferiores sunt tributarii[2] suo superiori, ut recognoscant se tenere[3] et habere quod habent a superioribus suis, sic et nos que tenemus et habemus a Deo recepimus,[4] iuxta illud prima ad Corinthios[5] IV: 'Quid habes quod non accepisti?' Dignum est ergo quod de omnibus nostris rebus simus tributarii ipsi Deo. Est enim ipse Deus, ut in alia sciencia scribitur, dives[6] per se ipsum, ceteri[7] autem sunt divites ex mutuatis; mutuavit enim Deus nobis[8] quecumque habemus. Quare non est mirum nec preter racionem si exinde simus[9] censuarii et tributarii ipsi Deo.

Terrena itaque et temporalis potestas, ut terrena est, id est ut fructus terre recipit, et ut temporalis est, id est ut bona temporalia habet, est tributaria et censuaria ecclesiastice potestati, quam, vice Dei recognoscens,[10] in recognicione[11] proprie servitutis debet ei[12] decimas exhibere. Tota ergo terrena potestas est sub ecclesiastica potestate, et specialiter sub Summo Pontifice, qui in ecclesiastica hierarchia est apicem Ecclesie assecutus, sub quo omnes debent esse subiecti, sive reges quasi precellentes sive quicumque alii.

Secunda via ad hoc idem sumitur ex benediccione et sanctificacione; et ista est[13] via Hugonis in *De sacramentis* libro secundo et parte secunda, dicentis[14] quod in Ecclesia Dei sacerdotalis dignitas regalem potestatem sacrat et benedicit. 'Si ergo,' ut ait Apostolus ad Hebreos VII, '"qui benedicit maior est et qui benedicitur minor," constat absque omni[15] dubitacione quod terrena potestas, que a spirituali benediccione accipit, iure inferior estimatur.'

Tercia via sumitur ex ipsius potestatis institucione. Et istam eciam viam tangit Hugo eodem libro et eadem parte, dicens: 'Quod autem spiritualis potestas maior sit dignitate et potestate terrena in illo antiquo Veteris Testamenti[16] populo manifeste declaratur, ubi primum a Deo sacerdocium institutum est, postea vero per sacerdocium,[17] iubente Deo, regalis potestas est ordinata.' Debet ergo regalis potestas sacerdotalem dignitatem superiorem recognoscere tamquam eam per quam, Deo iubente, est[18] instituta. Et[19] si dicatur quod non omnis potestas regia est per sacerdocium instituta, dicemus[20] quod nulla est potestas regia non per sacerdocium instituta que vel[21] non[22] fuerit non[23] recta, propter quod magis erat[24] latrocinium quam potestas; vel[25] non fuerit[26] sacerdocio coniuncta; vel non fuerit[27] institucionem per[28] sacerdocium subsecuta.[29] Nam in lege nature, ubi fuerunt regna gentilium, omnia quasi huiusmodi regna per invasionem et usurpacionem habita sunt. Unde[30] Neroth, quem primum legimus fuisse regem, ut potest haberi Geneseos X, cuius regni principium fuit in Babylone,[31] per invasionem et usurpacionem fecit se regem; unde ibidem dicitur

---

1: ergo] *om.* F   2: tributarii] cubicularii F   3: tenere] *om.* FV[2]   4: recepimus] recipimus F 5: prima ad Corinthios] ad Corinthios prima C   6: dives] autem *add.* FV[2]   7: ceteri] sancti F 8: nobis] *om.* PV[1]   9: simus] sumus FV[2]   10: recognoscens] cognoscens C   11: recognicione] recognitionem C   12: ei] eis *mss*   13: est] *om.* PV[1]   14: dicentis] dicens CFPV[1]   15: omni] *om.* C   16: Testamenti] testamento C   17: est, postea ... sacerdocium] *om.* F   18: est] sit F 19: Et] *om.* F   20: dicemus] ergo *add.* F   21: vel] *del.* F   22: non] nunc V[2]   23: fuerit non] fuit C   24: erat] erit *mss*   25: vel] si F   26: non fuerit] fuit C   27: non fuerit] fuit C 28: institucionem per] institucione post F   29: subsecuta] assecuta C insecuta V[1]   30: Unde] de *add.* C et *add.* FV[2]   31: Babylone] ubi *add.* F

the servant of God. Therefore, just as inferiors are tributaries to their superiors so that they may acknowledge themselves to hold and possess what they have from their superiors, so also have we received from God what we hold and possess, according to I Corinthians 4: 'What have you that you have not received?'[1] It is fitting, therefore, that we be tributaries to God Himself for all our possessions. For, as is written in another science,[2] God Himself is rich in Himself, but others are rich from loans, for God has lent us whatever we have. And so it is neither strange nor beyond reason if, on this account, we should be taxpayers and tributaries to God Himself.

Earthly and temporal power, then, as earthly (that is, inasmuch as it receives the fruits of the earth) and as temporal (that is, inasmuch as it possesses temporal goods), is a tributary and taxpayer to the ecclesiastical power, to which, acknowledging that it stands in the place of God, it is bound to pay tithes in recognition of its own servitude. Every earthly power, therefore, is under the ecclesiastical power, and especially under the Supreme Pontiff, who, in the ecclesiastical hierarchy, has attained to the summit of the Church, and under whom all men — kings, as excelling,[3] and all others — must be subject.

The second way towards the same conclusion is derived from blessing and sanctification; and this is Hugh's way at *De sacramentis* 2:2, where he says that, in the Church of God, the priestly dignity consecrates and blesses royal power. 'Therefore, if "he who blesses is greater and he who is blessed is less,"' as the Apostle says at Hebrews 7, 'it is established beyond all doubt that the earthly power, which receives blessing from the spiritual, is rightly deemed inferior.'[4]

The third way is derived from the institution of power itself. And, in the same book and in the same part, Hugh touches upon this way also, saying: 'Moreover, that the spiritual power is greater in dignity and might than the earthly is manifestly shown among that ancient people of the Old Testament, where, first, priesthood was instituted by God and, subsequently, royal power was ordained through priesthood at the command of God.' Royal power must therefore acknowledge priestly dignity as superior, as being that through which it was instituted at the command of God. And if it be said that not all royal power was instituted through priesthood, we shall reply that any royal power not instituted through priesthood was either not rightful, in that it was more robbery than power; or was united with priesthood; or was the successor of that which had been instituted through priesthood. For where there were kingdoms of the gentiles under the law of nature, almost all such kingdoms came into being through invasion and usurpation. Thus Nimrod, of whom we read that he was the first king, whose reign began in Babylon, as can be gathered from Genesis 10, made himself king by invasion and usurpation; and so it is said of him in the same

1. I Cor. 4:7.
2. The phrase suggests a philosophical source, but I have not managed to find it. It may also be that Giles is half remembering Augustine, *Sermo* 86:3 (PL 38:525); and cf. I Chron. 29:14.
3. Cf. I Pet. 2:13.
4. *De sacramentis* 2:2:4 (PL 176:418), quoting Heb. 7:7.

quod ipse cepit esse potens in terra. Per civilem itaque potenciam, non per iusticiam, regnum obtinuit. Sed secundum Augustinum, *De civitate Dei*, regna sine iusticia sunt magna latrocinia. Tales autem, etsi vocantur reges, non sunt reges, sed fures et latrones.

Regnum ergo non per sacerdocium institutum vel non fuit regnum sed latrocinium, vel fuit sacerdocio coniunctum. Nam et antequam per Samuelem tamquam per[1] sacerdotem Dei institueretur Saul et preficeretur in regem, fuit Melchisedech rex Salem. Sed huiusmodi Melchisedech, cum hoc quod erat rex, erat eciam sacerdos. Unde ibidem dicitur quod erat sacerdos[2] Dei altissimi. Ibi ergo regnum non fuit sine sacerdocio, sed fuit sacerdocio coniunctum, ut principalius esset ibi sacerdocium quam regnum. Regna vero moderna sequuntur regna instituta per sacerdocium,[3] ut[4] prius fuit regnum per sacerdocium institutum quam essent huiusmodi regna. Et quia priora sunt exemplaria et speculum posteriorum, omnia posteriora referenda sunt ad primum regnum, quod iubente Deo fuit per sacerdocium institutum. Cum igitur loquimur de regno, loquimur de regno recto et ut est divisum a sacerdocio.

Invenimus autem, ut patet per habita, quadruplicem modum regnorum: videlicet, regnum usurpatum, quod est latrocinium; regnum sacerdocio coniunctum; regnum per sacerdocium institutum; et regnum huiusmodi institucionem subsecutum. Si itaque sit regnum usurpatum, non est regnum de quo loquimur,[5] quia non est rectum.[6] Regnum vero quod est sacerdocio coniunctum non est de quo loquimur, quia non est a sacerdocio divisum. Sed loquimur de regno quod est per sacerdocium institutum vel huiusmodi institucionem subsecutum. Propter quod patet quod inicium regendi[7] recte, prout regnum et sacerdocium sunt duo gladii divisi,[8] a sacerdocio sumpsit originem. Recognoscant se ergo reges esse per sacerdocium instituti. Quare si diligenter advertimus unde venit potestas regia et unde est instituta, quia instituta est per sacerdocium, consequens est quod potestas regia subesse debeat potestati sacerdotali, et specialiter potestati Summi Sacerdotis.

Quarta via sumitur ex ipsa rerum gubernacione. Si ergo videre volumus que potestas sub qua potestate existat, attendere debemus ad universalis mundi machine gubernacionem. Videmus autem in gubernacione universi quod tota[9] corporalis substancia per spiritualem gubernatur. Reguntur quidem inferiora corpora[10] per superiora et grossiora per subtiliora[11] et minus potencia per potenciora. Tota tamen corporalis substancia regitur per spiritualem, et universa spiritualis substancia per Summum Spiritum,

---

1: per] *om.* F   2: Unde ibidem ... sacerdos] *om.* FV²   3: sacerdocium] subsecuta *add.* PV¹
4: ut] quia V²   ergo F   5: loquimur] quia non est a sacerdocio divisum *add.* P   6: rectum] regnum *add.* F   7: regendi] regnandi FV²   8: divisi] quod *add.* FV²   9: tota] *om.* C   10: corpora] *om.* CFV²   11: et grossiora per subtiliora] *om.* FV²

place that he began to be mighty on earth: he acquired his kingdom through civil might and not through justice.[1] But according to Augustine in *De civitate Dei,* kingdoms without justice are great bands of robbers.[2] And although such men [as Nimrod] are called kings, they are not kings, but thieves and robbers.

Kingship not instituted through priesthood, therefore, was either not kingship, but robbery, or was united with priesthood. For even before Saul was instituted and appointed as king through Samuel as through a priest of God,[3] Melchizedek was king of Salem.[4] But this Melchizedek, while he was a king, was also a priest. And so, in the same place, it is said that he was a priest of the Most High God. In this case, therefore, kingship did not exist without priesthood, but was united with priesthood, so that priesthood might here be superior to [mere] kingship [by virtue of the combination of spiritual and temporal power]. But modern kingships are the successors of kingships instituted through priesthood. For the kingship [of Saul] was instituted through priesthood before such kingships were in being. And since former things are the patterns and a mirror of later, all later kingships must be referred back to the first, which was instituted through priesthood at the command of God. When we speak of kingship, then, we are speaking of rightful kingship and of that which is separate from priesthood.

But, as is clear from what has been said, we find four kinds of kingship, namely: the kingship of usurpation, which is robbery; kingship united with priesthood; kingship instituted through priesthood; and kingship which is the successor of that so instituted. Thus, if there be a kingship of usurpation, it is not the kind of kingship of which we are speaking, because it is not rightful. Moreover, kingship which is united with priesthood is not that of which we are speaking, because it is not separate from priesthood. Rather, we are speaking of kingship which has been instituted through priesthood or which is the successor of that so instituted. Hence it is clear that the beginning of right rule, insofar as kingship and priesthood are two separate swords, derives its origin from priesthood. Let kings therefore acknowledge themselves to be instituted through priesthood. For if we give diligent attention to whence royal power has come and to whence it has been instituted, it follows that, because it has been instituted through priesthood, royal power should be subject to priestly power, and especially to the power of the Supreme Priest.

The fourth way is derived from the government of things themselves. Therefore, if we wish to see which power stands under which power, we must pay attention to the government of the whole mechanism of the world. And we see in the government of the universe that the whole of corporeal substance is governed through the spiritual. Inferior bodies are indeed ruled through superior, and the more gross through the more subtle and the less potent through the more potent; but the whole of corporeal substance is nonetheless ruled through the spiritual, and the whole of spiritual substance by the Supreme Spirit: that is, by

1. Gen. 10:8–10; cf. Peter Comestor, *Historia scholastica,* PL 198:1088.
2. *De civitate Dei* 4:4 (CCSL 47:101).
3. I Sam. 10:1.
4. Gen. 14:18.

videlicet per Deum. Unde Augustinus, III *De Trinitate* capitulo IV, dicit quod 'quedam corpora grossiora et inferiora per subtiliora et potenciora quodam ordine reguntur; omnia autem corpora[1] per spiritum, ac universa creatura per creatorem suum.' Et quod videmus in ordine et in[2] gubernacione universi debemus imaginari in gubernacione rei publice et in gubernacione tocius populi Christiani. Nam ipse idem Deus qui est universalis rector tocius machine mundi est specialis[3] gubernator[4] Ecclesie et suorum fidelium.

Quapropter, si totum universum, de quo Deus habet generalem curam, est sic bene ordinatum quod corpora inferiora sunt sub superioribus et universa corpora sunt sub spirituali, ipsa autem spiritualis substancia sub[5] Summo Spiritu, scilicet sub Deo, dicere[6] quod fidelis populus, et quod ipsa Ecclesia quam sibi elegit Deus non habentem maculam neque rugam, non sit bene ordinata, et quod non sit[7] tota secundum[8] totum sic[9] coniuncta et connexa, et quod ordo universi, qui est ordo pulcherrimus,[10] ut vult Augustinus in *Enchiridion*, et est admirabilis pulchritudo: quod illa pulchritudo admirabilis, quod ille ordo pulcherrimus, non refulgeat in Ecclesia, est omnino inconsequens.[11] Quare sicut in ipso universo corpora inferiora reguntur per superiora et infirmiora[12] per potenciora,[13] sic in ipso populo Christiano, inter ipsos fideles, domini temporales inferiores reguntur per superiores et minus potentes per potenciores.[14] Et sicut in ipso universo tota corporalis substancia regitur per spiritualem, quia ipsi celi, qui sunt supremi[15] inter corporalia et qui habent influenciam super omnia corpora, gubernantur per spirituales substancias, ut per intelligencias moventes eos, sic inter ipsos fideles universi domini temporales et universa potestas terrena[16] debet regi et gubernari per potestatem spiritualem[17] et ecclesiasticam, et specialiter per Summum Pontificem, qui in Ecclesia et in spirituali potestate tenet apicem et supremum gradum. Ipse autem Summus Pontifex a solo Deo habet iudicari. Ipse est enim, ut supra diximus, qui iudicat omnia et iudicatur a nemine: id est, a nullo puro[18] homine, sed a solo Deo.

Si deviat ergo potestas terrena, iudicabitur a potestate spirituali tamquam a suo superiori; sed si deviat potestas spiritualis, et potissime potestas Summi Pontificis, a solo Deo poterit iudicari. Unde Hugo in *De sacramentis* libro II et parte II, cum prius dixisset quod potestas terrena iudicatur[19] a potestate spirituali, postea subdit de potestate spirituali quod ipsa vero a Deo primum instituta est, et cum deviat a solo Deo iudicari potest.

Bene ergo ordo pulcherrimus universi relucet in Ecclesia et inter fideles, ut sicut ibi corpora inferiora reguntur per superiora et tota substancia corporalis per spiritualem, ipsa autem spiritualis per Deum, sic et in Ecclesia domini temporales et inferiores

---

1: corpora] corporalia FV[2]   2: in] *om.* V[1]   3: specialis] spiritualis V[1]   4: gubernator] sue *add.* C
5: sub] a FV[2]   6: dicere] ergo *add.* C   autem *add.* FV[2]   7: sit] *om.* CFV[2]   8: secundum] sed CF
9: sic] sit FV[2]   10: pulcherrimus] pulchritudinis CF   11: inconsequens] inconveniens CF
12: infirmiora] infimiora C   inferiora V[2]   13: potenciora] pociora FV[2]   14: per potenciores]
om. V[2]   per potentes F   15: supremi] superni F   16: potestas terrena] terrena potestas V[1]
17: potestatem spiritualem] spiritualem potestatem F   18: puro] *om.* F   19: iudicatur] iudicabitur FV[2]

God. Hence Augustine, at *De Trinitate* 3:4, says that 'certain more gross and inferior bodies are ruled in a certain order through the more subtle and the more potent;
but all bodies through spirit, and the whole of creation by its Creator.' And what we
see in the order and government of the universe we must picture to ourselves in
the government of the commonwealth and in the government of the whole Christian people. For that same God Who is the universal Director of the whole mechanism of the world is the special governor of His Church and of His faithful people.

And so if the whole universe, of which God has the general care, is so well
ordered that inferior bodies are under superior and all bodies are under the spiritual and spiritual substance itself is under the Supreme Spirit, that is, under God,
then it is wholly inconsistent to say that the faithful people, and the Church herself, whom God has chosen for Himself, having neither spot nor blemish,[1] is not
well ordered, and that she is not wholly and entirely united and joined in the same
way, and that the order of the universe, which, as Augustine maintains in the *Enchiridion*, is a most beautiful order and an astonishing beauty:[2] that this astonishing beauty, this most beautiful order, is not reflected in the Church. And so just as,
in the universe itself, inferior bodies are ruled through superior and the weaker
through the more potent, so, among the Christian people, among the faithful
themselves, inferior temporal lords are ruled through superiors and the less potent
through the more potent. And just as, in the universe itself, the whole of corporeal
substance is ruled through spiritual — for the heavens themselves, which are supreme among corporeal substances and which have influence over all bodies, are
governed through spiritual substances: through the intelligences which move
them;[3] so, among the faithful themselves, all temporal lords and every earthly
power must be ruled and governed through the spiritual and ecclesiastical power,
and especially through the Supreme Pontiff, who holds the supreme and highest
rank in the Church and in spiritual power. But the Supreme Pontiff himself must
be judged only by God. For, as we have said above,[4] it is he who judges all things
and is judged by no one: that is, by no mere man, but by God alone.

If the earthly power goes astray, therefore, it will be judged by the spiritual
power as by its superior. But if the spiritual power, and especially the power of
the Supreme Pontiff, goes astray, it will be able to be judged by God alone. And
so Hugh, at *De sacramentis* 2:2, having first said that the earthly power is judged
by the spiritual power, then added, as to the spiritual power, that it was truly first
instituted by God and that, when it goes astray, it can be judged by God alone.[5]

Therefore the most beautiful order of the universe is well reflected in the
Church and among the faithful in that, just as inferior bodies are there ruled
through superior and the whole of corporeal substance through spiritual and the
spiritual itself by God, so also, in the Church, temporal and inferior lords are ruled

1. Cf. Eph. 5:27.
2. *Enchiridion* 3:10 (CCSL 46:53).
3. Cf Aquinas, *Summa theologiae* Ia 115:3.
4. Ch. II.
5. *De sacramentis fidei Christianae* 2:2:4 (PL 176:418).

reguntur per superiores, universa autem temporalis et terrena potestas per spiritualem, et potissime per Summum Pontificem; Summus autem Pontifex a solo Deo poterit iudicari.

Nec valeret si quis diceret quod universa terrena potestas debet esse sub spirituali sed hoc est intelligendum[1] spiritualiter[2] et[3] quantum ad articulos fidei, non autem quantum ad temporalem et terrenam potestatem. Quia isti sic dicentes vim racionis non capiunt. Quia corpora, secundum quod corpora, subsunt spiritibus, ut ipsi corporales motus, et potissime motus superiorum corporum, sunt per spiritus moventes et per intelligencias motrices orbium, sic temporales potestates, ut temporales sunt, et potissime potestates temporales supreme, per potestatem spiritualem, et potissime per potestatem Summi Pontificis, qui[4] in Ecclesia est potestas spiritualis sublimior et suprema, poterunt iudicari.[5] Inferiores domini temporales, si delinquant,[6] iudicari poterunt per dominos temporales superiores.[7] Sed ipsi domini temporales superiores, quia inter temporales dominos non habent superiores, per potestatem spiritualem poterunt iudicari. Sed ipsa spiritualis potestas, et potissime potestas Summi Sacerdotis,[8] quia non habet superiorem hominem, sed Deum, a nemine, sed a solo Deo poterit iudicari.

CAPITULUM VI: *Quod sacerdotalis potestas non solum dignitate sed tempore prior est regia potestate.*

Intendimus in hoc capitulo declarare quod sacerdotalis potestas non solum dignitate sed tempore precedit regiam potestatem. Sed videtur quod intencio huius capituli precedenti capitulo et eciam sibi ipsi liquido contradicat. Ostendebatur enim in precedenti capitulo quod sacerdotalis potestas[9] est dignior, et per consequens dignitate est prior, regia potestate; et hoc idem in hoc capitulo repetitur, et additur quod non solum dignitate sed eciam[10] tempore hec[11] potencia precedit[12] illam. Sed ista duo sibi videntur contradicere: quod unum et idem sit prius altero dignitate et tempore. Quia, si est prius dignitate, consequens est, ut videtur, quod sit posterius tempore; quia[13] imperfecciora sunt priora tempore et posteriora dignitate, perfecciora autem econverso. Videmus autem naturaliter quod natura incipit ab imperfecto ad perfectum, ut[14] prius est aliquid tempore imperfectum et postea perficitur et fit perfectum. Ipsum ergo dominium temporale[15] prius fuit imperfectum et postea perfectum; et quia regia potestas non est dominium ita perfectum sicut dominium[16] Summi Sacerdocii, consequens est quod tempore hoc precessit illud.

Videtur[17] eciam hoc[18] concordare ipsis rebus gestis. Nam etsi in populo Iudaico potestas sacerdotalis precessit potestatem regiam, quin[19] prius[20] fuit sacerdos Hely et eciam Samuel quam esset Saul inunctus in regem, simpliciter tamen potestas sacerdocii non videtur quod precesserit tempore potestatem regiam. Nam antequam inciperet

1: intelligendum] intelligimus V[2]   2: sed hoc … spiritualiter] *om.* F   3: et] *del.* F   4: qui] que FV[2]
5: iudicari] nam *add.* C   6: delinquant] delinquunt F   7: superiores] *om.* V[1]   8: Sacerdotis]
sacerdocii FV[2]   9: potestas] *om.* V[1]   10: eciam] et *add.* PV[1]V[2]   11: hec] huiusmodi F
12: precedit] precedat F   13: quia] nam FV[2]   14: ut] et F   15: temporale] tempore FV[2]
16: ita perfectum … dominium] *om.* F   17: Videtur] videbitur F   18: hoc] hic V[1]   19: quin]
quia C   20: prius] prior F

through superiors and all temporal and earthly power through the spiritual, and especially through the Supreme Pontiff; but the Supreme Pontiff will be subject to the judgment of God alone.

Nor would it avail if anyone were to say that, though the whole of earthly power must be under the spiritual, this is to be understood with respect to the articles of faith, and not with respect to temporal and earthly power. For those who speak thus do not grasp the force of the argument. For bodies, inasmuch as they are bodies, are placed under spirits. And just as the movements of bodies themselves, and especially the movements of the higher bodies, are governed through ruling spirits and through the intelligences which move the spheres, so temporal powers, inasmuch as they are temporal, and especially the supreme temporal powers, will be subject to judgment by the spiritual power, and especially by the power of the Supreme Pontiff, who is the most sublime and supreme spiritual power in the Church. Inferior temporal lords, if they offend, will be subject to the judgment of superior temporal lords. But superior temporal lords themselves, because they have no superiors among temporal lords, will be subject to the judgment of the spiritual power. But the spiritual power itself, and especially the power of the Supreme Priest, will be subject to judgment by no one except God alone; for it has no man, but God, as its superior.

CHAPTER VI: *That priestly power is prior to royal power not only in dignity, but also in time.*

In this chapter, we intend to declare that priestly power precedes royal power not only in dignity, but also in time. It seems, however, that the intention of this chapter clearly contradicts the previous chapter and itself also. For it was shown in the previous chapter that priestly power is greater in dignity than, and consequently is prior in dignity to, royal power; and this same assertion is repeated in this chapter; yet it is added that the one power precedes the other not only in dignity, but also in time. But these two statements, that one and the same thing is prior to another both in dignity and in time, appear to contradict themselves. For if something is prior in dignity, it seems to follow that it is posterior in time, since more imperfect entities are prior in time and posterior in dignity, whereas the converse is true of more perfect entities. For we see by the evidence of nature that nature proceeds from the imperfect to the perfect, so that anything which is prior in time is imperfect, and is completed and made perfect subsequently.[1] Temporal lordship itself, therefore, was at first imperfect and subsequently perfected; and since royal power is not so perfect a lordship as the lordship of the Supreme Priest, it [seemingly] follows that it preceded it in time.

Again, this seems to agree with established facts. For although priestly power preceded royal power among the Jewish people, since Eli, and Samuel also, was a priest before Saul was anointed as king, it nonetheless does not seem that priestly power considered absolutely preceded royal power in time. For before the Jewish

---

1.   Cf. Aristotle, *Physics* 2:8 (199ª15); Aquinas, *Summa theologiae* Ia 85:3; IIIa 1:5 ad 3 & 6.

populus Iudaicus, et antequam Abraham esset, [1] erant[2] reges qui regnabant[3] in nacionibus aliis; propter quod antequam Saul, qui fuit primus rex Iudeorum, esset rex, congregati[4] universi maiores natu Israel venerunt ad Samuel dixeruntque ei: 'Constitue nobis regem, ut iudicet nos, sicut[5] habent universe naciones.' Ante ergo, ut videtur, fuerunt reges quam sacerdotes, licet in populo Iudaico incepisset regnum post sacerdocium. Immo, si bene consideramus dicta canonis Biblie, prius fit[6] mencio de regno, sicut de Neroth, cuius regnum incepit in Babilone, ut habetur Geneseos X, et postea fit mencio de sacerdote, ut de Melchisedech, qui erat sacerdos Dei altissimi, ut habetur Geneseos XIV. Ergo et racioni concordat quod regnum precesserit sacerdocium tempore, quia imperfectum tempore precedit perfectum,[7;8] et rebus gestis videtur hoc congruere,[9] quia prius[10] legimus mencionem factam de regno quam de sacerdocio.

Et eciam auctoritati videtur hoc consonare, quia potestas regia est potestas terrena et super corporalia, potestas sacerdotalis est potestas super spiritualia. Sed ut habetur Geneseos II: 'Formavit igitur[11] Dominus[12] Deus hominem de limo terre et inspiravit in faciem eius spiraculum vite, et factus est homo in animam viventem.' Prius ergo factus est homo de limo terre, quod competit corpori; postea spiravit Deus in faciem eius spiraculum vite, quod competit anime. Quare ex auctoritate Geneseos, sicut prius formatum est corpus humanum et postea recepit spiraculum vite et animam viventem, sic potestas regia, que est super corporalia, videtur quod precesserit tempore potestatem sacerdotalem, que est super spiritualia.

Hiis itaque prelibatis que videntur esse contraria nostro proposito, volumus declarare quod et racioni et rebus gestis et auctoritati concordat quod potestas sacerdotalis non solum dignitate sed eciam tempore precesserit[13] regiam potestatem. Itaque volumus solvere ad ea que in contrarium sunt obiecta;[14] quibus solutis quesita, veritas apparebit.

Sciendum ergo quod que dicebantur de perfecto et imperfecto[15] et de rebus gestis et de auctoritate Geneseos, quod corpus prius tempore est formatum et postea recepit spiraculum vite, nostro proposito non obviant nec eciam contradicunt. Ad quorum evidenciam advertendum quod in uno et[16] eodem generabili et corruptibili, vel in quolibet[17] creabili seu factibili, potencia[18] eciam tempore seu duracione[19] precedit actum. Quodcumque enim huiusmodi[20] factibile,[21] loquendo de 'faccione' large, sive sit factibile solum secundum potenciam agentis, sicut est in Creacione, ubi factum,

1: esset] om. V[2]   2: Abraham esset, erant] esset Abraham erant F   3: regnabant] regebant FV[2]
4: congregati] sunt add. F sunt add. and del. PV[1]   5: sicut] et add. FV[2]   6: fit] fuit V[1]   7: tempore precedit perfectum] precedit perfectum tempore C   8: perfectum] perfectionem F   9: congruere] quod imperfectum precedit perfectum tempore add. F   quod imperfectum precedit perfectum tempore add. and del. V[2]   10: prius] primo CF   11: igitur] om. V[1]   12: Dominus] om. C   13: precesserit] precessit C   14: obiecta] subiecta FV[2]   15: et imperfecto] om. V[1]   16: et] in add. F
17: quolibet] quocumque FV[2]   18: potencia] om. C   19: duracione] potencia add. C   20: huiusmodi] sit add. C   21: potencia eciam ... factibile] om. V[1]

people began, and before Abraham was, there were kings who ruled in other nations; for before Saul, who was the first king of the Jews, was king, the whole assembly of the elders of Israel came to Samuel and said to him: 'Appoint a king for us, to judge us, as all the nations have.'[1] It seems, therefore, that kings existed before priests, even though, among the Jewish people, kingship had begun after priesthood. Indeed, if we consider well what is said in the canon of the Bible, mention is first made of kingship, that of Nimrod, whose reign began in Babylon, in Genesis 10;[2] yet mention is made of priesthood, that of Melchizedek, who was a priest of the Most High God, only subsequently, in Genesis 14.[3] It therefore seems to accord with reason that kingship preceded priesthood in time, since the imperfect precedes the perfect in time; and this also seems to be congruent with established facts, since we read that mention is made of kingship before priesthood.

And again, this seems to be consonant with authority, because royal power is an earthly power and over bodily things, whereas priestly power is a power over spiritual matters. But, as is established in Genesis 2: 'The Lord therefore formed man from the slime of the earth and breathed into his face the breath of life; and man was made a living soul.'[4] First, therefore, man was made from the slime of the earth, which composes body; subsequently, God breathed into his face the breath of life, which composes soul. And so it seems from the authority of Genesis that, just as the human body was formed first and received the breath of life and a living soul subsequently, so royal power, which is over bodily things, preceded priestly power, which is over spiritual things, in time.

Thus, having first touched upon these considerations which seem to be contrary to our proposition, we wish to declare that it is in accordance with reason and established facts and authority alike that priestly power preceded royal power not only in dignity, but also in time. We wish, then, to solve those objections which have been put forward to the contrary; and, when such solutions have been discovered, the truth will appear.

It must be known, therefore, that what has been said concerning the perfect and the imperfect, and concerning established facts and the authority of Genesis — that the body was formed first in time and received the breath of life subsequently — neither opposes nor at all contradicts our proposition. As evidence of this, it must be noted that, in one and the same thing which is capable of coming into being or passing away, or in anything which can be created or made, potentiality certainly precedes actuality in time or duration.[5] For, speaking of 'making' in a large sense, this is true of whatever can be made. It is true of that which can be made only according to the potentiality of an agent, as in the Creation, where what was made did not exist in the potentiality of matter before it was made; for whatever

1. I Sam. 8:5.
2. Gen. 10:8–10.
3. Gen. 14:18.
4. Gen. 2:7.
5. See especially Aristotle, *Metaphysics* θ:7 (1049ª1).

antequam fiat, non est in potencia materie, quia quicquid[1] creatur non fit ex materia
preiacenti, sed tota racio facti est potencia facientis; vel, secundo, si huiusmodi
factibile sit eciam in potencia materie secundum racionem obediencialem, prout
habet esse in operibus miraculosis, ut puta si Deus de trunco faceret vitulum: in
ipsa enim materia trunci, etsi non est in ea racio seminalis ut de ea fiat vitulus,
est tamen in ea racio obediencialis ut materia trunci obediat[2] Creatori suo, ut de
ea, cum Creator voluerit, faciat inde[3] vitulum; sive, tercio, huiusmodi factibile
sit in potencia materie secundum racionem seminalem, sicut fiunt[4] effectus per
agencia naturalia que per[5] raciones seminales[6] agunt quecumque agunt,[7] ita quod
agens naturale per raciones seminales[8] quasi de potencia materie producat[9] suos
effectus. De quibus racionibus seminalibus loquitur Augustinus, III *De Trinitate*
capitulo VIII, quod sicut matres gravide sunt fetibus, sic iste mundus causis nas-
cencium.

Quocumque[10] ergo modo loquamur[11] de factibili, semper unum et idem prius fuit
in potencia quam in actu, ut si aliquid fit per Creatorem, prius fuit in potencia[12]
agentis quam esset in actu. Si autem fiat et educatur de potencia[13] materie secundum
racionem obediencialem, ut puta in operibus miraculosis, velut si de trunco fieret
vitulus, ille vitulus factus prius fuit in potencia obedienciali materie et postea fuit
factus in actu. Ita eciam si tercio[14] modo fieret factibile, ut quod educeretur de potencia materie secundum raciones seminales, secundum quem modum agunt agencia
naturalia et secundum quem modum Deus obiecit materiam agentibus naturalibus:[15]
illud sic productum prius fuit in potencia[16] materie secundum rationes seminales et
postea factum fuit in actu. Hoc ergo modo, in eodem et respectu eiusdem, potencia
precedit actum et imperfectum potest precedere perfectum. Et sic concederetur de
regno et de sacerdocio, quod imperfectum precedat perfectum, ut quod prius fuit
regnum imperfectum quam perfectum et prius sacerdocium imperfectum quam
perfectum.

Quod ergo regnum per successionem temporum profecerit, sic eciam quod sacerdocium profecerit, ut quod inceperit[17] sacerdocium in lege nature et perfeccius fuerit
in lege scripta et adhuc perfeccius in lege gracie, in qua lege sacramenta sunt perfecta

1: quicquid] quodcumque F   2: obediat] obedit F   3: inde] *om.* F   4: fiunt] sunt F   5: per]
om. FV[2]   6: seminales] sensibiles FV[2]   7: quecumque agunt] *om.* V[1]   8: agunt quecumque ...
seminales] *om.* FV[2]   9: producat] producunt V[1]   10: Quocumque] quomodocumque F
11: loquamur] loquitur V[1]   12: quam in ... potencia] *om.* F   13: ut si ... potencia] *om.* V[1]
14: eciam si tercio] et si in tercio V[1]   15: et secundum ... naturalibus] *om.* FPV[1]V[2]   16: fuit in
potencia] in potencia fuit F   17: inceperit] incepit CPV[1]

was created was not made from a pre-existing matter: rather, the whole principle of its making was the potentiality of the Maker.[1] Or, second, if that which can be made also exists in the potentiality of matter according to a principle of obedience, as occurs in miraculous works — for instance, if God were to make a calf out of a block of wood — then, in the matter of the block of wood itself, even though there is no seminal principle in it such that a calf might be made from it, there is nonetheless a principle of obedience in it such that the matter of the block of wood may obey its Creator, so that, when the Creator wills, He makes a calf from it. Or, third, that which can be made may exist in the potentiality of matter according to a seminal principle, as when effects are brought about by natural agents, which accomplish whatever they accomplish through seminal principles, so that a natural agent may produce its effects through seminal principles as through the potentiality of matter. And of these seminal principles Augustine says at *De Trinitate* 3:8 that, just as mothers are great with young, so is this world pregnant with causes.[2]

In whatever way we speak of that which can be made, therefore, one and the same thing always existed potentially before it existed actually, as with anything made by the Creator, which existed in the potentiality of the Agent before it existed in actuality. And if a thing is made and derived from the potentiality of matter according to a principle of obedience, as in miraculous works, such as a block of wood made into a calf, that calf would first exist in the potentiality of matter to obey, and afterwards would be made in actuality. So too if something were able to be made in the third way, by being derived from the potentiality of matter according to seminal principles, according to which mode natural agents act and according to which mode God exposes matter to natural agents: the thing so produced would first exist in the potentiality of matter according to seminal principles, and would be made in actuality subsequently. In this way, therefore, within the same thing, and with respect to that thing, potentiality precedes actuality and the imperfect can precede the perfect. And so it might be conceded with respect to kingship and priesthood that the imperfect preceded the perfect: that kingship was imperfect before it was perfect, and priesthood was imperfect before it was perfect.

It is, therefore, not at all incorrect to say that, as kingship has advanced with the passage of time, so also has priesthood advanced, in that priesthood began under the law of nature and was made more perfect under the Written Law and more perfect still under the Law of Grace, in which Law the sacraments are perfected and

---

1. Cf. Augustine, *De anima et eius origine* 2:3:5 (CSEL 25(2):855); *Confessiones* 11:5 (CCSL 27:197); 12:7 (CCSL 27:219); *De Genesi ad litteram* 7:2 (CSEL 28(1):201); *De natura boni* 1 (CSEL 25(2):855); *De civitate Dei* 12:2 (CCSL 48:356).
2. Augustine, *De Trinitate* 3:8 (CCSL 50:143). 'Seminal principle' (*ratio seminalis*) is a *terminus technicus* of Augustinian metaphysics, exactly translating the Stoic term λόγος σπέρματικος. Seminal principles are 'hidden "seeds" which contain everything future ages are to see unfolded'; and so 'the world created by God may be said to be pregnant with causes of beings still to come' (E. Gilson, *The Christian Philosophy of Saint Augustine* (London: Gollancz, 1961), p. 206; see pp. 206–208 of Prof. Gilson's work for more discussion; also F. Coplestone, *A History of Philosophy*, vol. 2 (London: Burns, Oates & Washbourne, 1959), ch. 6.)

et non sunt egena, sicut erant in lege scripta, de quibus sacramentis et 'elementis egenis' loquitur Apostolus ad Galatas IV: 'Quomodo convertimini iterum ad infirma[1] et egena elementa?' — id est, ad sacramenta veteris legis: nullum est inconveniens.[2]

Sic ergo in eodem, potencia precedit actum. Absolute tamen et[3] simpliciter, actus precedit[4] potenciam et perfectum imperfectum. Quia si res essent in potencia et non precederet actus qui faceret potencia talia actu, talia, cum nihil se moveat de potencia ad actum, encia forte possent esse, sed non essent absolute. Itaque et simpliciter, et[5] tempore et duracione actus precedit potenciam et perfectum imperfectum, licet in eodem sit econverso.

Racio itaque illa quod regnum tempore precessit sacerdocium tamquam imperfectum perfectum, si argueret de eodem, ut puta de eodem regno vel de eodem sacerdocio, quod prius fuit regnum aliquod imperfectum quam perfectum vel eciam sacerdocium, racio forte concluderet veritatem. Sed cum non arguat de eodem, nec arguat de regno respectu regni nec de sacerdocio respectu sacerdocii, sed[6] arguat de diversis, ut de regno respectu sacerdocii et econverso, quia, ut dicebatur, in eodem potencia precedat[7] actum et imperfectum perfectum, in diversis vero et simpliciter est econverso: patet quod racio prius facta[8] magis[9] concludit oppositum quam propositum.

Quod vero addebatur de rebus gestis, quod fuit prius[10] regnum[11] in nacionibus quam eciam sacerdocium in populo Iudaico, et prius fuit regnum simpliciter quam eciam sacerdocium, quia eciam[12] Geneseos X prius fit mencio de regno Neroth et postea Geneseos XIV fit mencio de sacerdocio Melchisedech: dicemus quod forte nomen sacerdocii non precessit nomen regni, sed res ipsa que est sacerdocium precessit eciam tempore rem que est regnum. Nam ante diluvium nec de re nec de nomine regni aliquid legimus, post diluvium vero ipsa res que est[13] sacerdocium precessit rem que est regnum. Nam statim post diluvium, egressis de archa Noe et filiis eius et uxoribus illorum, edificavit Noe altare Domino, et tollens de cunctis pecoribus et volucribus mundis,[14] obtulit holocausta super altare, odoratusque est Deus odorem suavitatis. Offerre autem super altare holocausta in odorem suavitatis est opus sacerdocii. Statim ergo post diluvium fuit sacerdocium, ut potest haberi Geneseos VIII;[15] non statim autem post diluvium fuit[16] regnum. Immo, incepit regnum a Neroth, qui per multas generaciones[17] post diluvium descendit de stirpe Noe. Sacerdocium ergo, secundum[18] res gestas, precessit regnum, quia fuit statim post diluvium, non autem regnum.

1: infirma] infima F   2: inconveniens] eciam conveniens V[1]   3: et] eciam *add.* CF
4: actum. Absolute ... precedit] *om.* V[2]   5: et] eciam PV[1]   6: sed] quia *add.* V[1]
7: precedat] precedit C   8: facta] vel tacta *add.* PV[1]   9: magis] pocius C   10: fuit prius]
prius fuit CFV[2]   11: regnum] quam sacerdocium *add.* CPV[1]V[2]   12: eciam] *om.* CFV[2]
13: est] *om.* F   14: mundis] mundi FPV[1]V[2]   15: VIII] x FPV[1]V[2]   16: sacerdocium, ut ...
fuit] *om.* F   17: generaciones] naciones C   18: secundum] per F

are not lacking as they were under the Written Law, of whose sacraments and 'beggarly elements' the Apostle speaks in Galatians 4: 'How turn ye again to the weak and beggarly elements?'[1] — that is, to the sacraments of the Old Law.

Within the same thing, therefore, potentiality precedes actuality. In an absolute and complete sense, however, actuality precedes potentiality and the perfect the imperfect. For if things were to exist potentially, and if the actuality which might cause such potentiality to become actuality did not precede it, then such entities might perhaps be able to exist, but they would not exist absolutely; for nothing moves itself from potentiality to actuality. In an absolute sense, then, actuality precedes potentiality and the perfect the imperfect in time and duration, even though, within the same entity, the converse is true.

Thus, the argument that kingship precedes priesthood in time as the imperfect does the perfect might perhaps be true if it concerned one and the same thing: that is, one and the same kingship or priesthood, where the kingship or priesthood was imperfect before it was perfect. But since it does not concern the same thing (either kingship as kingship or priesthood as priesthood) but different things (the relation of kingship to priesthood and the converse); and because, as we have said, potentiality precedes actuality and the imperfect the perfect within the same thing but the converse is true as among different things and absolutely: then it is clear that the previous argument [i.e. all that has been said about potentiality and actuality] rather supports the opposite view [that priesthood precedes kingship in time as well as in dignity] than the proposition [that one and the same thing cannot be prior to another in both time and dignity].

But because it has also been said, with reference to established facts, that kingship existed among the nations before there was also a priesthood among the Jewish people, and that kingship considered absolutely existed before there was priesthood, since mention is indeed first made of the kingship of Nimrod in Genesis 10 and mention is made of the priesthood of Melchizedek only subsequently, in Genesis 14: we shall say that the name of priesthood perhaps did not precede the name of kingship, but that the fact of priesthood did indeed precede the fact of kingship in time. For, before the Flood, we do not read anything of either the fact or the name of kingship, whereas, after the Flood, the fact of priesthood certainly preceded the fact of kingship. For immediately after the Flood, when Noah and his sons and their wives came forth from the Ark, Noah built an altar to the Lord and, taking of all the cattle and birds that were clean, offered burnt offerings upon the altar, and God smelt a sweet savour.[2] But to offer burnt offerings in a sweet savour upon the altar is a work of priesthood. It can be gathered from Genesis 8, then, that there was priesthood immediately after the Flood. But there was no kingship immediately after the Flood. Rather, kingship began with Nimrod, who had descended from the stock of Noah through many generations after the Flood. According to established facts, therefore, priesthood preceded kingship, since it existed immediately after the Flood, but kingship did not.

---

1. Gal. 4:9.
2. Gen. 8:20.

Immo, sacerdocium non solum fuit[1] post diluvium, sed eciam fuit ante diluvium. Nam de ipso Abel legimus Geneseos IV quod erat pastor ovium et quod obtulit Domino de primogenitis gregis sui et de adipibus eorum; et subditur quod 'respexit Dominus[2] ad Abel et ad munera eius.' Sed offerre holocausta sive primogenita gregum[3] est opus sacerdocii. Ergo in ipso Abel precessit sacerdocium. Dicere eciam[4] possumus quod in ipso Adam, primo parento nostro, sacerdocium precessit. Credibile enim est quod, postquam Adam penituit de suo peccato,[5;6] in recognicionem sue servitutis et uxoris eius[7] et suorum posteriorum, obtulit holocausta Domino: quod erat opus sacerdocii. Ante ergo diluvium, etsi non erat in usu nomen sacerdocii, fuit tamen res ipsa que est[8] sacerdocium. Sed nec nomen regni nec rem que est regnum legimus ante diluvium. Itaque et[9] post diluvium[10] et ante, res que est sacerdocium precessit regnum; et quia non est curandum de nomine cum constat de re, dicere possumus quod res gesta asserunt sacerdocium precessisse regnum.[11]

Quod autem dicebatur tercio de auctoritate Geneseos, quod prius formatum est corpus et postea recepit spiraculum vite, ita quod formacio corporis videtur precessisse tempore infusionem anime, dicere possumus quod Augustinus, libro[12] VII *Super Genesim*, videtur asserere quod anima primi parentis fuit creata ante corpus sive ante formacionem corporis. Unde[13] ait:[14] 'Tollerabiliter dici videtur Deum in illis primis operibus, per[15] que simul omnia creavit, animam eciam humanam creasse, quam suo tempore membris ex limo formati corporis inspiraret.' Verum, quia Augustinus ibi loquitur arguendo et disputando, propter quod ipsemet in eodem libro questionem huiusmodi post prefata verba insolutam relinquit, dicens quod 'De anima quam Deus inspiravit homini sufflando in eius faciem nihil confirmo,' sustinendo ergo quod primum formatum fuerit corpus et in ipsa complecione formacionis infusa fuerit anima, sicut in completa disposicione materie inducitur forma, non tamen propter hoc habetur propositum, sed oppositum. Nam ex illo corpore et illa anima factum fuit unum et idem, et in uno et eodem non est inconveniens quod origine vel tempore imperfectum precedat perfectum, in diversis tamen et simpliciter est econverso, ut supra diffusius diximus. Et quia hic de diversis est questio, ut de regno respectu sacerdocii et econverso, ideo prefata auctoritas nobis minime contradicit. Immo, si consideramus auctoritates Geneseos res gestas iuxta facti seriem describentes, sacerdocium tempore precessit regnum.

Ergo et racio et res gesta et auctoritas arguunt et declarant quod sacerdocium tempore precessit regnum. Precessit itaque simpliciter sacerdocium regnum. Sed quod precesserit non solum simpliciter sed eciam quantum ad divinam institucionem, Hugo de Sancto Victore in libro *De sacramentis* libro II, parte II asserit, dicens:

---

1 fuit] statim *add.* C   2: Dominus] deus C   3: gregum] gregis FV²   4: eciam] *om.* C
5: suo peccato] peccato suo F   6: peccato] quod *add. mss*   7: uxoris eius] eius uxoris F
8: est] erat C   9: et] *om.* C   10: Itaque et post diluvium] *om.* F   11: et quia ... regnum] *om.* PV¹
12: libro] *om.* F   13: Unde] ut V² *om.* F   14: ait] *om.* V²   15: per] *om.* C

Indeed, there was priesthood not only after the Flood, but before the Flood also. For in Genesis 4 we read of Abel that he was a keeper of sheep and that he offered to the Lord the firstborn of his flock and of their fat; and it is added that 'the Lord had respect unto Abel and to his offering.'[1] But to offer burnt offerings or the firstborn of the flock is a work of priesthood. In Abel himself, therefore, priesthood came first. Also, we can say that priesthood came first even in Adam, our first parent. For it is possible to believe that, after Adam repented of his sin, he offered burnt offerings to the Lord in recognition of his servitude and that of his wife and their posterity: which was a work of priesthood. Before the Flood, therefore, though the name of priesthood was not in use, there was still a priesthood in fact. But we read of neither the name nor the fact of kingship before the Flood. Thus, both after the Flood and before it, the fact of priesthood preceded kingship; and because no notice is to be taken of a name when the fact is clear, we can say that established facts show that priesthood preceded kingship.

But because, third, it has been said on the authority of Genesis that the body was formed first and received the breath of life subsequently, so that the formation of the body seems to have preceded the infusion of the soul in time, we can reply that in *De Genesi ad Litteram*, Book 7, Augustine appears to assert that the soul of our first parent was created before the body, or before the formation of the body. For he says: 'It may permissibly be said that, in His first works, by which He created all things together, God seems also to have created the human soul which, in His own time, He breathed into the members of the body formed from the slime.' But because Augustine is here speaking in a manner open to argument and dispute — for, in the same book, after the words just quoted, he himself leaves this question unresolved, saying: 'I can say nothing certain about the soul which God inspired into man by breathing into his face'[2] — even, therefore, by maintaining that the body was formed first and the soul infused into it at the completion of its formation as form is imposed upon matter at the completion of its disposition, the proposition [that priesthood cannot be prior in both time and dignity] is not thereby proved, but its opposite. For from that body and that soul one and the same thing was made; and, although it is not incorrect to say that the imperfect precedes the perfect in origin or time in one and the same thing, the converse is true as among different things and absolutely, as we have said at greater length above. And since the question here is one of different things — of kingship in relation to priesthood and the converse — the authority cited above [i.e. Genesis 2:7] therefore does not contradict us in the least. On the contrary, if we consider the authorities of Genesis according to the series of established facts which they describe, priesthood preceded kingship in time.

Reason, established facts, and authority, therefore, all argue and declare that priesthood preceded kingship in time. Thus, considered absolutely, priesthood preceded kingship. But that it preceded it not only considered absolutely, but also inasmuch as it is of divine institution, Hugh of Saint Victor has asserted at *De*

1. Gen. 4:4.
2. *De Genesi ad litteram* 7:24; 28 (CSEL 28(1):222; 228).

'Quod autem spiritualis potestas, quantum ad divinas instituciones spectat, eciam prior sit tempore et maior dignitate,[1] in illo antiquo Veteris Testamenti populo manifeste declaratur, ubi primum a Deo sacerdocium institutum est, postea vero per sacerdocium, iubente Deo, regalis potestas est ordinata.'

CAPITULUM VII: *Quod, sicut in homine est duplex substancia, corpus et spiritus, et sicut est dare duplicem cibum, corporalem et spiritualem, sic est ponere duplicem gladium, quorum unus alteri debet esse subiectus.*

Quilibet autem potest sensibiliter experiri quod homo est compositus ex duplici substancia: ex carne videlicet et spiritu; quod satis Dominus dedit intelligere Matth. XXVI, cum dixit:[2] 'Spiritus quidem promptus est, caro vero[3] infirma.' Et hoc idem clare habere potest ex eo quod dicitur Genes. II, quod 'Formavit igitur Deus hominem de limo terre,'[4] quantum ad corpus, 'et spiravit in faciem eius spiraculum vite,' quantum ad spiritum sive quantum ad animam. Et sicut duo sunt in homine, corpus et[5] spiritus, sic homo indiget duplici cibo, corporali et spirituali; ideo dicit Dominus Matth. IV: 'Non in[6] solo pane vivit homo, sed in omni verbo quod procedit de ore Dei.' Homo quidem, quia non est corpus tantum, sed est corpus et anima sive corpus et spiritus, ideo non vivit ex solo pane, id est in solo cibo corporali, ut per 'panem' intelligatur quilibet corporalis cibus, sed vivit ex verbo[7] Dei: id est ex[8] cibo[9] spirituali. Quia, sicut corpus indiget pane tamquam suo cibo corporali, ita[10] spiritus indiget verbo Dei tamquam suo cibo spirituali. Homo itaque, quia non est simplex, sed est compositus ex duobus, ideo non nutritur uno solo cibo, sed duplici: corporali videlicet[11] et spirituali. Sic gubernatur et regitur sub duplici gladio, terreno et ecclesiastico, regali et sacerdotali,[12] materiali et spirituali.

Primum itaque fundamentum distinccionis tam ciborum quam gladiorum, ut quod homo indigeat duplici cibo et regatur sub duplici gladio, est distinccio quantum ad partes ex quibus componitur homo, ut ideo indiget illo duplici cibo et regitur sub duplici gladio, corporali et spirituali, quin est compositus ex corpore et spiritu. Et quia, si quis habet edificare[13] domum debet[14] a fundamento incipere, sic qui vellet tractare de huiusmodi duplici cibo sive de huiusmodi duplici gladio deberet incipere a fundamento: videlicet, a partibus ex quibus componitur homo. Et sicut videret et[15] per racionem prospiceret quomodo se haberent hee due partes, sic posset iudicare de huiusmodi duobus cibis et[16] gladiis. Sumus enim creatura Dei et factura Dei, et fecit et formavit nos Deus ex duobus, corpore videlicet et spiritu. Et ideo ordinavit et propinavit nobis duplicem cibum: corporalem, per quem sustentaretur corpus, et spiritualem, per quem reficeretur anima. Et quia homo poterat impediri in utroque,

1: dignitate] suple [suppleo *or* supplevi] quam potestas terrena *add. mss*   2: dixit] dicit CFV²
3: vero] autem CFV²   4: hominem de limo terre] ex limo terre hominem FV²   5: et] *om.* FV²
6: in] ex FPV¹V²   7: verbo] cibo FV²   8: ex] a F   9: Dei: id est ex cibo] *om.* V²   10: ita] sic C
11: videlicet] *om.* CFV²   12: regali et sacerdotali] sacerdotali et regali C   13: habet edificare]
edificare habet C   14: debet] deberet FV²   15: videret et] *om.* C   16: et] duobus *add.* C

sacramentis 2:2, saying: 'Inasmuch as it looks to divine origins, the spiritual power is both prior in time and greater in dignity, as is manifestly shown among that ancient people of the Old Testament, where, first, priesthood was instituted by God and, subsequently, royal power was ordained at the command of God.'[1]

CHAPTER VII: *That just as in man there is a twofold substance, body and spirit, and just as it is necessary to give a twofold food, bodily and spiritual, so is it necessary to posit two swords, one of which must be subject to the other.*

Anyone can discover by the evidence of the senses that man is composed of a twofold substance: that is, of flesh and spirit. The Lord gave us to understand this sufficiently in Matthew 26, when He said: 'The spirit indeed is willing, but the flesh is weak';[2] and this same conclusion can be inferred clearly from what is said in Genesis 2: that 'God therefore formed man from the slime of the earth,' as regards body, 'and breathed into his face the breath of life,' as regards spirit or as regards soul.[3] And just as there are two elements in man, body and spirit, so does man need a twofold food, bodily and spiritual; and so the Lord says in Matthew 4: 'Man shall not live by bread alone, but by every word that proceeds out of the mouth of God.'[4] Indeed, because he is not only body, but body and soul or body and spirit, man therefore shall not live by bread alone (that is, by bodily food; for 'bread' may be taken to mean any kind of bodily food), but he shall live by the word of God: that is, by spiritual food. For just as the body needs bread as its bodily food, so does the spirit need the word of God as its spiritual food. Thus, because he is not simple, but is composed of two elements, man is therefore not nourished by a single, but by a twofold, food: namely, bodily and spiritual. So also is he governed and ruled under a twofold sword: earthly and ecclesiastical; royal and priestly; material and spiritual.

The first foundation of the distinction between foods and swords alike, then, such that man needs a twofold food and is ruled under a twofold sword, is a distinction as between the parts of which a man is composed, in that, because he is composed of body and spirit, he therefore needs this twofold food and is ruled under a twofold sword, bodily and spiritual. And since, if anyone intends to build a house, he must begin from the foundation, so he who wished to treat of this twofold food or of this twofold sword would have to begin from the foundation: that is, from the parts of which a man is composed. And just as he would see and perceive by reason how these two parts are related, so could he judge concerning these two foods and swords. For we are the creatures of God and are made by God, and God has made and formed us of two elements, namely, of body and spirit. And so He has ordained and provided a twofold food for us: a bodily, by which the body is sustained, and a spiritual, by which the soul is refreshed. And because a man might be impeded with respect to each of these, bodily

1. *De sacramentis fidei Christianae* 2:2:4 (PL 176:418).
2. Matt. 26:41.
3. Gen. 2:7.
4. Matt. 4:4.

et in[1] corporali cibo et in[2] spirituali, ordinavit duplicem gladium: materialem, ne impediremur in corpore nec in corporali cibo, et hoc spectat ad potestatem terrenam, cuius est defendere et tueri corpora et possessiones ex quibus habet esse corporalis cibus; ordinavit nihilominus eciam[3] gladium spiritualem, id est potestatem ecclesiasticam et sacerdotalem, ne impediremur in spirituali cibo et in hiis que spectant ad bonum anime.

Iuxta igitur hoc fundamentum, dicemus quod, sicut sunt res[4] differentes corpus et anima, cibus corporalis et spiritualis, sic sunt res differentes gladius materialis et spiritualis. Sed quantumcumque sint res differentes corpus et anima, possumus tamen dicere quod habent triplicem unionem. Una[5] quidem secundum composicionem, quia ex illis duobus componitur unus homo, unum suppositum, una persona humana, ita quod quilibet unus et idem homo, quelibet una et eadem persona humana, est composita ex illis duobus, ex anima videlicet[6] et corpore. Hec est[7] ergo prima unio anime et corporis: secundum composicionem.

Secunda unio anime et corporis est secundum adhesionem et subieccionem de iure et de facto, ut in hominibus[8] rectis[9] et studiosis, in quibus non solum de iure sed de facto corpus adheret et subicitur animo, caro spiritui et sensualitas racioni. Homines enim boni conantur corpus subicere anime et carnem spiritui, ut si aliquos impetus habet caro contra spiritum, impetus illos boni et studiosi mortificare student, iuxta illud ad Romanos VIII: 'Si enim secundum carnem vixeritis, moriemini; si autem spiritu[10] facta carnis mortificaveritis, vivetis.'

Tercia unio anime et corporis est adhesio et subieccio corporis de iure, sed non de[11] facto. Prima quidem et secunda unio est approbanda, licet, adaptata ad gladios, alio et alio tempore alium et alium habuerit vigorem.[12] Sed hec tercia unio est mala et reprobanda, et est in hominibus[13] non rectis, sed perversis, in quibus corpus de iure debet adherere et esse subiectum anime et caro spiritui, de facto tamen corpus rebellat anime et caro spiritui, nec vivere volunt secundum spirituales leges. Hec autem unio corporis et anime et hoc debitum numquam potest tolli quin corpus de iure sit subiectum anime; et ab hoc debito numquam potest corpus absolvi quin debeat esse anime subiectum. Absolvitur tamen de facto, prout actu rebellat anime.

Iuxta igitur tria hec[14] que videmus inter animam et corpus, ex quibus sumitur distinccio utriusque gladii, possumus loqui de utroque gladio; quia sicut anima est

1: in] *om.* V[1]   2: in] *om.* V[1]   3: eciam] *om.* PV[1] ei V[2]   4: sunt res] res sunt F   5: Una] unam C
6: videlicet] *om.* F   7: est] *om.* V[2]   8: hominibus] omnibus F   9: rectis] bonis *add.* CFV[2]
10: spiritu] spiritus F   11: de] *om.* FPV[1]V[2]   12: habuerit vigorem] vigorem habuerit CFV[2]
13: hominibus] omnibus F   14: tria hec] hec tria CFV[2]

food and spiritual alike, He has ordained two swords: a material, lest we be impeded in body or with respect to bodily food, and this belongs to the earthly power, whose task it is to defend and protect bodies and the possessions from which bodily food has its being; and He has moreover ordained a spiritual sword, that is, ecclesiastical and priestly power, lest we be impeded with respect to spiritual food and in those matters which relate to the good of the soul.

According to this foundation, then, we shall say that, just as body and soul and bodily and spiritual foods are different things, so are the material and spiritual swords different things. But however great may be the difference between body and soul, we can nonetheless say that they have a threefold union. One, indeed, is according to composition, since one man, one entity, one human person, is composed of these two elements, so that whoever is one and the same man, whoever is one and the same human person, is composed of these two elements: namely, of soul and body. This, therefore, is the first union of soul and body: according to composition.

The second union of soul and body is according to adherence and subjection both *de iure* and *de facto*, as in righteous and zealous men, in whom the body adheres to the soul and is subject to it, flesh to spirit and sensuality to reason, not only *de iure*, but *de facto* also. For good men endeavour to subject body to soul and flesh to spirit, so that, if the flesh has any impulses contrary to the spirit, these good and zealous men strive to mortify those impulses, according to what is said in Romans 8: 'For if you live after the flesh, you shall die; but if you through the spirit do mortify the deeds of the body, you shall live.'[1]

The third union of soul and body is the adherence and subjection of the body *de iure*, but not *de facto*. The first union is praiseworthy indeed; as is the second, even though, considered in relation to the swords, it will have had varying strength at different times. But this third union is evil and reprehensible, and occurs in men who are not righteous, but perverse: in whom, although the body should adhere and be subject to the soul *de iure*, and the flesh to the spirit, the body rebels against the soul and the flesh against the spirit *de facto*, and who are not willing to live according to spiritual laws. And this union of body and soul, and this obligation, can never be removed. Rather, the body is subject to the soul *de iure*, and from this obligation the body can never be released: rather, it must [always] be subject to the soul [in this sense]. Nonetheless, it is released *de facto* inasmuch as it rebels against the soul in actuality.[2]

We can speak of each sword, then, according to these three relations which we see between soul and body, from which the distinction between the two swords is

---

1. Rom. 8:13.
2. But the meaning here is not really that body and soul 'have a threefold union.' Rather, the point is (a) that they are united because of the way in which man happens to be made; (b) that it is always right for body to be subject to soul and that, in good men, it is so subject, even if its subjection must sometimes be strengthened by the power of the swords; but (c) that, although they cannot escape the obligation to be subject to it *de iure*, the bodies of the wicked rebel against the soul *de facto*. Thus, (b) and (c) are not 'kinds' of union, but moral dispositions: the good observe the proper relation of flesh to spirit and the wicked do not.

res distincta a corpore et econverso, sic gladius materialis est distinctus a spirituali
et econverso. Sunt enim hii duo gladii nunc in lege gracie, fuerunt in lege scripta,
fuerunt eciam in lege nature. Nam in lege nature fuerunt reges et sacerdotes et eciam
in lege scripta, et sunt nunc in lege gracie. Possumus itaque dicere quod sicut corpus
ad animam habet triplicem ordinem, ita gladius materialis ad spiritualem potest
habere triplicem ordinem.

Unus quidem ordo et una unio est secundum composicionem, quia, ut dicebatur,[1] ex anima et corpore fit unus homo et una persona humana,[2] sic et hii duo
gladii aliquando fuerunt in uno homine et in una persona humana. Nam Melchisedech, ut habetur Genes. XIV, fuit rex Salem et sacerdos Dei altissimi. Prout
ergo fuit rex, habuit usum gladii materialis; prout autem erat sacerdos, habuit usum
gladii spiritualis. Sic et Iob fuit rex et sacerdos. Fuit quidem rex, quia, ut dicitur
Iob XXIX: 'Cum sederem quasi rex circumstante[3] exercitu, eram[4] tamen merencium consolator'; ibi[5] 'quasi rex' non ponitur diminutive, sed expressive. Sedebat
ergo Iob quasi rex, id est sedebat ad modum regis; quod patet per verbum sequens,
quod sedebat 'circumstante exercitu,' id est sedebat cum magna civili potencia,
quod maxime spectat ad regem habere exercitum: gentem armatam et civilem
potenciam, ut possit vindictas corporales exercere et iudicium sanguinis facere. Et
secundum hunc modum debet esse rex 'merencium consolator,' puniendo corporaliter forefacientes in alios et contristantes[6] alios. Iste eciam idem Iob, qui erat rex,
fuit eciam sacerdos, quia, ut dicitur Iob primo: 'Consurgens diluculo offerebat Deo
holocausta,' quod est officium sacerdotis.

Itaque[7] hii duo gladii semper fuerunt et sunt res differentes, ita quod unus non est
alius, sicut anima non est corpus nec econverso. Sed ut patuit, licet sint res differentes, in lege tamen nature coniungebantur hii duo gladii, videlicet potestas regia et
sacerdotalis, in una et eadem persona, et potissime in bonis regibus, qui erant reges
et sacerdotes, ut patuit in Melchisedech et in Iob; nec erat preter racionem quod
utrumque gladium haberet unus et idem homo, cum ex anima et corpore constituatur
unus homo et una persona humana.

In lege autem scripta, cum regebatur populus Iudaicus per iudices et sacerdotes,
hii duo gladii erant aliqualiter distincti et aliqualiter uniti. Erant enim[8] uniti quia
sacerdotes,[9] una cum iudice qui erat pro tempore, audiebant causas non solum spirituales, quia iudicabant inter lepram et lepram et inter peccatum et peccatum, sed eciam

---

1: ut dicebatur] *om.* V[1]   2: humana] *om.* V[1]   3: circumstante] *om.* V[2]   4: eram] *om.* V[2]
5: ibi] ubi F   6: contristantes] contrastantes F   7: Itaque] ita C   8: enim] quidem V[2] quidam F
9: sacerdotes] sacerdos F

derived. For just as the soul is a thing distinct from the body and conversely, so is the material sword distinct from the spiritual sword and conversely. For these two swords exist now, under the Law of Grace; they existed under the Written Law; and they existed under the law of nature. For under the law of nature, and under the Written Law also, there were kings and priests, as there are now under the Law of Grace. We can say, then, that just as the body has a threefold order in relation to the soul, so can the material sword have a threefold order in relation to the spiritual.

One order and one union is, again, according to composition. For, as has been said, one man and one human person is made from soul and body, and so also were these two swords once in one man and in one human person. For, as is established in Genesis 14, Melchizedek was king of Salem and a priest of the Most High God.[1] Inasmuch as he was a king, therefore, he had the use of the material sword; inasmuch as he was a priest, he had the use of the spiritual sword. So too, Job was both king and priest. He was a king indeed; for, as is said in Job 29: 'When I sat as a king with an army standing round about, I was nonetheless the comforter of those who mourned';[2] and 'as a king' is there used not diminutively, but expressively.[3] Job, therefore, sat as a king: that is, he sat in the manner of a king. And it is clear from the words which follow — that he sat 'with an army standing round about': that is, he sat with great civil might — that it belongs especially to the king to have an army: armed men and civil might, so that he may be able to inflict bodily punishments and execute the judgment of blood. And it is in this way that the king must be 'the comforter of those who mourned': by inflicting bodily punishment upon those who injure others and who bring sorrow to others. Moreover, that same Job who was a king was also a priest; for, as is said in Job 1, he 'rose up early in the morning and offered burnt offerings to God,'[4] which is a priestly office.

These two swords, then, always were and are different things. Thus, the one is not the other, just as the soul is not the body and conversely. But it has become clear that, although they are different things, these two swords — that is, royal and priestly power — were nonetheless united under the law of nature in one and the same person, and especially in good kings who were kings and priests, as has become clear in the case of Mechizedek and Job. Nor was it beyond reason that one and the same man should possess both swords, since one man and one human person was composed of soul and body.

But, under the Written Law, when the Jewish people were ruled by judges and priests, these two swords were in some measure distinct and in some measure united. For they were united in that the priests, together with whoever was judge at that time, heard not only spiritual causes, since they judged between leprosy and leprosy and between sin and sin; but they also heard criminal causes

1.　Gen. 14:18.
2.　Job 29:25 (Vulgate).
3.　I.e. *quasi rex* there means 'as a king,' not 'like a king.'
4.　Job 1:5.

audiebant causas criminales inter sanguinem et sanguinem. Ideo dicitur Deuter. XVII: 'Si difficile et[1] ambiguum apud te iudicium esse prospexeris inter sanguinem et sanguinem,'[2] quantum ad corpora, 'causam et causam,' quantum ad res possessas, 'lepram et lepram,' quantum ad animam sive quantum ad peccata prout habent inficere animam, 'venies[3] ad sacerdotes Levitici generis et ad iudicem qui fuerit[4] in illo tempore, qui iudicabunt tibi iudicii veritatem, et facies quodcumque[5] dixerint.' Aliqualiter ergo sacerdotes Veteris Testamenti habebant utrumque gladium, quia non solum audiebant causas inter lepram et lepram, quod potest referri ad potestatem et gladium spiritualem, sed eciam audiebant causam inter sanguinem et sanguinem, quod potest referri ad potestatem terrenam et ad gladium materialem. Erant ergo tunc hii duo gladii in persona sacerdotis aliqualiter uniti. Erant eciam aliqualiter distincti, quia ipsam sentenciam sanguinis, si non obediebatur[6] sacerdoti, non videbatur proferre sacerdos, sed iudex. Propter quod ibidem dicitur quod[7] 'Qui autem superbierit, nolens obedire sacerdotis imperio, qui ministro[8] Domino Deo tuo, decreto iudicis morietur homo ille.'

Postmodum vero in eodem populo fuerunt hii duo gladii magis distincti, quoniam populus petiit constitui sibi regem, qui iudicaret eos, ut habetur primo Regum VIII capitulo. Nunc eciam in lege gracie sunt hii duo gladii distincti, potestas videlicet regia et sacerdotalis.

Sed dicet aliquis quod semper hii duo gladii debent esse coniuncti in una persona, quia, cum unus gladius respiciat animam et alius corpus, quia ex[9] anima et corpore semper fit una persona humana,[10] videtur quod in uno homine semper debet[11] residere[12] utraque potestas. Ad quod quidem dicere possumus quod anima, intenta rebus spiritualibus et eternis, videtur non esse in mundo, iuxta illud Augustini IV[13] *De Trinitate*: quod, secundum quod mente aliquid eternum quantum possumus capimus, non in hoc mundo sumus, et omnium iustorum[14] spiritus, eciam adhuc in carne vivencium, in quantum divina sapiunt non sunt in hoc mundo. Sacerdotes ergo legis nove, habentes statum perfecciorem quam sacerdotes veteris legis, et exinde quasi totaliter sancti et divinis dediti et per hoc non existentes in mundo, iudicium sanguinis non debuerunt sibi retinere, sed mundane potestati ac seculari committere.

Sed si bene considerant potestates terrene, potestas potissime commissa est eis ut, cum non obeditur sacerdotibus, et potissime Summo Pontifici, ipse potestates terrene contra inobedientes debent iudicium sanguinis exercere,[15] iuxta illud[16] quod habetur in Deuteronomio: quod inobediens sacerdoti decreto iudicis occidebatur, ut et[17]

1: et] *om.* FV[1]   2: et sanguinem] *om.* F   3: venies] veniensque V[2]   veniesque F   veniens P
4: iudicem qui fuerit] iudices qui fuerint F   5: quodcumque] quecumque FPV[1]V[2]   6: obediebatur] obediebant F   7: quod] *om.* F   8: ministro] ministrabat F   eo tempore *add.* V[2]   9: ex] et F
10: humana] *om.* C   11: debet] debeat C   12: residere] recidere P   13: IV] ix FPV[1]V[2]
14: iustorum] sanctorum F   15: iudicium sanguinis exercere] exercere iudicium sanguinis C
16: illud] istud FV[2]   17: et] *om.* CFV[2]

as between blood and blood. And so it is said in Deuteronomy 17: 'If you shall perceive there to be a difficult and doubtful matter among you as between blood and blood' as regards bodies, 'cause and cause,' as regards items of property, 'or leprosy and leprosy' as regards the soul, or as regards sins inasmuch as they have the capacity to infect the soul, 'come to the priests of the tribe of Levi and to whoever shall be judge at that time, and they will judge you with true judgment; and you are to do whatever they say.'[1] In some measure, therefore, the priests of the Old Testament had both swords. For not only did they hear causes as between leprosy and leprosy, which can be referred to the spiritual power and sword; but they also heard causes as between blood and blood, which can be referred to the earthly power and to the material sword. Therefore, these two swords were then in some measure united in the person of the priest. Also, they were in some measure distinct; for if obedience was not given to the priest, the priest was not seen to pronounce the sentence of blood itself, but the judge. For it is said in the same place: 'And whoever shall be proud, refusing to obey the command of the priest who is the minister of the Lord your God, that man shall die by the decree of the judge.'[2]

These two swords were subsequently distinguished more clearly among the same people, however; for, as is established in I Samuel 8, the people petitioned to have a king appointed for them, to judge them.[3] And now these two swords, that is, royal and priestly power, are distinct under the Law of Grace.

But someone will say that these two swords must always be united in one person; for, since the one sword is concerned with the soul and the other with the body, and since one human person is always made from soul and body, it seems that both powers must always reside in one man. To this, however, we can reply that the soul, being intent upon spiritual and eternal things, seems not to be in the world, according to what Augustine says in *De Trinitate* 4: that, insofar as our minds are able to grasp something of the eternal, we are not in this world, and that, even while they are alive and in the flesh, the spirits of all just men are not in this world insofar as they understand the divine.[4] The priests of the New Law therefore, since their condition is more perfect than that of the priests of the Old Law, and since they are therefore almost entirely holy and dedicated to the divine, and, for this reason, are not in the world, should not retain the judgment of blood to themselves, but must entrust it to worldly and secular powers.

But if the earthly powers consider matters well, [they will see that] power has been entrusted to them especially so that, when obedience is not given to the priests, and especially to the Supreme Pontiff, those earthly powers should execute the judgment of blood against the disobedient according to what is established in Deuteronomy: that those who disobeyed the priest should be slain by the

---

1. Deut. 17:8–10; but the quotation is inexact.
2. Deut. 17:12; but, again, inexact.
3. I Sam. 8:5.
4. Perhaps *De Trinitate* 4:18 (CCSL 50:191). The weight of MSS evidence favours the reading 'ix De Trinitate'; but this reading makes no sense, and 'ix' as a scribal misreading for 'iv' is palaeographically not unlikely.

cunctus populus, hoc audiens, timeret sacerdotis imperio contraire.

Patefactum est itaque, quantum ad primum ordinem quem habet anima ad corpus, ut quia ex ea et corpore fit una persona, quod[1] hii duo gladii aliquando hunc ordinem habuerunt, quia in una et eadem persona primitus residebant; sed racione cuiusdam decencie, et ut magis essent de divinis dediti, prelati ecclesiastici nove legis gladium materialem[2] et iudicium[3] sanguinis secularibus principibus commiserunt; vel, quod idem est, approbaverunt et voluerunt huiusmodi gladium et iudicium sanguinis talibus principibus fore commissum. Vel possumus dicere[4] quod in prelato ecclesiastico adhuc residet uterque gladius, ut sequenti capitulo apparebit.

Declarata itaque unione istorum duorum gladiorum quantum ad unitatem[5] et pluralitatem personarum, volumus agere de unione et ordine ipsorum, quarum[6] una est de iure et non de facto, alia de facto et[7] de iure.

Dicebatur quidem quod hii duo gladii sic se habent quod unus respicit animam et alius respicit corpus. Sed cum corpus habeat hanc unionem et hunc ordinem ad animam, quod semper de iure sibi debet esse subiectum, et ab hoc iure et ab hoc debito, quamdiu vivit corpus,[8] non[9] potest absolvi, ideo in hominibus bonis sicut est de iure, sic est de facto, quod toto posse conantur corpus subicere anime et carnem spiritui. Eodemque modo se habet in hiis gladiis quod[10] gladius materialis de iure debet esse subiectus spirituali et ab hoc iure et ab hoc debito non potest absolvi. Et sicut boni homines habent corpus subiectum anime, mali autem non habent, sic bene principantes secundum secularem potenciam sunt subiecti[11] sacerdocio, et potissime Summo Pontifici; quod si rebellent, non bene principantur.[12] Nec mirum si male principantes hoc aliquando faciunt,[13] quando[14] et contra Dominum non bene principantes aliquando rebellaverunt, sicut legitur de Ieroboam, quod surrexit et rebellavit contra Dominum.

CAPITULUM VIII: *Quomodo hii duo gladii in una et eadem persona, videlicet in Summo Pontifice, per quandam excellenciam reservantur.*[15]

Diximus hos gladios esse distinctos et has potestates esse differentes et quod potestas terrena reservatur in rege, ecclesiastica in sacerdote, et potissime in Summo Sacerdote. Videtur ergo ex hoc quod gladius materialis et terrena potestas non reservaretur in ecclesiastica potestate, et exinde posset ulterius argui quod sacerdotes in lege gracie essent imperfecciores sacerdotibus in lege nature, quia illi erant reges et sacerdotes, habentes utrumque gladium et utramque potenciam. Si igitur potencia est de genere bonorum et aliquam potenciam habebant[16] sacerdotes in lege nature quam non habent sacerdotes in lege[17] gracie, quia illi habebant potestatem terrenam et gladium

---

1: quod] quia PV²   2: gladium materialem] materialem gladium C   3: et iudicium] *om.* C
4: dicere] habere F   5: unitatem] unionem FV²   6: quarum] quorum C   7: et] non *add.* C
8: corpus] *del.* C   9: non] numquam FV²   10: quod] quia F   11: subiecti] subditi V¹
12: principantur] principentur F   13: faciunt] statuunt F   14: quando] quoniam V²
15: *reservantur*] reserventur F   16: habebant] habent V²   habebunt F   17: nature quam ...
lege] *om.* FV²

decree of the judge, so that, hearing this, the whole people should indeed fear to contravene the command of the priest.

Having regard, then, to the primary order which the soul has in relation to the body in that, from it and body, one person is made, it has been shown that these two swords also once had this order because they originally resided in one and the same person; but that, by reason of a certain fittingness, and so that they might be more fully dedicated to the divine, the prelates of the Church under the New Law have entrusted the material sword and the judgment of blood to secular princes: or, which comes to the same thing, have willed that this sword and the judgment of blood be entrusted to such princes. Alternatively, we can say that both swords still reside in the ecclesiastical prelate, as will appear in the following chapter.

Having declared the union of these two swords in relation to the unity and plurality of persons, then, we wish to deal with their union and order considered in themselves: which, on the one hand, is *de iure* and not *de facto* and, on the other, is both *de iure* and *de facto*.

It has indeed been said that these two swords are such that the one is concerned with the soul and the other is concerned with the body. But since the body is united with the soul and ordered in relation to it in such a way that it must always be subject to it *de iure* and cannot be absolved from this right and from this obligation for as long as the body lives, it is therefore true in the case of good men that they endeavour, as far as possible, to make body subject to soul and flesh to spirit not only *de iure*, but *de facto* also. And, in the same way, it is true of these swords that the material sword must be subject to the spiritual *de iure* and cannot be released from this right and from this obligation. And just as good men have a body which is subject to the soul and wicked men do not, so those who rule well according to secular power are subject to the priesthood, and especially to the Supreme Pontiff; because, if they rebel, they do not rule well. But it is not surprising if wicked rulers sometimes do this, when those who do not rule well have sometimes rebelled even against the Lord: as we read of Jeroboam, that he rose up and rebelled against the Lord.[1]

CHAPTER VIII: *How these two swords are reserved in one and the same person, namely, in the Supreme Pontiff, by reason of a certain excellence.*

We have said that these swords are distinct and that these powers are different, and that the earthly power is contained in the king and the ecclesiastical in the priest, and especially in the Supreme Priest. From this, therefore, it seems that the material sword and earthly power are not contained in the ecclesiastical power, and that, accordingly, it is also possible to argue that priests under the Law of Grace are less perfect than were priests under the law of nature, since the latter were kings and priests, having both swords and both powers. Thus, if power is a member of the class of goods, and if priests had a kind of power under the law of nature which priests under the Law of Grace do not have, since the former had earthly

---

1. I Kings 12:28–14:20.

materialem quem non habent sacerdotes in lege gracie, consequens est quod aliqua potencia, ac per consequens aliquod bonum et aliqua perfeccio, competebat sacerdotibus in lege nature vel eciam[1] in lege scripta que non competit sacerdotibus Novi Testamenti. Perfecciores ergo erant illi quam isti; quod est inconveniens.

Dicemus ergo quod sacerdotes, et potissime Sacerdos Summus, debet in lege nova habere gladium spiritualem et[2] non gladium materialem non quia[3] nullo modo habeat talem gladium, sed quia non habet materialem gladium ad usum, sed ad nutum, et quia decet Ecclesiam et Summum Pontificem habere materialem gladium ad nutum, non ad usum. Et quia habere huiusmodi gladium ad nutum est habere ipsum perfecciori modo quam ad usum, dicemus quod Ecclesia et Summus Pontifex excellenciori et perfecciori modo habet gladium materialem quam habeant reges et terreni principes. Habet itaque Ecclesia gladium spiritualem eciam ad usum, cum quo ferit et percutit,[4] et cum quo maiorem lesionem infert quam inferre possit materialis gladius, quanto lesio anime est multo maior quam lesio corporis. Ipsum autem gladium materialem non habet ad usum, sed ad nutum, ut est communis doctorum sentencia et ut Bernardus ait: 'Utrumque ergo gladium habet Ecclesia, sed non eodem modo; quia spiritualem habet ad usum, materialem ad nutum.'

Intendimus ergo[5] in hoc capitulo declarare[6] quod Ecclesia habet[7] utrumque gladium: alterum ad usum, alterum ad nutum. In sequenti autem[8] capitulo declarabimus quod expedit Ecclesie et decet eam habere gladium materialem non ad usum, sed ad nutum.[9] Insuper, in eodem capitulo ostendemus quod habere materialem gladium ad nutum est habere ipsum perfecciori modo quam ad usum. Propter quod non possunt reges et principes insultare contra Ecclesiam, dicentes se ex hoc esse excellenciores ea quia habent usum materialis gladii et quia habent dominium temporalium ac[10] terrenorum; quia huiusmodi gladium et huiusmodi dominium excellenciori modo habet Ecclesia quam habeant principes seculares.

Primum autem quod intendimus in hoc capitulo, videlicet quod Ecclesia habeat utrumque gladium, ut quod eciam habeat[11] ipsum materialem gladium ad nutum, de quo possent forte magis homines dubitare, tripliciter declarabimus. Primo ex ipso Moyse iuxta consilium sibi dato[12] a Iethro, cognato eius;[13] secundo ex ipso Summo Sacerdote ad quem appellabatur a iudicibus; tercio ex ipso rege qui preficiendus erat in populo, qui non debebat recedere a consilio Summi Sacerdotis.

Prima via sic patet. Dicitur enim Exodi XVIII[14] quod sedit Moyses ut iudicaret populum, qui assistebant[15] Moysi de mane usque ad vesperam; cui Iethro ait: 'Stulto labore consumeris. Esto tu populo in hiis que ad Deum[16] pertinent, ostendasque populo cerimonias et ritum colendi viamque per quam ambulent; provideque[17] de omni

---

1: eciam] *del.* F   2: et] *om.* C   3: quia] quod CPV¹V²   4: percutit] percussit F   5: ergo] *om.* FV²
6: in hoc capitulo declarare] declarare in hoc capitulo C   7: habet] habebat *mss*   8: autem]
om. FV²   9: non ad usum, sed ad nutum] ad usum, non ad nutum PV¹   10: ac] et FV²
11: utrumque gladium ... habeat] *om.* C   12: dato] datum C   13: eius] *om.* C   14: XVIII]
xvii C   15: assistebant] assistebat F   16: Deum] dominium P   17: provideque] autem *add.* F

power and the material sword, which priests under the Law of Grace do not have, then it follows that a kind of power, and consequently a kind of good and a kind of perfection, belonged to priests under both the law of nature and the Written Law which does not belong to the priests of the New Testament. The former, therefore, were more perfect than the latter; which is inconsistent.

Therefore, although, under the New Law, priests, and especially the Supreme Priest, must have the spiritual sword and not the material sword, we shall say not that there is no sense in which he may have the latter sword, but that he has the material sword not to use, but to command; and that it is fitting for the Church and the Supreme Pontiff to have the material sword to command, not to use. Also, since to have that sword to command rather than to use is to have it in a more perfect way, we shall say that the Church and the Supreme Pontiff have the material sword in a more excellent and perfect way than kings and earthly princes may have it. Thus, the Church indeed has the spiritual sword to use: with which she strikes and punishes, and with which she inflicts a more grievous wound than the material sword can inflict, inasmuch as a wound to the soul is far more grievous than a wound to the body. But she has the material sword itself not to use, but to command, as is the unanimous judgment of the learned and as Bernard says: 'The Church therefore has both swords, but not in the same way; for she has the spiritual to use and the material to command.'[1]

In this chapter, therefore, we intend to declare that the Church has both swords, the one to use and the other to command. And in the next chapter we shall declare that it is expedient for the Church and fitting for her to have the material sword not to use, but to command. Further, we shall show in the same chapter that to have the material sword to command rather than to use is to have it in a more perfect way. For this reason, kings and princes cannot rail against the Church, pronouncing themselves to be more excellent than she because they have the use of the material sword and because they have a temporal and earthly lordship; for the Church has that sword and such lordship in a more excellent way than secular princes may have it.

First, then, as to what we intend in this chapter, namely, that the Church may have both swords, so that (which men may perhaps be more able to doubt) she also has the material sword itself to command: we shall show this in three ways. The first is from Moses himself, according to the counsel given to him by his kinsman Jethro; the second is from the Supreme Priest to whom appeal was made from the judges; and the third is from the king who was to be set over the people yet who was obliged not to recede from the counsel of the Supreme Priest.

The first way appears thus. It is said in Exodus 18 that 'Moses sat to judge the people, who stood by Moses from morning till night'; and Jethro said to him: 'You are consumed by foolish labour. Be for the people in those things which pertain to God, and show the people the ceremonies and rites of worship and the path in which they are to walk; and provide from the whole people tribunes, rulers

---

1. *De consideratione* 4:3.

plebe tribunos, centuriones, quinquagenarios et decanos qui iudicent populum.' Primitus ergo ipse Moyses sedebat ut iudicaret populum, et exercebat in populo[1] non solum ea que sunt ad Deum, quod pertinet ad gladium spiritualem, sed eciam sedebat audiens causas et litigia quorumcumque de quibuscumque, quia quantum ad iudicium sanguinis et quantum ad litigia inter personas laicas pertinebat ad gladium materialem. Et quia stulto labore consumebatur nec poterat sufficienter exercere opera utriusque gladii, retento sibi quod spirituale erat in hiis que sunt ad Deum, audicionem causarum commisit iudicibus, quibus iudicibus, quantum ad eam partem que est de iudicio sanguinis et de questionibus temporalium inter laicas personas, succedunt[2] reges et principes seculares, et universaliter locum dictorum iudicum quantum ad iudicium sanguinis et litigia inter personas laicas tenent[3] terreni principes et domini seculares.

Propter quod, sicut inter ipsos iudices aliqui erant tribuni, id est millenarii, aliqui centuriones, aliqui quinquagenarii, aliqui decani, quia aliqui eorum habebant plurimam gentem[4] ad iudicandum et aliqui parviorem,[5] et sicut uni eorum erant sub aliis: sic[6] inter ipsos dominos seculares aliqui sunt[7] sub aliis et aliqui habent maiorem principatum et aliqui minorem. Quod ergo huiusmodi iudices possent sic iudicare populum, hoc erat ex commissione ipsius Moysis.

Quare, sicut et tunc iudices erant sub Moyse, et si qua insolita[8] et maiora occurrerent referenda erant ipsi Moysi, sic universaliter[9] terreni principes, si volunt salutem consequi, debent esse sub Summo Pontifice, et si aliqua magna et insolita[10] occurrerent referenda essent ipsi Summo Pontifici, et potissime si talia essent illa magna, quantumcumque essent secularia vel terrena, que possent Ecclesiam perturbare. Potest enim dici nunc[11] Summo Pontifici quod dictum fuit[12] Moysi Exod. XVIII: 'Quicquid autem maius[13] fuerit, referatur ad te.' Quod potissime, ut dicebamus,[14] de tali litigio magno intelligendum est, sive illud litigium sit in temporalibus sive in spiritualibus, quod potest Ecclesiam perturbare.

Ex ipso itaque Moyse, sub quo erant iudices quibus quantum ad aliquam partem succedunt[15] terreni principes, habentes iudicium sanguinis et gladium materialem, patet quod huiusmodi materialem gladium habet Ecclesia, etsi non ad usum, ad nutum: quod ideo dicitur talem gladium habere ad nutum[16] quia[17] sub ea et sub eius imperio debent esse principes seculares usum huius[18] gladii exercentes. Sicut ergo primitus iudices erant sub Moyse non solum in spiritualibus et in hiis que sunt ad Deum, que[19] Moyses retinuit sibi, sed eciam in hiis que pertinebant ad gladium materialem; sic et modo principes seculares in hiis que pertinent ad materialem gladium debent esse sub Ecclesia, quia ad opus Ecclesie, in bonum fidei, in augmentum[20] spiritualium bonorum, debent uti huiusmodi gladio.

1: populo] populum F   2: succedunt] subcedunt et FV²   3: tenent] tenentes PV² omnes *add.* CFV²
4: gentem] et *add.* F   5: parviorem] pauciorem C   6: sic] sicut F   7: sunt] *om.* C   8: insolita] insoluta CF   9: universaliter] item F   10: insolita] insoluta CF   11: nunc] nostro F
12: fuit] est C   13: maius] magnum C   14: dicebamus] dicebatur C   15: succedunt] subcedunt F
16: quod ideo ... nutum] *om.* PV¹   17: quia] *om.* PV¹   18: huius] huiusmodi F   19: que] quod PV¹   20: augmentum] augumentum F

of hundreds, rulers of fifties and rulers of tens, to judge the people.'[1] At first, therefore, Moses sat to judge the people himself, and he occupied himself among the people not only with those things which are of God, which pertain to the spiritual sword, but he also sat hearing the causes and disputes of all men concerning all things, which, insofar they involved the judgment of blood, and insofar as they were disputes between lay persons, pertained to the material sword. And because he was consumed by foolish labour and could not sufficiently perform the work of both swords, he entrusted the hearing of [temporal] causes to judges, retaining to himself that which was spiritual in those things which pertain to God. And to those judges, insofar as they were concerned with the judgment of blood and with temporal disputes between lay persons, kings and secular princes have succeeded; and, as regards the judgment of blood and disputes between lay persons, earthly princes and secular lords now everywhere hold the place of those who were called judges.

And so it is that, just as, among the judges themselves, some were tribunes — that is, rulers of thousands — some rulers of hundreds, some of fifties and some of tens, since some of them had jurisdiction over more people and some over fewer; and just as some of them were under others: so, among secular lords themselves, some are under others and some have a greater ruling power and some a lesser. Therefore it was by the commission of Moses himself that such judges were able to judge the people.

Hence, just as, even then, the judges were under Moses and, if any unusual and great matters occurred, they were to be referred to Moses himself, so earthly princes universally, if they wish to obtain salvation, must be under the Supreme Pontiff, and, if any great and unusual matters occur, they must be referred to the Supreme Pontiff himself: especially if those great matters, however secular or earthly they may be, are such as may disturb the Church. For what was said to Moses in Exodus 18 can be said now to the Supreme Pontiff: 'And whatever great matter shall arise, let it be referred to you.'[2] And, as we have said, this must be understood especially of any such great dispute, be it a dispute in the sphere of temporal or spiritual things, as can disturb the Church.

From Moses himself, then, under whom were the judges to whom earthly princes have in some part succeeded inasmuch as they have the judgment of blood and the material sword, it is clear that the Church has that material sword to command, even though not to use: that she is said to have such a sword to command because the secular princes who make use of that sword must be under her and under her command. Therefore, just as the judges were at first under Moses not only in spiritual matters and in those things which are of God, which Moses retained to himself, but also in those things which pertained to the material sword, so, in the same way, secular princes must be under the Church in those things which pertain to the material sword. For they must use that sword for the Church's work, for the good of the faith, and for the increase of spiritual goods.

1. Paraphrased from Exodus 18:13–22.
2. Exodus 18:22.

Nam sicut corpus, secundum quod corpus,[1] est propter animam et ordinatur ad animam, sic omnia terrena et temporalia, secundum quod huiusmodi sunt, ordinantur ad spiritualia, et de iure debent eis esse subiecta: a quo debito, ut supra tetigimus, numquam possunt absolvi. Terreni itaque principes, secundum quod huiusmodi sunt et ut habent materialem gladium, debent esse subiecti potestati spirituali, et potissime potestati Summi Pontificis: quod debitum sive[2] iugum non possunt a se abicere,[3] quod iugum non est servitus, sed libertas; quia iugum Christi suave est et onus[4] eius leve. Quare, si terreni principes, ut habent materialem gladium, Ecclesie sunt subiecti, quia rem subiectam quilibet dicitur[5] habere ad nutum, quia si non habet ad nutum non est sibi subiecta, bene dictum[6] est quod materialem gladium, etsi non ad usum, ad nutum habet Ecclesia.

Secunda via ad hoc idem, quod Ecclesia ad nutum habeat temporalem gladium, ostendi potest ex appellacione que fiebat a iudicibus ad Summum Sacerdotem Deuteronomio XVII. De difficili et ambiguo non solum inter causam et causam quantum ad temporalia, et inter lepram et[7] lepram quantum ad spiritualia, sed eciam inter sanguinem et sanguinem, recurrebatur[8] ad iudicem qui erat pro tempore et ad sacerdotes Levitici generis. Quod, ut intelligatur, sciendum quod, sicut[9] Iosephus ait et Magister tangit in *Historiis*, in singulis civitatibus septem eligebantur iudices, virtute et studio iusticie prediti, qui sedebant in portis audientes placita: qui[10] ideo[11] sedebant in portis ut possent iudicare intrinsecos et extrinsecos. Cuilibet autem iudici, ut magister in *Historiis* tangit, addebantur duo ministri de genere Levitarum. Si ergo inter iudices illos oriretur[12] aliquid difficile vel ambiguum, fiebat appellacio vel recursus ad Summum Sacerdotem. Unde et capitulum illud Deuteronomii ubi de hoc agitur intitulat Magister in *Historiis* 'De appellacione ad Summum Sacerdotem.'[13] Et quod Summus Sacerdos iudicabat, hoc tenebatur pro sentencia, cui nolens obedire decreto iudicis moriebatur, id est[14] occidebatur. Summus ergo Sacerdos ad nutum habebat materialem gladium, cum[15] nolens sibi obedire decreto iudicum, quibus quantum ad iudicium sanguinis et[16] secularia litigia succedunt[17] terreni principes, moriebatur propter inobedienciam ad Summum Pontificem. Hinc[18] ergo animadvertere debent cuncti fideles quam periculosum sit nolle obedire Summo Pontifici et nolle stare sentencie eius, quando de mandato Domini non obedientes ei morti tradebantur.

Tercia via sumitur ex ipso rege qui preficiendus erat in populo. Unde Deuter. XVII[19] scribitur:[20] 'Non poteris alterius gentis hominem regem facere.' De quo rege

---

1: secundum quod corpus] *om.* FV[2]   2: sive] seu C   3: a se abicere] adabiicere F   4: onus] honus P   5: dicitur] debet F   6: dictum] dicendum F   7: et] non *add.* P   8: recurrebatur] recurrebam F   9: sicut] *om.* CFV[2]   10: qui] quod FV[2]   11: ideo] *om.* V[1]   12: oriretur] daretur F   13: Sacerdotem] pontificem C   14: id est] et F   15: cum] quum *mss*   16: et] *om.* F   17: succedunt] subcedunt CF   18: Hinc] hic PV[1]   19: XVII] *om.* F   20: scribitur] quia *add.* PV[1]

For just as body, inasmuch as it is body, exists for the sake of the soul and is ordered towards the soul, so all things earthly and temporal are, as such, ordered towards spiritual things and must be subject to them *de iure*; from which obligation they can never be released, as we have noted above.[1] Earthly princes, then, since they are such, and since they have the material sword, must be subject to the spiritual power, and especially to the power of the Supreme Pontiff: they cannot rid themselves of this obligation or yoke. But this yoke is not servitude, but liberty; for the yoke of Christ is pleasant, and His burden light.[2] And so, if earthly princes, as having the material sword, are subject to the Church, then, since anyone to whom a thing is subject is said to have it to command — for it is not subject to him if he does not have it to command — it is well said that the Church has the material sword to command even though not to use.

The second way towards the same conclusion, that the Church has the material sword to command, can be shown from the appeal which was made from the judges to the Supreme Priest in Deuteronomy 17.[3] Anything difficult and doubtful not only between cause and cause, as regards temporal cases, and between leprosy and leprosy, as regards spiritual cases, but also between blood and blood, was remitted to whoever was judge at that time and to the priests of the tribe of Levi. And, so that this may be understood, it must be known that, as Josephus says, and as the Master mentions in the *Historia*,[4] seven judges distinguished by their virtue and zeal for justice were appointed in each of the cities, who sat at the gates hearing pleas: who sat at the gates, then, so that they might judge those who came in and went out. And to each of those judges, as the Master mentions in the *Historia*, two assistants from the tribe of Levi were added. If, therefore, anything difficult or doubtful arose among those judges, appeal was made, or recourse had, to the Supreme Priest. And so, in the *Historia*, the Master gives to that chapter of Deuteronomy in which this is discussed the title, 'Concerning Appeal to the Supreme Priest.' And the judgment which the Supreme Priest gave was held to be final, and anyone refusing to obey it died, that is, was slain, by the decree of the judge. The Supreme Priest therefore had the material sword to command; for anyone refusing to obey him died for his disobedience of the Supreme Pontiff by the decree of the judges to whom, as regards the judgment of blood and secular disputes, earthly princes have succeeded. Hence, therefore, all faithful people must note how perilous it is to refuse to obey the Supreme Pontiff and to refuse to stand by his decisions, when, at the Lord's command, those who did not obey him were handed over to death.

The third way is derived from the king himself, who was to be set over the people. Hence it is written in Deuteronomy 17: 'You may not make a man of another

1. Ch VII, p. 41.
2. Cf. Matt. 11:30.
3. There is, of course, no mention of any appeal to the 'Supreme Priest' in Deuteronomy 17. The argument here is derived not from scripture directly, but from the discussion in the *Historia scholastica* of Peter Comestor as cited in the following note.
4. Josephus, *Antiquitates iudaicae*, ed. and trans. H. Thackeray et al. (London: Loeb, 1930–1965), 4, p. 214; Peter Comestor, *Historia scholastica*, PL 198:1253.

preficiendo addit Magister in *Historiis* quod sine consilio Pontificis nihil debebat ordinare. Dicitur autem de huiusmodi rege preficiendo in eodem Deut. quod[1] 'Postquam sederit[2] in solio regni sui describet sibi Deuteronomium legem,[3] accipiens exemplar a sacerdotibus, et habebit secum omnibus diebus vite sue, ut discat timere Dominum Deum[4] suum.' Tria ergo dicta sunt de rege preficiendo: primo, quod nihil debet ordinare sine consilio Pontificis; secundo, quod semper debet habere secum Deuteronomium ubi[5] tradita erat divina lex,[6] et legem ipsam debebat habere secum omnibus diebus vite sue; tercio,[7] exemplar Deuteronomii et exemplar legis debebat[8] accipere a sacerdotibus.

Cum ergo regis sit exercere iudicium sanguinis et habere materialem gladium, quid est quod Dominus[9] mandavit, quod non deberet assumptus in regem ordinare aliquid sine consilio Pontificis, nisi quod[10] materialis gladius quo utitur rex ad nutum Summi Pontificis debet esse subiectus? Et quid eciam est quod rex semper debet habere secum legem Deuteronomii et divinam legem, nisi quia temporalis gladius et lex imperialis divine legi et statuto Ecclesie debent esse subiecta? Et tercio, quid est quod assumptus in regem debebat accipere exemplar legis a sacerdotibus, nisi quia in iudicando et in exercendo materialem gladium debet id sentire quod senciunt sacerdotes et non deviare a mandatis Ecclesie?

Utrumque ergo gladium habet Ecclesia: non solum spiritualem,[11] sed eciam materialem, etsi non ad usum, ad nutum. Est enim maioris et excellencioris potencie, ut in sequenti patebit capitulo,[12] habere materialem gladium ad nutum, prout habet potestas sacerdotalis, quam habere ipsum ad usum, prout habet potestas regalis vel[13] imperialis.

CAPITULUM IX: *Quod decet Ecclesiam habere materialem gladium non ad usum, sed ad*[14] *nutum; et quod sic habere huiusmodi gladium est maioris perfeccionis et excellencie pocioris.*

Duo autem intendimus in hoc capitulo declarare[15] circa materialem gladium: primo,[16] quod ad maiorem decenciam Ecclesie est habere materialem gladium ad nutum quam ad usum; et quod sic habere talem gladium est maioris perfeccionis et alcioris excellencie quam habere ad usum. Et quia unum istorum sequitur ad aliud possumus[17] tripliciter declarare. Sumetur[18] enim prima via ad hoc ostendendum[19] ex parte ipsius[20] potencie, secunda ex parte finis, tercia ex parte materialis gladii.

1: quod] sed F   2: sederit] sedit C   3: legem] *om.* F legis V²   4: Dominum Deum] deum dominum CFV¹   5: ubi] et sibi F   6: divina lex] lex divina C   7: tercio] quod *add.* C   8: debebat] dicebat F   9: Dominus] deus C   10: quod] eciam *add.* FV²   11: spiritualem] temporalem CFV²   12: patebit capitulo] capitulo apparebit CFV²   13: vel] et FV²   14: ad] *om.* F
15: in hoc capitulo declarare] declarare in hoc capitulo FV²   16: primo] quidem *add.* CF   17: possumus] hoc *add.* CFV²   18: Sumetur] sumitur F   19: ad hoc ostendendum] *del.* C *om.* FV²   20: ipsius] spiritualis *add.* C

nation your king.'[1] Concerning the king who was be set over them, the Master adds in the *Historia* that he was to ordain nothing without the counsel of the Pontiff.[2] And in the same chapter of Deuteronomy it is said of the king who was to be set over them that 'after he is seated upon the throne of his kingdom he shall transcribe for himself the Law of Deuteronomy, taking a copy of it from the priests; and he shall have it with him all the days of his life, so that he may learn to fear the Lord his God.'[3] Three things, therefore, are said of the king who was to be set over them: first, that he should ordain nothing without the counsel of the Pontiff; second, that he should have always with him the Deuteronomy in which the Divine Law was delivered, and should have that Law with him all the days of his life; and, third, that he should take a copy of the Deuteronomy and a copy of the Law from the priests.

Therefore, since it is the king's task to execute the judgment of blood and to have the material sword, what is it that the Lord has commanded — that one who has been received as king should not ordain anything without the counsel of the Pontiff — if not that the material sword which the king uses must be subject to the Supreme Pontiff's command? And again, what is meant when it is said that the king must have the Law of Deuteronomy and the Divine Law always with him if not that the temporal sword and the imperial law must be subject to the Divine Law and the statute of the Church? And, third, what is meant when it is said that one who has been received as king must take a copy of the Law from the priests if not that, in judging and in wielding the material sword, he must decide what the priests decide and not turn aside from the commandments of the Church?

The Church, therefore, has both swords: not only the spiritual, but the material also, to command even though not to use. For, as will appear in the following chapter, it is a thing of greater and more excellent power to have the material sword to command, as the priestly power has it, than to have it to use, as the royal or imperial power has it.

CHAPTER IX: *That it is fitting for the Church to have the material sword not to use, but to command, and that to have such a sword in this way is a thing of greater perfection and more excellent power.*

We intend in this chapter to make two things clear concerning the material sword: first, that is it more fitting for the Church to have the material sword to command than to use; and that to have such a sword in this way is a thing of greater perfection and loftier excellence than to have it to use. And we can show in three ways that one of these statements follows from the other. For the first way towards such a demonstration will be derived from a consideration of power itself; the second from a consideration of purpose; the third from a consideration of the material sword.

1. Deut. 17:15.
2. *Historia scholastica*, PL 198:1253.
3. Paraphrased from Deut. 17:18–19.

Prima quidem via sic[1] patet. Nam quodlibet[2] agens agit secundum modum sue nature. Si ergo volumus videre quomodo potestas spiritualis et sacerdotalis, et potissime potestas Summi Pontificis, habeat materialem gladium, videamus quomodo ista materialia et ista corporalia se habeant[3] ad ipsos spiritus et ad ipsas spirituales substancias.

Videmus autem quod ista corporalia obediunt spiritibus sive intelligenciis quas communi nomine vocamus angelos secundum eorum nutum et voluntatem. Non enim angeli habent manus nec pedes quibus attingant corporalia et attingendo moveant ea; sed solum secundum nutum et secundum voluntatem angeli moventur tantum corpus et tanta materialis substancia quanta est nata obedire ipsi angelo. Nam inter ipsos angelos sunt gradus, quia aliqui sunt superiores et habent virtutem et potenciam excellenciorem, aliqui inferiores, habentes virtutem et potenciam minus excellentem. Cuilibet autem secundum suam virtutem et potenciam est aptum natum obedire vel[4] tam magnum materiale vel tam magnum corpus. Ideo[5] dicitur in libro[6] *De celo et mundo* quod si primo orbi adderetur una stella, motor eius moveret cum labore et pena: id est, huiusmodi mobile esset improporcionatum suo motori. Supposita itaque proporcione inter spiritum moventem et corpus motum ut quod non sit tam magnum corpus quod excedat potenciam motoris, ipsum corpus et ipsa materialis substancia ad nutum obedit substancie spirituali.

Ex ipsa itaque potencia spirituali, cui obedit materialis substancia ad nutum, possumus cognoscere quante excellencie sit et quante perfeccionis habere materialem gladium ad nutum magis quam habere ipsum ad usum. Quia habere huiusmodi gladium ad nutum est ipsum habere eo modo que agunt spiritualia, qui[7] agunt perfecciori modo et excellenciori. Perfeccius ergo et excellencius est, ut patet ex parte ipsius spiritualis potencie, habere materialem gladium ad nutum quam ad usum.

Possumus autem hoc idem ex parte potencie ipsius,[8] quod perfeccius et excellencius sit habere materialem gladium ad nutum quam ad usum, aliter declarare. Nam principes seculares, habentes materialem gladium ad usum, habent dominium et potenciam super huiusmodi gladium et habent exercicium ipsius gladii. Sed potestas sacerdotalis, et potissime potestas Summi Pontificis, habens materialem gladium ad nutum, habet dominium super eum seu[9] super ipsum principem cuius est exercere materialem gladium. Nam hoc est habere materialem gladium non[10] ad usum sed ad nutum: non per se ipsum exercere huiusmodi gladium, sed habere dominium super eum qui exercet ipsum. Et quia longe est excellencior et potencior potencia[11] sub qua est exercens gladium quam sit potencia[12] super ipsum gladium, patet ex parte ipsius

1: sic] *om.* FV[2]   2: quodlibet] quodcumque FV[2]   3: habeant] habeat F   4: vel] *om.* CFV[2]
5: Ideo] secundo F   6: libro] *om.* FV[2]   7: qui] et quia spiritualia F   8: potencie ipsius] ipsius
potencie FV[2]   9: seu] sum F sive V[2]   10: non] *om.* PV[1]   11: potencia] potestas F   12: po-
tencia] potestas F

The first way appears thus. For each agent acts according to the measure of its nature. If, therefore, we wish to see how spiritual and priestly power, and especially the power of the Supreme Pontiff, has the material sword, let us consider how material and corporeal substances stand in relation to spirits and spiritual substances.

We see, then, that these corporeal substances obey the spirits or intelligences which we commonly call by the name of angels according to their command and will. For angels do not have hands or feet with which to touch corporeal substances and, by touching, move them. Rather, it is according to command and according to will alone that a body and a material substance is moved by an angel in proportion as it is fitted by nature to be moved by that angel. For there are degrees among the angels themselves; for some are superior and have a more excellent strength and power, whereas others are inferior and have a less excellent strength and power. And corresponding to each, according to its strength and power, there is a material substance of such magnitude, or a body of such magnitude, as is fitted by nature to obey it. And so it is said in the book *De caelo et mundo* that if a single star were added to the primary heaven, its mover would move it only with labour and pain: that is, the body to be moved would be disproportionate with its mover.[1] Assuming, then, a proportion between the moving spirit and the body to be moved such that the magnitude of the body is not so great that it exceeds the mover's power, the body itself and the material substance itself will obey the command of the spiritual substance.

From spiritual power itself, then, whose command material substance obeys, we can understand how much more excellent and how much more perfect it is to have the material sword to command than to have it to use. For to have that sword to command is to have it in the manner in which spiritual substances act, which act in a more perfect and excellent way. Therefore, as is clear from a consideration of spiritual power itself, it is more perfect and more excellent to have the material sword to command than to use.

But there is another way in which, from a consideration of power itself, we can make the same thing clear: that it is more perfect and more excellent to have the material sword to command than to use. For secular princes, having the material sword to use, have lordship and power over that sword, and have the wielding of that sword. But priestly power, and especially the power of the Supreme Pontiff, having the material sword to command, has lordship over it or over the prince himself whose task it is to wield the material sword. For this is what it is to have the material sword not to use but to command: not to wield that sword as such, but to have lordship over him who does wield it. And since the power under which he who wields a sword stands is far more excellent and mighty than is power over the sword itself, it is clear from a consideration of power itself that it

1. In this paragraph, Giles seems chiefly to have in mind Aquinas, *Summa theologiae*, Ia 110:1–3. See Aristotle, *De caelo*, passim, for the kind of cosmology he accepts. Scholz suggests that he is here thinking of *De caelo* 2:6 or 12, but neither is entirely satisfactory. Cf. *Metaphysics* Λ 8 (1073ᵃ15).

potencie quod perfeccius et excellencius est habere materialem gladium ad nutum quam ad usum.

Secunda via ad hoc idem sumitur ex parte finis. Quia quando[1] finis est sub fine, potestas est[2] sub.potestate, et per consequens potestas superior eo ipso, quod est superior et excellencior, est perfeccior alia. Ait enim Augustinus, VI *De Trinitate*, quod in hiis que non mole[3] magna sunt, idem est[4] esse 'maius' quam[5] esse 'melius'. Sic et in proposito: dicere possumus quod in hiis que non corporali situ superiora sunt, idem est esse 'superius' quam[6] esse 'perfeccius' et 'excellencius'. Cum enim dicimus spiritualem potestatem esse 'superiorem' potestate terrena, non intelligitur[7] secundum ordinem corporalem, ut quod una sit in turri, alia in plano,[8] sed hoc intelligimus secundum excellenciam et perfeccionem.

Respondeamus ergo ad propositum et dicamus quod finis et intencio principis secularis habentis materialem gladium ad usum est et esse debet inducere homines ad virtutem. Sed homines virtuosi sunt apti nati et sunt dispositi ad obediendum[9] potencie spirituali.[10] Ergo potestas secularis, habens usum materialis gladii, videtur[11] intendere tamquam finem disponere cives, et disponere suos subiectos, ut obediant spirituali potencie habenti materialem gladium ad nutum. Finis ergo utentis et exercentis materialem gladium est sub fine spiritualis potencie. Ex parte itaque ipsius finis patet quod alcior et potencior est potestas spiritualis quam terrena, et quod excellencius et perfeccius est habere materialem gladium ad nutum quam ad usum.

Tercia via ad hoc idem[12] sumitur ex parte ipsius materialis gladii. Quia secundum[13] Dionysium in libro[14] *De divinis nominibus*, capitulo VII,[15] per suprema infimorum attinguntur ultima supremorum,[16] ut, si spiritus sunt supra[17] corporalia,[18] ultimi spiritus habent movere suprema corpora. Angeli enim et spirituales substancie habentes exercicium immediate super corporalia sunt inferiores aliis angelis qui non mittuntur ad hoc corporalia et inferiora; non decet enim superiores spiritus habere immediatum[19] exercicium super hec corporalia. Sic non decet spiritualem potestatem tamquam superiorem et excellentem habere immediatum exercicium super materialem gladium; nec[20] decet eam habere huiusmodi gladium ad usum, sed ad nutum. Est hoc[21] ergo maioris decencie, et si maioris decencie, per consequens est maioris excellencie perfeccionis [habere materialem gladium ad nutum quam ad usum]. Illa ergo duo que dicebamus declaranda, unum sequitur ex alio; quia, si habere materialem gladium ad nutum quam ad usum est maioris perfeccionis et excellencie, consequens est quod sit maioris decencie et econverso.

1: quando] quantum V²   2: est] *om.* V²   3: mole] male F in V²   4: est] quod *add.* FV²
5: quam] quod PV¹   6: quam] quod C   7: intelligitur] intelligimus F   8: plano] palacio
PFV¹V²   9: obediendum] obedientiam F   10: spirituali] spiritualis F   11: videtur] debet FV²
12: idem] *om.* PV¹   13: secundum] *om.* C   14: libro] *om.* FV²   15: VII] vult quod *add.* C
16: supremorum] superiorum F   17: supra] super F   18: corporalia] corpora C   19: immediatum] immediate C   20: nec] non C   21: hoc] *om.* FPV¹V²

is more perfect and more excellent to have the material sword to command than to use.

The second way towards the same conclusion is derived from a consideration of purpose. For when one purpose is under another, one power is under another; and, consequently, the power which is superior in itself, which is the higher and more excellent, is more perfect than the other. For Augustine says in *De Trinitate* 6 that among those things which are not great in magnitude, to be 'greater' is the same as to be 'better.'[1] So also in our proposition: we can say that among those things which are not located in a higher bodily position, to be 'superior' is the same as to be 'more perfect' and 'more excellent.' For when we say that the spiritual power is 'superior' to the earthly power, this is not meant according to a bodily order such that one man is in a tower and the other on level ground. Rather, we understand this according to excellence and perfection.

Let us return to our proposition, therefore, and say that the purpose and intention of the secular prince in having the material sword to use is and must be to induce men to virtue. But virtuous men are fitted by nature and are disposed to obey the spiritual power. The secular power, therefore, having the use of the material sword, seems to intend as its purpose to dispose citizens and to dispose its subjects so that they may obey the spiritual power, which has the material sword to command. The purpose, therefore, for which the material sword is used and wielded is under the purpose of the spiritual power. Thus, from a consideration of purpose itself, it is clear that the spiritual power is loftier and mightier than the earthly, and that it is more excellent and more perfect to have the material sword to command than to use.

The third way towards the same conclusion is derived from a consideration of the material sword itself. For according to Dionysius in the book *De divinis nominibus*, 7, the lowest parts of the highest are touched by the highest parts of the lowest; so that, if spirits are above corporeal things, the lowest spirits must move the highest bodies.[2] For the angels and spiritual substances which act immediately upon corporeal things are inferior to the other angels who are not sent forth to these corporeal and inferior things; for it is not fitting for superior spirits to act immediately upon these corporeal things. Thus, it is not fitting for the spiritual power, as superior and excellent, to act immediately upon the material sword; nor is it fitting for it to have that sword to use rather than to command. It is a thing of greater fitness, therefore, and if of greater fitness, consequently of more excellent perfection, to have the material sword to command than to use. Therefore, as to the two things which we said were to be declared, the one follows from the other since, if it is a thing of greater perfection and excellence to have the material sword to command than to use, it follows that it is of greater fitness, and conversely.

1. I.e. 'better' rather than 'larger.' Cf. *De Trinitate* 6:7 (CCSL 50:237).
2. Ps.-Dionysius, *De divinis nominibus* 7 (PG 3:865). See also Aquinas, *Expositio in Dionysium De divinis nominibus*, Opera Omnia (Parma 1852–73) vol. 15, p. 388; cf. *Summa theologiae* Ia 110:3.

Propter quod tam ex parte ipsius potencie, ut dicebat[1] via prima, quam eciam ex[2] parte ipsius finis, ut dicebat racio secunda, quam eciam tercio ex parte ipsius materialis gladii, quia non decet spiritualem potenciam tamquam potenciam[3] supremam habere immediatum exercicium super materialem gladium, sicut non decet supremos spiritus sive supremos angelos habere immediatum exercicium super corporalia: est evidenter ostensum quod maioris perfeccionis et excellencie, et per consequens maioris decencie, est habere materialem gladium ad nutum, secundum quem modum habet potestas ecclesiastica, quam habere ipsum ad usum, prout habet potestas terrena.[4]

Explicit prima pars huius operis, in qua agitur de potestate Summi Pontificis respectu materialis gladii et respectu potencie secularis.

1: dicebat] dicebatur F   2: ex] *om.* F   3: tamquam potenciam] *om.* F   4: potestas terrena] terrena potestas F

And so, since we have shown equally by the first way, a consideration of power itself; and by the second argument, a consideration of purpose; and by the third, a consideration of the material sword, that it is not fitting for the spiritual power, as the supreme power, to act immediately upon the material sword, just as it is not fitting for supreme spirits or supreme angels to act immediately upon corporeal substances: it is evidently demonstrated that it is a thing of greater perfection and excellence, and consequently of greater fitness, to have the material sword to command, in which manner the ecclesiastical power has it, than to have it to use, as the earthly power has it.

Here ends the first part of this work, in which the power of the Supreme Pontiff has been discussed with respect to the material sword and with respect to secular power.

[SECUNDA PARS]

Incipiunt capitula secunde partis[1] huius operis, ubi agitur de Ecclesie potestate quantum ad hec temporalia que videmus.

CAPITULUM I: Quod liceat Ecclesie et universaliter clericis habere temporalia.

CAPITULUM II: In quo solvuntur dicta Evangelii que videntur nostro proposito contraria, quod non liceat clericis temporalia possidere.

CAPITULUM III: In quo solvuntur dicta et auctoritates Veteris Testamenti, quod non liceat clericis temporalia possidere.

CAPITULUM IV: Quod omnia temporalia sub dominio et potestate Ecclesie et potissime Summi Pontificis collocantur.

CAPITULUM V: Quod potestas regia per potestatem ecclesiasticam et a potestate ecclesiastica constituta est et[2] ordinata in opus et[3] obsequium ecclesiastice potestatis; propter quod clarius apparebit quomodo temporalia sint sub dominio Ecclesie collocata.

CAPITULUM VI: Quod terrena potestas, tum quia particularior est,[4] tum quia materiam preparans, tum eciam quia longinquius attingit optimum, secundum se et secundum sua spirituali potestati iure et merito famulatur.

CAPITULUM VII: Quod omne dominium cum iusticia, sive sit rerum sive personarum, sive sit utile sive potestativum, nonnisi sub Ecclesia et per Ecclesiam esse potest.

CAPITULUM VIII: Quod nullus est dignus hereditate paterna nisi sit servus et filius Ecclesie et nisi per Ecclesiam sit dignus hereditate eterna.

CAPITULUM IX: Quod licet non sit potestas nisi a Deo, nullus tamen est dignus aliqua potestate nisi sub Ecclesia et per Ecclesiam fiat dignus.

CAPITULUM X: Quod in omnibus temporalibus Ecclesia habet dominium universale, fideles autem de iure et cum iusticia dominium particulare habere possunt.

CAPITULUM XI: Quod infideles omni possessione et dominio et[5] potestate qualibet sunt indigni.

CAPITULUM XII: Quod in omnibus temporalibus Ecclesia habet dominium superius; ceteri autem solum dominium inferius habere possunt.

CAPITULUM XIII: Quare sunt duo tantum[6] gladii in Ecclesia, et quomodo hii duo gladii sunt sumendi.

1: Incipiunt … partis] Incipit secunda pars PV[1]   2: est et] et est C   3: et] *add.* in C   4: est] *om.* C
5: et] ac C   6: duo tantum] tantum duo C

[PART TWO]

Thus begin the chapters of the second part of this work, in which is discussed the power of the Church with respect to those temporal things which we see.

CHAPTER I: That the Church and clerics generally may have temporal possessions.

CHAPTER II: In which the sayings of the Gospel are explained which, contrary to our proposition, seem to show that clerics may not have temporal possessions.

CHAPTER III: In which the sayings and authorities of the Old Testament are explained which seem to show that clerics may not have temporal possessions.

CHAPTER IV: That all temporal things are placed under the lordship and power of the Church, and especially of the Supreme Pontiff.

CHAPTER V: That royal power is appointed through the ecclesiastical power and by the ecclesiastical power, and is ordained to the work and service of the ecclesiastical power; from which it will appear more clearly how temporal things are placed under the lordship of the Church.

CHAPTER VI: That the earthly power is rightly and properly the servant of the spiritual power in itself and in what belongs to it, because it is more particular, and because it prepares material, and because it comes less close to attaining what is best.

CHAPTER VII: That there can be no lordship with justice over things or persons, either of use or of power, except under the Church and through the Church.

CHAPTER VIII: That no one is worthy of a paternal inheritance unless he is the servant and son of the Church, and unless, through the Church, he is worthy of an eternal inheritance.

CHAPTER IX: That although there is no power except of God, no one is worthy of any power unless he is made worthy under the Church and through the Church.

CHAPTER X: That the Church has a universal lordship in all temporal things, but that, as of right and with justice, the faithful can have only a particular lordship.

CHAPTER XI: That unbelievers are all unworthy of any possession, lordship, and power.

CHAPTER XII: That the Church has a superior lordship in all temporal things, but that others can have only an inferior lordship.

CHAPTER XIII: Why there are only two swords in the Church, and how these two swords are to be understood.

CAPITULUM XIV: Quod cum duo gladii sint in Ecclesia, quinque de causis gladius inferior non superfluit propter superiorem, sed hii[1] duo gladii decorant et ornant Ecclesiam Militantem.

CAPITULUM XV: Ubi plenius agitur quomodo duo gladii qui sunt in Ecclesia adaptantur ad duos gladios in Evangelio nominatos.

CAPITULUM I: *Quod liceat Ecclesie et universaliter clericis habere temporalia.*

Superioris partis digesta materia quia[2] egimus de potestate Ecclesie quantum ad materialem gladium et quantum ad dominos temporales, ostendentes Ecclesiam habere utrumque gladium, spiritualem ad usum, materialem ad nutum, et omnes dominos temporales sive terrenos Ecclesie debere esse subiectos, sine quo salutem consequi nullatenus[3] possunt. Nam nulli fuerunt salvati[4] tempore diluvii nisi qui fuerunt in archa et sub Noe, sic[5] in hoc diluvio, in hac inundacione aquarum et procellarum, id est in hoc seculo, in hoc mari magno et spacio,[6] ubi non solum sunt procelle sed eciam sunt reptilia[7] quorum non est numerus, id est diversa genera inimicorum, nullus salvabitur, nullus potest consequi salutem, nisi per archam Noe, id est per Ecclesiam, et nisi sit sub Noe, id est sub Summo Pontifice. Hiis[8] itaque expeditis, nunc[9] in hac secunda parte tractare volumus de potestate ecclesiastica[10] respectu rerum temporalium, propter quosdam temere asserentes quod non liceat Ecclesie aliqua temporalia possidere. Videntur autem sic dicentes inniti auctoritate[11] Novi et Veteris Testamenti. Dicitur enim Luce X: 'Nolite portare sacculum neque peram,' ubi videtur Dominus[12] prohibere ne habeamus pecuniam, quia prohibet habere sacculum. Videtur eciam prohibere non solum[13] habere possessiones, ex quibus habemus cibos, sed eciam prohibet ne habeamus peram, ubi reservantur cibi.

Quare, ut videtur, non licet Ecclesie, ad quam spectat predicare verbum Dei, nec eciam, ut videtur, licet clericis, qui debent laicos docere et seminare inter eos verbum Dei, habere aliqua temporalia nec eciam aliquam reservanciam temporalium, quia non licet eis habere sacculum, ubi reservantur denarii, nec peram, ubi reservantur cibi. Istud idem universaliter quantum ad clericos, ut videtur, potest haberi Numeri XVIII, ubi Aaron et filiis eius, et eciam Levi et filiis eius, non est permissum quod habeant partem hereditatis in populo Iudaico, sed dictum est eis[14] quod[15] vivant de decimis et[16] primiciis et de[17] oblacionibus. Cum

---

1: hii] *om.* C   2: quia] quam F   3: consequi nullatenus] nullatenus consequi C   4: fuerunt salvati] salvati fuerunt F   5: sic] et *add.* C   6: spacio] spacioso C   7: reptilia] rectilia CPV[2]
8: Hiis] his F   9: nunc] autem *add.* V[1] *del.* P   10: ecclesiastica] ecclesie C   11: auctoritate] auctoritati C   12: Dominus] deus C   13: solum] non *add.* CFV[2] *del.* P   14: eis] omnibus F
15: quod] ut C   16: et] *om.* F   17: de] *om.* C

CHAPTER XIV: That, although there are two swords in the Church, there are five reasons why the inferior sword is not superfluous to the superior, but why these two swords decorate and adorn the church militant.

CHAPTER XV: In which the question of how the two swords which are in the Church are related to the two swords mentioned in the Gospel is more fully discussed.

———————— ✳ ————————

CHAPTER I: *That the Church and clerics generally may have temporal possessions.*

In the preceding part, we have arranged all the material that we need concerning the Church's power in relation to the material sword and in relation to temporal lords, showing that the Church has both swords, the spiritual to use and the material to command, and that all temporal or earthly lords must be subject to the Church or else they cannot by any means achieve salvation. For just as none were saved at the time of the Flood except those who were in the Ark and under Noah, so in this flood, in this inundation of waters and storms — that is, in this world, in this great and spacious sea, where there are not only storms but also creeping things without number, that is, enemies of many different kinds — no one will be saved, no one can achieve salvation, except through the Ark of Noah, that is, through the Church,[1] and unless he is under Noah, that is, under the Supreme Pontiff. Having dealt with these matters, then, we now wish, in this second part, to treat of ecclesiastical power with respect to temporal things. For there are certain persons who assert without cause that the Church may not have any temporal possessions;[2] and those who speak thus appear to rely on the authority of the New and Old Testaments. For it is said in Luke 10, 'Carry neither purse nor bag,'[3] where the Lord seems to forbid us to have money, since He forbids us to have a purse. Also, He seems not only to forbid us to have the possessions by means of which we obtain food; but He even forbids us to have a bag, in which food is stored.

And so, as it seems, neither the Church, with whom it rests to preach the Word of God, nor, as it seems, the clergy, who must teach the laity and sow the Word of God among them,[4] may have any temporal possessions or any store of temporal goods. For they may have neither a purse, in which coins are stored, nor a bag, in which food is stored. And the same prohibition, applying to clerics generally, can, as it seems, be inferred from Numbers 18, where Aaron and his sons, and also Levi and his sons, were not permitted to have a portion of the inheritance of the Jewish people: rather, it was said to them that they were to live by means of tithes and first-fruits

1. Cf. I Peter 3:20–21; Augustine, *De civitate Dei* 15:26 (CCSL 48:493). The analogy also occurs in the Bull *Unam sanctam.*
2. See Introduction, p. xxviii.
3. Luke 10:4.
4. Cf. Mark 4:14.

ergo per populum Iudaicum figuraretur[1] populus Christianus, et cum per Aaron[2] et
Levi et per eos qui erant de stirpe eorum figurentur et significentur universaliter
clerici, videtur quod omnes clerici in populo Christiano nullam partem, nullam
hereditatem, nullas possessiones habere debeant; sed vivere debent de primiciis,
decimis et oblacionibus. Propter quod dicitur Num. XVIII quod: 'Dixitque Dominus[3] ad Aaron in terra eorum,' id est[4] in terra populi Iudaici vel in terra populi fidelis sive in terra fidelium, 'nihil possidebitis nec habebitis partes[5] inter eos. Ego
pars et hereditas tua in medio filiorum Israel.' Ibidem eciam dicitur quod: 'Filiis
autem Levi dedi[6] omnes decimas'; et subditur: 'Nihil aliud possidebunt, decimarum oblacione contenti.'[7] Ergo[8] omnes servientes altari, cuiusmodi sunt alii clerici
qui figurantur per Aaron et Levi, non debent habere partem nec hereditatem in[9]
populo fideli, sed decimis et oblacionibus debent esse contenti.[10]

Sed omnia hec suum intellectum habent. Nam si sic vellemus intelligere verba
Scripture Sacre, et non vellemus ea fideliter exponere, diceremus quod nulli[11]
Christiano et nulli fideli licet aliquid possidere, dicente Domino: 'Qui non renun-
ciabit omnibus que possidet, non potest esse meus[12] discipulus.' Et quia omnes
fideles, omnes Christiani, sunt discipuli Christi, nullo Christiano, sive clerico sive
laico, licet aliquid possidere. Sed obmissis hiis[13] obieccionibus, de quibus in sequenti capitulo intendimus agere, dicemus quod non est contra mandatum Domini
quod Ecclesia et universaliter clerici possessiones habeant rerum temporalium.
Eciam ille qui voto se astringit[14] ad non habendum proprium potest habere
dominium rerum temporalium si fiat sponsus alicuius ecclesie, cuius est temporalia aliqua possidere: ut puta si religiosus fiat episcopus, habebit dominium omnium illorum temporalium que sunt possessiones ecclesie quam sibi desponsavit
episcopatum accipiendo. Et ne videamur solum verbis[15] inniti et non auctoritatibus Sacre Scripture,[16] dicemus[17] quod super illud Apostoli II ad Corinthios VI,
'Tamquam nihil habentes et omnia possidentes,' ait glossa, et est Ambrosii: 'Non
solum spiritualia, sed eciam[18] temporalia, quia timentibus Deum nihil deest.' Ipsa
ergo temporalia possunt possidere clerici et Ecclesia. Immo, ut ibidem dicit
glossa, quod ista fuit gloria apostolorum, sine sollicitudine esse et tam res quam
dominos earum possidere, quia omnia ad pedes apostolorum mittebantur, sicut
legitur in Actibus.[19]

Si ergo 'possessio' dicat ipsam 'sollicitudinem,' clerici nihil debent possidere, ut
possint cum modica vel eciam, si possibile esset, cum nulla sollicitudine esse, ut[20]

1: figuraretur] significaretur FV²   2: Aaron] figuraretur *add.* C   3: Dominus] deus C   4: id
est] *om.* C   5: partes] partem C   6: dedi] dedit C   7: contenti] erunt sacerdotes *add.* CFV²
8: Ergo] eorum et V² ergo et C   9: in] *om.* F   10: contenti] contempti C   11: nulli] nullo F
12: esse meus] meus esse CFV²   13: hiis] his F   14: astringit] astrinxit F   15: solum verbis]
verbis solum V¹   16: Sacre Scripture] scripture sacre C   17: dicemus] dicamus F   18: eciam]
et CF   19: legitur in Actibus] in actibus legitur CFV²   20: ut] *om.* F

and offerings.[1] Therefore, since the Christian people was prefigured by the Jewish people, and since clerics generally were prefigured and signified by Aaron and Levi and by those who were of their stock, it seems that no clerics may have any portion, any inheritance, any possessions, among the Christian people, but must live by means of first-fruits, tithes, and offerings. For it was said in Numbers 18: 'And the Lord said to Aaron, You shall possess nothing in their land,' that is, in the land of the Jewish people or in the land of the faithful people or in the country of the faithful; 'neither shall you have a portion among them. I am your portion and inheritance in the midst of the Children of Israel.' And, in the same place, it is said: 'And I have given to the sons of Levi all tithes.' And it is added: 'Content with the offering of tithes, they shall possess nothing else.' All who serve the altar, therefore, of which kind are the various clerics prefigured by Aaron and Levi, must [apparently] have neither portion nor inheritance among the faithful people, but must be content with tithes and offerings.

But all these sayings have their own proper meaning. Now, if we wished to understand the words of the Sacred Scriptures in such a way, and if we did not wish to expound them faithfully, we should [indeed] say that no Christian and no faithful man may possess anything. For the Lord said: 'He who does not renounce all that he has cannot be my disciple.'[2] And since all faithful men, all Christians, are Christ's disciples, [this too seems to indicate that] no Christian, whether cleric or layman, may possess anything. But leaving aside these objections, which we intend to discuss in the following chapter, we shall [here simply] say that it is not contrary to the Lord's command that the Church and clerics generally should have temporal things as their possessions. Even he who has bound himself by vow to have nothing of his own can have lordship over temporal things if he becomes the bridegroom of some church whose duty it is to possess certain temporal goods. If, for example, a member of a religious order becomes a bishop, he will have lordship over all those temporal goods which are the possessions of the church which he has espoused to himself by receiving the episcopate. And lest we seem to be relying upon mere words and not upon the authorities of Sacred Scripture, we shall say that a gloss (and this is from St. Ambrose) on the Apostle's words in II Corinthians 6, 'As having nothing and possessing all things,'[3] says: 'Not only spiritual things, but temporal things also; for those who fear God lack nothing.'[4] Clerics and the Church, therefore, can have temporal possessions. Indeed, as a gloss on the same passage says, it was the glory of the apostles to be without anxiety yet to possess both things and their lords;[5] for, as we read in the Acts, all things were laid at the feet of the apostles.[6]

Therefore, if 'possession' means 'anxiety,' the clergy must possess nothing, so that they may be little — or, indeed, if possible not at all — burdened with anxiety,

---

1. Num. 18:20–24.
2. Luke 14:33.
3. II Cor. 6:10.
4. Peter Lombard, *Collectanea in omnes de Pauli apostoli epistolas*, PL 192:48.
5. *Glossa ordinaria*, PL 114:560.
6. Matt. 6:33.

divinis liberius vacare possent. Sed si 'possessio' dicat ipsum 'dominium rerum temporalium,' quis diceret quod spiritualis potestas non debeat temporalia possidere, cuius est omnibus dominari? Unde et glossa super illo verbo 'Nihil habentes,' etc., dicit quod 'gloria fuit apostolorum nihil omnino possidere et sine sollicitudine esse,' et statim post subdit quod gloria apostolorum fuit 'tam res quam[1] dominos earum possidere.' Ergo gloria fuit apostolorum nihil omnino possidere quantum ad sollicitudinem, et omnia possidere quantum ad dominium.

Est enim Deus hereditas nostra et pars nostra, quia in eo debemus principaliter spem ponere. Temporalia autem hec possidere possumus et quasi additamenta et quasi adiecciones,[2] iuxta illud Matth. VI: 'Primum querite regnum Dei, et postea omnia hec adicientur vobis.' Abraham eciam, pater noster, cui Dominus Gen. XV dicit 'Ego protector tuus, et merces tua magna nimis,' fuit dives valde, iuxta illud Gen. XIII: quod 'Abraham erat dives valde'; et ita erat dives, et tanta fuit possessio eius, quod ipse et Loth non poterant cohabitare simul, ut potest haberi Gen. XIII.

Dicemus ergo quod religio[3] Christiana vel non[4] posset stare et non posset[5] habere sufficienciam vite nisi aliqui Christianorum essent solliciti circa temporalia, ut ad mercancias faciendum. Quia, cum alique regiones ubi Christiani habitant abundant[6] in uno et deficiunt[7] in alio, ut puta abundant in bonitate lane, deficiunt in ubertate vini, alique econverso, necessarium fuit humanum genus quantum ad alios[8] ex eis mercancias facere, quantum ad alios[9] terras arare, vineas colere. Et hoc modo habere temporalia, quantum ad istam sollicitudinem, competit laicis.[10] Sed[11] quantum ad dominium et sustentacionem vite, potest licite competere clericis, ut clerici debent esse solliciti in hiis que sunt ad Deum non solum pro se, sed eciam pro laicis, orando et[12] interpellando ad Deum et sacrificia offerendo. Et vice versa, sicut clerici pro laicis debent solliciti in hiis que sunt[13] ad Deum,[14] sic[15] laici pro clericis debent esse solliciti circa hec terrena et temporalia, prout satisfaciunt necessitati vite et subveniunt indigencie nature.

Nisi ergo se astrinxerint[16] voto, utrique, tam clerici quam laici, possunt habere temporalia et agros et vineas et possessiones alias. Sed decet clericos, dominium temporalium sibi retinendo,[17] curam et sollicitudinem committere aliis, ut circa ea que sunt Dei[18] liberius vacare possint. Nec tamen dicimus quod nihil habere in proprie non sit opus supererogacionis, cum Dominus dixerit Matth. XIX[19] adolescenti: 'Si vis perfectus esse, vade et vende omnia que habes,[20]

1: quam] tam temporalia C　　2: adiecciones] adiectionis F　　3: religio] religioso F　　4: non] *om.* V²
5: stare et non posset] *om.* F　　6: abundant] habundent C　　7: deficiunt] deficient C　　8: alios] aliquos C　　9: alios] aliquos C　　10: laicis] habere temporalia *add.* FV²　　11: Sed] *om.* FV²　　12: et] *om.* FV²　　13: in hiis que sunt] *om.* FV²　　14: sicut clerici … Deum] *om.* PV¹　　15: sic] sicut FV²
16: astrinxerint] abstrinxerint PV¹　　17: retinendo] accipiendo FV²　　18: sunt Dei] dei sunt C
19: XIX] IX FV²　　20: habes] possides C

and so that they may have greater liberty for things divine. But if 'possession' means 'lordship of temporal things,' who would say that the spiritual power, whose lordship extends to all things, should not have temporal possessions? Hence, the gloss on the words 'As having nothing,' and so on, both says that 'It was the glory of the apostles to possess nothing at all and to be without anxiety,' yet immediately afterwards adds that it was the glory of the apostles 'to possess both things and their lords.' It was, therefore, the glory of the apostles to possess nothing at all in the sense of being anxious, yet to possess all things in the sense of exercising lordship [i.e. to own and control all things, but to be free from the day-to-day care of them].

For God is our inheritance and our portion, since it is in Him that we must chiefly place our hope. But we can have temporal possessions both as additions and as increments, according to Matthew 6: 'First seek the Kingdom of God, and afterwards all these things will be added to you.'[1] Our father Abraham also, to whom the Lord said in Genesis 15, 'I am your protector and your very great reward,'[2] was exceedingly rich, according to what is said in Genesis 13: that 'Abraham was very rich.'[3] Indeed, so rich was he, and so great was his property, that, as can be gathered from Genesis 13, he and Lot could not both live together.[4]

We shall say, therefore, that the Christian religion could not even survive, and could not have the necessaries of life, if some Christians were not anxious with regard to temporal matters and so engaged in business. For since some regions in which Christians dwell abound in one commodity and are deficient in another — for example, some abound in excellent wool but are deficient in fruitful vines, while the converse is true of others — it was necessary that some members of the human race should engage in business and that others should plough the land and cultivate the vineyards. And the possession of temporal goods in this way — in the sense of being anxious for them — is the province of the laity; but, in the sense of exercising lordship, and for the sustaining of life, it can properly be the province of the clergy. For the clergy must be anxious with respect to those things which are of God, praying to God and calling upon Him and offering sacrifices not only for themselves, but for the laity also. And, on the other hand, just as the clergy must be anxious on behalf of the laity in those things which are of God, so must the laity be anxious on the clergy's behalf for earthly and temporal goods, inasmuch as, by so doing, they satisfy the needs of life and supply the requirements of nature.

Therefore, unless they have bound themselves by vow, both clerics and laymen alike can have temporal goods and farms and vineyards and other possessions. But it is fitting that the clergy, while retaining temporal lordship to themselves, should entrust care and anxiety to others, so that they may attend more freely to those things which are of God. Certainly, we do not say that it is not a work of supererogation to have nothing of one's own; for the Lord said to the young man in Matthew 19, 'If you would be perfect, go and sell all that you have,

1. Gen. 15:1.
2. Gen. 13:2.
3. Gen. 13:6.
4. Gen 13:7–11.

et da pauperibus.' Nihil itaque habere in proprio est opus supererogacionis et est organum deveniendi ad perfeccionem. Habere tamen possessiones non tamquam res suas, sed tamquam res Ecclesie, in nullo derogat perfeccioni.[1] Propter quod si religiosi fiant sponsi ecclesiarum[2] et hoc modo non tamquam res suas sed tamquam res Ecclesie possessiones habeant, in nullo derogatur eorum perfeccioni.[3]

Concludamus ergo et dicamus, quod omnes tenentur ad illud quod dicitur in psalmo: 'Divicie si affluant, nolite cor apponere'; et omnes tenentur ad illud Evangelii: 'Nisi quis renunciaverit omnibus que possidet, non potest meus esse[4] discipulus.' Non apponere ergo cor in diviciis, quod non queramus eas tamquam rem principalem et tamquam rem ubi ponendus est finis, et renunciare omnibus que possidemus, non ponendo in eis finalem intencionem nostram, omnes tenentur et obligantur. Habere tamen huiusmodi possessiones ad[5] dominium et sustentacionem vite licet[6] tam clericis quam laicis. Sollicitudinem autem circa eas decet clericos committere laicis, ut possint magis vacare divinis. Possunt autem laici huiusmodi sollicitudinem per seipsos habere, ut in hoc eciam[7] serviant clericis, ne[8] retrahantur a sollicitudine divinorum.[9]

CAPITULUM II: *In quo solvuntur dicta Evangelii que videntur nostro proposito contraria, quod non liceat clericis temporalia possidere.*

Dicebatur autem in precedenti capitulo tam per auctoritatem Novi Testamenti quam eciam Veteris quod non liceat clericis temporalia possidere. Dicebatur enim in Evangelio quod predicatores Evangelii non debeant habere sacculum ad retinendum[10] pecuniam neque peram ad conservandum cibaria, ut glosse exponunt. Et quia, ut dicebamus, clerici debent esse doctores laicorum et debent[11] eis annunciare verbum Dei, videtur ex hoc quod non liceat eis aliqua temporalia possidere. Et in libro Numerorum, ut dicebatur, illi de stirpe Aaron et Levi, per quos intelliguntur qui altari serviunt, non debebant habere hereditatem nec possessionem in populo Dei. Clerici ergo non debent habere aliam sortem nec aliam partem quam Deus, quia Deus est eorum sors. Unde Ieronimus ait quod 'cleros' grece latine 'sors' appellatur, et dicit quod propterea dicti sunt 'clerici' quia sunt de sorte Domini. Deus itaque est sors eorum: non debent aliam sortem querere.

Possumus autem primo[12] ad auctoritatem Evangelii solvere et dicere[13] illud Evangelii, quod predicatores non debent habere sacculum neque peram, propter septem dictum fuisse,[14] iuxta varias exposiciones doctorum atque sanctorum: primo quidem,[15] ut possimus adversarios convertere; secundo, ut possimus ipsos terrere; tercio, ut discant predicatores de Deo confidere; quarto, ut[16] in seipsis non debeant

1: perfeccioni] perfeccionem FV² 2: ecclesiarum] ecclesie C 3: perfeccioni] perfeccionem V² 4: meus esse] esse meus F 5: ad] usum *add.* C 6: vite licet] videlicet F 7: eciam] *om.* F 8: ne] ut F 9: divinorum] *om.* FV² 10: retinendum] recuperandum CFV² 11: debent] debemus *mss* 12: primo] *om.* F 13: dicere] quod *add.* FV² 14: fuisse] fuit CF 15: quidem] *om.* F 16: ut] *om.* F

and give to the poor.'[1] To have nothing of one's own, then, is a work of supererogation and is a means of achieving perfection. Nonetheless, to hold possessions not as one's own property, but as the property of a church, in no way detracts from perfection. And so, if members of religious orders become bridegrooms of churches and hold possessions in this manner — not as their own property, but as a church's property — this in no way detracts from their perfection.

Let us conclude, therefore, and say that all are bound by what is said in the Psalm: 'If riches abound, do not set your heart on them';[2] and that all are bound by what is said in the Gospel: 'He who does not renounce all that he has cannot be my disciple.' Therefore, we are all bound and obliged not to set our heart on riches: not to seek them as a thing of sovereign good and as an end in themselves, and to renounce all our possessions [in the sense of] not making them our ultimate goal. Nonetheless, clerics and laymen alike may hold such possessions as their lords and for the sustaining of life. It is fitting, however, that the clergy should entrust anxiety for them to the laity, so that they themselves may attend more freely to things divine. And laymen can have such anxiety on their own account so that, in this way, they may also serve the clergy, lest they be distracted from anxiety for things divine.

CHAPTER II: *In which the sayings of the Gospel are explained which, contrary to our proposition, seem to show that clerics may not have temporal possessions.*

Now it was said in the preceding chapter, on the authority of both the New Testament and the Old, that clerics [apparently] may not have temporal possessions. For, as the glosses explain, it was said in the Gospel that the preachers of the Gospel should have neither a purse for the keeping of money nor a bag for the storing of food. And since, as we have said, the clergy must be teachers of the laity and must proclaim the Word of God to them, it seems from this that they may not have any temporal goods. Again, it was said in the book of Numbers that those who were of the stock of Aaron and Levi, by whom are meant those who serve the altar, should have neither inheritance nor possession among the people of God. The clergy, therefore, must have no other portion or other share apart from God, for God is their portion. Hence, Jerome says that the Greek word 'cleros' is 'portion' in Latin; and he says that it is for this reason that 'clerics' are so called, because they are of the portion of the Lord.[3] God, then, is their portion: they must seek no other portion.

First, however, we can resolve the authority of the Gospel and say that, according to the various interpretations of learned and holy men, the Gospel statement that preachers must have neither purse nor bag was made for the sake of seven purposes: first, that we might be able to convert those who are against us; second, that we might be able to astonish them; third, that preachers might learn to trust in God; fourth, that they might not place hope in themselves;

1. Matt. 19:21.
2. Psalm 62:10.
3. *Epist.* 52 (*ad Nepotianum*), 5 (PL 22:531).

spem ponere; quinto, ut sciant homines excellenciam predicacionis cognoscere; sexto, ut varios status Ecclesie valeant previdere; septimo, ut cognoscant predicatores racione sui officii alios sibi debitores esse.

Propter primum, sciendum quod, ut Gregorius Nazianzenus exponit dictum passum Evangelii et habetur in glossa,[1] adeo[2] virtuosi debent esse predicatores evangelizantes verbum[3] Dei quod non minus propter vite modum quam propter eorum verbum proficiat Evangelium. Voluit ergo Deus, secundum hanc exposicionem, quod evangelizantes verbum Dei non portarent sacculum neque peram nec[4] eciam calciamenta ut in illo primordio evangelizacionis homines, videntes eos esse tante vite et tante virtutis, non minus converterentur propter ea que viderent in eorum vita[5] quam propter ea que audirent[6] per eorum verba. Mandavit ergo hoc Deus non quod ad hoc tenerentur predicatores vel clerici, sed[7] propter hanc spiritualem causam, ut in illo primordio, quando omnes erant adversi, cicius converterentur.

Secundo, possunt[8] exponi prefata verba ut sint dicta non solum ad adversarios convertendum sed ad eos terrendum; et sic aliqui doctores notaverunt, ut quia mittebat Dominus discipulos ad predicandum Iudeis, qui erant nimis[9] dure cervicis, et qui nimis confidebant de temporalibus, ut ipsi Iudei terrerentur considerando magnitudinem virtutis Christi, qui mittens ad predicandum discipulos sine sacculo et pera et sine sumptibus, et tamen, cum nullos sumptus haberent, ita abundabant quod nihil deficiebat eis. Ideo dicitur Luce XXII: 'Quando misi vos sine sacculo et pera et calciamentis, numquid aliquid defuit vobis? At illi dixerunt: Nihil.' Casu ergo speciali tunc emergente mandavit hoc Dominus discipulis suis, non quod posteriores ad hoc obligentur. Nam et ipsi discipuli non fuerunt postmodum ad hoc obligati, cum Dominus dixerit[10] Luce XXII: 'Sed nunc qui habet sacculum, tollat similiter et peram.' Ergo et sacculum ad pecuniam reponendam et peram ad cibaria reservanda[11] voluit Dominus discipulos suos habere.

Tercio, possunt exponi prefata verba ut non solum dicta sint ad adversarios convertendum et terrendum sed eciam ad de Deo confidendum.[12] Et ista est exposicio Gregorii, qui super dicto passu ait quidem quod 'tanta enim predicatori[13] debet[14] in Deo[15] esse fiducia, ut presentis vite sumptus, quamvis non prevideat, hoc tamen sibi non deesse certissime sciat.' Ipsi enim discipuli Christi non providebant sibi sumptus, quia ibant sine sacculo et pera et eciam[16] sine calciamentis, et tamen nil deerat eis. Non ergo mandavit Dominus predicatores vel discipulos suos non habere

---

1: glossa] quod *add. mss*   2: adeo] a deo *mss*   3: verbum] *om.* F   4: nec] neque F   5: in eorum vita] *om.* F   6: propter ... audirent] *om.* F   7: sed] vel FV²   8: possunt] possent F   9: nimis] *om.* CFV²   10: dixerit] dicit F dixit V²   11: reservanda] reservandum C   12: confidendum] confitendum P   13: predicatori] predicari FV²   14: debet] debent F   15: in Deo] *om.* C   16: eciam] *om.* F

fifth, that men might come to know the excellence of preaching; sixth, that they might be able to foresee the various conditions of the Church; and seventh, that preachers might understand others to be their debtors by reason of their ministry.

As to the first, it must be known that, as Gregory Nazianzenus explains in his interpretation of the Gospel saying, and as we gather from a gloss,[1] the preachers who proclaim the Word of God must be men of such virtue that the Gospel may benefit no less from their manner of life than from their words. According to this interpretation, therefore, God wished that those who proclaimed the Word of God should carry neither purse nor bag nor even shoes so that, at the very beginning of the proclamation of the Gospel, men might be converted no less by what they saw in their lives than by what they heard through their words, seeing them to be men of such great [frugality of] life and such great virtue. God commanded this, therefore, not because preachers or clerics were [all henceforth] to be bound by it, but for this spiritual cause: that, at the very beginning, when all men were against them, they might be the more speedily converted.

Second, we can interpret the foregoing statement as having been made not only so that those who were against them might be converted, but also that they might be astonished. And a number of teachers have noted this: that the Lord sent the disciples out to preach to the Jews, who were excessively stiff-necked and who trusted excessively in temporal possessions, in such a way that the Jews themselves might be astonished by contemplating the greatness of Christ's power, Whose disciples, sent forth to preach without purse and bag and without the means of support, still prospered so much even when they had no means of support that they lacked nothing. And so it is said in Luke 22: 'When I sent you out without purse or bag or shoes, did you lack anything? But they said, Nothing.'[2] The Lord gave His disciples this commandment, therefore, not because all who came after them were to be bound by it, but in the special circumstances then prevailing. And, indeed, the disciples themselves were not subsequently bound by it, when, in Luke 22, the Lord said: 'But now let whoever has a purse, and a bag also, take it.'[3] Therefore, [despite the initial prohibition,] the Lord wished His disciples to have both a purse for the keeping of money and a bag for the storing of food.

Third, we can interpret the foregoing statement as having been made not only so that those who were against them might be converted and astonished, but also that trust might be inspired in God. And this is Gregory's interpretation, who, expounding those words, says: 'For so great must be the preacher's trust in God that, even though he can see no way of supporting his present life, he still knows most certainly that he does not lack it.'[4] For the disciples of Christ did not provide themselves with the means of support, for they went out without purse and bag and without even shoes; yet, nonetheless, they lacked nothing. The Lord, therefore, did not command His preachers or disciples to have neither purse nor bag nor

1.   *Apud* Aquinas, *Catena Aurea* (Opera omnia, Parma, 1852–73) 12:115.
2.   Luke 22:35.
3.   Luke 22:36.
4.   *Apud* Aquinas, loc. cit.; cf. *Glossa ordinaria*, PL 114:284.

sacculum neque peram neque calciamenta quod clericis et hiis qui tenent locum illorum discipulorum secundum se sit illicitum aliquid possidere. Sed hoc mandavit, ut patuit per Gregorium, ut nos doceret et instrueret quanta debet esse fiducia predicatorum et evangelizancium verba divina in Deo, qui sine sumptibus et[1] sine calciamentis et nullam provisionem habentes, nullum paciebantur defectum. Hoc quidem non posset facere mundus, quod non calciatus et ad frigus expositus non haberet defectum caloris qui ei esset necessarius ad commoditatem vite. Fiducia ergo ista non poterat esse in mundo, sed in Deo.

Quarta vero exposicio esse potest: ut ipsi predicatores in seipsis spem non ponerent;[2] et ista est exposicio Chrysostomi, qui ait: 'Et quidem, quando nec calciamenta nec zonam habebant nec baculum nec es,[3] nullius sunt passi penuriam; ut autem marsupium concessit eis et peram, esaurire[4] videntur et sitire[5] et nuditatem pati,[6] ac si eis Dominus diceret: Actenus cuncta vobis uberrime affluebant, nunc autem volo vos inopiam experiri; ideo non addico vos pristine[7] necessitati, sed mando et loculum habere ad conservandam pecuniam et peram ad conservanda[8] cibaria.' Nullus ergo potest de seipso confidere. Nam hec est confidencia nostra secundum mundum: quando habemus loculos plenos pecunia, quando habemus peram[9] et horrea cibariis referta.[10] Discipuli vero, quando fuerunt sine sacculo et pera, nihil eis defuit;[11] quando concessit eis Dominus sacculum et peram, multas penurias[12] sunt experti. Non ergo inhibuit Dominus sacculum et peram quod secundum se esset illicitum clericis, predicatoribus et prelatis ecclesiasticis aliqua possidere, quia, si[13] secundum se hoc esset illicitum, numquam postea Dominus mandasset discipulis et sacculum et peram tollere. Sed inhibuit Dominus peram et sacculum ut homines, et specialiter clerici, in seipsis spem non ponerent, cum discipuli sine sacculo et pera multo magis abundaverunt quam[14] quando eis illa fuerunt concessa.

Quinta quidem exposicio est ut sciant homines excellenciam predicacionis et Evangelii cognoscere; quia tanta est huius[15] excellencia quod pro bene exercendo huiusmodi officio omnis alia cura et sollicitudo est pretermittenda. Homo enim, quantum ad presens spectat, potest comparari ad quatuor: primo, ad propriam substanciam sive ad[16] proprium corpus; secundo, ad bona exteriora, sicut ad pecuniam et cibaria; tercio, ad ea que adherent corpori, ut ad calciamenta; quarto, ad ipsos proximos cum[17] quibus conversamur. Circa omnia autem hec quatuor contingit homines esse sollicitos. Nam aliqui sunt solliciti de proprio subiecto et de proprio corpore, ita quod numquam irent ad aliquem locum ubi crederent posse esse periculum perdendi corpus. Aliqui vero sunt solliciti circa pecuniam et cibaria, quod semper vellent habere pecuniam in sacculo et cibaria in pera vel eciam in horreis; nam pera est quasi parvum horreum[18] ubi modica[19] possunt recondi cibaria,

---

1: et] *om.* C   2: ponerent] ponent FV²   3: es] eciam F   4: esaurire] *om.* PV¹   5: sitire]
sciture V²   6: pati] patiat V²   7: pristine] pecunie F   8: conservanda] conservandum C
9: peram] peras F *om.* V²   10: referta] refecta V²   11: eis defuit] defuit eis FV²   12: penurias]
pecunias F   13: si] *om.* V¹   14: quam] quod F   15: huius] huiusmodi C   16: propriam ...
ad] *om.* F   17: cum] *om.* C   18: horreum] locum FV²   19: modica] pauca FV²

shoes because it is unlawful in itself for clerics and those who hold the place of the disciples to possess anything. Rather, as Gregory makes clear, He commanded this in order to teach and instruct us how great must be the trust in God of preachers and those who proclaim the Divine Word; for, without the means of support, and without shoes, and having no provision, they suffered no lack. This, indeed, the world could not accomplish: that one without shoes and exposed to the cold should have no lack of the heat necessary to him for the comfort of life. Therefore, such trust could not be in the world, but in God.

A fourth explanation is also possible: that [temporal possessions were forbidden so that] preachers might not place hope in themselves. And this is the interpretation of Chrysostom, who says: 'And indeed, when they had neither shoes nor a girdle nor a staff nor money, they suffered no hardship; yet when pouch and bag were granted to them, they seem to have hungered and thirsted and suffered nakedness, as though the Lord had said to them: "All things have thus far come to you most abundantly; but I now desire that you be tried by want. And so I do not sentence you to your former necessity [of having no possessions] but I command that you have a purse for the keeping of money and a bag for the keeping of food."'[1] No one, therefore, can trust in himself. For this is our trust according to the world: when we have purses full of money and when we have a bag and barns stuffed with food. The disciples indeed lacked nothing while they were without purse and bag; yet, when the Lord granted them a purse and bag, they were tried by many hardships. Therefore, the Lord did not forbid purse and bag because it was unlawful in itself for clerics, preachers, and the prelates of the Church to possess anything; for, if this were unlawful in itself, the Lord would not subsequently have commanded the disciples to take both purse and bag. Rather, the Lord forbade bag and purse so that men, and especially the clergy, might not place hope in themselves, when the disciples prospered so much more without purse and bag than when these things were granted to them.

The fifth explanation is that [temporal possessions were forbidden so that] men might come to understand the excellence of preaching and of the Gospel. For so great is this excellence that all other care and anxiety must be set aside for the sake of performing this ministry well. For, so far as our present discussion is concerned, a man can be considered under four aspects: first, in relation to his own substance or his own body; second, in relation to such external goods as money and food; third, in relation to those articles which attach to the body, such as shoes; and, fourth, in relation to the neighbours with whom he has dealings. And it is a characteristic of men to be anxious in all four of these respects. For some are anxious with respect to their own person and their own body, and so would never go into any place where they believed there to be a possible danger of bodily harm. And some are anxious with respect to money and food, and so always desire to have money in their purse and food in their bag, or, indeed, in their barns; for a bag is like a small barn in which small quantities of food can be kept,

---

1. *Apud* Aquinas, *Catena aurea* 12:230.

et horreum est quasi magna pera ubi multa possunt cibaria reservari. Aliqui vero sunt solliciti circa tercium, ut puta circa ea que adherent corpori et que ornant et tegunt corpus, ut puta circa calciamenta. Sunt autem[1] aliqui solliciti circa quartum, ut puta circa consocios et circa[2] proximos, volendo delectabilia verba loqui eis et salutare ipsos. Voluit ergo Dominus[3] docere quanta deberet esse[4] sollicitudo Evangelii et predicacionis, pro qua homo debet dimittere omnem aliam sollicitudinem, sive sit proprii corporis sive bonorum exteriorum, sicut est sollicitudo pecunie vel cibariorum, sive sit bonorum ornancium et tegencium corpus, cuiusmodi sunt calciamenta, sive sit delectabiliter convivendi cum alio, sicut quod aliqui sunt multum solliciti salutare alios et delectabilia verba habere cum eis. Voluit ergo Dominus omnem huiusmodi sollicitudinem pretermitti per sollicitudinem evangelizandi.

Propter quod, volens suos discipulos ad evangelizandum mitti,[5] ait: 'Ecce, ego mitto vos sicut agnos inter lupos'; id est, pro sollicitudine predicacionis debetis[6] dimittere[7] sollicitudinem proprii corporis, quia eritis inter lupos et in[8] periculo[9] mortis. 'Nolite portare sacculum neque peram': id est, pro sollicitudine predicacionis dimittatis sollicitudinem exteriorum bonorum, ut pecunie et cibariorum. 'Neque calciamenta': id est, pro sollicitudine predicacionis dimittatis sollicitudinem calciamentorum, id est eorum que ornant et tegunt[10] corpus. 'Et neminem per viam salutaveritis': id est, non sitis vagi, sicut sunt homines qui sunt multum solliciti et intenti ad salutandum istos vel illos et quoscumque per viam inveniunt; sed solum sitis intenti et solliciti ad officium evangelizandi, quod est vobis commissum, pro qua sollicitudine debetis pretermittere sollicitudinem salutandi alios et delectabiliter[11] convivendi cum eis.

Cum ergo inhibuit Dominus[12] ne temporalia possideremus et ne sacculum vel peram haberemus, inhibuit ne aliquem per viam salutaremus, nulli autem dubium esse debet quod non est de se illicitum homines per viam salutare nec clericis nec laicis. Sic nec clericis nec laicis[13] est de se illicitum temporalia possidere. Utrumque tamen inhibuit Dominus non quasi essent illicita, sed quia erant pro illo tempore opportuna et erant in illo primordio predicandi Evangelium[14] ad cognoscendam[15] excellenciam Evangelii ordinata. Et ista est via Cyrilli, cuius verba ponere longum est.

Sexta via est ut diversos status Ecclesie[16] cognoscamus. Nam sicut medicus pro varietate temporum alia et alia dat infirmis,[17] sic Christus, medicus noster, secundum varios Ecclesie status alia et alia ordinavit, ut prius, tempore pacifico,[18] mandavit suos discipulos nec sacculum habere neque peram; instante vero tempore

---

1: autem] eciam *add.* C   2: circa] *om.* FV²   3: Dominus] deus C   4: deberet esse] esse deberet C   5: mitti] mittere FV²   6: debetis] debemus F   7: dimittere] dimitte C   8: in] in *add.* C (*by dittography*)   9: periculo] periculis FV²   10: tegunt] regunt FV²   11: delectabiliter] diligenter FV²   12: Dominus] deus C   13: Sic ... laicis] *om.* CFV²   14: predicandi Evangelium] *del.* C *om.* FV²   15: cognoscendam] recognoscendum FV² agnoscendum V¹   16: Ecclesie] *om.* C   17: infirmis] interius F   18: pacifico] pacifice F

and a barn is like a large bag in which large quantities of food can be stored. And some are anxious in the third way: namely, with respect to those articles which attach to the body and which adorn and clothe the body, such as shoes. And some are anxious in the fourth way: namely, with respect to companions and neighbours, desiring to have pleasant conversation with them and to greet them. Therefore, the Lord wished to teach us how great should be our anxiety for proclaiming the Gospel and for preaching, for the sake of which a man must put aside all other anxiety: whether for his own body, or for external goods, such as anxiety for money and food, or for the goods of bodily adornment and clothing, such as shoes, or for the pleasant company of another, as with those who are greatly anxious to greet others and to have pleasant conversation with them. Therefore, the Lord wished all such anxiety to be set aside in favour of anxiety for proclaiming the Gospel.

And so, desiring to send out His disciples to proclaim the Gospel, He said, 'See, I send you out as lambs among the wolves': that is, you must set aside anxiety for your own bodies in favour of anxiety for preaching, for you will be among wolves and in danger of death. 'Carry neither purse nor bag': that is, you are to lay aside anxiety for such external goods as money and food in favour of anxiety for preaching. 'Nor shoes': that is, you are to set aside anxiety for shoes — that is, for those things which adorn and clothe the body — in favour of anxiety for preaching. 'And greet no one on the road':[1] that is, do not be distracted as are men who are greatly anxious for and intent upon greeting all and sundry whom they find on the road. Rather, be wholly intent upon and anxious for the ministry of proclaiming the Gospel which is entrusted to you: in favour of which anxiety you must set aside anxiety for greeting others and taking pleasure in their company.

Therefore, although the Lord has forbidden us to possess temporal goods and to have purse or bag, and has forbidden us to greet anyone on the road, there should be no doubt that it is not unlawful in itself for either the clergy or the laity to greet men on the road. So too, it is not unlawful in itself for either clerics or laymen to have temporal possessions. Rather, the Lord forbade both these things not as if they were unlawful [as such], but because it was opportune at that time to do so and, when the Gospel was first beginning to be proclaimed, conducive to an understanding of the excellence of the Gospel. And this is the way of Cyril, whose words are too lengthy to quote.[2]

The sixth way [of explaining why the disciples were forbidden to have possessions] is that we might understand the various conditions of the Church. For just as a physician treats the sick in different ways to suit changing times, so Christ, our Physician, has ordered the condition of the Church differently according to different circumstances. Thus, at first, when the time was peaceful, He commanded His disciples to have neither purse nor bag; but, when the time of the

1. Luke 10:3–4.
2. See Aquinas, *Catena aurea* 12:115.

passionis, persecucione[1] Iudeorum, utrumque concessit. Et hec est via Bede expo-
nentis[2] verba. Unde ait quod 'non esse[3] eandem[4] vivendi regulam[5] persecucionis
tempore[6] quam[7] pacis discipulos Dominus informat; misit quidem discipulos ad
predicandum, ne quid in via tollerent precepit; instante vero mortis articulo et tota
illa gente pastorem et gregem,' id est Christum et discipulos, 'simul persequente,
congruam temporis regulam decernit, permittens ut tollerent victui necessaria, donec sopiatur persecutorum insania.' Pro illo ergo tempore, antequam esset nota[8]
Evangelii virtus, quia homines nimis confidebant de temporalibus, expediebat ut
tempore[9] pacifico discipuli non portarent sacculum neque peram; instante autem
persecucione Dominus concessit utrumque. Nunc autem, quia iam est virtus
Evangelii nota,[10] quantumcumque tempus sit[11] pacis, non solum licet clericis temporalia habere, sed eciam expedit, ne a laicis vilipendatur Ecclesia.

Septima via ad exponendum prefata verba[12] est ut cognoscant predicatores racione sui officii alios sibi debitores esse. Unde quod Dominus dicit,[13] 'Nolite portare sacculum neque peram,' magis hoc dicit permissive quam preceptive; quod
patet per[14] hoc, quod in Evangelio subditur: 'Dignus est enim operarius mercede
sua,' quasi diceret: 'Cum itis ad predicandum, non oportet quod vivatis propriis
sumptibus nec quod portetis sacculum neque peram, sed edatis et bibatis que sunt
apud illos quibus predicabitis, quia dignus est operarius mercede sua. Non enim
est magnum, si eis seminatis spiritualia, si comeditis et bibitis de bonis eorum et
metitis temporalia.' Qui ergo propriis sumptibus predicaret, sicut faciebat Paulus,
ut non esset onerosus Corinthiis,[15] de quo dicitur quod in die predicabat et nocte
operabatur[16] manibus ut sustentamenta vite haberet, opus supererogacionis faceret.
Qualitercumque ergo predicator vel per operacionem manuum vel per sumptus
proprios officium exerceret, non accipiendo ab aliis necessaria vite, non solum
non peccaret, sed pocius, quantum ad presens spectat, supererogaret.

Cum ergo in Evangelio vel in aliis locis Scripture Sacre interdicuntur clericis
possessiones et temporalia, ut puta quia debemus renunciare omnibus que possidemus, omnia huiusmodi dicta referenda sunt quantum ad finalem intencionem, quia
in possessionibus terrenis et in omnibus temporalibus rebus finaliter[17] intencionem[18]
nostram[19] ponere non debemus. Spirituali tamen[20] modo, ut dicebatur, clerici debent
temporalia respuere, quia spirituali modo,[21] ut tangebatur, clericus dicitur a 'cleros'
grece, latine 'sors,' quia spirituali modo Deus pars et sors esse dicitur clericorum.

1: persecucione] persecucionis CF   2: exponentis] prefata *add.* C   3: esse] enim FV²   4: ean-
dem] eadem FV²   5: vivendi regulam] verendi regula F   6: tempore] *om.* CFV²   7: quam]
quia F qua V²   8: nota] nata FV²   9: tempore] *om.* F   10: nota] nata F   11: tempus sit] sit
tempus CF   12: verba] *om.* C   13: dicit] ostendit FV²   14: per] ex F de V²   15: Corinthiis]
Corinciis FPV¹   16: operabatur]operabat F   17: finaliter] finalem C   18: quia in possessionibus ... intencionem] *om.* FV²   19: nostram] quam in his *add.* F   20: tamen] enim F   21: ut
dicebatur ... modo] *om.* F

Passion and the persecution of the Jews drew near, He granted both. And this is the way in which Bede interprets the words in question. Thus, he says that: 'The Lord did not intend the disciples to live by the same rule in time of persecution as in time of peace. He indeed sent the disciples out to preach and instructed them to take nothing on the way. But when the time of death drew near and that whole people [i.e. the Jews] persecuted Shepherd and flock' — that is, Christ and His disciples — 'together, He changed the rule to suit the time, allowing them to carry the necessary means of support until the madness of the persecutors should subside.'[1] At that time, therefore, before the strength of the Gospel was known and because men trusted excessively in temporal possessions, it was expedient, given that the time was peaceful, that the disciples should carry neither purse nor bag; but, when persecution drew near, the Lord granted both. And now, since the strength of the Gospel has long been known, it is not only lawful, but also expedient, for clerics to have temporal goods no matter how peaceful the time may be, lest the Church be held in low esteem by the laity.

The seventh way in which the words in question may be explained is that [temporal possessions were forbidden so that] preachers might understand others to be their debtors by reason of their ministry. Thus, when the Lord said, 'Carry neither purse nor bag,' He spoke more by way of permission than instruction, as is clear from this statement which is added in the Gospel: 'For the labourer is worthy of his hire.'[2] It is as if He said: 'When you go out to preach, you ought not to live by your own resources or carry purse or bag. Rather, you should eat and drink of what is already present among those to whom you preach; for the labourer is worthy of his hire. For if you sow spiritual things for them, it is no great matter if you eat and drink of their goods and reap temporal things.'[3] Therefore, he who preaches at his own expense performs a work of supererogation, as did Paul, of whom it is said that he preached by day and worked with his hands by night in order to have the means of sustaining life, so that he might not be a burden to the Corinthians.[4] So far as the present time is concerned, therefore, if any preacher supports his ministry either by the work of his hands or out of his own resources, not accepting the necessaries of life from others, he not only does not sin but, rather, does more than his duty.

Therefore, when, in the Gospel or at other places in Sacred Scripture, possessions and temporal goods are forbidden to clerics — for example, because [it is said that] we must renounce all that we possess — all such statements are to be understood with reference to our ultimate goal: for we must not have earthly possessions and any temporal goods as our ultimate goal. As has been said, however, the clergy must renounce temporal goods in a [further] spiritual sense; for, in a spiritual sense, the Greek word 'cleros' is 'portion' in Latin, as we have noted: for, in a spiritual sense, God is said to be the share and portion of clerics.

1. Bede, *In Lucae evangelium expositio* 10 (PL 92:462); cf. *Glossa ordinaria*, PL 114:339.
2. Luke 10:7.
3. Cf. I Cor. 9:11.
4. Acts 18:3.

Sed cum[1] dicimus quod spirituali modo clerici debent temporalibus renunciare, non est intelligendum quantum ad finalem intencionem,[2] quia ad hoc ita tenentur laici sicut et clerici. De utriusque enim, ut tetigimus, verum est quod divicie, si affluant,[3] non debent cor apponere. Nec est intelligendum quantum ad possessionem et dominium, quia non solum eque, sed eciam magis, ut infra patebit, clerici quam laici temporalibus dominantur. Sed intelligendum est quantum ad curam et sollicitudinem, quia 'nemo militans[4] Deo implicet[5] se negociis secularibus.' Significantur enim clerici per Mariam, que sedens secus pedes Domini audiebat verbum illius; laici[6] per Martam, que sollicita circa temporalia erga plurima turbabatur. Propter quod, cum clerici habent dominium et possessionem temporalium, ut liberius spiritualibus vacare possint, et ut, sedentes secus pedes Domini, divinis vacent misteriis et sanctarum studio scripturarum, quia ut dicitur Deuter. XXXIII,[7] 'Qui appropinquant pedibus eius, accipient de doctrina illius,' ideo curam et sollicitudinem temporalium[8] possessionum debent clerici per ministros alios exercere.

CAPITULUM III: *In quo solvuntur dicta et auctoritates Veteris Testamenti, quod non liceat clericis temporalia possidere.*

Non solum autem Evangelii dicta sonare videntur quod clerici non debent temporalia possidere, quia Dominus suis discipulis dixit quod non deberent portare sacculum neque peram, sed eciam auctoritates Veteris Testamenti hoc idem sonare cernuntur. Nam, ut supra tetigimus, dicit Dominus ad Aaron in terra filiorum Israel: 'Nihil possidebitis nec[9] habebitis partem inter eos. Ego pars et hereditas tua in medio filiorum Israel,' ut dicitur Num. XVIII. Si filii Aaron, qui serviebant altari et erant[10] ministri[11] Ecclesie, non debebant habere possessionem nec hereditatem, ergo nec clerici, qui altari serviunt et ministri Ecclesie nuncupantur. Sic eciam Numeri eodem capitulo dictum est filiis Levi, qui serviebant in tabernaculo federis, quod nihil aliud possiderent, sed decimarum oblacione contenti essent. Cum ergo per tabernaculum federis intelligatur templum et Ecclesia, igitur clerici, qui serviunt templo et Ecclesie, nil[12] possidere poterunt, sed decimarum oblacione et hiis que offeruntur in Ecclesia debent esse contenti.

Sciendum ergo, quod Novum et Vetus Testamentum sunt quasi rota in medio rote, quia unum continetur in alio, iuxta visionem que habetur Ezechielis I, ubi

1: Sed cum] sed tamen C tamen FV²   2: intencionem] nostram *add.* F   3: affluant] affluent CFV²
4: militans] militat V²   5: implicet] implicat CF   6: laici] vero *add.* FV²   7: XXXIII] xxiii PV¹
8: temporalium] et *add.* F   9: nec] nichil C   10: erant] ecclesie F   11: ministri] et *add.* F
12: nil] nichil C

But when we say that the clergy must renounce temporal goods in a spiritual sense, this is not to be understood with reference to their ultimate goal; for, in this respect, laymen are just as much bound as the clergy. For, as we have noted, it is true of both that, when riches abound, they must not set their heart on them.[1] Nor must it be understood with reference to possession and lordship; for, as will appear below, the clergy have lordship over temporal things not only equally with, but indeed more extensively than, the laity. Rather, it must be understood with reference to care and anxiety; for 'No soldier of God engages himself in the affairs of the world.'[2] For the clergy are signified by Mary, who, sitting at the Lord's feet, heard His words; and the laity by Martha, who was troubled by anxiety for many temporal responsibilities.[3] And so, when clerics have lordship and temporal property, those clerics must therefore exercise care and anxiety for temporal possessions through other ministers, so that they may attend more freely to spiritual matters, and so that, sitting at the Lord's feet, they may have leisure to study the Divine Mysteries and Sacred Scriptures. For, as is said in Deuteronomy 33, 'Those who approach His feet shall receive His teaching.'[4]

CHAPTER III: *In which the sayings and authorities of the Old Testament are explained which seem to show that clerics may not have temporal possessions.*

But not only do passages of the Gospel seem to proclaim that clerics must not have temporal possessions (for the Lord said to His disciples that they might carry neither purse nor bag): the authorities of the Old Testament are also understood [by some] to state the same principle. For, as we have noted above, the Lord said to Aaron in the land of the Children of Israel: 'You shall possess nothing, nor shall you have a portion among them. I am your portion and inheritance in the midst of the Children of Israel,' as is said in Numbers 18.[5] Therefore, if the sons of Aaron, who served the altar and were ministers of the Church, might have neither possession nor inheritance, then [it seems that] nor may the clergy who serve the altar and are called to be ministers of the Church. So also, in the same chapter of Numbers, it was said to the sons of Levi who served in the Tabernacle of the Congregation that they were to possess nothing else, but were to be content with the offering of tithes.[6] Therefore, since by the Tabernacle of the Congregation may be understood the Temple and the Church, [it seems that] the clergy who serve the Temple and the Church will thus be able to possess nothing, but must be content with the oblation of tithes and with those things which are offered in the Church.

It must be known, therefore, that the Old and New Testaments are as it were a wheel in the midst of a wheel; for the one is contained in the other according to the

1. Psalm 62:10.
2. II Tim. 2:4.
3. Luke 10:39–42.
4. Deut. 33:3.
5. Num. 18:20–21.
6. Num. 18:23–24.

dicitur: 'Quasi sit rota in medio rote.' Que enim hic sunt clara, ibi erant figurative; propter quod hiis que videmus in Testamento Novo, ut plurimum respondent similia in Testamento Veteri vel secundum figuram quantum ad cerimonialia, secundum que quod figurabatur[1] in Veteri verificatur in Novo, ut agnus immolatus figurabat Christum in Veteri qui[2] secundum veritatem immolatus est in Novo;[3] vel huius continencia est secundum rem quantum ad moralia, que in Novo non sunt evacuata sed adimpleta,[4] iuxta illud Matthaei V: 'Nolite putare quod[5] veni solvere legem aut prophetas; non enim veni solvere, sed adimplere.'

Propter quod de non habendo clericos vel eos qui serviunt templo et altari possessiones et temporalia, quasi similia habentur in Novo et in Veteri.[6] Nam, ut diximus, Luce X Dominus[7] mandavit discipulis non portare peram neque sacculum;[8] postea Luce XXII Dominus dixit eis: 'Qui habet sacculum, tollat similiter et peram.' Primo ergo Dominus inhibuit discipulis habere temporalia, postea concessit. Sic et[9] Num. XVIII Dominus filiis Aaron et Levi inhibuit habere partem et hereditatem in terra,[10] postea Num. XXXV Dominus[11] mandavit filiis Israel ut darent Levitis[12] de possessionibus suis[13] urbes ad habitandum[14] et suburbana[15] earum[16] per circuitum. Ita[17] quod Dominus concessit Levitis[18] ut haberent de possessionibus filiorum Israel urbes et suburbana: urbes quidem ad habitandum et suburbana[19] ad animalia nutriendum. Et quia similiter mandatum est de possessione temporalium in Veteri et in[20] Novo, omnia illa que dicta sunt ad exposicionem Novi, qui bene vellent[21] laborare aliqualiter adaptare[22] possent[23] ad exposicionem Veteris. Sed ut[24] in summa[25] sit dicere quod tam in Veteri quam in Novo prius inhibuit possessionem temporalium et postea concessit non quod ipsa temporalia secundum se sint illicita clericis ad possidendum, sed hoc prius fuit inhibitum et postea concessum quia sic expediebat priori tempori ut inhiberetur, et sic posteriori ut concederetur. Chrysostomus tamen, exponens illud Luce XXII, 'Qui habet sacculum, tollat similiter et peram,' refert inhibicionem ad concessionem et adsimilat[26] hoc et illud[27] natacioni,[28] dicens quod: 'Sicut[29] qui docet alium natare prius quidem supponit manus suas, postea subtrahens relinquit eum[30] quem[31] docet[32] natare proprie virtuti,[33] ut ipse sibi opituletur, ut ipse seipsum iuvet, ita[34] Dominus, temporalia inhibens[35] discipulis, eis[36] manum suam supposuit, concedens

1: figurabatur] figurabuntur C   2: qui] sic C   3: immolatus est in Novo] est in novo immolatus C
4: adimpleta] adimplecta C   5: quod] quoniam PV[1]   6: in Novo et in Veteri] in veteri et in novo CFV[2]   7: Dominus] deus C   8: peram neque sacculum] saculum neque peram CFV[2]
9: sic et] sicut F sic V[2]   10: terra] filiorum israel add. C   11: Dominus] deus C   12: Levitis] leviticis C   13: suis] om. FV[2]   14: habitandum] hereditandum FV[2]   15: suburbana] eciam add. F
16: earum] eorum PV[1]   17: Ita] item F   18: Levitis] leviticis C   19: urbes quidem ... suburbana] om. F   20: in] om. C   21: vellent] vellet mss   22: adaptare] adaptari auct   23: possent] possunt F   24: ut] om. V[2]   25: summa] summo F   26: adsimilat] ad similia F ad similias V[2]
27: illud] aliud CF   28: natacioni] vacacione F   29: Sicut] autem add. CFV[2]   30: eum] cum FV[2]   31: quem] que F   32: docet] nocet F   33: proprie virtuti] propria virtute F
34: ita] om. CF et add. V[2]   35: inhibens] iubens V[2]   36: eis] om. C

vision recorded in Ezekiel 1, where it is said: 'As it were a wheel in the midst of a wheel';[1] for those things which are now clear were there prefigured. And so, to those things which we see in the New Testament, many similar things in the Old Testament correspond: either figuratively, as with the ceremonies according to which what is fulfilled in the New was prefigured in the Old (for example, the lamb which was sacrificed in the Old prefigured Christ, Who was in truth sacrificed in the New); or literally, as when its content consists of moral teachings which are not abolished in the New, but fulfilled, according to Matthew 5: 'Do not suppose that I came to destroy the Law or the prophets; for I came not to destroy, but to fulfil.'[2]

And so, as to the question of whether clerics and those who serve in the Temple and at the altar may not have possessions and temporal goods, almost similar teachings are found in the New Testament and the Old. For, as we have said, in Luke 10 the Lord commanded His disciples to carry neither bag nor purse; yet subsequently, in Luke 22, the Lord said to them: 'Let whoever has a purse, and a bag also, take it.'[3] At first, therefore, the Lord forbade the disciples to have temporal possessions, but subsequently He granted them. And so too, in Numbers 18, the Lord forbade the sons of Aaron and Levi to have a portion and an inheritance in the land of the Children of Israel; yet subsequently, in Numbers 35, the Lord commanded the Children of Israel to give to the Levites from their possessions towns to dwell in and the lands surrounding them on every side.[4] Thus, from the possessions of the Children of Israel, the Lord granted the Levites towns and the lands surrounding them: the towns themselves to dwell in, and the surrounding lands for the support of their cattle. And since a similar commandment is given in the Old and New Testaments concerning the possession of temporal things, those who wish to perform the work [of scriptural exegesis] well can in some manner apply all that has been said in expounding the New Testament to the interpretation of the Old. In short, then, it may be said that, in the Old and New Testaments alike, the Lord first forbade and then granted the possession of temporal goods, but not that the possession of temporal goods by the clergy is unlawful in itself. Rather, this was at first forbidden and subsequently granted because it was expedient that it should be thus forbidden at the earlier time and thus granted at the later. Hence Chrysostom, expounding that verse of Luke 22 — 'Let whoever has a purse, and a bag also, take it' — considers the prohibition in relation to the permission and compares the one and the other to swimming, saying that: 'Just as someone who is teaching another how to swim at first places his hands beneath him and then, withdrawing them, leaves the one whom he is teaching to swim to his own devices, so that he may fend for himself and help himself, so, when the Lord forbade temporal things to His disciples, He was supporting them with His hand

1. Ezek. 1:16.
2. Matt. 5:17.
3. Luke 22:36.
4. Num. 35:2–8.

autem, subtraxit.' Est ergo intencio sua quod Dominus, cum prius inhibuit possidere temporalia et postea concessit, quasi docuit natare suos discipulos in hoc mari
magno et spacioso, id est in hoc seculo. Nam cum eis inhibuit temporalia, nihil eis
defuit, ita quod tunc Dominus supponebat manum suam et sustentabat eos, ut sine
cura et sine sollicitudine temporalium nihil eis deficeret, ita quod nihil habendo
omnibus abundabant; et postea, quando concessit eis sacculum et peram, aliqualiter subtraxit manum suam, ut discipuli ipsi,[1] cum hoc quod previdissent[2] sibi
de pecunia in sacculo et de cibariis in pera, ut sibi ipsis subvenirent et sibi ipsis
opitularentur, tunc, quia Dominus aliqualiter subtraxerat manum suam, passi sunt
discipuli sitim,[3] famem et nuditatem.

Numquam enim quis natare disceret[4] si semper sustentaretur manibus aliorum;
sed quando natare nesciens et volens hoc addiscere, si prius sustentatur[5] manibus
aliorum et postea sibi ipsi relinquitur, hoc modo iuvat seipsum et discit qualiter
natare debeat. Pari eciam modo in Veteri Testamento, quia Levitis in tabernaculo
federis ministrantibus prius hereditatem et partem possessionum temporalium[6]
Dominus inhibuit et postea concessit, et forte plus abundaverunt ipsi Levite cum
fuerunt eis possessiones temporalium inhibite quam quando fuerunt eis concesse,
ut sit rota in rota et Novum Testamentum in Veteri. Propter quod id quod dicit
Chrysostomus in Testamento Novo, quod discipuli, quando eis fuerunt inhibite
possessiones temporalium, quia Dominus sustentabat eos, abundabant, ut nil[7] de-
esset eis, quando autem eis fuerunt concesse, penuriam paciebantur, quia relicti
fuerunt proprie virtuti, subtrahente aliqualiter Domino manum suam: forte eciam
simile contingebat in Veteri, ut plus abundarent Levite possessione carentes quam
eam habentes.

Non ergo aliquo tempore secundum se fuerunt clericis illicite possessiones temporalium, sed pro casu imminente aliquando fuerunt inhibite, aliquando fuerunt
concesse. Sed quando casu imminente aliquid fit, ad posteriores trahi non debet. Et
ut clare quesiti veritas patefiat quantum ad Novum Testamentum spectat, distinguemus triplex tempus in Ecclesia:[8] unum quantum ad temporalia sive quantum ad
immediatam possessionem temporalium, ut sit primum tempus, quando fuerunt
temporalia[9] inhibita discipulis, quando manus Domini fuit eis supposita; quod, secundum unum modum exponendi,[10] tunc factum est quando Luce X dicit Dominus:
'Nolite portare sacculum neque peram.' Fuerunt enim, ut aliqui sancti exponunt,
tunc temporalia eis inhibita, sed manus Domini fuit eis supposita, quia cum nil[11]
haberent, omnibus abundabant, quod sine supposicione divine manus et sine divino
auxilio fieri non poterat. Secundum autem tempus fuit quando temporalia fuerunt

1: discipuli ipsi] ipsi discipuli CFV[2]   2: previdissent] providissent F   3: sitim] statim C
4: disceret] diceret V[2]   5: sustentatur] sustentaretur F   6: temporalium] om. C   7: nil] nichil C
8: in Ecclesia] om. PV[1]   9: sive quantum ... temporalia] om. CPV[1]   10: exponendi] exponendum F   11: nil] nichil C

and, when He granted them, He withdrew it.'[1] His intention, therefore, is this: that when, at first, the Lord forbade the possession of temporal goods and subsequently granted it, He was as it were teaching His disciples to swim in this great and spacious sea; that is, in this world. For when He forbade them to have temporal possessions, they lacked nothing, for the Lord was then supporting and sustaining them with His hand so that, without care and without temporal anxiety, they might want nothing: and indeed, possessing nothing, they prospered in all things. But when He subsequently granted them purse and bag, He in some measure withdrew His hand, so that, when the disciples had provided themselves with money in their purse and food in their bag in order that they might supply themselves and fend for themselves, the disciples then suffered thirst, hunger and nakedness, because the Lord had in some measure withdrawn His hand.

For no one would ever learn to swim if he were always supported by the hands of others. But when he does not know how to swim and wishes to learn, if he is at first supported by the hands of others and subsequently left to himself, he in this way helps himself and learns how to swim. And so it is also in the Old Testament. For the Lord first forbade and subsequently granted an inheritance and a portion of temporal possessions to the Levites who ministered in the Tabernacle of the Congregation; and perhaps those Levites prospered more when temporal possessions were forbidden them than when they were granted to them: for the New Testament is in the Old like a wheel in the midst of a wheel. And so what Chrysostom says of the New Testament — that the disciples prospered so that they lacked nothing when temporal possessions were forbidden them, for the Lord sustained them, yet suffered poverty when they were granted them, for they were left to their own devices when the Lord in some measure withdrew His hand — perhaps also has a counterpart in the Old, in that the Levites may have prospered more when they were without possessions than when they had them.

Temporal possessions were therefore not at any time unlawful in themselves for the clergy, but were sometimes forbidden and sometimes granted, according to the specific circumstances. But when something is done in specific circumstances, it ought not to bind those who come afterwards. And in order to show the truth of this matter clearly insofar as it relates to the New Testament, we shall distinguish three periods of time in the Church. So far as temporal possessions are concerned, or as regards the immediate possession of temporal goods, the first such period was that during which temporal things were forbidden to the disciples: when the hand of the Lord was their support. And, according to one mode of interpretation, this was brought about when, in Luke 10, the Lord said, 'Carry neither purse nor bag.' For, as some of the saints have explained, temporal possessions were then forbidden them, but the hand of the Lord was their support, because, while having nothing, they prospered in all things: which would not have been possible without the support of the Divine Hand and without Divine aid. And the second period was that during which temporal possessions were granted to the

---

1. *Apud* Aquinas, *Catena aurea* 12:231.

discipulis concessa sed manus Domini fuit eis aliqualiter subtracta; quod tunc impletum est quando Luce XXII dicit Dominus:[1;2] 'Qui habet sacculum, tollat similiter et peram'; quod Chrysostomus exponens ait, ut supra tetigimus, quod Christus, docens discipulos suos natare inter[3] procellas seculi, manum suam eis subtraxit. Nam, cum prius nec calciamenta nec zonam haberent nec es,[4] nullius penuriam passi sunt; postquam autem marsupium concessit et peram, esurire[5] videntur, sitire et nuditatem pati.

In primo ergo tempore fuit temporalium possessionum inhibicio et divine[6] manus supposicio; in secundo vero econverso, fuit enim tunc burse concessio et divine manus[7] aliqualiter subtraccio. Sed quis diceret quod divine manus supposicio vel divinum auxilium secundum se esset malum? Constat autem quod divinum auxilium secundum se bonum est; tamen hominibus ad tempus subtraccio huiusmodi auxilii potest esse bona,[8] ut homines sibi ipsis derelicti infirmitatem suam cognoscant. Et sic eciam quis diceret quod ipsa temporalia secundum se sint mala, cum a Deo[9] creata sint, et ut habetur Geneseos primo, quod 'vidit Deus cuncta que fecerat, et erant valde bona'? Ita quod unumquodque secundum se bonum est, omnia autem simul sumpta sunt valde bona, ut dicit Augustinus in *Enchiridion*, quod ex omnibus constat universitatis[10] admirabilis pulchritudo.

Dicemus ergo quod ipsum divinum auxilium secundum se est bonum; subtraccio tamen eius ad tempus potest nobis esse proficua. Sic ipsa temporalia secundum se sunt bona; inhibicio tamen eorum ad tempus potest nobis esse utilis et iuvativa. Hec ergo duo, videlicet divine manus supposicio et[11] temporalium possessio, respiciunt illa duo tempora divisim, ut in primo tempore, quando inhibita sunt sacculus et pera, esset divine manus supposicio[12] sine temporalium possessione; in secundo vero tempore, quando talia sunt concessa, fuit econverso, quia fuit temporalium concessio et divine manus aliqualiter subtraccio, ut est per habita declaratum.

Sed quia utrumque illorum bonum est, nullum illorum secundum se debuit[13] perpetuo prohiberi nec perpetuo subtrahi. Propter quod est dare tercium tempus, in quo tempore[14] nunc sumus,[15] ubi et temporalia sunt concessa viris[16] ecclesiasticis[17] et manus Domini est supposita.[18] In hoc ergo[19] tercio tempore utroque est Ecclesia dotata, quia gaudet[20] et temporalium[21] subsidio et divino auxilio, ut se possit in suo[22] statu regere et conservare. Habuit enim prius Ecclesia inicium, postea incrementum, nunc autem habet perfeccionem et statum; propter quod, ut in statu huiusmodi

---

1: 'Nolite portare ... dicit Dominus] *om.* FV[2]   2: Dominus] deus C   3: inter] per FPV[1]V[2]
4: es] *om.* C eis F   5: esurire] exurire C   6: divine] dominice F   7: in secundo ... manus]
marg., in a later hand C   8: bona] bonum PV[1]   9: a Deo] adeo C   10: universitatis] universitas CF   11: et] *om.* C   12: et temporalium ... supposicio] *om.* FV[1]   13: debuit] debet F
14: tempore] *om.* V[1]   15: nunc sumus] nos sumus CF sumus nunc V[1]   16: viris] iuris F
17: ecclesiasticis] ecclesiastici F   18: supposita] primitus quando fuit possessio temporalium inhibita et manus domini supposita ut discipuli nichil habentes et in omnibus habundantes disceret domino confidere postea fuerunt temporalia concessa et manus domini aliqualiter subtracte ne in temporalibus spem ponere nec de nobis deberemus presumere *add.* C   19: ergo] autem FV[2]
20: gaudet] gaudit F   21: temporalium] temporali F   22: suo] subsidio *add.* C

disciples, but the hand of the Lord in some measure withdrawn from them. And this came to pass when, in Luke 22, the Lord said, 'Let whoever has a purse, and a bag also, take it.' Interpreting this, Chrysostom says, as we have noted above, that Christ, teaching His disciples to swim in the midst of the storms of this world, withdrew His hand from them. For when, at first, they possessed neither shoes nor a girdle nor money, they suffered no hardship; yet, when pouch and bag were subsequently granted, they seem to have suffered hunger, thirst, and nakedness.

During the first period, therefore, the possession of temporal things was forbidden and the support of the Divine Hand given. In the second, however, the converse occurred: for, then, a money bag was granted and the Divine Hand in some measure withdrawn. But who would say that the support of the Divine Hand or Divine aid are in themselves evils? For it is clear that Divine aid is good in itself; but it can also be good for such aid to be withdrawn from men for a time so that, left to their own devices, men may understand their own infirmity. And again, who would say that temporal things are in themselves evil when they were created by God and when, as is established in Genesis I, 'God saw all the things that He had made, and they were very good'?[1] Thus, each thing is good in itself, and all things taken together are very good;[2] for, as Augustine says in the *Enchiridion*, the astonishing beauty of the universe is demonstrated in all things.[3]

We shall say, therefore, that Divine aid is good in itself, but that its withdrawal for a time can be of advantage to us. So too, temporal possessions are good in themselves, but their prohibition for a time can be useful and helpful to us. These two things, therefore — namely, the support of the Divine Hand and the possession of temporal goods — correspond to these two distinct periods. In the first period, when purse and bag were forbidden, the support of the Divine Hand was given without the possession of temporal goods. But, in the second period, when such possessions were granted, the converse occurred; for, as is clear from what has been said, temporal possessions were granted and the Divine Hand in some measure withdrawn.

But, since both these things are good, neither of them should be permanently prohibited or permanently withdrawn as such. For this reason, we must suppose there to be a third period, in which period we now are, in which temporal possessions are granted to the men of the Church yet the support of the Lord's hand is also given. In this third period, therefore, the Church is endowed with both; for she rejoices both in temporal support and in Divine aid, so that she may be able to govern and preserve herself in her own condition. For the Church first had a beginning and subsequently an increase, but now she has perfection and stature. For this reason, so that she may maintain herself in this stature, she needs

1. Gen. 1:31.
2. Cf. Rom 8:28.
3. *Enchiridion* 3:10 (CCSL 46:53).

se[1] conservet, et indiget divino auxilio, ne naufragium paciatur, et temporalium subsidio, ne a laicis vilipendatur.

CAPITULUM IV: *Quod omnia temporalia sub dominio et potestate Ecclesie et potissime Summi Pontificis collocantur.*

Intendimus in hoc capitulo declarare quod omnia temporalia sub dominio et potestate Ecclesie collocantur; nec per hoc intendimus potestati terrene et secularibus principibus sua iura subtrahere, sed pocius conservare. Non enim presentem tractatum suscepimus ut velimus[2] quorumcumque iura[3] solvere, sed pocius adimplere. Ostendamus[4] quidem in sequenti capitulo quod, quamvis omnia temporalia sub potestate Ecclesie collocentur,[5] laici tamen et seculares principes propter hoc suis iuribus non privantur. Immo, ut infra diffusius disseremus,[6] sic omnia temporalia sub dominio Ecclesie collocantur quod potestati ecclesiastice a potestate terrena possint[7] temporalia elargiri; quia ius quod habet terrena potestas potest ecclesiastice potestati donare, et huiusmodi ius potest Ecclesia a seculari principe recognoscere tamquam ei exhibitum et donatum.

Possumus autem quatuor viis nostrum propositum declarare, ut prima sumatur ex ipsis temporalibus, ut sunt temporalia; secunda vero ex corporibus nostris ad que ordinantur temporalia; tercia quidem ex ipsis dominis terrenis qui potestatem habent super temporalia; quarta autem ex ipso censu sive ex ipsis decimis ad que obligantur temporalia.

Prima autem via sic patet. Nam oportet quidem ipsa temporalia, ut huiusmodi sunt, ad spiritualia ordinari;[8] nam in rebus temporalibus non est ponenda felicitas, quia, cum sint transitoria et caduca, in nullo eorum[9] felicitas est ponenda. Immo, cum sint bona extrinseca et non possint[10] animam saciare, in talibus bonis beatitudo nostra esse non poterit. Nam cum dicatur in psalmo 'Saciabor[11] cum apparuerit gloria tua,' non poterit esse gloria et felicitas nostra nisi in eo quod[12] potest saciare[13] animam nostram. Velle autem saciare et replere animam nostram de temporalibus rebus, que non sunt res intra animam, sed sunt extrinseca,[14] est velle replere archam de eo quod non intrat archam. Sicut ergo reputaretur demens et fatuus qui semper poneret res extra archam[15] et hoc modo vellet[16] replere et saciare archam, sic est demens et fatuus reputandus qui temporalia temporalibus cumulando intendit[17] suam animam saciare, cum nihil illorum animam intret, sed quodlibet eorum extra animam reservetur.

In spiritualibus itaque bonis que possunt esse intra[18] animam et animam saciare

---

1: se] *om.* V[1]   2: velimus] in eo *add.* CF   3: quorumcumque iura] iura quorumcumque FV[2]
4: Ostendamus] ostendemus C   5: collocentur] collocantur CF   6: disseremus] dicemus F   dixerimus V[2]   7: possint] possunt C   8: Nam oportet ... ordinari] *om.* C   9: eorum] rerum PV[1]
10: possint] possunt C   11: Saciabor] saciabitur F   12: quod] quid FV[2]   13: saciare] salvare FV[2]
14: extrinseca] anime *add.* FV[2] *del.* C   15: Sicut ergo ... archam] *marg., in a later hand* C
16: vellet] velle C   17: intendit] intendat CFV[2]   18: intra] infra PV[1]V[2]

both Divine aid, lest she suffer shipwreck, and temporal support, lest she be held in low esteem by the laity.

CHAPTER IV: *That all temporal things are placed under the lordship and power of the Church, and especially of the Supreme Pontiff.*

In this chapter, we intend to show that all temporal things are placed under the lordship and power of the Church. By this, however, we do not intend to remove their rights from earthly powers and secular princes, but rather to protect them. For we have not undertaken the present treatise as wishing to destroy the rights of any persons whatsoever, but rather to fulfil them.[1] Indeed, we shall show in a subsequent chapter that, even though all temporal things are placed under the Church's power, laymen and secular princes are nonetheless not on this account deprived of their rights. On the contrary, as we shall discuss at greater length below,[2] all temporal things are placed under the lordship of the Church in such a way that temporal possessions can be bestowed upon the ecclesiastical power by the earthly power: for the earthly power can give a right which it has to the ecclesiastical power, and the Church can acknowledge that she holds such a right from a secular prince as a gift and grant to her.

Now we can make our proposition [that all temporal things are placed under the lordship of the Church] clear in four ways. The first is derived from temporal things themselves, inasmuch as they are temporal; and the second from our bodies, to which temporal possessions are ordered; and the third from earthly lords themselves, who have power over temporal things; and the fourth from that tax, or from those tithes, to which temporal goods are subject.

The first way proceeds as follows. Temporal things, as such, must indeed be ordered towards spiritual ends. For the hope of happiness must not be placed in temporal things: they are frail and transitory, and so the hope of happiness must not be placed in any of them. On the contrary, since they are external goods and cannot satisfy the soul, our blessedness cannot be in such goods. For when it is said in the Psalm, 'I shall be satisfied when Thy Glory shall appear,'[3] [what is meant is that] it will not be possible for our glory and happiness to be in anything except that which can satisfy our soul. But to wish to satisfy and fill up our soul by means of temporal things, which are not within the soul but external to it, is like wishing to fill up a box with that which does not go into the box. Therefore, just as he who always placed objects outside a box and wished in this way to fill up and occupy the box would be considered senseless and foolish, so he who strives to satisfy his soul by piling temporal goods upon temporal goods must be considered senseless and foolish. For none of these goods may enter the soul, but each of them is placed outside the soul.

Thus, the hope of happiness must be placed in spiritual goods, which can exist

1.   Cf. Matt. 5:17.
2.   See esp. Pt. III, Ch. XI.
3.   Psalm 17:15.

felicitas est ponenda. Et quia, ut dicit ille Commentator[1] super[2] II *Metaphysice*, finis et bonum idem et qui tollit finem tollit omne bonum, oportet quod quicquid habet[3] racionem boni habeat hoc ex fine. Et inde sumpsit originem illa maxima quod cuius finis bonus[4] est ipsum quoque bonum est; nam quicquid est bonum vel est bonum quod est finis vel est ad[5] bonum huiusmodi ordinatum. Si ergo non est ponendus finis nec beatitudo nostra in temporalibus sed in spiritualibus, oportet quod temporalia non aliter bona sint nisi prout ad spiritualia ordinantur.

Bona itaque temporalia sunt organa adminiculancia et deserviencia spiritualibus bonis; quod si servire desinant, desinunt esse bona. Nam temporalia bona non ordinata ad spiritualia et non deserviencia eis, etsi sunt bona in se, non sunt bona nobis. Quod adeo notorium est ut et[6] philosophi, ductui racionis inherentes,[7] veritatem huiusmodi protestentur.[8] Innuit enim[9] Philosophus in V *Eth.* quod homines nesciunt orare. Orant autem ut habeant bona fortune sive ut habeant[10] divicias; deberent autem orare ut divicie et bona fortune, que sunt bona in se, sint bona[11] eis. Propter quod in eodem V[12] dicitur quod que sunt bona simpliciter alicui autem[13] non bona semper:[14] id est, aliquid est bonum in se quod, non bene ordinatum, non est bonum huic.

Temporalia ergo, etsi sunt bona in se quia omne quod est, in quantum est, bonum est, ut vult[15] Augustinus, *De doctrina Christiana*, temporalia tamen non bene ordinata non sunt bona huic: id est, non sunt bona habenti illa. Et quia numquam temporalia sunt[16] bene[17] ordinata nisi ordinentur ad spiritualia, quia universa natura corporalis ordinatur ad spiritualem, ut vult Augustinus, III *De Trinitate* cap. IV, consequens est quod princeps[18] vel quicumque homo habens temporalia, nisi ordinet ea[19] ad spiritualia, illa temporalia non sunt bona sibi, quia non sunt ei[20] ad salutem sed ad damnacionem anime. Temporalia itaque, quia secundum se ordinantur ad spiritualia et debent obsequium spiritualibus et ancillari eis, Summus Pontifex, qui in corpore mystico universaliter dominatur spiritualibus, manifestum est quod eciam omnibus temporalibus dominatur,[21] ut sit dominus temporalium, ut temporalia sunt, cum temporalia eciam secundum quod huiusmodi spiritualibus famulentur.

Secunda via ad hoc idem sumitur ex parte corporum nostrorum, in[22] quorum

---

1: Commentator] isto *add.* C   2: super] *om.* C   3: quicquid habet] quisquis habet P quisquis habeat V[1]   4: bonus] bonum F   5: ad] *om.* F   6: et] *om.* F   7: inherentes] innitentes FV[2]
8: protestentur] attestentur F   9: enim] *om.* F   10: bona ... habeant] *om.* F   11: bona in ... bona] *om.* F   12: V] VI° FPV[1]V[2]   13: autem] aut F   14: bona semper] semper bona C
15: vult] *om.* FV[2]   16: non bene ... temporalia sunt] *om.* F   17: bene] ad bonum F   18: princeps] principes FV[2]   19: ordinet ea] ordinent eum FV[2]   20: ei] ea F   21: spiritualibus, manifestum ... dominatur] *om.* F   22: in] ad F

within the soul and satisfy the soul. And since, as the Commentator[1] says on *Metaphysics* II, 'end' and 'good' are the same and he who takes away 'end' takes away all 'good,' it must be that whatever has the capacity for good derives this from an end. And hence comes the origin of the maxim that whatever has a good end is itself also good; for whatever is good is either a good which is an end or is ordered towards such a good.[2] Therefore, if neither our end nor our hope of blessedness is to be placed in temporal things, but in spiritual, then it must be that temporal things are not good except insofar as they are ordered towards spiritual ends.

Thus, temporal goods are instruments for the aid and devout service of spiritual goods. And if they cease to serve, they cease to be goods; for temporal goods which are not ordered towards spiritual ends and which do not devoutly serve them are not goods for us, even though they are good in themselves. And this is so well known that even the philosophers, cleaving [only] to the guidance of reason, attest it to be the truth. For the Philosopher suggests in *Ethics* 5 that men do not know how to pray. For they pray that they may have the goods of fortune or that they may have riches; but they ought to pray that riches and the goods of fortune, which are good in themselves, may be goods for them.[3] For it is said in Book 5 of the same work that those things which are good in an absolute sense are not always goods for a particular individual: that is, something is good in itself which, when not well ordered, is not a good for him.[4]

Therefore, even though temporal things are good in themselves — for, as Augustine maintains in *De doctrina christiana*, everything which exists is good insofar as it exists[5] — temporal goods which are not well ordered are nonetheless not goods for him: that is, they are not goods for him who has them. And since temporal goods are never well ordered unless they are ordered towards spiritual ends — for, as Augustine maintains at *De Trinitate* 3:4, the whole of corporeal nature is ordered towards the spiritual[6] — it follows that, when a prince or any man possesses temporal things, those temporal possessions are not goods for him unless he orders them towards spiritual ends; for they lead not to salvation, but to the damnation of the soul. And so since, of themselves, temporal things are appointed to spiritual ends and must obey spiritual things and serve them, it is clear that the Supreme Pontiff, who has lordship of spiritual things universally within the Mystical Body, also has lordship of all temporal things: that he is lord of temporal things inasmuch as they are temporal, because temporal things as such are the servants of spiritual ends.

The second way towards the same conclusion is derived from a consideration of

1. I.e. Averroes, on Aristotle, *Metaphysics* α:2 (994^{b}10) (*Aristotelis opera cum Averrois commentariis* (repr. Frankfurt: Minerva 1962), 8:33.
2. Cf. Aristotle, *Nicomachean Ethics* 1:1 (1094^{a}1); 1:7 (1097^{a}15).
3. *Nicomachean Ethics* 5:1 (1129^{b}5).
4. Ibid.
5. *De doctrina Christiana* 1:32 (PL 34:32).
6. CCSL 50:135–136.

subsidium sunt temporalia ordinata. Sumus enim, ut in alia sciencia probatur, quodammodo finis omnium, ut omnia in nostrum obsequium ordinentur. Corporalium ergo sumus finis, in quantum ipsa corporalia[1] famulantur corporibus nostris[2] et subveniunt nobis quantum ad necessitatem[3] corporalis vite. Et quia anima dominatur et quia[4] dignum et[5] iustum est ut[6] dominetur corpori, cum experimentaliter videamus[7] quod nostra corporalia membra moventur secundum nutum et voluntatem anime, ut sicut vult anima, sic moventur pedes, sic digiti constringuntur et aperiuntur, sic moventur manus et brachia, sic et ipsum caput:[8] consequens est quod sacerdotalis potestas, et potissime potestas Summi Pontificis, que super nostris animabus noscitur habere dominium, corporibus nostris et temporalibus rebus que ordinantur ad corpora principetur et dominetur.

Erit ergo hic ordo: quod potestas Summi Pontificis dominatur animabus, anime dominantur[9] vel de iure dominari debent[10] super corpora, male ordinatum est corpus quantum ad illam partem secundum quam[11] non obedit anime[12] et[13] menti et racioni. Ipse autem res temporales nostris corporibus famulantur. Consequens est quod sacerdotalis potestas, que dominatur animabus, corporibus et rebus temporalibus principetur. Quando quidem dictum fuit Petro 'Tu es Petrus, et super hanc petram edificabo Ecclesiam meam,' sensum[14] exponendo, prout ibi pro petra significetur Christus, iuxta illud Apostoli, 'Petra autem erat Christus,' ut sit sensus quod dicat Christus, 'Ego sum petra, et tu es Petrus dictus ab hac petra, et super hanc petram, id est super me ipsum, edificabo Ecclesiam meam. Tu igitur Petrus, qui a me petra nomen accepisti, totam Ecclesiam super me fundatam reges et gubernabis. Tu pasces oves meas: non has vel illas tantum, sed omnes universaliter. Aliis quidem commisse sunt oves iste vel ille; tibi autem, sine contraccione, sine diminucione,[15] oves universaliter sunt commisse.' Non est quidem Petro dictum, 'Pasce[16] has oves vel illas,'[17] sed simpliciter: 'Pasce oves.'[18] Dicimus autem oves esse 'istas,' ut puta Christianos existentes in hac parte mundi, et oves 'illas' existentes in alia parte mundi. Tolle 'istas' et tolle 'illas,' et intelligas ipsas oves[19] ipsos Christianos universaliter, non contractos ad 'hos' vel 'illos.' Sic intelliges potestatem Summi Pontificis non contractam, non diminutam, sed universaliter super omnes.

Ergo, quia Christus, cuius erat committere regnum sue Ecclesie, cuius vicarius fuit Petrus et cui commisit regimen Ecclesie sue,[20] tunc dedit sibi claves Ecclesie

1: corporalia] temporalia *corr. to* corporalia *in a later hand* C   2: corporibus nostris] nobis C
3: necessitatem] necessitates F   4: anima ... quia] *om.* F   5: et] est FV²   6: ut] anima *add.* F
7: videamus] videmus C   8: et ipsum caput] eciam capitulum F   9: dominantur] debent V¹
dominentur FV²   10: debent] *om.* PV²   11: quam] quod F   12: anime] a se FV²   13: et] *om.* C
14: sensum] sive C   15: diminucione] dominacione F   16: Petro dictum, 'Pasce] dictum petro
pasceas F   17: illas] oves *add.* V²   18: vel illas ... oves] *om.* F   19: oves] et *add.* CF
20: Ecclesiae sue] sue ecclesie CF

our bodies, for whose support temporal possessions are appointed. For, as is proved in another science, we are, in a sense, the end of all things, for all things are appointed to serve us.[1] We are the end of corporeal things, therefore, inasmuch as corporeal things themselves are the servants of our bodies and assist us with respect to the necessaries of bodily life. And since the soul has lordship, and since it is right and fitting that it should be lord of the body — for we may see by experience that our bodily members are moved according to the command and will of the soul: that, as the soul wills, so are the feet moved, and so are the fingers clenched and unclenched, and so are the hands and arms moved, and also the head itself — it follows that the priestly power, and especially the power of the Supreme Pontiff, who is known to have lordship over our souls, may be the ruler and lord of our bodies and of the temporal things which are ordered to bodies.

There will, therefore, be this order: the power of the Supreme Pontiff has lordship over souls; souls have lordship over bodies, or should have lordship *de iure*, or the body will be ill ordered with respect to that part of it which does not obey the soul and mind and reason; but temporal things themselves are the servants of our bodies, and it follows that priestly power, which has lordship over souls, may rule bodies and temporal things. Indeed, when it was said to Peter, 'You are Peter, and upon this Rock I will build my Church,'[2] insofar as it is Christ Who is here signified by 'Rock' (for the sense of this must be interpreted according to what the Apostle says: 'And this Rock was Christ'[3]), it is as though Christ said: 'I am the Rock, and you are Peter, named from this Rock; and upon this Rock, that is, upon my very self, I will build my Church. And so you, Peter, who have received from me the name "Rock," will rule and govern the whole Church founded upon me. You will feed my sheep — not only these or those, but all of them universally. To others, indeed, are these sheep or those entrusted; but to you are the sheep entrusted universally, without contraction or diminution.' For it was not said to Peter, 'Feed these sheep or those,' but simply: 'Feed my sheep.'[4] But we say that 'these sheep' — that is, Christians — dwell in this part of the world, and that 'those sheep' dwell in another part of the world. Take away the 'these,' and take away the 'those,' and consider the sheep themselves — the Christians themselves — universally, not contracted into 'these' or 'those.' Thus, you will understand that the power of the Supreme Pontiff is not contracted, not limited, but extends universally over all.

Therefore Christ, Whose prerogative it was to entrust the rule of His Church, Whose vicar was Peter, and to whom He entrusted the government of His Church, gave the keys of the Church to him on that occasion when He said, 'You

1.   Perhaps Aristotle, *Politics* 1:8 (1256^b10); cf. Gen. 1:28–30.
2.   Matt. 16:18. This and the following paragraph cannot be rendered into English with total success, thanks to the untranslatable word-play on *petra* ('rock') and *Petrus* ('Peter'); but the pun is so familiar that this will not be too severe a drawback.
3.   I Cor. 10:4.
4.   John 21:15.

quando[1] dixit 'Tu es Petrus,' qui dicitur a petra, id est a Christo, super quem Ecclesia est fundata, si bene consideremus[2] verba Christi, quomodo[3] Petro tradite sunt claves et regimen Ecclesie prout Ecclesia fundata est super petram: quis[4] ergo unquam[5] diceret quod quilibet fidelis secundum se totum, tam secundum animam quam secundum corpus, quam[6] eciam[7] secundum omnia que habet, sive sint temporalia sive alia, non sit fundatus super Christum? Et quis ergo diceret quod quilibet fidelis secundum se totum et secundum omnia que habet[8] non sit sub regimine Petri? Anime ergo nostre, corpora nostra, temporalia nostra omnia sunt sub regimine Petri et per consequens sub regimine[9] et gubernacione Summi Pontificis, qui in potestate et regimine Ecclesie Petro noscitur successisse.

Idem est enim nunc papa et idem Summus Pontifex qui fuit a tempore Petri, sicut idem est populus Romanus nunc qui fuit iam sunt plus[10] quam mille anni; et eciam idem est Tiberis, et[11] idem Romanus[12] fluvius, qui fuit a principio. Homines enim sunt alii et alii, quia hii fluunt et refluunt qui constituunt Romanum populum; attamen idem est Romanus populus. Sic alia et alia[13] aqua, que fluit et refluit, que constituit Romanum fluvium; semper est tamen idem[14] Romanus fluvius, quia semper est idem formaliter, licet semper non sit idem materialiter, quia aqua que est materia huius fluvii semper fluit et refluit et est alia et alia. Et quia a forma est principaliter esse et denominacio rei, non autem a materia, semper est idem fluvius et idem populus, licet non sit semper eadem aqua et non sint idem homines. Sic semper est idem[15] Summus Pontifex, licet non semper sit idem homo in huiusmodi officio[16] constitutus.

Non ergo plus habuit de potestate Petrus quam nunc habeat Summus Pontifex. Et sicut Petro fuit commissa potestas Ecclesie prout Ecclesia est fundata super Christum, et per consequens fuit ei commissa potestas super animas, super corpora et super omnia temporalia que habent, quia omnes fideles secundum se totos et secundum omnia sua fundati sunt super Christum: sic et Summo Pontifici qui nunc est, quia est idem pontifex qui prius fuit licet non sit[17] idem homo, omne[18] huiusmodi regimen est commissum.[19] Et sicut Petrus immediate habuit a Christo regimen Ecclesie, sic et Summus Pontifex qui nunc est, quia est idem Summus Pontifex qui tunc fuit, immediate a Deo sive a Christo, qui erat verus Deus,[20] habere huiusmodi noscitur potestatem.

Sed si immediate a Deo sive immediate a Christo habet Summus Pontifex potestatem super Ecclesiam et super fideles prout huiusmodi fideles fundati super Christum, quia, ut dictum est, omnes fideles secundum se totos et secundum omnia sua debent inniti Christo tamquam vero fundamento et se totos et omnia sua debent

---

1: quando] cum F   2: consideremus] consideramus F   3: quomodo] eo modo C   4: quis] quid F
5: unquam] om. C   6: tam secundum ... quam] om. F   7: eciam] et F   8: sive sint temporalia ...
que habet] om. F   9: Anime ergo ... sub regime] om. FV[2]   10: plus] pluries F   11: et] ut C
velut F   12: Romanus] pontifex add. FV[2]   13: alia] est add. C   14: idem] om. C   15: est
idem] idem est F   16: officio] om. PV[1]   17: sit] fit F   18: omne] esse F   tunc V[2]   19: commissum] concessum FV[2]   20: Deus] summus pontifex qui nunc est add. FV[2]

are Peter,' so named from the Rock: that is, from Christ, upon Whom the Church is founded. And so, if we give due consideration to the words of Christ — to the way in which the keys and government of the Church were delivered to Peter inasmuch as the Church was founded upon a Rock — who, therefore, would ever say that any one of the faithful is not founded upon Christ in his whole self: in soul and body alike, and also in all that he possesses, temporal or otherwise? And who, therefore, would say that any one of the faithful is not under the government of Peter in his whole self and in all that he possesses? Therefore, our souls, our bodies and our temporal possessions are all under the government of Peter, and, in consequence, under the government and direction of the Supreme Pontiff, who is known to have succeeded Peter in power and in the government of the Church.

For the Pope is the same, and the Supreme Pontiff is the same, now as in the time of Peter: just as the Roman people is the same now as it was a thousand and more years ago, and the Tiber also is the same Roman river as it was from the beginning. The men who comprise the Roman people are different at different times, for they come and go; yet the Roman people is the same. So too the water which comprises the Roman river is different at different times, for it comes and goes; but the Roman river is nonetheless always the same. For it is always the same formally, even though it is not always the same materially, since the water which is the matter of that river is always coming and going and is different at different times. And since the essence and character of a thing is principally derived from its form and not its matter, the river is always the same and the people always the same, even though the water is not always the same and the persons are not always the same. Thus, the Supreme Pontiff is always the same, even though the man appointed to the office is not always the same.[1]

Peter, therefore, had nothing more in the way of power than the Supreme Pontiff has now. And just as the power of the Church was entrusted to Peter inasmuch as the Church was founded upon Christ [Who delivered it into Peter's custody], and, consequently, power over souls, over bodies, and over all the temporal goods which they possess was entrusted to him, since all faithful men are founded upon Christ in their whole selves and in all that is theirs: so also he who is now Supreme Pontiff, since there has been the same Pontiff from the beginning, even though not the same man, is entrusted with the government of all such things. And just as Peter received the government of the Church immediately from Christ, so too he who is now Supreme Pontiff, since the Supreme Pontiff is the same now as then, is known to have received such power immediately from God or from Christ, Who was the True God.

But if the Supreme Pontiff has power over the Church and over the faithful immediately from God, or immediately from Christ inasmuch as the faithful people are founded upon Christ, then, since, as has been said, all faithful people, in their whole selves and in all that is theirs, must rest upon Christ as their true foundation and order their whole selves and all that is theirs towards Christ, it

---

1. On the development of this important theme, especially during the pontificate of Leo I (440–461) see W. Ullmann, *The Growth of Papal Government*, Introduction.

ordinare ad Christum, consequens est quod secundum se totos et secundum omnia
sua imperio Summi Pontificis sint subiecti.

Tercia via sumi potest[1] ex parte dominorum sive ex parte regum et principum,
quia habent materialem gladium et super temporalia potestatem. Nam semper imperfecciora ordinantur ad perfecciora et obsecuntur perfeccioribus, ut non vivencia, cuiusmodi sunt terra et aqua et huiusmodi talia,[2] obsecuntur et famulantur
plantis,[3] quia sunt imperfecciora quam sint plante et arbores et universaliter vegetabilia, que vivunt et nutriuntur. Ipsa eciam vegetabilia,[4] quamvis vivant, tamen,
quia non senciunt, sunt imperfecciora quam sint animalia, que non solum vivunt,
sed eciam senciunt, ideo obsequi eis. Ipsa eciam animalia racione carencia, licet
vivant et senciant,[5] tamen, quia non intelligunt, sunt imperfecciora quam homines
et obsecuntur hominibus,[6] qui vivunt, senciunt et intelligunt.

Videmus ergo totum universum sic connexum, sic ordinatum, quod[7] semper
imperfecciora subsunt perfeccioribus et sunt in amminiculum ipsorum, ut terra et
aqua tamquam non vivencia sunt in amminiculum arborum et plantarum et universaliter vegetabilium que nutriuntur et vivunt;[8] ipsa vegetabilia subsunt animalibus et sunt in eorum amminiculum; animalia vero omnia, sive sint volatilia celi
sive pisces maris sive bestie terre sive reptilia[9] que moventur super terram tamquam imperfecciora hominibus, quia carent intellectu, universa huiusmodi sunt in
obsequium hominis et sub dominio eius.[10] Unde et Geneseos I dicitur quod:
'Creavit Deus hominem ad imaginem et similitudinem suam, masculum et femi-
nam creavit eos[11] et ait: Crescite et multiplicamini, et replete terram, et subicite
eam et dominamini piscibus maris et volatilibus[12] celi et universis animantibus[13]
que moventur super terram.'

Tota ergo racio quare homo subicit sibi terram et dominatur omnibus que
moventur super terram est quia factus est ad imaginem Dei. Sed secundum
Augustinum in pluribus locis in libro *De Trinitate*, homo factus est ad imaginem
Dei secundum mentem et racionem. Sicut igitur non vivencia sunt imperfecciora
viventibus, ideo sunt in eorum obsequium ordinata; et sicut[14] non senciencia sunt
imperfecciora sencientibus, ideo sunt in eorum obsequium constituta; et sicut
non intelligencia et que non sunt facta ad imaginem Dei sunt imperfecciora in-
telligentibus, ideo sunt sub eorum dominio stabilita: sic universaliter omnia imperfecciora debent obsequi perfeccioribus et sunt in eorum obsequium constituta. Et
quia nullus dubitat quin divina sint perfecciora humanis et celestia terrenis et spiritualia corporalibus, ergo nil conveniencius quam[15] quod[16] potestas regia, que est
potestas[17] humana et terrena et[18] super corporalia, subsit et sit ordinata in obsequium

---

1: sumi potest] sumitur FV²   2: talia] *om.* F   3: obsecuntur et famulantur plantis] *marg.* C
om. PV¹   4: que vivunt ... vegetabilia] *om.* F   5: ideo obsequi ... senciant] *om.* PV¹   6: et
obsecuntur hominibus] *om.* PV¹   7: quod] et FV²   8: universaliter ... vivunt] *om.* F   9: rep-
tilia] rectilia F   10: dominio eius] eius dominio C   11: eos] *om.* C   12: et volatilibus] volatili-
busque C   13: animantibus] animalibus FV²   14: sicut] et *add.* P   15: quam] *om.* F
16: quod] *interlin.* C *om.* PV¹V²   17: potestas] *om.* F   18: et] est *add.* C

follows that they are subject in their whole selves and in all that is theirs to the command of the Supreme Pontiff.

The third way [of showing that the Church is lord of temporal things] can be derived from a consideration of [temporal] lords or from a consideration of kings and princes, since they possess the material sword and power over temporal affairs. For more imperfect creatures are always subordinated to the more perfect, and serve the more perfect. Thus, such non-living things as earth and water and so forth serve and minister to plants, since they are more imperfect than plants and trees and non-sentient beings generally, which live and are nourished. And non-sentient beings themselves, because they do not have sensation even though they are alive, are more imperfect than animals, and so serve them; for the latter not only live, but also have sensation. And the animals, lacking reason even though they live and have sensation, nonetheless, because they have no intelligence, are more imperfect than men, who live and have sensation and intelligence; and so they serve men.

We see, therefore, that the whole universe is so connected and so ordered that more imperfect creatures are always placed under the more perfect and are their supports. Thus, earth and water, as non-living things, are the supports of trees and plants and non-sentient beings generally, which are nourished and alive. The non-sentient beings themselves are placed under the animals and are their support; and all animals — whether the birds of the heaven or the fish of the sea or the beasts of the earth or the creeping things which move upon the earth — are everywhere the servants of man, and are under his lordship; for they are less perfect than men because they lack intelligence. And so it is said in Genesis I that: 'God created man in His own image and likeness: male and female' created He them, and said, 'Increase and multiply, and replenish the earth and subdue it, and have lordship over the fish of the sea and the birds of the heaven and all the creatures which move upon the earth.'[1]

The whole reason, therefore, why man may subdue the earth to himself and have lordship over everything which moves upon the earth is that he was made in the image of God. But, according to Augustine in several places in the book *De Trinitate*, man was made in the image of God with respect to mind and reason.[2] Thus, just as non-living things are more imperfect than living, and are therefore ordained to serve them; and just as non-sentient beings are more imperfect than sentient, and are therefore appointed to serve them; and just as those creatures which have no intelligence and which are not made in the image of God are more imperfect than the intelligent, and are therefore established under their lordship: so all imperfect creatures generally must serve the more perfect and are appointed as their servants. And since there is no doubt that the divine is more perfect than the human and the heavenly than the earthly and the spiritual than the bodily, nothing is more consistent, therefore, than that royal power, which is a human and earthly power and over bodies, should be subject to and ordered towards the service of the

1. Gen. 1:28–30; cf. Aristotle, *Politics* 1:8 (1256ᵇ10).
2. See, e.g., *De Trinitate* 12:7 (CCSL 50:366).

potestatis sacerdotalis, et potissime potestatis Summi Pontificis, que est potestas quodammodo divina et celestis et super spiritualia.

Dicamus itaque hec quatuor se habere per ordinem, videlicet: potestatem sacerdotalem, potestatem regiam, corpora nostra[1] et hec temporalia que sunt ordinata ad supplendam indigenciam corporalis vite. Potestas ergo sacerdotalis, tamquam perfeccior, ordinata est ut dominetur potestati regie:[2] aliter negaremus illam communem dignitatem, illam generalem[3] maximam quod imperfecciora sunt ad perfecciora ordinata et in eorum obsequium stabilita. Ipsa autem potestas regia, tamquam habens materialem gladium, ordinata est ut dominetur corporibus; ipsa autem temporalia sunt in obsequium corporum constituta. Quare, si temporalia ordinata sunt in obsequium corporum, corpora autem subsunt regie potestati, regia autem potestas sub sacerdotali, ipsa sacerdotalis potestas est omnibus superior, ut omnibus dominetur. Ipsa itaque[4] temporalia, tamquam infima in hoc regimine, sunt sub pedibus et sub[5] dominio Summi Pontificis constituta.

Quarta quidem via sumi potest ex censu quem debent temporalia ipsi Ecclesie. Dicimus autem[6] quod 'res transit cum onere[7] suo'; sed sub quocumque sint temporalia et qualitercumque se transferant, sive sint[8] hodie huius sive cras illius, semper debent censum ipsi[9] Ecclesie, quia semper de eis[10] iure divino accipienda est decima. Ergo hoc est onus temporalium, ut temporalia sunt, a quo onere non possunt absolvi: quia qualitercumque transferantur[11] et qualitercumque transeant, cum hoc onere transeunt, quod debent[12] decimam Ecclesie. Quis ergo diceret agrum aliquem non esse sub dominio illius qui haberet censum annuum super ipsum? Et quis diceret temporalia non esse sub dominio Ecclesie, super quibus habet censum annuum iure et mandato divino?

Sed quia cor hominis non quiescit, ut[13] dicamus temporalia esse sub potestate regia, et cum plures doctores notaverint, quod Ecclesia ab imperio et a regibus et a principibus temporalia recognoscit, ideo in sequentibus capitulis declarabimus quomodo et qualiter hec omnia[14] veritatem habent et quomodo et qualiter veritate carent. Nam et rex posset a suo milite aliqua temporalia recognoscere, si ius quod haberet miles in temporalibus illis[15] regi donaret. Sed hec inferius diffusius tractabuntur. Ad presens autem scire sufficit quod propter ipsa temporalia, ut dicebat racio prima, et propter corpora nostra ad que ordinantur temporalia, ut dicebat secunda, et propter potestatem que est ordinata super ipsa temporalia, ut dicebat tercia,

---

1: corpora nostra] nostra corpora C   2: regie] vel *add.* FV²   3: generalem] generaliter FV²
4: ipsa itaque] ita quod F   5: sub] *om.* C   6: autem] ergo F   7: onere] humore F   honere P
honore V²   8: sint] sit F   9: ipsi] illius F   10: de eis] *om.* F   11: transferantur] transferatur FV²
12: debent] debeant F   13: ut] quod F   14: hec omnia] omnia hec FV²   15: illis] vel F

priestly power, and especially the power of the Supreme Pontiff, which is in some measure a divine and heavenly power and over spiritual things.

Let us say, then, that these four things stand in the following order, namely: priestly power, royal power, our bodies, and those temporal possessions which are appointed to meet the needs of bodily life. The priestly power, therefore, as the more perfect, is ordained to have lordship over the royal power: otherwise, we should be denying what is universally fitting — the general principle that more imperfect creatures are subordinated to the more perfect and are established as their servants. And the royal power itself, as possessing the material sword, is ordained to have lordship over bodies; and temporal things themselves are appointed to the service of bodies. And so, if temporal things have been appointed to the service of bodies, and if bodies are subject to royal power and royal power is under priestly, then the priestly power itself is superior in all respects, as having lordship over all things. And so temporal things, since they are the lowest in this scheme, are placed beneath the feet and under the lordship of the Supreme Pontiff.

The fourth way can be derived from the tax which temporal goods owe to the Church. And we say that 'an article passes with its burden,'[1] so that, regardless of who is the owner of temporal goods — whether one man today or another tomorrow — or of how they change hands, they always owe a tax to the Church, for she must always receive a tithe from them under the Divine Law. This, therefore, is a burden which attaches to temporal possessions as such; and from this burden they cannot be released, for, however they may be transferred and however they may pass, they pass with the burden of owing a tithe to the Church. Therefore, who would say that a farm is not under the lordship of one who is entitled to an annual tax upon it? And who would say that temporal possessions are not under the lordship of the Church, when she is entitled to an annual tax upon them under the Divine Law and commandment?

But because the heart of man does not rest [i.e. because no one will be content to leave the matter here], and since many learned men will have noted that the Church acknowledges that she holds temporal possessions from the empire and from kings and princes, we shall therefore show in subsequent chapters how and in what way all these things have truth, and how and in what way they lack truth, so that we may say [precisely in what sense it is] that temporal things are under royal power.[2] For even the king could acknowledge that he held temporal possessions from one of his knights if the knight were to give the right which he had in those temporal possessions to the king. But these matters will be treated at greater length below. For the time being, suffice it to know that from temporal things themselves, as the first argument stated; and from our bodies, to which temporal possessions are ordered, as the second stated; and from the power which is appointed over temporal things, as the third stated; and from the tax and

1. X.3:30:33: *Quum non sit* (CIC 2:568).
2. See Chaps. VII–XII, below; Pt, III, Ch. XI.

et propter censum et[1] decimam quam debent ipsi Ecclesie temporalia, ut dicebat racio quarta, patet quod omnia temporalia sunt sub dominio Ecclesie collocata; et si non de facto, quia multi forte huic iuri et veritati[2] rebellant, de iure tamen et ex debito temporalia Summo Pontifici sunt subiecta, a quo iure et a quo debito nullatenus possunt absolvi.

CAPITULUM V: *Quod potestas regia per potestatem ecclesiasticam et a potestate ecclesiastica constituta est et ordinata in opus et[3] obsequium ecclesiastice potestatis; propter quod clarius apparebit quomodo temporalia sint sub dominio Ecclesie collocata.*

Voluerunt autem aliqui dicere quod utraque potestas, tam sacerdotalis quam regalis sive imperialis, sit immediate a Deo, et quod una non sit per aliam nec una sit ab alia; et ex hoc volunt ulterius concludere quod papa non habeat utrumque gladium. Sed quod[4] potestas regia sit per potestatem ecclesiasticam constituta sic patere potest.

Nam qui fuerunt reges in lege nature vel fuerunt mali et[5] fecerunt se reges per invasionem et usurpacionem, sicut legimus de Neroth, cuius regnum incepit in Babilone, ut habetur Geneseos X,[6] ubi dicitur quod Neroth erat robustus venator, id est, ut exponit magister in *Historiis*, erat hominum extinctor et oppressor; vel si fuerunt boni reges, ut supra tetigimus, fuerunt eciam sacerdotes, sicut patuit de Melchisedech et de Iob. Nec tamen legimus eos fuisse factos reges mandato Domini. Licet enim non sit potestas nisi a Deo et qui potestati resistit Dei ordinacioni resistit,[7] ut dicitur ad Romanos XIII, ita quod et ipsi mali potestatem quam habent a Deo habent, iuxta responsionem quam Christus[8] fecit Pilato cum ait: 'Non haberes super me potestatem ullam, nisi esset tibi datum desuper.' Sed aliud est esse a Deo prout agit generaliter[9] in rebus, et aliud est esse ab ipso prout speciale[10] mandatum facit.[11]

De hoc ergo est nostra quaestio: qualiter Deus mandavit quod constitueretur rex super fideli populo. Nam in hoc tractatu hominibus fidelibus loquimur, quia nihil ad nos de hiis[12] que foris sunt. Propter quod videndum est qualiter de mandato Domini constitutus sit rex super fideli populo; quia illud debet esse exemplar regum omnium christianorum et omnium regum fidelium, ut eo modo se credant esse reges, quo mandavit Dominus regem fieri. Dicitur autem I Regum VIII capitulo quod congregati in unum omnes maiores natu Israel venerunt ad Samuelem, quod constitueret eis regem, et cum orasset Samuel ad Dominum, dixit ei Dominus:

1: et] *om*. FV²   2: et veritati] *om*. V¹   3: et] in *add*. CFV²   4: quod] si V²   5: et] vel FV²
6: X] xiiii C   7: Dei ordinacioni resistit] *om*. F   8: Christus] dominus FV²   9: generaliter]
naturaliter F   10: speciale] specialem F   11: facit] de quo *add*. F de aliquo *add*. CV²
12: hiis] his F

tithe which temporal goods owe to the Church, as the fourth argument stated: it is clear that all temporal things are placed under the lordship of the Church. Even if this is not so *de facto*, for there are perhaps many who rebel against justice and truth, nonetheless, as of right and obligation, temporal things are subject to the Supreme Pontiff; and from this right and from this obligation they can never be released.

CHAPTER V: *That royal power is appointed through the ecclesiastical power and by the ecclesiastical power, and is ordained to the work and service of the ecclesiastical power; from which it will appear more clearly how temporal things are placed under the lordship of the Church.*

Some have wished to say that both powers, the priestly and the royal or imperial alike, come immediately from God, and that the one does not come into being through the other and that the one is not appointed by the other; and they wish moreover to conclude from this that the pope may not have both swords.[1] But that royal power is appointed through the ecclesiastical power can be shown in the following way.

For those who were kings under the law of nature were either wicked men, and made themselves kings by invasion or usurpation (as we read of Nimrod, whose reign began in Babylon, as is established in Genesis 10, where it is said that Nimrod was a mighty hunter: that is, as the Master explains in the *Historia*, he was a slayer and oppressor of men[2]); or, if they were good kings, as we have noted above, they were also priests, as has become clear in the case of Melchizedek and Job.[3] We do not read, however, that the former were made kings by the Lord's command. For although there is no power except of God, and he who resists the power resists the ordinance of God, as is said in Romans 13[4] (so that even the wicked receive the power which they have from God, according to the reply which Christ made to Pilate when He said: 'You would have no power over me at all, had it not been given to you from above'[5]), it is nonetheless one thing to derive existence from God inasmuch as He acts generally in all things, and another to derive existence from Him inasmuch as He has given a special command.

From this, therefore, comes our question: that of how God has commanded that a king should be appointed over the faithful people (for, in this treatise, we are speaking of faithful men; for those who are outside [the faith] do not concern us). And so we must take note of the way in which a king was appointed over the faithful people at the Lord's command. For this must be the pattern of all Christian kings and of all faithful kings, so that they may believe themselves to be kings only insofar as the Lord has commanded that a king be made. And it is said in I Samuel 8 that the whole assembly of the elders of Israel came to Samuel so that he might appoint a king for them; and when Samuel had prayed to the Lord, the Lord said to

1. See Introduction, p. xxii.
2. Gen. 10:9; Peter Comestor, *Historia scholastica*, PL 198:1088.
3. Genesis 14:18; Job 29:25. See Pt. I, Ch. VII, p. 43.
4. Rom. 13:2.
5. John 19:11.

'Audi vocem populi in omnibus que loquuntur[1] tibi.' Samuel ergo de mandato Domini constituit primum regem Saulem super fideli populo. Potestas ergo regia non fuit constituta de mandato Domini nisi per potestatem ecclesiasticam. Unde Hugo in libro[2] *De sacramentis*, libro II, parte II, capitulo IV, ait quod primum a Deo sacerdocium institutum est, postea vero per sacerdocium, iubente Deo, regalis potestas est ordinata.

Errant itaque dicentes quod eque immediate a Deo sint sacerdocium et imperium vel sacerdocium et potestas regia, cum iubente Deo primus rex in populo fideli fuit per sacerdocium institutus. Regebatur quidem primo populus Iudaicus, qui erat populus tunc fidelis, cui nunc[3] succedit populus Christianus,[4] per iudices qui per sacerdotem[5] instituebantur. Propter quod dicitur I Regum capitulo VIII quod Samuel posuit filios suos iudices Israel. Nam primitus, antequam essent iudices, ipse Moyses regebat[6] fideliter populum, et erat eorum rector et iudex non solum in hiis que sunt ad Deum, que spectant[7] ad spiritualem potestatem[8] et ad gladium spiritualem, sed eciam in aliis que spectant[9] ad potestatem terrenam et ad gladium materialem. Sed quia stulto labore consumebatur et opus ultra suas vires agebat, ductus consilio Iethro, cognati sui, constituit viros alios a se, timentes Deum, odientes avariciam, sequentes veritatem, qui iudicarent Israel. Hiis[10] autem iudicibus, quantum ad temporales causas inter personas laicas, succedit imperator, succedunt reges et terreni principes, ut supra tetigimus. Hos autem iudices constituebat potestas sacerdotalis et ecclesiastica, quia Moyses, retinens sibi potestatem in hiis que sunt ad Deum, in quo significatur potestas ecclesiastica, constituit huiusmodi iudices, qui modo quo dictum est exercebant officium potestatis terrene, ut habetur Exodi XVIII; et Samuel, ut diximus, I Regum VIII suos filios constituit iudices super Israel.

Ergo, antequam populus fidelis haberet regem,[11] regebatur per iudices, et huiusmodi iudices[12] erant per potestatem ecclesiasticam constituti vel erant constituti per sacerdocium. Postquam autem populus fidelis habuit regem, ut patuit, primus rex eorum,[13] videlicet Saul, fuit per sacerdotem iubente Domino constitutus. Potestas ergo regia et universaliter potestas terrena, si refert se ad suam originem, prout incepit esse in populo fideli, fuit per sacerdocium vel per potestatem ecclesiasticam constituta.[14]

Omnes reges Christiani, omnes fideles principes, debent in se advertere unde venit potestas regia et quomodo mandavit Dominus quod constitueretur rex super fideli populo. Invenient autem[15] clare et manifeste, ut patuit, quod talis potestas fuit per sacerdocium instituta. Non ergo eque immediate a Deo est hec potestas et

1: loquuntur] loquitur F   2: libro] *om.* FV[2]   3: nunc] vero F   4: Christianus] primo *add. mss*
5: sacerdotem] sacerdotium C   6: Moyses regebat] regebat Moyses F   7: que spectant] quod spectat *mss*   8: spiritualem potestatem] potestatem spiritualem CF   9: spectant] spectabunt CF
10: Hiis] his F   11: regem] et *add.* CF   12: et huiusmodi iudices] *om.* F   13: eorum] earum F
14: constituta] et quia *add.* CFV[2]   15: autem] enim CF

him: 'Hear the voice of the people in all that they say to you.'[1] At the Lord's command, therefore, Samuel appointed Saul as the first king over the faithful people.[2] Royal power, therefore, was appointed at the Lord's command, but only through the ecclesiastical power. And so Hugh, in the book *De sacramentis* 2:2:4, says that the priesthood was instituted by God first and that royal power was subsequently ordained through the priesthood at God's command.[3]

They err, then, who say that priesthood and imperial authority, or priesthood and royal power, both come immediately from God in the same fashion; for the first king of the faithful people was instituted through the priesthood at God's command. In the beginning, indeed, the Jewish people, which was then the faithful people, to whom the Christian people has now succeeded, was first ruled by judges who were instituted through a priest. For it is said in I Samuel 8 that Samuel appointed his sons as judges over Israel.[4] But originally, before there were judges, Moses himself faithfully ruled the people and was their guide and judge not only in those things which are of God, which belong to the spiritual power and to the spiritual sword, but also in other matters which belong to the earthly power and to the material sword. But because he was consumed by foolish labour and occupied with a task beyond his powers, guided by the counsel of his kinsman Jethro he appointed men other than himself, who feared God, hated avarice and followed truth, who judged Israel.[5] And to these judges, as regards temporal causes between lay persons, the emperor has succeeded and kings and earthly princes have succeeded, as we have noted above.[6] And priestly and ecclesiastical power appointed those judges; for Moses, retaining to himself power in those things which are of God, by which is signified ecclesiastical power, appointed such judges, who discharged the office of the earthly power in the manner stated, as is established in Exodus 18. And, as we have said, Samuel, in I Samuel 8, appointed his sons as judges over Israel.

Before the faithful people had a king, therefore, they were ruled by judges, and such judges were appointed through the ecclesiastical power, or were appointed through the priesthood. And subsequently, as has become clear, when the faithful people had a king, their first king, namely Saul, was appointed through a priest at the Lord's command. If we refer it back to its origin, therefore — to the manner of its inception among the faithful people — royal power, and earthly power generally, was appointed through the priesthood or through the ecclesiastical power.

Thus, all Christian kings, all faithful princes, must pay attention to whence royal power comes and to how the Lord has commanded that a king should be appointed over the faithful people; and they will discover clearly and manifestly that, as has been shown, such power was instituted through the priesthood. It is not the case, therefore, that the one power and the other both come immediately

1. I Sam. 8:7.
2. I Sam. 10:1.
3. PL 176:418.
4. I Sam. 8:1.
5. Exod. 18:13–26.
6. Pt. I, Ch. VIII, pp. 49–51.

illa. Immo, est hec per illam, et per consequens est hec sub illa.

Sed non esset potestas regia sub potestate ecclesiastica constituta nisi et ipsa temporalia, quibus preest potestas regia, essent sub potestate Summi Pontificis collocata. Et quod tangebatur in primordio huius capituli, quod Summus Pontifex non habet nisi alterum gladium, dicemus quod terrena potestas habet gladium[1] materialem tantum, et[2] nullo modo, nec ad usum nec ad nutum, habet spiritualem; sed potestas ecclesiastica habet utrumque gladium, ut supra tetigimus:[3] spiritualem ad usum, materialem ad nutum. Nam et discipuli Domini, quibus succedunt prelati ecclesiastici, duos gladios se habere professi sunt, iuxta illud Luce XXII: 'Ecce gladii duo hic,' per quos duos gladios possunt intelligi due potestates, spiritualis et terrena. Utrumque ergo gladium habebant discipuli, et utrumque gladium habet Ecclesia.

Et si bene considerentur verba Evangelii, optime figuratum est per illos duos gladios[4] quomodo utrumque gladium Ecclesia habeat; quia, ut Beda ait, alter illorum gladiorum extractus est, alter in vagina remansit. Nam, cum duo essent gladii, non legimus nisi unum gladium fuisse extractum,[5] cum quo percussit Petrus servum principis sacerdotum[6] et amputavit eius auriculam[7] dextram. Quid ergo est quod, cum[8] duo sunt gladii, unus extractus alter in vagina remanens,[9] nisi quod[10] Ecclesia duos habet gladios: spiritualem quantum ad usum, quod figuratur per gladium extractum, et materialem non quantum ad usum sed quantum ad nutum, quod figuratur per gladium non extractum? Cum gladio itaque extracto, et[11] cum gladio spirituali quem[12] habet Ecclesia ad usum, 'servi,' id est peccatoris — quia qui facit peccatum servus est peccati — amputatur 'auricula dextra,' per quam audiuntur[13] verba Dei, sicut cum sinistra audiuntur verba seculi: id est, separatur a communione fidelium, ut verba divina non possit audire ad salutem suam, et anima eius in[14] verbis que 'procedunt[15] ore Dei' vivere nequaquam potest.

Sed quis usus est hoc gladio et quis amputavit auriculam dextram? Petrus. Quare[16] Summus Pontifex, qui succedit Petro, habet huiusmodi gladii usum, quia eius est habere potestatem ecclesiasticam et posse expellere alios per ecclesiasticam censuram[17] et separare eos a communione fidelium. Alii autem, si utuntur hoc gladio, auctoritate Summi Pontificis hoc exercent. Discipuli ergo habebant utrumque gladium, sed solum altero usi sunt;[18] alterum autem non habuerunt ad usum, sed

---

1: dicemus quod ... gladium] *om.* F   2: tantum, et] tamen F   3: tetigimus] *om.* FV²
4: gladios] *om.* FV²   5: extractum] tractum FV²   6: sacerdotum] sacerdotes C   7: eius auriculam] auriculam eius CFV²   8: cum] *om.* CF   9: remanens] remansit CFV²   10: quod] quia F
11: et] id est F   12: quem] quam FV²   13: audiuntur] audiunt F   14: in] ex F   15: procedunt] ex *add.* C de *add.* F   16: Quare] quia C   17: ecclesiasticam censuram] censuram ecclesiasticam C   18: usi sunt] utebantur F

from God in the same fashion. On the contrary, the one comes into being through the other; and it follows that the one is under the other.

But royal power would not be set under the ecclesiastical power if the temporal things over which royal power rules were not themselves also placed under the power of the Supreme Pontiff. And so to what was touched upon at the beginning of this chapter — that the Supreme Pontiff has nothing if not both swords — we shall add that the earthly power has the material sword only, and does not have the spiritual in any way, either to use or to command. But, as we have noted above, the ecclesiastical power has both swords: the spiritual to use and the material to command.[1] For even the Lord's disciples, to whom the prelates of the Church have succeeded, declared themselves to have two swords, according to Luke 22: 'Behold, here are two swords';[2] by which two swords can be understood the two powers, spiritual and earthly. The disciples, therefore, had both swords, and [so] the Church has both swords.

And if due consideration is given to the words of the Gospel, the way in which the Church has both swords is perfectly illustrated by the two swords [there mentioned]. For, as Bede says, one of those swords was drawn and the other remained in its sheath.[3] And so, although there were two swords, we read that only one sword was drawn, with which Peter struck the servant of the High Priest and cut off his right ear.[4] What, therefore, does this mean — that while there were two swords, the one was drawn and the other remained in its sheath — if not that the Church has two swords: the spiritual to use, which is represented by the drawn sword, and the material not to use, but to command, which is represented by the undrawn sword?[5] Thus, with the drawn sword and with the spiritual sword, which the Church has for use against the 'servant' — that is, the sinner, for he who commits sin is the servant of sin — his 'right ear' is cut off, by which the words of God are heard, just as the words of this world are heard by the left. That is, he is separated from the communion of the faithful, so that he may not hear the Divine words for his salvation, and his soul cannot by any means live by the words which 'proceed out of the mouth of God.'[6]

But who made use of this sword, and who cut off the right ear? Peter. And so the Supreme Pontiff, who has succeeded Peter, has the use of that sword; for it belongs to him to exercise ecclesiastical power, and he can expel others by means of ecclesiastical censure and separate them from the communion of the faithful. And if others make use of this sword they accomplish this [only] by the authority of the Supreme Pontiff. The disciples, therefore, had both swords, but they made use of only one; and they had the other not to use, but to command. And

1. Pt. I, Chaps. VIII & IX.
2. Luke 22:38.
3. *In Lucae evangelium expositio* 6 (PL 92:601).
4. Matt. 26:51; Mark 14:47; Luke 22:50; John 18:10. Only in St John's Gospel is Peter named as the disciple who cut off the servant's ear.
5. The obvious difficulties to which this argument is subject will be discussed in Ch. XV, below.
6. Cf. Matt. 4:14.

ad nutum. Sic et Ecclesia utrumque gladium habet, [1] quod non esset nisi terreni principes, habentes usum materialis gladii et habentes iudicium sanguinis, essent[2] sub famulatu et sub obsequio ecclesiastice potestatis. Et si terreni principes sunt sub famulatu ecclesiastice potestatis,[3] consequens est ergo[4] quod et temporalia, quibus principatur potestas terrena, sint sub dominio Ecclesie collocata.

Hiis[5] itaque prelibatis, adhuc[6] ut evidencius nostrum propositum declaretur, dato quod concederemus eis qui negant temporalia sub dominio Ecclesie collocari quod potestas terrena eque[7] immediate esset a Deo sicut ecclesiastica, et quod una non esset per alteram constituta, quamvis hoc concedere sit negare que in[8] canone Biblie continentur: nihilominus tamen hoc concesso, adhuc quesita veritas manet, videlicet quod potestas terrena est sub ecclesiastica et temporalia sub dominio Ecclesie collocantur;[9] quod potest leviter declarari.

Nam hii duo gladii sumpti sunt propter duas partes que sunt in homine: propter animam videlicet et corpus, ut spiritualis gladius respiciat animas, materialis quidem, qui[10] habet[11] iudicium sanguinis, videtur[12] propter corpora[13] et propter temporalia[14] constitutus. Sed si Deus eque immediate faceret corpus humanum et animam humanam,[15] numquam ex illo corpore et ex illa anima constitueretur homo nisi esset corpus[16] in potencia respectu anime, et anima esset actus et perfeccio corporis. Numquam autem ex duobus in actu fit unum neque ex duobus in potencia, sed semper[17] fit unum ex potencia et[18] actu, ut in naturali physica diffusius declaratur. Si ergo ex anima et corpore fit unum, quia constituitur[19] inde unus homo, oportet quod unum sit sub alio, quod unum perficiatur per aliud, quod unum alteri famuletur. Corpus itaque est sub anima, perficitur per animam, et ordinatum est ut anime famuletur.[20]

Hii ergo duo gladii sunt propter regimen humani generis et propter regimen hominum. Si igitur hominis sic se haberent quod corpora essent ex una parte et anime ex alia, ita quod nullum dominium, nullam presidenciam haberent anime supra corpora,[21] forte et hii duo gladii sic se haberent quod unus non famularetur alii nec esset sub alio. Sed cum sic se habeant quod anime et corpora, ad quorum regimen[22] ordinantur hii duo gladii,[23] habent ad invicem hanc unionem et coniunccionem quod ex[24] eis fit unum aliquid,[25] et corpora sunt sub animabus et famulantur eisdem, oportet quod et hii gladii hunc ordinem teneant, quod unus sit sub alio et alteri famuletur. Dato ergo quod uterque gladius esset eque immediate a Deo, tamen[26] unus est ordinatus ad regimen corporum, alter vero ad regimen animarum: sicut corpus est sub anima, sic gladius erit sub gladio, et potestas terrena erit sub

---

1: habet] ut sepe iam diximus spiritualem ad usum materialem ad nutum *add. and del.* C
2: essent] erunt C   3: Et si ... potestatis] *om.* C   4: ergo] *om.* FV²   5: Hiis] his F   6: adhuc] *om.* F   7: eque] eis PV¹   8: in] *interlin.* C *om.* FV²   9: collocantur] collocata FV²   10: qui] *om.* FV²   11: habet] habere F   12: videtur] videatur F   13: corpora] corpus F   14: temporalia] spiritualia F   15: et animam humanam] *om.* F   16: esset corpus] corpus esset CF   17: sed semper] *om.* CFV²   18: et] *om.* F   19: constituitur] constitutus CFV²   20: anime famuletur] famuletur anime F   21: corpora] corpus C   22: regimen] regnum C   23: duo gladii] *om.* PV¹   24: ex] *om.* F   25: aliquid] aliud F   26: tamen] quia *add.* PV¹

so the Church has both swords, which would not be so if earthly princes, having the use of the material sword and having the judgment of blood, were not in the service of and under obedience to the ecclesiastical power. And if earthly princes are in the service of the ecclesiastical power, it therefore follows that the temporal things over which the earthly power presides are also placed under the lordship of the Church.

Thus, having first touched upon these considerations in order to make our argument more clearly evident, it can easily be shown that even if, to those who deny that temporal things are placed under the lordship of the Church, we concede that earthly and ecclesiastical power both came immediately from God in the same fashion and that the one was not appointed through the other (although to concede this is to deny what is contained in the canon of the Bible), this much nonetheless stands revealed as the truth regardless of this concession: namely, that the earthly power is under the ecclesiastical and that temporal things are placed under the lordship of the Church.

For these two swords are provided for the two parts which are in man: that is, for soul and body; so that the spiritual sword is concerned with souls while the material, which has the judgment of blood, is seen to be appointed for bodies and for temporal matters. But although God made the human body and the human soul equally immediately,[1] man would never have been composed from that body and from that soul unless the body existed potentially in relation to the soul and the soul was the actuality and perfection of the body. For a single entity is never made either from two actualities or from two potentialities. Rather, as is more extensively shown in natural science, a single entity is always made from potentiality and actuality.[2] Therefore, if a single entity is made from soul and body — for a single man is constituted in this way — then it must be that the one is under the other, that the one is perfected through the other, and that the one is the servant of the other. Thus, the body is under the soul, is perfected through the soul, and is appointed to serve the soul.

Therefore, these two swords exist for the government of the human race and for the government of men. Thus, if men were composed in such a way that bodies and souls were separate parts, so that souls had no lordship, no presiding power, over bodies, then these two swords would perhaps also be such that the one was not the servant of the other nor under the other. But since they are such that souls and bodies, for the government of which these two swords are ordained, are mutually united and conjoined in such a way that a single entity is made from them, and since bodies are under souls and are their servants, it must be that these two swords also exhibit this order: that the one is under the other and is the servant of the other. Even if we grant, therefore, that both swords have come immediately from God in the same fashion, the one sword will nonetheless be under the other and the earthly power will be placed under the ecclesiastical

1.   That is, He made body and soul directly, without any intermediate power, even if not both at the same time: see Pt. I, Ch. VI, p. 31.
2.   See Pt. I, Ch. VI, pp. 31–35.

potestate[1] ecclesiastica collocata.[2] Cum ergo probatum sit quod potestas regalis est per sacerdocium constituta et cum ordinetur ad regimen corporum, illa, scilicet[3] spiritualis, potestas ad regimen animarum, ex utroque[4] sufficienter concluditur quod altera sub altera collocetur.

Sed ad quid[5] ulterius racionibus indigemus? Constat quod potestas Summi Pontificis non est directe super animabus separatis. Rogare quidem[6] potest[7] Ecclesia[8] pro illis qui[9] sunt in purgatorio, cum quibus est caritate coniuncta. Sed directam potestatem et directam iurisdiccionem habet super animabus coniunctis que presunt corporibus, ad quarum nutum moventur corpora. Unde glossa super illo verbo Matthaei XVI, 'Quodcumque ligaveris super terram'[10] etc., ait quod 'Non enim data est potestas hominibus ligandi vel solvendi mortuos sed vivos;[11] qui autem mortuos solveret vel ligaret[12] non super terram sed post terram hoc faceret.' Habet ergo ecclesiastica potestas auctoritatem directam super animabus ut sunt coniuncte corporibus et ut presunt corporibus et ut ad nutum earum[13] moventur corpora.

Consequens ergo est quod, sicut auctoritas spiritualis est[14] super animabus, ut presunt corporibus et ut ad nutum earum moventur corpora, sic huiusmodi potestas hoc modo est super animabus, ut eis subsit corporalis et terrena, et huiusmodi potestas sic habet spiritualem gladium, ut ei[15] subsit gladius materialis, et ut habeat[16] materialem gladium, etsi non ad usum, ad nutum. Ex hiis ergo manifeste patet quod omnia temporalia sub dominio Ecclesie collocantur.[17]

Declaratum est ergo[18] quomodo potestas terrena est per ecclesiasticam constituta; et ex hoc est ulterius patefactum quomodo temporalia sub dominio Ecclesie collocantur. Quod autem potestas terrena non solum ex speciali mandato divino sit[19] per ecclesiasticam, sed eciam[20] sit ab ecclesiastica constituta, non est difficile declarare.

Nam inter potestates terrenas imperialis dicitur esse maior, et tamen huiusmodi potestatem potestas ecclesiastica, si expedit[21] communi bono, potest transferre, et iam transtulit de oriente in occidentem. Est eciam terrena potestas ordinata ad opus ecclesiastice potestatis. Nam imperator hoc modo consuevit iurare pape, quod si Romam veniat et adeptus[22] sit imperium, secundum suum posse Romanam Ecclesiam exaltabit.[23] Maiores ergo inter potestates terrenas iurant Romane

---

1: potestate] *del.* C   2: collocata] *del.* C   3: illa, scilicet] *del.* C   4: ex utroque] *om.* F
5: quid] quod CF   6: rogare quidem] *om.* FV[2]   7: potest] autem pro animabus separatis rogare *add.* FV[2]   8: Ecclesia] et specialiter *add.* FV[2]   9: qui] que C   10: super terram] *om.* F
11: sed vivos] *om.* FPV[1]V[2]   12: ligaret] ligaverit C   13: earum] eorum FPV[2]   14: est] *om.* F
15: ei] eis CFV[2]   16: et ut habeat] habeat ergo C   17: collocantur] Nam si terrena potestas constituta est per ecclesiasticam et per consequens subest ecclesiastica apte concludit ut quod temporalia quibus preest terrena potestas sub potestate ecclesiastica collocentur rursus si potestas ecclesiastica preest animabus ut sunt coniuncti corporibus et ut presunt corporibus temporalia non ordinata sunt in amminiculum et in obsequium corporum nisi dominio potestatis ecclesiastice ordinantur et terrena potestas que preest corporibus oportet quod sit sub ecclesiastica collocata *add. and del.* C   18: est ergo] ergo est F   19: sit] *om.* F   20: eciam] quod simpliciter *add.* FV[2]
21: expedit] expediat FV[2]   22: adeptus] ad tempus FV[2]   23: exaltabit] exaltare PV[1]

power, just as the body is under the soul; for the one is ordained to rule bodies and the other to rule souls. When, therefore, it is proved that royal power is appointed through the priesthood and that it is ordained to rule bodies as the spiritual power clearly is to rule souls, then it is sufficiently shown in both ways that the one is placed under the other.

But what need have we of further arguments? It is clear that the Supreme Pontiff has no direct power over departed souls. The Church can indeed only intercede for those who are in purgatory, with whom she is united in love. But he does have direct power and direct jurisdiction over the souls which are united with and rule bodies, at whose command bodies are moved. Hence, a gloss on those words of Matthew 16 — 'Whatever you shall bind on earth,'[1] and so on — says that 'Power has not been given to men to bind or release the dead; for he who bound and released the dead would do this not on earth, but after it.'[2] The ecclesiastical power, therefore, has direct authority over souls insofar as they are united with bodies, and insofar as they rule bodies, and insofar as bodies are moved at their command.

Therefore, as spiritual authority is over souls insofar as they rule bodies and insofar as bodies are moved at their command, so it follows that this power is over souls in such a way that it may rule bodily and earthly things through them; and that this power has the spiritual sword in such a way that it may rule the material sword with it, and so may have the material sword to command even if not to use. It is manifestly clear from these considerations, therefore, that all temporal things are placed under the lordship of the Church.

It has been shown, then, how the earthly power is appointed through the ecclesiastical and, from this, it has been made clear in addition how temporal things are placed under the lordship of the Church. Moreover, it is not difficult to show that the earthly power is appointed not only through the ecclesiastical by special divine command, but actually by the ecclesiastical.

For, among earthly powers, the imperial is said to be greater; yet, nonetheless, if it is expedient for the common good, the ecclesiastical power can transfer such power, and has already transferred it from the east to the west.[3] Also, the earthly power is ordained to the work of the ecclesiastical power. For the emperor customarily takes an oath to the pope to this effect: that if he comes to Rome and the imperial authority is conferred, he will exalt the Roman Church to the best of his power.[4] Among earthly powers, therefore, the greater swear an oath to the Roman

---

1. Matt. 16:19.
2. Cf. Aquinas, *Catena aurea* 11:199.
3. See Introduction, n. 41.
4. Cf. Dist. 63, c. 33: *Tibi domino* (CIC 1:246), recording the oath sworn by Otto I to Pope John XII in 962. What Giles has in mind here is the fact that the emperor, though entering upon his powers from the time of his election by the German princes, was called 'king of the Romans' until his coronation at Rome. His point is that though, strictly speaking, the emperor is appointed by God *through* the pope, the *translatio imperii* and the coronation oath show that there is an immediate sense in which he is appointed *by* the pope: to whom he (and, *a fortiori,* every lesser power) therefore owes a personal allegiance. Cf. Professor Watt's comment: 'It

Ecclesie.[1] Sed ad hoc omnes fideles tenentur, et quanto maiores sunt, magis tenentur Romanam Ecclesiam exaltare. Nam ipse Deus noster, Iesus Christus, qui[2] 'exauditus' est 'pro sua reverencia,' oravit pro Petro ut non deficeret fides sua. Numquam[3] ergo deficere poterit in fide sedes Petri et Romana Ecclesia. Et si quilibet fidelis loco et tempore tenetur eciam se exponere morti pro fide, et quanto maiores sunt, magis tenentur, consequens est ut omnes fideles debeant secundum suum posse sedem Petri et Romanam Ecclesiam exaltare. Ad hoc ergo[4] tenentur omnes reges et principes et omnes terrene potestates, si velint esse fideles. Bene itaque dictum est quod terrena potestas est per ecclesiasticam et ab ecclesiastica et in opus ecclesiastice constituta.[5]

Quo posito, consequens est quod ipsa temporalia quibus dominatur terrena potestas sub ecclesiastice potestatis imperio necessario collocantur. Nam[6] ad ecclesiasticam potestatem spectat[7] dominos quam res eorum possidere. Ideo super illo verbo II ad Corinthios VI, 'Tamquam nihil habentes et omnia possidentes,' dicit glossa, exponens hoc de apostolis, quod 'eorum fuit possidere non solum spiritualia, sed eciam temporalia,' et subditur ibi in glossa quod 'gloria fuit[8] apostolorum tam res quam dominos earum possidere.' Ecclesia ergo debet omnia possidere et nihil possidere. Nam, quantum ad dominium, ut supra tetigimus, omnia possidet, quia super omnibus habet auctoritatem, tam super spiritualia quam super temporalia,[9] 'tam super res quam super dominos,' ut patuit ex glossa iam allegata. Nihil autem debet possidere quantum ad sollicitudinem; et hinc est quod si esse non potest quin[10] Ecclesia nullam sollicitudinem habeat[11] de temporalibus, ipsa tamen, quantum potest, debet se abstrahere ab huiusmodi sollicitudine, ut spiritualibus liberius vacare possit, ut ipsa, militans Deo, non implicet se negociis secularibus.

Non tamen propter hoc colligitur[12] quod in nullo casu sit licitum Ecclesie habere huiusmodi sollicitudinem. Si enim videat quod expediat communi bono, potest tali sollicitudini aliquod opus[13] dare, salvata congruencia sui status. Nam et Dominus mandavit discipulis suis[14] tollere sacculum et peram, quod non erat sine sollicitudine temporalium. Unde Beda, exponens huiusmodi dictum Evangelii et huiusmodi

---

1: Romane Ecclesie] romanam ecclesiam exaltare CF   2: qui] in omnibus *add.* C   3: Numquam] numquid FPV[1]   4: ergo] enim PV[1]   5: constituta] cum quelibet terrena potestas debeat potestatem ecclesiasticam et ei subesse et ipsum pro viribus exaltare et si sic se habet potestas terrena ad eccles *add. and del.* C   6: Nam] nec non FV[2]   7: spectat] spectet FV[2]   8: gloria fuit] fuit gloria F   9: quam super temporalia] *om.* F   10: quin] quod V[1] in *add.* FPV[2]   11: habeat] eciam *add.* P   12: colligitur] tollitur FV[2]   13: opus] tempus FV[2]   14: suis] *om.* FV[2]

Church. All faithful men are bound to do this [i.e. exalt the Roman Church]; but the greater they are, the more are they bound to exalt the Roman Church. For our God Himself, Jesus Christ, 'Who was heard for his reverence,'[1] prayed for Peter, that he might not lack faith.[2] Therefore, it will never be possible for the See of Peter and the Roman Church to lack faith. And if each faithful man is everywhere and always bound to expose himself even to death for the faith, and if the greater are the more bound, then it follows that all faithful men must exalt the See of Peter and the Roman Church to the best of their power. Therefore, all kings and princes and all earthly powers are bound to do this if they wish to be faithful men. It is well said, therefore, that the earthly power is appointed through the ecclesiastical and by the ecclesiastical, and for the work of the ecclesiastical power.

But, having established this, it follows that even temporal things, over which earthly power has lordship, are of necessity placed under the command of the ecclesiastical power. For it rests with the ecclesiastical power to possess both lords and their goods. Hence a gloss on the words of II Corinthians 6, 'As having nothing and possessing all things,' interpreting this in relation to the apostles, says that it fell to them to possess 'not only spiritual things, but temporal things also';[3] and to this it is added in a gloss that it was the glory of the apostles 'to possess both things and their lords.'[4] The Church, therefore, must possess all things, yet she must have nothing. For she may possess all things with regard to the exercise of lordship, as we have noted above;[5] for she has authority over all things both spiritual and temporal, over 'both things and their lords,' as is clear from the gloss just cited. But she must have nothing in the sense of being anxious. And so, even if it is not possible for the Church to have [absolutely] no anxiety for temporal matters, she must still withdraw herself from such anxiety as far she can, so that she may attend more freely to spiritual matters and so that, being a soldier of God, she may not involve herself in worldly affairs.[6]

It is not to be inferred from this, however, that there is no case in which the Church may have such anxiety. For if it should seem expedient to the common good, she can devote such anxiety to some task, provided that this is consistent with her standing. For the Lord Himself commanded His disciples to take purse and bag;[7] for [even] He was not without temporal anxiety. Thus, interpreting this saying of the Gospel and this command of the Lord — that the disciples were to take purse

---

[i.e. Dist 63, c. 33] might even be read occasionally, and crudely, as a feudal oath, thus making the emperor "homo papae"' (J.A. Watt, *The Theory of Papal Monarchy in the Thirteenth Century*, New York: Fordham University Press, 1965, p. 26).

1. Heb. 5:7.
2. Luke 22:32.
3. Peter Lombard, *Collectanea in omnes de Pauli apostoli epistolas*, PL 192:48.
4. *Glossa ordinaria*, PL 114:560.
5. Ch. I.
6. Cf. II Tim. 2:4.
7. Luke 22:36.

mandatum Domini, quod tollerent discipuli sacculum et peram,[1] ait quod Dominus dat nobis exemplum quod nonnumquam iusta[2] causa instante quedam[3] de nostri proposti rigore possunt[4] sine culpa intermitti.[5] Rigor ergo propositi discipulorum requirebat ut[6] tantam[7] haberent[8] sollicitudinem evangelizandi quod omnem aliam sollicitudinem[9] pretermittere,[10] ut non haberent sollicitudinem nec de sacculo nec de pera. Iusta[11] tamen causa instante poterat iuste[12] rigor intermitti, ut haberent sollicitudinem eciam de sacculo et de pera.[13]

Sic et Ecclesia quantum ad dominium omnia possidet, sed tanta debet esse eius sollicitudo circa spiritualia ut committat aliis sollicitudinem quantum ad temporalia,[14] ut ipsa quantum ad sollicitudinem non habeat sacculum neque peram, et quantum ad huiusmodi sollicitudinem sit[15] quasi nihil possidens. Propter quod illa eadem glossa II ad Corinthios VI que dixit Apostolos omnia possidere, quantum tamen ad sollicitudinem dixit eos nihil debere possidere, ideo ait quod 'gloria fuit apostolorum nihil omnino possidere, et sine sollicitudine esse.' Rigor itaque propositi ecclesiastici est se abstrahere a cura et sollicitudine temporalium, ut magis possit curam spiritualium exercere. Iusta[16] tamen causa instante secundum documenta Bede potest iste rigor intermitti, ut eciam de temporalibus et de pera et de sacculo Ecclesia sollicitudinem gerat.

CAPITULUM VI: *Quod* [17] *terrena potestas, tum quia*[18] *particularior, tum quia materiam preparans, tum eciam quia longinquius attingit optimum, secundum se et secundum sua spirituali potestati iure et merito famulatur.*

Quia[19] potestas terrena temporalibus dominatur, ideo in variis capitulis huius opusculi conati sumus apercius declarare quomodo huiusmodi potestas potestati spirituali iure et merito est subiecta, ut exinde habere possimus quod spiritualis potestas non solum potestati terrene, sed eciam rebus temporalibus dominetur, cum auctoritas ecclesiastica et res temporales et earum dominos ostendatur habere subiectos.

Tetigimus autem in rubrica huius capituli quasi tria per que poterit nostrum propositum declarari; que tria[20] sumpta sunt ex[21] hiis que videmus in aliis potestatibus. Nam ne aliqui in hac materia valeant resistere, volumus per ea que videmus in aliis potestatibus ostendere quod potestas terrena spirituali potestati debet esse subiecta, ut ex hoc eciam ulterius concludamus quod ipsa terrena et ipsa temporalia iurisdiccioni et dominacioni Ecclesie supponuntur.[22] Ex quibus poterit ulterius[23] declarari quod, Deo disponente, hee due potestates sic sunt ad invicem ordinate quod una non impedit aliam, sed iuvat, et una non tollit ius alterius, sed quelibet

---

1: quod non erat ... peram] *om.* FV² 2: iusta] iuxta FV² 3: quedam] que FV² 4: possunt] posset FV² 5: intermitti] pretermitti FV² 6: ut] non *add.* V¹ 7: tantam] curam F 8: haberent] et *add.* F 9: evangelizandi ... sollicitudinem] *om.* V¹ 10: pretermittere] pretermittent C 11: Iusta] iuxta F 12: iuste] iste F 13: Rigor ergo ... pera] *om.* V² 14: ut committat ... temporalia] *om.* F 15: sit] fit V¹ 16: Iusta] iuxta C 17: *Quod*] quia P 18: *quia*] *om.* P 19: Quia] *om.* F 20: tria] *del.* C 21: ex] in FV² 22: supponuntur] supponantur F 23: poterit ulterius] ulterius poterit F

and bag — Bede says that the Lord gives to us an example that sometimes, for some just and urgent cause, the strictness of our duty can be set aside without fault.[1] The strictness of the disciples' duty, therefore, required that they should have so great an anxiety for proclaiming the Gospel that they put aside all other anxiety, so that they should have anxiety for neither purse nor bag. Nonetheless, for just and urgent cause, they could justly set aside this strictness, and so have anxiety even for purse and bag.

So also, the Church may possess all things in the sense of exercising lordship; but so great must be her anxiety for spiritual matters that she entrusts anxiety for temporal matters to others, so that, in the sense of being anxious, she may have neither purse nor bag and, so far as such anxiety is concerned, may be as though having nothing. Hence, that same Gloss on II Corinthians 6 which said that the apostles possessed all things nonetheless said of them that, in the sense of being anxious, they were to have nothing. And so it asserts that 'It was the glory of the apostles to have nothing at all and to be without anxiety.' Thus, it is the strict duty of the Church to withdraw herself from care and temporal anxiety, so that she may be the more able to exercise care over spiritual matters. For just and urgent cause, however, according to the teaching of Bede, this strictness can be set aside, so that the Church may display anxiety even for temporal things and for bag and purse.

CHAPTER VI: *That the earthly power is rightly and properly the servant of the spiritual power in itself and in what belongs to it, because it is more particular, and because it prepares material, and because it comes less close to attaining what is best.*

Because the earthly power has lordship over temporal things, we have therefore endeavoured in the various chapters of this short work to show more clearly how such power is rightly and properly subject to the spiritual power, so that we may be able to infer from this that the spiritual power will have lordship not only over the earthly power, but also over temporal things, since ecclesiastical authority is shown to have both temporal things and their lords as its subjects.

Now in the heading of this chapter we have noted some three ways in which our proposition can be made clear, which three ways are derived from what we see in other powers. For, in order that it may not avail anyone to resist us in this matter, we wish to show through what we see in other powers that the earthly power must be subject to the spiritual power, so that, from this, we may draw the further conclusion that earthly and temporal things are themselves placed under the jurisdiction and lordship of the Church. Furthermore, it will be possible to show from these observations that, by the disposition of God, these two powers are mutually ordered in such a way that the one does not impede the other, but assists it, and that the one does not take away the right of the other, but that each,

---

1. *In Lucae evangelium expositio* 6 (PL 92:601).

modo debito[1] observato[2] gaudet et utitur iure suo, ut si potestas terrena famulatur spirituali, in hoc ius potestati terrene non tollitur, quia tenetur spirituali potestati iure et merito famulari. Et si iusta causa imminente de rebus imperii vel de ipso imperio se intromittat Ecclesia, eciam si iusta imminente causa ipsum imperium transferat, nulli ex hoc iniuriam faceret,[3] cum hoc de iure sibi competat, et nulli dicatur iniuriam facere[4] qui[5] utitur iure suo. Dicebatur enim in precedenti capitulo quod hoc exigit rigor ecclesiastice potestatis, quod si omnia possideat omnibus dominando, et ut liberius spiritualibus vacet, nihil possideat temporale, scilicet circa illud sollicitando, sed sollicitudo temporalium est laicis committenda, iusta tamen imminente causa, ut probavimus per auctoritatem Bede, iste rigor potest aliquando intermitti, ut de ipsis temporalibus et de hiis que spectant ad ius imperii[6] iuste se Ecclesia intromittat.[7]

Descendamus ergo ad propositum, declarantes que in rubrica capituli continentur. Eapropter distinguemus[8] quatuor genera potestatum et in quolibet huiusmodi genere ostendemus aliquas potestates esse superiores, aliquas inferiores, et in quolibet eciam huiusmodi genere[9] semper inferiores potestates superioribus famulantur. Describentes itaque potestatem, dicamus quod nihil[10] aliud est potestas nisi per quam aliquis dicitur esse potens. Sicut ergo hec est albedo per quam aliquid[11] dicitur esse album,[12] et hec nigredo per quam aliquid[13] dicitur esse nigrum,[14] sic hec est[15;16] potestas, per quam aliquis dicitur esse potens.

Videmus autem quod per virtutes naturales sunt potentes naturales cause, ut ignis per calorem et per virtutem calefactivam quam habet potest calefacere, et aqua per virtutem infrigidativam potest infrigidare, et celum per virtutem quam habet potest in ista inferiora influere, ita ut quelibet res naturalis per suam virtutem et per suam potenciam sit potens. Et sicut per virtutes naturales sunt potentes naturales[17] cause, sic per artes sunt potentes[18] artifices, ut per artem citharizandi potest citharista debite citharizare, qui autem illa arte caret debite citharizare non potest. Tercio, per sciencias sunt potentes sapientes, ut per naturalem philosophiam fit quis potens cognoscere partes et passiones corporis mobilis, et per alias sciencias fit aliquis potens speculari et cognoscere que in illis scienciis declarantur. Per principatus vero sunt potentes principes, sive sint illi principatus materiales sive spirituales, ut quilibet suo iure gaudeat, et suo principatu quilibet principetur.

Distincta ergo sunt quatuor genera potestatum, ut unum genus potestatum sint[19] virtutes naturales, aliud sint[20] artes, tercium[21] sint sciencie, quartum[22] sint principatus et gubernaciones hominum. Et quelibet harum potestatum in quadam

1: modo debito] debito modo F   2: observato] observata CF   3: faceret] facit FV[2]   4: cum hoc ... facere] om. FV[2]   5: qui] quia F   6: imperii] ut de ipsis temporalibus add. CPV[1]V[2]   7: imperii ... intromittat] imperii ut de ipsis temporalibus et de hiis que spectant ad ius imperii et de ipsis temporalibus et de hiis que spectant ad ius imperii et de ipsis temporalibus iuste se ecclesia intromittat F   8: distinguemus] distingue F   9: genere] om. F   10: nihil] enim add. F   11: aliquid] aliquis F   12: album] albus CF   13: aliquid] aliquis CF   14: nigrum] niger F   15: hec est] est hoc F   16: est] om. V[2]   17: sunt potentes naturales] om. F   18: naturales cause ... potentes] om. V[2]   19: potestatum sint] potestatis sit F   20: sint] sunt F   21: tercium] tercia FV[2]   22: quartum] quarta FV[2]

by observing its proper limit, enjoys and uses its own right: so that, if the earthly power serves the spiritual, the right of the earthly power is not taken away by this, since it is rightly and properly bound to serve the spiritual power. And if, for just and urgent cause, the Church were to concern herself with the affairs of the empire, or with the empire itself, or even, for just and urgent cause, were to transfer the empire, she would inflict injustice on no one by this. For she is competent to do this as of right, and he who makes use of his own right is said to inflict injustice on no one.[1] For it was said in the previous chapter that the strict duty of the ecclesiastical power requires this: that, though it may possess all things in the sense of exercising lordship, it may have nothing temporally — that is, in the sense of being anxious. Rather, it must entrust anxiety for temporal possessions to the laity, so that it may attend more freely to spiritual matters. Nonetheless, for just and urgent cause, as we have proved by the authority of Bede, this strict duty can sometimes be set aside, so that the Church may justly concern herself even with temporal matters and with those things which belong to the right of the empire.

Let us come, therefore, to our proposition, and make clear the statements contained in the heading of this chapter. To this end, we shall distinguish four kinds of power, and we shall show that, in each kind, some powers are superior and others inferior, and also that, in each such kind, the inferior powers are always the servants of the superior. By way of describing power, then, let us say that power is nothing other than that through which someone is said to be powerful. Therefore, just as whiteness is that through which something is said to be white and blackness is that through which something is said to be black, so power is that through which someone is said to be powerful.

Moreover, we see that it is through natural forces that natural causes are powerful. For example, fire is able to heat through heat and through the heating force which it has; and water is able to cool through a cooling force; and the heaven is able to influence these inferior agents through the force which it has. Thus, each natural thing is powerful through its force and through its potency. And just as natural causes are powerful through natural forces, so artists are powerful through the arts: for example, a lute-player is able to play the lute properly through the art of lute-playing, but he who lacks this art cannot play the lute properly. Third, the wise are powerful through the sciences: for example, one man may be powerful in understanding the parts and properties of body in motion through natural philosophy, and another may be powerful, through the other sciences, in examining and understanding those phenomena which are explained by the other sciences. And princes are powerful through the ruling powers, whether these ruling powers be material or spiritual, so that each may enjoy his own right and each may rule by virtue of his own ruling power.

Therefore, four kinds of power have been distinguished. One kind of power consists in natural forces, another in the arts, a third in the sciences, and a fourth in the ruling powers and governments of men. And each of these powers consists

1.   Cf. Justinian, *Digesta*, ed. T. Mommsen (repr. Philadelphia: University of Pennsylvania Press, 1985), 50:17:55.

ordinacione et proporcione consistit: ut potestas naturalis sit proporcionata faccio effectuum naturalium; potestas autem artificialis sit recta racio vel ordinata faccio factibilium artificialium; potestas quidem scientifica sit recta racio consideracionum speculabilium; potestas autem principatuum sit ordinata et recta racio gubernacionis hominum. Et quia presentem tractatum suscepimus[1] ut de ipsis principatibus, qui sunt potestates quedam, aliqua pertractemus, si volumus diligenter videre quis[2] ordo sit in principantibus[3] et in gubernacionibus hominum, que gubernaciones sunt potestates quedam, debemus in potestatibus aliis[4] aspicere;[5] et prout videbimus in potestatibus aliis, poterimus de principantibus[6] et gubernacionibus[7] hominum aliqua declarare.

Sic[8] autem videmus in potestatibus naturalibus quod alique sunt ibi superiores, alique inferiores; ut virtutes celestes sunt superiores[9] quam elementares, nam[10] elementares virtutes non agunt nisi in virtute celi, quia, ut in naturali philosophia traditur, ignis non ageret ad generacionem ignis, vel non posset generare ignem, nisi in virtute celi, ita quod celum et ignis generant ignem. Et quod dictum est de elementis intelligendum est de elementatis,[11;12] ita quod secundum istum[13] ordinem quem[14] videmus, equus non posset generare equum nisi in virtute solis; et sic de animalibus aliis, ita quod[15] sol et equus generant equum, et sol et leo generant[16] leonem, ut habet in naturalibus declarari. Virtus ergo celestis, tamquam communior et universalior, omnibus aliis virtutibus dominatur, sive virtutes ille sint elementorum sive elementatorum.

Et sicut in rebus naturalibus videmus aliquas superiores, aliquas inferiores, sic et in artibus alique sunt superiores, alique inferiores, ut sicut est quedam ars facere frena, ita est quedam ars[17] scire uti milicia, et hee due artes non comparantur ad paria,[18] sed est ars sub arte, ut frenifactiva est sub militari, ut frenifactiva tale facit frenum quale expedit militi. Sed non[19] secundum eandem racionem virtutes iste inferiores famulantur celestibus.[20] Nam virtutes iste inferiores famulantur celestibus eo quod particularius agunt; frenifactiva vero obsequitur militari eo quod materiam preparat. Nam celi est in omnia influere, omnia iuvare. Iuvat enim elementa et elementata: iuvat enim aquam ad infrigidandum, ignem ad calefaciendum; equum iuvat ut generet equum, leonem ut generet leonem. Nam nec leo nec equus nec[21] alia elementa possent naturaliter aliquid facere nisi[22] virtute celi, nec aqua nec ignis nec alia elementa[23] possent naturaliter aliquid facere nisi in virtute celi.

Virtus itaque celi est generalis, et ideo dominatur; virtutes autem istorum

---

1: suscepimus] suscipimus FV²   2: quis] quid F   3: principantibus] principatibus CFV²
4: aliis] alii F   5: aspicere] et add. FV²   6: principantibus] principibus CFPV²   7: gubernacionibus] gubernatoribus P   8: Sic] si FV²   9: ut virtutes ... superiores] om. PV¹   10: nam]
PV¹   11: elementatis] elementis F   12: intelligendum est de elementatis] marg. C   13: istum]
hunc FV²   14: quem] quam V²   15: ita quod] itaque F   16: generant] om. C   17: facere ...
ars] om. F   18: paria] ipsa F pia V²   19: Sed non] om. F   20: celestibus] celesti FV² et frenifactiva obsequitur militari add. CF   21: nec] ut F   22: nisi] in F in nisi V²   23: elementa]
elementata C

in a certain order and proportion. Thus, natural power is the proportionate production of natural effects; and artistic power is right reason or order applied to the production of that which can be made by art; and scientific power is right reason applied to the study of that which can be investigated; and the power of ruling is ordered and right reason applied to the government of men. And because we have undertaken the present treatise in order to say something of the ruling powers, which are powers of a kind, we must also consider the other powers if we wish diligently to examine what order there may be among the ruling powers and governments of men. For, to the extent that we examine the other powers, we shall be able to show something of the ruling powers and governments of men.

And so we see, among the natural powers, that some of them are superior and others inferior: that the forces of heaven are superior to those of the elements. For the forces of the elements do not act except by the force of heaven since, as is taught in natural philosophy, fire would not act in such a way as to generate fire, or would not be able to generate fire, except by the force of heaven; and so the heaven and fire generate fire.[1] And what has been said of the elements must be understood to be true also of compounds. For example, according to the order which we see, a horse would not be able to generate a horse except by the force of the sun. And so too with the other animals: sun and horse generate a horse, and sun and lion generate a lion, as it is the task of the natural sciences to show. The force of heaven, therefore, as more general and more universal, is lord of all other forces, whether these forces be those of elements or of compounds.

And just as among natural things we see that some are superior and others inferior, so also among the arts some are superior and others inferior. For example, just as there is a certain art of bridle-making, so also is there a certain art of knowing how to make use of an army; and these two arts are not to be linked together as equals. Rather, the one art is under the other: bridle-making is under warfare, for the art of bridle-making is that of making such a bridle as will be of use to the soldier.[2] It is not in this way, however, that the inferior [natural] forces serve the heavenly; for those inferior forces serve the heavenly in that they act more particularly, whereas bridle-making is subservient to warfare in that it prepares its material. But the heaven exerts influence upon all things and assists all things, for it assists both elements and compounds: it assists water to cool and fire to heat; it assists the horse to generate a horse and the lion to generate a lion. For neither the lion nor the horse nor the other compounds could produce anything naturally except by the force of heaven; and neither water nor fire nor the other elements could produce anything except by the force of heaven.

The force of heaven, then, is general, and so has lordship, whereas those inferior

---

1.   Cf. Averroes, commentary on Aristotle, *De caelo* 2:1 (284ª) (*Aristotelis opera cum Averrois commentariis* 5:125) and *Metaphysics* Λ:3 (1070ª) (*Aristotelis opera cum Averrois commentariis* 8:304); Aquinas, *Summa theologiae* Ia 115:3.
2.   Cf. Aristotle, *Nicomachean Ethics* 1:1 (1094ª10).

inferiorum, sive[1] sint elementorum sive[2] elementatorum, sunt particulares et ideo famulantur. In artibus vero, ut[3] frenifactiva famulatur militari, potes[4] assignare racionem et causam magis ex preparacione materie quam ex particularitate agentis, quia possent aliis et aliis animalibus ab equo fieri frena, que animalia non essent organum ad militandum nec ad bellandum. Licet ergo ista inferiora sint sicut virtutes particulares respectu celi, ut nihil agant nisi in virtute eius, non tamen oportet quod frenifactiva sit sic particularis respectu militaris quod nihil agat nisi quod expedit militi. Famulatur tamen frenifactiva militari materiam sibi preparando, et ut sibi materiam preparat se et sua ad militarem ordinat. Dicemus ergo quod equus est quedam materia circa quam se exercitant milites; sed equus non est materia preparata et disposita ut serviat militi nisi habeat frenum, sicut nec navis esset disposita ut famuletur[5] naute nisi haberet temonem.[6] Frenifactiva itaque famulatur militari materiam preparando; sic eciam dolativa famulatur[7] domifactive materiam disponendo, nam ille qui dolat lapidem[8] obsequitur edificatori sibi materiam preparando.

Assignate itaque sunt raciones et cause in rebus naturalibus et in artibus quare una alteri famuletur.[9] In scienciis vero possumus terciam racionem et causam assignare quare una famuletur alteri,[10] ut inter sciencias humanitus inventas omnis famulatur metaphysice, non solum quia metaphysica est generalior et universalior[11] quam alie sciencie, sed eciam quia magis attingit optimum. Inter sciencias enim humanitus inventas metaphysica magis habet considerare de Deo, qui est optimum inter encia, quam aliqua alia sciencia considerare possit.[12] Et inde est quod[13] theologia est domina[14] scienciarum et omnibus scienciis utitur in obsequium suum, ut ipsa[15] metaphysica sit eius ancilla et famula, quia magis attingit optimum quam metaphysica et quam aliqua sciencia. Nam metaphysica vel aliqua sciencia humanitus inventa, si considerat de Deo, hoc est prout illa consideracio haberi potest ductu racionis. Sed theologia considerat de Deo ut habetur eius cognicio cum adiutorio divine revelacionis; et quia[16] plura possunt haberi, ut habentur, de Deo per revelacionem quam per previam[17] racionem, consequens est quod theologia magis attingat optimum et plura possit considerare de Deo quam aliqua alia sciencia; et exinde est dea et domina scienciarum, omnes autem alie sciencie sibi ancillantur. Ideo omnes eas tamquam ancillas mittit vocare ad arcem et ad menia civitatis, nam omnibus eis utitur in obsequium suum, ut omnes defendant arcem et menia civitatis: id est, ut omnes defendant theologiam, quam dicimus esse quandam arcem et quandam civitatem cum suis meniis, ut non possit ab adversariis impugnari. Unde in Canticis assimilata est turri[18] David, que edificata est cum propugnaculis, ubi sunt varii clipei et omnis armatura[19] forcium, ut argumenta

---

1: sive] cum PV[1]   2: sive] sint add. F   3: ut] quod add. C   4: potes] poteris CF   5: famuletur] famularetur FV[2]   6: temonem] remum FV[2]   7: famulatur] om. PV[1]   8: lapidem] lapides C   9: famuletur] famulatur C   10: famuletur alteri] alteri famuletur CFV[2]   11: universalior] utilior F   12: considerare possit] del. C   13: quod] om. FV[2]   14: domina] divina F   15: ipsa] eciam add. FV[2]   16: quia] multo add. C   17: previam] viam, altered from previam C   18: turri] domum C   19: omnis armatura] armatura omnis FV[2]

forces which are either of elements or of compounds are particular, and are therefore servants. But, in the arts, you can assign the reason and cause whereby bridle-making serves warfare rather to the preparation of material than to the particularity of the agent. For there may be various other animals apart from horses for which bridles can be made, which animals may not be the instruments of war or battle. Therefore, although the inferior [natural] forces are particular in relation to the heaven and so can do nothing except by its force, it nonetheless cannot be that bridle-making is particular in relation to warfare in the sense of producing nothing except that which is of use to the soldier. Bridle-making does indeed serve warfare; but by preparing material for it. And, in order to prepare material for it, it orders itself and what belongs to it towards warfare. Therefore, we shall say that a horse is a kind of material with which soldiers occupy themselves; but a horse is not a kind of material prepared and disposed in such a way as to serve the soldier unless it has a bridle, just as a boat would not be disposed in such a way as to serve the sailor unless it had a rudder. Thus, bridle-making serves warfare by preparing material. So also stone-cutting serves building by disposing material, for he who cuts stone serves the builder by preparing material for him.

The reasons and causes have been assigned, then, whereby, among natural things and in the arts, one agent serves another. And, in the sciences, we can assign a third reason and cause whereby one is the servant of another. For, among the sciences discovered by man, each is the servant of metaphysics: not only because metaphysics is more general and more universal than the other sciences, but also because it more completely attains what is best. For, among the sciences discovered by man, metaphysics is more able to contemplate God, Who is the most perfect among beings, than any of the other sciences. And so it is that, since theology attains what is best more completely than metaphysics and any other science, she is mistress of the sciences and makes use of all the sciences in her service, so that metaphysics herself is her handmaid and servant. For if metaphysics, or any science discovered by man, contemplates God, this is so only to the extent that He can be contemplated by rational means; but theology contemplates God as He is known with the aid of Divine revelation. And since many more things can be known, and are known, of God through revelation than by effort of reason, it follows that theology attains what is best more completely, and can contemplate many more aspects of God, than any other science, and so is goddess and mistress of the sciences, all of which other sciences are her handmaids. And so she sends to summon them all to the citadel and to the walls of the city as handmaids; for she makes use of them all in her service, so that they may all defend the citadel and the walls of the city: that is, so that they may all defend theology, which we are calling a kind of citadel and a kind of walled city, lest she be attacked by her adversaries. Thus, in the Song of Songs,[1] she is likened to the Tower of David which was adorned with battlements upon which were many bucklers and all the arms of valiant men, so that the arguments of the

1. Cf. Cant. 4:4.

philosophorum non possint eam dirimere nec sufficienter invadere. Que omnia possunt et ad theologiam et ad Ecclesiam adaptari.

Distinximus[1] ergo quatuor genera potestatum; quia dicimus[2] alias potestates esse virtutes naturales, alias res artificiales, alias raciones scienciales[3] et alias principatuum et[4] hominum gubernaciones. In tribus quidem primis generibus assignavimus tres raciones et causas subieccionis et dominacionis: ut in virtutibus naturalibus, quare dominantur[5] virtutes celestes, assignavimus racionem et causam[6] generalitatem[7] et contraccionem, ut ideo virtutes celestes dominantur[8] quia sunt generales, ideo autem iste virtutes inferiores[9] famulantur quia sunt contracte et particulares. In rebus quidem artificialibus assignavimus[10] huiusmodi racionem et causam materie preparacionem, ut ideo dolativa famulatur domifactive et frenifactiva militari quia eis materiam preparant et disponunt. In racionibus quidem sciencialibus assignavimus[11] racionem et causam appropinquacionem ad optimum, ut illa que magis[12] attingit[13] optimum[14] dominatur et cetere ancillantur.

In quarto vero genere potestatum, ut in principantibus[15] et gubernacionibus hominum[16;17] dicemus omnes has tres causas simul concurrere. Dicemus enim quod potestas et principatus terrenus debet obsequi et famulari potestati et principatui spirituali propter omnia prefata tria: et[18] quia particularior, et quia materiam disponens et preparans, et quia non[19] ita appropinquat nec[20] attingit optimum potestas hec sicut illa.

Est autem potestas ecclesiastica universalior quam terrena, quia ipsa Ecclesia dicitur esse Catholica, id est universalis, ut dicit Isidorus, *Etymol.* libro VII, capitulo ultimo, propter quod ait quod 'catholicus' 'universalis' sive 'generalis' interpretatur, et subdit quod Greci 'universale' 'catholicum' vocant. Si ergo est articulus fidei quod debemus credere Sanctam Ecclesiam Catholicam, non est vere fidelis qui non credit Ecclesiam esse Catholicam, id est[21] universalem, et Sanctam, id est sancitam et firmam, quia fundata est supra firmam petram, vel Sanctam, id est puram et immaculatam, iuxta illud ad Ephesios V: 'ut exhiberet ipse Christus sibi gloriosam Ecclesiam, non habentem maculam aut[22] rugam.'[23] Ecclesia ergo est Sancta et Catholica, id est universalis; vere autem universalis non esset nisi omnibus universaliter preesset.

Ceteri autem principatus sunt particulares, quia nullus est principatus sine quo non possit quis salutem consequi, et maxime si loquamur de principatibus secularibus et de potestatibus terrenis, a quibus quis se abstrahens fit saluti propinquior. Nam clerici, qui non sunt sub potestate terrena, sunt in statu perfecciori

1: Distinximus] diximus FV[2]   2: dicimus] diximus FV[2]   3: scienciales] seminales *mss*
4: principatuum et] *om.* C   5: dominantur] dirigantur C   6: assignavimus ... causam] alligavimus causam et rationem C   7: generalitatem] *om.* V[1]   8: dominantur] dominarentur PV[1]
9: virtutes inferiores] inferiores virtutes F   10: assignavimus] alligavimus C   11: sciencialibus assignavimus] seminalibus alligavimus C   12: magis] appropinquat ad optimum et magis *add.* F
13: attingit] appropinquat V[2]   14: optimum] et magis attingit optimum *add.* C   15: principantibus] principatibus FV[1]V[2] principalibus P   16: hominum] *om.* PV[1]   17: et gubernacionibus hominum] hominum et gubernacionibus C   18: prefata tria: et] tria prefata C   19: non] *om.* FV[2]
20: nec] et F   21: id est] *om.* PV[1]   22: aut] neque FV[2]   23: rugam] *om.* V[2]

philosophers might not disturb nor suffice to invade her. And all these remarks can be applied to theology and to the Church alike.[1]

Therefore, we have distinguished four kinds of power. For we have said that some powers are natural forces, others are the creations of art, others are the rational operations of the sciences, and others are the ruling powers and governments of men. And, as to the first three kinds, we have assigned three reasons for their subjection and lordship, and three causes. As to the natural forces, we have assigned generality and limitation as the reason and cause by virtue of which they are under the lordship of the forces of heaven. Thus, the forces of heaven have lordship because they are general, whereas the inferior forces serve because they are limited and particular. And, as to the creations of art, we have assigned the preparation of materials as such a reason and cause. Thus, stone-cutting is the servant of building and bridle-making of warfare because they prepare and dispose material for them. And, as to the rational operations of the sciences, we have assigned nearness to what is best as the reason and cause; for that science which attains what is best more completely is lord, and the others are its handmaids.

But in the case of powers of the fourth kind — the ruling and governing powers — we shall say that all three of these causes come together at once. For we shall say that earthly power and rule must obey and serve spiritual power and rule for all three of the reasons so far given: because it is more particular, and because it disposes and prepares material, and also because the one does not come near to or attain what is best as does the other.

Now the ecclesiastical power is more universal than the earthly because the Church herself is said to be Catholic, that is, universal, as Isidore says in the final chapter of *Etymologiae* 7; for he says that 'catholic' is to be translated as 'universal' or 'general', and he adds that 'catholic' is the Greek word for 'universal'.[2] Therefore, if it is an article of faith that we must believe in the Holy Catholic Church, he is not truly faithful who does not believe the Church to be Catholic, that is, universal, and Holy, that is, established and made firm because founded upon a firm Rock; or Holy, that is, pure and spotless, according to what is said in Ephesians 5: 'That Christ might present it to Himself as a glorious Church, having no spot or blemish.'[3] The Church, therefore, is Holy and Catholic, that is, universal; but she would not be truly universal if she did not rule universally over all things.

But the remaining ruling powers are particular, for none of them is a power without which a man cannot obtain salvation. And this is especially so if we speak of secular rulers and earthly powers, for he who withdraws himself from these comes nearer to salvation. For the clergy, who are not under the earthly power, are

1. The thought of this paragraph seems somewhat confused, but the point is evidently that just as metaphysics, though the highest of the sciences discovered by man, is nonetheless subject to theology, so even the highest of earthly powers is subject to the Church. Cf. Aquinas, *Summa theologiae* Ia 1:6. See also p. 129, below.
2. *Etym.* 7:14:4 (PL 82:294).
3. Eph. 5:2.

quam laici, qui sub potestate terrena[1] collocantur. Potestas itaque terrena non est universalis ut, nisi quis sit sub ea, non possit salutem consequi. Immo, ut diximus, clerici, qui non sunt sub potestate terrena, sunt in statu perfecciori quam laici.[2]

Semper enim voluit Dominus non clericos solum[3] liberos esse a potestate terrena, sed eciam confugientes ad clericos voluit immunitatem et libertatem consequi. Nam Numeris penultimo mandavit Deus[4] quod Levitis qui serviebant altari, per quos, secundum Hugonem, intelliguntur clerici, darentur quadraginta octo urbes sive quadraginta octo oppida. Mandavit eciam quod non solum darentur eis oppida et urbes ad habitandum, sed eciam suburbana ad animalia nutriendum. Voluit eciam quod huiusmodi suburbia se protenderent contra[5] omnem plagam celi sive contra[6] omnem partem, videlicet contra[7] orientem, occidentem, meridiem et septentrionem. Mandavit insuper quod de huiusmodi quadraginta octo urbibus sive quadraginta octo oppidis sex deberent esse separata in auxilium fugitivorum, ut fugerent ad ea qui fuderint sanguinem.

Habentes ergo gladium materialem et iudicium sanguinis non habebant auctoritatem exercendi huiusmodi iudicium contra fugientes[8] ad illa sex oppida Levitarum, id est[9] clericorum; per quod sufficienter monstratur quod non solum nunc in lege gracie, ubi sacerdocium est longe dignius quam esset in lege scripta — quia hic est veritas, ibi autem erat figura, nunc autem in altari vere continetur Christus, vere est ibi corpus quod traxit Christus de virgine,[10] est ibi et[11] suus proprius sanguis, licet[12] non sub propria specie, sed sub specie panis et vini; secundum virtutem[13] tamen est ibi Christus et secundum propriam substanciam, qui in sacramentis veteris legis solum erat secundum figuram: si ergo tunc in lege veteri sacerdocium et clerus[14] erant tante dignitatis quod non solum ipsi erant exempti a potestate laicali, sed eciam confugientes ad ipsos secundum determinata oppida, dato quod effudissent sanguinem et quod merita eorum exigerent, quod subirent iudicium sanguinis, nihilominus tamen salvi erant a[15] dicto iudicio,[16] multo itaque forcius nunc, ubi[17] sacerdocium est dignius[18] et[19] status clericalis[20] perfeccior, clerus non est subiectus potestati terrene.[21] Immo, et[22] confugientes[23] ad clericos, et potissime fugientes ad loca Deo[24] dedicata,[25] in quibus locis serviunt clerici, dato quod incurrerent mortis iudicium, terrena potestas non poterit in eos suam exercere[26] potenciam.[27] Que omnia particularitatem potestatis terrene et libertatem et immunitatem clericorum arguunt et demonstrant.

Est ergo particularis terrena potestas, quia non habet super omnibus potestatem; potestas autem ecclesiastica est universalis. Quod figuratum[28] fuit in libro

---

1: sunt in statu … terrena] *om.* F   2: Ceteri autem … laici] *om.* C   3: clericos solum] solum clericos CF   4: Deus] Dominus CF   5: contra] circa FV[2]   6: contra] circa F *om.* V[2]
7: contra] circa FPV[1]V[2]   8: fugientes] fugitivos RV[1]   9: id est] vel F   10: virgine] et *add.* FV[2]
11: et] *om.* FV[2]   12: licet] sed F si V[2]   13: virtutem] veritatem FV[2]   14: clerus] clerum F
15: a] *om.* F   16: a dicto iudicio] *om.* C   17: ubi] est *add.* FV[2]   18: dignius] dignior F
19: et] *om.* FV[2]   20: clericalis] et *add.* FV[2]   21: potestati terrene] terrene potestati F   22: et] *om.* C   23: confugientes] fugientes F   24: Deo] Domino F   25: dedicata] dicata FV[2]
26: exercere] extendere CF   27: potenciam] potestatem F   28: Quod figuratum] que figurata C

in a more perfect state than are the laity, who are placed under the earthly power. Thus, the earthly power is not universal in such a way that no one can obtain salvation unless he is under it. On the contrary, as we have said, the clergy, who are not under the earthly power, are in a more perfect state than the laity.

For the Lord always willed not only that the clergy should be exempt from earthly power, but He willed also that those who take refuge with the clergy should obtain immunity and liberty. For in the penultimate chapter of Numbers, God commanded that the Levites who served the altar — by whom, according to Hugh, we are to understand the clergy[1] — should be given forty-eight towns or forty-eight strongholds.[2] Also, He commanded not only that these strongholds and towns were to be given to them as dwelling-places, but the surrounding lands also, for the support of their cattle. Moreover, He desired that these surrounding lands should extend in every direction under heaven or towards all the corners of the earth: that is, to the east, west, south, and north. Furthermore, He commanded that, of these forty-eight towns or forty-eight strongholds, six were to be set aside for the aid of fugitives, so that those who had shed blood might flee to them.[3]

Therefore, those who had the material sword and the judgment of blood had no authority to execute such judgment against those who fled to the six strongholds of the Levites, that is, of the clergy. And it is sufficiently demonstrated by this that if, even then, under the Old Law, the priesthood and clergy were so great in dignity that not only were they themselves exempt from lay power, but even those who took refuge with them in their appointed strongholds — even though they had shed blood and deserved to suffer the judgment of blood — were protected from that judgment: then now, when priesthood is still greater in dignity and the clerical state still more perfect, the priest is certainly not subject to the earthly power. For priesthood is now far greater in dignity under the Law of Grace than it was under the Written Law; for what was there prefigured is now established in truth. Now Christ truly rests upon the altar; the body which Christ received from the Virgin is truly there; His own Blood is there: not, indeed, under their own species, but under the species of bread and wine; yet Christ is there in His strength and in His own substance, Who was only prefigured in the sacraments of the Old Law. Indeed, the earthly power will not be able to exercise its authority even against those who have incurred the judgment of death if they take refuge with the clergy, and especially if they flee to the places dedicated to God, in which places the clergy serve. And all these things argue and demonstrate the particularity of the earthly power and the liberty and immunity of the clergy.

The earthly power, therefore, is particular, because it does not have power over all men; but the ecclesiastical power is universal. This was prefigured in the book

1. Hugh of Saint Victor, *De sacramentis fidei christianae* 2:2:3 (PL176:417).
2. Num. 35:2–8.
3. Num. 35:6.

Numerorum, quando Levitis, id est clericis, data fuerunt suburbia versus omnem partem celi; in quo figurabatur quod Ecclesia, que succedere debebat Levitis qui serviebant altari, in universo orbe et in omni parte dominari debebat. Nam quilibet de iure est sub illo, sub quo non existens non potest salutem consequi. In universo itaque orbe debet Ecclesia dominari et omnes debent esse sub ea, sub qua non existentes clausas invenient celi ianuas, ut ad regna celorum non valeant introire.

Hoc eciam universale dominium Ecclesie non solum fuit figuratum in lege veteri,[1] sed fuit expressum[2] inter articulos fidei, qui non sunt restringendi, sed dilatandi, cum super eis fundentur omnia que sunt credenda et tota Christiana fides. Quilibet autem verus Christianus debet confiteri hunc articulum, quod Ecclesia est Sancta et Catholica. Non autem esset Catholica, id est universalis, nisi omnibus, tam fidelibus quam rebus fidelium, dominaretur. Nam Ecclesia est Catholica universaliter dominando, et ipsi fideles ex hoc sunt Catholici universaliter se Ecclesie subiciendo. Nullus autem se dicat esse Catholicum nisi universali[3] Ecclesie sit subiectus, et nullus confiteatur Ecclesiam esse Catholicam nisi confiteatur eam universaliter dominari. Non est autem quis universaliter subiectus Ecclesie nisi se et sua Ecclesie subiciat, primo quidem se et postea sua; quia, ut habetur Geneseos IV, quod respexit Dominus ad Abel et ad munera eius: prius ergo ad Abel, et postea ad munera. Primo ergo fideles debent se subicere Ecclesie, et postea sua. Utraque autem sunt Ecclesie, et fideles et res fidelium, et apostoli utrumque[4] volebant possidere et utrisque[5] volebant dominari non ut seipsos exaltarent, sed ut Ecclesiam dilatarent et eam universalem et Catholicam facerent. Ideo dicit glossa ad [II] Corinthios VI,[6] gloriam fuisse apostolorum 'tam res quam dominos earum[7] possidere.'

Revertamur ergo ad propositum et dicamus quod quasi singula[8] verba huius racionis concludunt terrenam potestatem, tam secundum se quam secundum sua, potestati ecclesiastice debere esse subiectam. Tamen, ut prosequamur nostram materiam prout in rubrica capituli est descripta, dicemus, ut est[9] per habita manifestum,[10] quod dominium ecclesiasticum est universale, dominium terrenum est particulare.

Propter quod dominium ecclesiasticum imitatur virtutes celestes, quarum est in omnia influere. Dominium vero terrenum imitatur virtutes istas inferiores, quarum est particulares effectus efficere, ut ignis ita calefacit, quod per se loquendo non infrigidat, et aqua ita infrigidat, quod per se loquendo non calefacit. Virtus autem celestis utrumque peragit, quia iuvat aquam ad infrigidandum, quia virtute celi subtracta, secundum hunc ordinem quem videmus, aqua non posset infrigidare; hoc eciam modo iuvat ignem ad calefaciendum. Omnes enim

---

1: veteri] in quocumque loco *add.* F   2: expressum] in lege nova et non fuit expressum in quocumque loco sed fuit expressum *add.* CV²   3: universali] universaliter F   4: utrumque] utraque FV²   5: utrisque] utrorumque F   6: VI] VII CPV¹V²   XI F   7: dominos earum] earum dominos CFV²   8: singula] signacula FV²   9: est] *om.* C   10: manifestum] est *add.* C

of Numbers, when the Levites, that is, the clergy, were given the surrounding lands under every part of heaven. In this it was prefigured that the Church, who was to succeed to the Levites who served the altar, was to have lordship over the whole world and in every part thereof. For, as of right, every man is under that without which he cannot obtain salvation. Thus, the Church must have lordship over the whole world, and all men must be under her; for those who are not under her will find the gates of heaven closed, and so will not gain entry into the Kingdom of Heaven.

And this universal lordship of the Church was not only prefigured in the Old Law, but has been made manifest among the articles of faith: which must be interpreted not narrowly, but broadly, since upon them are founded all the things which are to be believed and the entire Christian faith. And every true Christian must confess this article: that the Church is Holy and Catholic. But she would not be Catholic — that is, universal — if she did not have lordship equally over all the faithful and over all the possessions of the faithful. For the Church is Catholic because she exercises a universal lordship, and the faithful themselves are Catholics because of their universal subjection to the Church. Let no one say that he is a Catholic, then, if he is not subject to the Universal Church; and let no one confess the Church to be Catholic unless he confesses that she has a universal lordship. But no one is universally subject to the Church unless he places himself and what is his under the Church: first himself, indeed, and then what is his. For, as is established in Genesis 4, the Lord was mindful of Abel and of his offerings:[1] of Abel first, therefore, and of his offerings afterwards. Therefore, the faithful must subject first themselves and then what is theirs to the Church; for both belong to the Church: the faithful and the possessions of the faithful. The apostles also desired to have both and to be lords of both: not in order to exalt themselves, but in order to extend the Church and to make her universal and Catholic. And so a gloss on II Corinthians 6 says that it was the glory of the apostles 'to possess both things and their lords.'[2]

Let us turn again to our proposition, therefore, and say that almost every word of this argument supports the conclusion that the earthly power, both in itself and in what belongs to it, must be subject to the ecclesiastical power. Nonetheless, in order to pursue our subject matter as described in the heading of this chapter, we shall [adduce still further arguments to] indicate that, as is clear from what has been said, ecclesiastical lordship is universal whereas earthly lordship is particular.

For ecclesiastical lordship imitates the forces of heaven, whose task it is to exert influence over all things; but earthly lordship imitates those inferior forces whose task it is to bring about particular effects. Thus, fire heats in such a way that it cannot of itself be said to cool; and water cools in such a way that it cannot of itself be said to heat. But the force of heaven accomplishes both. For it assists water to cool since, according to the order that we see, water could not cool if the force of heaven were withdrawn. And, in the same way, it assists fire to heat. For all these

1.   Gen. 4:4.
2.   *Glossa ordinaria*, PL 114:560.

iste virtutes inferiores, tamquam famulantes celo, quecumque agunt, illa efficiunt in virtute celi. Sic et terreni domini, tamquam famulantes Ecclesie, in omnibus suis actibus et in omnibus que ad ipsos spectant debent recognoscere Ecclesiam Catholicam et universalem, id est universaliter dominantem. Erit igitur terrena potestas sub ecclesiastica sicut particularis sub universali; quam subieccionem habent virtutes inferiores ad celestes.

Secundo, erit terrena potestas sub ecclesiastica sicut preparans materiam est sub ea cui preparat. Nam ad terrenam potestatem pertinet per Ecclesiam et sub Ecclesia accipere gladium materialem et dominari rebus materialibus et rebus temporalibus et eciam humanis corporibus, quantum ad personas laicas et ad res earum super quibus potenciam acceperunt.[1] Erit ergo potestatis terrene officium super hiis iusticiam facere ut nullus iniurietur alteri[2] in proprio corpore nec in propriis rebus, sed quilibet civis[3] et quilibet fidelis gaudeat bonis.[4] Officium ergo terrene potestatis est materiam preparare ne princeps ecclesiasticus[5] in spiritualibus impediatur.[6:7] Nam corpus factum est ut serviat anime, et temporalia ut deserviant[8] corpori. Tunc est ergo bene dispositum corpus quando bene deservit anime, et tunc sunt bene disposita et ordinata temporalia quando ordinantur ad sufficienciam vite corporalis et ad indigenciam humanorum corporum. Totum ergo officium potestatis terrene est[9] ista bona exteriora[10] et materialia sic gubernare et regere ut non impediantur fideles in pace consciencie et in pace animi et in tranquillitate mentis. Hoc enim modo iusticia et pax osculate sunt non solum in hiis que sunt ad Deum, quia nisi nos vivamus iuste cum Deo non habebimus pacem cum ipso,[11] sed eciam iusticia in istis exterioribus multum facit ad tranquillitatem animi et ad pacem mentis. Si omnes enim[12] essent ita perfecti sicut dicitur Matth. V, 'Si quis te percusserit[13] in dexteram maxillam, prebe illi et alteram, et ei qui vult tecum in iudicio contendere et tunicam tuam tollere, dimitte[14] ei et pallium,' quantum ad pacientes iniuriam forte non esset opus iusticie terrene. Sed quia non sunt omnes ita perfecti, et quia non solum bonum est reprimere iniurias ne offendantur pacientes, sed eciam ne offendant agentes, opus fuit instituere potestatem terrenam propter servandam iusticiam in[15] corporibus et in rebus temporalibus, ad salvandam tranquillitatem animi et pacem mentis,[16] ad salvandam tranquillitatem[17] in rebus spiritualibus.

Hoc ergo potissime faciunt principes terreni, quod disponunt et preparant materiam principi ecclesiastico. Illi ergo salvant iusticiam in rebus temporalibus et materialibus, ut salvetur pax mentis et tranquillitas in rebus spiritualibus, ut ille qui spiritualiter dominatur possit liberius dominari. Sicut ergo frenifactiva, imponens frenum equo, preparat equum militi ut ei liberius famuletur, sic[18] potestas terrena,

1: acceperunt] accipiunt F   2: alteri] ei PV[1]   3: civis] del. C   4: bonis] suis add. C   5: princeps ecclesiasticus] om. C   6: Officium ... impediatur] et materiam preparare ne officium ergo terrene potestatis in spiritualibus impediatur FV[2]   7: impediatur] impediantur C   8: deserviant] serviant C   9: est] om. C   10: exteriora] temporalia C terrena FV[2]   11: non habebimus ... ipso] om. F   12: omnes enim] enim omnes F   13: percusserit] percussit F   14: dimitte] remitte CFV[2]   15: in] om. F   16: mentis] et add. C   17: animi et ... tranquillitatem] om. F   18: sic] et add. F

inferior forces, as servants of heaven, effect whatever they accomplish through the power of heaven. And so earthly lords, as the Church's servants in all their actions and in everything that belongs to them, must acknowledge that the Church is Catholic and universal: that is, universal in lordship. Thus, the earthly power will be under the ecclesiastical as the particular is under the universal, which form of subjection is displayed by the inferior [natural] forces relative to the heavenly.

Second, the earthly power will be under the ecclesiastical as an art which prepares material is under that for which it prepares it. For it pertains to the earthly power to receive the material sword through the Church and under the Church, and to exercise lordship over material things and temporal affairs, and, so far as lay persons and the property over which they have received power are concerned, over human bodies also. Therefore, it will be the duty of the earthly power to do justice in these respects, so that no one may injure another in his own body or in his own property, but every citizen and every faithful man may enjoy his goods. Therefore, it is the duty of the earthly power to prepare material so that the ruler of the Church may not be impeded in spiritual tasks. For the body was made to serve the soul and temporal goods to serve the body. The body is therefore well disposed when it serves the soul well, and temporal goods are well disposed and ordered when they are ordered to the requirements of bodily life and the needs of human bodies. Therefore, the whole duty of the earthly power is to govern and rule these external and material goods in such a way that the faithful are not impeded in the peace of conscience and in peace of soul and in tranquillity of mind. For, in this way, not only have justice and peace kissed[1] in those things which are of God — since unless we live justly with God we shall not have peace with Him — but also justice among these external goods conduces greatly to tranquillity of soul and to peace of mind. For if all men were perfect in their suffering of injustice in the way described in Matthew 5 — 'If someone shall strike you on your right cheek, turn to him the other also; and if someone shall sue you at law and take away your coat, let him have your cloak also'[2] — then perhaps there would be no need of earthly justice. But since not all men are thus perfect, and since it is good to restrain injustice not only so that victims may not suffer harm, but also so that offenders may not inflict it, there was a need to institute the earthly power to preserve justice as between bodies and temporal things, to preserve tranquillity of soul and peace of mind, and to preserve tranquillity in spiritual matters.

Above all, therefore, the task of earthly princes is to dispose and prepare material for the ruler of the Church. Therefore, they preserve justice in the temporal and material spheres so that peace of mind and tranquillity may be preserved in the spiritual, and so that he who exercises lordship spiritually may exercise lordship more freely. Therefore, just as bridle-making, by placing a bridle on a horse, prepares the horse for the soldier so that it may serve him more freely, so the earthly

1. Cf. Psalm 85:10.
2. Matt. 5:39–40.

imponens frenum laicis ne forefaciant in Ecclesiam nec in se ipsos, disponit eos[1] ut potestati ecclesiastice liberius sint subiecti. Et sicut dolativa, dolans lapides, disponit eos ut edificator ex ipsis lapidibus possit debitam et ordinatam domum facere, sic, quia fideles sunt membra ex quibus conficitur corpus Ecclesie et sunt lapides ex quibus conficitur spirituale templum quod est Ecclesia, cuius lapis angularis et fundamentum est Christus, iuxta illud ad Ephesios II, 'Ipso summo angulari lapide Christo Iesu, in quo omnis edificacio constructa[2] crescit in templum sanctum in Domino, in quo vos coedificamini,' etc.: terrena potestas, per iusticiam in exterioribus bonis, dolat et disponit istos lapides ad pacem mentis et ad tranquillitatem animi, ut ex ei[3] spirituale templum liberius et facilius construatur.

Patet ergo quod terrena potestas et ars gubernandi populum secundum terrenam potestatem est ars disponens materiam ad disposicionem[4] ecclesiastice potestatis. Quare, sicut frenifactiva supponitur militari, et sicut dolativa est subiecta domifactive, ut omnia agant secundum earum nutum[5] et voluntatem, et ut omnia instrumenta earum et omnia earum organa ordinent ad nutum et ad voluntatem superiorum arcium, sic ars dominandi secundum terrenam potestatem et ipsa terrena potestas debet sic esse subiecta potestati ecclesiastice ut seipsam et omnia organa et instrumenta sua ordinet ad obsequium et ad nutum spiritualis potencie. Et quia organa et instrumenta potestatis terrene sunt civilis potencia, arma bellica,[6] bona temporalia que habet,[7] leges[8] et constituciones quas condit,[9] ideo seipsam et omnia hec tamquam eius organa et instrumenta ordinare debet ad obsequium et voluntatem ecclesiastice potestatis. Ipsa itaque secularis potestas, secundum se et secundum omnia prefata organa, subicitur ecclesiastice potestati.

Tercio, erit[10] terrena potestas sub ecclesiastica tamquam[11] attingens optimum sub ea que magis attingit; quem modum subieccionis videmus in scienciis, ut quia metaphysica, que est de[12] Deo, est dea scienciarum inventarum ab homine, et omnes alie huiusmodi[13] sciencie sunt sub metaphysica et famulantur sibi, et ipsa dirigit alias sciencias. Secundum hunc eundem modum potestas ecclesiastica, que est spiritualis et in hiis que sunt ad Deum, est domina potestatis terrene, et ad eam spectat potestatem huiusmodi[14] dirigere, et potestas terrena debet sacerdotis imperio esse subiecta.

Aperi ergo oculos tuos et vide;[15] interroga virtutes naturales et annunciabunt tibi; considera modos artificiales[16] et dicent tibi; animadverte[17] consideraciones scienciales et manifestabunt tibi. Vides[18] in virtutibus naturalibus quod particulares virtutes et terrene subiciuntur secundum se et secundum sua virtutibus universalibus et celestibus; vides eciam in artificialibus quod artes preparantes materiam subiciuntur secundum se et secundum[19] sua hiis quibus materiam preparant; vides insuper

---

1: eos] *om.* PV[1]   2: constructa] constituta C   3: eis] ipsis C   4: disposicionem] gubernacionem CFV[2]   5: nutum] virtutum F   6: bellica] et *add.* F   7: que habet] *om.* C   8: habet, leges] habent reges F   9: condit] ostendit FV[2]   10: erit] erat *mss*   11: tamquam] minus *add.* C   12: de] a FV[2]   13: alie huiusmodi] huiusmodi alie F   14: potestatem huiusmodi] huiusmodi potestatem CF   15: vide] inde F   16: artificiales] naturales F   17: animadverte] animadvertere F   18: Vides] vide PV[1]   19: secundum] *om.* CF

power, by placing a bridle on the laity so that they may not offend against the Church or each other, disposes them so that they may be the more freely subject to the ecclesiastical power. And just as stone-cutting, by cutting stones, disposes them so that the builder may make from those stones a commodious and well-arranged house, so — since the faithful people are the members of which the body of the Church is composed, and are the stones of which the spiritual temple which is the Church is assembled, whose cornerstone and foundation is Christ, according to Ephesians 2: 'Christ Jesus Himself being the chief cornerstone, upon Whom the whole building grows into a holy temple in the Lord, upon Whom also you are built together,' and so on[1] — the earthly power, by means of justice in external goods, cuts and disposes these stones for the sake of peace of mind and tranquillity of soul, so that a spiritual temple may be the more freely and easily built from them.

It is clear, therefore, that earthly power and the art of governing a people by earthly power is the art of disposing material for the sake of the disposition of the ecclesiastical power. And so, just as bridle-making is subordinate to warfare, and just as stone-cutting is subject to building, so that all that they do is subject to the command and will of the superior arts and they subordinate all their tools and all their instruments to their command and will: so the art of exercising lordship by means of earthly power, and the earthly power itself, must be so subject to the ecclesiastical power that it subordinates itself and all its instruments and tools to the service and to the command of the spiritual power. And because the instruments and tools of the earthly power are civil might, the weapons of war, the temporal goods which it has, and the laws and constitutions which it establishes, it must therefore subordinate itself and all these things which it has as instruments and tools to the service and will of the ecclesiastical power. Thus, secular power, in itself and with all the instruments just mentioned, is subject to the ecclesiastical power.

Third, the earthly power will be under the ecclesiastical as that which attains what is best is under that which attains it more completely. We see this mode of subjection in the sciences; for metaphysics, which is concerned with God, is the goddess of the sciences discovered by man, and all other such sciences are under metaphysics and serve her, and she herself directs the other sciences. According to this same mode, the ecclesiastical power, which is spiritual and concerned with those things which are of God, is mistress over the earthly power, and it rests with her to direct such power; and the earthly power must be subject to the command of the priest.

Open your eyes, therefore, and see: ask the forces of nature and they will proclaim it to you;[2] consider the ways of the arts and they will tell you; attend to the investigations of the sciences and they will show you. You see, among the forces of nature, that the particular and earthly forces are subject in themselves and in what belongs to them to the universal and heavenly forces. You see also in the arts that those arts which prepare material are subordinate in themselves and in what belongs to them to those for which they prepare material. You see moreover,

1. Eph. 2:20–22.
2. Cf. Deut. 32:7; II Kings 19:16.

in consideracionibus sciencialibus quod sciencia magis attingens optimum omnibus aliis scienciis dominatur. Et quia omnia ista concurrunt in potestate ecclesiastica respectu terrene, quia terrena est particularior, disponens materiam et[1] est[2] minus attingens optimum, exinde claro clarius arguitur et concluditur quod huiusmodi potestas, et[3] secundum se et secundum sua, potestati ecclesiastice subdatur et obsequatur.

CAPITULUM VII: *Quod omne dominium cum iusticia, sive sit[4] rerum sive personarum, sive sit utile sive potestativum, nonnisi sub Ecclesia et per Ecclesiam esse potest.[5]*

Declaravimus in precedenti capitulo quod sicut virtutes terrene secundum totum illud[6] quod sunt sunt subdite celestibus, et quod[7] sicut alie sciencie humanitus invente sunt subdite metaphysice, et sicut artes preparantes[8] materiam secundum se et secundum omnia sua organa superioribus artibus[9] supponuntur, sic potestas terrena, secundum se et secundum totum id quod est et secundum omnia sua organa, sacerdocio debet esse subiecta. Dicebamus eciam quod organa potestatis terrene sunt civilis potencia, temporalia, arma bellica,[10] constituciones et leges condite ab huiusmodi potestate. Non ergo secundum se et secundum omnia sua organa[11] hec potestas illi subicitur nisi constituciones et leges condite a potestate terrena ad canones ecclesiasticos ordinentur, et nisi civilis potencia temporalia et arma bellica et quecumque possidet potestas terrena ad adminiculum et ad[12] famulatum iurisdiccionis ecclesiastice disponantur.

In presenti autem capitulo volumus declarare quod nullum est dominium cum iusticia, sive sit dominium super res temporales sive super personas laicas, de quo magis posset dubium exoriri, nisi sit sub Ecclesia et per Ecclesiam institutum. Probabimus[13] enim racionibus et auctoritatibus quod non sufficit quod quicumque[14] sit generatus carnaliter, nisi sit per Ecclesiam regeneratus spiritualiter, quod[15] possit cum iusticia rei alicui dominari nec rem aliquam possidere, ut hic homo qui est a patre carnali generatus, nisi sit per Ecclesiam regeneratus, in hereditatem paternam[16] non potest cum iusticia subcedere nec dominium rerum paternarum poterit cum iusticia obtinere. Si igitur inicium[17] habendi hereditatem paternam et subcedendi in dominium hereditatis paterne habet quis ex eo, quod est a patre carnaliter generatus, complementum tamen huiusmodi dominii[18] et perfeccionem sic subcedendi habet ex eo, quod est per Ecclesiam regeneratus. Quare, si pater habet dominium hereditatis cum filio et habet dominium superius[19] quam habeat filius, Ecclesia habet dominium cuiuscumque[20] hereditatis et quarumcumque rerum, et habet superius et excellencius huiusmodi dominium quam habeant ipsi fideles. Et[21] quia, ut tangebamus, subcedendi in hereditatem paternam quia a patre generatus est

---

1: et] *om.* C   2: est] *om.* F   3: et] *om.* CF   4: *sit*] *om.* P   5: *esse potest*] potest esse C
6: illud] id CFV² 7: quod] *om.* C   8: preparantes] preparantur FV²   9: artibus] quibus *add.* F
10: bellica] et *add.* CFV²   11: sua organa] organa sua F   12: ad] *om.* FV²   13: Probabimus]
prohibimus F   14: quicumque] quilibet FV²   15: quod] non *add.* F   16: hereditatem paternam]
hereditate paterna F   17: inicium] *om.* PV¹   18: dominii] dominium C   19: dominium superius] superius dominium F   20: cuiuscumque] cuiusque F   21: Et] *om.* CFV²

in the investigations of the sciences, that the science which attains what is best more completely is mistress of the other sciences. And since all these things come together in the ecclesiastical power in relation to the earthly — because the earthly power is more particular, disposes material, and attains what is best less completely — it is thus demonstrated and shown clearer than clearly that such power is, in itself and in what belongs to it, subject and subservient to the ecclesiastical power.

CHAPTER VII: *That there can be no lordship with justice, whether over things or persons, either of use or of power, except under the Church and through the Church.*

We have shown in the preceding chapter that, just as [the natural] earthly forces are subject in all that they are to the heavenly, and just as the other sciences discovered by man are subject to metaphysics,[1] and just as the arts which prepare material are, in themselves and with all their instruments, placed under the superior arts, so must the earthly power, in itself and in all that it is and with all its instruments, be subject to the priesthood. Also, we have said that the instruments of the earthly power are civil might, temporal goods, the weapons of war, and the constitutions and laws established by such power. Therefore, the one power would not be subject in itself and with all its instruments to the other if the constitutions and laws established by the earthly power were not subordinated to the canons of the Church, and if civil might and temporal goods and the weapons of war and whatever else the earthly power may have were not disposed in such a way as to aid and serve the Church's jurisdiction.

Now in the present chapter we wish to show that there is no lordship with justice, whether it be a lordship over temporal things or (and here there is more possibility that doubt may arise) over lay persons, except under the Church and as instituted through the Church. For we shall prove by arguments and authorities that for a man to be carnally begotten does not suffice to enable him to be the lord of anything or to possess anything with justice unless he is also spiritually regenerated through the Church; so that the man who is begotten of a carnal father cannot with justice succeed to a paternal inheritance, and cannot with justice acquire lordship of the paternal estate, unless he is also regenerated through the Church. Thus, if his possession of the paternal inheritance and his succession to the lordship of the paternal inheritance has its origin in the fact that he has been carnally begotten of a father, such lordship is nonetheless completed and his succession made perfect by the fact that he is regenerated through the Church. And so, if a father [in a sense] holds the lordship of an inheritance [jointly] with his son [who will succeed to it], yet has a superior lordship to that which his son has, the Church has lordship over every inheritance and over all things, and has such lordship in a superior and more excellent manner than do the faithful people. And since, as we have noted, to succeed to a paternal inheritance because begotten of a father is the beginning

1. See p. 119 and n. 1 on p. 121.

iusticia iniciata, sed subcedendi in talem hereditatem quia est quis per Ecclesiam regeneratus est iusticia perfecta et consummata, et in tantum ista iusticia quam dicimus esse perfectam consummativam,[1] est fecundior et universalior quam illa[2] quod, si ista desit, illa tollatur.[3] Nam, ut clare patebit, si quis a patre esset[4] carnaliter generatus et non esset eciam[5] per Ecclesiam spiritualiter regeneratus, dominium hereditatis paterne non posset cum iusticia possidere.

Hiis itaque prelibatis ut nostrum propositum liquido declaretur, incipiamus a sacramentis tam legis nature quam scripte[6] quam eciam legis gracie, quia ex differencia horum sacramentorum accipietur via et fundamentum ad declarandam propositam veritatem.

Videtur autem Hugo aperte asserere quod dominium temporalium et terrenorum, sive sit utile sive potestativum, Ecclesia a[7] secularibus principibus recognoscat,[8] et pia largicione fidelium Ecclesia incepit temporalia dominia possidere: quod[9] videtur nostro proposito contrarium, cum dixerimus[10] quod dominium quodcumque cum iusticia nonnisi per Ecclesiam haberi potest. Sed si distinguatur inter dominia, patebit quomodo potestates terrene dominium, quodcumque habent,[11] per Ecclesiam acceperunt; patebit eciam quomodo verificari potest quod Ecclesia a[12] principibus rerum temporalium dominia[13] recognoscat. Sed de hiis in sequentibus capitulis intendimus diffusius pertractare.[14] Nam sic volumus iura ecclesiastica describere et reddere que sunt Dei Deo, ut eciam reddantur que sunt Cesaris Cesari, et ut reges et principes habentes materialem gladium suis iuribus non priventur.

Redeamus ergo ad propositum et dicamus quod ex differencia sacramentorum poterit proposita veritas declarari; quia sacramenta legis nature erant indeterminata et voluntaria, sed in lege scripta fuerunt sacramenta determinata et particularia, in lege quidem gracie sunt sacramenta non solum determinata et certa, sed eciam sunt[15] generalia et universalia.[16] Quilibet enim sub lege nature, secundum[17] quod Dominus sibi inspirabat,[18] sic offerebat oblaciones et sacrificia. Propter quod sacramenta illa voluntaria erant, quia quilibet id agebat pro libito voluntatis. Unde Hugo, in libro[19] *De sacramentis* libro I, parte XI, ait quod inter sacramenta sub naturali lege et sub lege scripta et sub gracia, 'hoc interesse conspicimus, quod illa voluntatis magis esse videntur, ista necessitatis. Illa,' videlicet sacramenta in lege nature, 'ex voto celebrata' fuerunt,[20] 'ista,' videlicet in lege scripta et sub gracia, 'ex precepto. In lege' itaque nature 'neque sacramenta neque decima neque sacrificia neque oblaciones,' ut ipse Hugo ait, 'ita homini ex necessitate sunt indicta[21] ut qui ea non executus fuisset reatum prevaricacionis

1: consummativam] consummatam FV[2]   2: illa] *om.* C   3: illa tollatur] tollatur et illa C

4: a patre esset] esset a patre CF   5: eciam] *om.* CF   6: scripte] scripture F   7: a] *om.* F

8: recognoscat] cognoscat FV[2]   9: quod] ut C   10: dixerimus] diximus F   11: habent] *om.* F

12: a] *om.* F   13: dominia] temporalia CPV[1]V[2]   14: pertractare] declarare C   15: sunt] *om.* F

16: generalia et universalia] universalia et generalia CF   17: secundum] *om.* CF   18: sibi inspirabat] inspirabat sibi CF   19: libro] *om.* FV[2]   20: fuerunt] sunt CFV[2]   21: indicta] indita FV[2]

of justice, but to succeed to such an inheritance because regenerated through the Church is justice perfected and consummated, then that justice which we say is thus perfected and consummated is so much more fruitful and universal than the former that, if it is lacking, the former is annulled. For, as will become clear, if a man were carnally begotten of a father but not also spiritually regenerated through the Church, he could not with justice have lordship over the paternal inheritance.

Thus, having first touched upon these considerations in order to make our proposition clear, let us begin by considering the sacraments of the law of nature and of the Written Law and of the Law of Grace in turn. For, by so distinguishing these sacraments, a way towards and a foundation for the truth of our argument may be discovered.

Hugh, however, seems clearly to assert that the Church may acknowledge that she holds temporal and earthly lordships, both of use and of power, from secular princes, and that the Church began to have temporal lordships by the pious gift of the faithful.[1] And this seems to contradict our argument; for we have said that no lordship can be held with justice except through the Church. If a distinction is made between kinds of lordship, however, the way in which earthly powers have received through the Church whatever lordship they hold will become clear, and the way in which it can be confirmed that the Church may acknowledge that she holds lordship over temporal things from princes will also become clear. But we intend to treat of these questions at greater length in subsequent chapters.[2] For we wish to describe ecclesiastical rights, and to render to God those things which are God's, in such a way that those things which are Caesar's may also be rendered to Caesar,[3] and so that kings and princes, having the material sword, may not be deprived of their rights.

Let us return to our proposition, therefore, and say that it will be possible to show the truth of our argument by distinguishing the sacraments. For the sacraments of the law of nature were indeterminate and voluntary, but, under the Written Law, the sacraments were determinate and particular, and, under the Law of Grace, the sacraments are not only determinate and certain, but are also general and universal. For, under the law of nature, each man offered oblations and sacrifices as the Lord inspired him. And so those sacraments were voluntary, since each man acted of his own free will. Hence, in the book *De sacramentis*, Book 1, Part 2, Hugh says that: 'We perceive there to be this difference' between the sacraments under the natural law and under the Written law and under Grace; 'that the former appear to be more a matter of will and the latter of necessity. The former,' that is, the sacraments under the law of nature, were 'celebrated from desire; the latter,' that is, under the Written Law and under Grace, 'from precept.' Under the law of nature, then, as Hugh himself says, 'neither sacraments nor tithes nor sacrifices were so imposed upon man from necessity that he who did not perform them

1. Hugh of Saint Victor, *De sacramentis fidei christianae* 2:2:7 (PL 176:420).
2. See Chaps. VIII–XII; Pt. III, Ch. XI.
3. Cf. Matt. 22:21.

incurreret.'[1] Fuerunt ergo illa sacramenta non ex mandato, ut qui ea non faceret[2] reatum incurreret prevaricacionis, sed fuerunt ex voluntate et ex voto, ut qui ea fideliter coleret inveniret meritum devocionis.[3]

Sed in lege quidem veteri sive in lege scripta fuerunt sacramenta determinata et distincta, sed non fuerunt universalia, sed particularia. Erant enim sacramenta illa sub precepto, sed non omnes tenebantur ad illa sacramenta, sed solus Iudaicus populus. Pactum enim fuit inter Deum et Abraham et semen eius quod circumcideretur omne masculum et quod[4] debebat fieri talis circumcisio octava die. Ideo dicitur Geneseos XVII: 'Infans octo dierum circumcidetur in vobis et omne masculinum in generacionibus vestris'; et sequitur quod masculus cuius prepucii caro circumcisa non fuerit delebitur anima illa de populo suo. Igitur si distinctum et si preceptum erat, quid[5] deberent facere, quia infans octo dierum debebat circumcidi, non tamen hoc preceptum erat universale, quia non tangebat nisi masculos tantum, nec tangebat omnes masculos, sed solum masculos de populo Iudaico. Masculi autem alii de populo gentilium eciam post preceptum de circumcisione salvabantur, vel salvari poterant, in fide parentum, nec tenebantur circumcidi, quia non erat eis[6] datum illud preceptum. Ideo Geneseos XVII non mandabatur circumicidi omnis masculus[7] in quibuscumque generacionibus, sed 'in generacionibus vestris,' id est in generacionibus Abrahe.

Sed in lege gracie sunt[8] sacramenta non solum[9] distincta et sub precepto, sed eciam sunt universalia. Ideo dicitur Iohannis III: 'Nisi quis renatus[10] fuerit ex aqua et Spiritu Sancto, non potest introire in regnum Dei'; et[11] Marci ultimo dicitur: 'Euntes in mundum universum predicate evangelium omni creature. Qui crediderit et baptizatus fuerit, salvus erit, qui autem non crediderit, condemnabitur.' Non autem distinguitur hic inter generacionem Abrahe et generaciones alias, nec eciam[12] inter masculos et feminas, sed mandatur quod predicetur evangelium in 'universo mundo' et 'omni creature,' id est omni homini, tam masculo quam femine. Sacramentum ergo universale est baptismus[13] omni tempore, quia[14] si ante octavam diem moriatur infans non baptizatus, de[15] iure communi non dicitur esse salvus. Est eciam universale hoc sacramentum omni generacioni et omni sexui, cum nullus posset consequi salutem sine eo vel in re vel in voto. Et[16] quia hoc sacramentum[17] datur in Ecclesia, ideo Ecclesia est Catholica, id est universalis, et est mater

1: incurreret] incurrerent F   2: faceret] facerent F   3: devocionis] donacionis F   4: quod] om. FV²   5: quid] quia FV²   6: eis] ei F   7: omnis masculus] omnes masculos F   8: sunt] om. C   9: solum] sunt add. C   10: renatus] regeneratus F   11: et] in add. F   12: eciam] om. FV²   13: universale est baptismus] est universale baptismum FV²   14: quia] et add. C   15: de] om. F   16: Et] hoc add. C   17: hoc sacramentum] sacramentum hoc PV¹

incurred the guilt of having failed in his duty.'[1] These sacraments, therefore, were not commanded in such a way that he who did not perform them incurred the guilt of having failed in his duty. Rather, they were celebrated from wish and from desire, so that he who offered them faithfully might earn the reward of devotion.

But under the Old Law or under the Written Law, the sacraments were indeed determinate and distinct, though they were not universal, but particular. For those sacraments were defined by precept, although not all men were bound to [perform] those sacraments, but only the Jewish people. For there was a covenant between God and Abraham and his seed that all males were to be circumcised and that such circumcision should be performed on the eighth day. Thus, it is said in Genesis 17: 'An infant of eight days shall be circumcised among you, and every male of your generations'; and it is added that if any male were not circumcised in the flesh of his foreskin, that soul should be blotted out from among his people.[2] Thus, although what they ought to do was specified and taught — that an infant of eight days was to be circumcised — this precept was nonetheless not universal; for not only did it apply exclusively to males, but it also applied not to all males, but only to the males of the Jewish people. Even after the precept concerning circumcision was given, other males — those of the people of the gentiles — were saved, or could be saved, by the faith of their fathers, and were not bound to be circumcised, since that precept was not given to them. For, in Genesis 17, it was not commanded that all males of whatever generations should be circumcised, but 'of your generations': that is, of the generations of Abraham.

But under the Law of Grace, the sacraments are not only distinct and defined by precept, but they are also universal. And so it is said in John 3: 'Unless a man be born again of water and the Holy Spirit, he cannot enter into the Kingdom of God.'[3] And in the final chapter of Mark it is said: 'Go into all the world and preach the Gospel to every creature. Whoever believes and is baptized will be saved, and whoever does not believe will be condemned.'[4] Here, then, no distinction is made between the generations of Abraham and other generations, or even between males and females. Rather, it is commanded that the Gospel be preached in 'all the world' and 'to every creature': that is, to every human being, whether male or female. Baptism, therefore, is a universal sacrament for all time; for, if an infant should die unbaptized before the eighth day, it is not generally said to be saved as of right.[5] This sacrament is also universal for all generations and for each sex, since no one may obtain salvation without having received it either in fact or by desire. And since this sacrament is conferred in the Church, the Church is therefore Catholic — that is, universal — and is the mother

---

1. *De sacramentis* 1:11:3 (PL 176:344).
2. Gen. 17:12–14.
3. John 3:5.
4. Mark 16:15–16.
5. That is, rather than by the kind of special Divine grace which it is not in the Church's power to confer: see Pt. III, Ch. IX, p. 367.

omnium, cum nullus possit consequi salutem nisi sit subiectus Ecclesie[1] et nisi sit
eius filius. Hanc autem universalitatem habuit Ecclesia et habuit hoc sacramentum
a passione[2] et post passionem Christi. Nam ante passionem currebant legalia et
evangelia, ut[3] et circumcisi salvarentur et eciam baptizati; sed post passionem
Christi legalia fuerunt mortua, ut ex tunc nullus salvaretur nisi baptizatus. Ideo ex
latere Christi dicitur esse formata Ecclesia, quia a passione Christi habent virtutem
sacramenta Ecclesie. Et quia tunc cepit[4] Ecclesia esse[5] universalis, ut nullus salvaretur nisi per sacramenta Ecclesie, quando Christus fuit passus,[6] quia ante passionem, ut diximus, eciam absque hoc sacramento poterat esse salvus,[7] ideo[8] super
illo verbo ad Romanos V, quod Adam est forma futuri Ade, vult glossa quod primus Adam gerebat formam, id est typum et similitudinem, futuri Ade, id est
Christi: ait glossa quod Adam dicitur forma Christi quia sicut ille est pater omnium secundum carnem, sic Christus est pater omnium secundum fidem; et sicut
ex latere Ade dormientis formata est Eva, sic ex latere Domini dormientis in cruce
fluxerunt sacramenta per que salvatur Ecclesia.

Hiis ergo declaratis, volumus descendere ad propositum et ostendere quod
nullum sit dominium cum iusticia, nec rerum temporalium nec personarum lai-
carum nec quorumcumque, quod non sit sub Ecclesia et per Ecclesiam, ut agrum
vel vineam vel quodcumque aliud quod habet hic homo vel ille non potest habere
cum iusticia nisi habeat illud sub Ecclesia et per Ecclesiam.

Dicemus enim cum Augustino II[9] *De civitate Dei*, capitulo XXII, quod vera[10]
iusticia non est nisi in ea republica cuius est[11] conditor rectorque Christus. Vide-
bantur enim Romani gentiles multum de iusticia loqui et de republica magnum
sermonem facere. Sed illa respublica, ut Augustinus ait prefato libro,[12] non erat
viva moribus, sed picta coloribus. Nam quia Romani mutaverunt gloriam incor-
ruptibilis Dei in similitudinem imaginis corruptibilis hominis et volucrum et
quadrupedum et serpentum, ideo, dicentes se esse sapientes, stulti facti sunt, nec
vera iusticia in eorum republica esse poterat, ubi non colebatur verus Deus. Et
post passionem Christi nulla respublica potest esse vera ubi non coleretur[13]
sancta mater Ecclesia, et ubi non est conditor et rector Christus. Unde Augustinus
XIX *De civitate Dei*, capitulo XXI, vult quod respublica Romanorum non fuit vera
respublica, quia numquam fuit ibi vera iusticia.

1: subiectus Ecclesie] ecclesie subiectus C　　2: passione] Christi *add.* CFV[2]　　3: ut] *om.* C
4: cepit] incepit CFV[2]　　5: Ecclesia esse] esse ecclesia CFV[2]　　6: fuit passus] passus fuit F
7: salvus] salus C　　8: ideo] item PV[1] non V[2]　　9: II] *om.* C　　10: vera] autem *add.* FV[2]
11: est] *om.* PV[1]　　12: libro] capitulo FV[2]　　13: coleretur] colatur F

of all, since no one may obtain salvation unless he is subject to the Church and unless he is her son. And the Church has received this universality, and she has received this sacrament, from the Passion, and after the Passion, of Christ. For, before the Passion, the provisions of the Law and the Gospel ran side by side, so that men might be saved both by circumcision and by baptism. But, after the Passion of Christ, the provisions of the Law were dead,[1] so that, from then on, no one could be saved unless he were baptized. And so the Church is said to have been formed from the side of Christ, because it is from the Passion of Christ that the Church's sacraments derive their power.[2] And because it was then, when Christ had suffered, that the Church began to be universal, so that no one could be saved except through the Church's sacraments (for, as we have said, it was possible before the Passion to be saved even without this sacrament [of baptism]), a gloss on the words of Romans 5 — that Adam is the form of the future Adam[3] — maintains that the first Adam bore the form, that is, the type and similitude, of the future Adam: that is, of Christ.[4] The gloss asserts that Adam is called the form of Christ because, just as he was the father of all according to the flesh, so Christ is the Father of all according to the faith. And just as Eve was formed from the side of the sleeping Adam, so from the side of the Lord sleeping upon the Cross there flowed the sacraments through which the Church is saved.

Having made these things clear, therefore, we wish to come down to our proposition and show that there may be no lordship with justice over temporal things or lay persons or anything else which is not under the Church and through the Church: for example, this man or that cannot with justice have a farm or a vineyard or anything else which he has unless he holds it under the Church and through the Church.

For we shall say with Augustine at *De civitate Dei* 2:22 that there is no true justice save in that commonwealth whose Founder and Ruler is Christ.[5] For the Roman people seemed to have much to say about justice, and they made a great boast of their commonwealth. But that commonwealth, as Augustine says in the book just cited, was not a living moral entity but a coloured picture. For the Romans changed the glory of the incorruptible God into a likeness of the image of corruptible man and of birds and four-footed beasts and serpents; and so, declaring themselves wise, they were made foolish;[6] nor could there be true justice in their commonwealth, where the true God was not worshipped. And after the Passion of Christ, no commonwealth can be truly such in which Holy Mother Church is not cherished and of which Christ is not the Founder and Ruler. Hence Augustine, at *De civitate Dei* 19:21, maintains that the commonwealth of the Romans was no true commonwealth, because true justice was never there.[7]

1. Cf. Rom. 7:4–6.
2. Cf. Aquinas, *Summa theologiae* IIIa 62:5.
3. Rom. 5:14.
4. *Glossa ordinaria*, PL 114:486.
5. CCSL 47:55.
6. Cf. Rom. 1:22–23.
7. CCSL 48:687.

Et quia forte alicui auctoritates[1] non sufficiunt, volumus raciones[2] adducere quod nullus possit cum iusticia de aliqua re habere dominium nisi sit regeneratus per Ecclesiam. Nam,[3] ut dicit Augustinus predicto libro et capitulo, iusticia[4] est virtus que sua distribuit unicuique. Nisi ergo reddatur unicuique quod suum est, vera iusticia non est. Cum ergo[5] tu debeas esse sub Deo et sub Christo, nisi sis sub eo, iniustus es, et quia iniuste es[6] subtractus a Christo[7] Domino tuo,[8] iuste quelibet res subtrahitur a dominio[9] tuo. Qui enim non vult esse sub domino[10] suo, nullius rei cum iusticia potest habere dominium. Si enim miles nollet esse sub rege, dignum esset ut subditi eius non deberent esse sub milite. Si ergo[11] miles se subtrahit iniuste a domino suo, iuste privatur omni dominio suo. Sed quicumque non est regeneratus per Ecclesiam non est sub Christo Domino suo. Digne igitur privatus est omni dominio suo, ut nullius rei iuste dominus esse possit.

Vides ergo quod ad iustam et dignam possessionem rerum plus facit regeneracio per Ecclesiam, que est spiritualis, quam generacio paterna,[12] que fuit carnalis. Nam ex eo, quod quis est generatus per patrem carnaliter, est natura filius ire, iuxta illud Apostoli ad Ephesios II:[13] 'Eramus natura[14] filii ire'; et in Psalmo dicitur: 'Ecce iniquitatibus conceptus sum.' Ergo, nati carnaliter, sumus natura filii ire, sumus iniquitatibus concepti, et per consequens non sumus[15] sub Domino nostro,[16] ut diximus. Dignum est quod privetur omni dominio suo iste qui est carnaliter a patre generatus, nec[17] potest subcedere iuste in dominium hereditatis paterne nisi sit per Ecclesiam regeneratus; per[18] quam regeneracionem collocatur sub Christo Domino suo, propter quod non privatur dominio suo, sed iuste debetur sibi dominium hereditatis sue. Igitur, si, quia es filius patris, ex hoc arguere possumus quod pater est magis dominus illius hereditatis quam tu, cum ad possidere iuste quamcumque[19] possessionem magis faciat Ecclesia que, te regenerans, facit te esse sub Christo Domino tuo, sub quo non existens nihil iuste possidere potes, sub qua et per quam es filius misericordie,[20] quam faciat pater tuus carnalis, sub quo iniquitatibus conceptus es et es natura filius ire, magis itaque[21] erit Ecclesia domina possessionis tue quam tu ipse.

Concludamus ergo[22] et dicamus quod si nullum est dominium, nec utile, cuiusmodi est dominium fructiferum, nec potestativum, cuiusmodi est[23] dominium iurisdiccionem habens,[24] quod cum iusticia possideatur nisi possidens sit subiectus Deo, quia[25] Deo quis subiectus esse non potest nisi per sacramenta Ecclesie, ideo, ut dicebamus, magis es dominus possessionis tue et cuiuscumque rei quam

---

1: alicui auctoritates] auctoritates alicui FV² 2: raciones] alias *add.* C 3: Nam] iusticia *add.* C 4: iusticia] *om.* C 5: ergo] *om.* F 6: es] est F 7: Christo] *om.* V² 8: Christo Domino tuo] domino christo tuo F 9: dominio] domino *mss* 10: domino] dominio FV² 11: ergo] enim FV² 12: paterna] prima F 13: II] *om.* C 14: Eramus natura] natura eramus V² 15: natura filii ire … sumus] *om.* C 16: nostro] et quia quod non est sub domino nostro *add.* C 17: nec] non C 18: per] propter F 19: quamcumque] *om.* F 20: misericordie] iusticiae F 21: itaque] *del.* C 22: ergo] *om.* FV² 23: est] *om.* F 24: habens] *del.* C 25: quia] ut diximus qui non est subiectus deo qui est dominus eius dignum est quod privetur omni dominio et omni possessione *add. and del.* C

And since there is perhaps someone for whom authorities are not enough, we wish to adduce arguments to show that no one may with justice have lordship over anything unless he is regenerated through the Church. For, as Augustine says in the book and chapter cited above, justice is the virtue which distributes to each what is due to him.[1] There is no true justice, therefore, unless what is due to each is rendered to him. Therefore, since you should be under God and under Christ, you are unjust if you are not under Him and, since you are unjustly withdrawn from Christ your Lord, everything is justly withdrawn from your own lordship. For he who refuses to be under his lord cannot with justice have lordship over anything. For if a knight were to refuse to be under the king, it would be fitting that those subject to the knight should themselves not be under him. Therefore, if a knight unjustly withdraws himself from his lord, he is justly deprived of all his own lordship. But whoever is not regenerated through the Church is not under Christ his Lord; and so he is properly deprived of all his own lordship, so that he may not justly be lord of anything.

You see, therefore, that, so far as the just and worthy possession of things is concerned, regeneration through the Church, which is spiritual, accomplishes more than generation through a father, which was carnal. For by reason of carnal generation through a father, a man is by nature a child of wrath, according to what the Apostle says in Ephesians 2: 'We were by nature children of wrath.'[2] And it is said in the Psalm, 'Behold, I was conceived in iniquities.'[3] Carnally born, therefore, we are by nature children of wrath: we were conceived in iniquities. And it follows, as we have said, that we are not under our Lord. Thus, it is fitting that he who is carnally begotten of a father should be deprived of all his lordship; nor can he justly succeed to the lordship of a paternal inheritance unless he is regenerated through the Church, by which regeneration he is brought under Christ his Lord. In this event, he is not deprived of his lordship; rather, the lordship of his inheritance is justly due to him. Thus, if, from the fact that you are the son of a father, we can argue that your father is more lord of the inheritance than you, then, since the ownership of whatever you have justly is rather conferred upon you by the Church than by your carnal father — under whom you were conceived in iniquities and are by nature a child of wrath — the Church will therefore be more the lord of your possessions than you are yourself. For she regenerates you and causes you to be under Christ your Lord, without Whom you can have nothing justly; and under her and through her you are a child of mercy.

Let us conclude, therefore, and say that if no lordship either of use, which is a lordship over fruits, or of power, which is a lordship involving jurisdiction, may be had with justice unless its possessor is subject to God, then, because, as we have said, no one can be subject to God except through the sacraments of the Church, you are lord of your possessions and of all that you have rather because

1. I.e. *De civitate Dei* 19:21 (CCSL 48:688).
2. Eph. 2:3.
3. Psalm 51:5.

habes quia es Ecclesie filius spiritualis quam quia es filius patris carnalis. Consequens ergo est quod hereditatem tuam et omne dominium tuum et omnem possessionem tuam magis debes recognoscere ab Ecclesia et per Ecclesiam et quia es filius Ecclesie quam a patre tuo carnali et per ipsum et quia es filius eius. Consequens est eciam quod si pater, eo vivente,[1] est magis dominus hereditatis quam tu, Ecclesia, que non moritur, est magis domina rerum tuarum quam tu.[2]

Animadvertendum[3] tamen quod, licet dicamus Ecclesiam omnium possessionum et omnium temporalium esse matrem et[4] dominam, non tamen propter hoc privamus fideles[5] dominiis suis et possessionibus suis,[6] quia, ut infra patebit, et Ecclesia habet huiusmodi dominium et eciam fideles huiusmodi dominium habent; sed Ecclesia habet tale dominium universale et superius, fideles vero particulare et inferius. Reddimus[7] ergo que sunt Cesaris Cesari, et que sunt Dei Deo, quoniam[8] ipsorum[9] temporalium dominium universale et[10] superius Ecclesie tribuimus, dominium autem particulare et inferius fidelibus elargimur.

CAPITULUM VIII: *Quod nullus est dignus hereditate paterna nisi sit servus et filius Ecclesie et nisi per Ecclesiam sit dignus hereditate eterna.*

Ex precedenti quidem capitulo satis haberi potest quod in presenti capitulo continetur. Ad maiorem tamen declaracionem proposti dicemus quod, loquendo eo modo secundum quem Sapiencie III scribitur, quod Deus invenit illos, id est homines iustos et habentes graciam, dignos se, id est dignos[11] participacione beatitudinis sue, ut exponit glossa interlinearis, dicemus quod omnes habentes graciam sunt digni hereditate eterna.

Nam nullus potest habere[12] graciam nisi sit in caritate, quia nullus potest esse gratus Deo sine caritate. Nullus autem est in caritate nisi sit filius regni eterni, iuxta illud Augustini XV *De Trinitate* capitulo XVIII: 'Nullum est donum excellencius caritate; solum autem est[13] istud donum[14] quod dividit inter filios regni eterni et filios perdicionis eterne.' Si ergo, habentes graciam et caritatem, sumus filii Dei et filii regni eterni, quia, ut arguit Apostolus ad Romanos VIII, si sumus filii, consequens est quod simus[15] heredes, quia filiis debetur hereditas, omnes itaque habentes graciam et caritatem sunt filii Dei et sunt heredes hereditatis eterne et sunt digni hereditate eterna, et nisi simus digni hereditate[16] spirituali et eterna, non[17] possumus esse digni hereditate temporali et paterna.

Dupliciter autem sumus indigni hereditate eterna, et per consequens dupliciter

---

1: vivente] invente C   2: Consequens est ... quam tu] *marg.* C   3: Animadvertendum] advertendum FV[2]   4: et] *om.* C   5: fideles] *om.* F   6: et possessionibus suis] *om.* C   7: Reddimus] reddemus F   8: quoniam] quando F   9: ipsorum] *om.* C   10: et] *om.* P   11: dignos] *om.* F   12: habere] habet CPV[1]   13: autem est] est autem CFV[2]   14: donum] dominium FV[2]   15: simus] sumus FV[2]   16: nisi simus ... hereditate] *om.* F   17: eterna, non] *om.* F

you are the spiritual son of the Church than because you are the son of a carnal father. It follows, therefore, that you should acknowledge that your inheritance and all your lordship and all that you have come rather from the Church and through the Church and because you are a son of the Church than from your carnal father and through him and because you are his son. And it follows also that if your father, while he lives, is more lord of the inheritance than you, then the Church, who does not die, is more lord of your possessions than you.

It must be noted, however, that, although we say that the Church is the mother and mistress of all possessions and of all temporal goods, we nonetheless do not on this account deprive the faithful of their lordships and possessions. For, as will appear below, both the Church and the faithful have lordship of this [i.e. of a temporal] kind. But the Church has such lordship universally and in a superior manner, whereas that of the faithful is particular and inferior.[1] Therefore we render to Caesar that which is Caesar's and to God that which is God's; for to the Church we attribute a universal and superior lordship of temporal things, and to the faithful we assign a particular and inferior lordship.

CHAPTER VIII: *That no one is worthy of a paternal inheritance unless he is the servant and son of the Church, and unless, through the Church, he is worthy of an eternal inheritance.*

What is contained in the present chapter can indeed be sufficiently inferred from the previous chapter [without further discussion]. Nonetheless, in order to make our argument clearer, we shall say that, if we speak according to what is written in Wisdom 3 — that 'God found them' (that is, just men and those who had grace) 'worthy of Himself'[2] (that is, as the interlinear gloss explains, worthy of participation in His blessedness) — we shall show that all who have grace are worthy of an eternal inheritance.

For no one can have grace [*gratia*] except with love; or no one can be pleasing [*gratus*] to God without love. But no one has love unless he is a child of the Eternal Kingdom, according to Augustine at *De Trinitate* 15:18: 'There is no gift more excellent than love; for it is this gift alone which distinguishes the children of the Eternal Kingdom from the children of eternal loss.'[3] If, therefore, having grace and love, we are sons of God and children of the Eternal Kingdom, then all who have grace and love are sons of God and heirs to an eternal inheritance, and are worthy of an eternal inheritance; for, as the Apostle argues in Romans 8, if we are sons it follows that we are heirs, because it is to sons that the inheritance is due.[4] And, unless we are worthy of a spiritual and an eternal inheritance, we cannot be worthy of a temporal and paternal inheritance.

But there are two ways in which we are unworthy of an eternal inheritance and

1. See Chaps. X & XII below; see also Pt. III, Ch. XI.
2. Wisd. 3:5.
3. CCSL 50(A):507.
4. Rom. 8:17.

sumus indigni quolibet dominio et qualibet possessione, et per consequens dupliciter sumus indigni qualibet hereditate temporali sive paterna: videlicet, per peccatum originale, secundum quod peccavimus in Adam, iuxta illud ad Romanos V, 'In quo,' scilicet in Adam, 'omnes peccaverunt'; et per peccatum actuale, secundum quod peccamus[1] in nobis ipsis.

Si enim rex dedisset militi aliquod castrum possidendum ab eo et a tota posterioritate eius, filius[2] qui descenderet ex milite dupliciter posset perdere castrum et hereditatem illam:[3] vel per peccatum patris vel per peccatum proprium. Si enim ille miles pater eius forefaceret contra regem, iuste rex acciperet sibi castrum, quo accepto filius per peccatum patris[4] perderet hereditatem castri. Sed dices, Quomodo rex esset iustus, qui, peccante patre, non[5] peccante filio, acciperet filio hereditatem castri? Dicemus quod iste filius militis vel consideratur in se vel consideratur ut est filius patris. Si consideratur in se, non peccat nec punitur, quia, si non succederet in hereditatem[6] castri, nulla punicio est huic filio secundum se, quia ei secundum se[7] considerato non debetur hereditas castri. Sed si consideratur ut est filius patris, debetur sibi hereditas castri.[8] Si ergo non debetur ei[9] huiusmodi hereditas nisi quia est filius patris, sufficit quod peccaverit pater, vel sufficit quod ipse peccaverit in patre, ad hoc, quod perdat hereditatem castri. Alio modo potest hic filius perdere hereditatem castri non solum per peccatum patris, sed eciam per peccatum proprium, ut si postquam devenit ad filium[10] hereditas castri, si ipse peccet in regem, iuste privabitur castro.

Sic et in proposito. Dicitur[11] iuste privamur hereditate eterna vel per peccatum Ade, quod dicitur peccatum originale, quia est peccatum quod ex[12] origine nostra contrahimus, vel per peccatum proprium, quod dicitur actuale, quod est peccatum quod actu et opere nostro committimus. Dederat enim Deus Ade quoddam donum supernaturale,[13] quod dicebatur originalis[14] iusticia, per quam originalem iusticiam Adam erat subiectus Deo et omnia sua[15] inferiora erant subiecta sibi. Quod donum non erat datum Ade tamquam singulari persone, sed, tamquam capiti, tocius posterioritatis sue. Ideo donum illud dicebatur iusticia originalis, quia, si non peccasset, transfudisset per originem huiusmodi donum in omnes suos posteros, ita quod omnes fuissent nati Deo subiecti et omnes fuissent nati cum huiusmodi iusticia. Sed Adam peccante et per peccatum se a Deo avertente, iuste perdidit huiusmodi donum, quo perdito non potuit ipsum in posteros[16] transfundere, quia non habebat tale donum, sed perdiderat ipsum. Nemo autem dat quod non habet. Ergo non dedit[17] Adam tale donum suis filiis, quia ipsum non habebat. Filii ergo Ade et nos omnes, qui, si Adam non peccasset, fuissemus nati cum[18] originali iusticia et fuissemus nati Deo subiecti, Adam peccante nascimur sine tali iusticia et nascimur a Deo aversi. Ideo ait Apostolus quod nascimur natura filii ire et

---

1: peccamus] peccavimus FV²   2: filius] filium F   3: et hereditatem illam] *om.* F   4: patris] iuste *add.* C   5: non] nec FV²   6: succederet in hereditatem] succedit in hereditate FV²
7: quia ei secundum se] *om.* F   8: Sed si … castri] *om.* F   9: ei] *om.* FV²   10: filium] eum C
11: Dicitur] dicit FV²   12: ex] *om.* PV¹   13: supernaturale] super F   14: originalis] originaliter F
15: iusticia, per … sua] *om.* F   16: posteros] posteris F   17: ergo non dedit] non ergo dabit FV²
18: cum] *om.* PV¹

consequently two ways in which we are unworthy of any lordship and any possession, and consequently two ways in which we are unworthy of any temporal or
paternal inheritance — namely, through original sin, since we have sinned in
Adam, according to what is said in Romans 5: 'In whom,' that is, in Adam, 'all
have sinned';[1] and through actual sin, since we are sinners in ourselves.

For if a king were to give a castle to a knight as his own possession and as that
of all his posterity, a son who had descended from the knight might be liable to
lose that castle and inheritance in two ways: either through his father's sin or
through his own sin. For if his father the knight were to offend against the king,
the king might justly receive the castle back to himself, by which reception the
son would lose the inheritance of the castle through the sin of his father. But, you
say, How would the king be just if he were to receive back the inheritance of the
castle from the son not for the son's sin, but for the sin of the father? We shall reply that this son of the knight may be considered either in himself or insofar as he
is his father's son. If he is considered in himself, he neither sins nor is punished;
for although he will not now succeed to the inheritance of the castle, this is not a
punishment to the son in himself, because it is not to him considered in himself
that the inheritance of the castle is due. Rather, the inheritance of the castle is due
to him considered insofar as he is his father's son. Therefore, if that inheritance is
due to him only because he is his father's son, then the fact that the father has
sinned, or that he has sinned in his father, is a sufficient ground for his losing the
inheritance of the castle. Then again, this son can lose his inheritance in the castle
not only through his father's sin, but also through his own sin; so that if, after the
inheritance of the castle had passed to the son, he himself were to sin against the
king, then he might justly be deprived of the castle.

So also in our proposition. It is said that we are justly deprived of an eternal
inheritance either through Adam's sin, which is called original sin because it is the
sin which we contract from our origin, or through our own sin, which is called
actual because it is the sin which we commit by our own act and deed. For God
had given to Adam a certain supernatural gift which was called original justice;
and, through this original justice, Adam was made subject to God and all His inferior creatures were made subject to him. And this gift was not given to Adam as to
a single person, but as the head of his whole posterity. And so that gift was called
original justice; for, had he not sinned, he would have transferred this gift origi-
nating thus to all his offspring, and so all would have been born with such justice.
But Adam, by sinning and by turning himself away from God through sin, justly
lost that gift, and, having lost it, could not transfer it to his posterity, for he no
longer possessed such a gift, but had lost it; for no one can give what he does not
have. Therefore, Adam did not give such a gift to his sons, for he did not have it.
Therefore, the sons of Adam and all of us who, had Adam not sinned, would have
been born with original justice and would have been born subject to God, are, because of Adam's sin, born without such justice, and are born turned away from
God. And so the Apostle says that, by nature, we are born children of wrath, and

1.   Rom. 5:12.

nascimur indigni hereditate eterna. Nam licet non nascamur digni pena sensus, quia ex peccato originali non debetur nobis pena sensibilis, nascimur tamen digni pena damni, quia nascimur digni ut privemur vita eterna. Nascimur itaque per peccatum originale natura filii ire, et nascimur Deo non subiecti, sed pocius a Deo aversi, quia quilibet in[1] iniquitatibus[2] concipimur et in peccatis nascimur, et per consequens nascimur[3] indigni hereditate eterna.

Secundo modo sumus indigni hereditate eterna per peccatum actuale, prout peccantes mortaliter avertimur a Deo nostro, et iniquitates nostre dividunt inter nos et Deum nostrum; et quia sic peccantes non sumus subiecti Deo, consequens est quod non simus digni Deo nec hereditate divina.[4]

Dupliciter ergo, ut patuit, sumus non subiecti Deo et sumus indigni hereditate eterna: per peccatum originale et eciam actuale. Et sicut dupliciter sumus[5] non subiecti Deo et sumus indigni hereditate eterna, sic dupliciter sumus indigni hereditate paterna et sumus indigni quacumque possessione et quocumque dominio, ut eciam ipsis temporalibus non sumus digni dominari nisi simus Deo subiecti. Nam si miles nollet esse subiectus regi, iuste perderet et iniuste possideret omne illud quod habet a rege. Igitur, cum omnia habeamus a Deo, iuxta illud Apostoli — 'Quid habes quod non accepisti?' — nam ipse Deus est dives per seipsum, nos autem sumus divites ex mutuatis et ex hiis que ipse Deus nobis mutuat, qui ergo non est subiectus Deo iuste perdit et iniuste possidet omne illud quod habet a Deo. Sive enim sint reges, per Deum regnant et a Deo habent quod regnent; sive sint principes, per Deum imperant et a Deo habent quod imperant,[6] iuxta illud Proverbia[7] VIII: 'Per me reges regnant, et per me principes imperant'; sive sint possessores alii, totum a Deo habent. Immo, nos[8] ipsi non sumus nostri,[9] sed sumus ipsius Dei,[10] quia Domini[11] est 'terra et plenitudo eius, orbis terrarum et universi[12] qui habitant in eo.' Qui ergo non est subiectus Deo[13] iuste perdit et iniuste possidet omne illud quod habet ab eo. Non dicant reges, Iuste regnamus;[14] non dicant principes, Iuste imperamus; non dicant quicumque fideles, Iuste aliquid possidemus: quia nisi sint subiecti Deo, nihil cum iusticia possident.

Sed forte dices cum Apostolo: 'Non est potestas nisi a Deo'; et dices cum Apostolo Petro: 'Subditi estote in omni timore dominis,[15] non tantum bonis et modestis,

---

1: in] *om.* C   2: iniquitatibus] suis *add.* FV[2]   3: et per ... nascimur] *om.* C   4: divina] eterna FV[2]

5: dupliciter sumus] sumus dupliciter C   6: imperant] imperavit F   7: Proverbia] sapiencie *mss*

8: nos] *om.* F   9: nostri] *interlin., in another hand* C   10: nostri, sed ... Dei] ipsius Dei Dei V[2]

11: Domini] dictum F   12: orbis terrarum et universi] et omnes C   13: Deo] quia *add.* C

14: regnamus] regnavimus FV[2]   15: dominis] domini F

are born unworthy of an eternal inheritance.[1] For although it may be that we are not born worthy of the pain of sense because the pain of sense is not due to us from original sin, we are nonetheless born worthy of the pain of loss, since we are born worthy to be deprived of eternal life.[2] Thus, through original sin, we are by nature born children of wrath, and we are born not subject to God, but rather turned away from Him, since we are all conceived in iniquities and born in sin, and consequently are born unworthy of an eternal inheritance.

The second way in which we are born unworthy of an eternal inheritance is through actual sin, insofar as, being mortal sinners, we are turned away from our God and our iniquities divide us from our God. And since, as sinners, we are not subject to God, it follows that we are not worthy of God or of a Divine inheritance.

As has become clear, therefore, there are two ways in which we are not subject to God and are unworthy of an eternal inheritance: through original sin and also through actual. And just as there are two ways in which we are not subject to God and are unworthy of an eternal inheritance, so are there two ways in which we are unworthy of a paternal inheritance and unworthy of any possession and any lordship: for we are not worthy to have lordship even of temporal possessions unless we are subject to God. For if a knight were to refuse to be subject to the king, he would justly lose and unjustly possess all that he held of the king. Thus, since we hold all things of God, according to what the Apostle says: 'What have you that you have not received?'[3] — for God Himself is rich in Himself, but we are rich from loans and from those things which God Himself has lent us[4] — he who is not subject to God therefore justly loses and unjustly possesses all that he holds of God. For if men are kings, they reign by God and receive their reign from God; and if they are princes, they rule by God and receive their rule from God, according to Proverbs 8: 'By me, kings reign, and by me princes rule.'[5] And if they are possessors of another kind, they receive everything from God. Indeed, not even our own selves are ours: rather, we belong to God Himself, for 'the earth and its fullness' are the Lord's, 'the whole world and all who dwell in it.'[6] He who is not subject to God, therefore, justly loses and unjustly possesses all that he holds of Him. Let not kings say, We reign justly; let not princes say, We rule justly; and let none of the faithful say, We possess something justly. For they possess nothing with justice unless they are subject to God.

Perhaps, however, you will say with the Apostle, 'There is no power except of God,'[7] and with the apostle Peter, 'Be subject to your lords in all fear: not only to

---

1. Eph. 2:3.
2. The oblique reference here is to the opinion — widely held, though never defined as a dogma of the Church — that the souls of infants who die unbaptized do not go to hell but enter a state, usually called *limbus infantium* or *puerorum*, in which they suffer no pain of sense but are consciously deprived of the Vision of God, and so suffer the pain of loss.
3. I Cor. 4:7.
4. See n. 2 on p. 23.
5. Prov. 8:15–16.
6. Psalm 24:1.
7. Rom. 13:1.

sed eciam discolis.' Ergo et malis dominis subiecti esse debemus, quod non esset nisi potestatem haberent a Deo et nisi iusta esset eorum potestas. Nam et Augustinus III *De Trinitate* capitulo VIII[1] vult quod iniqui voluntatem habent[2] iniustam, sed potenciam non recipiunt nisi iustam. Ergo iniqui iuste habent potestatem quam habent, licet non iustam habeant voluntatem.

Sed de hoc in sequentibus capitulis plenius agemus[3] et ostendemus omnia hec non esse contraria nostro proposito. In presenciarum autem dictum sit quod qui non est subiectus Deo digne perdit et iniuste possidet omne illud quod habet a Deo. Nam quantum distat rex eternus a rege temporali, tanto liquido magis manifestum est quod qui non est subiectus Deo magis est dignus perdere et magis iniuste possidet quod habet a Deo quam qui[4] non est subiectus regi temporali iuste debeat perdere omne illud quod habeat ab huiusmodi rege. Nam si crimen lese maiestatis facit te dignum morte et[5] indignum vita et omni possessione tua, quia per antonomasiam maiestas reservatur in Deo, qui non est subiectus Deo indignus est seipso et omni possessione sua. Et quia per peccatum originale nascimur non subiecti Deo et per peccatum actuale sumus non subiecti sibi, per utrumque peccatum sumus digni perdere et indigne possidemus omne illud quod habemus a Deo, ut dicamus[6] secundum sanctorum sentenciam: quod peccator non sit dignus pane quo vescitur. Et si ab indigno possessore tollitur possessio et ab indigno dominatore tollitur[7] dominium, nil dignius et nil iustius poterit iudicari. Quare si per peccatum originale nascitur quis non subiectus Deo, et per peccatum actuale mortale fit non subiectus,[8] consequens est quod peccatum tam originale quam actuale omnium rerum tuarum possessorem te facit indignum.

Ergo per sacramentum baptismi, quod est directum remedium contra [peccatum] originale, et per sacramentum penitencie, quod est remedium contra peccatum actuale, efficeris dignus dominator et dignus princeps et possessor rerum. Et quia hec sacramenta non nisi in Ecclesia et per Ecclesiam tribuuntur, quia nullus potest suscipere baptismum nisi velit se subicere Ecclesie et esse filius Ecclesie, cum Ecclesia sit Catholica, id est universalis, sine qua salus esse non potest; et cum nullus recipiat sacramentum penitencie nisi sub Ecclesia et per Ecclesiam, dicente Domino Petro 'quodcumque ligaveris' etc., nullus efficitur dignus dominator nec dignus princeps nec possessor rerum nisi sub Ecclesia et per Ecclesiam.

Clare itaque vides quod reges regnorum,[9] principes principatuum[10] et alii fideles possessionum suarum sunt magis digni possessores per suam matrem Ecclesiam, per quam sunt spiritualiter regenerati,[11] quam[12] per suos patres et per hereditatem

---

1: VIII] vii *mss*   2: habent] habeant F   3: plenius agemus] agemus plenius CF   4: qui] *om.* C
5: dignum morte et] *om.* F   6: dicamus] dicatur CFV[2]   7: tollitur] totaliter *add.* F   8: subiectus] deo *add.* C, *then the following words add. and del.*: per utrumque peccatum efficiatur quis indignus dominator et indignus possessor cuiuscumque rei que habet a domino et quia nichil habes quod non accepisti et omnia habes a deo   9: regnorum] et *add.* C   10: principatuum] principantium F   11: regenerati] per quam sunt sacramenta ecclesiastica accepti per que sacramenta fuit subiecti deo quod fuit digni possessores per suos patres et per hereditatem paternam *add. and del.* C
12: quam] *om.* C

the good and moderate, but also to the spiteful.'[1] [And so you will say that] we must therefore be subject even to wicked lords, which would not be so unless they held their power of God and unless their power were just. For Augustine himself maintains in *De Trinitate* 3:8 that, although the wicked have an unjust will, they do not receive an unjust power.[2] Therefore, the wicked justly hold whatever power they have, even though they do not have a just will.

But we shall deal more fully with this in the following chapters, and show that none of these things is contrary to our argument. For the time being, it may be said that he who is not subject to God worthily loses and unjustly possesses all that he holds of God. For the difference between the Eternal King and a temporal king is so great that, if he who is not subject to a temporal king is justly liable to lose all that he holds of that king, it is manifestly clear that he who is not subject to God is still more liable to lose, and more unjust in possessing, that which he holds of God. For if the crime of treason [*lese maiestatis*] renders you worthy of death and unworthy of life and of all your property, then, since majesty [*maiestas*] is an attribute reposed pre-eminently in God, he who is not subject to God is unworthy of himself and of all his possession. And since, through original sin, we are born not subject to God and, through actual sin, we are [also] not subject to Him, then, through both kinds of sin, we are worthy to lose and unworthily possess all that we hold of God. And so, according to the judgment of the saints, we say that the sinner is not worthy of the bread which he eats.[3] And if his property is removed from the unworthy possessor, and if his lordship is removed from the unworthy lord, nothing could be deemed more fitting and more just. And so if a man is born not subject to God through original sin, and if through actual mortal sin he becomes not subject, then it follows that both original and actual sin render you an unworthy possessor of all your goods.

Therefore, through the sacrament of baptism, which is the direct remedy against original sin, and through the sacrament of penance, which is the remedy against actual sin, you will be made a worthy lord and a worthy prince and possessor of things. And since these sacraments are not conferred except in the Church and through the Church, no one is made a worthy lord or a worthy prince or possessor of things except under the Church and through the Church. For no one can receive baptism unless he desires to subject himself to the Church and to be a son of the Church, for the Church is Catholic, that is, universal, and there can be no salvation outside her; and no one may receive the sacrament of penance except under the Church and through the Church, for the Lord said to Peter, 'Whatever you shall bind,' and so on.

You see clearly, then, that kings are worthy possessors of their kingdoms, princes of their principalities, and other faithful people of their possessions, rather through their mother the Church, by whom they are spiritually regenerated, than through their fathers and by paternal inheritance, from which carnal

1.   I Peter 2:18.
2.   CCSL 50:141.
3.   Cf. perhaps II Thess. 3:10; *Glossa ordinaria*, PL 114:624.

paternam,[1] a quibus patribus carnalibus[2] et per quos nascuntur in peccato originali:[3] nascuntur non subiecti Deo, sed pocius aversi[4] ab eo. Cum ergo queritur a
principe, Unde habes tuum principatum? et cum queritur ab aliquo fideli, Unde
habes tuam hereditatem? respondet princeps quod habet eam a suo progenitore et
a suo patre et dicit quod iure hereditario subcedit in hereditatem patris. Et sicut
respondet princeps de principatu suo, sic[5] respondet quilibet fidelis de hereditate
sua. Sed si dicit princeps vel fidelis aliquis se habere hereditatem aliquam, sive sit
principatus sive hereditas alia, a suo patre, a quo[6] est genitus carnaliter, magis debet dicere se habere huiusmodi principatum et hereditatem a sua matre Ecclesia,
per quam est regeneratus spiritualiter et absolutus sacramentaliter, cum sic[7] regeneratus[8] et absolutus incipiat esse dignus hereditate et possessione sua qui[9] prius
erat indignus, et ex tunc[10] incipiat iuste possidere qui prius poterat iuste privari.

Sic enim videmus in naturalibus rebus quod, si materia fiat indisposita ad formam quam habet, expoliatur illa forma ad quam est indisposita, quia non est illa
forma ulterius digna, et induitur forma ad quam est disposita, qua forma[11] dicitur
esse digna: ut si corpus per infirmitatem egrotat et ulterius non sit dispositum ut
possit agere opera vivi, expoliatur forma vivi, qua expoliata dicitur mortuum.[12] In
omnibus enim naturalibus rebus, tamdiu materia est sub forma, quamdiu est disposita ad illam formam, et quamdiu potest facere opera eius. Cum ergo indisposita
non possit facere opera sue forme, dignum est quod expolietur huiusmodi forma.

Sic et in proposito: tunc es iustus possessor tue hereditatis cum possidere
digne potes[13] illam, et tamdiu es iustus possessor, quamdiu eam digne possidere
vales. Si autem sis vel efficiaris indignus, dignum et iustum est quod illa priveris. Et quia, natus in [peccato] originali et carnaliter es indignus, regeneratus
spiritualiter factus es dignus, unde dictum est quod magis debes recognoscere
huiusmodi hereditatem ab Ecclesia, per cuius regeneracionem factus es dignus,
quam a patre tuo carnali, per cuius generacionem[14] natus eras indignus. Rursus,
si ab originali [peccato] absolutus et regeneratus[15] spiritualiter, cum venis[16] ad
etatem et incipis habere racionis usum[17] agis contra Deum et peccas mortaliter,
quia sic peccans avertisti et subtraxisti te a Deo Domino tuo, dignum est ut[18]
careas omni dominio tuo[19;20] et quod subtrahatur a te omnis possessio tua.
Noluisti enim servire Deo, dignum est quod nihil serviat vel famuletur tibi. Et
quia tota hereditas tua data est tibi ut servias Deo, dignum est quod, si es aversus
a Domino Deo tuo,[21] priveris omni hereditate tua. Et quia, sicut ab originali [pec-
cato] fuisti absolutus per baptismum et ex hoc factus eras dignus hereditate eterna et
eciam hereditate paterna, sic quia per penitencie sacramentum absolveris a peccato

---

1: et per ... paternam] *om.* C   2: patribus carnalibus] *om.* C   3: originali] et *add.* CFV²
4: aversi] adversi P   5: sicut respondet ... sic] *om.* F   6: a quo] *om.* P   7: sic] sit CFV²
8: regeneratus] generatus FPV¹V²   9: qui] quia V²   10: tunc] nunc FV²   11: forma] *del.* C
12: mortuum] mortuus F   13: possidere digne potes] potes digne possidere C digne potes possidere F   14: generacionem] regeneracionem P   15: et regeneratus] *om.* F   16: venis] veneris FV²
17: racionis usum] usum racionis C   18: ut] *om.* F   19: tuo, dignum ... tuo] *om.* V²   20: tuo]
suo P   21: tuo] quod *add. mss*

fathers and through whom they were born in original sin: they were born, not subject to God, but rather turned away from Him. Therefore, when a prince is asked, From whom do you receive your principality? and when any one of the faithful is asked, From whom do you receive your inheritance? the prince replies that he receives it from his forebears and from his father, and says that he succeeds to the inheritance of his father by right of succession. And just as the prince says this of his principality, so every one of the faithful says this of his own inheritance. But if a prince or any one of the faithful says that he receives whatever inheritance he has — whether it be a principality or any other inheritance — from his father, by whom he was carnally begotten, he ought rather to say that he receives that principality and inheritance from the Church, through whom he is spiritually regenerated and sacramentally absolved. For, by this regeneration and absolution, he who formerly was unworthy begins to be worthy of his inheritance and possession, and he who was once justly liable to be deprived then begins justly to possess.

For we see also in natural things that, if matter becomes indisposed to the form which it has, it is deprived of the form to which it is indisposed because it is no longer worthy of that form; and it takes on a form to which it is disposed, of which form it is said to be worthy. For example, if a body is so much worn out by illness that it is no longer so disposed as to be able to continue with the task of living, it is deprived of the form of a living being and, being thus deprived, is said to be dead. For, in all natural things, matter is under a form for as long as it is disposed to that form and for as long as it is able to accomplish its tasks. But when it is not disposed to its form and not able to accomplish its tasks, it is fitting that it be deprived of that form.

So also in our proposition. You are the just possessor of your inheritance while you are able to possess it worthily, and you are its just possessor for as long as you are fit to possess it worthily. But if you are or become unworthy, then it is right and just that you should be deprived of it. And since, born in original sin and carnally, you are unworthy, you are made worthy [only] by spiritual regeneration; and so it is said that you must acknowledge such inheritance to come rather from the Church, through whose regeneration you are made worthy, than from your carnal father, through whose generation you were born unworthy. Furthermore, if, absolved from original sin and spiritually regenerated, you act against God and commit mortal sin when you come of age and begin to have the use of reason, then, since by so sinning you turn away and withdraw yourself from the Lord your God, it is fitting that you should be stripped of all your lordship and that all your property should be withdrawn from you. For, having refused to be subject to God, it is fitting that nothing should be subject to or serve you. And since all your inheritance is given to you so that you may serve God, it is fitting that, if you are turned away from the Lord your God, you should be deprived of all your inheritance. Also, just as you were absolved from original sin through baptism and thereby made worthy of an eternal inheritance and also of a paternal inheritance, so you will be absolved from

mortali, quociens de peccatis tuis es contritus et per penitenciam absolutus, quia
hoc non fit, nisi per Ecclesiam et ab Ecclesia, tociens debes recognoscere omnia
bona tua[1] ab Ecclesia et per Ecclesiam, quociens per eam efficeris dignus primo
hereditate eterna et postea hereditate paterna et quacumque alia possessione, sive
a patre sive aliunde proveniat.

Bene itaque dictum est quod in rubrica capituli dicebatur, quod nullus est dignus hereditate paterna nec quacumque alia possessione et quocumque alio principatu vel dominio nisi sit servus et filius Ecclesie, et nisi per Ecclesiam fiat dignus
hereditate eterna. Claram itaque veritatem continet quod dicitur Matthei VI: 'Querite autem primum regnum Dei et iusticiam eius, et hec omnia adicientur vobis.'
Nisi ergo queras primum regnum Dei, et nisi sis sub Deo, non es dignus quod ista
adiciantur tibi. Immo, ut Chrysostomus ait, hoc exponens: 'Terra[2] propter peccata
hominum maledicitur, iuxta illud: "Maledicta terra in opere tuo."' Maledicitur
ergo terra in opere peccatoris quia non est dignus peccator quod sibi serviat terra.[3]
Et si non est dignus quod sibi serviat terra,[4] que est fex elementorum, non est dignus quod sibi serviat quecumque res alia.

Dignus est quidem quod omnibus privetur qui Domino[5] omnium servire contempsit. Igitur non sunt digni hereditate paterna nec re alia qui non sunt servi Dei.[6]
Et quia[7] non possumus fieri servi Dei nisi[8] simus absoluti per Ecclesiam sacramentaliter, omnia que habemus ab Ecclesia et per Ecclesiam debemus recognoscere per cuius sacramenta, que sunt vasa gracie, suscipimus divinam graciam
et fimus[9] filii et heredes Dei.[10]

Advertendum tamen nos dixisse baptismum esse remedium contra originale
peccatum,[11] quia contra tale peccatum est remedium directum. Tamen, si baptiza-
retur[12] adultus et non accederet[13] fictus ad baptismum,[14] quia impium[15] est a Deo
dimidiam sperare[16] veniam, ille sic[17] baptizatus absolveretur a peccato originali[18]
et eciam ab omni peccato mortali quod ante baptismum commisisset. Contra [pec-
catum] originale itaque est ordinatum sacramentum baptismi; sed baptismus,[19] si
qua alia peccata cum originali invenit, omnia illa simul cum originali diluit.

Advertendum eciam nos dixisse per baptismum collatum per Ecclesiam et in
forma Ecclesie[20] absolvi a peccato originali, per sacramentum autem penitencie a

---

1: tua] *om.* F   2: Terra] quod *add.* C   3: serviat terra] terra serviat F   4: serviat terra] terra
serviat CPV[1]V[2]   5: Domino] dominio F   6: Dei] nec sunt digni hereditate eterna *add.* C
7: non sunt ... quia] non sunt servi Dei nec sunt digni hereditate eterna et quia F   non sunt digni
hereditate eterna et quia V[2]   8: nisi] nec filii eius nisi regenerati per ecclesiam *add. and del.* C
9: fimus] sumus F   10: Dei] Concludamus ergo et dicamus quod quia ab originali peccato solus
sint inter mortuos liber quibus ante alius fuit in originali conceptus si ab huiusmodi peccato et ab
aliis peccatis per que efficiamur indigni hereditate eterna et paterna et quacumque re paterna alia
non nisi per ecclesiam et potestatem ecclesie absolvi possumus ab ecclesia matri nostra ut sepius
dictum est debemus omnes res magis recognoscere per quam fimus digni quacumque possessione
nostra *add. and del.* C   11: peccatum] *om.* FV[2]   12: baptizaretur] baptizetur CFV[2]   13: acced-
eret] accideret V[1]   14: ad baptismum] *del.* C   15: impium] imperatum F   16: sperare]
separare *mss*   17: sic] sit F   18: a peccato originali] ab originali peccato PV[1]   19: baptismus]
om. C   20: Ecclesie] homines *add.* C

mortal sin through the sacrament of penance as often as you show contrition for your sins and are released through penitence. And because this does not come about except through the Church and by the Church, you must acknowledge that you hold all your goods from the Church as often as you are made worthy by her, first, of an eternal inheritance, and then of a paternal inheritance and of every other kind of possession, whether it comes to you from your father or from elsewhere.

Thus, what was said in the heading of this chapter was well said: that no one is worthy of a paternal inheritance or of any other possession or of any other principality or lordship unless he is the servant and son of the Church, and unless, through the Church, he is made worthy of an eternal inheritance. The truth is clearly contained, then, in what is said in Matthew 6: 'Therefore seek first the Kingdom of God and His justice, and all these things will be added to you.'[1] Unless you seek first the Kingdom of God, therefore, and unless you are under God, you are not worthy to have these things added to you. On the contrary, as Chrysostom says in his interpretation of this, 'The earth is cursed by the sins of men, according to what is written: "The earth shall be cursed by your work."'[2] The earth is cursed, then, by the work of the sinner, for the sinner is not worthy that the earth should serve him. And if he is not worthy that earth, which is the basest of the elements, should serve him, nor is he worthy that anything else should serve him.

It is indeed fitting that he who is contemptuous of serving the Lord of all things should himself be deprived of all things.[3] Thus, those who are not the servants of God are not worthy of a paternal inheritance nor of anything else. And because we cannot become the servants of God unless we are sacramentally absolved through the Church, we must acknowledge that we hold all that we possess from the Church and through the Church, by whose sacraments, which are the vessels of Grace, we receive the Divine Grace and are made the sons and heirs of God.

It must be noted, however, that, although we have said that baptism is the remedy against original sin — for it is the direct remedy against such sin — if an adult were to be baptized, and did not come to baptism falsely, then, because it is impious to hope for only half a pardon from God, he who was thus baptized would be absolved both from original sin and also from every mortal sin which he had committed before baptism. Thus, the sacrament of baptism is directed against original sin; but, if it finds any other sins present with the original, baptism washes away all these simultaneously with the original.

It must be noted also that we have said that original sin is absolved through baptism conferred by the Church and in the Church's prescribed form, and that the

---

1. Matt. 6:33. 'These things' are food, drink and clothing (see vs. 31): i.e. temporal possessions generally.
2. *Homilia in Genesim* 18 (PG 53-54:146), quoting Gen. 3:17.
3. The use of *contempsit* here is perhaps intended to echo Augustine's *amor sui usque ad contemptum Dei* (*De civitate Dei* 14:28 (CCSL 48:451)); and cf. *Epistulae* 93:12:50 (CSEL 34(2):494).

peccato mortali quod baptizati[1] post baptismum commiserint; cui non obstat quod in sola contricione dimittuntur peccata. Quia nullus vere contritus est[2] nisi habeat sacramentum penitencie in voto, id est in voluntate et proposito, id est nisi proponat confiteri, et cum adest locus et tempus, si vult vere esse[3] absolutus, tenetur confiteri, quia ficta reputaretur voluntas, et Deus iudicat illam voluntatem fictam esse quam, cum adest locus et tempus, quis non implere procurat. Si ergo dicis te contritum et proposuisse te[4] confiteri, iudicabit Deus tuum propositum fictum fuisse si non implevisti illud propositum[5] cum locus affuit atque[6] tempus. Ab Ecclesia itaque, cuius est dare sacramenta penitencie et alia sacramenta, debes recognoscere quod factus es Dei filius et Dei servus, cui serviens[7] dignus es ut res tue tibi famulentur et serviant.

CAPITULUM IX: *Quod licet non sit potestas nisi a Deo, nullus tamen est dignus aliqua potestate nisi sub Ecclesia et per Ecclesiam fiat dignus.*

Tam auctoritates canonis quam sanctorum de potestate loqui diversimode invenimus. Nam ad Romanos XIII scribitur quod 'non est potestas nisi a Deo.'[8] Osee autem VIII legitur: 'Ipsi regnaverunt, et non ex me.' Videtur itaque Apostolus[9] velle quod non sit potestas nisi a Deo, et Osee videtur asserere quod aliqui regnent non ex Deo. Gregorius eciam, exponens prefatam Osee auctoritatem, ait quod 'ex se et non ex arbitrio Summi Rectoris regnant qui nullis virtutibus subditi, nequaquam divinitus vocati, sed sua cupiditate accensi culmen regiminis rapiunt.' Videtur ergo in hiis verbis innuere Gregorius quod duplex sit potestas et duplex regnum, unum a[10] Deo collatum et aliud a cupiditate dominandi usurpatum; ut ex hoc videatur non omnis potestas esse a Deo, sed aliqua est per rapinam et violenciam usurpata. Cui videtur contradicere Augustinus III *De Trinitate* capitulo VIII, ubi ait quod iniqui voluntatem habent iniustam, potestatem autem nonnisi iuste accipiunt; et quia non acciperent nisi[11] a Deo ipsam[12] haberent,[13] non erit potestas nisi a Deo, cum eciam iniqui nonnisi a Deo potestatem accipiant,[14] dicente Domino ipsi Pilato: 'Non haberes potestatem adversus me ullam, nisi datum esset tibi desuper.'

Ut ergo talis controversia dissolvatur, sciendum quod potestas de genere bonorum est. Nullum autem bonum alicui datum est vel concessum nisi a Summo

---

1: baptizati] *del.* C baptisandi PV[1]   2: contritus est] est contritus CF   3: vere esse] esse vere F
4: te] *om.* C   5: propositum] *om.* C   6: atque] adest FV[2]   7: serviens] servus F   8: Deo] et
add. FV[2]   9: Apostolus] apostolum F   10: a] *om.* C   11: nisi] ipsam *add.* C   12: ipsam] *om.* C
13: ipsam haberent] haberent illam F   14: accipiant] accipient FV[2]

mortal sin which the baptized commit after baptism is absolved through the sacrament of penance: to which it is no objection to say that contrition alone is the ground upon which sins are forgiven. For no one is truly contrite unless he has the sacrament of penance by desire — that is, in will and purpose: that is, unless he intends to confess. And, when the time and place is at hand, he is bound to confess if he truly wishes to be absolved; for his wish would be deemed false, and God judges that wish to be false, if he does not bring it to completion when the time and place is at hand. If, therefore, you say that you are contrite and that you had intended to make your confession, God will judge your intention to have been false if you did not fulfil that intention when the place and time was at hand. Thus, you must acknowledge that it is by the Church, in whose power it is to give the sacrament of penance and the other sacraments, that you are made a son of God and a servant of God: serving Whom, you are worthy that your own possessions should serve and be subject to you.

CHAPTER IX: *That although there is no power except of God, no one is worthy of any power unless he is made worthy under the Church and through the Church.*

We find that the authorities of the [Biblical] canon and of the saints alike speak of power in different ways. For in Romans 13 it is written that 'There is no power except of God.'[1] In Hosea 8, however, we read: 'They have reigned, but not from me.'[2] The Apostle, then, appears to maintain that there is no power except of God; yet Hosea seems to assert that there are some who reign [even though their power is] not of God. And Gregory, interpreting the authority of Hosea just cited, says: 'Those who, inflamed by their own greed, seize the pinnacle of rule, reign of themselves and not by the will of the Supreme Ruler: they are sustained by no virtues, nor are they in any way divinely called.'[3] In these words, therefore, Gregory appears to suggest that power is twofold and kingship is twofold: that one kind is conferred by God and the other usurped out of greed for lordship. Thus, it would seem from this that not all power is of God, but that some is usurped by robbery and violence. Yet Augustine seems to contradict this at *De Trinitate* 3:8, where he says that although the wicked have an unjust will, they nonetheless receive power justly.[4] And, because they would not receive it [justly] unless they had it from God, there will [after all] be no power except of God, for even the wicked receive power from God alone. For the Lord said to Pilate: 'You would have no power against me at all had it not been given to you from above.'[5]

That such controversy may be settled, therefore, it must be known that power is a member of the class of goods. And no good is given to anyone or conferred except

1. Rom. 13:1.
2. Hos. 8:4.
3. *Regula pastoralis* 1:1 (PL 77:14).
4. CCSL 50:141.
5. John 19:11.

Bono, qui est omnis boni Bonum. Sed quamvis potestas sit bonum[1] et a Deo data, usus tamen potestatis potest esse non bonus. Dicemus ergo quod potestatem quam habes a Deo habes,[2] et membra que habes a Deo habes. Sicut igitur membris que a Deo habes potes male uti et peccare, sic potestate quam a Deo habes potes male uti et demereri. Unde et Dominus, respondens Pilato, cum prius dixisset quod non haberet adversus eum[3] potestatem ullam nisi esset sibi[4] datum desuper, postea subdit: 'Propterea qui tradidit me tibi maius peccatum habet.'[5] Quod Chrysostomus exponens ait: 'Vide qualiter Pilatus seipsum condemnat. Si enim in eo totum positum erat, quia potestatem habebat crucifigere eum et dimittere eum, quare nullam causam inveniens non absolvebat[6] eum? A Deo itaque habebat[7] huiusmodi potestatem, sed male utebatur huiusmodi potestate, cum sedens pro tribunali iudicaret interfici innocentem.' Iudas igitur et populus Iudaicus a Deo habuerunt istam potestatem ut possent tradere Iesum Pilato[8] ad iudicandum; et Pilatus a Deo habuit istam potestatem ut posset tradere Iesum[9] militibus ad crucifigendum. Eapropter utrique abusi sunt huiusmodi potestate, quia nec illi innocentem debuerunt tradere Pilato ad iudicandum, nec Pilatus debuit ipsum tradere[10] ad[11] crucifigendum. Sed Iudas hoc fecit amore pecunie, populus Iudaicus hoc livore invidie, Pilatus[12] hoc egit timore Cesaree potestatis. Cum ergo peius[13] sit peccare cupiditate et invidia quam timore, tam Iudas, qui per cupiditatem, quam populus Iudaicus, qui per invidiam tradidit, maius peccatum habuit quam Pilatus, qui timens Cesarem Iesum innocentem iudicavit.

Omnes ergo sunt sub potestate, tam boni quam mali, et ipsa potestas est sub potestate, et a Deo est quod sit potestas sub potestate. Unde Augustinus, hoc exponens, ait quod talem, quippe Deus, Pilato dederat[14] potestatem ut esset sub Cesaris potestate. Populus quidem Iudaicus et Pilatus abusi sunt potestate sibi tradita, quia uterque peccavit; sed magis populus, qui fecit hoc invidendo, quam Pilatus, qui hoc egit metuendo. Unde Augustinus, exponens prefata verba, ait: '"Propterea qui tradidit me tibi maius peccatum habet," quia ille, id est populus Iudaicus, tradidit me[15] potestati tue invidendo; tu vero eandem potestatem in me executurus[16] es metuendo.'

Erit[17] itaque una distinccio: quod aliud est potestas, aliud potestatis usus; nam potestas, licet secundum se semper sit bona, usus tamen potestatis potest esse non bonus.

Alia autem distinccio esse potest: quod, licet omnis potestas sit a Deo, non tamen omnis huiusmodi potestas est a Deo iussa, sed alia[18] est a Deo iussa,[19] ut illa

1: bonum] bona FV²   2: a Deo habes] habes a deo C   3: eum] ullam *add.* C   4: sibi] ei C
5: habet] habuit FV²   6: absolvebat] absorbebat F   7: eum? A ... habebat] *om.* F   8: Pilato]
om. V²   9: Pilato ad ... Iesum] *om.* F   10: Pilato ad ... tradere] *om.* F   11: ad] *om.* C
12: Pilatus] quidem *add.* FV²   13: peius] prius F   14: dederat] dederit PV¹   15: tradidit me]
me tradidit F   16: executus FV¹V²   17: Erit] fuit PV¹   18: alia] aliqua F   19: sed alia ...
iussa] *om.* V²

by the Supreme Good, who is the Good of all goods. But although power is a good and is given by God, the use of such power can nonetheless be not good. We shall say, therefore, that you receive the power which you have from God, and that you receive the bodily members which you have from God. Thus, just as you can put the bodily members which you receive from God to evil use, and sin, so can you put the power which you receive from God to evil use, and deserve ill. And so, answering Pilate, when the Lord Himself had first said that he would have no power against Him had it not been given to him from above, He afterwards added: 'Therefore he who has delivered me to you has the greater sin.' And Chrysostom, interpreting this, says: 'See how Pilate condemns himself. For if it rested entirely with him, since he had power, to crucify Him and pardon Him, why did he not release Him when he found no cause against Him? He had such power from God, then; but he made evil use of this power when, sitting at the tribunal, he judged that an innocent man was to be slain.'[1] Thus, Judas and the Jewish people had from God a power such that they could deliver Jesus to Pilate to be judged; and Pilate had from God a power such that he could deliver Jesus to the soldiers to be crucified. But both abused that power; for the former should not have delivered an innocent man to Pilate to be judged, and Pilate should not have delivered Him to be crucified. But Judas did this from love of money, the Jewish people from the malice of envy, and Pilate acted thus from fear of the power of Caesar.[2] Therefore, since it is worse to sin from greed and envy than from fear, both Judas, who acted from greed, and the Jewish people, who delivered Him out of envy, had a greater sin than Pilate, who judged the innocent Jesus while fearing Caesar.

All men, therefore, good and evil alike, are under a power, and that power is [in turn] under a power, [as in the case of Pilate, whose power was under Caesar's]; and it is of God that one power is under another. Hence Augustine, interpreting this [i.e. John 19:11–15], says that God indeed gave to Pilate a power such that he should be under the power of Caesar; and, although both the Jewish people and Pilate abused the power given to them — for both sinned — the people, who did this from envy, [sinned] more than Pilate, who acted thus out of fear. And so Augustine, interpreting the words already cited, says: '"Therefore he who has delivered me to you has the greater sin": for he (that is, the Jewish people) delivered me into your power out of envy, but you will exercise the same power against me out of fear.'[3]

This, then, will be one distinction: that power is one thing and the use of power another. For though, in itself, power is always a good, the use of power can nonetheless be not good.

And another distinction is possible: that although all power is of God, not all such power is given by God's command. Rather, some is given by God's command,

1. *Homiliae in Ioannem* 84 (PG 59:457).
2. Cf. John 19:12, 15.
3. *In Ioannis evangelium* 116:19:5 (CCSL 36:648–649.); although the words in question apply more obviously to Judas than to 'the Jewish people.'

que data est bonis, et aliqua a Deo permissa, ut illa que data est malis. Quod satis innuit Augustinus III *De Trinitate* capitulo VIII,[1] ubi ait quod nec boni hoc agunt,[2] id est suam potestatem exercent, nisi in quantum Deus iubet, nec mali hoc iniuste faciunt nisi in quantum[3] iuste ipse permittit. Potestas igitur a Deo data numquam est ex omni parte iniusta, sed vel est ex omni parte iusta quantum ad bonos, quibus Deus potestatem iuste dat, et ipsi secundum eam iuste agunt; vel est[4] quantum ad malos[5] iusta ex parte dantis, in quantum Deus hoc[6] iuste permittit, et iniusta ex parte recipientis, in quantum mali secundum eam iniuste faciunt. Quod expresse Augustinus innuit in prelibata auctoritate, ubi ait quod mali secundum potenciam eis datam iniuste faciunt, ipse autem Deus iuste permittit.

Omnis itaque[7] potestas est a Deo vel iussa vel permissa; vel omnis potestas est a Deo quia omnis potestas est quid[8] bonum. Usus autem vel execucio potestatis bona et mala esse potest. Non igitur omnes merentur per huiusmodi potestatem sibi a Deo datam, sicut divicias, membra corporis et alia quecumque bona a Deo habemus. Sed non semper per huiusmodi bona meremur,[9] quia non semper bene utimur huiusmodi bonis.

Bonum est enim ingenium naturale, industria, sciencie; bone sunt[10] artes; facultates,[11] membra corporis; bona est aqua; bonus est et[12] ignis. Hiis tamen qui suffocantur non est bona aqua, et hiis qui comburuntur non est bonus ignis. Bonum enim esset[13] ad opus suffocatorum quod aqua non fuisset. Ideo dicitur VII *Ethicorum* quod quando aqua suffocat non est opus bibere. Si enim quis sitiret, melius esset quod abstineret a potu quam quod tantum biberet quod suffocaretur. Bona est ergo[14] aqua, sed non ad opus suffocatorum, et bonus est ignis, sed non ad opus combustorum; bona sunt membra corporis, sed male utentibus non sunt bona: ut si quis per oculos sic scandalizatur quod per eos peccat mortaliter, in quo peccato moriens vadit in gehennam, bonum fuisset ei quod esset natus cecus et non peccasset per oculos nec ivisset in gehennam. A Deo itaque habemus membra non ut eis male utamur, sed ut per ea Deo serviamus; et quanto meliora et pulchriora membra habemus, tanto magis tenemur Deo servire, cui non serviendo, gravius peccamus. Hoc eciam modo bone sunt facultates et bona est sanitas corporis; sed si per hec[15] bona ad malum inducimur, melius esset nobis quod essemus infirmi et pauperes et essemus Deo subiecti, quam sani et divites et essemus[16] a Deo aversi.

Isto eciam modo bone sunt artes, sciencie bone,[17] ingenium bonum,[18] [bona est] industria naturalis. Sed si per hec[19] inclinaris ad peccandum, bonum esset tibi quod esses simplex, grossus,[20] ignarus et iners, et a peccato caveres, quam

---

1: VIII] vii *mss*   2: hoc agunt] agunt hoc F   3: nisi in quantum] nunquam FV[2]   4: est] *del.* C
5: malos] est *interlin. add.* C   6: Deus hoc] hoc deus C   7: itaque] *om.* FV[2]   8: est quid] *om.* C
9: meremur] merentur F   10: bone sunt] *om.* CFV[2]   11: facultates] sunt bone *add.* PV[1]
12: et] *om.* FV[1]V[2]   13: enim esset] esset enim F   14: ergo] *om.* F   15: hec] *om.* F
16: essemus] *om.* C   17: bone] *om.* FV[2]   18: bonum] *om.* FV[2]   19: hec] hoc *mss*   20: grossus] et *add.* C

as is that which is given to good men; and some is given only by God's permission, as is that which is given to the wicked. This is suggested plainly enough by Augustine at *De Trinitate* 3:8, where he says that 'Good men do not do this' — that is, do not exercise their power — 'except insofar as God commands, while wicked men do not commit injustice except insofar as He justly permits.'[1] Thus, a power given by God is never unjust in all respects. Rather, it is either just in all respects, as in the case of good men, to whom God justly gives power and who act justly by means of it; or, in the case of evil men, it is just on the part of the Giver, inasmuch as God justly permits it, and unjust on the part of the recipients, inasmuch as wicked men commit injustice by means of it. And Augustine expressly suggests this in the place just cited, where he says that wicked men commit injustice by means of the power given to them, but that God Himself justly permits this.

All power, then, is of God, whether by command or permission; or all power is of God since all power is a kind of good: but the use or exercise of power can be either good or evil. Thus, not all men earn merit by such power as is given to them by God, just as, though we receive riches, the parts of the body and all other goods from God, we do not always earn merit by means of such goods, for we do not always use such goods well.

For natural ability, diligence and the sciences are good; the arts are good; riches and the parts of the body are good; water is good; and fire is good. But water is not a good for those who are drowning, and fire is not a good for those who are burning: for the need of the drowned, it would have been good if there had been no water. Thus, it is said in *Ethics* 7 that, when water drowns, there is no need to drink.[2] For, if anyone thirsts, it would still be better for him to abstain from drink than to drink so much that he drowns. Water is good, therefore; but not for the need of the drowned. And fire is good, but not for the need of the burnt. And the parts of the body are good, but they are not goods for those who use them ill. Thus, if anyone is led astray by his eyes so that, through them, he commits mortal sin and, dying in such sin, goes to hell, it would have been good for him to have been born blind and so neither to have sinned through his eyes nor gone to hell.[3] Thus, we receive the parts of our bodies from God not so that we may put them to evil use, but so that we may serve God through them; and the better and more admirable the parts of our bodies are, the more are we bound to serve God by means of them, and the more grievously do we sin by not serving Him. In the same way, riches are good and bodily health is good. But if we are led into evil by these goods, then it would be better for us to have been ill and poor, yet subject to God, than healthy and rich and turned away from God.

In the same way again, the arts are good, the sciences are good, mental ability and natural diligence are good. But if you are drawn into sin by these goods, then it would be good for you if you were simple, dull, ignorant, and idle, yet without

1.   CCSL 50:141.
2.   *Nicomachean Ethics* 7:2 (1146ª35).
3.   Cf. Matthew 18:9.

hec[1] habendo peccato[2] servires. Si enim intellectus te sufflat[3] et ostendit tibi vias per quas potes malum facere, et tuum ingenium te ad peccandum inducit, peior es quam bestia, que non habens[4] intellectum nescit hec mala excogitare. Ideo dicitur VII *Ethicorum* quod decies millies utique plura mala faceret homo malus quam bestia, et I *Politicorum* scribitur quod sicut homo perfectus virtutibus est animalium optimum, sic separatus a lege et iusticia est animalium pessimum. Habet enim, ut ibi dicitur, homo sevissima arma; appellantur enim ibi[5] 'sevissima arma' intellectus et racio, per que omnia nequissima possunt excogitari. Ideo si hiis armis, videlicet intellectu et racione, homo vult uti ad bonum, homo est[6] animalium[7] optimum, si ad malum, est animalium pessimum.

Clare itaque apparet quod omnia preassignata bona a Deo sunt, qui est Summum Bonum et omnis boni Bonum; sed male utentibus non bona sunt,[8] nec sunt ad salutem, sed ad dampnacionem, iuxta[9] Gregorii sentenciam:[10] 'Cum enim crescunt dona, raciones eciam crescunt donorum; unde[11] tanto humilior, eciam ad[12] serviendum[13] Deo promotior[14] quisque debet esse ex munere, quanto obligaciorem se esse conspicit in reddenda racione.' Data itaque sunt tibi membra corporis, facultates et cetera huiusmodi bona, ut eis[15] utaris non ad iniusticiam[16] et impietatem, sed ad divinum obsequium et ad opera pietatis.

Quod ergo dictum est de omnibus prefatis bonis[17] de ipsa eciam potestate verum est: quod non est potestas nisi a Deo, sed quanto potencior es et[18] bene uteris potestate tibi tradita, tanto magis mereris, quia, ut dicitur Iob XXXVI, Deus potentes[19] non abicit, cum et ipse sit potens. Sed si qui male utantur potestate sibi tradita, quanto potenciores sunt, potenciora tormenta pacientur, et quanto magis presunt, durius iudicium fiet eis. Ideo dicitur Sapiencie VI quod 'iudicium durissimum hiis qui presunt fiet'; et ibidem subditur quod 'potentes[20] potenter tormenta pacientur.' Es igitur princeps, es rex, habes potenciam magnam, a Deo illam potenciam habes: ex hoc debes esse[21] Deo magis subiectus. Sed si Deo subiectus non es, indignus es illa potencia, et quia, ut dicebamus, generatus a patre carnaliter nasceris filius ire et non ens[22] Deo subiectus, peccans eciam mortaliter, te avertis a Deo et non es subiectus sibi, indignus es potestate illa. Et quia nil dignius[23] quam privari indignum, debent parentes pro filiis ad devocionem surgere et ad Ecclesiam recurrere, ut spiritualiter regenerentur, per quam regenerati fient digni hereditate paterna[24]

1: hec] hoc *mss*   2: peccato] peccando FV[2]   3: sufflat] suffocat *mss*   4: habens] habet PV[1]
5: ibi] *om.* F   6: homo est] est homo C   7: homo est animalium] animalium est F   8: bona sunt] sunt bona CF   9: iuxta] illud *add.* C   10: sentenciam] *om.* C   11: unde] ut C   12: eciam ad] et FV[2]   13: serviendum] serviendo F   14: promotior] propinquior FV[2]   15: ut eis] *om.* F ut V[2]   16: iniusticiam] instanciam F   17: bonis] *om.* PV[1]   18: et] *om.* F   19: potentes] potestates FV[2]   20: potentes] potestates FV[2]   21: debes esse] esse debes FV[2]   22: ens] es F
23: dignius] est *add.* FV[2]   24: paterna] eterna C

sin, than, having these goods, were the servant of sin. For if the intellect puffs you up and shows you ways in which you can do evil, and if your ability leads you into sin, then you are worse than a beast which, having no intellect, does not know how to devise evil deeds. Thus, it is said in *Ethics* 7 that a wicked man will do ten thousand times more harm than a beast, and in *Politics* 1 it is written that, just as man is the best of animals when perfected by the virtues, so is he the worst of animals when separated from law and justice.[1] For, as is said there, man has the most formidable arms (for intellect and reason are there called 'the most formidable arms') by which all manner of iniquities can be devised. And so, if man desires to use these arms — that is, intellect and reason — for good, he is the best of animals; if for evil, he is the worst of animals.

It appears clearly, then, that all the goods so far mentioned come from God, Who is the Supreme Good and the Good of all goods. But they are not goods for those who use them ill, and they lead not to salvation, but to damnation, according to what Gregory says: 'For when gifts increase, the duties of those gifts increase also; and so the more obliged each man perceives himself to be in rendering an account [to God for a gift], the more humble must he be, and the more ready to serve God through that gift.'[2] Thus, the parts of your body, your riches, and other such goods are given to you so that you may use them not for injustice and impiety, but in the Divine service and for works of godliness.

Therefore, what has been said of all the goods so far mentioned is also true of power itself: that there is no power except of God. But the mightier you are, and the better use you make of the power delivered to you, the more merit you deserve, since, as is said in Job 36, God does not overthrow the mighty, for He Himself is mighty.[3] But if those to whom power is given use it ill, then, the mightier they are, the mightier will be the torments which they will suffer, and the greater their rule the more harshly will they be judged. Thus, it is said in Wisdom 6 that 'a most harsh judgment awaits those who rule'; and, in the same place, it is added that 'the mighty will be mightily tormented.'[4] You are a prince, then; you are a king; you have great power: you have that power from God, and so you must be the more subject to God. But if you are not subject to God you are unworthy of that power. And, as we have said,[5] because, carnally begotten of a father, you were born a child of wrath[6] and a being not subject to God, and because you have turned away from God by sinning mortally and are not subject to Him, you are [indeed] unworthy of that power. And since nothing is more fitting than for the unworthy to be deprived, parents must rise up in devotion for their children's sake and hasten to the Church so that they [i.e. the children] may be spiritually regenerated and, through this regeneration, be made worthy of a paternal inheritance and

---

1. *Nicomachean Ethics* 7:6 (1150ᵃ5); *Politics* 1:2 (1253ᵃ30).
2. *Homiliae XL in evangelia* 1:9:1 (PL 76:1106).
3. Job 36:5.
4. Wisd. 6:6–7.
5. Ch. VII, p. 139.
6. Cf. Eph. 2:3.

et omni potestate et dominio.[1]

Potentum itaque[2] principum heredes et quorumcumque fidelium filii hereditatem quam habent, potenciam et dominium, ut supra sufficienter tetigimus, magis debent recognoscere ab Ecclesia, per quam[3] spiritualiter regenerati fiunt talibus honoribus, potestatibus et facultatibus digni, quam a parentibus carnalibus, a quibus nascuntur indigni; et quilibet fideles,[4] quociens in peccatum mortale labuntur et per Ecclesiam absolvuntur, tociens omnia bona sua, omnes honores,[5] omnes[6] potestates et facultates suas debent recognoscere ab Ecclesia, per quam absoluti facti sunt talibus digni, quibus, cum peccato serviebant, erant indigni. Et quia nulli sunt digni nec honore nec dominio nec potestate nec aliquo alio[7] bono nisi per sacramenta ecclesiastica et per Ecclesiam et sub Ecclesia,[8] bene dictum est, ut in rubrica capituli dicebatur, quod, licet non sit potestas nisi a Deo, nullus tamen est dignus aliqua potestate nisi sub Ecclesia et per Ecclesiam fiat dignus.

Ex dictis autem sequendo distincciones superius factas, quod aliud est potestas, aliud potestatis usus, et quod[9] potestas aliqua est iussa, aliqua est permissa, possumus solvere omnes prefatas contrarietates. Nam si loquamur[10] de ipsa potestate secundum se, que bonum quid est, verum est quod ait Apostolus, quod non est potestas nisi a Deo. Sed si loquamur[11] de ipso potestatis usu, verum est quod dicitur in Osee, quod 'ipsi regnaverunt, sed non ex me.' Nam regnare est potestate uti. Illi ergo non regnant ex Deo, qui non bene utuntur potestate sibi data a Deo. Vel dicere possumus quod et mali habent iustam potestatem, quia, licet ipsi ea iniuste utantur, tamen non habent aliquam potestatem nisi quantam Deus eis iuste permittit. Et si queratur quare Deus permittit malos potestatem habere cum sciat eos male usuros, dicemus quod aliquando hoc est[12] propter peccata populi, iuxta illud Iob XXXIV: 'Qui regnare facit[13] hominem hypocritam propter peccata populi'; et Osee XIII scribitur:[14] 'Dabo tibi regem in furore meo.' Vel possumus dicere quod, etsi nulla essent peccata populi, sinit Deus quod mali habeant potestatem, sicut sinit quod habeant membra corporis et[15] facultates et divicias et alia huiusmodi bona, que bonis et malis possunt esse communia. Omnis ergo potestas est a Deo,[16] si consideretur ipsa potestas que est quid bonum; et tamen regnant mali non ex Deo, si consideretur potestatis abusus, qui[17] est quid malum. Vel omnis potestas est a Deo aut iussa aut permissa, ut dicit Augustinus; et mali cupiditate dominandi usurpant sibi potestatem, ut dicebat[18] Gregorius. Nam usurpare sibi potestatem dicuntur mali, quia hoc non agunt divina iussione, sed permissione.

1: dominio] quod per huismodi hereditatem et hec possunt *add. and del.* C   2: itaque] eciam *add.* C   3: quam] ecclesiam F   4: fideles] fidelis F   5: honores] humores *del.* C   6: omnes] *om.* CFV[2]   7: aliquo alio] alio aliquo C   8: et sub Ecclesia] *om.* F   9: quod] *om.* F   10: loquamur] loquimur F   11: loquamur] loquimur F   12: est] *om.* F   13: regnare facit] facit regnare F   14: scribitur] *om.* F   15: et] *om.* CF   16: Deo] sed *add.* FV[2]   17: qui] que C   18: dicebat] dicuntur *del.* C

of all power and lordship.

Thus, as we have sufficiently shown above, the heirs of mighty princes and the sons of all faithful men must acknowledge that they receive the inheritance, power and lordship which they have rather from the Church, through whom, being spiritually regenerated, they are made worthy of such honours, powers and riches, than from the carnal parents through whom they were born unworthy. And all faithful men, as often as they are plunged into mortal sin and receive absolution through the Church, must acknowledge that they hold all their goods, all their honours, all their powers and riches, of the Church, through whose absolution they have been made worthy of those things of which, for as long as they served sin, they were unworthy. And since none are worthy of honour or lordship or power or of any other good except through the sacraments of the Church and by the Church and under the Church, what was said in the heading of this chapter was well said: that, although there is no power except of God, no one is worthy of any power unless he is made worthy under the Church and through the Church.

Also, by observing the distinctions made above — that power is one thing and its use another, and that one kind of power is commanded and the other permitted — we can resolve all the contradictions previously mentioned. For if we speak of power in itself, which is a kind of good, then what the Apostle says is true: that there is no power except of God. But if we speak of the use of such power, then what is said in Hosea is true: that 'They have reigned, but not from me.' For to reign is to make use of power. Therefore, those who do not use the power given to them by God well do not reign from God. Alternatively, we can say that even the wicked have a just power since, though they use it unjustly, they nonetheless have no power except insofar as God justly permits it to them. And if it be asked why God permits the wicked to have power when He knows that they will use it ill, we shall reply that this sometimes comes about because of the sins of the people, according to Job 34: 'Who causes a hypocrite to reign because of the people's sins.'[1] Again, it is written in Hosea 13: 'I will give you a king in my wrath.'[2] Or we can say that, even if there were no sins of the people, God permits the wicked to have power just as He permits them to have bodily members and riches and wealth and other such goods, which can be common to good and evil men alike.[3] Therefore, if we consider power, which is a kind of good, all power is of God. And even if we consider the abuse of power, which is a kind of evil — for wicked men do not reign from God — all power is nonetheless still of God, either by command or by permission, as Augustine says. And, as Gregory has said, the wicked usurp power to themselves out of greed for lordship; but those who usurp power to themselves are called wicked men, for they do this not by divine command, but [only] by permission.

1. Job 34:30.
2. Hosea 13:11.
3. Cf., e.g., Augustine, *Sermo* 50:2–7 (CCSL 41:625–629).

CAPITULUM X: *Quod in omnibus temporalibus Ecclesia habet dominium universale, fideles autem de iure et cum iusticia dominium particulare habere possunt.*

Quia hanc secundam partem huius operis prosecuti sumus et prosequimur propter dominium temporalium quod habet Ecclesia, ideo in hoc capitulo volumus declarare quod Ecclesia in temporalibus omnibus habet ius et dominium universale, fideles autem in ipsis temporalibus nonnisi dominium particulare de iure et cum iusticia habent vel habere possunt, infideles autem cum iusticia nullum habent dominium. Duo itaque in hoc capitulo circa temporalia intendimus declarare: primo quidem, quale sit dominium Ecclesie circa hec temporalia, quia est universale; secundo, quale est dominium ipsorum fidelium, quia de iure et cum iusticia est particulare. Dicimus autem 'de iure et cum iusticia' quia de facto posset potestas terrena super temporalibus non divina iussione sed pocius permissione sibi dominium universale usurpare; quo facto non esset illud dominium de iure et cum iusticia, sed magis esset de facto et cum iniuria. Esset autem tercio declarandum[1] quale sit dominium ipsorum infidelium, quia vere et ex utraque parte cum iusticia tale dominium[2] esse non potest. Dicimus quidem 'ex utraque parte cum iusticia,' quia non est potestas nisi a Deo. Ipsa itaque potestas quam habent infideles super temporalia a Deo est.[3] Duo ergo est considerare in huiusmodi potestate, videlicet, Deum eam iuste permittentem, et ipsum hominem infidelem secundum huiusmodi potestatem permissam iniuste operantem, ut patuit per Augustinum *De Trinitate* libro III capitulo VIII, qui ait quod nec mali hoc, id est secundum hoc, sive secundum potestatem eis permissam, iniuste faciunt nisi quantum ipse iuste permittit.[4] Huiusmodi potestas ergo[5] non est ex omni parte iusta, quia, etsi est iusta ex parte Dei permittentis, non est iusta ex parte operantis et abutentis. Hec itaque tria intendimus per ordinem declarare; sed prima duo in hoc capitulo declarabimus, tercium vero poterit in sequenti capitulo declarari.

Propter primum, sciendum quod Hugo, *De sacramentis* parte II, capitulo VII, circa temporalia distinguit duplex dominium: utile et potestativum. Appellat autem dominium utile illud quod est fructiferum, dominium autem potestativum vocat illud quod est iurisdiccionale, ad quod spectat iusticiam exercere. Secundum autem utrumque dicimus Ecclesiam in temporalibus dominium habere[6] universale. Ostendemus ergo de utroque dominio, tam potestativo quam fructifero, quod Ecclesia habet dominium universale in omnibus temporalibus.[7] Sciendum est[8] ergo quod in nobis tria[9] est considerare: animam, corpus et res exteriores que communi nomine temporalia nominantur. Tribus itaque viis[10] propositum ostendemus.

1: declarandum] declarandam P　2: tale dominium] *del.* C　3: est] habent F　4: permittit] deus ergo iuste permittit potestatem aliquam secundum quam malus homo etsi fidelis iniuste facit *add. and del.* C　5: potestas ergo] ergo potestas CFV²　6: dominium habere] habere dominium FV²　7: temporalibus] temporibus P　8: est] *om.* FV²　9: tria] *om.* V²　10: viis] iuris V²

CHAPTER X: *That the Church has a universal lordship in all temporal things, but that, as of right and with justice, the faithful can have only a particular lordship.*

Since we have carried forward, and are carrying forward, the second part of this work for [the purpose of elucidating] the temporal lordship which the Church has, we therefore wish to show in this chapter that the Church has a universal right and lordship in all temporal things, but that, as of right and with justice, the faithful have, or can have, no more than a particular lordship in such temporal things; and [in the next chapter we shall show] that unbelievers can have no lordship with justice at all. In this chapter, then, we intend to make two matters clear concerning temporal things: first, the nature of the Church's lordship with respect to these temporal things, for this is universal; and, second, the nature of the lordship of the faithful themselves, for, as of right and with justice, this is particular. And we say 'as of right and with justice' because, *de facto*, an earthly power might usurp to itself a universal temporal lordship: not by divine command, but only by permission. But, if this were done, such lordship would not be held as of right and with justice; rather, it would be held only *de facto* and with injustice. And, third, we must discuss the nature of the lordship of unbelievers; for such lordship cannot be held truly and with justice in both respects. We say indeed 'with justice in both respects,' for there is no power except of God. Thus, even that power which unbelievers have over temporal things is of God. There are, therefore, two aspects to consider in relation to such power: namely, God's having justly permitted it, and the unjust use made of such power by the unfaithful men to whom it is permitted. And this was made clear by Augustine, who says at *De Trinitate* 3:8 that with this — that is, by means of this, or by means of the power permitted them — wicked men can commit no injustice except insofar as God justly permits.[1] Therefore, such power is not just in every respect; for, though it is just in respect of God's permitting it, it is not just in respect of his [i.e. the wicked man's] using and abusing it. We intend, then, to make these three matters [i.e. the lordship of the Church, of the faithful, and of unbelievers] clear in turn. But we shall deal with the first two in this chapter, and we shall be able to deal with the third in the next chapter.

As to the first, it must be known that Hugh, in *De sacramentis*, Part 2, Chapter 7, distinguishes two kinds of lordship in temporals: of use, and of power.[2] And that which he calls a lordship of use consists in the right to enjoy fruits; but that which he calls a lordship of power is jurisdictional, and to it belongs the execution of justice. And we say that the Church has a universal temporal lordship in both these ways. Therefore, we shall show that the Church has a universal lordship in all temporal things by considering the two kinds of lordship: of power, and of enjoyment. It must be known, therefore, that we must consider three things: the soul, the body, and the external goods which are commonly called temporals. Thus, we shall demonstrate our proposition in three ways.

---

1. CCSL 50:141.
2. *De sacramentis fidei Christianae* 2:2:7 (PL 176:420).

Prima autem via sumitur ex parte animarum sive ex parte substanciarum spiritualium; nam anime humane inter spirituales substancias numerantur. Dicebatur autem supra quod tota corporalis substancia per spiritualem gubernatur et regitur, ut patuit per Augustinum, *De Trinitate* libro III capitulo IV. Ille ergo qui spiritualem habet potenciam, consequens est quod omnibus corporibus dominetur, et quia temporalia quedam[1] corporalia sunt, spiritualis potestas, cuiusmodi est ecclesiastica, omnibus temporalibus dominatur. Et ut hoc[2] melius patefiat,[3] dicemus quod si iuxta tria assignata essent tres gladii in Ecclesia, unus quidem qui solum[4] preesset rebus exterioribus, alius vero qui preesset humanis corporibus, et tercius qui preesset animabus et spiritibus, ille quidem gladius qui preesset rebus exterioribus de humanis corporibus se non posset intromittere, dicente Domino in evangelio quod corpus est plus quam esca et anima plus quam vestimentum. Immo, cum esca et vestimentum ordinentur[5] ad corpus, quia anima secundum se nec[6] tegimento nec alimento indiget, consequens est quod ipsum corpus plus sit quam esca et vestimentum. Et quia nil agit ultra suam speciem, gladius ille qui preesset rebus exterioribus que ordinantur ad victum et tegumentum corporis de ipso corpore humano, quod est alcius et excellencius, se intromittere non valeret, quia hoc faciendo ultra suam speciem ageret; nihil autem ultra suam speciem agit nisi hoc faciat in virtute superioris agentis.

Ille ergo gladius qui preesset rebus exterioribus non posset se intromittere de humano corpore nisi hoc faceret in virtute et ex commissione superioris gladii. Sed gladius qui preesset humanis corporibus de rebus exterioribus se intromitteret, et preesset hic gladius illi gladio. Hoc enim faciendo et de rebus exterioribus se intromittendo non ageret ultra vel supra suam speciem, quia res exteriores non sunt supra corpora humana, sed pocius infra. Immo, secundum regulam Boecii, quia quicquid potest virtus inferior potest et superior, quicquid posset gladius qui preesset rebus exterioribus posset et[7] gladius qui preesset corporibus, licet forte non eodem modo, quia non oportet quod secundum eundem modum agat virtus inferior et superior, sed id quod agit virtus inferior modo inferiori potest agere virtus superior modo superiori.

Modus autem superiorum[8] est supplere defectum inferiorum.[9] Rursus, superiorum modus est inferiora dirigere. Spectat et tercio ad superiora intendere bono publico et communi, ut etsi idem agit virtus celestis et virtus particularis, ut quia sol et

---

1: quedam] *del.* C   2: hoc] hec C   3: patefiat] patefiant C   4: solum] solus F   5: ordinentur] ordinantur FV²   6: nec] *om.* C   7: et] *om.* F   8: superiorum] superior F   9: inferiorum] inferiori F

The first way is derived from a consideration of souls or of spiritual substances; for human souls are numbered among spiritual substances. Now we have said above that all corporeal substance is governed and ruled through spiritual, as was made clear by Augustine at *De Trinitate* 3:4.[1] He who has spiritual power, therefore, consequently has lordship of all bodies; and since, in a manner of speaking, temporal goods are bodily things, spiritual power, of which kind is the ecclesiastical, has lordship over all temporal goods. And, to show this more clearly, we shall say that if there were three swords in the Church answering to the three things just mentioned — one to rule external goods only, one to rule human bodies, and a third to rule souls and spirits — the sword which ruled external goods would not be able to concern itself with human bodies.[2] For the Lord said in the Gospel that the body is more than food and the soul more than clothing.[3] Indeed, since it is to the body that food and clothing are ordered (for the soul, as such, has need of neither covering nor nourishment), it follows that the body by itself is more than food and clothing. And because nothing acts beyond what is proper to its kind, the sword which ruled the external goods appointed to feed and clothe the body would not be able to concern itself with the human body as such, which is higher and more excellent: for, by doing this, it would act beyond what is proper to its kind; and nothing acts beyond what is proper to its kind unless it does so through the power of a superior agent.

Therefore, the sword which ruled external goods would not be able to concern itself with the human body unless it did so through the power and by the commission of a superior sword. The sword which ruled human bodies, however, would concern itself with external goods, and so the one sword would rule the other sword; for, by doing this and by concerning itself with external goods, it would not act beyond what is proper to its kind: for external goods are not above human bodies, but, rather, beneath them. Indeed, according to the rule of Boethius,[4] because a superior power can do whatever an inferior can, the sword which ruled bodies would be able to do whatever the sword which ruled external goods could do: although not, perhaps, in the same way, for it is not fitting that an inferior power and a superior should both act in the same way. Rather, what an inferior power accomplishes in an inferior way, a superior power can accomplish in a superior way.

But it is the mode of superiors to supply the defects of inferiors; also, it is the mode of superiors to direct inferiors; and, third, it rests with superiors to strive towards a general and common good. For example, although the force of heaven and a particular force act in the same way, as when the sun and a horse produce a

1. CCSL 50:135–136; cf. Ch. IV, p. 91.
2. The distinction between the rule of human bodies and that of external goods is evidently a distinction as between civil and criminal jurisdiction. The argument of this and the following paragraphs therefore seems to be that, just as criminal jurisdiction overrides civil jurisdiction because of the nature of what it governs, so, for the same reason, spiritual jurisdiction overrides both; though criminal and civil jurisdiction are not, in fact, separate 'swords', but different functions of the same material sword. See also Ch. XIII and n. 4 on p. 211–213.
3. Cf. Matt. 6:25.
4. Possibly *Consolatio philosophiae* 3, pr. 12; but the correspondence is not close.

equus generant equum, virtus tamen particularis existens in semine equi intendit participare[1] aliquid, ut conservacionem[2] huiusmodi[3] speciei, scilicet equine, vel conservacionem horum generabilium et corruptibilium, videlicet equorum; sed virtus celestis sive virtus solis intendit generacionem[4] omnium specierum et omnium generabilium et corruptibilium: ideo sol non solum facit ad generacionem equi, sed eciam ad generacionem hominis, bovis, leonis et omnium aliorum. Sicut ergo in istis naturalibus ad superiores virtutes spectat defectum inferiorum virtutum supplere, eas[5] dirigere et bonum publicum intendere, sic et in gubernacione hominum se habet, ut si potestates inferiores deficerent vel oblique agerent vel bonum publicum non attingerent, potestas superior in omnes inferiores habet animadvertere, et de omnibus habet iudicare. Et inde est quod multa fuerint sine culpa que tamen non fuerint sine causa. Nam deficere, quod[6] est peccatum omissionis, vel oblique[7] agere, quod est peccatum commissionis, non sunt[8] sine culpa; sed non attingere publicum[9] bonum potest esse sine culpa, quia potest esse per impotenciam vel per[10] invincibilem[11] ignoranciam vel multis aliis modis. Eapropter sine omni culpa potestatis inferioris potestas superior potest in ipsam animadvertere, si bono communi et reipublice hoc videat expedire.

Omnia itaque spectancia ad virtutem inferiorem potest agere virtus superior, et potissime si illa deficiat, si non recte se habeat et si bono publico expediat. Quare, si essent duo gladii, quorum unus preesset rebus exterioribus, alter[12] humanis corporibus, esset gladius sub gladio, potestas sub potestate, et quod posset gladius inferior, posset[13] superior, ut et[14] ipse gladius corporibus presidens de rebus exterioribus iudicaret.

Quare autem[15] super corpora et super res[16] exteriores non sunt hii duo gladii, sed unus gladius? Et quare, sicut est alius gladius spiritualis et alius corporalis,[17] non est alius gladius temporalis[18] et alius corporalis,[19] ut dicatur corporalis, qui preest humanis corporibus, et[20] temporalis qui preest exterioribus rebus? Sed est unus et idem gladius temporalis et corporalis,[21] quia unus et idem gladius est[22] qui habet iudicium sanguinis et iudicat de corporibus et iudicat eciam de rebus temporalibus[23] sub sua potestate[24] constitutis: ita quod in Ecclesia non sunt tres gladii, sed duo gladii, ut infra patebit.

In presenciarum autem sit dictum[25] quod si circa corpora humana et res exteriores essent duo gladii, ut diximus, esset[26] gladius sub gladio, et[27] gladius qui[28] preesset corporibus de ipsis rebus exterioribus iudicaret; ergo a simili, cum sint

---

1: participare] particulare C   2: conservationem] conservaciones FV[1]V[2]   3: huiusmodi] *om.* FV[2]
4: generacionem] generacioni F   5: eas] eos F   6: quod] quidem F   7: oblique] aliqua F
8: sunt] est F   9: attingere publicum] attingit cum publicum F   attingeret cum publicum P
10: per] *om.* F   11: invincibilem] immutabilem F   12: alter] alterum F   13: posset] et *add.* F
14: et] *om.* FV[2]   15: Quare autem] *om.* F   16: res] corporales *add.* F   17: corporalis] quare
add. CF   18: temporalis] corporalis C   19: corporalis] temporalis C   quare non est alius gladius
corporalis et alius temporalis *add.* V[1]   20: et] *om.* FV[2]   21: temporalis et corporalis] corporalis
et temporalis FV[2]   et temporalis sive terrenis *add. and del.* C   22: gladius est] est gladius FV[2]
23: temporalibus] et terrenis *add. and del.* C   24: potestate] potencia C   25: sit dictum] dictum
sit C   26: esset] esse CF   27: et] *om.* FV[2]   28: gladius qui] qui gladius FV[2]

horse, the particular force existing in the seed of the horse nonetheless strives to participate in some particular end: to wit, the preservation of a species, namely the equine, or the preservation of certain creatures capable of coming into being or passing away, namely horses. But the force of heaven, or the force of the sun, strives towards the generation of all species and of everything capable of coming into being or passing away. Thus, the sun brings about not only the generation of horses, but also the generation of men, cattle, lions, and all other creatures. Therefore, just as, in these natural phenomena, it belongs to the superior forces to supply the deficiencies of the inferior forces and to direct them and strive towards a general good, so it is also in the government of men: that, if inferior powers are deficient or act dishonestly or do not achieve the public good, a superior power must correct all such inferiors and judge them in all respects. And so many things will be without fault which will not, however, be without cause. For to be deficient, which is a sin of omission, or to act dishonestly, which is a sin of commission, are not without fault; but it is possible to fail to achieve the public good without fault, for this can come about through lack of power or through invincible ignorance[1] or in many other ways. Therefore, [even] without any fault on the part of an inferior power, a superior power can correct it if this should seem expedient to the common good and to that of the commonwealth.

A superior power, then, can act in relation to all that pertains to an inferior power; and especially if it is deficient, if it does not act rightly, and if this is expedient to the public good. And so, if there were two [material] swords, one of which ruled external goods and the other human bodies, the one sword would be under the other, the one power would be under the other, and the superior sword would be able to do whatever the inferior sword could do. And so the sword which ruled bodies would also judge matters involving external goods.

Why, then, are there not these two swords over bodies and over external goods [respectively], but only the one [material] sword? And, just as there is a bodily sword distinct from the spiritual, why is there not also a temporal sword distinct from the bodily: the one called bodily to rule human bodies, and the temporal to rule external goods? But the temporal and bodily sword is [in fact] one and the same thing, for it is one and the same sword which has the judgment of blood and judges bodies and also judges the temporal things placed under its power, so that there are not three swords in the Church, but two swords, as will appear below.[2]

For the present, however, it may be said that if there were two swords concerned with human bodies and external goods [respectively], then, as we have argued, the one sword would be under the other and the sword which ruled bodies would also judge matters involving external goods. By the same token, therefore,

---

1. I.e. a condition of ignorance which, despite righteous intent and the use of reasonable diligence and moral prudence, is unavoidable or incurable: cf. Aquinas, *Summa theologiae* Ia IIae 76:2 *responsio.*
2. See Ch. XIII.

duo gladii in Ecclesia, unus materialis, alter spiritualis, quia materialia et corpora-lia[1] et omnia[2] ista sensibilia ad spiritualia ordinantur,[3] oportet quod sit gladius sub gladio, et quod possit[4] gladius inferior possit superior, ut et[5] de ipsis temporalibus spiritualis gladius habeat[6] iudicare. Qui enim spiritualia iudicat multo magis potest materialia iudicare; qui enim subtiliora videt et iudicat grossiora eum latere non debent,[7] nec iudicium eius possunt effugere. Et sicut qui spiritualia iudicat potest materialia iudicare, sic et qui spiritualia seminat potest et[8] carnalia et temporalia[9] metere. Unde per locum a minori arguit Apostolus I ad Corinthios IX:[10] 'Si nos vobis spiritualia seminamus, magnum[11] est si vestra carnalia,' id est[12] temporalia, 'metamus?' Et ex ipsis ergo animabus sive ex ipsis substanciis spiritualibus et ex hoc, quod gladius Ecclesie est gladius spiritualis, habet dominium super ipsis temporalibus et super ipsis rebus exterioribus tam potestativum quam fructiferum: potestativum quidem, quia ad spiritualem gladium spectat iudicare de temporali-bus rebus, quia ad quem spectat iudicare de rebus spiritualibus et subtilibus, eius iudicium, ut dicebamus, materialia et grossa non possunt effugere. Nam intelli-gens et sapiens gubernacula possidebit, iuxta illud Proverbiorum I: 'Audiens sapiens sapiencior erit et intelligens gubernacula possidebit.' Immo, si consideras in naturali regimine, semper vides quod sapienciora et industriora aliis preponun-tur,[13] ut si homines presunt bestiis, mares feminis[14] et[15] viri[16] pueris, hoc est, quia magis industria et cognicione vigent homines quam bestie, mares quam femine, viri quam pueri. In gubernacione enim hominum plus est attendenda sapiencia quam civilis potencia, iuxta illud Ecclesiastis IX: 'Melior est sapiencia quam arma bellica'; et Ptolomeus ait quod 'sapiens dominabitur astris'; et Philosophus in suis *Politicis* probat quod qui viget racione et intellectu, naturale est quod debeat dominari. Nec oportet in hoc multum insistere, quia huic vero et isti veritati omnia consonant.

Revertamur ergo ad propositum et dicamus quod in gubernacione hominum et in dominio rerum potissime est[17] industria et sapiencia attendenda.[18] Et ideo, sicut videmus in iudicio sapienciali et speculativo, sic in iudicio potestativo et guberna-tivo considerare debemus. Sic autem videmus in iudicio sapienciali et speculativo quod cum intellectus intellexerit maxime intelligibilia, ut probatur in tercio *De an-ima*, non minus intelligit infima. Qui enim superiora videt, si vult se avertere,[19] eum[20] inferiora non latent. Si ergo sic[21] est in iudicio speculativo, sic erit et in iudicio

1: corporalia] ordinent oportet quod sit gladius *add. and del.* C   2: omnia] alia FV²   3: ordi-nantur] ordinentur C   4: possit] potest CFV²   5: et] habeat FV²   6: habeat] *om.* FV²
7: debent] preesset C   8: et] *om.* CFV²   9: temporalia] spiritualia F   10: IX] *om.* F
11: magnum] magis FV²   12: id est] et F   13: preponuntur] proponuntur FV²   14: feminis] presunt *add. and del.* C   15: et] si CFV²   16: viri] presunt *add. and del.* C   17: est] et F
18: attendenda] est *add.* F   19: avertere] convertere FV²   20: eum] *om.* FV²   21: sic] *del.* C

since there are only two swords in the Church — the one material and the other spiritual — then, since material and corporeal creatures and all sentient beings are ordered towards spiritual ends, it must be that the one sword is under the other and that the superior sword may do whatever the inferior may. Thus, the spiritual sword must judge even temporal matters. For he who judges spiritual matters is all the more able to judge those involving material things; for, since he sees and judges those things which are more subtle, those which are more gross should not be hidden from him, and cannot escape his judgment. And just as he who judges spiritual matters can judge those involving material things, so he who sows spiritual things can reap both fleshly and temporal things. Hence, in I Corinthians 9, the Apostle argues from the greater to the lesser: 'If we have sown spiritual things for you, is it a great matter if we reap your fleshly things?'[1] — that is, your temporal goods. Therefore, from a consideration of souls or spiritual substances, and from the fact that the Church's sword is a spiritual sword, it follows that she has a lordship both of power and enjoyment over temporal things and over external goods. Of power indeed, since it rests with the spiritual sword to judge matters involving temporal goods; for, as we have said, since it rests with it to judge matters involving spiritual and subtle things, material and gross things cannot escape its judgment. For he who understands and is wise shall possess governments, according to Proverbs 1: 'The wise man shall hear and be wiser, and he who understands shall possess governments.'[2] Indeed, if you consider the government of nature, you will always see that the wiser and more capable are placed over others; so that, if men rule over the beasts, husbands over their wives, and adults over boys, this is because men are greater in capacity and understanding than the beasts, husbands than wives, and adults than boys. For, in the government of men, more attention must be given to wisdom than to civil might, according to Ecclesiastes 9: 'Wisdom is better than the weapons of war.'[3] Ptolemy, too, says that 'the wise man will rule the stars';[4] and the Philosopher, in his *Politics*, shows that it is natural that he who is great in reason and intellect should have lordship.[5] Nor is it here necessary to cite many examples, for all agree as to the truth of these things.

Let us return to our proposition, therefore, and say that in the government of men and in the lordship of things, attention must be given especially to capability and wisdom. And so what we see in learned and speculative judgment we must also consider in relation to the judgment of those invested with power and government. And, as is shown in *De anima* 3, we see in learned and speculative judgment that when the intellect considers the highest objects of enquiry, it no less considers the lowest also.[6] For even if he wishes to turn himself away, inferior things are not concealed from him who perceives superior things. Therefore, if this is so in the case of speculative judgment, it will also be so in the case of judgment involving

1. I Cor. 9:11.
2. Prov. 1:5.
3. Eccles. 9:18.
4. *De iudiciis astrologiae libri IV* (Nuremberg, 1535), f. 13ʳ6.
5. *Politics* 1:2 (1252ᵃ30).
6. Aristotle, *De anima* 3:4 (429ᵇ1).

gubernativo et potestativo, ut cuius est superiora iudicare, eius iudicium inferiora non possunt effugere, quod[1] potissime verum est quando talia sunt inferiora quod ad superiora directe et per se sunt ordinata. Et quia omnia materialia et omnia temporalia directe ad spiritualia ordinantur, quia non est rectus usus temporalium si non sit ad spiritualia ordinatus, consequens est quod spiritualis gladius, cuius est spiritualia iudicare,[2] et super temporalia poterit proferre iudicia.[3]

Concludamus itaque et dicamus quod spiritualis gladius, quia omnia spiritualia iudicat, potest de omnibus temporalibus iudicare, et quia omnia spiritualia seminat, potest de omnibus temporalibus metere, ut supra per Apostolum probabatur. Quia ergo spiritualis gladius potest de omnibus temporalibus iudicare, habet super temporalibus universale dominium iurisdiccionale et potestativum; quia vero potest de omnibus temporalibus metere, habet[4] universale dominium utile et fructiferum.[5]

Secunda via ad hoc idem sumitur ex parte ipsorum corporum, ad que alenda et fovenda[6] omnia temporalia ordinantur. Nam, ut Augustinus ait X *Confessionum*, sic sumenda sunt alimenta quasi medicamenta; quod veritatem habet quantum ad sanitatem corporis, et multo magis quantum ad sanitatem anime. Immo, ubi una sanitas alteri repugnaret, ut si sanitas corporis repugnaret[7] sanitati anime, pretermittenda est[8] sanitas corporis propter sanitatem anime. Bona quidem est sanitas corporis, et bona est fortitudo; sed si sanitas et fortitudo corporis te inclinant ad peccandum, bonum esset tibi quod esses infirmus, ut a peccato caveres et in te gracia Christi et virtus eius habitaret, ut posses dicere cum Apostolo II ad Corinthios XII: 'Libenter igitur[9] gloriabor in infirmitatibus, meis, ut inhabitet in me virtus Christi.' Sumenda itaque sunt alimenta ut medicamenta et ut adminiculancia utrique sanitati, corporali et spirituali.[10] Verum quia per hec corporalia manuducimur in spiritualia, ut possimus de spirituali sanitate aliqua cernere, de corporali sanitate primitus est dicendum.

Advertendum ergo[11] quod qui vellet per medicum sanitatem recuperare vel in sanitate recuperata conservari, oporteret[12] ipsum uti alimentis et uti rebus exterioribus que temporalia nuncupantur secundum quod medicus imperaret.[13] Habet itaque medicus corporalis[14] super omnibus hiis qui volunt sani fieri imperium quantum ad usum alimentorum et eciam operimentorum, quia sicut ad sanitatem corporis facit debitus usus alimentorum, sic et ad sanitatem facit debitus usus operimentorum et vestimentorum. Posset enim sic corpus onerari vestibus, quod nimis[15] calefieret, et sic denudari, quod nimis[16] infrigidaretur. Et quia omnia temporalia, ut patet, ordinantur ad corpus, aliqualiter potest se intromittere medicus

---

1: quod] et FV[2]   2: iudicare] quod *add.* CFV[2]   3: iudicia] iudicium F   4: habet] super omnibus temporalibus *add. and del.* C   5: fructiferum] est autem predicta racio quasi pregnans dupliciter concludens intentum tam ex parte superioritatis quam ex parte industrie unde sumitur racio dominandi nam spiritus est superior corpore et quicquid industrie et prudencie competit homini simpliciter et formaliter est ex spiritu sive ex anima materialiter autem secundum quid est ex corpore *add.* C (*marg.*) PV[1]   6: alenda et fovenda] alendum et fovendum C   7: ut si … repugnaret] *om.* F   8: est] esset FV[2]   9: igitur] sibi F   10: spirituali] et pocius spirituali quam corporali *add.* FV[2]   11: ergo] *om.* V[2]   12: oporteret] oportet PV[1]   13: imperaret] impetraret FP   14: corporalis] super cibus *add.* F   15: nimis] minus F   16: nimis] minus F

government and power: inferior things cannot escape the judgment of him who judges superior things. And this is especially so when such inferior things are appointed directly and as such for the sake of superior things. And since all material and all temporal things are appointed directly for the sake of spiritual things — for no right use can be made of temporal possessions unless it is ordered towards spiritual ends — it follows that the spiritual sword, whose task it is to judge spiritual matters, will also be able to pass judgment upon temporal matters.

Let us conclude, then, and say that the spiritual sword, since it judges all spiritual matters, can judge all temporal matters also; and that, since it sows all spiritual things, it can reap all temporal things, as was shown above by reference to the Apostle. Therefore, since the spiritual sword can judge all temporal matters, it has a universal lordship of jurisdiction and power over temporal things; and since it can also reap all temporal things, it has a universal lordship of use and enjoyment.

The second way towards the same conclusion is derived from a consideration of bodies themselves, for the sake of whose growth and support all temporal things are appointed. For, as Augustine says in *Confessions* 10, nourishment must be taken as though it were a medicine.[1] And if this is true of bodily health, it is much more so of the health of the soul. Indeed, if one form of health were to oppose the other, so that bodily health were opposed to the health of the soul, bodily health would have to be disregarded in favour of the health of the soul. Bodily health is indeed a good, and strength is a good also. But if the health and strength of the body lead you into sin, it would be a good for you to be ill, that you might abstain from sin, and that the grace and strength of Christ might dwell in you, and that you might say with the Apostle in II Corinthians 12: 'Gladly, therefore, will I glory in my infirmities, that the power of Christ may dwell in me.'[2] Thus, nourishment must be taken as a medicine and as an aid to both bodily and spiritual health. But since it is through bodily things that we are conducted towards spiritual ends, we must speak of bodily health first, in order that we may be able to understand something of spiritual health.

It must be noted, therefore, that he who wishes to recover health through a physician or, having recovered health, to preserve it, must make use of nourishment, and must make use of the external goods which are called temporal, according to the directions of the physician. Thus, the bodily physician has power over all who wish to become healthy as regards the use of nourishment, and also of clothing. For just as bodily health is achieved through the proper use of nourishment, so too health is achieved through the proper use of clothing and garments; for the body could be so weighed down by clothes as to be too hot, or be so scantily clad as to be too cold. And since it is clear that all temporal goods are ordered to the body, the bodily physician can to that extent concern himself with these temporal

1. *Conf.* 10:31 (CCSL 27:178).
2. II Cor. 12:9.

corporalis super istis temporalibus. Differt tamen medicus corporalis[1] a[2] spirituali quantum ad presens spectat, quia sic[3] aliqualiter potest se intromittere corporalis medicus super temporalibus quod dominus temporalium dici non debet; sed spiritualis medicus, cuiusmodi est potestas sacerdotalis et potissime potestas Summi Sacerdocii, sic[4] habet imperium super temporalibus quod dominus temporalium dici debet. Nam medicus corporalis habet aliquale imperium in temporalibus prout spectant[5] ad sanitatem corporalem. Sed que quis possideat et que non, hoc non spectat ad sanitatem corporalem, sed solum quibus utatur et quibus non: spectat autem ad sanitatem spiritualem. Sed si non spectat[6] ad sanitatem corporalem[7] licita possessio rerum, nec spectat[8] ad medicum corporalem[9] se intromittere qualiter curandi corporaliter facultates proprias debeant possidere, spectat tamen[10] hoc ad sanitatem spiritualem, quia non est sanus spiritualiter qui aliena usurpat et qui suas non licite possidet facultates. Spectabit itaque ad medicum spiritualem curam habere, quod iusticia observetur, quod unicuique quod suum est tribuatur, quia non potest[11] aliter spiritualis sanitas conservari.

Unde multociens iuste et pie interponit Ecclesia suum spiritualem gladium, suam censuram ecclesiasticam, contra usurpatores et contra aliquarum rerum indebitos[12;13] retentores, et precipue[14] in arduis casibus ubi pax publica et bonum publicum perturbatur. Plus ergo habet de dominio Ecclesia in possessionibus fidelium et in ipsis temporalibus rebus quam habeant ipsi[15] fideles. Nam semper qui iudicat rem aliquam dominus est rei iudicate, iuxta illud Apostoli I ad Corinthios IV:[16] 'Qui enim[17] me iudicat, Dominus est.' Iusticia enim non est res corporis, sed est res anime, et non est perfeccio rerum[18] corporalium, sed est[19] perfeccio[20] appetitus intellectivi, qui nec[21] quid corporale nec quid organicum dici debet.

Ad medicum itaque corporalem non spectabit iudicare de iusta possessione rerum, sed ad spiritualem.[22;23] Immo, si bene considerantur que dicuntur, ipsa potestas terrena, cuiusmodi est potestas regalis vel imperialis, non habebit iudicare quid iustum nec quid non iustum nisi in quantum hoc agit in virtute potestatis spiritualis. Nam si iusticia res est[24] spiritualis et est perfeccio anime et non corporis, ad potestatem spiritualem spectabit iudicare de ipsa iusticia; potestas autem terrena et corporalis non habebit iudicare de ea nisi hoc agat in virtute spiritualis potestatis.[25] Propter quod omnes leges imperiales et[26] potestatis terrene sunt ad ecclesiasticos canones ordinande,[27] ut inde sumant robur et eciam firmitatem; vel omnes tales leges a potestate terrena edite, ut robur et firmitatem habeant, non debent contradicere ecclesiasticis legibus, sed pocius sunt per potestatem spiritualem et ecclesiasticam confirmande. Est enim iusticia res spiritualis,

---

1: super istis ... corporalis] *om.* F   2: a] in F   3: sic] cum FV[2]   4: sic] sicut FV[2]   5: spectant] spectat *mss*   6: spectat] peccat F   7: corporalem] *om.* CPV[1]V[2]   8: nec spectat] spectaret FV[2] 9: licita possessio ... corporalem] *om.* C   10: tamen] autem C   11: potest] est PV[1]   12: indebitos] indebite F   13: et contra ... indebitos] *om.* V[2]   14: precipue] potissime FV[2]   15: habeant ipsi] habent ipsum F habent ipsi V[2]   16: IV] X P   17: enim] autem FV[2]   18: rerum] virtutum FV[2] 19: sed est] sicut F   20: perfeccio] ipsius *add.* CFV[2]   21: nec] non CF   22: sed ad spiritualem] *om.* F   23: spiritualem] spiritualium P   24: res est] est res CF et res V[2]   25: spiritualis potestatis] potestatis spiritualis F   26: et] *om.* PV[1]   27: ordinande] sunt *add.* C

goods. For our present purpose, however, there is a difference between the bodily physician and the spiritual. For the bodily physician cannot concern himself with temporal goods in such a way that he must be called the lord of temporal goods. But the spiritual physician — the priestly power, and especially the power of the Supreme Priest — has power over temporal goods in such a way that he must be called the lord of temporal goods. For the bodily physician has a kind of power over temporal goods insofar as they bear upon bodily health. But what a man does or does not possess does not bear upon bodily health: only what he does or does not use; whereas this does bear upon spiritual health. If, however, the question of whether goods are lawfully possessed does not bear upon bodily health, then nor does it rest with the bodily physician to concern himself with how those who need a bodily cure should possess their property. But this question does bear upon spiritual health; for he who usurps what belongs to another and who does not possess his property lawfully is not healthy in spirit. Thus, it will rest with the spiritual physician to take care that justice is observed and that to each is given what is due to him, since, otherwise, spiritual health cannot be preserved.

Hence, on many occasions the Church intervenes justly and piously by bringing her spiritual sword — her ecclesiastical censure — to bear against usurpers and against those who retain anything improperly; and especially in serious cases where public peace and the public good is disturbed.[1] Therefore, the Church has a greater lordship over the possessions of the faithful, and over temporal things as such, than the faithful themselves have. For he who judges a thing is always lord of the thing judged, according to the Apostle in I Corinthians 4: 'And he who judges me is the Lord.'[2] For justice is not a bodily property, but a property of the soul; and it is not a perfection of bodily things, but the completion of an intellectual desire, which may not be said of anything which is either bodily or instrumental.

Thus, it will not rest with the bodily physician to judge whether things are possessed justly, but with the spiritual. Indeed, if due consideration is given to what has been said, [it will be seen that] the earthly power, being itself a royal or imperial power, will have no capacity to judge what is just or unjust except insofar as it does this by virtue of [a delegated] spiritual power. For if justice is a spiritual property and a perfection of soul and not of body, then it will rest with the spiritual power to judge concerning such justice; and earthly and bodily power will have no capacity to judge concerning it unless it does so by virtue of spiritual power. And so all imperial laws and those of the earthly power must be ordered to the canons of the Church, so that they may derive strength from them and also firmness. Again, all such laws enacted by the earthly power must not contradict the ecclesiastical laws, but must rather be confirmed by the spiritual and ecclesiastical power, so that they may have strength and firmness. For justice is a spiritual property,

1. See esp. Pt. III, Ch. VI.
2. I Cor. 4:4.

quia est rectitudo quedam sola mente perceptibilis. Sensu enim possumus iudicare quid factum vel quid non factum; sed per intellectum iudicabimus quid iustum vel quid non iustum.

Redeamus ergo ad propositum et dicamus quod quia omnia alimenta et omnia temporalia sunt possidenda prout sunt quedam medicamenta et prout sunt quedam[1] adminiculancia ad sanitatem anime pocius quam ad sanitatem corporis, medicus spiritualis, et potissime Summus Sacerdos, habet[2] imperium et eciam dominium super omnibus temporalibus rebus. Nam medicus corporalis non habet dominium[3] super temporalibus rebus, sed spiritualis tantum,[4] quia non habet[5] intromittere se[6] de iusta possessione rerum, sed spiritualis; tum[7] quia eciam[8] infirmitas et mala disposicio corporis non est rebellis Deo, sed infirmitas et mala disposicio anime, quia, ut dicebatur,[9] si iniusta possessio rerum facit ad infirmitatem anime et non corporis, cuius est curare animas et cui commissa est animarum cura et iurisdiccio spiritualis, ad iurisdiccionem eius spectat[10] agere de omnibus que possunt animam infirmare. Et quia huiusmodi est iniusta possessio rerum, spectabit ad potestatem spiritualem possessioni iniuste[11] rerum temporalium obviare et in eis iusticiam fovere, quod sine iurisdiccione super rebus temporalibus et sine earum dominio esse non potest.

Rursus, ut dicebamus, ex eo quod aliquis est male[12] dispositus in corpore non est a Deo aversus,[13] sed ex[14] eo quod est male dispositus in anima. Qui autem est[15] a Deo aversus est iniustus possessor cuiuscumque[16] rei. Nam qui iuste privandus est aliqua re iniuste possidet rem illam.[17] Sed qui avertit se a Deo et non vult esse sub dominio Dei, iustum est quod non habeat dominium, ut supra tetigimus,[18] alicuius rei. Quare, si homo a Deo[19] aversus est iniustus possessor rerum, conversus autem ad Deum ex tunc efficitur iustus possessor facultatum suarum, quia ad Ecclesiam pertinet iudicare de spirituali lepra, id est de peccato, et ad eam spectat iudicare propter que homines dicantur a Deo aversi et ad Deum conversi: ad eam spectabit iudicare de iusta et iniusta possessione quarumcumque rerum; quod esse non posset nisi super ipsis rebus et super ipsis temporalibus haberet universale dominium.

Nec obstat quod potestates terrene habent huiusmodi iudicium, ut puta quia in foro eorum[20] litigatur de iusta et iniusta possessione rerum. Quia et Ecclesia habet dominium temporalium et potestates terrene habent tale dominium et tale iudicium. Sed Ecclesia habet huiusmodi dominium et iudicium universale, potestates autem terrene particulare. Ideo si fideles inferiores delinquant circa aliqua particularia bona vel si usurpent sibi prout non debent aliqua particularia bona, poterit iudicare de eis potestas terrena.[21] Sed si ipsa terrena potestas[22] delinquat in usurpando sibi temporalia bona, animadvertere poterit in eam potestas ecclesiastica, que habet universalius dominium eciam in ipsis temporalibus quam habeat terrena potestas.

1: quedam] om. FV²   2: habet] habebit CFV²   3: dominium] nisi add. F   4: tantum] tamen F
5: habet] medicus corporalis add. and del. C   6: intromittere se] se intromittere om. CF
7: tum] cum F   8: quia eciam] eciam quia CF   9: dicebatur] dicebamus CFV²   10: spectat]
spectabit CFV²   11: iniuste] om. FV²   12: male] valde FV²   13: aversus] conversus FV²
14: ex] om. FV²   15: est] om. FV²   16: cuiuscumque] cuiusque F   17: rem illam] illam rem F
18: ut supra tetigimus] om. FV²   19: a Deo] om. C   20: eorum] om. FV²   21: potestas terrena]
terrena potestas CF   22: ipsa terrena potestas] om. F

since it is a kind of rectitude perceptible only to the mind. For we can judge by means of sense what is done or what is not done; but it is with the intellect that we shall judge what is just and what is not just.

Let us return to our proposition, therefore, and say that, since all nourishment and all temporal things must be possessed as a kind of medicine and as a kind of aid to the soul's health rather than to the health of the body, the spiritual physician, and especially the Supreme Priest, has supreme power, and lordship indeed, over all temporal things. For the bodily physician does not have lordship over temporal things, but only the spiritual; for it is not he, but the spiritual physician, who must concern himself with the just possession of things. For it is not the infirmity and ill disposition of the body which is a revolt against God, but the infirmity and ill disposition of the soul. And so, as has been said, if unjust possession renders the soul infirm and not the body, it will rest with whoever has jurisdiction over the care of souls, and to whom is entrusted the cure of souls and spiritual jurisdiction, to have jurisdiction to act upon all those things which can render the soul infirm. And since unjust possession is such a thing, it will rest with the spiritual power to prevent the unjust possession of temporal goods and to foster justice among them; which, without jurisdiction over temporal things, and without lordship over them, it cannot do.

Again, as we have said, it is not because anyone is ill disposed in body that he is turned away from God, but because he is ill disposed in soul. And he who is turned away from God is an unjust possessor of everything; for he who should justly be deprived of something possesses that thing unjustly. But, as we have noted above, it is just that he who turns himself away from God and refuses to be under the lordship of God should have no lordship over anything.[1] And so, if a man who is turned away from God is an unjust possessor of things, and is made a just possessor of his property as soon as he is turned towards God, then, because it pertains to the Church to judge matters of spiritual leprosy — that is, of sin — and because it rests with her to judge in those matters by reason of which men are said to be turned away from God or towards God, it will also rest with her to judge concerning the just and unjust possession of all things; which she could not do if she did not have a universal lordship over such things and over temporal affairs themselves.

Nor is it an objection to say that earthly powers possess such jurisdiction: that is, because disputes concerning the just and unjust possession of things are heard in their courts. For the Church has temporal lordship, and earthly powers also have such lordship and such jurisdiction: but the Church has such lordship and jurisdiction universally, whereas the earthly powers have them particularly. And so, if lesser members of the faithful offend with respect to some particular goods, or if they usurp to themselves some particular goods which are not due to them, then the earthly power will be able to judge them. But if the earthly power itself offends by usurping temporal goods to itself, then the ecclesiastical power, which has a more universal lordship even in temporal matters than the earthly power has,

---

1. See Chaps. VII and VIII.

Unde Hugo in *De sacramentis* libro II, parte II, ut superius diximus, plane[1] ait quod potestas spiritualis potestatem terrenam iudicare habet.

Sed dices quod tam spiritualis gladius quam temporalis intromittet se de utroque, de spiritualibus et[2] temporalibus, cum ex anima et corpore fiat unum, et cum agens de uno oportet quod agat[3] de alio et converso. Ad quod dici potest quod materialis gladius intromittere[4] habet se[5] de iniusto,[6] et inducet[7] homines ad virtutes, et intromittet[8] se de iis que sunt anime. Sed hoc erit modo famulativo, quia corpus comparatur ad animam tamquam id quod debet anime famulari. Et spiritualis gladius intromittet se de corporalibus non modo famulativo, sed dominativo, quia spiritus corporalibus dominatur.[9]

Declaratum est igitur duplici via quod Ecclesia habet universale dominium super omnibus temporalibus rebus. Prima quidem via sumpta est ex parte animarum sive ex parte spirituum, quia spiritualis potestas habet corporalia gubernare; secunda quidem via sumpta est[10] ex parte corporum, quia temporalia sic sunt alimenta et medicamenta corporum et sic sunt ad recuperandam vel conservandam sanitatem corporum, quod sunt[11] ordinata ad sanitatem animarum. Ideo spiritualis potestas de omnibus temporalibus se[12] potest intromittere, prout sunt ad infirmitatem vel sanitatem[13] animarum, prout aliquis iuste vel iniuste possidet.

Hiis itaque prelibatis,[14] declarabimus hoc idem via tercia sumpta ex parte ipsarum rerum. Nam omnes res[15] temporales sunt incensive[16] Ecclesie, et census quem debent sunt[17] ipse decime, ita quod hoc onus videtur esse rerum temporalium, ut temporalia sunt, cum semper, ut iam tetigimus, transeant temporalia cum hoc onere, ut si aliquis vendat temporalia alii, decimas quas prius debebat[18] venditor, debebit postea emptor. Ergo si omnia temporalia, ut temporalia sunt, debent censum Ecclesie et sunt incensiva[19] Ecclesie, patet ex parte ipsorum temporalium quod Ecclesia habet universale dominium super ipsis.

Patefacta quidem prima parte capituli, quia ostensum est triplici via Ecclesiam super temporalibus habere dominium universale, volumus prosequi secundam partem capituli,[20] videlicet quod fideles super eis habent vel habere possunt dominium particulare. Quod[21] eciam via triplici ostendemus, ut prima via sumatur ex ipsis rebus possessis, secunda ex ipsis possidentibus, tercia ex ipso modo possidendi.

Prima via sic patet. Nam dictum est quod ipse possessiones et ipsa temporalia debent censum Ecclesie. Sed accipiens censum dicitur racione census super totam rem habere dominacionem; dans autem censum dicitur de tota re illa debere

---

1: plane] plene FV²   2: et] de *add.* F   3: agat] agas F   4: intromittere] intromitteret V¹
5: habet se] se debet FV²   6: iniusto] iusto F   7: inducet] inducit FV² induceret V¹   8: intro-
mittet] intromittere F intromitteret V¹   9: Sed dices ... dominatur] *marg.* C   10: via sumpta est]
om. CFV²   11: sunt] pocius *add.* CF   12: se] *om.* P   13: infirmitatem vel sanitatem] sanitatem
vel infirmitatem CF   14: prelibatis] declaratis F   15: res] *om.* FV²   16: incensive] in censura
CFV²   17: sunt] *om.* FV²   18: debebat] debebit P   19: incensiva] in censura CFV²   20: ca-
pituli] *del.* C   21: Quod] *om.* F

will be able to punish it. And so, as we have said above, Hugh, in *De sacramentis,* Book 2, Part 2, plainly asserts that the spiritual power must judge the earthly power.[1]

But you will say that the spiritual and temporal swords will each concern themselves with both spiritual and temporal matters; for a single entity is made from both soul and body, and what acts upon the one must act upon the other and conversely. To this, we can reply that the material sword must concern itself with the unjust, and that it will induce men to be virtuous, and that it will concern itself with matters pertaining to the soul: but that this will be in the manner of a servant; for the body is joined to the soul as that which must serve the soul. The spiritual sword, however, will concern itself with the affairs of the body not in the manner of a servant, but in that of a lord: for spirit has lordship over bodily things.

It has been shown in two ways, then, that the Church has a universal lordship over all temporal things. The first way was derived from a consideration of souls or from a consideration of spirits, since the spiritual power must govern corporeal things; and the second way was derived from a consideration of bodies, since temporal possessions exist for the nourishment and medication of bodies, and for the recovery and preservation of the health of bodies, in such a way that they are ordered to the health of souls. The spiritual power, therefore, can concern itself with all temporal things, since the just or unjust possession of such things are matters which bear upon the infirmity or health of souls.

Having first touched upon these considerations, then, we shall now show a third way towards the same conclusion, derived from a consideration of things themselves. For all temporal things are subject to the assessment of the Church, and tithes themselves are a tax which they are bound to pay. And so this burden is seen to attach to temporal things as such; for, as we have already noted, temporal possessions always pass with their burdens, so that, if anyone sells temporal goods to another, the tithes which were originally due from the seller will then become due from the purchaser.[2] Therefore, if all temporal things, as such, owe a tax to the Church and are subject to the Church's assessment, it is clear from a consideration of temporal things themselves that the Church has a universal lordship over them.

Thus, having made clear in the first part of this chapter — for this has been shown in three ways — that the Church has a universal lordship over temporal things, we wish to proceed to the second part of this chapter: that is, to showing that the faithful have or can have only a particular lordship over them. And this also we shall show in three ways: the first way being derived from things possessed, the second from those who possess them, and the third from the manner in which they are possessed.

The first way proceeds as follows. It has been said that possessions and temporal goods owe a tax to the Church. But he who receives a tax is said to have lordship over the whole property by reason of the tax; and he who pays the tax is said to be

---

1. *De sacramentis fidei Christianae* 2:2:4 (PL 176:418); cf. Pt. I, Ch. IV.
2. Cf. Ch. IV, p. 99, above.

subieccionem. Dato itaque quod unus homo omnia temporalia possideret et de omnibus eis deberet censum, non diceretur de eis habere dominium totale, cum super ipsum censum non haberet dominium, et cum racione rei censate competeret sibi subieccio. Haberet ergo homo ille de possessionibus illis non totaliter dominium utile, quia non haberet inde totam utilitatem, cum deberet inde censum; nec haberet dominium totaliter potestativum, cum propter possessiones illas diceretur alteri esse subiectus. Fideles itaque eciam super ipsis temporalibus, racione census quem inde debent, non dicuntur[1] habere dominium universale et totale, sed magis particulare et aliquale.

Utrum[2] autem posset Ecclesia aliquas decimas donare, ut quod aliqui laici reciperent aliquas decimas, vel posset aliquas decimas donare,[3] quod de aliquibus possessionibus vel de aliquibus fructibus non deberentur decime, non est presentis speculacionis tales questiones decidere.[4] Dato tamen quod ista fierent, totum esset ex indulgencia Ecclesie, et totum esset ad Ecclesiam referendum, ut ex hoc Ecclesia dici non posset quod universale dominium temporalium perderet, sed pocius quod haberet.

Secunda via ad hoc idem sumitur ex parte ipsorum possidencium. Nam, sicut omnes possessiones debent esse subcensive[5] Ecclesie, sic omnes possidentes debent esse[6] tributarii Ecclesie. Nam, cum ipsi fideles sint redempti a potestate diaboli per Ecclesiam, debent recognoscere se esse servos ascripticios[7] Ecclesie; et quia servus lucratur domino suo, et ideo de se ipsis et de iis que habent et de hiis que lucrantur debent recognoscere esse dominam Sanctam[8] Matrem Ecclesiam, per cuius[9] sacramenta sunt redempti et a servitute diaboli exempti. Et exinde potest sumi racio quare preter decimas quas debent ipse possessiones, ordinate sunt oblaciones et alia que fiunt in templis, ut homines fideles non solum sint censuarii Ecclesie dando de suis fructibus decimas, sed eciam sint tributarii et sicut servi empticii Ecclesie recognoscendo se esse servos Ecclesie, ut pro se ipsis et pro omnibus[10] que habent offerant aliquid Ecclesie in recognicionem proprie servitutis. Sed ista servitus, si debeat esse meritoria,[11] magis est amoris quam timoris, magis est devocionis quam coaccionis. Pro ista servitute nihil perditur, sed multum acquiritur, quia de omnibus hiis que dant fideles ipsi Ecclesie centuplum accipient et vitam eternam possidebunt. Nam ex tali dacione temporalia multiplicantur et eterna[12] acquiruntur, ut pro illo modico quod das Ecclesie, Deus[13] multiplicat tibi[14] fructus tuos, segetes tuas et alia[15] bona tua, ut ex hoc centuplum accipias, et quia si cum devocione das, mereris inde vitam eternam.[16] Ideo vides

---

1: dicuntur] dicantur F   2: Utrum] utrumque C   3: vel posset ... donare] *om.* F   4: non est ... decidere] *om.* V¹   5: subcensive] subcensiva P   6: subcensive Ecclesie ... esse] *om.* FV² 7: ascripticios] emptivos F empticios CV²   8: Sanctam] suam FV²   9: cuius] *om.* FPV¹V² 10: omnibus] hiis *add.* FV²   11: meritoria] *om.* F   12: eterna] terrena C   13: Deus] *om.* C 14: tibi] deus *add.* C   15: alia] omnia C   16: vitam eternam] vita eterna F

subject with respect to the whole property. Suppose, then, that a single man possessed all temporal goods and that he owed a tax on all of them: he would not be said to have a total lordship of them, for he would not have lordship of the tax payable on them and, with respect to the taxable part of the property, he would himself be subject. That man would therefore not have a total lordship of use over his possessions, for he would not have the use of them in their totality, because he would owe a tax on them. Nor would he have a total lordship of power, since he would be said to be subject to another with respect to those possessions. The faithful, then, are not said to have a universal and total lordship even over temporal possessions, but only a particular and partial one, by reason of the tax which they owe from them.

But whether it might be possible for the Church to give away any tithes so that some lay persons might receive those tithes, or to give away any tithes so that tithes were not due from certain possessions or fruits, are questions which it is not part of our present enquiry to decide. Suppose, however, that these things were done: this would come about solely by the Church's indulgence and would be entirely attributable to the Church; and so it could not be said on this ground that the Church had lost, but rather that she possessed, a universal lordship over temporal things.[1]

The second way towards the same conclusion is derived from a consideration of possessors themselves. For, just as all possessions must be subject to the assessment of the Church, so must all possessors be tributaries of the Church. For since the faithful are redeemed from the power of the devil through the Church, they must acknowledge that they are bound to the Church as servants; and, because the servant makes profit for his lord, they must therefore acknowledge that they themselves and all that they have and all that they earn are subject to the lordship of Holy Mother Church, through whose sacraments they are redeemed and released from bondage to the devil. And, from this, it is also possible to understand the reason why, in addition to the tithes which are due from possessions, offerings and other benefactions are appointed to be made in churches: so that faithful men may be not only taxpayers to the Church, paying tithes from their fruits, but may also be tributaries, who, as servants purchased by the Church, acknowledging that they are the Church's servants, offer something for themselves and for all that they have in recognition of their own servitude. But if such servitude is to be meritorious, it must be given more from love than from fear, and more from devotion than compulsion. Nothing is lost by this servitude, but much gained; for the faithful will receive back an hundredfold from all that they give, and will possess eternal life.[2] For, from such giving, temporal goods are multiplied and eternal goods acquired; for from the little you give to the Church, God will multiply your fruits, your lands, and all your goods, so that you may receive an hundredfold and so that, if you give with devotion, you may deserve eternal life. You see, then,

---

1. The allusion is to the many cases in which popes had apparently given away tithes by authorising their payment to kings as aids, as Boniface VIII had effectively been forced to do in 1297. Giles's point is that such gifts do not amount to a permanent alienation of ecclesiastical property. They are *ad hoc* exceptions to a general law, made entirely at the Church's discretion.
2. Cf. Matt. 19:29.

quam benedicta sit ista servitus, et quam bonum sit sic Ecclesie de bonis tuis offerre et dare, cum[1] eciam in temporalibus centuplum recipiamus, et post hec temporalia vitam eternam possideamus.[2]

Patet ergo ex parte ipsorum possidencium quod eciam fideles non habent universale[3] nec totale dominium super ipsis temporalibus, sed magis particulare et
aliquale, cum[4] de se ipsis et de[5] omnibus hiis que habent et que lucrari possunt
debeant esse servi et tributarii Ecclesie. Tales itaque eciam quantum ad ipsa temporalia, si referantur[6] ad Ecclesiam, possunt dici totaliter subiecti eo, quod de habitis et habendis servitutem et tributa debeant.

Tercia via ad hoc idem sumitur ex ipso modo possidendi. Nam Ecclesia dicitur
Catholica, id est universalis, et quilibet fidelis dicitur Catholicus, id est universalis. Sed esse non potest quod duo aliqua relata ad invicem sint eodem modo
Catholica sive universalia, ut quod quilibet eorum respectu alterius sit universaliter superius, quia tunc idem esset superius se ipso, vel quod quodcumque illorum respectu alterius sit universaliter[7] inferius,[8] quia tunc idem esset inferius se
ipso. Oportet itaque illa duo sic se habere quod unum sit universaliter superius et
universaliter dominus, et aliud sit universaliter inferius et universaliter serviens.
Sic ergo Ecclesia est Catholica et universalis,[9] quia est universaliter dominans, et
fideles sunt Catholici, id est universalis, quia debent esse universaliter subiecti
Ecclesie[10] et servientes. Fideles itaque, si sunt vere Catholici, vere debent esse subiecti universaliter[11] Ecclesie, ut modus possidendi seipsos et quecumque habent
sit quod et[12] de seipsis et de omnibus que habent Ecclesie sint subiecti fideles.
Ergo ex ipso modo possidendi, quia debent possidere suas possessiones ut subiecti
Ecclesie, super ipsis possessionibus fidelium Ecclesia habebit dominium universale[13] et totale; ipsi autem fideles dominium quod habent[14] poterit esse[15] particulare et aliquale.

CAPITULUM XI: *Quod infideles omni possessione et dominio et potestate
qualibet sunt indigni.*[16]

Videtur fortasse multis quod fideles essent peioris[17] condicionis quam infideles,
cum sint censuarii et tributarii Ecclesie et cum ipsi de seipsis et de omnibus hiis
que habent Ecclesie debeant[18] esse subiecti. Dicamus ergo quod infideles sunt
servi Belial, fideles vero, ut sunt subiecti Ecclesie, sunt servi Christi: infideles
vero[19] sunt tenebre, fideles vero, ut serviunt[20] Ecclesie, sunt lux in Domino, iuxta
illud ad Ephesios V: 'Eratis enim aliquando tenebre, nunc autem lux in Domino.'
Et quia iuxta sentenciam Apostoli nulla est comparacio Christi ad Belial, nec lucis
ad tenebras, nulla erit comparacio infidelium ad fideles. Sed videamus et caveamus

---

1: cum] bonis tuis *add.* FV[2]   2: possideamus] possidemus F   3: universale] dominium *add.* FV[2]
4: cum] ipsi *add.* FV[2]   5: de] *om.* F   6: referantur] reservantur FV[2]   7: superius, quia … uni-
versaliter] *om.* PV[1]   8: inferius] et *add.* PV[1]   9: universalis] universaliter P   10: Ecclesie]
om. CFV[2]   11: subiecti universaliter] universaliter subiecti FV[2]   12: et] *om.* C   13: univer-
sale] *om.* PV[1]   14: habent] domini *add.* F   15: esse] dici PV[1]V[2]   16: *indigni*] privati F
17: peioris] peiores   18: debeant] debent F   19: vero] autem C eciam F   20: serviunt] serviant F

what a blessing such servitude is, and how good it is that you should thus offer and give of your goods to the Church, since we may receive an hundredfold even in temporal goods and, after those temporal goods, we may possess eternal life.

It is clear from a consideration of possessors, therefore, that the faithful do indeed have neither a universal nor a total, but only a particular and partial, lordship over temporal things, since, in themselves and in all that they have and which can be of profit to them, they must be servants and tributaries of the Church. Such possessors, then, if they are considered in relation to the Church, can be said to be wholly subject even with respect to temporal possessions themselves; for they owe service and tribute to her from what they have and are.

The third way towards the same conclusion is derived from the manner in which things are possessed. For the Church is said to be Catholic, that is, universal; and each of the faithful is said to be Catholic, that is, universal. But two mutually related things cannot both be Catholic or universal in the same way, so that each of them is universally superior with respect to the other (for then the same thing would be superior to itself) or so that each of them is universally inferior with respect to the other (for then the same thing would be inferior to itself). It must be, then, that these two things are such that one of them is universally superior and universally lord and the other universally inferior and universally subservient. If, therefore, the Church is Catholic and universal because her lordship is universal, then the faithful are Catholic, that is, universal, because they must be universally subject and subservient to the Church. The faithful, then, if they are truly Catholic, must be truly subject to the Church universally, so that their manner of possessing themselves and whatever they have is such that they are faithful subjects of the Church in themselves and in all that is theirs. Therefore, from the manner in which things are possessed — since men must hold their possessions as the Church's subjects — the Church will have a universal and total lordship over the possessions of the faithful, but the lordship which the faithful themselves have will be able to be [only] particular and partial.

CHAPTER XI: *That unbelievers are all unworthy of any possession, lordship, and power.*

Perhaps it seems to many that the faithful are in a worse condition than unbelievers are, since they are taxpayers and tributaries to the Church and since they must be subject to the Church in themselves and in all that they have. Let us say, therefore, that unbelievers are the servants of Belial, whereas the faithful, because they are the Church's subjects, are the servants of Christ — that unbelievers are darkness, whereas the faithful, because they serve the Church, are light in the Lord, according to Ephesians 5: 'For you were once darkness, but now you are light in the Lord.'[1] And because, according to what the Apostle says, there is no agreement between Christ and Belial or light and darkness,[2] nor will there be any agreement between unbelievers and the faithful. But let us be vigilant, and take

1. Eph. 5:8.
2. II Cor. 6:15.

et[1] diligenter attendamus,[2] ne lumen quod in nobis est fiat tenebre.[3] Si ergo, quia subiectus es Ecclesie, et es[4] conversus ad Deum, vide ne contra Ecclesiam erectus et per consequens a Deo aversus tenebre fias.

Recordemur que dicta sunt: quam laudabilis sit ista servitus per quam eruimur[5] a potestate diaboli; quam utilis,[6] per quam centuplum accipimus et vitam eternam possidemus; quam nobilis, per quam non servimus[7] homini, sed Deo. Ille enim[8] qui sic nobis dominatur, non dominatur[9] ut homo mortalis sed ut vicarius Dei eterni et immortalis. Sed ut non plures sermones fiant quam requirit materia, volumus ad ipsam possessionem et dominium et potestatem infidelium nos convertere, ostendentes quod nullam possessionem, nullum dominium, nullam potestatem possunt infideles habere vere et cum iusticia, sed usurpando[10] et cum iniusticia.[11] Nam etsi Deus iuste permittit infideles dominari, potenciam et possessionem habere, ipsi tamen abutentes potestate, non recognoscentes inde Deum Creatorem suum, sed veritatem Dei in mendacium commutantes et demonibus inde sacrificantes, iniuste dominantur, possident et potestatem habent.

Volumus autem via triplici declarare quale sit dominium infidelium et qualis eorum possessio, quia vere et iuste non dominantur nec possessiones possident; ut prima via sumatur ex parte ipsius Dei, a quo possessiones habent, secunda ex parte ipsorum possidencium, tercia ex parte ipsarum possessionum.

Prima via sic patet. Nam a Deo habemus quecumque habemus; ipse enim est dives per se ipsum, nos autem sumus divites ex hiis que ipse prestat nobis[12] et mutuat nobis. Unde cum Deo offerimus aliqua, ea que de manu sua recipimus sibi damus, iuxta[13] verbum David quod habetur primo Paralipomenon ultimo: 'Tua sunt omnia, et que de manu tua accepimus, dedimus tibi.' Nos enim ipsi sumus factura Dei,[14] et res quas habemus ab ipso habemus. Servus itaque qui omnia sua habet a domino suo, si non vult subesse ei et[15] non est[16] subiectus sibi, iniuste possidet omnia que habet ab eo. Et quia quilibet infidelis est aversus a Deo et non placens Deo, quia sine fide impossibile est placere Deo, ut dicitur ad Hebreos XI, ideo quilibet infidelis iniuste possidet quicquid habet a Deo. Sed a Deo habemus res[17] temporales et dominia et potestates, quia non est potestas nisi a Deo. Quanto[18] ergo magis, si hec omnia habemus a Deo, tanto sumus magis iniusti possessores si inde non servimus Deo.

1: et] *del.* F *om.* V[2]   2: attendamus] *del.* C   3: fiat tenebre] tenebre fiat C   4: es] *om.* F
5: eruimur] erudimur C educimur F   6: utilis] utiliter P utilius V[2]   7: servimus] sumus F
8: enim] *om.* FV[2]   9: non dominatur] *om.* F   10: usurpando] usurpative FV[2]   11: iniusticia] iusticia FV[2]   12: nobis] *om.* C   13: iuxta] illud *add.* FV[2]   14: Dei] et possessio Dei *add.* FV[2]
15: et] aut F   16: est] esse FV[2]   17: res] *om.* FV[2]   18: Quanto] *om.* FV[2]

care, and strive diligently, lest the light which is in us become darkness. If, there-fore, because you are the Church's subject, you are indeed turned towards God, see to it that you be not raised up against the Church and consequently turned away from God and made darkness.

Let us recollect what has been said: how praiseworthy is that subjection whereby we are set free from the devil's power; how beneficial, since we receive an hundredfold from it and possess eternal life; how noble, since, through it, we serve not men, but God. For he who thus has lordship over us does not have lord-ship as a mortal man, but as the Vicar of the Eternal and Immortal God. But in order not to prolong this discourse beyond what the subject matter requires, we wish to turn to the possession and lordship and power of unbelievers, showing that unbelievers can have no property, no lordship, and no power truly and with jus-tice, but only by usurpation and with injustice. For although God justly permits unbelievers to have lordship, power, and property, they are nonetheless abusers of such power. From it, they do not acknowledge God as their Creator, but, ex-changing the truth of God for lies, and thence sacrificing to demons, they exercise lordship, have possession, and wield power unjustly.[1]

We wish, then, to show in three ways the nature of the lordship of unbelievers and the nature of their possession; for they neither exercise lordship nor hold pos-sessions truly and justly. The first way is derived from a consideration of God Himself, of Whom they hold their possessions; the second from a consideration of possessors; and the third from a consideration of possessions.

The first way proceeds as follows. For we hold of God whatever we have; for He is rich in Himself, but we are rich from those things which He entrusts to us and lends us.[2] Hence, when we offer anything to God, we are giving to Him what we have received from His hand, according to what David says in the final chapter of I Chronicles: 'All things are Yours, and we have given to You what we have received from Your hand.'[3] For we ourselves are made by God, and we hold the goods which we have of Him. Thus, if the servant who holds all that is his of his lord refuses to be subject to him and is not subject to him, he unjustly possesses all that he holds of him. And since every unbeliever is turned away from God and is not pleasing to God — for, as is said in Hebrews 11, it is impossible to please God without faith[4] — every unbeliever therefore unjustly possesses whatever he holds of God. But it is of God that we hold temporal goods and lordships and powers, because there is no power except of God.[5] Therefore, if we hold all these things of God, the more we have them the more unjust are we as possessors if we do not serve God by means of them.

---

1. Cf. Rom. 1:23. This, incidentally, is the most 'reactionary' of all Giles's chapters. Its thesis explicitly contradicts, for example, the statements of Innocent IV (*Apparatus ad quinque li-bros decretalium* (Venice, 1578) 3:34:8) and Aquinas (*Summa theologiae* IIa IIae 10:10) con-cerning the legitimacy of pagan governments.
2. See n. 2 on p. 23.
3. I Chron. 29:14.
4. Heb. 11:6.
5. Rom. 13:1.

Secunda via ad hoc idem sumitur ex parte ipsorum possidencium. Nam, ut dicebamus, ipsi possidentes de se ipsis et de quibuscumque possident debent esse tributarii Ecclesie. Ideo, ut dicebamus, preter decimas fiunt oblaciones in ecclesiis in recognicionem proprie servitutis, ut recognoscamus nos ipsos servos Ecclesie et de omnibus hiis que habemus, recognoscamus Ecclesie nos esse subiectos. Sed qui de iure debet esse tributarius alicui de se et de omnibus que habet, nisi tributum solvat, iniuste possidet quicquid habet. Possumus autem hanc eandem conclusionem aliter deducere. Nam quicumque tenet possessionem aliquam non eo modo quo debet, vel non reddit inde suo superiori quod debet, et maxime si sit talis[1] superior quod non possit ei preiudicari ex quacumque diuturnitate temporis, ille iniuste tenet possessionem illam. Immo, quodcumque sit illud, unde[2] debet aliquis se[3] recognoscere servum sui superioris, si non se recognoscat et non reddat inde quod debet, erit iniustus possessor et iniustus detentor illius rei. Sed quilibet debet tributum Deo et de se ipso, quia est servus Dei, et de omnibus,[4] quia[5] omnia habet a Deo.

Ideo, ut supra tetigimus, preter decimas, que sunt census possessionum nostrarum, debemus offerre oblaciones quasi tributum quoddam, ut simus tributarii et censuarii ipsius Dei et per consequens ipsius Ecclesie, quia non possumus reconciliari Deo nisi per Ecclesiam et sub Ecclesia. Dicimus autem quod pro nobis ipsis et pro omnibus rebus nostris debemus offerre oblaciones Deo et Ecclesie, ita quod prius debemus offerre nos ipsos subiciendo nos ipsos, devocionem habendo ad Ecclesiam, quam offerre res nostras. Immo, nihil prodest nobis offerre res[6] nostras nisi offeramus nos ipsos prius. Ideo dicitur Geneseos IV quod ad Cain et ad munera eius Dominus non respexit;[7] quod Magister in *Historiis* exponens ait quod Cain non recte obtulerat[8] nec recte diviserat. Non[9] recte quidem obtulerat,[10] quia se ipsum, qui erat melior oblacione, non obtulit Deo, sed diabolo; nec recte diviserat, quia meliora sibi retinebat et peiora Deo dabat. Nam cum esset agricola, spicas attritas et corrosas, ut puta spicas que erant secus viam, offerebat Deo, reliquas autem bonas spicas[11] retinebat sibi. Debemus itaque esse tributarii Ecclesie per rectam oblacionem offerendo nos ipsos prius, devocionem habendo et nos subiciendo Ecclesie, et per rectam divisionem dividendo et discernendo que Deo damus et que Ecclesie tribuimus, quia non de peioribus, sed de melioribus dare debemus.

Redeamus ergo ad propositum et dicamus quod cum nihil possumus possidere recte et sine peccato nisi simus inde tributarii Deo et Ecclesie, ideo infideles, vel eciam fideles contra Ecclesiam delinquentes, nec se ipsos recte habent nec suas facultates debite tenent. Unde Augustinus ait, VI *Confessionum,* quod mali

---

1: talis] *om.* F   2: unde] vere FV^2 3: aliquis se] se quis F quis se CV^2 4: omnibus] que habet *add.* F   5: quia] que C   6: res] *om.* C   7: Dominus non respexit] non respexit deus C   8: non recte obtulerat] *om.* F   9: Non] nec F   10: obtulerat] *om.* F   11: spicas] *om.* C

The second way towards the same conclusion is derived from a consideration of possessors themselves. For, as we have said,[1] possessors must be tributaries of the Church for themselves and for whatever they possess. As we have said, then, in addition to tithes, offerings are made in churches in recognition of due servitude, so that we may acknowledge ourselves to be the servants of the Church for all that we have, and may acknowledge that we are the Church's subjects. But he who, *de iure*, must be a tributary to another for himself and for all that he has, unjustly possesses whatever he has if he does not pay tribute. And we can deduce this same conclusion in another way. For if whoever holds some possession does so in an improper manner, or does not render from it what is due to his superior (especially if the superior is such that his claim cannot be prejudiced by any lapse of time), then he holds that possession unjustly. Indeed, if anyone is bound to acknowledge that he is the servant of his superior with respect to something, whatever it may be, and does not acknowledge this, and does not render what is due from it, then he will be an unjust possessor and holder of that thing. But each man owes tribute to God: both for himself, since he is the servant of God, and for everything else, for he holds all things of God.

And so, as we have noted above, in addition to the tithes which are a tax on our possessions, we must make offerings as a kind of tribute, so that we may be the tributaries and taxpayers of God Himself, and consequently of His Church; for we cannot be reconciled to God except through the Church and under the Church. But we say that we must make offerings to God and to the Church for ourselves and for all our goods. Thus, we must first offer ourselves, by subjecting ourselves to and having devotion for the Church, before we offer our goods. Indeed, it is profitless to offer our goods unless we first offer ourselves. For it is said in Genesis 4 that the Lord was not mindful of Cain and of his gifts;[2] and, interpreting this, the Master says in the *Historia* that Cain had neither offered rightly nor divided rightly.[3] He had indeed not offered rightly, for he did not offer himself, which was better than an offering, to God, but to the devil. Nor had he divided rightly, for he kept the better for himself and gave the worse to God. For, since he was a farmer, [we may suppose that] he offered to God the ears of corn which were rubbed away and torn — that is, the ears which were beside the path — and kept the remaining good ears for himself. We must, then, be tributaries of the Church by making right offerings of ourselves first — by having devotion for and subjecting ourselves to the Church — and by rightly dividing and separating what we give to God and what we pay as tribute to the Church [from what we keep for ourselves]; for we must give not the worse, but the better.

Let us return to our proposition, therefore, and say that since we can possess nothing rightly and without sin unless we pay tribute from it to God and the Church, unbelievers, and the faithful also, if they offend against the Church, therefore do not possess themselves rightly nor hold their property worthily. Hence, Augustine says

1. See Pt. I, Ch. V, pp. 21–23; Pt. II, Ch. IV, p. 99; Pt. II, Ch X, pp. 177–179.
2. Gen. 4:5.
3. Peter Comestor, *Historia scholastica*, PL 198:1077.

homines eciam se ipsos non habent.

Tercia via sumitur ex parte ipsarum possessionum, de quibus debemus esse censuarii Ecclesie et de quibus debemus decimas dare. Infideles ergo, vel eciam fideles contra Ecclesiam delinquentes et ipsi Ecclesie quod debent non reddentes eamque non Catholicam et universalem dominam recognoscentes, omnium[1] que habent, tam propriarum personarum[2] quam eciam facultatum necnon dominiorum et potestatum, sunt indebiti possessores.

Sed queres, Unde habet Ecclesia quod sic sit Catholica et plena et universalis domina? Dicemus quod hoc habet a sacramentis, que sunt plena et universalia:[3] plena quidem, quia sunt vasa plena[4] gracie; universalia vero, quia sine eis nullus[5] potest salutem consequi. Et potissime hoc habet a sacramento baptismi, quod est ianua omnium sacramentorum, iuxta illud Psalmi:[6] 'Dominabitur a mari usque ad mare, a flumine usque ad terminos orbis terrarum.' In quibus verbis prius describitur Ecclesie universalis dominacio, secundo describitur[7] universalitatis causa et racio. Universalis quidem dominacio Ecclesie describitur[8] cum dicitur 'Dominabitur a mari,' id est a quolibet fine terre, 'usque ad mare,' id est usque[9] ad quemlibet finem terre, ut glossa exponit. Tota enim terra est circumdata maribus. Dominari ergo a mari usque ad mare est dominari super[10] universam terram, vel est dominari usque ad omnes terminos[11] terre, cum ipsa maria sint termini terre. Bene itaque dictum est quod describitur Ecclesie universalis dominacio cum dicitur 'Dominabitur a mari usque ad mare.' Sed huius universalis dominii describitur causa et racio cum subditur 'et a flumine usque ad terminos orbis terrarum,' quasi dicat quod hec est causa quare Ecclesia dominatur a mari usque ad mare: quia dominatur[12] a flumine, id est a Iordane, ut exponit glossa, ubi fuit baptizatus Christus, usque ad terminos orbis terrarum. A flumine igitur, id est a baptismo, qui est ianua omnium sacramentorum, habet Ecclesia quod dominetur a mari usque ad mare sive[13] ad terminos orbis terrarum. Nam cum nullus possit consequi salutem sine baptismo, quilibet est filius ire et est aversus a Deo nisi sit baptizatus.

Sed, ut sepe et[14] sepius dictum est, qui non est subiectus Deo et non est possessione[15] Dei dignus,[16] nihil subiciatur sibi et nulla sit possessio eius. Omnes ergo homines et omnes possessiones sunt sub dominio Ecclesie, ita quod ipsius Ecclesie est orbis terrarum et universi qui habitant in eo. Si ergo per baptismum ipsi habitantes terram eripiuntur a potestate diaboli, consequens est quod omnes habitantes terram debeant esse servi empticii Ecclesie, ut[17] per eam redimantur a diabolica potestate. Rursus, quia baptizati per Ecclesiam fiunt suarum possessionum iusti possessores, qui non baptizati et non subiecti Deo erant[18] possessores iniusti, consequens est quod omnes possessiones nostras et omnia temporalia nostra

---

1: omnium] omnia FV²   2: personarum] *om.* FV²   3: universalia] et *add.* F   4: plena] *om.* C
5: nullus] nullum F   6: Psalmi] in psalmis F   7: describitur] huius *add.* FV²   8: Universalis
quidem ... describitur] *om.* PV¹   9: usque] *om.* F   10: super] usque C   11: terminos] orbis
add. F   12: dominatur] dominabitur FV²   13: sive] usque *add.* CF   14: et] *om.* FV²   15: possessione] possessio F   16: dignus] est qui *add.* C dignum CPV¹V²   17: ut] cum C   18: erant]
erunt FPV¹V²

in *Confessions* 6 that wicked men do not possess even themselves.[1]

The third way is derived from a consideration of possessions themselves, from which we must be taxpayers to the Church and from which we must pay tithes. Therefore, unbelievers, and the faithful also, if they offend against the Church, not rendering to the Church what they owe and not acknowledging her Catholic and universal lordship, are unworthy possessors of all that they have: of their own persons and property alike, and also, indeed, of their lordships and powers.

But, you will ask, Whence has the Church this Catholic and full and universal lordship? We shall reply that she has it from the sacraments, which are full and universal: full indeed, for they are vessels full of grace; and universal, for, without them, no one can obtain salvation. And, above all, she has it from the sacrament of baptism, which is the gateway to all the sacraments, according to the Psalm: 'He shall rule from sea to sea, from the river to the ends of the earth.'[2] For, in these words, there is described, first, the Church's universal lordship, and, second, there is described the cause and reason of this universality. The Church's universal lordship is indeed described when it is said, 'He shall rule from sea to sea': that is, as a gloss explains, from one end of the earth to the other.[3] For all the earth is surrounded by seas. To rule from sea to sea, therefore, is to have lordship over the whole earth or to have lordship extending to all the ends of the earth, for those seas are the ends of the earth. It is well said, then, that the Church's universal lordship is described when it is stated, 'He shall rule from sea to sea.' But the cause and reason of this universal lordship is described when it is added, 'And from the river to the ends of the earth.' It is as if it said that the cause whereby the lordship of the Church extends from sea to sea is that she rules from the river, that is, as the gloss explains, from the Jordan, where Christ was baptized, to the ends of the earth. Thus, the Church derives her lordship from sea to sea, or to the ends of the earth, from the river, that is, from baptism, which is the gateway to all the sacraments. For since no one may obtain salvation without baptism, every man is a child of wrath and turned away from God if he is not baptized.[4]

But, as has been said again and again, he who is not subject to God and not worthy to possess God may have nothing subject to him and nothing as his own possession. Therefore all men and all possessions are under the lordship of the Church, for the earth and all who dwell therein belong to the Church. Therefore, if those who dwell upon the earth are set free through baptism from the power of the devil, it follows that, inasmuch as they are redeemed through her from the devil's power, all who dwell upon the earth must be bound to the Church as servants. Again, since those who are baptized through the Church are made just possessors of their possessions who, when they were not baptized and not subject to the Church, were unjust possessors, it follows that we must acknowledge that we hold all our

1. Nothing to this effect is found in *Confessions* 6. Possibly Giles is here half-remembering *Tractatus in Ioannem evangelium* 6:25-26 (CCSL 36:66–67).
2. Psalm 72:8.
3. *Glossa ordinaria*, PL 113:954.
4. Cf. Eph. 2:3.

recognoscamus ab Ecclesia, per quam baptizati et spiritualiter regenerati ac per alia sacramenta a peccatis liberati fimus[1] bonorum nostrorum iusti et debiti possessores.

Sed dices quod auctoritates Psalterii allegate indebite sunt inducte,[2] nam, cum dicitur 'dominabitur a mari usque ad mare' etc., dices hoc non esse dictum de Ecclesia, sed de Christo; et quod eciam in Psalterio legitur, 'Domini est orbis terrarum et omnes[3] qui habitant in eo,' hoc dictum est de Deo, non de Ecclesia. Sed tales obiecciones nulle sunt. Nam non est inconveniens quod multis modis simus debitores alicuius, et quod multis modis alicui domino debeamus esse subiecti. Inter alios autem modos quare debeamus esse servi Christi et quare ipse debeat dominari a mari usque ad mare, id est in universa terra, exprimit David hunc modum: quod dominatur a flumine, id est a Iordane, ubi Christus fuit baptizatus, usque ad terminos orbis terrarum. Christus enim baptizatus in Iordane tactu sue mundissime carnis vim regenerativam contulit aquis, ut ex tunc aque haberent hanc vim[4] regenerativam, ut possent sic[5] corpus attingere, quod eciam suam animam lavarent. Et quia istam vim et istam virtutem non possunt aque exercere nisi per[6] baptismum factum in forma Ecclesie, si Christus conferens huiusmodi virtutem aquis dicitur ex hoc esse Dominus universe terre, Ecclesia, que confert baptismum et in cuius forma baptismus datur, quia nonnisi per baptismum possent[7] aque istam virtutem exercere, ut animas humanas lavent et homines regenerent, consequens est quod Ecclesia, cuius est dare baptismum et in cuius forma baptismus datur, quod ipsa a flumine, id est a baptismo, hoc habeat quod[8] dominetur usque ad terminos orbis terrarum. Et quia ipsa ex hoc est Catholica et universalis domina, consequens eciam est[9] quod suus sit orbis terrarum et universi qui habitant in eo. Habuit autem Ecclesia huiusmodi formam baptizandi a Christo, quia a Christo habet quod sic dominetur.

CAPITULUM XII:[10] *Quod in omnibus temporalibus Ecclesia habet dominium superius; ceteri autem solum dominium inferius habere possunt.*

Forte videbitur multis quod non sit in hoc opere latitudo sermonis secundum exigenciam rei, sed sunt[11] ibi plures sermones quam presens requirat[12] materia, eo quod videatur unum et idem multociens repetitum. Sed, ut sapientes notaverunt,[13] finis imponit necessitatem hiis que sunt ad finem, ut si finis serre est secare dura, necesse est quod sit ferrea et dentata, quia aliter non posset apte dura secare. Finis autem huius operis est omnes fideles sive totum populum Christianum erudire quia toti populo expedit scire ecclesiasticam potestatem, ne per tam periculosam ignoranciam ignoraretur a Domino in futuro[14] iudicio. In

1: fimus] simus F   2: inducte] adducte CFV² 3: omnes] universi C   4: vim] vitam F   5: sic] sicut F   6: per] sit C   7: possent] possunt CF   8: quod] ut F   9: eciam est] est eciam F 10: XII] xiii C   11: sunt] sint F   12: requirat] requirit F   13: notaverunt] noverunt F 14: ignoraretur a ... futuro] a domino in futuro ignoretur FV²

possessions and all our temporal goods of the Church, through whom we are baptized and spiritually regenerated, and, by the other sacraments, set free from sin and made just and worthy possessors of our goods.

But you will say that we have cited the authorities of the Psalter improperly. For, you will say, when it is stated that 'He will rule from sea to sea,' and so on, this is said not of the Church, but of Christ; and also that what we read in the Psalter — that 'The earth is the Lord's and all who dwell therein'[1] — is said of God, not of the Church. But such objections are of no significance. For it is not inconsistent to say that we are debtors to someone for many reasons and that we should be subject to some lord for many reasons. And from among the various reasons why we must be servants of Christ and why He should rule from sea to sea, that is, over the whole earth, David chose this reason: that He rules from the river — that is, from the Jordan, where Christ was baptized — to the ends of the earth. For when Christ was baptized in the Jordan, He conferred a regenerative power upon water by the touch of His most pure flesh, so that water might thenceforth have the regenerative power of also washing the soul by touching the body. And since water cannot exert this force and this power except through baptism in the form prescribed by the Church; and if Christ, Who has conferred such power upon water, is thereby said to be Lord of the whole earth: then the Church, who confers baptism and in whose form baptism is given because water cannot exercise the power of washing souls and regenerating men except through baptism — then it follows[2] that the Church, to whom it belongs to give baptism and in whose form baptism is given, has it from the river, that is, from baptism, that she possesses lordship over all the ends of the earth. And since her lordship is Catholic and universal by reason of this, it follows that the earth and all who dwell therein are hers. And the Church has received this form of baptism from Christ, for she has it from Christ that she thus possesses lordship.

CHAPTER XII: *That the Church has a superior lordship in all temporal things, but that others can have only an inferior lordship.*

Perhaps it will seem to many that the extent of the discussion in this work is not suitable to the needs of the subject, but that much more has here been said than the present question requires; for it may seem that one and the same argument has been frequently repeated. As wise men have noted, however, an end imposes a necessity upon those things which are ordered to that end.[3] Thus, if the end of a saw is to cut hard material, it is necessary that it be made of iron and have teeth, for it would not otherwise be adapted to the cutting of hard material. And the end of this work is the education of all the faithful or of the whole Christian people; for it is expedient for the whole people to understand ecclesiastical power lest, through such dangerous ignorance, they be ignored by the Lord at the future

1. Psalm 24:1.
2. The evident confusion here may be due to an early textual corruption; but all the MSS exhibit it, and conjecture seems unwise. Perhaps Giles has simply got lost in his own knotty sentence.
3. Cf. Aristotle, *Physics* 2:9 (200ª10).

toto autem populo multi sunt quorum intellectus est hebes et grossus, et quia tales sunt parvuli in Christo, non esca sed, secundum Apostoli sentenciam, lac est eis pocius tribuendum. Tales autem tamquam parvuli et non habentes dentes non possunt dura frangere nec duram escam edere. Horum autem doctores debent esse velut nutrices, que prius cibum masticant quam ipsum suo tribuant alumno. Sic et isti nonnisi doctrinam masticatam capere possunt. Non tamen propter hoc sunt despiciendi, quia et[1] inferiores angeli indigent 'masticata' doctrina; unde et[2] Dionysius in libro[3] *De angelica hierarchia* probat[4] metaphorice loquendo: 'Angeli superiores habent dentes, quia frangunt et dividunt species et conceptus, que indivisa non possent capere inferiores angeli; divisa autem et quasi masticata capiunt.'

Et ut hoc nostro proposito adaptemus, dicamus quod non omnes sunt ita acuti et subtilis quod propositis principiis ita ingrediantur in ea et ita penetrent ipsa quod possint[5] ex eis omnes conclusiones elicere. Est enim[6] acuti ingredi, penetrare et scindere, quod grossi non possunt facere. Et ideo, quando ex uno principio possunt multe conclusiones elici, populo, qui est auditor grossus, ut in *Rhetoricis*[7] declaratur, tociens illud principium est repetendum quociens inde nove conclusiones exprimi possunt. Immo, non solum ad novam conclusionem, sed eciam[8] ad sufficienciorem[9] deduccionem non inaniter sunt eadem principia repetenda. Et quia numquam eadem pluries repetimus nisi vel ut nova haberetur conclusio vel ut sufficiencior narraretur deduccio, nugacionem que est inutilis unius et eiusdem repeticio hec[10] faciendo in hoc opere credimus evitasse. Semper enim dicendus est nova dicere qui sive eadem sive alia semper ad nova cernitur ordinare.

Ad excusacionem nostram hiis itaque prelibatis, volumus exequi que[11] in rubrica capituli continentur.[12] Nam licet per superiora dicta sufficienter haberi possit quod Ecclesia habeat in temporalibus dominium superius, ceteri vero[13] inferius — quia in multis superioribus capitulis probatum est terrenam potestatem sub ecclesiastica collocari; est eciam paulo ante ostensum quod Ecclesia in temporalibus habet dominium universale, ceteri vero particulare; quia ergo particularia sub universalibus continentur, satis ostensum esse videtur quod Ecclesia habeat dominium superius, ceteri vero inferius — volumus tamen[14] nihilominus ad hanc conclusionem[15] novas raciones adducere vel aliqualiter iam adductas novo modo deducere, ut nostrum propositum clarius elucescat.

Probabimus autem quatuor viis propositum prelibatum, ut prima via sumatur ex ecclesiastico iudicio sive iurisdiccione; secunda vero ex Ecclesie generali

---

1: et] *om.* C   2: unde et] ut F   3: libro] *om.* CF   4: probat] quod *add.* C   5: possint] possunt C
6: enim] *om.* F   7: *Rhetoricis*] Rhetorica F   8: eciam] et PV[1]V[2]   9: sufficienciorem] suffocatiorem F   10: hec] hoc C   11: que] quod F   12: continentur] continetur F   13: vero] autem F
14: tamen] *om.* FV[2]   15: conclusionem] controversiam F

judgment.[1] But, among the whole people, there are many whose intellect is dull and gross; and, because such persons are infants in Christ, milk must be given to them rather than solid food, according to what the Apostle says.[2] And such persons, as infants who have no teeth, cannot bite what is hard or eat hard food; and their teachers must be like nurses who first chew the food before they give it to their charge. So also, these cannot grasp our teaching unless it is chewed. They are not to be despised on this account, however; for even the lower angels need doctrines which are 'chewed,' as Dionysius himself proves metaphorically in the book *De angelica hierarchia*, saying: 'The higher angels have teeth; for they bite and divide the forms and concepts which, undivided, the lower angels could not grasp; and the latter grasp what is divided and, as it were, chewed.'[3]

And, so that we may apply this to our proposition, let us say that not all men are so sharp and subtle that they can enter into the principles of an argument and penetrate them so as to elicit all conclusions from them. For sharp instruments can enter and penetrate and cut, but dull ones cannot. And so, when many conclusions can be elicited from one principle, that principle must be repeated to the populace — which, as is shown in the *Rhetoric*, is a dull audience[4] — as often as is necessary to enable them to infer new conclusions from it. Indeed, it is not in vain that the same principles should be repeated not only to reach new conclusions, but also to establish a more sufficient chain of reasoning. And because we never repeat the same argument several times unless either to infer a new conclusion or to explain a chain of reasoning more sufficiently, we believe that, by doing this in the present work, we have avoided the triviality which is the useless repetition of one and the same argument. For what is always said in order to distinguish either the same or a different argument in a new way must itself always be called new.

Thus, having first touched upon these considerations in our own defence, we wish to pass to the matters contained in the heading of this chapter. For although it may be sufficiently inferred from what has been said already that the Church has a superior and that others have only an inferior lordship in temporal things (for it has been proved in many of the foregoing chapters that the earthly power is placed under the ecclesiastical, and also, a short while ago,[5] it was shown that the Church has a universal, and others only a particular, lordship in temporal things: since, therefore, particulars are contained under universals, this seems to be enough to show that the Church has a superior lordship and others only an inferior), we nonetheless wish to adduce further arguments for this conclusion, or to deduce in some new way those already adduced, so that our proposition may be revealed in a clearer light.

And we shall demonstrate the proposition just touched upon in four ways. The first will be derived from ecclesiastical judgment or jurisdiction; the second from

---

1. I Cor. 14:38; Peter Lombard, *Collectanea in omnes de Pauli apostoli epistolas*, PL 191:1672.
2. I Cor. 3:1–2.
3. *De caelesti hierarchia* 15 (PG 3:332).
4. Perhaps Aristotle, *Rhetoric* 3:4 (1406^{b}35), referring to Plato, *Republic* 488A.
5. Ch. X.

solucione[1] et ligacione, prout sic ligatus privatur communione fidelium; tercia eciam sumitur ex[2] eadem ligacione, prout sic ligatus privatur communione sacramentorum; quarta quidem sumitur ex ligacione eadem, prout sic ligatus privatur communione eternorum bonorum.

Propter primum sciendum quod aliud est habere aliquid ex officio, aliud ex personali perfeccione. Multi enim sciunt canere qui in aliqua ecclesia non habent officium cantorie, et multi optime sciunt iura qui non sunt iudices in aliqua causa. Habentes itaque perfeccionem personalem ad aliquid agendum, nullam ex hoc habent iurisdiccionem et auctoritatem, sed habent idoneitatem quandam ut sibi tale officium committatur. Sed ex eo quod sibi est commissum[3] officium, et ex eo quod aliquis est in statu prelacionis, dato quod non haberet personalem perfeccionem secundum quod res commissa exigeret, iuxta tamen suum statum et iuxta commissionem sibi factam habet iurisdiccionem vel auctoritatem.

Cum ergo supra diximus, et cum pluries repetimus, quod Summus Pontifex est ille spiritualis homo qui iudicat omnia et ipse a nemine iudicatur, intelligendum est secundum officium sibi traditum[4] et secundum exigenciam sui status. Est enim in statu tam alto, et sic est in apice Ecclesie collocatus, ut ipse iudicet omnia et a nemine iudicetur. Illud ergo iudicium non erit speculativum tantum, sed erit auctoritativum et iurisdiccionale. Scientes enim iura habent in decidendis causis iudicium speculativum vel consiliativum si ab eis consilium postuletur; sed decidere causas, et auctoritatem[5] et iurisdiccionem habere in eis, habent qui sunt iudices in quantum sunt iudices constituti. Itaque, si Summus Pontifex iudicat omnia et huiusmodi iudicium non est solum secundum perfeccionem personalem, ut sit solum speculativum, sed est ut suum officium postulat et ut exigit suus status, et exinde est iurisdiccionale et auctoritativum, consequens est ut eo[6] modo iudicet omnia, quod auctoritatem et iurisdiccionem habeat in omnibus. Sed qui 'omnia' dicit nihil excipit. Totus itaque, ut dicebamus, est suus orbis terrarum et universi qui habitant in eo. Quia ergo in omnibus possidentibus et possessionibus iurisdiccionem et auctoritatem habet, cum tam possidentes quam possessiones inter omnia computentur, nam non omnes iudicaret nisi[7] super omnibus iurisdiccionem haberet, dicamus ergo [quod] ille qui sic spiritualis est, si est homo, habebit iurisdiccionem super omnes homines et super omnia que hominibus sunt subiecta. Non enim posset intelligi quod homo ex sua spiritualitate super spiritualiora[8] se iurisdiccionem haberet, cum iurisdiccio et auctoritas

---

1: solucione] absolucione F   2: ex] *om.* F   3: commissum] aliquod *add.* F   4: traditum] creditum CFV[2]   5: auctoritatem] auctoritates FPV[1]V[2]   6: eo] eodem F   7: nisi] ubi C   8: spiritualiora] spiritualia et ora F

the Church's general power of releasing and binding, inasmuch as whoever is so bound is deprived of the communion of the faithful; the third will be derived from the same power of binding, inasmuch as whoever is so bound is deprived of the communion of the sacraments; and the fourth will, again, be derived from the same power of binding, inasmuch as whoever is so bound is deprived of the communion of eternal goods.

As to the first, it must be known that it is one thing to have something by reason of office and another to do so by reason of personal perfection. For there are many who know how to sing who do not hold the office of cantor in any church, and there are many who understand the laws excellently who are not judges in any cause. Thus, although they have a personal perfection in relation to some activity, they do not on this account have jurisdiction and authority: rather, they have a certain competence by reason of which such an office might be entrusted to them. But it is from the fact that an office has [actually] been entrusted to someone, and from the fact that he occupies a position of eminence, that he has jurisdiction or authority according to his status and according to the task entrusted to him, even supposing that he does not have the personal perfection which the matter entrusted to him requires.[1]

Therefore, what we have said above and several times repeated, that the Supreme Pontiff is that spiritual man who judges all things and is himself judged by no one, must be understood in terms of the office delivered to him and in terms of what is needful to his status [rather than in terms of personal perfection or expertise]. For he occupies so high a status, and is thus placed at the summit of the Church, in order that he himself may judge all things and be judged by no one. His judgment, therefore, will not be merely speculative: rather, it will be authoritative and jurisdictional. For those who understand the laws must contribute a speculative and advisory judgment to the decision of a cause if advice is sought from them. But it is because they have been appointed as judges [and not because of their legal expertise] that those who are judges [as distinct from expert counsellors] have in themselves both the authority and the jurisdiction to decide causes. Thus, if the Supreme Pontiff judges all things, and if such judgment is not simply a matter of personal perfection, as is a merely speculative judgment, but is as his office demands and as his status requires, and so is jurisdictional and authoritative, then it follows that he may judge all things in the sense of having authority and jurisdiction in all things. He who says 'all things,' however, excludes nothing.[2] Thus, as we have said, the whole earth is his and all who dwell therein. Therefore, since he has jurisdiction and authority over all possessors and possessions — for possessors and possessions alike are to be included in 'all things,' and he would not be able to judge all men unless he had jurisdiction over all things — let us say, then, that he who is thus spiritual, if he is a man, will have jurisdiction over all men and over all things which are subject to men. (For we could not suppose that, by reason of his spirituality, a man might have jurisdiction over things more spiritual than himself; for jurisdiction

---

1. Cf. Pt. I, Ch. II, where 'personal perfection' denotes moral goodness rather than competence or expertise; but the point is the same in both cases.
2. Cf. X. 1:33:6: *Solitae* (CIC 2:198).

secundum quod huiusmodi ad inferiora referantur.[1]

Sufficienter itaque probatum est quod[2] ex iudicio et iurisdiccione Ecclesie, cum iurisdiccio inferiora respiciat, omnia sunt sub Ecclesia. Habet itaque Ecclesia super omnibus dominium superius, ceteri vero inferius. Ex hiis autem[3] apparet clarius quod dicebatur supra, capitulo X: quomodo Summus Pontifex, quia est spiritualis medicus, ideo habet iudicare de omnibus hiis que spectant ad salutem animarum, et exinde auctoritatem et iurisdiccionem habet super temporalibus omnibus. Nam quia huiusmodi iudicium non est speculativum tantum, ut est per habita manifestum, sed est auctoritativum et iurisdiccionale, cum temporalia possint haberi debite et indebite et cum salute et non salute animarum, eapropter qui habet iudicare de salute animarum et de omnibus temporalibus iudicabit, ut iudicando de iusta possessione rerum, quantum ad hoc, omnes animas salvas faciat.[4,5] Et si illud iudicium non est speculativum tantum, sed auctoritativum et iurisdiccionale, cuiusmodi est iudicium Summi Pontificis, consequens erit quod ipse super omnibus temporalibus auctoritatem et iurisdiccionem habebit.

Secunda autem[6] via ad hoc idem sumitur ex Ecclesie generali[7] solucione et ligacione. Non enim dixit Dominus Petro 'Si hunc vel illum ligaveris erit super terram, erit ligatus[8] et in celis,' sed universaliter protulit: 'Quecumque[9] ligaveris super terram.' Volumus autem clare ostendere quod quicumque est ligatus ab Ecclesia vel excommunicatus ab ea, nihil potest dicere quod sit suum; vel si potest hoc dicere, hoc erit solum ex indulgencia Ecclesie. Quo ostenso, erit liquido declaratum quod Ecclesia sic habet dominium superius super omnia temporalia et super omnes possessiones, quod quemcumque ligat, nisi ex indulgencia Ecclesie fiat, nihil sibi remanebit quod sit suum.

Sciendum ergo quod primitus non fuit de iure hec possessio huius et[10] illa illius, quod aliquis posset dicere 'hoc est meum,' nisi ex convencione et pacto quod habebant ad invicem. Que convencio et pactum ad particionem et divisionem orbis terrarum se solummodo extendebat[11] ut Ade filii hoc modo appropriassent possessiones aliquas et hoc modo proprium habuissent, prout divisissent terras, et ex convencione[12] et ex[13] pacto concessissent hoc esse huius, hoc illius. Multiplicatis tamen hominibus, oportuit pacta et convenciones magis extendi ut non solum ad[14] terrarum divisionem,[15] sicut[16] fuit in filiis Ade, et post diluvium in filiis Noe — de quibus secundum unum modum dicendi ait Magister in *Historiis* quod tres filii Noe disseminati sunt in tribus partibus orbis, quia Sem Asiam, Cham Africam, Iaphet

---

1: referantur] referatur FV²   2: quod] et F   3: autem] itaque F   4: faciat] faciet F   5: ut iudicando ... faciat] *marg.* C   6: autem] *om.* F   7: Ecclesie generali] generali ecclesie F   8: ligatus] ligatum CPV¹   9: Quecumque] quicumque F   10: et] vel FV²   11: extendebat] ostendebat FV²   12: convencione] convencionibus FV²   13: ex] *om.* CFV²   14: ad] ex *mss*   15: divisionem] divisione *mss*   16: sicut] sic F

and authority as such relate to inferiors.)

It has been sufficiently proved from the judgment and jurisdiction of the Church, then, that, since jurisdiction relates to inferiors, [and since no one on earth occupies a status superior in jurisdiction to that of the Supreme Pontiff,] all things are under the Church. Thus, the Church has a superior lordship over all things, and others only an inferior. And, from these remarks, what was said above, in Chapter X, becomes clearer: how, since he is a spiritual physician, the Supreme Pontiff must therefore judge all those things which bear upon the health of souls, and so has authority and jurisdiction over all temporal things. For since, as is clear from what has been said, such judgment is not merely speculative, but is authoritative and jurisdictional, and since temporal things may be possessed worthily and unworthily and healthily and unhealthily for souls, he who must judge in matters concerning the health of souls will therefore also judge all temporal things in such a way that, by giving judgment as to the just possession of things, he may in this way save all souls. And if this form of judgment, of which kind is the judgment of the Supreme Pontiff, is not merely speculative, but is authoritative and jurisdictional, it will follow that he will have authority and jurisdiction over all temporal things.

The second way towards the same conclusion is derived from the Church's general power of releasing and binding. For the Lord did not say to Peter, 'If you shall bind this man or that on earth, he will be bound in heaven.' Rather, He said generally: 'Whatever you shall bind on earth.'[1] And we wish to show clearly that whoever is bound by the Church or excommunicated by her can say of nothing that it is his own, or, if he can say so, that this will be only by the Church's indulgence. And, when this has been shown, it will be very clear that the Church has so superior a lordship over all temporal goods and over all possessions that nothing will remain as his own to one whom she binds except by the indulgence of the Church.

It must be known, therefore, that, in the beginning, this or that possession of this or that man was not a matter of law; so that no one could say 'this is mine' except by mutual covenant and pact. And this covenant and pact extended only to the partitioning and division of the earth. For the sons of Adam had appropriated certain possessions, and had in this way possessed them as their own, inasmuch as they had divided the lands and agreed by covenant and pact that one part should belong to one and another to another.[2] But, as men multiplied, it became necessary for such pacts and agreements to be wider in extent, so as to include not only the division of the lands (as was the case among the sons of Adam and, after the Flood, the sons of Noah,[3] of whom, according to one manner of speaking, the Master says in the *Historia* that the three sons of Noah were scattered to three parts of the earth; for Asia was allotted to Shem, Africa to Ham, and Europe to Japheth[4])

1. Matt. 16:18–19.
2. A process not recorded in scripture, but inferred from Gen. 4–5.
3. Cf. Gen. 9:18–19.
4. Peter Comestor, *Historia scholastica*, PL 198:1087.

Europam sortitus est — [sed ad divisionem omnium temporalium]. Sed de modo divisionis nihil ad propositum. Sufficit enim scire quod non poterat aliquis illorum iuste appropriare sibi aliquam partem terre nisi ex pacto et convencione[1] habita cum aliis, ita[2] quod prima appropriacio fuit secundum pacta et convenciones, vel secundum assensum in divisionibus terrarum, prout filii Ade vel Noe, eis assencientibus,[3] vel saltem non contradicentibus, sortiti sunt sibi terras, et unus appropriavit sibi hanc partem, alius vero illam. Sed postea, ut diximus, multiplicatis iam hominibus, oportuit huiusmodi convenciones et pacta multiplicari, ut fieret possessio terrarum et agrorum non solum secundum[4] particionem[5] prout fit in filiis eiusdem patris, sed secundum empcionem, donacionem, commutacionem vel aliis modis qui sub convencione vel animorum consensu cadere possunt; quia nec empcio nec communicacio nec donacio fieret nisi animorum consensus ibi concurreret.

Postquam autem inceperunt homines dominari super terram et fieri reges, supervenerunt leges que et hoc continebant et alia superaddebant. Volunt autem leges quod licita pacta et licite convenciones et liciti contractus observentur; ex quibus licitis pactis[6] et convencionibus[7] et contractibus[8] potest aliquis dicere 'hoc est meum, hoc est tuum.' Superaddiderunt autem leges alia preter convenciones, contractus et pacta, per que potest aliquis[9] dicere 'hoc est meum': ut puta si tanto tempore fuit illius[10] rei possessor pacificus, vel si concurrerunt ibi condiciones alie quas leges assignant. Leges ergo et iura continent omnia per que potest quis dicere 'hoc est meum,' quia continent contractus licitos, convenciones et pacta, et continent alia per que quis iudicatur iustus possessor rerum. Et inde forte venit illud verbum quod si tollerentur leges, tolleretur quod aliquis posset[11] dicere 'hoc est meum, hoc est tuum.'

Incipiamus ergo a fundamento et dicamus quod quando tollitur fundamentum, totum edificium ruit, ut nihil remaneat in edificio illo, ut edificium est.[12] Fundamentum autem omnium istorum est communicacio hominum ad invicem; inde enim exorte sunt particiones, inde donaciones, commutaciones et empciones. Proinde[13] eciam composite sunt leges, quia, ut probat Philosophus in *Ethicis*, nullus potest sibi ipsi iniustum[14] facere. Si igitur homines nullo modo communicarent ad invicem, sed quilibet solum sibi ipsi viveret, leges quarum est discernere quid iustum et quid[15] non iustum nullo modo essent necessarie.[16] Hoc eciam posito, quod homines ad invicem non communicarent, non essent particiones, empciones et cetera huiusmodi. Si ergo potest facere Ecclesia quod iste privetur communione hominum vel communione fidelium,[17] potest facere quod iste privetur fundamento ubi omnia ista fundantur.[18] Huic ergo sic privato non proderunt particiones, empciones,

1: convencione] aliqua *add.* C   2: ita] vel FV²   3: assencientibus] consencientibus C   4: secundum] sed F   5: particionem] protensionem V¹   6: pactis] contractis *add.* C   7: convencionibus] questionibus *mss*   8: et contractibus] *om.* C   9: aliquis] quis C   10: illius] alicuius FV²   11: posset] possit F   12: in edificio … est] *del.* C   13: Proinde] provide FV¹   14: sibi ipsi iniustum] iniustum sibi F   15: quid] quis F   16: necessarie] necesse F   17: vel communione fidelium] *om.* FV²   18: fundantur] fundatur F

but also the division of all temporal things. But the manner of this division is no part of our present argument. For it may suffice to know that no one could justly appropriate any part of the earth to himself other than by pact and covenant concluded with others. Thus, at first, appropriation took place according to pacts and covenants, or according to agreements as to the division of the lands, inasmuch as the sons of Adam or Noah, agreeing as to these divisions, or at least not disagreeing, acquired lands for themselves, and one appropriated this part to himself and another that. Subsequently, however, as we have said, when men were multiplied it became necessary for such covenants and pacts to be multiplied. And so there came to be possession of lands and fields not only according to partition, as among the sons of the same father, but also according to purchases, gifts, exchanges, or in the other ways which can be reckoned as a covenant or consensus of minds; for neither purchase nor exchange nor gift could take place if there were not at the same time a consensus of minds in the matter.

But after men had begun to be lords over the earth and had become kings, there then arose laws which contained all this and added more besides. And the laws intend that lawful pacts and lawful covenants and lawful contracts shall be observed; by virtue of which lawful pacts and covenants a man is able to say 'This is mine; this is yours.' And the laws added other provisions as well as covenants, contracts and pacts, through which, for example, a man can say 'this is mine' if he has been the peaceable possessor of the goods in question for a sufficiently long time, or if other conditions which the laws stipulate are also there present. Therefore, the laws and rules of justice contain everything by reason of which a man can say 'This is mine': for they contain lawful contracts, covenants, and pacts, and they contain the other provisions by virtue of which a man is judged to be the just possessor of things. And hence, perhaps, came the saying that to remove the laws would be to remove the possibility of anyone's saying, 'This is mine; this is yours.'[1]

Let us begin from the foundation, therefore, and say that when the foundation is removed the whole building collapses, so that nothing remains of that building as such. And the foundation of all these [property laws] is the communion of men with one another; for from this have come partitions, gifts, exchanges and purchases. And, consequently, the laws were composed; for, as the Philosopher shows in the *Ethics*, no one can do injustice to himself.[2] Thus, if men did not communicate with one another in any way, but if each man lived only to himself, then the laws, whose purpose it is to discern what is just and what is not just, would not be in any way necessary. Also, supposing this — that men did not communicate with one another — there would be no partitions, purchases, and other such transactions. If, therefore, the Church can cause a man to be deprived of communion with men or of the communion of the faithful, then she can cause him to be deprived of the foundation upon which all these transactions are grounded. Therefore, to anyone thus deprived, partitions, purchases,

---

1. Cf. Dist. 8, c. 1: *Quo iure* (CIC 1:12f).
2. *Nicomachean Ethics* 5:6 (1134ᵇ10).

donaciones, commutaciones nec quecumque leges. Nihil ergo poterit dicere quod sit suum, cum omnia prefata, ex quibus alicui[1] competit vel potest competere[2] aliquid esse suum, super communicacionem fundentur.

Sed dices quod non ex hoc, quod quis est excommunicatus et privatus communicacione aliorum, privatur possessione sua, eciam secundum iura que dicuntur concedere quod excommunicatus possit se defendere, licet forte non possit agere. Sed qui potest defendere bona sua non videtur privatus iure bonorum suorum. Immo, qui talis est, ex hoc ipso, quod potest bona sua defendere, potest dicere 'hoc est meum.' Cuius contrarium superius dicebatur, videlicet quod excommunicatus nihil de iure potest dicere quod sit suum.

Sciendum ergo quod aliud est quod competit rei secundum se, aliud vero quod[3] competit ei ex benignitate vel ex indulgencia sive ex permissione potestatis superioris. Statim enim, cum quis mortaliter peccat, si Deus secum ageret prout secundum se dignus est, statim[4] eum exterminaret vel eum statim morti adiudicaret. Sicut enim habetur Geneseos II: 'De ligno autem sciencie boni et mali ne comedas; in quacumque enim die comederis ex eo, morte morieris.' Si enim Deus egisset cum Adam prout dignus erat, statim privasset eum vita cum ipse contempsisset mandatum Dei. Dixit ergo Deus quod quacumque die comederet, morte moreretur; nec tamen mortuus fuit Adam illa die qua comedit.

Que controversia multipliciter[5] potest solvi. Primo, ut dicatur 'quacumque die comederis, morte[6] morieris,' id est[7] 'habebis necessitatem moriendi'; nam ex tunc factus est Adam mortalis, ut necesse esset ipsum mori. Ergo et mortuus fuit illa die qua comedit, et non fuit mortuus. Mortuus quidem fuit, quod illa die incurrit necessitatem moriendi, cum necesse esset ipsum debitum mortis exsolvere.[8] Non autem fuit mortuus, quia huiusmodi debitum non exsolvit, sed per multa tempora postea vixit.

Secundo, solvitur dicta controversia ut intelligatur de morte spirituali, videlicet, quod quacumque die comederet, morte moreretur, quia peccaret mortaliter et esset mortuus secundum animam. Has autem duas exposiciones tangit Magister in *Historiis.*

Possumus autem nos tercio modo hanc[9] controversiam solvere, qui modus tercius deserviret nostro proposito: videlicet, 'quacumque die comederis, morte morieris,' id est 'eris morte dignus.' Quia si Deus attendisset ad merita sua, statim privasset eum vita. Quod autem statim Adam non fuit mortuus nec statim fuit privatus vita, hoc fuit ex benignitate Dei et ex indulgencia et ex permissione eius. Nam non solum qui facit mortale peccatum, sed eciam qui consentit facienti,[10]

1: alicui] aliquid *mss*　　2: potest competere] competere potest F　　3: quod] *om.* FV[2]　　4: statim] *om.* CFV[2]　　5: multipliciter] *om.* FV[2]　　6: morte] *om.* FV[2]　　7: id est] et FV[2]　　8: exsolvere] solvere C　　9: hanc] *om.* F　　10: facienti] pacienti FV[2]

gifts, exchanges, and laws of any kind are profitless. Therefore, he will not be able to say of anything that it is his own, since all the provisions just mentioned, by virtue of which anything is capable, or anything can be capable, of being his, are founded upon communication.

But you will say that a man who is excommunicated and deprived of communion with others is certainly not thereby deprived of his property according to the laws, which are said to grant that, even though he perhaps may not sue, an excommunicate may defend himself:[1] for he who can defend his goods does not seem to be deprived of his goods by the law. Indeed, such a man is able to say 'This is mine' by virtue of the fact that he can defend his own goods; and this is contrary to what was said above: namely, that the excommunicate cannot say that anything belongs to him as a matter of law.

It must be known, therefore, that what belongs to something in its own right is one thing, and that what belongs to it through the kindness or through the indulgence or through the permission of a superior power is another. For if God were to treat a man according to his deserts He would destroy him instantly, or pronounce him worthy of instant death, as soon as he committed mortal sin. For we read in Genesis 2: 'You shall not eat of the Tree of Knowledge of Good and Evil; for on the day that you eat of it you shall die the death.'[2] Thus, if God had treated Adam according to his deserts, He would have deprived him of life as soon as he had displayed contempt for God's commandment. God, therefore, said that he would die the death on the day he ate: yet Adam did not die on the day he ate.

There are many ways in which this difficulty can be resolved. First, it may be said that 'On the day that you eat you shall die the death' means 'You will be under the necessity of dying'; for, from that time forth, Adam was made mortal, so that it was necessary that he should die. Therefore, on the day he ate he both died and did not die. He died in the sense that, on that day, he incurred the necessity of dying, for it was necessary that he should pay the penalty of death. But he did not [actually] die, for he did not pay that penalty [there and then], but lived for many years thereafter.

The second way in which this difficult saying may be resolved is by understanding it to refer to spiritual death: that is, as meaning that on the day he ate he would die the death since he would commit mortal sin and so would be spiritually dead. And the Master touches upon these two interpretations in the *Historia*.[3]

But there is a third way in which we can solve this difficulty, and this third way is directly to our purpose: namely, by saying that 'On the day that you eat you shall die the death' means 'You shall be worthy of death.' For if God had looked to his deserts, He would instantly have taken away his life. But the fact that Adam did not instantly die, or was not instantly deprived of life, was due to the benevolence of God and His indulgence and permission. For not only he who commits mortal sin, but also he who consents to one who does so, is worthy of

1. X. 2:1:7: *Intelleximus*(CIC 2:241); X. 2:25:11: *Significaverunt*(CIC 2:381).
2. Gen. 2:17.
3. Peter Comestor, *Historia scholastica*, PL 198:1069.

secundum Apostoli sentenciam dignus est morte. Sed quod non statim moritur, hoc est ex benignitate Dei, qui vult sibi tempus penitencie concedere. Sic et in proposito. Cum enim quis est excommunicatus, quantum est de se privatus est[1] iure quod habet in omnibus bonis suis, quia, ut dictum est, privatus est communione fidelium, et quia, ut supra diffusius dicebatur, omne ius quod habemus in possessionibus nostris, ut possimus dicere 'hoc est meum' vel 'hoc est tuum,' fundatum est super communicacione[2] quam habemus cum aliis, unde ortum habent hereditatum particiones, donaciones, commutaciones, empciones, legum ediciones et cetera talia, unde quis allegare posset de possessione aliqua quod esset sua.

Excommunicatus ergo, quia privatus est[3] communione fidelium, privatus est omnibus bonis que possidet ut est fidelis et ut est inter fideles. Et multo magis privatus esset si fieret infidelis et esset[4] inter infideles, quia illi omni possessione et omni dominio sunt indigni. Sed quod Ecclesia non statim promulgat[5] contra excommunicatos, qui privati sunt omnibus bonis et omnibus possessionibus suis, et quod non statim dat licenciam aliis fidelibus quod possint invadere bona excommunicatorum et ea accipere tamquam sua, hoc est ex indulgencia et ex[6] benignitate Ecclesie, que non vult totam suam potenciam in suos eciam malos et degeneres filios exercere, sed vult parcere omnibus, quoniam omnia sunt sua,[7] imitatrix et[8] emulatrix[9] existens Dei patris omnipotentis, qui non statim in peccatores exercet omnia mala quibus digni essent.

Quod ergo dicebatur, quod excommunicati secundum iura possunt se defendere, sed non possunt agere: utrum autem hec iura dicant vel non dicant[10] nihil ad nos. Nam claro clarius est quod excommunicati, si considerentur secundum se, nec possunt de iure in aliquo foro agere nec eciam se defendere; cum et agere et se defendere sit cum aliis communicare, et ipsi extra aliorum communionem sint positi. Sed si leges sunt eis benigne et permittunt quod se defendant per se vel per alios, vel eciam indulgent quod alique persone vel in aliquo casu cum excommunicatis communicent, hoc est ex indulgencia vel ex permissione superioris potestatis. Ipsi tamen, nisi in casu conversionis et nisi se convertant, sunt omnino indigni communicare cum quocumque fideli homine. Quod si ex hoc vellent se ad infideles convertere, magis essent digni omni malo, quia magis peccarent et magis suam matrem Ecclesiam contemnerent.

Concludamus ergo et dicamus quod ex ipsius Ecclesie generali ligacione, quia quodcumque ligaverit[11] super terram erit ligatum et in celis, prout sic ligati sunt privati communione aliorum, quia super tali communione fundantur omnia iura de

---

1: est] *om.* CF omni *add.* C   2: communicacione] communione FV^2 3: est] *om.* C   4: esset] infidelis *add.* F   5: promulgat] promulget V^1 6: ex] *om.* CF   7: sunt sua] sua sunt CF   8: et] *om.* FV^2 9: imitatrix et emulatrix] imitates et emulates C   10: vel non dicant] *om.* FV^2
11: ligaverit] ligaveris FV^2

death, according to what the Apostle says.[1] But the fact that he does not instantly die is due to the benevolence of God, Who wishes to grant him time for repentance. And so too in our proposition. For when anyone is excommunicated, he is in himself deprived of the right which he has over all his goods because, as has been said, he is deprived of the communion of the faithful, and because, as was said at greater length above, all the right which we have in our possessions, so that we may say 'This is mine' or 'This is yours,' is founded upon the communication which we have with others, from which arise the division of inheritances, gifts, exchanges, purchases, codes of law and other such provisions, by reason of which a man can claim of some possession that it is his own.

The excommunicate, therefore, because he is deprived of the communion of the faithful, is deprived of all the goods which he possesses as a faithful man and among faithful men. He would be even more liable to be deprived if he were to become an unbeliever and were among unbelievers, for these are unworthy of all property and all lordship. But the fact that the Church does not immediately declare the excommunicate deprived of all their goods and all their possessions, and does not immediately give licence to other members of the faithful to invade the goods of the excommunicate and receive them as their own, is due to the indulgence and benevolence of the Church, who does not wish to bring all her power to bear against even her wicked and degenerate children, but wishes to spare all men because all men are her own, being the imitator and emulator of God the Almighty Father, Who does not immediately inflict upon sinners all the evils which they might deserve.

Therefore, as to the statement that, according to the laws, the excommunicate can defend themselves even though they cannot sue: whether the laws say this or not is neither here nor there. For it is clearer than clear that, *de iure* [and regardless of what is permitted *de facto*], the excommunicate, if they are considered as such, can neither sue nor even defend themselves in any court. For both to sue and to defend oneself involves communion with others, and such men are placed outside communion with others. But [as to what is allowed *de facto*,] if the laws are kind to them and allow them to defend themselves either in person or through others, or even grant an indulgence such that certain persons may in some cases communicate with the excommunicate, this comes about through the indulgence or permission of a superior power. [Considered as such,] however, unless their circumstances change and unless they are converted, these persons are wholly unworthy to communicate with any faithful man. And if, for this reason, they should wish to turn themselves into unbelievers, they would be even more deserving of every evil, since their sin and their contempt for their mother the Church would itself be greater.

Let us conclude, therefore, and say that from the Church's general power of binding — for whatever she binds on earth will be bound in heaven — [it follows that,] inasmuch as those who are so bound are deprived of communion with others, and inasmuch as all property rights are founded upon such communion, the

---

1. Rom. 1:32.

proprietatibus possessionum, excommunicati,[1] quia sunt privati hoc fundamento, quod non debeant cum aliis communicare, si considerentur secundum se, erunt privati bonis suis et possessionibus suis et dominiis suis, ut de nullo tali possint[2] dicere quod sit suum.[3]

Tercia via ad hoc idem sumitur ex eadem ligacione Ecclesie, prout sic ligati sunt privati communione sacramentorum. Nam cum sacramenta sint vasa gracie, quia nullum est Ecclesie sacramentum, quod si devote recipiatur, quod non tribuatur ibi aliqua gracia vel aliqua pulchritudo anime, oportet[4] sacramenta nove legis in se ipsis causaliter[5] graciam continere, ut eciam in matrimonio gracia conferatur.

Non tamen propter hoc dicimus quod quilibet debeat nubere, quantumcumque matrimonium sit quoddam sacramentum Ecclesie, et quantumcumque[6] confertur in eo gracia vel augmentum gracie.[7] Nam qui vult nubere, devote proponens ab omnibus aliis mulieribus abstinere et cum sua tantummodo conversari, in hoc bono proposito Deus auget sibi graciam. Sed qui vult virginitatem tenere et cum nullis mulieribus conversari, sed ab omnibus abstinere,[8] iste melius habet propositum, et[9] in hoc proposito Deus,[10] ceteris aliis paribus, paratus est dare maiorem graciam. Et inde est quod ait Apostolus, quod qui nubit bene facit, et qui non nubit melius facit.

Redeamus ergo ad propositum[11] et dicamus quod omnia[12] sacramenta Ecclesie sunt quedam vasa gracie. Excommunicato ergo, quia proiectus extra communionem Ecclesie, extra quam non est salus nec collacio gracie, nulla sacramenta sunt exhibenda. Inhibendum est ergo excommunicato, quamdiu vult in sua pertinacia permanere et non vult ad gremium Ecclesie redire, quod non nubat; debet enim sibi annunciari quod ei sic se habenti non licet nubere. Et si excommunicato non licet nubere, cum ex nupciis proveniant legitimi filii, quilibet excommunicatus, si comparatur ad filium, debet se reputare[13] indignum patrem, et si comparatur ad[14] patrem, debet se reputare[15] indignum filium.[16] Indignus est enim excommunicatus ut dicatur ortus ex nupciis, que sunt quoddam Ecclesie sacramentum, cum ipse sit privatus communione omnium sacramentorum. Nam si privatus est communione omnium sacramentorum Ecclesie, consequens est quod privatus sit omni bono quod potest sibi communicari per huiusmodi sacramentum.

Si ergo homo spurius non potest hereditare[17] hereditatem paternam, et si tota causa quare filius carnalis succedit in hereditatem paternam sumitur ex hoc, quod natus est[18] de legitimis nupciis, cum legitime nupcie sint quoddam sacramentum Ecclesie[19] iuxta illud Apostoli ad Ephesios V: 'Sacramentum hoc magnum[20] est in Christo et Ecclesia,' dicitur enim matrimonium[21] magnum sacramentum in Christo

---

1: excommunicati] *om.* FV²   2: possint] possit FV²   3: sit suum] suum est CF   4: oportet] quod *add.* V¹   5: causaliter] taliter F   6: quantumcumque] matrimonium sit quoddam sacramen *add. and del.* C   7: vel augmentum gracie] *om.* C   8: abstinere] abstinet C   9: et] deus *add.* CFV² 10: Deus] *om.* FV²   11: ad propositum] *om.* FPV¹V²   12: omnia] *om.* C   13: reputare] repugnare C   14: filium, debet ... ad] *om.* F   15: reputare] repugnare C   16: filium] quia si ille legitimus eo qui natus est de legitimis nuciis [*sic*] cum excommunicati sint indigni ad nuciis contrahendus quilibet excommunicatus est indignus ut sit filius nuciarum *add. and del.* C   17: hereditare] *om.* FV²   18: natus est] est natus V²   19: sacramentum Ecclesie] ecclesie sacramentum C 20: magnum] maximum FV²   21: matrimonium] et *add.* F

excommunicate, if they are considered as such — who, since they may not communicate with others, are deprived of this foundation — will be deprived of their goods and possessions and lordships, so that they may not say of any such thing that it is their own.

The third way towards the same conclusion is derived from the Church's same power of binding, inasmuch as those who are so bound are deprived of the communion of the sacraments. For since the sacraments are vessels of grace — because there is none of the Church's sacraments which, if received devoutly, does not confer some measure of grace or some beauty of soul — it must be that the sacraments of the New Law contain the cause of grace within themselves, so that grace is conferred even in matrimony.

We do not on this account say, however, that every man should marry, even though matrimony is one of the sacraments of the Church, and even though grace, or an increase of grace, may be conferred in it. For if a man wishes to marry, devoutly intending to abstain from all other women and to live only with his own wife, God will add grace to him in this good intention. But he who wishes to keep his virginity and to live with no women but to abstain from all, has the better intention; and, other things being equal, God is ready to give him the greater grace in this intention. And so it is that the Apostle says that he who marries does well, and he who does not marry does better.[1]

Let us return, therefore, and say that all the sacraments of the Church are like vessels of grace. To the excommunicate, then, because he is ejected from the communion of the Church, outside whom there is neither salvation nor reception of grace, the sacraments must not be permitted. Thus, for as long as he wishes to persist in his obstinacy and refuses to return to the bosom of the Church,[2] the excommunicate must be forbidden to marry; for it must be made clear to him that he may not marry while he remains as he is. And if the excommunicate may not marry, then, since it is from marriage that legitimate sons come, every excommunicate, if he is considered in relation to his son, must regard himself as an unworthy father and, if he is considered in relation to his father, must regard himself as an unworthy son. For the excommunicate is unworthy to have it said of him that he was born of matrimony, which is one of the Church's sacraments; for he himself is deprived of the communion of all the sacraments. And if he is deprived of the communion of all the Church's sacraments it follows that he is deprived of every good which can be communicated to him through this sacrament.

If, therefore, an illegitimate man cannot come into a paternal inheritance, and if the sole cause whereby a carnal son succeeds to a paternal inheritance is derived from the fact that he was born of lawful matrimony (for lawful matrimony is one of the sacraments of the Church, according to what the Apostle says in Ephesians 5: 'This is a great sacrament in Christ and the Church';[3] for matrimony is called a

---

1. I Cor. 7:38.
2. Cf. Durandus, *De origine iurisdictionum*, quaest. 3, quoted by Walter Ullmann, *Medieval Papalism*, p. 123, n. 2.
3. Eph. 5:32.

et Ecclesia, quia est magnum sacramentum, quantum ad hanc figuram, quia figurat hanc rem magnam, unionem videlicet Christi et Ecclesie: quare si excommunicatus positus est extra communionem sacramentorum Ecclesie, et bona que proveniunt ex huiusmodi sacramentis non debent sibi communicari, consequens est
quod in nullo suffragetur sibi et nullum emolumentum recipere debeat quia est ex
legitimis nupciis procreatus; quia hoc esset communicare sibi bona que proveniunt
per Ecclesie sacramenta,[1] quibus iam diximus eum esse privatum. Nam claro
clarius est quod qui est privatus aliquo agro vel aliqua vinea privatus est bonis que
possunt per illum agrum vel per illam vineam provenire.[2]

Ecclesia itaque, excommunicando aliquem, privat ipsum communione fidelium, ex qua communione proveniunt iura et raciones quod possessiones alique
sunt istius proprie vel illius. Rursus, sic excommunicatus privatur non solum
communione fidelium sed communione sacramentorum, ut ex hoc nullum
emolumentum habere debeat ex aliquo Ecclesie sacramento. Nihil ergo sibi proderit[3] quia natus est ex legitimis nupciis, cum legitime nupcie sint quoddam Ecclesie sacramentum. Utroque ergo modo Ecclesia excommunicando aliquem et[4]
privando eum[5] tam communione fidelium quam sacramentorum, reddit ipsum,
quantum est de se, privatum omni iure quod habet in temporalibus bonis; quod
esse non possit[6] nisi omnium temporalium bonorum esset Ecclesia domina et
magistra.

Quarta via ad hoc idem sumitur ex eadem ligacione, prout sic[7] ligatus est privatus communione eternorum bonorum. Sic enim dixit Dominus Petro, ut habetur
Matthei XVI: 'Quodcumque ligaveris super terram, erit ligatum et in celis'; quod
exponens Origenes ait: 'Vide quantam potestatem habet Ecclesia, ut eciam iudicia
eius maneant firma quasi Deo iudicante per eam.' Vult ergo Origenes quod qui
ligatur ab Ecclesia in terris est ligatus in celis, quia Deus[8] celi approbat tale iudicium; vel sic ligatus in terris est ligatus in celis, quia sic ligatus non potest intrare
celum. Ideo dicitur Ecclesia habere claves regni celorum, quia cui claudit celum
ipsum ligando et[9] excommunicando, illi clausum est, et cui aperit ipsum absolvendo,[10] illi apertum est, nisi ipse prebeat obicem.[11] Nam sicut materia existente
indisposita non introducitur ibi forma, ita si homo est indispositus et perseverat in
suo malo proposito, non prodest sibi[12] absolucio Ecclesie.

Ligatus itaque ab Ecclesia et excommunicatus ab ea est privatus communione
eternorum bonorum, ut si decedat in suo malo proposito, nolens[13] redire ad gremium
Ecclesie, non poterit intrare regnum celeste[14] nec poterit consequi hereditatem eternorum bonorum. Si enim nihil aliud esset in nobis nisi quia[15] nolumus subesse
Ecclesie et nolumus parere[16] mandatis eius, non proderit nobis passio Christi, de

---

1: sacramenta] sacramentum FV²　　2: provenire] pervenire C　　3: proderit] proderint V²
4: excommunicando aliquem et] *del.* C　　5: eum] aliquem C　　6: possit] posset V²　　7: sic] *om.* F
8: Deus] *om.* C　　9: ligando et] *om.* C　　10: absolvendo] solvendo F　　11: obicem] obicere V²
12: sibi] ipsi F　　13: nolens] volens F　　14: celeste] celi sic FV²　　15: quia] quam F　　16: parere]
om. V²

great sacrament in Christ and the Church because, considered figuratively, it is a great sacrament since it represents a great thing, namely, Christ's union with the Church), then, if the excommunicate is placed outside the communion of the Church's sacraments, and if the goods which proceed from those sacraments must not be communicated to him, it follows that he may derive no support for himself and may receive no gain from the fact that he was born of lawful matrimony. For this would be to communicate to him goods which proceed from the Church's sacraments, of which, as we have already said, he is deprived. For it is clearer than clear that he who is deprived of a field or a vineyard is deprived of the goods which can proceed from that field or from that vineyard.

By excommunicating a man, then, the Church deprives him of the communion of the faithful, from which communion come the laws and rules according to which possessions are the property of this man or that. Moreover, the excommunicate is thereby deprived not only of the communion of the faithful, but of the communion of the sacraments, so that he may derive no benefit from any sacrament of the Church. Therefore, it will profit him nothing to have been born of lawful matrimony, for lawful matrimony is one of the sacraments of the Church. By excommunicating a man, therefore, and by depriving him of the communion of the faithful and of the sacraments alike, the Church causes him to be deprived in both ways of all the right which, in himself, he has over temporal goods. And this could not be so if the Church were not the lord and director of all temporal goods.

The fourth way towards the same conclusion is derived from the same power of binding, inasmuch as he who is so bound is deprived of the communion of eternal goods. For, as is established in Matthew 16, the Lord spoke thus to Peter: 'Whatever you shall bind on earth shall be bound in heaven';[1] and Origen, interpreting this, says: 'See how great a power the Church has; for her judgment stands as firmly as though God Himself were judging through her.'[2] Origen, therefore, maintains that he who is bound by the Church on earth is bound in heaven because the God of heaven approves such judgment. Again, he who is thus bound on earth is bound in heaven because he who is so bound cannot enter heaven. And so the Church is said to hold the keys of the kingdom of heaven because, when she closes heaven by binding and excommunicating a man, it is closed to him, and when she opens it by releasing him, it is open to him (unless he places an obstacle in the way: for just as, when matter is ill disposed, no form comes into it, so too, if a man is ill disposed and perseveres in his wicked intention, the Church's absolution is of no profit to him).

He who is bound by the Church and excommunicated by her, then, is deprived of the communion of eternal goods, so that, if he dies in his wicked intention, refusing to return to the bosom of the Church, he will not be able to enter the Kingdom of Heaven, nor will he be able to obtain an inheritance of eternal goods. For if there were nothing else in us apart from a refusal to be under the Church and a refusal to keep her commandments, the Passion of Christ, from

1. Matt. 16:19.
2. *Commentaria in evangelium Mattheum*, 12 (PG 13:1014).

cuius latere, eo moriente in cruce, Ecclesia est formata. Sed passio Christi nobis aperuit ianuam celestem. Nam nullus, quantumcumque sanctus, ante passionem Christi intravit regnum celorum nec potuit frui[1] visione divina. Sed Christo passo et eo moriente statim fuit aperta celestis ianua; nam illo eodem die latro fuit in paradiso et vidit divinam essenciam. Igitur, si Christo paciente in cruce exinde formata est Ecclesia, ut vult glossa ad Romanos V, quicumque contemnit Ecclesiam repellit a se fructum quem potest habere ex passione Christi; et quia passio Christi nobis aperuit celestem ianuam, consequens est ergo[2] quod illi sit clausa celestis ianua.

Influencia enim passionis Christi non potest ad nos pervenire[3] nisi[4] per Ecclesiam. Sicut enim a capite non potest[5] venire influencia ad aliquod membrum nisi prout est coniunctum corpori, quia in membrum abscissum non potest caput influere, sic, quia Ecclesia est corpus Christi et[6] Christus est caput eius iuxta illud ad Ephesios I, 'Ipsum dedit caput[7] supra omnem Ecclesiam que est corpus ipsius,' ideo[8] nec[9] a Christo, tamquam a capite, nec a passione eius potest derivari aliqua influencia in aliquod membrum nisi ut est coniunctum Ecclesie. Ad personam itaque excommunicatam, quia est membrum abscissum, non derivabitur influencia capitis nec ei proderit passio Christi.

Manifeste ergo apparet quomodo Ecclesia habet claves regni celorum et quomodo potest celum[10] claudere et aperire. Nam quia passio Christi aperuit celestem ianuam, si ergo ad te perveniat influencia passionis Christi, est tibi celum apertum; si non potest ad te talis influencia pervenire, est tibi celum clausum. Et quia hoc non potest fieri nisi per Ecclesiam et sub Ecclesia,[11] bene dictum est quod Ecclesia habet claves regni celorum:[12] et si habet hec Ecclesia,[13;14] habet hec[15] Summus Pontifex, qui adeptus est apicem tocius Ecclesie. Immo, quod Summus Pontifex facit, dicitur Ecclesia facere, quia in eo reservatur auctoritas tocius Ecclesie. Ecclesia itaque, cum excommunicat aliquem, facit ipsum membrum abscissum,[16] ut non possit ad eum pervenire influencia capitis; quod faciendo, claudit sibi celestem ianuam et privat ipsum communione[17] eternorum bonorum, ut non sit dignus[18] hereditate eterna. Sed, ut supra dicebatur, qui non est dignus et est privatus hereditate eterna est indignus et de iure est privatus hereditate paterna.[19] Qui enim non est dignus Deo et est privatus eo, non est dignus aliquo bono quod sit[20] a Deo, et de iure est privatus omni tali bono.[21] Est enim Deus fons luminis et fons tocius bonitatis, ut non sit aliquod bonum quod non derivetur ab ipso. Ideo dicitur pater luminum et ab eo dicuntur descendere omnia data et omnia dona, que, ut[22] ab eo sunt, optima sunt et perfecta sunt, iuxta illud Iacobi I: 'Omne datum

---

1: frui] *om.* V[2]   2: est ergo] ergo est FV[2]   3: pervenire] *om.* F   4: ad nos ... nisi] *om.* V[2]
5: potest] est PV[1]   6: et] *om.* FV[2]   7: caput] *om.* C   8: ideo] *om.* F   9: nec] necnon F
10: et quomodo potest celum] *om.* F   11: Ecclesia] hec *add.* V[2] quia ad membrum abscissum
potest pervenire influencia capitis *add. and del.* C   12: claves regni celorum] regni celorum
claves V[1]   13: hec Ecclesia] ecclesia hec F   14: bene dictum ... Ecclesia] *om.* V[2]   15: hec]
hic FV[2]   16: abscissum] ab ecclesia *add. and del.* C   17: communione] fidelium et *add.* FV[2]
18: dignus] sed sit privatus *add. and del.* C   19: paterna] *om.* V[2]   20: sit] est C   21: bono]
quod est ab eo *add.* C   22: que, ut] ut que C

Whose side, as He died on the Cross, the Church was formed, would be of no profit to us. But the Passion of Christ has opened the gate of heaven to us. For before the Passion of Christ, no man, however holy, entered the Kingdom of Heaven or could enjoy the Divine Vision. But when Christ suffered and died, the heavenly gate was immediately opened; for, on that same day, the thief was in Paradise and saw the Divine Essence.[1] Thus, if the Church was formed from Christ's suffering on the Cross, as a gloss on Romans 5 maintains,[2] then whoever despises the Church thrusts away from himself the benefit which he can obtain from the Passion of Christ. And since the Passion of Christ has opened heaven's gate to us, it follows that, to him, the gate of heaven is therefore closed.

For the influence of Christ's Passion cannot come to us except through the Church. For just as the head can bring influence to bear upon a member only insofar as it is joined to the body (for the head can have no influence upon a severed member), so, since the Church is the body of Christ and Christ is her head, according to Ephesians 1: 'He gave Him to be the head of all things in the Church which is His body,'[3] no influence can accrue to any member, either from Christ as from a head or from His Passion, unless he is joined to the Church. To the excommunicate, then, since he is a severed member, there will accrue no influence from the Head, nor will the Passion of Christ profit him.

It is very clear, therefore, how the Church holds the keys of the kingdom of heaven and how she can close heaven and open it. For, because the Passion of Christ has opened the gate of heaven, heaven is therefore open to you if the influence of Christ comes to you; but, if such influence cannot come to you, heaven is closed to you. And since this could not come about except through the Church and under the Church, it is well said that the Church holds the keys of the kingdom of heaven. And if the Church holds them, the Supreme Pontiff holds them, for he has attained to the summit of the whole Church. Indeed, what the Supreme Pontiff does the whole Church is said to do, for in him is contained the authority of the whole Church. Thus, when the Church excommunicates a man, she causes him to become a severed limb, so that the influence of the Head cannot reach him. And, by doing this, she closes the gate of heaven to him and deprives him of the communion of eternal goods, so that he is not worthy of an eternal inheritance. But, as has been said above,[4] he who is not worthy and is deprived of an eternal inheritance is unworthy, and is deprived *de iure* of a paternal inheritance. For he who is not worthy of God and is deprived of Him is not worthy of any good which comes from God and is deprived *de iure* of every such good.

For God is the fount of light and the fount of all goodness, so that there is no good which is not derived from Him. Hence, He is called the Father of lights and, from Him, all gifts and all benefits are said to descend, which, since they are from God, are the highest and most perfect of gifts, according to James 1: 'Every good

1. Luke 23:43; cf. Aquinas, *Summa theologiae* IIIa 69:7.
2. *Glossa ordinaria*, PL 114:486 (on Rom. 5:14); cf. Aquinas, *Summa theologiae* IIIa 62:5.
3. Eph. 1:22–23.
4. Ch. VIII.

optimum et omne donum perfectum desursum est[1] descendens a patre luminum.'
Sed sic sensibiliter videmus quod qui se avertit a lumine est in tenebris et est
privatus lumine, ergo qui se avertit a[2] Deo, a quo est omne bonum, de iure est
privatus omni bono. Sed cuicumque est clausa ianua celestis, et quicumque est
indignus hereditate eterna, et quicumque est privatus communione eternorum
bonorum, ille est[3] aversus a Deo, a quo omne bonum est.[4] Igitur de iure ipse est
privatus omni bono.

Ad maiorem tamen intelligenciam dictorum, sciendum quod Magister IV
Sentenciarum innuit duplicem modum ligandi et solvendi: unum qui sit in foro
penitencie sive in foro consciencie, ubi agitur causa inter hominem et Deum;
alium autem modum[5] qui fit[6] per excommunicacionem in foro exterioris iudicii,
ubi agitur causa inter hominem[7] et hominem.[8] Utrumque autem modum ligandi
et solvendi possumus appropriare clavibus; sed distinguemus duplex genus cla-
vium. Quia[9] sunt claves ordinis,[10] quas habent sacerdotes soli,[11] et claves iurisdiccionis, quas habere possunt eciam non sacerdotes. Nam archidiaconi, legati et
electi,[12] eciam antequam fiant sacerdotes, excommunicant vel excommunicare
possunt, quia, etsi[13] non habent claves sacerdotalis ordinis, habent[14] claves iurisdiccionis. Sciencia quidem discernendi et potestas ligandi et solvendi in foro
iudicii, excommunicando vel ab excommunicacione absolvendo, possunt dici
claves celestis regni, quia sic excommunicati, contemnendo iurisdiccionem Ecclesiasticam et non celeriter redeundo ad gremium Ecclesie, mortaliter peccant.
Et ex hoc dicitur eis celum clausum, quia quodlibet mortale peccatum celum
claudit; redeundo autem celeriter ad Ecclesie gremium et absolucionis beneficium obtinendo vitant[15] prefatam mortalem culpam, ut quantum ad hoc dicatur
eis celum[16] esse apertum.

Ecclesia itaque, per claves quas habet claudendo tibi celestem ianuam, claudit
tibi[17] ianuam[18] omnium bonorum, ut non sis[19] dignus aliquo bono eciam temporali,[20]
sed de iure sis[21] privatus omni tali bono. Sed qui potest hoc facere, quod de iure
sis[22] privatus aliquibus bonis,[23] habet iurisdiccionem et auctoritatem super omnia
illa bona. Ecclesia itaque, te excommunicando, facit quod de iure sis[24] privatus
omnibus temporalibus bonis. Ergo[25] habet iurisdiccionem et auctoritatem super

---

1: desursum est] est desursum F   2: lumine, est ... a] *om.* F   3: est] autem FV[2]   4: omne bonum est] est omne bonum CF   5: modum] *del.* C   6: fit] sit F   7: hominem] homines F
8: et hominem] *om.* F   9: Quia] nam F   10: quia sunt claves ordinis] *om.* C   11: sacerdotes
soli] soli sacerdotes CF   12: electi] clerici F   13: etsi] si V[2]   14: habent] autem *add.* F
15: vitant] vacant F   16: eis celum] *om.* V[2]   17: tibi] *om.* V[2]   18: claudit tibi ianuam] *om.* F
19: sis] sit CF   20: eciam temporali] et temporalibus V[1]   21: sis] sit CF   22: sis] sit FV[2]
23: aliquibus bonis] omni tali bono F   24: sis] sit F   25: Ergo] *om.* F

gift, and every perfect gift, is from above and descends from the Father of lights.'[1] But just as, by reference to the senses, we see that he who turns himself away from the light is in darkness and is deprived of the light, so he who turns himself away from God, from Whom every good comes, is therefore deprived *de iure* of every good. But every man to whom the gate of heaven is closed, and every man who is unworthy of an eternal inheritance, and every man who is deprived of the communion of eternal goods, is turned away from God, from Whom every good comes; and so he is deprived *de iure* of every good.

For the sake of a greater understanding of these remarks, however, it must be known that the Master, in *Sententiae* 4, suggests a twofold mode of binding and releasing: one which occurs in the court of penance or in the court of conscience, where causes between man and God are tried; and another mode which is brought about by means of excommunication in a court of external judgment where causes between man and man are tried.[2] And we can assign keys to both modes of binding and releasing. But we shall distinguish keys of two kinds; for there are the keys of the priestly order, which only priests hold, and the keys of jurisdiction which even those who are not priests can hold. For those who are appointed and elected as archdeacons excommunicate, or can excommunicate, even before they are made priests; for although they do not hold the keys of the priestly order they hold the keys of jurisdiction. And the capacity to judge and the power to bind and release in a court of [external] judgment [as distinct from the court of penance] by excommunicating or releasing from excommunication can [also] be called the keys of the kingdom of heaven. For those who are thus excommunicated commit mortal sin by despising the jurisdiction of the Church and by not quickly returning to the bosom of the Church; and so heaven is said to be closed to them, because every mortal sin closes heaven. But if they return quickly to the bosom of the Church and obtain the blessing of absolution, they escape such mortal sin, so that heaven is for this reason said to be open to them.[3]

Thus, by closing the gate of heaven to you with the keys which she holds, the Church closes to you the gate of all goods, so that you are not worthy even of any temporal good, but are deprived *de iure* of every such good. But she who can cause you to be deprived *de iure* of all goods has jurisdiction and authority over all such goods. The Church, then, by excommunicating you so that you are deprived *de iure* of all temporal goods, therefore has jurisdiction and authority over

1. James 1:17.
2. Peter Lombard, *Sententiae* 4:18:102–103 (PL 192:887–888).
3. The point here is that the Church's binding and releasing power is not confined to the priest in the confessional. The same power, in a different form, is at the disposal of the ecclesiastical judge exercising jurisdiction in a public court. This observation is important in the light of the arguments which Giles intends to present in Pt. III; for if, in appropriate circumstances, the ecclesiastical judge can hear temporal cases, and if he too holds the keys of the kingdom of heaven, then his judgment even in secular matters has behind it all the authority conferred upon Peter at Matthew 16:18–19. We note also the further repetition of the principle that authority inheres in offices rather than in their holders. Ecclesiastical judges derive their authority not from the fact that they are priests (which medieval archdeacons in some cases were not), but from their having been appointed to a certain jurisdiction.

omnia temporalia bona.

Advertendum tamen quod cum dicimus[1] quod excommunicatus de iure est privatus omni bono et omni possessione sua,[2] ut non possit iuste de aliquo dicere quod sit suum, hoc intelligendum est, si consideretur excommunicatus secundum se, quia talis[3] existens factus est indignus Deo et est aversus a Deo, a quo est omne bonum, ideo de iure privatus est omni bono. Si autem non statim est sic privatus, sed potest in iudicio defendere sua bona, hoc est ex benignitate Ecclesie et ex eius indulgencia, ut superius dicebatur.

Ecclesia itaque, aliquem excommunicando, facit quod, si consideretur secundum se, de iure[4] sit privatus omnibus temporalibus bonis: tum quia talis existens est privatus a communione fidelium, tum eciam quia est privatus a communione sacramentorum, tum et tercio quia est privatus a communione eternorum bonorum. Ex quibus omnibus aperte concluditur quod Ecclesia iurisdiccionem et auctoritatem habeat super omnia temporalia bona, cum possit bonorum talium possessores indignos reddere ac[5] eciam[6] privare.[7]

CAPITULUM XIII: *Quare sunt duo tantum gladii in Ecclesia, et quomodo hii duo gladii sunt sumendi.*

Necessitas presentis capituli ex superioribus oritur. Habet enim hoc capitulum duas partes, quarum una est quare[8] sunt tantum duo gladii et non plures neque pauciores, secunda[9] quidem quomodo sumendi sunt huiusmodi gladii. Nam cum hii duo gladii, videlicet potestas sacerdotalis et regalis sive potestas spiritualis et terrena, figurati sint per illos duos gladios de quibus habetur in evangelio, 'Ecce gladii duo hic,' quorum unus fuit extractus, ille videlicet cum quo Petrus percussit servum principis sacerdotum,[10] alter autem non extractus, ut Beda ait, dicendum esset[11] in hoc capitulo quomodo sumendi sunt hii duo gladii et hee due potestates: utrum potestas[12] spiritualis figuretur per gladium extractum, terrena vero per non extractum vel econverso.

Dicamus ergo quod necessitas prime partis huius capituli, quare videlicet sunt tantum duo gladii, oritur ex decimo capitulo huius secunde partis, ubi dicitur quod, cum sub gubernacione hominum tria esse conspiciamus, videlicet animas, corpora et res exteriores, quare non sunt tres gladii, quorum unus presit animabus, alter corporibus, tercius rebus exterioribus, ut si iniuste agatur quantum ad res exteriores, corrigetur per gladium qui preest rebus exterioribus, si autem forefiat quoad corpora, rectificabitur per gladium qui preest corporibus, si quoad animas, per gladium qui preest animabus. Quod si dicatur quod res exteriores ordinantur ad

---

1: dicimus] diximus F　　2: sua] *om.* C　　3: talis] *om.* F　　4: de iure] *om.* C　　5: ac] *del.* C
6: ac eciam] et FV²　　7: privare] suis possessionibus et suis temporalibus bonis *add. and del.* C
8: quare] qua C　　9: Secunda] est *add.* CV²　　10: sacerdotum] sacerdotis FV²　　11: esset] est V²
12: utrum potestas] *om.* V²

all temporal goods.

It must be noted, however, that, when we say that the excommunicate is deprived of every good and of all his property *de iure*, so that he may not justly call anything his own, this must be taken to mean that, if the excommunicate is considered as such, he is deprived of every good *de iure* because one who is in such a condition has been made unworthy of God, from Whom every good comes. But if he is not immediately so deprived [*de facto*], but can defend his goods in court, this is due to the Church's benevolence and to her indulgence, as has been said above.

Thus, by excommunicating a man, the Church causes him, if he is considered as such, to be deprived of all temporal goods *de iure*: not only because one who is in such a condition is deprived of the communion of the faithful, but also because he is deprived of the communion of the sacraments and, third, because he is deprived of the communion of eternal goods. And from all these considerations the conclusion clearly follows that the Church has jurisdiction and authority over all temporal goods, since she may render the possessors of such goods unworthy, and also deprive them.

CHAPTER XIII: *Why there are only two swords in the Church, and how these two swords are to be understood.*

The need for the present chapter arises out of what has been said above. For this chapter has two parts, one of which deals with the question of why there are only two swords and neither more nor fewer, and the other with that of how those swords are to be understood.[1] For since these two swords — that is, priestly and royal power, or spiritual and earthly power — are signified by those two swords of which we read in the Gospel, 'Behold, here are two swords,'[2] one of which (namely, that with which Peter struck the servant of the High Priest) was drawn, whereas the other was not drawn, as Bede says,[3] we must in this chapter discuss how these two swords and these two powers are to be understood: whether the spiritual power is signified by the drawn sword and the earthly by the undrawn, or the converse.

Let us say, therefore, that the need for the first part of this chapter, namely, the discussion of why there are only two swords, arises from the tenth chapter of this second part. There, because we perceive three things to be under the government of men — that is, souls, bodies and external goods — it was asked why there are not three swords: one of which rules souls, another bodies, and the third external goods, so that if injustice is done with respect to external goods, this will be corrected by the sword which rules external goods, and if injury is done to bodies, this will be rectified by the sword which rules bodies, and if to souls by the sword which rules souls.[4] For if we say that it is because external goods are ordered to

---

1. The second question will not, in fact, be discussed here but in Ch. XV, below. It is a fair guess that Ch. XV was added as an afterthought, in view of the great length of the present chapter.
2. Luke 22:38.
3. *In Lucae evangelium expositio* 6 (PL 92:601–602).
4. See p. 165, above. But why is it so important to show that there are not three swords? All Giles's case requires him to prove, after all, is that the spiritual sword can do all things, that the material

corpora, ideo non est alius[1] gladius qui preest corporibus et rebus exterioribus, dicemus quod et corpora ordinantur ad animas. Non erit ergo alius gladius qui preest animabus et corporibus et rebus exterioribus. Erit itaque unus solus gladius in Ecclesia.

Necessitas vero secunde partis huius capituli, quomodo hii duo gladii sunt sumendi, oritur ex quinto capitulo secunde partis huius operis, ubi per gladium extractum, ut ibi dicitur, figuratur[2] potestas spiritualis, per non extractum materialis. Ideo merito dubitatur utrum standum sit in hac exposicione et adaptacione, vel possint aliter sumi hii duo gladii vel aliter adaptari.

Propter primum, sciendum quod ad videndum quare sunt duo gladii in Ecclesia et non plures neque pauciores, tria videntur facere dubium. Primum quidem est[3] quia cum potestas spiritualis extendat se ad omnia et iudicet omnia, non solum animas sed eciam corpora et res exteriores, videtur quod unus solus gladius sufficiat. Secundum vero[4] quod in hac materia potest nos facere dubitare est quod, cum corpora habeant alium gladium ab animabus, quare non habent alium gladium[5] a rebus exterioribus? Videretur quidem quod corpora magis deberent habere[6] alium gladium a rebus exterioribus quam ab animabus,[7] quia ex corpore et anima fit unum aliquid, ut unus homo. Non enim habent corpora esse per se et anime per se, sed est unum esse corporis et anime, et ille qui preest animabus non preest eis tamquam separatis, sed ut sunt coniuncte corporibus et ut presunt corporibus; et gladius qui preest corporibus[8] preest eis ut sunt coniuncta animabus et ut subsunt animabus. Et ex[9] hoc supra dicebatur quod gladius est sub gladio et potestas[10] sub potestate. Quare si ex corpore et anima fit unum aliquid et utriusque est unum[11] et idem esse, corporum autem et rerum exteriorum non est unum esse, videtur ex hoc quod corpora magis debent habere alium gladium a rebus exterioribus quam ab animabus. Tercium quod facit dubium in hac materia est, quid peccaverunt res exteriores quod non habuerunt proprium gladium et proprium principantem? Nam anime habent proprium gladium et proprium principem qui preest animabus; corpora eciam habent proprium principem et proprium gladium qui preest corporibus, qui exercet iudicium sanguinis. Res ergo exteriores proprium gladium et proprium principem habere[12] debebant.

Hiis itaque prelibatis, volumus triplici via declarare quare in gubernacione

---

1: alius] aliud F   2: figuratur] significatur CFV[2]   3: est] *om.* V[2]   4: vero] *om.* F   5: ab animabus ... gladium] *om.* F   6: habere] *om.* C   7: animabus] fit *add.* V[2]   8: et gladius ... corporibus] *om.* F   9: ex] ut F   10: potestas] est *add.* F   11: aliquid et ... unum] *om.* V[2]   12: habere] *om.* V[2]

bodies that there is therefore not one sword to rule bodies and another external goods [but only a single material sword to rule both], we shall also [have to] say that bodies are themselves [just as much] ordered to souls [as external goods are to bodies]. Therefore, [it seems that, on this showing] there will not be one sword to rule souls and another bodies and another external goods [but only the spiritual sword, ruling all three]. There will, then, be only one sword in the Church.

Moreover, the need for the second part of this chapter — the discussion of how these two swords are to be understood — arises from the fifth chapter of the second part of this work, where the spiritual power is signified by the drawn sword, as is said there, and the material by the undrawn. For it is justly doubted whether this exposition and interpretation should be accepted, or whether these two swords may be understood differently or differently interpreted.

As to the first [of these questions]: in order that it may be seen why there are two swords in the Church and neither more nor fewer, it must be known that three factors seem to give rise to doubt. The first is that, since the spiritual power extends itself to all things and judges all things — not only souls, but bodies and external goods also — it seems that only one sword may suffice. And the second factor which can give us cause for doubt in this matter is that, since bodies [do in fact] have a sword distinct from that of souls, why do they not have a sword distinct from that of external goods? [i.e. why are there not three swords altogether?] Indeed, because a single entity — that is, a single man — is made from both body and soul, it would [on the face of it] seem that bodies should have a sword which is more distinct from that of external goods than from that of souls. For bodies and souls do not each have a separate existence; rather, a single entity is composed of both body and soul. And that [sword] which rules souls does not rule them as separate, but as united with bodies and as ruling bodies; and the sword which rules bodies rules them as united with souls and as placed under souls. And, for this reason, it was said above that sword is under sword and power under power.[1] Thus, if a single entity is made from body and soul, and if both compose one and the same being, yet there is not one being composed of bodies and external goods, then it seems on this ground that bodies should have a sword which is more distinct from that of external goods than from that of souls. And the third factor which gives rise to doubt in this matter is: How have external goods sinned, that they have not received their own sword and their own ruler? For souls have their own sword and their own ruler, who rules souls; and bodies have their own ruler and their own sword, which rules bodies, which executes the judgment of blood. Therefore [consistency seems to require that] external goods should have their own sword and their own ruler.

Thus, having first touched upon these considerations, we wish to show in three

sword has been appointed as its assistant, and that secular power is therefore entirely subordinate to spiritual. This established, the separate question of how many forms secular power can take is surely irrelevant. Having introduced the notion of three swords in Ch. X, he evidently now feels obliged to treat the question in detail.

1. See, e.g., Pt. I, Ch. VII; Pt. II, Ch. V.

hominum et in regimine humani generis[1] sive in regimine fidelium sunt tantum
due potestates et duo gladii: potestas quidem sacerdotalis et regalis sive imperialis, gladius videlicet spiritualis et materialis. Prima autem via sumitur ex excellencia quam habent spiritualia ad corporalia, secunda ex differencia quam habent hec
ad illa, tercia vero ex ordine qui competit hiis et illis: ex qua triplici via prefata[2]
dubia dissolventur.

Prima quidem via sic patet. Nam tanta est excellencia spiritualium ad corporalia quod parvus defectus in spiritualibus preponderat omni defectui in corporalibus. Quod ergo in Ecclesia sunt duo gladii, spiritualis et materialis, non est quin[3]
Ecclesia habeat utrumque gladium, nec est quod potestas spiritualis non se extendat ad corporalia; sed ut potestas spiritualis[4] magis vacare posset rebus divinis,
circa quas maxime cavendum est, ne sit ibi defectus, bene se habuit statuere secundum gladium, qui preesset corporalibus[5] rebus. Sed quando due potestates ita
se habent quod una se extendit ad omnia, videlicet ad magis nobilia et ad minus
nobilia, sed, ut liberius vacare possit circa magis nobilia, instituitur secunda potestas que[6] specialiter[7] vacet circa minus nobilia, oportet tunc potestatem institutam ad vacandum[8] circa minus nobilia esse sub potestate altera;[9] et oportet eam
esse institutam per alteram et habere quod[10] habet ex commissione alterius potestatis. Sic et in proposito. Nam potestas spiritualis extendit se ad spiritualia tamquam ad magis nobilia, et ad corporalia tamquam ad[11] minus nobilia. Quoniam, ut
sepe sepius dictum est, cum potestas spiritualis presit animabus, ut sunt coniuncte
corporibus et ut presunt corporibus,[12] ideo clare patet quod huiusmodi potestas
eciam ipsis corporibus presit.

Que ergo fuit necessitas instituendi aliam potestatem et alium gladium? Dicemus ergo quod huiusmodi necessitas fuit nimia excellencia et nimia perfeccio rerum spiritualium. Quia tanta est nobilitas et tanta est excellencia rerum spiritualium quod, ne contingeret[13] defectus circa ea, bonum fuit instituere secundam
potestatem que specialiter[14] preesset rebus corporalibus ad hoc, quod spiritualis
potestas circa spiritualia liberius vacare posset. Potestas ergo spiritualis est potestas generalis et extensa, cum non solum ad spiritualia sed ad corporalia se extendat. Potestas autem materialis et[15] terrena est particularis et contracta, cum specialiter sit circa corporalia instituta.

Sed, ut tangebatur, cum due potestates sic se habent quod una est generalis et
extensa, alia particularis et contracta, oportet quod una sit sub altera, sit[16] instituta
per alteram et agat ex commissione alterius vel in virtute alterius, ut patuit in exemplo superius posito: ut si ad generacionem equi facit celestis potestas tamquam potestas generalis et potestas[17] que est in equo vel in semine equi [hoc facit tamquam

---

1: et in ... generis] *del.* C   2: prefata] tria *add.* CV[2]   3: quin] qui F   4: non se ... spiritualis]
om. F   5: corporalibus] ad hoc quod circa spiritualia spiritualis gladius liberius vacare posset *add.*
and del. C corporibus V[2]   6: que] quin FV[2]   7: specialiter] spiritualiter P   8: vacandum] *om.* P
9: altera] alia F   10: quod] quodlibet F   11: ad] *om.* FPV[1]   12: et ut presunt corporibus] *om.* V[2]
13: contingeret] contingerent F   14: specialiter] spiritualiter FV[2]   15: et] est C   16: sit] sic PV[1]
17: tamquam potestas ... potestas] *om.* V[2]

ways why, in the government of men and in the rule of the human race or in the rule of the faithful people, there are only two powers and two swords: namely, the priestly and the royal or imperial power; that is, a spiritual and a material sword. And the first way is derived from the excellence which spiritual things have in comparison with bodily; the second from the difference which holds as between the one and the other; and the third from the order which belongs to the one and to the other. By recourse to these three ways, the doubts stated above will be resolved.

The first way proceeds as follows. For so great is the excellence of spiritual things in comparison with bodily that the least defect in spiritual things outweighs any defect in bodily. Therefore, the fact that there are two swords in the Church, a spiritual and a material, does not mean that the Church may not hold both swords, nor that the spiritual power may not extend itself to bodily concerns. Rather, it was well to establish a second sword, to rule bodily affairs, so that the spiritual might be the more able to devote itself to things divine, of which it must take the greatest care so that there may be no defect among them. But when two powers are such that the one extends itself to all things — namely, to the more noble and less noble alike — but the second power has been instituted to devote itself especially to the less noble so that the former might be able to attend more freely to the more noble, then it must be that the power instituted to have care of the less noble is under the other power; and it must be that it is instituted through the other, and holds what it has by the commission of the other power. So also in our proposition: for the spiritual power extends itself to spiritual matters as to the more noble and to bodily as to the less noble. For, as has been said again and again, since the spiritual power rules souls as united with bodies and as ruling bodies, it is therefore clearly apparent that such power may also rule bodies themselves.

What need was there, then, to institute another power and another sword? We shall say, therefore, that such need arose from the very great excellence and the very great perfection of spiritual things. For so great is the nobility and so great is the excellence of spiritual things that it was good to institute a second power to rule bodily things, to this end: that the spiritual power might be able to attend more freely to spiritual matters, so that no defect should arise with respect to them. Therefore, the spiritual power is a general and extended power, since it extends itself not only to spiritual, but also to bodily matters. But the material and earthly power is particular and limited, since it is instituted specifically with respect to bodily matters.

But, as has been noted, when two powers are such that the one is general and extended and the other particular and limited, it must be that the one is under the other, is instituted through the other, and may act only by the commission of the other or through the other's power. This is clear from the example given above:[1] that if the heavenly power brings about the generation of a horse as a general power, and the power which is in the horse or in the seed of the horse does so as a

---

1. Ch. VI, p. 117; Ch. X, pp. 165–167.

potestas particularis], oportet quod hec sit sub illa et hec sit[1] instituta[2] per illam, quia non esset virtus in semine equi ad producendum equum nisi hoc[3] haberet a virtute celesti. Oportet et tercio quod et hoc agat in virtute alterius, quia virtus que est in semine equi[4] non ageret ad generacionem equi nisi hoc ageret in virtute celi; quia, ut probatur in II *De generacione*, ignis, qui inter hec inferiora est maxime activus,[5] non ageret ad generacionem alicuius rei nisi hoc faceret in virtute supercelestis corporis. Non erit ergo ponere duas potestates, unam generalem, alteram particularem, nisi una sit sub alia, sit[6] instituta per aliam et agat ex commissione alterius vel in virtute alterius.

Potestas itaque terrena est sub spirituali et[7] instituta per spiritualem et agit ex commissione[8] spiritualis potestatis. Unde primus rex qui regnavit in populo fideli institutus fuit per Samuelem. Ideo Dominus dixit Samueli: 'Constitue super eos regem,' ut habetur I Regum VIII. Si ergo non est potestas nisi a Deo, eo modo se[9] cognoscant[10] institutos esse reges et principes prout ore suo constituit eos Deus.[11] Hoc autem modo voluit Dominus[12] esse institutum regem, quia dixit[13] Samueli quod ipse constitueret eum.[14] Utrum autem ipse Dominus loqueretur Samueli vel angelus in persona Dei nihil ad propositum. Nam multa fiunt per inferiores que in Scriptura Sacra appropriantur superioribus; quia, ut habetur Isaie cap. VI, quod ad purgandum labia Isaie[15] volavit ad eum unus de seraphim, qui forcipe accepto calculo de altari, vel, ut habet[16] alia littera,[17] accepto carbunculo de altari, tetigit os eius et purgavit labia ipsius. Constat autem quod ille angelus non fuit seraphim, nam seraphim sunt supremus ordo supreme hierarchie, qui numquam ab intimis recedunt et numquam ad nos mittuntur, ut probat Dionysius in *De angelica hierarchia*. Tamen, quia 'seraphim' interpretatur 'incendentes',[18] et ille angelus qui volavit ad Isaiam per incendium purgavit labia eius, quia hoc fecit cum carbunculo, ideo fecit officium ipsius seraphim, et dictus est seraphim. Et Exodi III de rubo ardente dicitur quod apparuit Moysi Dominus[19] in flamma ignis de medio rubi: in Exodo[20] ergo dicitur quod Dominus locutus est Moysi; Actuum autem VII dicitur quod apparuit Moysi angelus in igne flamme rubi. Ergo fuit[21] Dominus et fuit angelus qui apparuit Moysi, quia[22] fuit angelus qui representabat ipsum Dominum sive ipsum Deum.[23] Sed[24] sive Dominus loqueretur ipsi Samueli

---

1: sub illa et hec sit] *om.* V[2]   2: instituta] sub illa et hec sit instituta *add.* V[2]   3: hoc] *om.* F
4: equi] *om.* F   5: activus] *om.* V[2]   6: sit] sic CPV[1]V[2]   7: et] est CP   8: commissione] institucione *mss*   9: se] *om.* CV[2]   10: cognoscant] se *add.* CV[2]   11: Deus] dominus FV[2]
12: Dominus] deus F   13: dixit] dicit FPV[1]   14: eum] *om.* V[2]   15: cap. VI ... Isaie] *om.* V[2]
16: habet] habetur F   17: alia littera] aliter PFV[2]   18: interpretatur 'incendentes'] interpretantur intendentes F   19: apparuit Moysi Dominus] dominus apparuit moysi F   20: in Exodo] et exodi PV[1]   21: fuit] *om.* FV[2]   22: quia] qui PV[1]   23: Deum] domino PV[1]   24: Sed] et F

particular power, then it must be that the one is under the other and that the one is instituted through the other. For there would be no power in the seed of a horse to produce a horse unless it had this from the power of heaven. And, third, it must be that the one achieves this through the power of the other, because the power which is in the horse's seed would not bring about the generation of a horse unless it did so through the power of heaven. For, as is proved in *De generatione* 2, fire, which is the most active element among inferior things, would not bring about the generation of anything unless it did so through the power of a body which is above the heaven.[1] Therefore, it will not be consistent to posit two powers, one general and the other particular, unless the one is under the other, is instituted through the other, and acts by the commission of the other or through the other's power.

Thus, the earthly power is under the spiritual, and is instituted through the spiritual and acts by the commission of the spiritual power. Hence, the first king who ruled among the faithful people was instituted through Samuel. And so the Lord said to Samuel, 'Appoint a king over them,' as is established in I Samuel 8.[2] If there is no power except of God, therefore, let kings and princes understand that they are as much instituted by God as if He had appointed them out of His own mouth, but that the Lord desired that a king should be appointed in this way [i.e. through the agency of the priesthood rather than from His own mouth], for He told Samuel that he himself was to appoint him. And whether the Lord Himself, or an angel as God's representative, spoke to Samuel is neither here nor there; for many things are done by inferiors which are attributed in Sacred Scripture to superiors. For according to Isaiah 6, one of the Seraphim flew down to Isaiah to purify his lips, and, taking a stone from the altar with the tongs — or, as another version has it, taking a coal from the altar — touched his mouth and purified his lips.[3] But it is clear that this angel was not one of the Seraphim; for the Seraphim are the highest order of the highest hierarchy, and never leave the inmost part, and are never sent forth to us, as Dionysius proves in *De angelica hierarchia*.[4] But because 'Seraphim' means 'burning ones', and because the angel who flew down to Isaiah purified his lips with fire — for he did this with a coal — he therefore performed the office of the Seraphim and [so] is called one of the Seraphim.[5] Also, in Exodus 3 it is said of the burning bush that 'the Lord appeared to Moses in a flame of fire out of the midst of a bush.' In Exodus, therefore, it is said that the Lord spoke to Moses. But in Acts 7 it is said that there appeared to Moses 'an angel in a flame of fire in a bush.'[6] Therefore, in one sense it was the Lord Who appeared to Moses and, in another, an angel; for it was an angel who represented the Lord Himself or God Himself. But whether it was the Lord who spoke to Samuel or an

---

1. Perhaps Aristotle, *De generatione et corruptione* 2:9 (336ª5).
2. I Sam. 8:22.
3. Isaiah 6:6–7 (the Septuagint has ἄνθραξ: 'coal', and the Vulgate *calculus*: 'stone').
4. *De caelesti hierarchia* 13 (PG 3:300); 7 (PG 3:205); cf. Hugh of Saint Victor, *Expositio in hierarchiam caelestem S. Dionysii areopagitae* 9 (PL 175:1111).
5. Cf. Aquinas, *Summa theologiae* Ia 112:2.
6. Exod. 3:4; Acts 7:30.

sive angelus qui representabat Dominum[1] nihil ad propositum; quia, quocumque modo factum fuit, constat quod fuit expressa voluntas Domini quod potestas terrena[2] constitueretur per spiritualem et potestas regia per sacerdotalem, cum dictum fuit Samueli a Domino, vel ab angelo in persona Domini, quod constitueret Iudeis[3] regem.

Redeamus ergo ad propositum et dicamus quod una racio[4] et[5] una causa quare preter potestatem spiritualem et sacerdotalem constituta est potestas regia et terrena est nobilitas et[6] excellencia rerum spiritualium: videlicet, ut[7] ne esset defectus circa eas et ut potestas spiritualis liberius vacare posset[8] circa spiritualia, instituta est alia potestas et alius gladius, qui dicitur materialis et corporalis, qui specialiter[9] circa materialia et corporalia debet esse intentus.

Ex hac autem causa et racione solvitur primum dubium. Nam cum dicebatur quod potestas spiritualis se extendit eciam[10] ad corporalia et habet eciam sub se non solum spiritualia, sed eciam corporalia, et ex hoc arguebatur quod sufficeret spiritualis gladius et superflueret alius, nam frustra fit per plura quod potest fieri per unum: verum est, si potest fieri per illud unum eque bene et eque decenter. Sed si non esset nisi unus gladius in Ecclesia, videlicet spiritualis, ea que agenda essent in gubernacione hominum non fierent eque bene, quia exinde spiritualis gladius multa[11] obmitteret que agenda essent circa spiritualia, ex eo quod oporteret[12] ipsum intendere circa materialia.[13] Non dicimus autem quod, si casus immineat,[14] non possit spiritualis gladius circa materialia intendere; sed ut possit liberius rebus spiritualibus vacare que sunt res excellentes et res nobiles, bonum fuit instituere secundum gladium, cui materialia essent commissa. Habet ergo spiritualis gladius posse super utraque,[15] tam super spiritualia quam super materialia.

Quod ergo institutus est secundus gladius, non est propter impotenciam spiritualis gladii, sed ex bona ordinacione et ex decencia.[16] Nam, ut vult Philosophus circa finem primi *De anima*, anima[17] magis continet corpus[18] quam corpus animam. Nam si separetur corpus ab anima, non propter hoc moritur anima; sed recedente[19] anima a corpore, corpus expirat et marcescit. Non ergo potest corpus subsistere[20] nisi innitatur anime. Sic potestas materialis[21] non potest subsistere[22] nisi innitatur potestati spirituali et nisi potestatem quam habet se recognoscat habere a spirituali. Corpus enim non potest vivere nisi per animam. Virtutem ergo operandi quam habet corpus, habet ab anima. Sic virtutem operandi quam habet materialis gladius, habet a spirituali. Non est ergo propter impotenciam spiritualis gladii quod institutus est

---

1: representabat Dominum] representat deum C   2: potestas terrena] terrena potestas CF
3: Iudeis] *om* F   4: racio] *del.* C   5: et] *om.* C   6: et] ex PV[1]   7: ut] *om.* FPV[1]V[2]   8: posset] possit FV[2]   9: specialiter] spiritualiter V[2]   10: eciam] et P   11: multa] *om.* F   12: que agenda ... oporteret] *om.* C   13: materialia] que agenda essent circa spiritualia ex eo quod oporteret ipsum intendere circa materialia *add.* C   14: immineat] quod *add. mss*   15: utraque] utrumque FV[2]   16: decencia] in omni gladium habet ecclesia *add. and del.* C   17: anima] *om.* C
18: corpus] anima *add.* C   19: corpus ab ... recedente] *om.* F   20: subsistere] substinere F
21: potestas materialis] materialis potestas CF   22: subsistere] substinere F

angel who represented the Lord is neither here nor there. For, however this was achieved, it is clear that it was the express will of the Lord that the earthly power should be appointed through the spiritual and royal power through the priestly, when it was said to Samuel, either by the Lord or by an angel as representing the Lord, that he should appoint a king for the Jews.

Let us return to our proposition, therefore, and say that one reason and one cause why royal and earthly power was appointed in addition to spiritual and priestly power is the nobility and excellence of spiritual things: that is, it is so that there should be no defect with respect to these, and so that the spiritual power might be able to attend more freely to spiritual matters, that another power and another sword has been instituted, which is called material and bodily, and which must be specifically intent upon material and bodily affairs.

And from an examination of this cause and reason, the first doubt is resolved. For when it was said that the spiritual power extends itself to bodily things also, and has under it not only spiritual but also bodily matters; and when it was argued on this ground that the spiritual sword would suffice and the other be superfluous, for it is vain to do with many instruments what can be done with one: this is true if the task in question can be done with one instrument equally well and equally fittingly. But if there were only one sword in the Church, namely, the spiritual, then those tasks which must be performed in the government of men would not be as well done; for the spiritual sword would then neglect many tasks which should be performed in the spiritual sphere, because it would itself be obliged to attend to material affairs. We do not, however, say that the spiritual sword could not attend to material affairs if a special case were to arise, but that, in order that it might be able to attend more freely to spiritual matters, which are excellent and noble things, it was good to institute a second sword to which material affairs were entrusted. Therefore, the spiritual sword has power over both spiritual and material things [but usually delegates its material power to the material sword].

Therefore, the fact that a second sword has been instituted is not because of any lack of power on the part of the spiritual sword; rather, it is for the sake of good order and for the sake of decency. For, as the Philosopher maintains towards the end of the first book of *De anima*, it is the soul which holds the body together rather than the body the soul.[1] For if the body is separated from the soul, the soul does not on that account die. Rather, when the soul is withdrawn from the body, the body expires and decays. Therefore, the body cannot continue to exist unless it is sustained by the soul. So too, material power cannot continue to exist unless it is sustained by spiritual, and unless it acknowledges that it receives the power which it has from the spiritual power. For the body cannot live except through the soul. The body, therefore, receives the power which it has to act from the soul. So too, the material sword receives the power which it has to act from the spiritual. Therefore, it is not because of any lack of power on the part of the spiritual sword that a second sword, which is called material, has been instituted.

---

1. Aristotle, *De anima* 1:5 (411ᵇ5).

secundus gladius, qui dicitur materialis, sed propter beneficium execucionis, quia non ita bene nec ita benefice posset spiritualis gladius exequi spiritualia et[1] vacare circa spiritualia si non haberet adiutorium materialis gladii qui vacaret circa materialia. Non ergo fuit[2] bonum spiritualem gladium esse solum, sed factus fuit materialis gladius in adiutorium sibi.

Si ergo non esset materialis gladius, execucio gubernacionis hominum non fieret eque[3] bene. Rursus, non fieret eque decenter. Nam non esset decens quod spiritualis gladius per se ipsum exerceret iudicium sanguinis. Ideo oportuit quod hoc iudicium a spirituali gladio committeretur materiali gladio.[4] Propter quod huiusmodi gladium exercentem iudicium sanguinis dicitur Ecclesia habere non ad usum, sed ad nutum, quia tale iudicium Ecclesia non exercet per seipsam, sed per alium, qui in omnibus debet Ecclesie famulari. Iste ergo alius gladius et ista potestas terrena sic debet uti materiali gladio, prout viderit Ecclesie expedire.

Secunda via ad hoc idem, quare sunt duo tantum[5] gladii in Ecclesia, sumitur ex differencia rerum spiritualium ad corporalia.[6] Nam spiritualia et corporalia non sunt sub eodem genere, quia corruptibile et incorruptibile[7] differunt genere, ut declarari habet in X *Metaphysice*; nec pertinet consideracio de hiis ad eandem[8] particularem scienciam, sed solum ad generalem. Illa ergo sciencia que considerat de corporibus, ut naturalis philosophia, non considerat de spiritibus,[9] quia[10] que non amplius mota movent, cuiusmodi sunt[11] substancie spirituales que movent immobiles, non amplius sunt philosophice consideracionis. Et si dicatur quod eciam philosophia naturalis considerat de anima, dicemus quod considerat de ea, ut est[12] actus corporis. Hoc eciam modo considerat de angelis, ut sunt motores orbium; de eis autem secundum se non considerat. Sed illa sciencia que considerat de spiritibus secundum se, considerat de corporibus, quia est sciencia generalis.[13] Metaphysica enim, que considerat de substancia intelligibili, ut patet ex XII [*Metaphysice*], considerat et de sensibili, ut patet ex dictis.[14]

Sic ergo est in scienciis, quod illa que considerat de substancia[15] spirituali est sciencia generalis,[16] quia considerat non solum de substancia spirituali, sed eciam[17] corporali et sensibili. Sed illa sciencia[18] que per se habet considerare de substancia sensibili, cuiusmodi est naturalis philosophia, est sciencia particularis, non valens[19] per se considerare de substanciis spiritualibus. Est itaque hic modus in scienciis, quod propter scienciam generalem non superfluunt sciencie particulares. Propter hoc enim quod metaphysica est sciencia generalis, considerans de spiritualibus et de corporalibus et de sensibilibus substanciis, non propter hoc superfluit naturalis philosophia, cuius consideracio restringitur[20] ad substancias corporales et sensibiles.

1: et] *om.* FPV[1]V[2]   2: ergo fuit] fuit ergo C   3: eque] et *add.* CFV[2]   4: committeretur materiali gladio] *om.* V[2]   5: duo tantum] tantum duo C   6: corporalia] corpora F   7: et incorruptibile] *om.* V[2]   8: eandem] quandam V[2]   9: spiritibus] spiritualibus FV[2]   10: quia] *om.* FV[2]   11: sunt] *om.* V[2]   12: est] *om.* F   13: sciencia generalis] generalis sciencia F   14: dictis] vii° C   15: substancia] *om.* FV[2]   16: sciencia generalis] generalis sciencia C   17: eciam] de *add.* CFV[2]   18: sciencia] *del.* C   19: valens] volens F   20: restringitur] restringatur F

Rather, this is to secure a benefit in the sphere of execution. For the spiritual sword could not execute spiritual tasks and devote itself to spiritual matters so well or so beneficially if it did not have the aid of the material sword which devotes itself to material affairs. Therefore, it was not good for the spiritual sword to be alone, but the material sword was made as its helper.[1]

If, therefore, there were no material sword, the execution of the government of men would not be as well performed. Also, it would not be as fittingly performed; for it would not be fitting if the spiritual sword were itself to execute the judgment of blood. Thus, it was necessary that this judgment should be entrusted by the spiritual sword to the material sword. And so the Church is said to have the sword which executes the judgment of blood not to use, but to command. For the Church does not execute such judgment herself, but through another, who must be the servant of the Church in all things. Therefore, this other sword and this earthly power must use the material sword in such a way as shall seem expedient to the Church.

The second way towards the same conclusion, that there are only two swords in the Church, is derived from the difference between spiritual and bodily things. For spiritual and bodily things do not fall under the same genus. For corruptible and incorruptible things are members of different genera, as has been declared in *Metaphysics* 10;[2] nor does the consideration of them pertain to the same particular science, but only to a general one. Therefore, that science which considers corporeal objects, natural philosophy, does not consider spirits. For those things which cause movement without themselves being moved (of which kind are spiritual substances, which cause movement while remaining unmoved) do not themselves come under the consideration of natural philosophy. And if it be said that natural philosophy does indeed consider the soul, we shall reply that it considers it only insofar as it produces corporeal actions. In this sense, it also considers the angels, as movers of the spheres; but it does not consider them in their own nature. But that science which does consider spirits in their own nature also considers bodies, because it is a general science. For metaphysics, which considers intelligible substance, as is clear from book 12 [of Aristotle's *Metaphysics*] also considers that which is sensible, as is clear from what we have said.[3]

So it is, therefore, among the sciences: that which considers spiritual substance is a general science, because it considers not only spiritual substances but also corporeal and sensible objects; but that science which has the task of considering sensible objects as such, of which kind is natural philosophy, is a particular science which cannot of itself consider spiritual substances. Among the sciences, then, there is an order such that the particular sciences are not superfluous to the general science. For although metaphysics is the general science, considering spiritual and corporeal and sensible substances alike, natural philosophy, whose field of study is restricted to corporeal and sensible substances, is

1. This allusion to Gen. 2:18 is perhaps intended to suggest that the relation of the material to the spiritual sword is analogous to that of wife to husband.
2. *Metaphysics* I:10 (1058^{b}30).
3. *Metaphysics* Λ:1 (1069^{a}20).

Sic et in proposito, idest in regimine et[1] gubernacione hominum, qui sunt compositi ex utraque substancia spirituali et corporali. Illa ergo potestas que est spiritualis erit generalis et extendet[2] se eciam ad corporalia; potestas autem illa que specialiter ordinata est circa corporalia erit particularis et contracta et[3] per se et secundum se de spiritualibus se intromittere non valebit; nec tamen propter potestatem spiritualem, que est generalis, superfluit potestas terrena, que est contracta et
particularis, sicut et in scienciis dicebamus non superfluere particularem scienciam propter generalem. Verumtamen de hoc infra clarius dicetur.

  Ex hoc autem patet quare Ecclesia dicta est[4] Catholica, idest universalis, quod
veritatem habet non solum racione sacramentorum, que sunt universalia et generalia, sine quibus non potest esse salus, sed eciam racione extensionis potencie,[5]
quia potencia ecclesiastica, que est potencia spiritualis, oportet quod ex hoc sit
generalis et quod[6] ad corporalia se extendat. Hunc ergo modum quem videmus in
scienciis videmus[7] eciam in naturalibus virtutibus sive potenciis. Nam corporalia
habent suas potencias et suas virtutes naturales, et spiritualia habent suas potencias et suas virtutes naturales.[8] Spiritualis autem virtus est generalis, ut supra aliqualiter tetigimus, cum se extendat eciam ad corporalia, quia oportet[9] corpora
spiritibus esse subiecta. Corporalis autem virtus est particularis et contracta, quia
huiusmodi virtus per se in spiritualia[10] agere[11] non potest. Dicimus autem 'per se',
quia in virtute alterius non est inconveniens corpus agere in spiritum, ut aqua baptismi in virtute divine misericordie animam lavat, et ignis inferni in virtute divine
iusticie[12] animam cruciat. Sicut ergo in virtutibus naturalibus virtus spiritualis est
generalis, extendens eciam se ad corporalia, virtus autem corporalis est particularis, non valens per se extendere se ad spiritualia; et sicut propter virtutem spiritualem non superfluit virtus corporalis: sic in gubernacione hominum potestas
spiritualis est[13] generalis, extendens se eciam ad corporalia, potestas autem terrena
est contracta et particularis, per se ad spiritualia non valens se extendere.[14] Quantum ad superfluere,[15] sicut est in virtutibus naturalibus et in scienciis, sic est in
gubernacione hominum: quod propter potestatem spiritualem, que est generalis,
non superfluit potestas terrena, que est particularis.

  Redeamus ergo ad propositum et dicamus quod tanta est differencia corporum et spirituum ut[16] sub una particulari sciencia non comprehendantur[17] hec et
illa, sed solum sub sciencia universali. Sic eciam in virtutibus naturalibus: si
virtutes spirituales que[18] naturaliter habent esse in spiritibus volumus appellare
generales, virtutes autem corporales que naturaliter habent esse in corporibus
volumus appellare particulares, sub una virtute particulari non cadent hec et illa.
Quod ergo videmus in virtutibus naturalibus et scienciis, que sunt quedam potencie,

---

1: et] in *add.* CFV[2] 2: extendet] extendit FV[2] 3: et] *om.* F 4: est] *om.* C 5: potencie] *del.* C
6: quod] *om.* F 7: in scienciis, videmus] *om.* F 8: et spiritualia ... naturales] *om.* F 9: opor-
tet] corporalia quia oportet *add.* V[2] 10: spiritualia] spiritualem FV[2] 11: agere] regere F
12: iusticie] iusticia V[2] 13: est] *om.* PV[1] 14: extendere] et *add.* C 15: superfluere] et *add.* V[1]
16: ut] quod CV[2] 17: comprehendantur] comprehenduntur CV[2] 18: que] eciam *add.* V[2]

not on this account superfluous. So also in our proposition: that is, in the rule and government of men, who are composed of both spiritual and corporeal substance. Therefore, that power which is spiritual will be general, and will extend itself to bodily things also. But that power which is especially appointed in relation to bodily things will be particular and limited and, of itself and as such, will not be able to concern itself with spiritual matters. Nonetheless, the earthly power, which is limited and particular, is not superfluous to the spiritual power, which is general, just as, as we have said with reference to the sciences, a particular science is not superfluous to the general. This, however, will be stated more clearly below.[1]

And it is clear from this why the Church is called Catholic, that is, universal: that this is true not only by reason of the sacraments, which are universal and general, without which there can be no salvation,[2] but also by reason of the extent of her power. For the ecclesiastical power, which is a spiritual power, must for this reason be general, and extend itself to bodily matters. Therefore, the order of operation which we see in the sciences we see also in natural forces or powers. For corporeal substances have their powers and their natural forces, and spiritual substances have their powers and their natural forces. But spiritual power is general, as we have in some measure noted above, since it extends itself to corporeal substances also: for bodies must be subject to spirits. Corporeal power, however, is particular and limited because, of itself, such power cannot act in spiritual matters. And we say 'of itself' because it is not incongruous for body to act upon spirit by virtue of some other power, as the water of baptism washes the soul by virtue of the Divine Mercy, and as the fire of hell tortures the soul by virtue of the Divine Justice. Therefore, just as, among natural powers, spiritual power is general, extending itself to corporeal substances also, and corporeal power is particular, not being able of itself to extend itself to spiritual substances; and just as corporeal power is not superfluous to spiritual power: so, in the government of men, the spiritual power is general, extending itself to bodily matters also, and the earthly power is limited and particular and, of itself, is unable to extend itself to spiritual matters. And, as to the question of superfluousness, just as it is among the natural powers and in the sciences, so is it in the government of men: that the earthly power, which is particular, is not superfluous to the spiritual power, which is general.

Let us return to our proposition, therefore, and say that the difference between bodies and spirits is so great that the one and the other may not be brought under one particular science, but only under a universal science. So also among natural forces: if we wish to call the spiritual forces which occur naturally in spirits general, and if we wish to call the corporeal forces which occur naturally in bodies particular, the one and the other will not both fall under one particular force. Therefore, what we see in the forces of nature and in the sciences — which are powers

1. Ch. XIV.
2. See Ch. XI, pp. 187–189 and Ch. XII, pp. 203–205.

quia sciencie sunt quedam potencie[1] ad speculandum, virtutes naturales sunt quedam potencie[2] ad agendum, sic arbitrari debemus in gubernacione hominum, quod sub potencia particulari et terrena non cadent spiritualia et corporalia. Erunt ergo due potencie et duo gladii: unus spiritualis, qui erit quasi generalis, extendens se ad spiritualia et corporalia; et alius materialis, qui erit contractus[3] et particularis, specialiter ordinatur ad corporalia. Sed cum spiritualis gladius sit generalis, quare[4] non superfluit materialis, quia frustra fit per plura quod potest fieri per unum, supra in hoc capitulo est patefactum et infra clarius patefiet.[5]

Dicimus autem potestatem spiritualem esse generalem non[6] quin una spiritualis potestas sit generalior alia et quin una potestas spiritualis sit sub alia, sed dicitur generalis quia non est sic contracta sicut potestas materialis et terrena, que per se solum ad materialia se extendit. Spiritualis vero et ad spiritualia et ad corporalia se potest extendere. Illa ergo potestas spiritualis, que in gubernacione fidelium est suprema, omnem habet potestatem in corpore mistico et omnia sunt subiecta sub pedibus eius, ut omnia possit imperare et precipere[7] que non obviant iuri naturali et fidei orthodoxe.

Sed dices quod sicut corpora sunt distincta a spiritibus,[8] sic res exteriores sunt separate[9] ab humanis corporibus. Si ergo corpora habent gladium distinctum a spirituali gladio, videtur quod debeant habere gladium distinctum ab exterioribus rebus. Sed, ut patet per habita, non sunt corpora humana sic[10] distincta ab exterioribus rebus[11] sicut sunt[12] distincta a[13] spiritualibus substanciis, quia corpora cum spiritualibus substanciis[14] non cadunt sub una particulari sciencia nec sub una particulari potencia; sed corpora cum exterioribus rebus cadunt sub una particulari sciencia[15] et sub una particulari potencia. Cadunt quidem sub una particulari sciencia, quia[16] si res exteriores sunt nostre facultates et nostre divicie, sive sint divicie naturales, sicut sunt animalia, vites, arbores, segetes, sive sint divicie artificiales, sicut sunt aurum et argentum et cetera[17] metalla que oriuntur in venis terre, de omnibus considerat una et eadem particularis sciencia, ut philosophia naturalis. Immo, quia divicie artificiales sunt propter naturales, una et eadem sciencia particularis et[18] subalterna, cuiusmodi est sciencia medicinalis, considerabit de omnibus talibus, tam de corporibus humanis quam eciam de diviciis naturalibus et de rebus quibus utitur humanum corpus; considerabit eciam et tercio una et eadem sciencia, ut puta sciencia moralis, de omnibus istis.

Sed aliter et aliter de omnibus hiis considerabit sciencia naturalis, medicinalis et moralis. Quia naturalis considerat de omnibus eis[19] ut sunt partes corporis mobilis, quod est subiectum in naturali philosophia, et eius[20] partes et passiones considerat. Sed medicinalis considerabit[21] de omnibus eis ut ordinantur ad sanitatem corporis

---

1: quia sciencie ... potencie] *om.* CF   2: ad speculandum ... potencie] *om.* V[1]   3: contractus] extractus V[2]   4: quare] quia V[2]   5: patefiet] patebit F   6: non] vero F   7: precipere] percipere F   8: spiritibus] spiritualibus FV[2]   9: sunt separate] separate sunt FV[2]   10: sic] *om.* V[2]   11: Sed, ut ... rebus] *om.* F   12: sunt] *om.* FV[2]   13: a] *om.* V[2]   14: spiritualibus substanciis] substanciis spiritualibus F   15: nec sub ... sciencia] *om.* FV[2]   16: quia] *om.* C   17: cetera] eciam PV[1]   18: et] eciam FV[2]   19: eis] iis F   20: eius] cuius FV[2]   21: considerabit] considerat V[2] moralis sciencia *add. and del.* C

of a kind, for the sciences are certain powers of investigation and the forces of nature are certain capacities for action — we must deem to be true of the government of men: that spiritual and bodily matters will not both fall under a particular and earthly power. There will, therefore, be two powers and two swords: one spiritual, which will be as it were general, extending itself to both spiritual and bodily things, and another material, which will be limited and particular, ordained especially with respect to bodily things. But since the spiritual sword is general, the reason why it does not render the material sword superfluous (since it is vain to do with many instruments what can be done with one) has been made clear earlier in this chapter, and will be made still clearer below.

But when we say that spiritual power is general, we do not mean that one spiritual power is not more general than another and that one spiritual power is not under another. Rather, it is called general because it is not limited in the way that material and earthly power is, which, of itself, extends itself only to material things, whereas spiritual power can extend itself to both spiritual and corporeal things. Therefore, that [holder of] spiritual power who is supreme in the government of the faithful has all power within the Mystical Body, and all things are placed beneath his feet, so that he may command and teach all things which are not contrary to natural law and to orthodox faith.[1]

But you will say that, just as bodies are distinct from spirits, so are external goods separate from human bodies. If, therefore, bodies have a sword which is distinct from the spiritual sword, it seems that they should also have a sword which is distinct from that of external goods. As is clear from what we have said, however, human bodies are not distinct from external goods in the way that they are distinct from spiritual substances. For bodies and spiritual substances do not both fall under one particular science or one particular power, whereas bodies and external goods do fall under one particular science and under one particular power. They do indeed fall under one particular science; for if external goods are our wealth and our riches — whether natural riches, such as animals, vines, trees and cornfields, or artificial riches such as gold and silver and the other metals which come from veins in the earth — one and the same particular science, natural philosophy, considers them all. Again, because artificial riches exist for the sake of natural riches [i.e. so that we can acquire natural riches by means of them], one and the same particular and subordinate science, of which kind is the science of medicine, will consider all such things equally: human bodies, natural riches, and those [artificial] things of which the human body makes use. Also, and third, one and the same science, to wit, moral science, will consider all of these.

But the natural, medical and moral sciences will consider all these things in different ways. For natural science considers all of them inasmuch as they are parts of body in motion, which is the subject of natural philosophy, which considers its parts and properties. But medical science will consider all of them inasmuch as they are ordered towards the health of the human body, which is the

---

1. Cf. Dist. 40, c. 6: *Si papa* (CIC 1:146).

humani, quod est subiectum in medicina, circa quod sanitatem et egritudinem considerat tamquam humani corporis proprias passiones. Moralis autem sciencia de humanis corporibus et de rebus exterioribus poterit considerare prout circa ea versantur actus humani, qui sunt subiectum in morali sciencia. Circa quos considerat sciencia[1] quid iustum et quid non iustum tamquam proprias passiones. Et sicut omnia hec cadunt sub una particulari sciencia, non solum naturali sed medicinali et morali, quamvis aliter et aliter, sic[2] omnia prefata cadunt sub una potencia particulari, quia eadem potencia et eadem virtus corporalis aget in corpora nostra et in res exteriores, sive ille res exteriores[3] sint divicie naturales sive artificiales. Idem enim ignis calefacere poterit corpora nostra et aurum et argentum et cetera metalla, que sunt divicie artificiales quia per artem hominum sunt invente ad sufficienciam humane[4] vite. Poterit eciam idem ignis calefacere fructus terre, qui[5] sunt divicie naturales, quoniam[6] ad sufficienciam vite nostre naturaliter ordinantur.[7] Corpora itaque nostra[8] cum rebus exterioribus non habent illam differenciam quam habent cum substanciis spiritualibus, quia nec sub una particulari sciencia nec sub una particulari sive corporali potencia[9] cadunt corpora nostra cum substanciis spiritualibus, sed sub una particulari sciencia et sub una particulari potencia cadunt corpora nostra cum[10] rebus exterioribus.

Quod ergo dicebatur, quod ex corporibus nostris et exterioribus facultatibus non fit unum secundum esse, et ideo non debent cadere sub uno gladio, sed ex corporibus nostris et spiritibus sive ex corporibus et animabus nostris fit unum secundum esse, ideo conveniencius poterunt cadere sub uno gladio: dicemus quod si loqueris de gladio[11] spirituali, qui dici debet[12] gladius generalis, omnia hec cadunt sub uno gladio, quia ille gladius poterit animadvertere in spiritualia, corporalia et temporalia. Habet enim iurisdiccionem super animas et[13] super corpora et super res exteriores, quamvis huiusmodi gladius super corporalia quantum ad iudicium sanguinis hanc iurisdiccionem non debeat per se, sed per alium exercere. Sed si loqueris de gladio particulari, cuiusmodi est gladius materialis,[14] non sunt omnia sub uno gladio. Corpora tamen et res exteriores possunt esse sub uno particulari gladio. Nam, licet res exteriores et corpora nostra non sint unum subiecto nec unum secundum esse, sunt tamen unum quantum ad consideracionem unius particularis sciencie, et sunt unum quia possunt esse sub accione unius particularis potencie. Sic possunt esse unum sub iurisdiccione unius particularis gladii.

Et quod dicitur de uno secundum esse, dicemus quod unitas secundum esse est unitas[15] suppositi sive unitas subiecti; sed in uno et eodem supposito possunt esse omnia predicamenta de quibus secundum se considerant diverse particulares sciencie. Ad esse ergo sub uno particulari gladio plus facit habere unitatem quantum ad consideracionem unius particularis sciencie vel quantum ad accionem unius particularis potencie quam habere unitatem quantum ad suppositum vel subiectum,

---

1: sciencia] *om.* F   2: sic] sicut F *om.* CV²   3: exteriores] *om.* C   4: humane] huius PV¹
5: qui] quia C   6: quoniam] quantum F   7: ordinantur] ordinatur FV²   8: itaque nostra] nostra itaque F   9: potencia] *om.* F   10: cum] ut CF in V²   11: dicemus quod ... gladio] *om.* F
12: debet] potest C   13: et] *om.* CFV²   14: materialis] et terrena potestas *add. and del.* C
15: secundum esse est unitas] *om.* F

subject of medicine, which considers health and illness as peculiar properties of the human body. And moral science will be able to consider human bodies and external goods insofar as they bear upon human acts, which are the subject of moral science: the science which considers such things with reference to the peculiar properties of justice and injustice.[1] And just as all these things fall under one particular science — not only the natural, but also the medical and moral, although in various ways — so all the things mentioned above fall under one particular power. For the same power and the same corporeal force will act upon our bodies and upon external goods, whether those external goods are natural or artificial riches. For the same fire will be able to warm our bodies and gold and silver and the other metals which are artificial riches discovered by the art of man to supply the necessities of human life. Also, the same fire will be able to warm the fruits of the earth, which are natural riches inasmuch as they are naturally appointed to supply the necessities of our life. Thus, our bodies do not differ from external goods in the way that they differ from spiritual substances. For our bodies do not fall either under one particular science or under one particular or corporeal power in company with spiritual substances; but our bodies do fall under one particular science and under one particular power in company with external goods.

Therefore, as to what has been said — that our bodies and external goods do not comprise an essential unity, and that therefore they should not fall under one sword, but that our bodies and spirits, or our bodies and souls, do comprise an essential unity and therefore can more appropriately fall under one sword: we shall reply that if you speak of the spiritual sword, which must be called a general sword, then all these things [i.e. souls, bodies and external goods alike] fall under the one sword. For this sword will be able to take action in relation to spiritual, bodily and temporal matters equally; for it has jurisdiction over souls, over bodies and over external goods, even though, so far as the judgment of blood is concerned, that sword may not exercise such jurisdiction over bodily matters of itself, but only through another. But if you speak of a particular sword, of which kind is the material sword, then not all things are under the one sword. Bodies and external goods, however, can be under the one particular sword; for, although external goods and our bodies do not form one entity or one essential unity, they are nonetheless one in the sense of falling under the consideration of one particular science, and they are one because they can be under the action of one particular power. Thus, they can be under the jurisdiction of one particular sword.

And to what has been said concerning essential unity, we shall reply that essential unity is [indeed] unity of underlying substance or unity as an entity, but that, in one and the same entity, there can be all the aspects which, as such, the various particular sciences consider. Thus, it is the possession of unity in the sense of falling under the consideration of one particular science, or in the sense of being subject to the action of one particular power, rather than the possession of the unity of

---

1. A rather restrictive definition of 'moral science', however; cf. Aristotle, *Nicomachean Ethics* 1:1 (1094a20).

in quo est unum et idem esse. Nam auctoritas gubernandi populum, quam videtur importare gladius, requirit consideracionem de hiis quos[1] habet gubernare; secundo, eciam requirit[2] accionem et[3] animadversionem in eos quos habet gubernare. Propter quod unitas huiusmodi auctoritatis vel huiusmodi gladii magis sumenda est ex consideracione unius sciencie, que habet considerare de suis sensibilibus,[4] sicut auctoritas gubernandi habet considerare de suis gubernabilibus,[5] vel pocius sumenda est ex accione unius potencie, que habet agere in sua obiecta,[6] sicut auctoritas gubernandi habet animadvertere et habet agere in sibi subiecta, quam sumenda sit[7] ex unitate unius suppositi, in quo possunt esse talia et tam diversa, quod per se loquendo nec ad consideracionem unius particularis sciencie nec ad accionem unius particularis potencie poterunt pertinere.

Patet ergo quod differencia quam habent spiritualia ad corporalia, quia non cadunt sub una particulari sciencia nec sub una particulari potencia, quam differenciam non habent corpora nostra et res exteriores, facit quod sint duo gladii in Ecclesia, unus spiritualis et unus materialis, et non facit quod sint tres gladii. Ex hac autem via solvitur secundum dubium: videlicet, quare corpora nostra habent alium gladium a gladio spirituali, non autem habent alium gladium a rebus exterioribus. Quia, ut patet per habita, tam corpora nostra quam res exteriores possunt sub eodem particulari gladio collocari, cum possint considerari sub una particulari sciencia et esse sub una particulari potencia.

Tercia via ad hoc idem sumitur ex ordine quem videmus in rebus spiritualibus et corporalibus. Agitur autem in hoc opere de regimine et gubernacione hominum prout homines hominibus presunt, sive istud[8] preesse fiat per potenciam spiritualem, sicut presunt prelati ecclesiastici, sive per potenciam terrenam, sicut presunt seculares principes. Sed cum loquimur de spirituali potencia, semper subintelligendum est quod sit generalis, ut eciam ad temporalia se extendat, ut replicatum est multipharie[9] multisque modis. Dicamus ergo quod omnis talis principatus qui est in hominibus, sive sit ecclesiasticus sive terrenus,[10] statutus et ordinatus est[11] propter electos. Immo, non solum in hominibus sunt tales principatus ordinati propter electos, sed eciam[12] in angelis et[13] demonibus. Quia quando completus erit numerus electorum, quod erit in fine mundi, tunc evacuabuntur omnes principatus, omnes potestates et virtutes, iuxta illud prime[14] ad Corinthios XV: 'Deinde finis,[15] cum tradiderit regnum Deo et Patri, cum evacuaverit omnem principatum et potestatem et virtutem.' Cum ergo Christus, in quantum homo, tradet regnum,[16] idest eos qui bene regnaverunt et bene vixerunt, hoc est electos, 'Deo et

1: quos] quas F   2: secundo, eciam requirit] requirit eciam C requirit eciam secundo FV²   3: et] ad V¹   4: sensibilibus] scibilibus F   5: gubernabilibus] gubernacionibus CFV²   6: obiecta] obiectus V²   7: sit] *om.* V²   8: istud] illud V²   9: multipharie] multipliciter F   10: terrenus] est *add.* C   11: est] *om.* C   12: sed eciam] sicut FV²   13: et] in *add.* CV²   14: prime] primo C   15: finis] fuit V²   16: regnum] *om.* FV²

underlying substance or [unity as an] entity which one and the same being has, which causes something to be under one particular sword. But the authority to govern a people, which seems to connote a sword, requires a consideration of those whom it has the task of governing; second, it also requires action and chastisement in relation to those whom it has the task of governing. And so the unity of such authority or of such a sword is to be understood rather by comparison with the subject matter of a single science (which must consider its sensible objects, just as governing authority must consider those whom it can govern), or rather by comparison with the action of a single [natural] power (which must act upon its objects, just as governing authority must act upon its subjects), than by reference to the unity of a single entity, in which there can be so many different aspects that, speaking of them as such, they will be able to pertain neither to the consideration of one particular science nor to the action of one particular power.

It is clear, therefore, that the difference which holds as between spiritual and corporeal things in that they do not fall under one particular science or under one particular power — which difference does not hold as between our bodies and external goods — means that there are two swords in the Church, the one spiritual and the other material, and does not mean that there are three swords. And, in this way, the second doubt is resolved: namely, that of why our bodies have a sword distinct from the spiritual sword but do not have a sword distinct from that of external goods. For, as is clear from what has been said, our bodies and external goods can equally be placed under the same particular sword, since they can be considered under one particular science and stand under one particular power.

The third way towards the same conclusion is derived from the order which we see among spiritual and bodily things. And the rule and government of men is discussed in this work insofar as it is men who rule over men, whether such ruling be effected by spiritual power, as the prelates of the Church rule, or by earthly power, as secular princes rule. But when we speak of spiritual power, it must always be taken as implied that it is general, in that it extends itself to temporal matters also, as has been repeated in a great many different ways. Let us say, therefore, that every such ruling power as exists among men, be it ecclesiastical or earthly, is established and appointed for the sake of the Elect. Indeed, not only among men, but also among the angels and demons, such ruling powers are appointed for the sake of the Elect. For when the number of the Elect is made up, which will occur at the end of the world, all principalities, all powers and virtues, will then be swept away, according to what is said in I Corinthians 15: 'Then will come the end, when He will have delivered up the Kingdom to God, to the Father Himself, when He will have swept away every principality and power and virtue.'[1] Therefore, when Christ, as Man, shall deliver the Kingdom — that is, those who have ruled well and lived well, that is, the Elect — 'to God, to the

---

1. I Cor. 15:24.

Patri,' idest Patri suo in quantum est Deus, tunc erit finis mundi: tunc ipse[1] evacuabit omnem prelacionem. Hoc[2] est ergo, quod glossa ibidem ait, quod quamdiu durat mundus, angeli angelis, demones demonibus et homines hominibus presunt; sed omnibus[3] collectis, idest quando completus erit numerus electorum, omnis prelacio cessabit. Tunc,[4] ut glossa exponit, Christus evacuabit omnem principatum, id est omnes prelaciones maiores et omnem potestatem, id est omnes[5] prelaciones minores, et omnem virtutem, id est omnes personas[6] forciores qui ex sua fortitudine et sua potencia subiciunt[7] sibi alios et[8] dominium sibi usurpant.[9] Omnis ergo prelacio, sive sit maior sive minor, sive iusta sive per fortitudinem usurpata, cessabit in fine seculi, quando completus erit numerus electorum.

Dicemus enim quod prelacio est quasi quidam caminus ignis et quasi quoddam prelum[10] et quasi quoddam flagellum sive quedam tribula.[11] Videmus autem quod sub eodem igne aurum rutilat et palea fumat; sub eodem pondere preli[12] oleum nitet,[13] amurca[14] fetet; sub eodem flagello sive sub eadem tribula stipula[15] comminuitur et frumentum purgatur. Sic sub eisdem flagellis, sub eisdem principibus,[16] boni purificantur et mali damnantur, ut innuit Augustinus primo *De civitate Dei* capitulo VIII.[17] Verum, quia, ut idem Augustinus vult, omnis malus vel ideo vivit ut corrigatur vel ut per eum bonus exerceatur, ideo omnes iste prelaciones, sive sint angelorum sive demonum sive hominum, Deus ordinavit eas[18] propter bonos et propter electos, cum et ipsos malos Deus ordinet id bonum electorum: videlicet, ut ipsi mali exerceant sive exercitent[19] electos.

Et ut discurramus per singula, ostendemus omnem[20] prelacionem propter electos esse, ut ex ipsis electis ostendamus quot prelaciones et quot gladii sunt in Ecclesia. Declarabimus enim ex hoc quod non sunt nisi duo[21] gladii, spiritualis et terrenus, et quod res exteriores proprium gladium habere non possunt.

Sciendum ergo quod cum hec tercia racio, ex ordine quem habent spiritualia et ex principatu quem videmus in eis, debeat probare[22] intentum. Nos enim videmus quod ordinatus principatus est in spiritualibus propter salutem electorum. Sunt enim in spiritibus[23] tam bonis quam malis ordines varii,[24] secundum quos[25] sibi invicem presunt, quod preesse ad bonum et ad salutem electorum ordinatur. Ideo igitur de[26] utroque fecimus mencionem: et de ipsis ordinibus secundum quod sibi invicem presunt et de ipsa salute electorum, ad quam ordinatur huiusmodi preesse, ut utroque modo nostrum propositum ostendamus. Dicemus ergo de ordinibus spirituum, et primo de ordinibus angelorum, secundo de ordinibus[27] demonum; ex quibus ordines

1: ipse] ergo *add.* C Christus V²   2: Hoc] hic F   3: presunt; sed omnibus] *om.* V²   4: Tunc] et C
5: omnes] principes *add.* FV²   6: prelaciones maiores ... omnes personas] *om.* FV²   7: subiciunt] subiciuntur FV²   8: et] eciam FV²   9: usurpant] usurpatum FV²   10: prelum] prelium FV²
11: tribula] tribulator V²   12: preli] pali F   13: nitet] et *add.* C   14: amurca] amurta F
15: stipula] sticula V²   16: principibus] principatibus C   17: VIII] vii *mss*   18: eas] *del.* C
19: exercitent] exercent F exercerent V²   20: omnem] *om.* F   21: gladii sunt ... duo] *om.* F
22: probare] plure C   23: spiritibus] spiritualibus FV²   24: ordines varii] varii ordines FV²
25: quos] quod V²   26: de] in FV²   27: spirituum, et ... ordinibus] *om.* V²

Father Himself,' that is, to His Father as God, then will come the end of the world: then will He sweep away all rule. So it is, therefore, as a gloss on the same passage says, that, for as long as this world endures, angels rule angels, demons demons and men men, but that when all are brought together — that is, when the number of the Elect is made up — all rule will cease.[1] Then, as the gloss explains, Christ will sweep away every principality, that is, all greater rulers; and every power, that is, all lesser rulers; and every virtue, that is, all mighty men who, by their force and power, subject others to themselves and usurp lordship to themselves. Therefore, all rule, whether greater or lesser, whether just or usurped by force, will cease at the end of the world, when the number of the Elect is made up.[2]

For we shall say that rule is like a kind of furnace of fire and like a kind of press and like a kind of flail or a kind of threshing-sledge. But we see that, under the same fire, gold shines and straw smokes; under the same weight of the press, oil glistens and the pulp reeks; under the same flail or under the same threshing-sledge the chaff is crushed and the grain purified. So, under the same flails, under the same princes, the good are purified and the wicked damned, as Augustine suggests at *De civitate Dei* 1:8.[3] Truly, because, as the same Augustine maintains, every wicked man lives either so that he may be corrected or so that, through him, the good man may be tried, God has therefore ordained all these rulers, whether of angels or of demons or of men, for the sake of the good and for the sake of the Elect: that is, so that the wicked may themselves try or tempt the Elect.[4]

And as we deal with each [i.e. with angels, demons and men] in turn, we shall show that all rule exists for the sake of the Elect, so that we may show from the Elect themselves how many rulers and how many swords there are in the Church. For we shall show from this that there are only two swords in the Church, the spiritual and the earthly, and that external goods cannot have a sword of their own.

It must be known, therefore, that our case may be proved from this third argument: from the order which spiritual beings have and from the ruling power which we see among them. For we see that ruling power is appointed among spiritual beings for the salvation of the Elect. For among spirits, whether good or evil, there are various orders according to which they mutually rule themselves; and this rule is ordered towards the good and towards the salvation of the Elect. So, then: we have made mention both of the orders according to which they mutually rule themselves, and of the salvation of the Elect for the sake of which such rule is appointed, so that we may demonstrate our proposition in two ways. We shall speak, therefore, of the orders of the spirits: first, of the orders of the angels and, second, of the orders of the demons. And, from these orders, and from

---

1.   *Glossa ordinaria*, PL 114:547.
2.   Cf. Rev. 7:3–9.
3.   CCSL 47:8.
4.   Cf. Peter Lombard, *Collectanea in omnes de Pauli apostoli epistolas*, PL 191:1504.

et ex salute electorum ad quam huiusmodi ordines ordinantur quesita veritas declaretur.

Advertendum itaque quod angeli sibi invicem presunt propter regimen universi, ut universum sic regatur et gubernetur quod electi salvi fiant.[1] Si enim aliquis[2] rex vellet regere aliquod regnum, primo essent illi qui semper essent circa regem; et tales tripartiti essent, quia vel essent[3] dilecti et amici regis,[4] vel essent sapientes et assisterent regi, vel tercio essent qui promulgarent aliis et publicarent iudicia et beneplacita regis.[5] Post istos essent illi qui se intromitterent de questionibus tocius regni. Tercio, essent illi qui non de toto regno, sed de partibus regni se intromitterent. Eodem eciam modo, si rex vellet facere aliquod edificium,[6] primo essent illi qui semper assisterent regi, qui, ut diximus, essent tripartiti, quia vel essent dilecti[7] et amici regis vel essent[8] sapientes vel essent regis[9] iudicia et beneplacita promulgantes. Per hos ergo sciretur quale edificium rex vellet[10] fieri.[11] Secundo, essent illi qui se intromitterent de toto edificio, qui eciam essent tripartiti, quia vel hoc facerent[12] precipiendo qualiter edificium fiat, sicut faciunt architectores, vel hoc agerent amminicula exhibendo, ut edificium promoveatur, vel impedimenta removendo, ne edificium detrimentum paciatur. Tercio, essent illi qui non se intromitterent de toto edificio, sed de partibus edificii, qui se[13] haberent sicut inferiores operarii. Et hii essent[14] tripartiti, quia aliqui facerent[15] principaliores partes, ut illi[16] qui componerent parietem vel[17] tectum, et aliqui operarentur particulares partes, ut hii[18] qui dolarent lapides et ligna, et isti essent[19] bipartiti, quia[20] aliqui dolarent lapides maiores et ligna excellenciora, aliqui lapides minores et ligna minus excellencia.

Sic et in proposito. In gubernacione mundi et in regimine universi aliqui sunt angeli qui[21] coniuncti Deo et in vestibulis Dei scientes voluntatem eius, qualiter vult quod universum regatur; et ista est hierarchia prima, que continet tres ordines: dilectos, sapientes et iudicia proferentes. Dilecti sunt seraphim, sapientes[22] cherubim, iudicia proferentes throni. Inter angelos quidem plus est[23] esse dilectum quam sapientem, quia ibi[24] dileccio est causa sciencie; nam ex eo quod quis est dilectus a Deo, ex hoc scit secreta Dei. Et plus est esse sapientem quam iudicantem, quia sciencia est causa iudicii, ut unusquisque bene iudicat de hiis que novit. Seraphim itaque sunt supra cherubim, et cherubim supra thronos. Seraphim ergo,

---

1: fiant] fient FV[2]   2: aliquis] aliquid V[2]   3: quia vel essent] *om.* V[2]   4: regis] regni V[2]
5: regis] regni FPV[1]V[2]   6: edificum] beneficium F   7: dilecti] electi P   8: essent] *om.* P
9: regis] regni FPV[1]V[2]   10: rex vellet] vellet rex CFV[2]   11: fieri] facere F   12: tripartiti, quia …
facerent] *om.* V[2]   13: se] *om.* V[2]   14: essent] sunt FV[2]   15: facerent] faciunt F   16: illi]
aliqui F   17: vel] *om.* F   18: hii] illi CFV[2]   19: essent] *om.* V[2]   20: quia] si V[2]   21: qui]
quia V[2]   22: sapientes] *om.* V[2]   23: est] autem *add. and del.* C   *add.* FV[2]   24: ibi] sapientem
add. and del. C

the salvation of the faithful for the sake of which such orders are appointed, the truth of the matter may be revealed.

Thus, it must be noted that the angels mutually rule themselves for the sake of the government of the universe, so that the universe may be ruled and governed in such a way that the Elect may be saved.[1] For if any king wished to rule a kingdom, in the first place there would be those who would be always near the king; and these would be of three kinds. For they would either be those whom the king loved and who were his friends; or they would be wise men, and would stand near the king; or, third, they would be those who promulgated and published to others the king's judgments and decrees. After these, there would be those who concerned themselves with questions affecting the whole kingdom; and, third, there would be those who concerned themselves not with the whole kingdom, but with the parts of the kingdom. And, in the same way, if the king wished to construct a building, in the first place there would be those who would stand always near the king, who, as we have said, would be of three kinds. For they would either be those whom the king loved and who were his friends; or they would be wise men; or they would be promulgators of the king's judgments and decrees. Through these, therefore, it would be made known what kind of building the king wished to be constructed. Second, there would be those who would concern themselves with the whole building; who, again, would be of three kinds. For they would either give instruction as to the construction of the building, as do architects; or they would act by giving assistance, so that the building might be expedited; or by removing obstacles, so that the building should not suffer detriment. Third, there would be those who would concern themselves not with the whole building, but with the parts of the building: who would act as lower workmen; and these would be of three kinds. For some would make the more important parts, as in the case of those who would construct the walls or the roof; and others would be occupied with particular parts, as in the case of those who would cut stone and wood, and these would be of two kinds, for some would cut the larger stones and the more excellent wood, and some the smaller stones and the less excellent wood.

So also in our proposition. In the government of the world and in the rule of the universe there are some angels who are united with God and who stand in the presence of God, knowing His will and how He wishes the universe to be governed. And this is the first hierarchy, which contains three orders: the Beloved, the Wise, and the Publishers of Judgments. The Beloved are the Seraphim, the Wise are the Cherubim, and the Publishers of Judgments are the Thrones. And, among the angels, it is greater to be beloved than to be wise; for love is there the cause of wisdom because one who is beloved of God for this reason knows the secrets of God. And it is greater to be wise than to be a judge, because wisdom is the cause of judgment, so that each judges well concerning those matters which he knows.[2] Thus, the Seraphim are above the Cherubim and the Cherubim above the Thrones. Therefore the

1. For the argument of this and the following paragraphs, see Ps.-Dionysius, *De caelesti hierarchia* 6 (PG 3:199).
2. Cf. Aristotle, *Nicomachean Ethics* 1:3 (1094^{b}25).

tamquam dilecti Dei et primo cognoscentes secreta Dei qualiter universum regi debeat ut salventur[1] electi, de illis secretis illuminant cherubim, ut et ipsi dicantur sapientes et scientes secreta Dei. Nam et 'cherub' 'sciens'[2] vel 'plenitudo sciencie' interpretatur. Cherubim vero, iam[3] illuminati per seraphim et iam scientes secreta et iudicia Dei, illuminant thronos, ut ipsi illa iudicia et illa secreta de regimine universi annuncient aliis et illuminent[4] alios. In thronis ergo dicitur sedere Deus et in eis sua iudicia proferre, quia iudicia Dei de regimine universi annunciant throni inferioribus hierarchiis.

Hec est itaque hierarchia prima, hos tres ordines continens, qui sciunt modo quo diximus[5] Dei secreta[6] de regimine universi propter salutem electorum, et annunciant hoc[7] aliis hierarchiis.

Secunda quidem hierarchia est se intromittens de ipso generali regimine universi. Et hec continet tres ordines, quia illi qui presunt toti operi vel presunt precipiendo qualiter omnia fiant, et iste sunt dominaciones, a 'dominando' dicte, quia dominantur et precipiunt qualiter in hoc regimine omnia fienda sunt; vel sic presunt toti operi adminicula exhibendo, et huiusmodi sunt virtutes, quibus tribuitur miracula facere in adminiculum gubernacionis mundi et salutis electorum; vel sic presunt impediencia removendo, et iste sunt potestates, cohercentes demones[8] et potestates tenebrarum, ne[9] impediatur regimen universi, et ne temptent electos et universaliter omnes homines[10] ultra id quod possunt.

Prima ergo hierarchia, quantum ad regimen universi, sunt sicut[11] secretarii et sicut illi qui prius sciunt secreta Dei et eius iudicia; secunda vero sunt quasi architectores, qui principalius se intromittunt[12] de regimine universi; tercia quidem sunt quasi inferiores operarii, quia sunt illi qui deputantur ad custodiendum partes universi. Sed huiusmodi partes vel est aliqua tota multitudo, ut aliqua tota provincia; et isti sunt principatus, de quorum numero erat[13] princeps Persarum qui preerat Persis, ut habetur in Daniele, vel princeps alius qui preest alii genti. Vel huiusmodi partes universi non sunt multitudo vel provincia, sed singulares persone, circa quas vel exercent que sunt maiora, quod faciunt archangeli, qui sunt[14] principaliores nuncii. 'Archos' enim 'princeps', 'angelus' vero 'nuncius' interpretatur, unde 'archangelus' quasi 'princeps nuncius'[15] vel 'principalis nuncius' esse dicitur. Vel exercent[16] que sunt minora: et hoc faciunt angeli, qui sunt quasi simplices nuncii.

1: salventur] salvetur et F   2: sciens] *om.* F   3: iam] *om.* V[1]   4: illuminent] illuminant P
5: diximus] *om.* FV[2]   6: secreta] scripta FV   7: hoc] et *add.* F   8: demones] dominationes V[2]
9: ne] magnum ut FV[2]   10: homines] et *add.* CFV[2]   11: sunt sicut] sicut sunt FV[2]   12: intromittunt] intromittant V[2]   13: erat] erit FV[2]   14: sunt] *om.* V[2]   15: nuncius] esse *add.* V[2]
16: exercent] exercet F

Seraphim, as the beloved of God and the first knowers of the secret intentions of God as to how the universe should be governed so that the Elect may be saved, enlighten the Cherubim concerning those secrets, so that they also may be called wise, and knowers of the secrets of God. For 'Cherub' also means 'knowing' or 'fullness of wisdom'. And the Cherubim, now enlightened by the Seraphim, and now knowing the secrets and the judgments of God, enlighten the Thrones, so that they themselves may announce those judgments and those secrets of the government of the universe to others, and enlighten others. God is therefore said to sit among the Thrones and to publish His judgments through them;[1] for the Thrones announce the judgments of God concerning the government of the universe to the lower hierarchies.

This, then, is the first hierarchy, containing these three orders, who, in the manner we have described, know the secrets of God concerning the government of the universe for the salvation of the Elect, and announce this to the other hierarchies.

And the second hierarchy is that which concerns itself with the general government of the universe. And this contains three orders. For there are those who rule over the whole work, or who rule by giving instruction as to how all things are to be done; and these are the Dominations [*Dominationes*], so called from 'ruling' [*a 'dominando' dicte*] because they are the lords who rule and give instruction as to how all things in the government must be accomplished. Or there are those who rule over the whole world by giving assistance; and these are the Virtues, to whom it is given to perform miracles for the aid of the government of the world and the salvation of the Elect. Or there are those who rule by removing impediments; and these are the Powers, who coerce the demons and the powers of darkness lest the government of the universe be impeded, and lest they tempt the Elect, and all men generally, to go beyond what they can [rightly do].

So far as the government of the universe is concerned, therefore, the members of the first hierarchy are like counsellors, and like those who first know the secrets of God and His judgments. And the members of the second are like architects, who concern themselves more principally with the government of the universe. And the members of the third are like lower workmen; for these are they who are charged with the custody of the parts of the universe. But such parts consist either of some whole multitude, for example, some whole region; and these are [entrusted to] the Principalities, of which number was the Prince of the Persians who, as is established in Daniel,[2] ruled Persia, or some other [angelic] prince who rules another nation. Or such parts of the universe consist not of a multitude or region, but of single persons, in relation to whom they [i.e. the angels] perform either the greater tasks which the Archangels, who are the more principal messengers, accomplish (for 'archos' is translated [from the Greek] as 'prince' and 'angelus' as 'messenger', so that 'Archangel' is to be rendered as 'prince-messenger' or 'principal messenger'); or they perform lesser tasks, and this is done by the Angels, who are as it were messengers merely.

1. Cf. Rev. 4:2–11.
2. Cf. Dan. 10:13.

Apparet ergo ex dictis quod omnes tres hierarchie celestium spirituum, ut[1] hierarchie sunt et[2] ut sacri principatus sunt, et omnes ordines ibi existentes, ordinati sunt et[3] sibi invicem presunt ut requirit[4] regimen universi et salus electorum.

Dictum est supra[5] de principatu angelorum quod ordinatus est propter[6] electorum salutem.[7] Dicendum est ergo de principatu demonum, qui eciam ordinatus est propter salutem electorum: non quod ipsi demones[8] salutem electorum[9] intendant, sed quia diligentibus Deum omnia cooperantur in bonum, ut dicitur ad Romanos VIII. Ideo ipse insidie demonum, quas demones ordinant in malum hominum,[10] cooperantur in bonum electorum, quia electi per demonum insidias exercitati[11] proficiunt et merentur. Nam non solum insidie demonum, sed tribulaciones quas paciuntur malis hominibus, diligentibus Deum[12] et hiis qui secundum propositum vocati sunt sancti, idest electis,[13] cooperantur in bonum. Immo, et peccata propria cooperantur[14] eis in bonum, prout resurgentes a peccatis humiliores et devociores fiunt.

Dicamus[15] ergo quod, sicut boni angeli sunt ad invicem ordinati propter salutem electorum, sic et demones ex sua nequicia seipsos ordinant ut hominibus magis nocere possint. Sed licet demones, et specialiter ille Lucifer draco, intendat nocere Ecclesie et electis, Deus tamen[16] illudit sibi, quia insidias eius convertit in bonum Ecclesie et electorum, iuxta illud Psalmi: 'Draco iste quem formasti ad illudendum ei'; quod exponens Augustinus XI[17] *Super Genesim* ait quod diabolo illuditur[18] cum de malevolencia ipsius Ecclesie Dei consulitur. Sed licet sic illudatur diabolus et convertatur in bonum Ecclesie quod ipse machinatur in malum, ipsi tamen demones ordinant[19] se[20] ut magis possint nocere nobis. Sciendum ergo quod in demonibus possumus distinguere quatuor ordines. Nam ordines prime hierarchie ibi esse non possunt, cum omnes illi ordines sint in vestibulis Dei et sint collaterales Dei. Nec dominaciones ibi sunt,[21] de quibus ait Dionysius quod sunt absoluti ab omni pedestri minoracione, id est ab omni depressione, ut exponit Hugo: quod demonibus non potest competere, cum sint sic depressi. Nec eciam sunt ibi virtutes, quarum est miracula facere. Alios autem ordines possumus ibi adaptare, ut sicut in bonis angelis sunt potestates, principatus, archangeli et angeli, sic et in[22] malis angelis sunt potestates, principatus,[23] archidemones

---

1: ut] vel F   2: et] *om.* F   3: et] ut C   4: requirit] requiratur FV[2]   5: supra] ergo FV[2]
6: propter] quod *add.* FV[2]   7: electorum salutem] salutem electorum FV[2]   8: salutem electorum ... demones] *om.* F   9: non quod ... electorum] *om.* V[2]   10: hominum] hominem V[2]
11: exercitati] exterriti F   12: diligentibus Deum] *om.* F   13: electis] electi F   14: in bonum ...
cooperantur] *om.* V[2]   15: Dicamus] dicimus FV[2]   16: tamen] cum *add. and del.* C cum F
17: XI] x *mss*   18: illuditur] illud dicitur F   19: ordinant] *om.* F semper armant *marg.* V[2]
20: se] exercent *add.* F   21: ibi sunt] *om.* F   22: in] *om.* V[2]   23: archangeli et ... principatus] *om.* F

From what has been said, therefore, it is clear that all three hierarchies of the heavenly spirits, inasmuch as they are hierarchies and inasmuch as they exercise a sacred power of ruling, and all the orders therein existing, are ordered, and mutually rule themselves, as the government of the universe and the salvation of the Elect requires.

We have said above of the ruling power of the angels that it has been appointed for the salvation of the Elect. Therefore, we must now speak of the ruling power of the demons, which is also appointed for the salvation of the Elect: not because the demons themselves intend the salvation of the Elect, but because, as is said in Romans 8: 'To those who love God, all things work together for good.'[1] Thus, even the snares of the demons, which the demons set for the harm of men, work together for the good of the Elect, because the Elect profit and earn merit when tempted by the snares of the demons. But not only do the snares of the demons work together for good to those who love God and to those who are called saints according to His purpose: so also do the tribulations which they suffer at the hands of wicked men. Indeed, even their own sins work together for good to them, in that, when they rise from sin, they are made the more humble and the more devout.

Let us say, therefore, that just as the good angels are mutually ordered for the salvation of the Elect, so also the demons, by their own wickedness, order themselves in such a way that men may be the more harmed. But although the demons, and especially that dragon Lucifer, intend to harm the Church and the Elect, God nonetheless makes sport of him, because He turns his snares towards the good of the Church and of the Elect, according to the Psalm: 'This dragon which You have formed to make sport therein.'[2] For, interpreting this, Augustine says in *De Genesi ad litteram* 11 that the devil is made sport of when the Church of God is mindful of his wickedness.[3] But although the devil is thus made sport of, and that which he devises for harm turned towards the good of the Church, the demons nonetheless order themselves in such a way that they may do us more harm. It must be known, therefore, that we can distinguish [only] four orders among the demons [as distinct from the nine orders of the angelic hierarchies]. For the orders of the first hierarchy cannot be there, since all those orders are in the courts of God and are the companions of God. Nor are there Dominations there, of which Dionysius says that they are absolved from all lowly servitude:[4] that is, as Hugh explains, from being in any way cast down;[5] which cannot be true of the demons, for they certainly are cast down. Nor again are there Virtues there, whose task it is to perform miracles. But we can find counterparts of the other orders there, so that, just as there are Powers, Principalities, Archangels, and Angels among the good angels, so also are there Powers, Principalities,

1.   Rom. 8:28.
2.   Psalm 104:26.
3.   *De Genesi ad litteram* 11:20; 22; 29 (CSEL 28(1): 352–353; 354–355; 361–362).
4.   *De caelesti hierarchia* 8 (PG 3:237).
5.   Hugh of Saint Victor, *Expositio in hierarchiam caelestem* 8 (PL 175:1075).

et demones, ut dicantur potestates in demonibus, qui de toto universo, ut obesse possint, se intromittunt; principatus autem,[1] qui non toti universo sed toti alicui provincie insidiantur; archidemones autem et demones dicantur, qui nec toti universo nec toti[2] provincie sed singularibus personis deputantur ad insidiandum: differenter tamen, quia[3] archidemones insidiantur circa maiora, simplices demones circa minora. Archidemones[4] enim et demones sic se habent insidiando sicut archangeli et angeli in proficiendo. Hos autem quatuor ordines demonum tangit Apostolus ad Ephesios VI, cum dicit quod 'non est nobis colluctacio adversus carnem et sanguinem, sed adversus principes et potestates, adversus mundi rectores, qui sunt rectores[5] tenebrarum harum, et contra spiritualia nequicie.' Quatuor ergo ordines tetigit: videlicet, principes,[6] potestates,[7] rectores mundi sive rectores tenebrarum, qui[8] sunt[9] dici archidemones, et spiritualia nequicie, idest spirituales nequam hostes, qui communi nomine possunt dici demones.

Hiis itaque prelibatis et distinctis ordinibus angelorum et demonum, dicemus quod ibi est considerare et eorum ordines et finem ad quem[10] ordinantur tales ordines; ex quolibet enim horum possumus descendere ad materiam nostram. Nam quod sunt plures hierarchie angelorum et quod in qualibet hierarchia sunt plures ordines, non est quod prima hierarchia non possit quod potest secunda, et quod secunda non possit quod potest tercia, quamvis non econverso. Quia non potest tercia quod potest secunda, nec potest secunda[11] quod potest prima. Sic et de ordinibus cuiuscumque hierarchie. Nam quicquid potest secundus ordo[12] hierarchie cuiuslibet[13] potest primus, sed non econverso; et[14] quicquid potest tercius potest secundus, sed[15] non econverso.

Si vero[16] angeli sic sunt ordinati et sic sunt distincti in salutem nostram et in nostrum bonum,[17] nec superfluunt ad regimen universi angeli inferiores propter superiores,[18] quamvis quicquid possunt inferiores, possint superiores, multo ergo magis debent esse distincti principatus et distincte potestates inter ipsos homines. Quia[19] si sunt angeli distincti et ordinati in bonum hominum,[20] ipsi homines in bonum suum proprium[21] non minus,[22] immo forte magis, debent esse sic distincti et ordinati; nec superfluet[23] potestas et gladius inferior propter potestatem et gladium superiorem, quantumcumque quicquid[24] potest gladius inferior, possit et superior. Hoc idem[25] et de demonibus dicimus, quia si sic se ordinant et distinguunt se in nostrum malum, bonum est quod et in nobis[26] sint ordinati et distincti principatus in nostrum bonum.

Angeli ergo in duas partes sunt divisi, quia aliqui fuerunt remanentes et

---

1: autem] dicantur add. CV²   2: universo nec toti] om. F   3: quia] om. FV²   4: circa minora. Archidemones] om. F   5: rectores] mundi add. FV²   6: principes] om. mss   7: potestates] potestas principatus CV²   8: qui] om. FPV¹V²   9: sunt] possunt C   10: quem] quam P   11: potest secunda] secunda potest F   12: ordo] vel tercius cuiuscumque add. F potest tercius add. V²   13: cuiuslibet] om. F   14: et] om. F   15: sed] et F   16: vero] ergo FV²   17: nostrum bonum] bonum nostrum CFV²   18: propter superiores] om. F   19: Quia] sint homines quia add. V²   20: hominum] om. V²   21: proprium] propositum FV²   22: minus] nimius V¹   23: superfluet] superfluit FV²   24: quicquid] interlin. C quod FV²   25: idem] om. V¹   26: nobis] ibi V²

Archdemons, and Demons among the wicked angels. Thus, there may be said to be Powers among the demons, who concern themselves with the whole universe so that they may obstruct it; and there are Principalities, who lay snares not for the whole universe, but for the whole of a certain region. And there may be said to be Archdemons and Demons, who are given the task of ensnaring neither the whole universe nor a whole region, but single persons: in differing ways, however, for the Archdemons lay snares in respect of greater matters and the mere Demons in respect of lesser; for the Archdemons and Demons act in the laying of snares as do the Archangels and Angels in the conferring of benefits. And the Apostle touches upon these four orders of demons in Ephesians 6, when he says that 'Our wrestling is not against flesh and blood, but against principalities and powers, against the rulers of the world, who are the rulers of darkness, and against the spirits of wickedness.'[1] He mentions four orders, therefore: namely, Principalities; Powers; the rulers of the world or the rulers of darkness, who can be called Archdemons; and the spirits of wickedness, that is, the wicked spiritual enemies who can be called by the general name of demons.[2]

Thus, having first touched upon these considerations and discerned the orders of the angels and of the demons, we shall say that it is here necessary to consider both their orders and the end to which such orders are directed. For we can pass to our subject matter from each of these [points of departure]. For the fact that there are several hierarchies of angels and that there are several orders in each hierarchy does not mean that the first hierarchy cannot do what the second can do and that the second cannot do what the third can do; although the converse is not true (for the third cannot do what the second can do and the second cannot do what the first can do). And so too with the orders of each hierarchy: for whatever the second order of each hierarchy can do the first can do, but not the converse; and whatever the third can do the second can do, but not the converse.

Thus, if the angels are so ordered and so ranked for the sake of our salvation and our good, yet the lower angels are not superfluous to the higher in the government of the universe even though the higher can do whatever the lower can, then the principalities and powers which exist among men themselves must be even more clearly ranked. For if the angels are ranked and ordered for the good of men, men themselves must be not less, but indeed more, ranked and ordered in this way for their own good. Nor will an inferior power and sword be superfluous to a superior power and sword, however much the superior sword can do whatever the inferior can. And we say this also of the demons; for if they so order and rank themselves for the sake of harming us, it is good that the ruling powers which exist among us should be ordered and ranked for our good.

The angels, therefore, are separated into two classes;[3] for some have remained

1. Eph. 6:12.
2. Cf. Aquinas, *Summa theologiae* Ia 114.
3. Cf. Aquinas, *Summa theologiae*, Ia 69:3.

aliqui cadentes, et tam in remanentibus quam in cadentibus distinguimus varios principatus et varios ordines. Hominum autem genus non distinguitur per cadentes et remanentes, ut quod aliqui homines fuerint eiecti de paradiso et aliqui ibi remanserint,[1] sicut aliqui angeli fuerunt[2] eiecti de celo empireo et aliqui ibi remanserunt; quia totum humanum genus quod primitus reservabatur in primis parentibus, in Adam videlicet et Heva, eiectum fuit de paradiso. Non ergo poterimus in hominibus distinguere principatus in[3] duas partes[4] modo quo distinguimus in angelis, quantum ad cadentes et remanentes. Sed distinguemus principatus in hominibus secundum ea[5] quibus componitur homo, qui compositus est ex corpore et spiritu.

Erunt itaque duo[6] gladii et due potestates in Ecclesia: gladius videlicet spiritualis, et corporalis sive materialis, ita quod,[7] si consideramus ipsos ordines angelorum, viam habemus ad distinguendum duos principatus in Ecclesia, sacerdotalem et regalem, spiritualem et terrenum, iuxta duas partes ex quibus componitur homo. In quolibet autem huiusmodi principatu, tam spirituali quam materiali, sunt diversi gradus et ordines; qui gradus et qui ordines, cum uterque principatus sit bonus, tam sacerdotalis quam regalis, non sunt accipiendi prout habent esse in malis angelis, sed prout habent in bonis esse.[8] Et sicut in bonis habent esse tres hierarchie et novem ordines, sic leviter adaptari posset ad principatum sacerdotalem sive ecclesiasticum ternarius hierarchiarum et novenarius ordinum.

Diceremus enim quod Summus Pontifex se habet[9] sicut Dei vicarius, respectu cuius sumitur, vel sumi potest, quasi triplex hierarchia. Nam primo sunt collaterales et semper assistentes sibi, et hii sunt tripartiti in episcopos, presbiteros et diaconos, et hoc dici poterit quasi hierarchia prima, quasi tres ordines continens; et ideo forte nullus subdiaconus fit cardinalis, quia[10] hierarchia illa contineret[11] quatuor gradus, quo posito non perfecte representaret hierarchiam celestem. Secundam autem quasi hierarchiam faciunt prelati per universum mundum sparsi, quorum[12] eciam sunt quasi tres gradus, quia quidam sunt primates sive patriarche, quidam autem archiepiscopi, quidam episcopi. Terciam autem quasi hierarchiam constituunt alii inferiores clerici, quam eciam possemus[13] distinguere in tres gradus. Quia quidam sunt habentes iurisdiccionem[14] in foro publico potentes excommunicacionis sentenciam ferre, et[15] huiusmodi sunt archidiaconi vel alii habentes personatus sive dignitates in ecclesiis, ad quos spectat in foro publico iurisdiccionem habere. In secundo autem gradu sunt sacerdotes curati, quibus non simpliciter in foro publico, sed in foro consciencie est commissa animarum cura. In tercio quidem gradu sunt alii clerici qui nec curam habent animarum in foro consciencie nec iurisdiccionem in foro publico, cuiusmodi sunt alii clerici, quorum aliqui, etsi

---

1: remanserint] remanserunt V² 2: fuerunt] sunt F 3: principatus in] *om.* F 4: partes] potestates F 5: ea] ex *add.* CV² 6: duo] et *add.* C 7: ita quod] itaque F 8: in bonis esse] esse in bonis CFV² 9: habet] habent P 10: quia] *om.* FP 11: contineret] continet FP continens V¹ 12: quorum] *om.* CFV² 13: possemus] possimus C 14: iurisdiccionem] iurisdicciones FV² 15: et] *om.* FV²

steadfast and others have fallen. And, among those who have remained steadfast and those who have fallen alike, we discern various ruling powers and various orders. But the human race is not divided into those who have fallen and those who have remained steadfast, as though some men had been expelled from Paradise and others remained there, just as some angels were expelled from the empyrean heaven[1] while others remained there; for the whole human race originally contained in our first parents — that is, in Adam and Eve — was expelled from Paradise. Among men, therefore, we shall not be able to distinguish the ruling powers into two classes as we can distinguish the angels in terms of those who have fallen and those who have remained steadfast. We can, however, distinguish the ruling powers [which exist] among men in terms of those elements of which man is composed; for he is composed of body and spirit.

Thus, there will be two swords and two powers in the Church: namely, a spiritual and a bodily or material sword. Hence, if we consider the orders of the angels themselves, we have a way of distinguishing the two ruling powers in the Church — priestly and royal, spiritual and earthly — in terms of the two parts of which man is composed. And in each of these ruling powers, whether spiritual or material, there are different ranks and orders; which ranks and orders, because both ruling powers, priestly and royal alike, are good, are not to be understood as resembling those which exist among the wicked angels, but as resembling those which exist among the good. And just as there are three hierarchies and nine orders among the good, so might a corresponding threefold hierarchy and ninefold order easily be identified in the priestly or ecclesiastical ruling power.

For we would say that the Supreme Pontiff stands as the Vicar of God, and that, around him, a kind of threefold hierarchy is provided or can be discerned. For the first consists of his counsellors and of those who stand always near him [i.e. the cardinals]; and these are divided in three ways: into bishops, priests, and deacons. And it will be possible to say that this is like the first hierarchy, containing some three orders. (And perhaps it is for this reason that no subdeacon becomes a cardinal; for this hierarchy would then contain four ranks and, this being so, would not perfectly reflect the celestial hierarchy.) And the second kind of hierarchy is made up of the prelates who are spread throughout the whole world, of whom, again, there are some three ranks. For some are primates or patriarchs, and some are archbishops, and some are bishops. And the third hierarchy includes all the lower clergy, which, again, we may divide into three ranks. For some have jurisdiction in a public court with power to impose a sentence of excommunication; and these are the archdeacons or other persons who hold offices or dignities in the churches whose task it is to have jurisdiction in a public court. And in the second rank are the priests who have the cure of souls: to whom the cure of souls is entrusted not directly in a public court, but in the court of conscience. And in the third rank are the remaining clergy, who have neither the cure of souls in the court of conscience nor jurisdiction in a public court. Of this kind are the rest of the clergy [monks or university teachers, for instance], some of whom, even though

---

1. Cf. Aquinas, *Summa theologiae* Ia 66:3.

sunt[1] magis[2] litterati, non est commissa eis[3] cura regiminis, nec Summo Pontifici assistendo nec in foro publico iurisdiccionem exercendo nec in foro consciencie curam animarum habendo; propter quod, quantum ad regimen[4] universi, prout tale regimen est sub principatu ecclesiastico infimum gradum tenent, quantumcumque sint magis[5] litterati.

Hiis[6] visis, dicamus quod sicut distinximus quasi tres hierarchias et quasi novem ordines sive novem gradus in clericis et in principatu ecclesiastico, ita possemus omnia hec aliqualiter invenire in laicis et in principatu imperiali, ut primus esset imperator, circa quem essent reges et[7] principes et duces, qui facerent quasi hierarchiam primam, et sic de aliis qui facerent hierarchias alias. Sed de hoc non sit nobis cure.

In tantum ergo dictum sit quod, si consideramus ipsos ordines angelorum, viam habemus ad distinguendum gladios qui sunt in Ecclesia. Habemus eciam viam ad hoc idem si consideramus[8] fines istorum ordinum. Nam finis ordinum angelorum est gubernacio mundi et salus electorum; finis eciam[9] ordinum in demonibus, non prout demones se ordinant et demones intendunt, sed prout Deus ordinat et prout Deus[10] illudit, est eciam salus et profectus[11] electorum, quia Deus maliciam demonum convertit in bonum nostrum, idest in bonum electorum. Ergo propter electos debent esse omnia ista regimina et omnes isti principatus: nam omnes huiusmodi principatus,[12] sive sint hominum sive angelorum sive demonum,[13] ordinati sunt modo quo diximus ad bonum electorum. Sed[14] ipsi electi resurgent in anima et corpore et habebunt illa et eadem corpora que nunc habent, iuxta illud Iob: 'Et in carne mea videbo Deum salvatorem meum,[15] quem visurus sum ego ipse et non alius.' Caro autem sine anima non posset videre Deum salvatorem suum. In utroque ergo resurgent electi, in corpore et anima. Rursus, si non resurgeret electus in eadem[16] carne et in eodem corpore, non videret 'ipsemet' qui prius fuit, sed esset factus 'alius.' Quilibet enim electus, ipse idem, '[et] non alius' factus, videbit Deum salvatorem suum. Corpora ergo et anime per se pertinent ad electos, quia omnes resurgent in corpore et anima.

Res autem exteriores, quas dicimus esse divicias, per se non pertinent ad electos, ideo per se non[17] debuerunt habere gladium. Nam divicie sive res exteriores sic sunt distincte, ut supra tetigimus, quia quedam sunt divicie artificiales, ut aurum, argentum et cetera metalla, et quedam naturales. Artificiales autem divicie sunt propter naturales. Divicie autem naturales quasi in quinque partes distinguuntur; quia vel sunt emolumentum quod habemus ex arboribus et plantis, vel amminiculum quod habemus ex vineis, vel sunt condimentum quod habemus ex olivis et fructibus pinguibus, vel cibus[18] quem habemus ex segetibus[19] et arvis, vel

---

1: sunt] sint F   2: magis] magni FV[2]   3: commissa eis] eis commissa CF eis tamen commissa V[2]
4: regimen] regimine C   5: magis] magni CFV[2]   6: Hiis] itaque *add.* FV[2]   7: et] *om.* CFV[2]
8: consideramus] consideremus FV[2]   9: eciam] autem C   10: Deus] eis *add.* C   11: et profectus]
om. FV[2]   12: nam omnes huiusmodi principatus] *om.* CFV[2]   13: demonum] nam omnes huiusmodi principatus *add.* C   14: Sed] si F   15: salvatorem meum] meum salvatorem C   16: eadem]
om. F   17: pertinent ad ... se non] *om.* F   18: cibus] cibum FV[2]   19: segetibus] sementibus F
seietibus V[2]

more learned [than those who hold judicial office or have benefices], are not entrusted with the business of government: neither with assisting the Supreme Pontiff, nor with exercising jurisdiction in a public court, nor with having the cure of souls in the court of conscience. Thus, with regard to the government of the universe, insofar as such government is subject to ecclesiastical rule these hold the lowest rank no matter how much more learned they may be.

Having looked into these matters, let us say that, just as we have distinguished some three hierarchies and some nine orders or nine ranks among the clergy and in the ruling power of the Church, so in some fashion can we discover all of these among the laity and in the ruling power of the empire. Thus, in the first place, there would be the emperor, around whom there would be the kings and princes and dukes who would as it were make up the first hierarchy; and so too there would be others, composing the other hierarchies. But of this it is not our business to speak.

In short, therefore, it may be said that, if we consider the orders of the angels themselves, we have a way of distinguishing the swords which are in the Church. Also, we have a way of making the same distinction if we consider the purposes of those orders. For the purpose of the orders of the angels is the government of the world and the salvation of the Elect. And the purpose of the orders which exist among the demons is also the salvation and benefit of the Elect: not because of how the demons order themselves and what the demons intend, but because of what God ordains and insofar as God makes sport of them. For God turns the malice of the demons to our good: that is, to the good of the Elect. Therefore, all these governments and all these ruling powers must exist for the sake of the Elect. For all such ruling powers, whether of men or of angels or of demons, are ordered, in the way that we have discussed, for the good of the Elect. But the Elect themselves will rise in body and soul, and will have exactly the same bodies then as they have now, according to Job: 'And in my flesh shall I see God my Saviour, Whom I myself, and no other, shall see.'[1] But flesh without soul could not see God its Saviour.[2] Therefore, the Elect will rise in both body and soul. Again, if one who was among the Elect did not rise in the same flesh and in the same body, he would not see 'himself,' as he was formerly: rather, he would have been made 'other.' For each of the Elect — he himself 'and no other' — will see God his Saviour. Therefore, body and soul as such pertain to the Elect, for they will all rise in body and soul.

But external goods, which we call riches, do not as such pertain to the Elect; and so they should not have a sword of their own. For as we have noted above, riches or external goods are distinguished in such a way that some, such as gold, silver and other metals, are artificial riches, and some are natural. But artificial riches exist for the sake of natural ones, and natural riches are divided into some five kinds. For they consist of the produce which we receive from trees and plants; or the sustenance which we receive from vines; or the seasoning which we receive from olives and oily fruits; or the food which we receive from cornfields and tillage;

1.   Job 19:26.
2.   Cf. Augustine, *De Trinitate* 2:6 (CCSL 50:94).

sunt aliqua subvencio quam habemus ex animalibus. Omnia autem[1] ista cessabunt in fine mundi, ita quod iste res exteriores et iste divicie[2] non sunt nisi per accidens et ad tempus. Corpora autem et anime erunt perpetua, quia, secundum sentenciam Apostoli, 'Oportet hoc corruptibile induere incorrupcionem et mortale hoc induere inmortalitatem.'

In die igitur tribulacionis sive in die ire, idest in die novissimo, qui erit dies tribulacionis et ire quantum ad malos, et erit dies quietis quantum ad bonos, resurgent electi cum animabus et corporibus, et omnes prefate divicie cessabunt. Hoc est ergo quod dicitur Abacuc III: 'Ut requiescam in die tribulacionis, idest in die iudicii, in die ire, ut ascendam ad populum accinctum nostrum,' id est ad populum[3] electorum, qui erit populus accinctus omni robore et omni fortitudine; et sequitur quomodo tunc cessabunt omnes iste divicie, unde subditur: 'Ficus enim non florebit.' Per ficum autem possumus intelligere omnes arbores et plantas; post diem enim iudicii non florebit ficus, quia cessabit omne emolumentum quod nunc habemus ex arboribus et plantis. Et[4] additur[5] postea, secundo: 'Et non erit germen in vineis,' id est, cessabit omne amminiculum quod ex vineis[6] nunc habemus. Additur et[7] tercio quod 'mentietur opus olive,' ut per olivam[8] intelligatur omnis fructus pinguis unde extrahi potest condimentum sive oleum: mentietur ergo tunc opus olive, quia cessabit omne condimentum quod habemus ex olivis et[9] fructibus pinguibus. Additur autem et quarto quod et 'arva non afferent cibum,' quia tunc cessabunt segetes et omnis cibus quem habemus ex arvis. Additur autem et quinto quod 'abscidetur de ovili pecus, et non erit armentum in presepibus,' quia cessabit omnis subvencio quam nunc habemus ex quibuscumque animalibus.[10] Totum autem gaudium nostrum erit tunc in Domino et tota exultacio nostra in Deo[11] Iesu nostro.[12] Ideo subditur: 'Ego autem in Domino gaudebo et exultabo in Deo Iesu meo.'[13] Vere ergo divicie sunt dicte[14] res[15] temporales, quia per accidens faciunt ad electos et non erunt sempiterne, sed omnes cessabunt in die iudicii. Et quia sunt per accidens et[16] ad tempus, de[17] eis non debuit per se esse cure arti nec per se debuerunt[18] habere gladium.

Sunt ergo tantum duo gladii, spiritualis et corporalis, sub quo corporali gladio eciam temporalia collocantur. Et quamvis spiritualis gladius se ad omnia extendat, non propter hoc superfluit gladius materialis, sicut et in regimine universi non superfluunt angeli inferiores, quamvis quicquid[19] possunt[20] inferiores[21] possint[22] superiores. Solutum est itaque tercium dubium, quare divicie et res exteriores sive temporalia per se habere gladium minime meruerunt.

Viso quomodo in Ecclesia sunt duo[23] gladii, unus spiritualis et alter materialis, restat videre quomodo hii duo gladii sunt sumendi. Dicemus quidem quod hii duo gladii figurati sunt per illos duos gladios de quibus in evangelio dicitur, 'Ecce gladii

1: autem] *om.* V² 2: divicie] *om.* F 3: accinctum ... populum] *om.* F 4: Et] *om.* CFV² 5: additur] enim *add.* C autem *add.* FV² 6: id est ... vineis] *om.* F 7: et] *om.* V² 8: olivam] oliva F 9: et] ex *add.* V² 10: animalibus] animabus FV² 11: Deo] domino F 12: nostro] christo F 13: meo] nostro F 14: sunt dicte] dicte sunt CFV² 15: res] *om.* F 16: et] *om.* V² 17: de] ad V² 18: debuerunt] debuit FV² 19: quamvis quicquid] quanquam eadem F 20: possunt] possint V¹ 21: inferiores] *om.* FV¹ 22: possint] *om.* F possunt V² 23: duo] tantum CV²

or the various aid which we receive from the beasts. And all these will cease at the end of the world; for these external goods and these riches exist only accidentally and for a time. But bodies and souls will be eternal; for, according to what the Apostle says, 'This corruptible must put on incorruption, and the mortal put on immortality.'[1]

Thus, on the day of tribulation, or on the day of wrath — that is, on the last day, which will be a day of tribulation and wrath for the wicked and a day of rest for the good — the Elect will rise with souls and bodies, and all the riches mentioned above will cease. This, therefore, is what is said in Habbakuk 3: 'That I may rest on the day of tribulation,' that is, on the day of judgment, on the day of wrath; 'that I may go up to our people who are girded,' that is, to the people of the Elect, who will be a people girded with all strength and with all fortitude. And, after this, on the subject of how all these riches will then cease, it is added: 'For the fig-tree will not blossom'; and by the fig tree we can understand all trees and plants. For the fig tree will not blossom after the day of judgment because all the produce which we now have from trees and plants will cease. Then, secondly, it is added: 'And there will be no bud upon the vines'; that is, all the sustenance which we now have from vines will cease. And, thirdly, it is added that 'The work of the olive will fail'; and by the olive may be understood every oily fruit from which seasoning or oil can be extracted. Therefore, the work of the olive will then fail, for all the seasoning which we receive from the olive or oily fruits will cease. And, fourthly, it is also added that 'The fields will not yield food'; for corn and all the food which we receive from the fields will then cease. And, fifthly, it is added that 'The flock will be cut off from the fold and there will be no herd in the stalls'; for all the aid which we now receive from the various beasts will cease. But all our joy will then be in the Lord, and all our exultation in God our Jesus. Thus, it is added: 'But I will rejoice in the Lord and I will exult in God my Jesus.'[2] Therefore, riches are truly called temporal things; for they accrue to the Elect accidentally, and they are not eternal, but will all cease on the day of judgment. And because they exist accidentally and for a time only, no art need be specifically devoted to their care, nor are they worthy to have a sword of their own.

Therefore, there are only two swords, the spiritual and the corporeal; and temporal things themselves are placed under the corporeal sword. And although the spiritual sword extends itself to all things, the material sword is not on this account superfluous, just as, in the government of the universe, the lower angels are not superfluous even though the higher can do whatever the lower can. Thus, the third doubt is resolved: that of why riches and external goods, or temporal things as such, have not in the least deserved to have a sword of their own.

Having looked into the question of how there are two swords in the Church, the one spiritual and the other material, it remains to see how these two swords are to be understood. We shall say, indeed, that these two swords are signified by those two swords of which it is said in the Gospel, 'Behold, here are two swords,'

1. I Cor. 15:53.
2. Hab. 3:16–17.

duo hic,' quorum unus fuit extractus, alter in vagina remansit. Cum ergo queris quomodo sunt sumendi hii duo gladii qui sunt in Ecclesia, utrum per gladium[1] extractum significetur gladius spiritualis per non extractum materialis vel econverso, dicemus quod per utrumque potest[2] uterque[3] gladius figurari. Sed hoc in ultimo capitulo huius secunde partis diffusius ostendemus.

CAPITULUM XIV: *Quod cum duo gladii sint*[4] *in Ecclesia, quinque de causis gladius inferior non superfluit propter superiorem, sed hii duo gladii decorant et ornant Ecclesiam Militantem.*

Forte multorum animum agitat que sit necessitas ponendi materialem gladium[5] in Ecclesia, cum dictum sit quod spiritualis gladius cuncta potest. Ideo volumus assignare sex raciones et sex causas; de quibus sex causis adaptabimus[6] quinque causas ad propositum, quare fuit utile et eciam[7] necessarium ponere secundum gladium in Ecclesia. Videmus autem quod[8] sex de[9] causis propter potestatem superiorem non superfluit potestas inferior.

Prima quidem causa est quoniam[10] aliquid potest superior[11] cum potestate inferiori et cum[12] agente instrumentali[13] quod non posset sine illo; secundum quem modum dicimus[14] propter fabrum non superfluit martellus. Non est enim martellus fabro superfluus; immo, necessarius. Quantumcumque[15] enim faber sit agens superior et principalis, martellus autem sit agens inferior et instrumentalis, non tamen est fabro martellus superfluus, quia aliquid potest faber cum martello quod non posset sine martello:[16] ut puta quia[17] potest extendere ferrum, quod[18] sine martello non posset. Habet enim aliquid[19] martellus[20] quod non habet a fabro. Habet autem martellus gravitatem et duriciem, quam non habet a fabro sed ex natura propria hoc habet, ut quia est de ferro. Quia igitur aliquid habet martellus quod non habet a fabro, ideo potest faber cum martello quod non posset sine eo.

Secunda causa ad hoc idem est quod,[21] etsi non est potencia in inferiori agente que non sit in superiori,[22] est tamen in inferiori ut non est in[23] superiori: ut si[24] nulla esset potencia in forcipibus que non esset in fabro, est tamen in eis potencia ut non est in fabro, quia possunt forcipes immediate capere ferrum ignitum sine sui lesione, quod non potest faber. Si enim faber movet ferrum ignitum per forcipes, plus movet faber quam moveant forcipes, et potencia ad movendum ferrum plus in fabro quam in forcipibus; sed illa potencia non est in fabro ut est in forcipibus.

Tercia causa quare non superfluit potestas inferior propter superiorem est quia,

1: gladium] *om.* V² 2: utrumque potest] utramque potes F 3: uterque] utrumque CV² 4: *sint*] sunt V² 5: gladium] *om.* V² 6: adaptabimus] adaptavimus F 7: eciam] immo F 8: quod] sex viis sive *add.* FV² 9: de] *om.* FV² 10: quoniam] *om.* V² 11: quidem causa ... superior] *om.* F 12: cum] *om.* CV² 13: potestate inferiori ... instrumentali] potestas inferior sit agens instrumentale F 14: dicimus] quod *add.* V² 15: Quantumcumque] quamquam F 16: quod non ... martello] *om.* V² 17: quia] qui F 18: quod] et FV² 19: aliquid] *om.* F 20: aliquid martellus] martellus aliquid V² 21: quod] quando FV² 22: in superiori] inferiori V² 23: Secunda causa ... est in] *om.* V¹ 24: ut si] etsi F

one of which was drawn while the other remained in its sheath.[1] Therefore, when you ask how these two swords which are in the Church are to be understood — whether the spiritual sword is represented by the drawn sword and the material by the undrawn, or the converse — we shall reply that each sword can be signified by either of them. But we shall deal with this more fully in the final chapter of this second part.

CHAPTER XIV: *That, although there are two swords in the Church, there are five reasons why the inferior sword is not superfluous to the superior, but why these two swords decorate and adorn the Church Militant.*

Perhaps it disturbs the minds of many that it should be necessary to place a material sword in the Church; for it has been said that the spiritual sword can do all things. And so we wish to assign six reasons and six causes, five of which six causes we shall apply to our question: why it was useful and indeed necessary to place a second sword in the Church. And we see from these six causes that an inferior power is not superfluous to a superior power.

The first cause is this: that there may be something which a superior power can do with an inferior and with an instrumental agent which it could not do without it. In this sense, we say that a hammer is not superfluous to the blacksmith; for the hammer is not superfluous, but necessary, to the blacksmith. For however much the blacksmith may be the superior and principal agent and the hammer the inferior and instrumental agent, the hammer is nonetheless not superfluous to the blacksmith, because there is something which the blacksmith can do with the hammer which he could not do without a hammer: that is, he can forge iron, which he could not do without a hammer. For the hammer has a certain quality which it does not receive from the blacksmith: it has a weight and hardness which it does not receive from the blacksmith. Rather, it has this from its own nature, since it is made of iron. Thus, because the hammer has a certain quality which it does not receive from the blacksmith, the blacksmith can therefore do with the hammer what he could not do without it.

The second such cause is this: that even if there is no power in an inferior agent which is not in a superior, it may nonetheless be in the inferior in a way that it is not in the superior. For example, although there is no power in a pair of tongs which is not in the blacksmith, power is nonetheless in them in a way that it is not in the blacksmith; for the tongs can grasp hot iron directly without damage to themselves, which the blacksmith cannot. Thus, if the blacksmith moves a piece of hot iron with the tongs, it is the blacksmith who accomplishes the movement more than the tongs, and the power to move the iron is more in the blacksmith than in the tongs; but that power is not in the blacksmith in the way that it is in the tongs.

The third reason why an inferior power is not superfluous to a superior is that

1. Luke 22:38.

etsi totum possit superior quod potest inferior, etsi nihil potest superior cum inferiori quod non possit sine[1] eo,[2] tamen non[3] ita commode nec ita bene potest superior sine inferiori sicut potest cum eo. Secundum quem modum Exodi XVIII
Iethro, cognatus Moysis,[4] reprehendit eum quod[5] stulto labore consumebatur et
negocium ultra vires assumpserat et solus non poterat illud implere. Ideo consuluit
dictus Iethro Moysi quod ipse esset pro populo in hiis que sunt ad Deum et
eligeret tribunos, centuriones et ceteros huiusmodi, qui populum iudicarent. Prius
ergo Moyses iudicabat sine illis et poterat totum facere sine illis inferioribus iudicibus, sed non ita bene nec ita commode.

Quarta causa ad hoc idem sumitur: si non ita decenter. Eciam[6] hoc modo non
superfluit preco principi, sed est sibi necessarius. Nam licet princeps posset ipse[7]
esse preco sui ipsius, tamen[8] non deceret eum officium preconis facere. Posset
ergo princeps sine precone quod potest cum precone,[9] sed non ita decenter.

Quinta causa ad hoc idem sumitur: si non ita ordinate. Nam in ipso ordine rerum refulget mirabilis prudencia et mirabilis pulchritudo. Ideo dicitur tercio
Regum X de regina Saba, quando venit ut[10] videret sapienciam Salomonis, quod,
videns[11] ordinem ministrancium, 'non habebat ultra spiritum': idest, expavit et[12]
admirata est[13] de[14] tanta ordinacione quam vidit in domo Salomonis. Ideo dicta
regina dixit ad regem: 'Verus est sermo quem audivi in terra mea super sermoni-
bus tuis et super sapiencia tua, et non credebam narrantibus mihi donec ipsa veni
et vidi oculis meis et probavi quod media pars mihi nunciata non fuerit.'[15] Dato
ergo quod unus minister posset totum facere, tamen,[16] ut[17] quia in ordine adminis-
trancium refulget admirabilis pulchritudo, non superfluit ordinata pluralitas min-
istrorum.

Sexta causa ad hoc idem sumitur: quia superior vult inferioribus suam dignitatem communicare; secundum quem modum, quantumcumque accio Dei se
possit extendere ad omnia, quia quicquid potest Deus cum creatura potest sine
creatura, et eque bene et eque decenter et eque ordinate, tamen, quia vult dignitatem suam communicare[18] creaturis, ideo non superfluit accio creature. Posset
enim Deus calefacere sine igne,[19] infrigidare sine aqua, salvare transfretantes[20] et
transeuntes mare sine ligno vel sine navi. Tamen, ut non essent supervacua opera sapiencie sue, voluit dignitatem suam communicare creaturis, et voluit quod
creature sue haberent acciones proprias et virtutes proprias et essent cause rerum:
ut ignis esset causa calefaciendi, aqua infrigidandi, lignum autem sive navis
esset causa salvandi navigantes et transeuntes aquam. Hoc est ergo quod dicitur

1: sine] sive F   2: eo] *om.* FV²   3: tamen non] totum cum F   totum non V²   4: Moysis]
Moysi V²   5: quod] *om.* V²   6: Eciam] ex FV²   7: ipse] ipsemet CV²   8: tamen] cum FV²
9: quod potest cum precone] *om.* CFV²   10: ut] *om.* V²   11: videns] videret FV²   12: et] *om.* PV¹
13: est] *om.* F   14: de] ex C   15: fuerit] fuerat *mss*   16: tamen] tum F   17: ut] *om.* C
18: communicare] cum *add.* FV²   19: igne] et *add.* C   20: salvare transfretantes] transfretantes
salvare F

even if the superior can do all that the inferior can, and even if there is nothing that the superior can do with the inferior that it cannot do without it, [it may nonetheless be that] the superior cannot act as conveniently or as well without the inferior as it can with it. In this sense, in Exodus 18, Jethro, the kinsman of Moses, reproached him because he was consumed by foolish labour and had assumed tasks beyond his powers which he could not accomplish alone. And so Jethro counselled Moses that he should act for the people in those things which are of God, and should appoint tribunes, rulers of hundreds, and others such, to judge the people.[1] At first, therefore, Moses judged without these, and could do all things without these lesser judges; but not so well or so conveniently.

The fourth such cause is derived from a consideration of what is fitting. In this way, again, the herald is not superfluous to the prince, but is necessary to him. For although the prince himself could be his own herald, it would nonetheless not be fitting for him to perform the office of herald. Therefore, the prince might do without the herald what he can do with the herald, but not so fittingly.

The fifth such cause is derived from a consideration of orderliness. For in the orderliness of things there is reflected a wondrous wisdom and a wondrous beauty.[2] And so it is said in I Kings 10, of the Queen of Sheba, that when she came to see the wisdom of Solomon, and saw the order of his ministers, 'She no longer had any spirit in her': that is, she was astounded and filled with admiration by the great orderliness which she saw in the house of Solomon. And so the said queen spoke to the king thus: 'The report which I heard of your words and your wisdom in my own country is true. I did not believe those who told me until I came myself and saw with my own eyes; and I have found that the half has not been told me.'[3] Even supposing, therefore, that a single minister could do all things, an orderly arrangement of many ministers would still not be superfluous, because a wondrous beauty is reflected in a well-ordered administration.

The sixth such cause is derived from the fact that a superior may wish to share his own dignity with his inferiors. In this sense, however much the agency of God may extend to all creatures — for whatever God can do with a creature He can do without a creature, and equally well and equally fittingly and in an equally well-ordered fashion — nonetheless, since He wishes to share His own dignity with His creatures, the agency of the creatures is therefore not superfluous. For God could warm without fire, cool without water, and preserve those who come and go upon the sea without wood or without boats. Nonetheless, so that the works of His wisdom should not be in vain, He has desired to share His own dignity with His creatures, and He has desired that His creatures should have their own activities and their own powers, and that they should be causes of things: for example, that fire should be the cause of heating, water of cooling, and wood or boats should be the means by which seamen and travellers upon water are preserved. This, therefore, is

1. Exod. 18:17–26.
2. Cf. Augustine, *Enchiridion* 3:10 (CCSL 46:53).
3. I Kings 10:5.

Sapiencie XIV: 'Tua autem Pater omnia gubernat providencia'; et sequitur: 'Quoniam potens es ex omnibus salvare eciam, quod sine rate quis adeat mare.' Posset[1] enim Deus facere quod sine rate quis mare transiret. Et sequitur: 'Sed ut non essent vacua opera sapiencie sue,[2] propter hoc eciam exiguo[3] ligno,' idest uni navicule, 'credunt homines animas suas[4] et[5] committunt homines vitas suas et[6] transeuntes mare per ratem liberati sunt.' Si ergo creature non haberent virtutes suas et acciones suas, sed Deus sine eis omnia faceret, essent creature ociose, et per consequens essent frustra et vacue. Si ergo queratur quare requiritur accio creature ad aliquid agendum cum Deus totum possit, dicemus quod non propter indigenciam vel insufficienciam Dei, sed propter benignitatem suam, et[7] quia vult dignitatem[8] suam communicare creaturis, ut opera sapiencie sue et ea que sunt creata ab eo non sint ociosa nec frustra nec vacua.

Hiis itaque prelibatis, volumus ad propositum descendere, quare non superfluit in Ecclesia materialis gladius[9] cum sit ibi spiritualis qui cuncta operari potest. Ideo prosequimur[10] causas tactas prout poterimus prosequi. Sed prima causa non potest simpliciter[11] adaptari ad nostrum propositum: videlicet, quod non superfluat[12] gladius materialis adiunctus spirituali quia aliquid possit spiritualis cum materiali quod non posset sine illo, sicut aliquid potest faber cum martello quod non posset sine eo.

Sed dices quod optime potest hoc adaptari ad propositum, quia iudicium sanguinis potest exercere potestas spiritualis mediante potestate terrena, quod non posset sine ea. Prohibitus[13] enim fuit Petrus[14] ne[15] uteretur materiali gladio, et[16] mandatum fuit sibi quod ipsum converteret[17] in vaginam. Ideo ait Bernardus, libro quarto ad[18] Eugenium papam: 'Quid tu denuo[19] usurpare gladium temptes, cum[20] semel iussus es reponere in vaginam?'

Advertendum ergo quod spiritualis gladius non potest cum materiali quod non possit sine materiali, sed potest cum materiali ut non potest sine materiali;[21] ita quod nulla impotencia est ex parte spiritualis gladii, sed quantum ad corpus misticum et[22] ad ea que agenda sunt in Ecclesia, omnis potencia[23] est in ipso. Data est enim huic gladio omnis potestas in celo et in terra: in celo quantum ad spiritualia et[24] in terra[25] quantum ad temporalia. Est enim Summus Pontifex Christi vicarius, qui Christus dicit Matthei ultimo: 'Data est mihi omnis potestas in celo et in terra.' Sed propter iam dicta, sciendum[26] quod qui emeret piscem crudum et comederet coctum non comederet quod non[27] emit, sed comederet ut non emit. Illud enim comederet quod

---

1: Posset] possit V[2]   2: sue] tue CV[2]   3: exiguo] ex V[2]   4: suas] salvare *add.* V[2]   5: et] id est V[2]
6: committunt homines ... et] *om.* F   7: et] ut CFV[2]   8: dignitatem] benignitatem PV[1]   9: gladius] *om.* FV[2]   10: prosequimur] prosequitur V[2]   11: simpliciter] *om.* C   12: superfluat] superfluit F   13: Prohibitus] prohibitum FV[2]   14: Petrus] Petro FV[2]   15: ne] ut F   16: et] *om.* V[2]
17: converteret] communicaret PV[1]   18: ad] *om.* V[2]   19: denuo] de uno V[2]   20: cum] quem V[2]
21: sed potest ... materiali] *om.* F   22: et] quantum *add.* F   23: potencia] potestas F   24: et] *om.* CF   25: in celo ... terra] *om.* V[2]   26: sciendum] est *add.* F   27: non] *om.* V[2]

said in Wisdom 14: 'But Your providence, Father, governs all things.' And it continues: 'For you can save men from all things, even if a man were to put to sea without a boat' (for God could so act that one might cross the sea without a boat). And it goes on: 'But that the works of Your wisdom should not be in vain, men entrust their souls and commit their lives to a little thing of wood,' that is, to a little boat, 'and, crossing the sea by ship, are saved.'[1] If, therefore, creatures did not have their own powers and their own actions, but if God did all things without them, the creatures would be idle, and consequently would be futile and empty. Therefore, if it be asked why, since God can do all things, there is need of action on the part of creatures to accomplish anything, we shall reply that this is not due to a lack or insufficiency on God's part, but to His benevolence, and because He wishes to share His dignity with His creatures, so that the works of His wisdom and those things which were created by Him should not be futile or idle or empty.

Thus, having first touched upon these considerations, we wish to come to our question: why the material sword is not superfluous in the Church when there is a spiritual sword there which can do all things. And so we shall pursue the causes already mentioned as far as we can pursue them. The first cause, however — namely, that [which would imply that] the material sword is not superfluous when joined to the spiritual because the spiritual can do with the material what it could not do without it — cannot as such be applied to our present argument.

But you will say that this can be applied to our argument perfectly well, since the spiritual power can execute the judgment of blood through the agency of the earthly power, which it could not do without it. For Peter was forbidden to use the material sword, and a command given to him to replace it in its sheath;[2] and so Bernard, in the fourth book of his work addressed to Pope Eugenius, says: 'Why should you again attempt to usurp the sword which you were once commanded to replace in its sheath?'[3]

It must be noted, therefore, that although it can act with the material sword in a way in which it cannot act without it, there is [nonetheless] nothing which the spiritual sword can do with the material which it cannot do without it. Thus, there is no lack of power on the part of the spiritual sword. On the contrary, so far as the Mystical Body and those things which must be done in the Church are concerned, all power is in it: all power in heaven and upon earth is given to that sword — in heaven as regards spiritual things and upon earth as regards temporal. For the Supreme Pontiff is the Vicar of Christ, and Christ said in the final chapter of Matthew: 'All power in heaven and upon earth is given to me.'[4] But in view of the above statement [that the spiritual sword can act with the material in a way in which it cannot act without it], it must be known that although he who bought a fish raw and ate it cooked would not eat what he had not bought, he would not eat it as he bought it. For he would eat what he had bought, but he would

---

1.   Wisd. 14:3–5.
2.   John 18:11.
3.   *De consideratione*, 4:3:7.
4.   Matt. 28:18.

emit, sed[1] non comederet ut emit, quia emit[2] crudum et comedit[3] coctum. Sic qui non habet unum solum denarium et dat unum solum denarium, non dat quod non habet, sed ut non habet, quia non habet denarium solum, sed habet ipsum cum alio. Dat tamen ipsum solum et non cum alio. Et si sol, qui[4] est calidus virtualiter, calefacit te formaliter, non dat tibi calorem quem non habet, sed ut non habet, quia habet[5] calorem virtualiter quem dat tibi formaliter. Alciori ergo modo habet sol calorem quem det tibi. Sic et in proposito: utrumque gladium habet Ecclesia; utriusque est claviger Petrus terreni et celestis regni; omne posse quod habet terrena potestas habet et ecclesiastica. Nulla est itaque potestas in materiali gladio que non sit in spirituali, sed est potestas in materiali gladio ut non est in spirituali; quia materialis gladius potest immediate exercere iudicium sanguinis, secundum quem modum non potest, idest non decet, quod exercet[6] gladius spiritualis. Ergo non potest[7] hic gladius quod non possit ille, sed potest hic gladius[8] ut non potest ille.

Unde doctores aliqui notaverunt quod auctoritate primaria et superiori utrumque gladium habet[9] Ecclesia. Ipsum ergo materialem gladium plus habet Ecclesia quam terrena potestas, quia plus est habere aliquid auctoritate primaria et superiori quam auctoritate secundaria et inferiori. Non est ergo simile de fabro respectu martelli et de gladio spirituali respectu gladii materialis, quia aliquid habet martellus quod non habet a fabro, sed potenciam et auctoritatem quam habet gladius secularis habet per spiritualem et a spirituali, sicut potenciam operandi quam habet corpus habet ab anima. Unde doctores nostre sciencie in suis questionibus notaverunt quod Christus Petro ambas claves[10] tradidit et duos gladios commisit, sic ut regimen universalis Ecclesie tam in spiritualibus quam in temporalibus ad ipsum pertineret. Ipsi eciam iuriste volunt quod Christus beato Petro, eterne vite clavigero, terreni simul et celestis imperii iura commisit.

Sed dices, ut et quidam doctores dicere videntur, quod licet utrumque gladium habeat Ecclesia, execucionem utriusque gladii non habet; quod si in hiis verbis staretur, bonum[11] intellectum huiusmodi verba habere possent. Sed sic dicentes plus addunt: videlicet, quod huiusmodi execucionem non habet materialis gladius sive imperator a papa concessam, sed a Christo commissam,[12] quia tunc, ut dicunt, passim[13] posset appellari in temporalibus a principibus secularibus[14] ad papam.

1: comederet ut … sed] *om.* V[2]   2: sed non … emit] *om.* F   3: comedit] comederit FV[2] sed ut non habet] *om.* F   4: qui] *om.* C   5: quia habet] *om.* F   6: exercet] exerceat CFV[2]   7: idest non … potest] *om.* PV[1]   8: quod non … gladius] *om.* F   9: habet] habeat V[2]   10: claves] clavas V[2]   11: bonum] *om.* F   12: sed a Christo commissam] *om.* V[2]   13: passim] *om.* F   14: secularibus] *om.* FV[1]

not eat it as he bought it because he bought it raw and would eat it cooked. So too, he who has more coins than one and gives away only one coin does not give what he does not have, but he does not give it as he has it. For he does not have the one coin only: he has it with another; but he gives it singly and not with the other. And if the sun, which is warm intrinsically, warms you superficially, it does not give warmth to you which it does not have, but as it does not have it. For it has warmth intrinsically which it gives to you superficially. Therefore, the sun has warmth in a higher way than that in which it gives it to you. So also in our proposition: the Church has both swords; Peter is the key-bearer of both the earthly and the heavenly kingdoms; all the might which the earthly power has the ecclesiastical has also. Thus, there is no power in the material sword which is not in the spiritual. But the power which is in the material sword is not there as it is in the spiritual; for the material sword can execute the judgment of blood directly, and the spiritual sword cannot act in this manner: cannot, that is, do so fittingly. Therefore, it is not the case that the one sword can do what the other cannot, but only that the one sword can act in a way that the other cannot.

Hence, certain teachers have noted that the Church has both swords with a primary and superior authority [since, even though she cannot fittingly act without it, the material sword is subject to her command]. It is the Church more than the earthly power, therefore, who has the material sword; for it is better to have something with a primary and superior than with a secondary and inferior authority. Therefore, there is no similarity between the blacksmith in relation to a hammer and the spiritual sword in relation to the material sword. For the hammer has some quality which it does not receive from the blacksmith; but the power and authority which the secular sword has it receives through the spiritual and from the spiritual, just as the capacity to act which the body has it receives from the soul. Hence, the teachers of our science [i.e. canon law] have noted in their enquiries that Christ delivered to Peter two keys and entrusted to him two swords, so that the government of the Church Universal should belong to him in spiritual and temporal matters alike.[1] Also, the jurists themselves maintain that Christ entrusted to the blessed Peter, bearer of the keys of eternal life, the laws of the earthly and heavenly empires together.[2]

But you will say, as, indeed, certain teachers are seen to say, that although the Church possesses both swords, she does not have the right to wield both swords. And if this were the only statement made, then such words could bear a proper meaning. But, having said this much, they add more: to wit, that the emperor does not receive the right to wield the material sword as a grant from the pope, but as a [direct] commission from Christ.[3] For otherwise, as they say, it would be possible to appeal indiscriminately from secular princes to the pope in temporal matters.

1. He evidently has in mind Hostiensis, Commentary on X. 4:17:13, *Summa Domini Henrici Cardinalis Hostiensis* (Lyons, 1537), p. 216, of which this sentence is a close paraphrase.
2. The grammar, and the use of the word *iuriste*, suggests an allusion to the civil as distinct from the canon lawyers; but the reference is clearly to Dist. 22, c. 1: *Omnes* (CIC 1:73), and the thirteenth-century civil lawyers certainly did not hold that the pope has a general authority in temporals.
3. See Introduction, n. 37, and Pt. III, Chaps. I and IV.

Advertendum ergo quod si[1] due potestates sunt in superiori agente, si aliqua illarum potestatum competit agenti inferiori, oportet quod ei conveniat per commissionem superioris; quod[2] ipsi non negant. Concedunt quidem quod potestas gladii materialis est a[3] gladio spirituali, sed non execucio potestatis. Dicamus ergo quod, sicut a virtute visiva est actus videndi et ab auditiva[4] actus audiendi, et sicut a potencia calefactiva est actus calefaciendi et ab infrigidativa actus infrigidandi,[5] sic in regimine hominum a potencia gubernativa et ab auctoritate gubernandi est ipsum gubernare et ipsum agere. Sed quis diceret quod res aliqua haberet ab aliquo agente potenciam calefaciendi et non haberet[6] ab eo quod calefaceret et quod ageret secundum illam potenciam?[7] Sic[8] si utrumque gladium habet Ecclesia, et terrena potestas suum gladium et suam potestatem habet ab ecclesiastica potestate, oportet quod exequi et agere secundum potestatem[9] illam ab Ecclesia recognoscat. In populo enim[10] fideli — quia de infideli nihil ad nos — terrena potestas est per ecclesiasticam instituta, per baptismum regenerata, et, si[11] in peccatum mortale incidit,[12] est per Ecclesiam sacramentaliter absolvenda.[13] Per hoc ergo, et[14] per alia multa que supra tetigimus, materialis gladius omnem[15] potestatem quam habet a spirituali habet; et si potestatem exequendi[16] et agendi habet materialis gladius a spirituali, oportet quod et ipsam execucionem et ipsum agere habeat a spirituali gladio.

Quod autem non passim nec indifferenter a principibus secularibus ad Summum Pontificem appellatur, hoc est[17] quia sacerdotalis potestas nimis et ultra suam decenciam negociis seculi se implicaret si passim et indifferenter in temporalibus appellaretur ad ipsum. Et forte non expediret hoc bono publico, quia ex hoc nimis turbari posset pax secularium principum. Nam multa licite et de iure fieri possunt que non expediunt quia forte turbarent pacem multorum; et multa sunt de iure simpliciter et absolute sumpto que non sunt[18] de iure consueto. Sic ergo passim et indifferenter a principibus secularibus ad Ecclesiam appellare non est consuetum; et forte non expediret paci[19] ipsorum secularium principum, et eciam[20] non expediret ipsi potestati ecclesiastice, que debet[21] esse intenta in hiis que sunt ad Deum, ea autem que[22] sunt mundi debet[23] aliis committere; sed si quid in eis difficile vel ambiguum fuerit, ad Sacerdotem Summum referri debet. Unde et[24] Exodi XVIII,[25] quando Iethro dedit consilium Moysi quod ipse esset[26] pro populo in hiis que sunt ad Deum et alia iudicibus committeret, dixit quod 'quicquid autem maius fuerit, referatur ad te, et ipsi minora

---

1: si] *om.* F   2: quod] et *add.* FV²   3: a] *om.* FV²   4: auditiva] auditia C est *add.* F   5: ab infrigidativa actus infrigidandi] *del.* C   6: et non haberet] et non haberet *dittog.* V²   7: potenciam] calefaciendi et non habet *add. and del.* C   8: Sic] sive F   9: suum gladium ... potestatem] *om.* C   10: enim] *om.* V²   11: si] *om.* C   12: incidit] incidat FV²   13: absolvenda] absoluta C   14: et] quod FV²   15: omnem] *om.* CFV²   16: exequendi] excercendi F   17: est] *om.* V²   18: que non sunt] quia sint F   19: paci] pari F pati V²   20: eciam] *om.* C   21: debet] dicitur F   22: que] *om.* P   23: debet] oportet F   24: et] *om.* V²   25: XVIII] octavo V²   26: esset] *om.* V²

It must be noted, therefore, that if there are two powers within a superior agent and if one of those powers devolves upon an inferior agent, this must come about by the commission of the superior; and this much they do not deny. Indeed, they concede that the power of the material sword comes from the spiritual sword, but not the execution of that power. Let us say, therefore, that just as the act of seeing comes from the power of sight and the act of hearing comes from the power to hear, and just as the act of heating comes from the power to heat and the act of cooling from the power to cool, so, in the government of men, the act of governing and directing comes from governing power and from the authority to govern. But who would say of something that it received from some agent the power of heating yet did not receive from it the capacity to heat and to act according to that power? Thus, if the Church possesses both swords, and if the earthly power holds its sword and its power from the ecclesiastical power, then it must also acknowledge that it receives the right to execute and to act according to that power from the Church. For among the faithful people (for unbelievers are of no concern to us),[1] earthly power is instituted through the ecclesiastical, regenerated through baptism and, if it falls into mortal sin, is sacramentally absolved through the Church. For this reason, therefore, and the many others which we have touched upon above, the material sword receives all the power which it has from the spiritual. And if the material sword receives the power to execute and to act from the spiritual, then it must also receive the right to execute and to act from the spiritual sword.

But the fact that appeal is not made indiscriminately or without distinction to the Supreme Pontiff from secular princes is due to this: that, if appeal were to be made to him indiscriminately or without distinction in temporal cases, the priestly power would involve itself excessively and beyond what is fitting in secular affairs. And perhaps also this would not be expedient to the public good since, by it, the peace of secular princes might be unduly disturbed. For many things can be rightly and lawfully done which, because they would perhaps disturb the peace of many, are not expedient.[2] And many things are lawful considered as such and in an absolute sense which are not lawful as a matter of ordinary practice.[3] Therefore, a practice is not made of indiscriminate and invariable appeal to the Church from secular princes. And [if it were] this would perhaps not be expedient to the peace of those secular princes, and indeed not expedient to the ecclesiastical power, which should be intent upon those things which are of God, and which should entrust the affairs of the world to others. If, however, there should be something difficult or doubtful in these affairs, it must be referred to the Supreme Priest. Hence, in Exodus 18, when Jethro gave it as his advice to Moses that he should act for the people in those things which are of God and entrust other matters to judges, he said: 'They shall refer to you whatever great matter shall arise,

1. See Ch. XI.
2. Cf. I Cor. 10:23.
3. Cf. Pt. I, Ch. IV, p. 21; Pt. III, Chaps. I–VIII.

tantummodo[1] iudicent'; et Deuteronomii XVII[2] in difficilibus et ambiguis appellabatur ad summum sacerdotem, ut Magister in *Historiis* notat. Si ergo consideramus ipsum ius simpliciter et absolute, non videmus quare possit[3] appellari in magnis et non in parvis, cum iudex possit forefacere tam in magnis quam in parvis.[4] Sed si consideramus decenciam et pacem offensorum, plane conspicimus non esse appellandum[5] in parvis, sed in magnis. Nam tantus homo cui tocius orbis cura committitur debet esse magnanimus; sed magnanimus est 'qui se ipsum magnis[6] dignificat,' ut dicitur[7] in IV *Ethicorum*. Et ibidem dicitur quod pro magnis se exponit magnanimus, non pro parvis; et ibidem traditur quod magnanimus est magnorum operativus, et ex hoc est operativus paucorum quia raro contingunt magna.[8] In his ergo que sunt mundi, ubi respectu spiritualium magna sunt parva, valde debent esse magna et ardua pro[9] quibus spiritualis homo qui iudicat omnia se intromittere debet. Itaque, si consideramus decenciam status, si advertimus pacem offensorum, indifferenter et passim in temporalibus non est ad Summum Pontificem appellandum. Sed si absolute et[10] simpliciter iura ipsius potencie advertere[11] volumus, ipsa naturalia nos docent[12] quod parva continentur in magnis, et qui humeres[13] sic[14] fortes habet quod possit magna onera[15] sustinere poterit multo amplius levia onera deportare. Sed forte non deceret eum ad parva se exponere quem Christus ordinavit ad magna.

Revertamur ergo ad propositum et dicamus quod prima racio et[16] causa quare non superfluunt inferiora propter superiora, videlicet[17] quia aliqua potestas potest[18] esse in inferioribus que non est in superioribus nec a superioribus, ut quia aliquid habet martellus quod non habet a fabro, sed habet ex natura ferri ex quo est compositus, proprie ad nostrum propositum adaptari non potest, quia utrumque gladium habet Ecclesia et utramque potestatem, sibique simul[19] terreni et celestis iura imperii sunt commissa, extra quam non est salus, 'sub qua curvantur[20] qui portant orbem.' Ipsi enim seculares principes qui gubernando et regendo mundum[21] ex hoc orbem portare[22] videntur, in statu salutis esse non possunt nisi sub Ecclesia[23] incur ventur.

Secundam quidem racionem et causam poterimus ad propositum applicare. Nam bona est potestas inferior que non superfluit sed multum expedit quod sit adiuncta superiori, dato quod nulla potestas sit in inferiori que non sit in superiori, cum[24] tamen sit in inferiori ut non est[25] in superiori.[26] Nam potestas ad capiendum

---

1: tantummodo] tantum F   2: XVII]xviii *mss*   3: possit] posset C   4: cum iudex … parvis] *om.* C si ergo consideramus ipsum ius simpliciter et absolute non videmus quare possit appellari in magnis et non in parvis F   5: appellandum] appellacio F   6: magnis] magnus FPV[1]   7: dicitur] videtur FV[2]   8: magna] maiora F   9: pro] de FV[2]   10: et] *om.* FV[2]   11: advertere] avertere PV[2]   12: docent] decent PV[2]   13: humeres] humores FV[2]   14: sic] sunt V[2]   15: onera] opera P   16: et] prima *add.* C   17: videlicet] est C   18: potest] *om.* V[2]   19: sibique simul] sibi quia simulque FV[2]   20: curvantur] incurvantur CFV[2]   21: mundum] et *add.* CV[2]   22: orbem portare] *om.* V[2]   23: Ecclesia] *om.* V[2]   24: cum] dum CFV[2]   25: est] *om.* F   26: ut non … superiori] *om.* V[2]

and they shall judge every small matter.'[1] And, according to Deuteronomy 17, appeal was made in difficult and doubtful cases to the Supreme Priest, as the Master notes in the *Historia*.[2] If, therefore, we consider the law itself, as such and in an absolute sense, we do not see why appeal may be made in great matters yet not in small; for a judge may err in great matters and in small alike. But if we consider [the question with regard to] fitness and the peace of those offended, we shall see plainly that appeal ought not to be made in small matters, but in great. For a man who is so great that the care of the whole world is entrusted to him must be great of soul; but, as is said in *Ethics* 4, a great-souled man is 'one who considers himself worthy of great things'[3] and, in the same place, it is said that he shows himself to be great of soul in great matters, not in small. In the same place again, it is taught that the great-souled man is concerned with great matters, and is concerned with small ones only because great matters seldom occur. In the affairs of the world, therefore, where, in comparison with spiritual things, great matters are small, those affairs with which the spiritual man who judges all things must concern himself should be very great and difficult. Thus, if we consider what is fitting to his status, and if we give attention to the peace of those offended, [we shall see that] appeal may not be made without distinction and indiscriminately to the Supreme Pontiff in temporal matters. But if we wish to give attention to the rights which attach to his power in an absolute sense and as such, then the facts of nature themselves teach us that the small are contained within the great and that he who is so strong of shoulder that he can sustain great burdens will be much the better able to sustain light ones. But it would perhaps not be fitting for one whom Christ has ordained to great tasks to occupy himself with small ones.

Let us revert to our proposition, therefore, and say that the first reason and cause why inferiors are not superfluous to superiors — that is, because there can be some power in inferiors which is neither in superiors nor from superiors, as with a hammer, which has some quality which it does not receive from the blacksmith but which it has from the nature of the metal of which it is composed — cannot appropriately be applied to our argument. For the Church has both swords and both powers, and the laws of both the earthly and the heavenly empires together have been entrusted to her, outside whom there is no salvation, and 'beneath whom those who bear up the world are bowed down.'[4] For the secular princes who, by their government and rule of the world, seem to bear up the world, cannot be in a state of salvation unless they are bowed down beneath the Church.

We shall, however, be able to apply the second reason and cause to our proposition. For an inferior power may be a good which is not superfluous, but which is greatly advantageous, when joined to a superior. For, granted that there is no power in the inferior which is not in the superior, it may nonetheless be in the inferior in a way in which it is not in the superior. For the power to grasp and move

1. Exod. 18:17–26.
2. Deut. 17:8–13; Peter Comestor, *Historia scholastica*, PL 198:1253. See also n. 3 on p. 53.
3. Aristotle, *Nicomachean Ethics* 4:3 (1123ª1).
4. Job 9:13 (Vulgate).

et movendum ferrum plus est in manu fabri quam[1] in forcipe. Huiusmodi ergo[2] potestas non est in forcipe que non sit in manu fabri, sed est in forcipe ut non est in manu fabri,[3] quia possunt forcipes[4] immediate attingere[5] ignitum ferrum, quod sine lesione non poterit manus fabri.[6] Sic et in proposito: non est potestas in gladio materiali que non sit in Summo Sacerdote[7] et a Summo Sacerdote;[8] sed est potestas in huiusmodi gladio ut non est in huiusmodi sacerdote; quia potest immediate iudicium sanguinis exercere, quod sacerdos non posset vel non cum decencia posset.

Et hoc modo verificari possunt verba quorumdam doctorum superius posita, quod Ecclesia habet utrumque gladium sed non habet utriusque gladii execucionem. Quod non est intelligendum quod nullo modo habeat execucionem materialis gladii, sed quod non habet eam, vel non est decens quod habeat eam,[9] immediatam.[10] Habet enim eam per vicarium vel per substitutum vel per interpositam personam, ut sit persona[11] interposita inter potestatem ecclesiasticam et iudicium sanguinis ad hoc, quod cum[12] decencia possit tale officium exerceri.[13]

Adaptavimus itaque secundam racionem et causam quare bonum fuit instituere materialem gladium et auctoritatem terrenam; quia, etsi nulla est potestas in huiusmodi gladio que non[14] sit in sacerdotali dignitate, est tamen potestas in tali gladio ut non est, vel eo modo quo non est, in huiusmodi dignitate.

Tercia autem causa, quia non ita commode nec ita bene gubernaretur mundus et[15] in temporalibus et in spiritualibus[16] nisi ecclesiastice potestati[17] adderetur materialis gladius; et causa[18] quarta, quia non ita decenter, superius tangebatur. Quinta vero causa, quia non ita ordinate,[19] de levi patet. Nam, ut ait Augustinus XIX *De civitate Dei*, capitulo XIII: 'Ordo est parium dispariumque rerum sua cuique loca tribuens disposicio.' Materialis enim gladius et spiritualis non sunt pares, sed impares, quia unus est superior, alter inferior. Bonum ergo fuit instituere secundum gladium, ut sibi proprius assignaretur locus et poneretur sub superiori gladio[20] ad hoc, quod omnia debite et secundum ordinem fiant. Si enim non esset dare secundum gladium in Ecclesia, sed Summus Pontifex sic haberet utrumque gladium quod materialem gladium[21] alteri non committeret,[22] consequens esset quod materialis gladius non haberet proprium et distinctum locum,[23] sed uterque gladius secundum quandam potestatem primariam reservaretur in Summo Sacerdote.[24] Non ergo refulgeret tantus ordo in Ecclesia, et per consequens nec tantus decor, quantus nunc refulget: videlicet, quod materialis gladius[25] commissus est terrene[26] potestati, ex qua commissione quidam decorus ordo relucet in Ecclesia, quia est gladius sub gladio et potestas sub potestate.

1: quam] sit *add.* FV[2]   2: ergo] *om.* FV[2]   3: sed est … fabri] *om.* V[2]   4: forcipes] in virtute *add. and del.* C   5: immediate attingere] attingere immediate C   6: manus fabri] fabri manus F
7: Sacerdote] pontifice FV[2]   8: Sacerdote] pontifice FV[2]   9: vel non … eam] *om.* F   10: immediatam] sed mediatam *add.* FV[2]   11: ut sit persona] *om.* V[2]   12: cum] *om.* V[2]   13: exerceri] exercere F   14: que non] quin F   15: et] *om.* CFV[2]   16: in temporalibus et in spiritualibus] in spiritualibus et temporalibus CFV[2]   17: potestati] potestate C   18: causa] *del.* C   19: ordinate] nominata FV[2]   20: ut sibi … gladio] *om.* C   21: materialem gladium] materialis gladius F
22: committeret] committeretur FV[2]   23: locum] *om.* V[2]   24: Sacerdote] pontifice C   25: gladius] *om.* F   26: terrene] in terre V[2]

iron is more in the hand of the blacksmith than in the tongs: there is, therefore, no power of this kind in the tongs which is not in the hand of the blacksmith. But it is not in the tongs in the way that it is in the hand of the blacksmith; for the tongs can touch hot iron directly, whereas the hand of the blacksmith will not be able to do so without injury. So also in our proposition: there is no power in the material sword which is not in the Supreme Priest and from the Supreme Priest; but power is not in that sword in the way that it is in the [Supreme] Priest, since it can execute the judgment of blood directly, which the [Supreme] Priest could not, or could not fittingly, do.

And in this way, the words of those teachers mentioned above can be shown to be true: that the Church has both swords, but that she does not have the right to wield both swords. For it is to be understood by this not that there is no sense in which she has the right to wield the material sword, but that she does not have it, or that it is not fitting for her to have it, directly. For she has it through a vicar or through a substitute or through a person interposed: a person interposed, that is, between the ecclesiastical power and the judgment of blood, so that such an office may be discharged fittingly.

Thus, we have applied [to our argument] the second reason and cause why it was good to institute a material sword and earthly authority. For although there is no power in that sword which is not in the priestly dignity, it is nonetheless in that sword not as it is in that dignity, but in a different way.

So too with the third cause, that the world could not be as conveniently or as well governed in both temporal and spiritual respects if the material sword were not added to the ecclesiastical power; and with the fourth cause, that of fitness, as has been touched upon above. And [the truth of] this [statement, that it was good to institute a material sword,] readily appears with the fifth cause, that of orderliness. For as Augustine says at *De civitate Dei* 19:13: 'Order is the distribution which assigns equal and unequal things each to its own proper place.'[1] For the material and spiritual swords are not equals, but unequals, since the one is superior and the other inferior. It was good, therefore, to institute a second sword, so that a proper place might be assigned to it, and so that it might be set under the superior sword, so that all things should be done decently and in order.[2] For if no second sword were appointed in the Church, but if the Supreme Pontiff possessed both swords in such a way that he did not entrust the material sword to another, then it would follow that the material sword would not have its proper and distinct place, but that each sword would be contained in the Supreme Pontiff according to some primary power. Therefore, so great an order would not be reflected, and consequently there would not be so great an adornment as is now reflected, in the Church: because, that is, the material sword is entrusted to the earthly power. For, by reason of this entrusting, a certain fitting order is reflected in the Church because sword is under sword and power under power.

1.   CCSL 48:679.
2.   Cf. I Cor. 14:40.

Sexta eciam causa potest ad hoc idem adaptari: videlicet, quod quantumcumque sit in Ecclesia spiritualis gladius cuncta potens, bonum fuit statuere secundum gladium qui[1] esset terrenus et materialis ad hoc, quod aliqua dignitas regiminis communicaretur laicis, ne in gubernacione populi laici totaliter se cernerent despectos et ex hoc esset murmur et litigium in Ecclesia inter laicos et clericos.[2] Simile autem habetur Actuum VI, quod, crescente numero discipulorum, factum[3] est murmur Grecorum adversus Hebreos, eo quod despicerentur in ministerio cotidiano vidue eorum; ubi Beda ait quod causa murmuris erat quia Hebrei viduas eorum in cotidiano ministerio preferebant viduis Grecorum. Sic, si in gubernacione populi solum preferentur clerici et nulla auctoritas daretur laicis, murmur et scissura contingeret in Ecclesia. Dicemus[4] ergo quod si nulla esset alia causa, cum plures sint alie cause assignate, hec sexta causa, quod aliqua dignitas regiminis et gubernacionis populi quantum ad temporalia communicaretur laicis, est satis sufficiens quod sit secundus gladius in Ecclesia, ut ex hoc in Ecclesia sit quedam imitacio omnipotentis Dei, qui, cum totum de se posset, noluit quod essent supervacua opera sapiencie sue, sed voluit dignitatem suam communicare creaturis, ut ipse creature non essent ociose sed haberent virtutes proprias et acciones proprias, per quas virtutes et acciones facerent ad gubernacionem et ad regimen universi.

Patet igitur,[5] quod cum sex sint[6] cause assignate quare agens inferior non superfluit sed competenter adiungitur agenti superiori, de illis sex causis et racionibus adaptate sunt quinque ad propositum nostrum, quod non superfluit gladius materialis[7] et inferior, sed decenter adiungitur spirituali gladio et superiori: per quos duos gladios totus fidelis populus decenter regitur, et per consequens totus huiusmodi populus ornatur[8] et decoratur.

CAPITULUM XV: *Ubi plenius*[9] *agitur*[10] *quomodo duo gladii qui sunt in Ecclesia adaptantur ad duos gladios in Evangelio nominatos.*

Quoniam in XIII capitulo non plene actum est de duobus gladiis qui sunt in Ecclesia quomodo adaptentur[11] ad duos gladios in evangelio nominatos, sed differebatur hec materia usque ad hoc capitulum ultimum, ideo in hoc capitulo intendimus hoc plenius declarare.

Dicebatur quidem in capitulo V huius secunde partis quod per gladium extractum figurabatur gladius spiritualis, per non extractum materialis. Bernardus tamen, libro quarto ad Eugenium, econtra adaptare videtur. Vult enim quod per gladium extractum significetur materialis; propter quod consequens erit quod per non

---

1: qui] quod F   2: laicos et clericos] clericos et laicos CFV²   3: factum] factus FV²   4: Dicemus] dicamus V²   5: igitur] ergo F   6: sint] sunt V²   7: gladius materialis] materialis gladius F   8: ornatur] honoratur C   9: *plenius*] planius FPV¹V²   10: *agitur*] ageretur C   11: adaptentur] adaptantur CFV²

The sixth cause can also be applied to the same conclusion: namely, that although the spiritual sword can do all things in the Church, it was good to establish a second sword, which should be earthly and material, so that some of the dignity of rule might be shared with the laity, lest the laity should otherwise perceive themselves to be wholly despised in the government of the people and that, for this reason, murmuring and dispute should arise within the Church as between laity and clergy. And something of a similar kind is recorded in Acts 6: that when the number of the disciples had increased, there arose a murmuring of the Greeks against the Hebrews because their widows were neglected in the daily ministry.[1] And Bede says that the cause of this murmuring was that the Hebrews gave preference to their own widows above the widows of the Greeks in the daily ministry.[2] Thus, if the clergy only were to be preferred, and no authority given to the laity in the government of the people, murmuring and division would arise within the Church. We shall say, therefore, since several other causes have been assigned, that, even if there were no other cause, this sixth cause — that some of the dignity of the rule and government of the people in the temporal sphere might be shared with the laity — would of itself be enough to show that there is a second sword in the Church so that, in the Church, there should be a kind of imitation of Almighty God, Who, though He could do all things Himself, did not desire that the works of His wisdom should be in vain: rather, He wished to share his dignity with His creatures in order that those creatures should not be idle, but should have their own powers and activities, through which powers and activities they might contribute to the government and rule of the universe.

. Thus, since six reasons have been assigned why an inferior agent is not superfluous to a superior agent, but may properly be added to it, five of which six causes and reasons have been applied to our proposition, it is clear that the material and inferior sword is not superfluous, but is fittingly joined, to the spiritual and superior sword, and that by these two swords the whole people is fittingly ruled and, consequently, that whole people is adorned and ornamented.

CHAPTER XV: *In which the question of how the two swords which are in the Church are related to the two swords mentioned in the Gospel is more fully treated.*

In chapter XIII, the question of how the two swords which are in the Church may be understood in relation to the two swords mentioned in the Gospel was not fully discussed. Rather, the question was deferred to this final chapter; and so, in this chapter, we intend to deal with it more fully.

Now it was said in chapter V of this second part that the spiritual sword was represented by the drawn sword and the material by the undrawn. Bernard, however, in Book 4 of his work addressed to Eugenius, seems to take a contrary view. For he maintains that the material sword is signified by the drawn sword; and so it

1. Acts 6:1.
2. *Super acta apostolorum* 6 (PL 92:956).

extractum significetur[1] spiritualis. Ait enim ad Eugenium papam: 'Aggredere eos,' idest homines tibi commissos, 'non ferro, sed verbo'; et subdit 'Quid[2] tu denuo usurpare gladium[3] temptas, quem semel iussus es reponere in vaginam?' Vult ergo quod Ecclesia non debeat uti ferro, idest gladio materiali, sed debeat uti verbo, idest gladio spirituali, iuxta illud ad Ephesios VI: 'Et gladium[4] spiritus, quod est verbum Dei.' Prelatus ergo ecclesiasticus non debet uti gladio ferreo, idest materiali, quem semel iussus est reponere in vaginam; quod factum est quando dixit[5] Dominus[6] Petro: 'Converte gladium tuum in locum suum,' ut habetur Matthei XXVI.[7]

Utrumque ergo gladium habet Ecclesia: et extractum, per quem, secundum Bernardum, significatur[8] gladius materialis, et non extractum, per quem significari[9] potest gladius spiritualis. Ideo in eodem libro Bernardus ait: 'Quem,' scilicet[10] gladium materialem et ferreum extractum a Petro,[11] 'qui tuum esse negant,' idest qui negant[12] quod ille gladius non sit Summi Pontificis, 'non satis videntur attendere verbum Domini[13] dicentis "Converte gladium tuum in vaginam." Tuus ergo et ipse,' gladius materialis, 'tuo forsitan nutu,[14] etsi non tua manu evaginandus. Alioquin, si nullo modo ad te pertineret,[15] dicentibus apostolis "Ecce gladii duo hic," non respondisset Dominus "Satis est,"[16] sed "Nimis[17] est." Uterque[18] ergo est Ecclesie, et spiritualis scilicet gladius et[19] materialis; sed is[20] quidem,' idest materialis gladius, 'pro Ecclesia,[21] ille vero,' videlicet spiritualis, 'ab Ecclesia exercendus, ille sacerdotis, is militis manu, sed sane ad sacerdotis nutum.'

Ex tribus[22] ergo colligi potest quod Ecclesia non solum habet spiritualem gladium, sed materialem; primo, ex eo quod Dominus[23] dixit Petro. Nam si per gladium extractum significatur gladius materialis, quando Dominus dixit Petro 'Converte gladium[24] tuum[25] in vaginam' sive 'in locum suum,' plane dedit intelligi quod gladius ille materialis erat Petri et quod gladius materialis ad Ecclesiam pertinebat. Secundo, hoc idem potest colligi ex eo quod discipuli dixerunt: 'Ecce gladii duo hic.' Si ergo tunc discipuli et apostoli representabant Ecclesiam, cum ibi dicerent esse duos gladios, sufficienter nos instruebant quod utrumque gladium habeat Ecclesia. Tercio, hoc idem colligi potest per responsionem Domini, cum dixit 'Satis est.' Non enim dixit 'Nimis[26] est'; nec dixit quod esset parum. Nam dicentibus apostolis[27] quod duo gladii erant ibi, idest in Ecclesia, si uterque gladius non pertineret ad Ecclesiam, nimis[28] fuisset, quia Ecclesia haberet plures gladios quam deberet habere; si autem plures gladios quam duos[29] deberet Ecclesia habere,[30] tunc

---

1: significetur] significatur C   2: Quid] cum *add.* C   3: usurpare gladium] gladium usurpare FV[2]
4: gladium] gladius F   5: dixit] dicit F   6: Dominus] deus FV[2]   7: XXVI] xxii FV[2] xxvii PV[1]
8: significatur] figuratur C   9: significari] figurari C   10: scilicet] idest quem CFV[2]   11: extractum a Petro] a Petro extractum CFV[2]   12: idest qui negant] *om.* F   13: Domini] dei V[2]
14: nutu] motu F   15: pertineret] pertingeret FV[2]   16: est] *om.* C   17: Nimis] minus FV[2]
18: Uterque] utrumque F   19: spiritualis scilicet gladius et] *om.* C   20: is] hic V[2]   21: pro Ecclesia] per ecclesiam F   22: tribus] utroque F   23: Dominus] deus C   24: gladium] *om.* P
25: gladium tuum] tuum gladium V[1]   26: Nimis] minus FV[2]   27: apostolis] discipulis CFV[2]
28: nimis] minus FV[2]   29: duos] duo C *om.* F   30: Ecclesia habere] habere ecclesia F

will follow that the spiritual is signified by the undrawn. For he says to Pope Eugenius: 'Come to them' — that is, to the men entrusted to you — 'not with iron, but with the word.' And he adds: 'Why should you again attempt to usurp the sword which you were once commanded to replace in its sheath?'[1] He maintains, therefore, that the Church may not use an iron — that is, the material — sword, but should use the word, that is, the spiritual sword, according to what is said in Ephesians 6: 'And the sword of the spirit which is the word of God.'[2] The ruler of the Church, therefore, must not use a sword of iron: that is, the material sword which he was once commanded to replace in its sheath; which came about when the Lord said to Peter, 'Put up your sword into its place,' as is established in Matthew 26.[3]

The Church, therefore, has both swords: the drawn, by which, according to Bernard, is signified the material sword, and also the undrawn, by which the spiritual sword can be signified. And so, in the same book, Bernard says: 'Those who deny that it,' that is, the material and iron sword drawn by Peter, 'is yours' — who deny, that is, that this sword belongs to the Supreme Pontiff — 'seem not to give sufficient attention to the words of the Lord when He said, "Put up *your* sword into its sheath." Therefore it,' the material sword, 'is yours: yours indeed to command, even though not yours to unsheathe with your own hand. For if there were no sense in which it belonged to you, then, when the apostles said, "Behold, here are two swords," the Lord would not have replied, "It is enough," but "It is too much."'[4] Both, therefore, belong to the Church: that is, the spiritual and the material sword alike. But the one,' that is, the material sword, 'must be wielded on behalf of the Church, and the other,' namely, the spiritual, 'by the Church: the one by the priest and the other by the hand of the soldier, but indeed at the command of the priest.'

From three statements, therefore, it can be inferred that the Church has not only the spiritual sword, but the material also. The first is what the Lord said to Peter. For if the material sword was signified by the drawn sword, then, when the Lord said to Peter, 'Put up your sword into its sheath' or 'into its place,' He plainly gave us to understand that the material sword was Peter's and that the material sword belongs to the Church. Second, the same inference can be drawn from what the disciples said: 'Behold, here are two swords.' Therefore, if the disciples and apostles then represented the Church, they taught us sufficiently that the Church has both swords when they said that there were two swords there. Third, the same inference can be drawn from the Lord's reply, when He said: 'It is enough.' For He did not say 'It is too much'; nor did He say that it was not enough. For when the apostles said that there were two swords there — that is, in the Church — and if both swords did not belong to the Church, then that would have been too much: for the Church would have had more swords than she should have. But if the Church should have more than two swords, then it would not have been enough

---

1. *De consideratione* 4:3:7.
2. Eph. 6:17.
3. Matt. 26:52.
4. Cf. Luke 22:38.

parum esset quod solum duos gladios haberet. Sed quia Dominus non dixit 'nimis'[1] nec 'parum,' sed dixit quod erat 'satis,' sufficienter datur intelligi quod utrumque gladium habet Ecclesia, et non plures neque pauciores. Ecclesia quidem, habendo duos gladios, non habet nimis, quia non habet plus quam debeat, nec habet parum, quia non habet minus quam debeat habere, sed habet satis, quia habet quantum habere debet.[2]

Hiis habitis, redeamus unde venit sermo[3] prius, quomodo per duos gladios in Evangelio nominatos figurantur duo gladii qui sunt in Ecclesia: utrum per gladium extractum significetur materialis, per non extractum spiritualis vel econverso. Sciendum ergo quod cum agimus de duobus gladiis in evangelio nominatis, vel[4] volumus sequi rem vel figuram. Si rem quidem sequi volumus, uterque[5] fuit materialis, et ille quem Petrus extraxit et ille qui non[6] extractus[7] in vagina remansit. Sed si figuram sequi volumus,[8] non est inconveniens quod una et eadem res secundum aliam et aliam condicionem possit opposita[9] figurare, ut leo figurat Christum et Belial sive Christum et diabolum. Leo quidem figurat Christum cum dicitur: 'Vicit leo de tribu Iuda'; figurat diabolum cum dicitur: 'Adversarius vester diabolus tamquam leo rugiens.' Sic et in proposito: gladius extractus aliter et aliter sumptus figurat gladium materialem et spiritualem,[10] et gladius non extractus aliter et aliter consideratus utrumque gladium figurare[11] potest.[12]

Nam gladius extractus et non extractus[13] dupliciter potest considerari: vel quantum ad usum, quia gladio extracto apostoli sunt usi,[14] non extracto non sunt usi;[15] vel quantum ad visionem, quia gladius extractus, eo quod extractus, erat visibilis, non extractus vero, secundum quod huiusmodi, non erat visibilis, sed erat occultus et in vagina absconsus. Si ergo consideramus usum[16] gladiorum, quia Ecclesia non habet usum vel immediatum exercicium gladii materialis, sed spiritualis, vel, quod idem est, quia gladius qui est creditus Ecclesie, ut cum eo ipsamet feriat, est spiritualis, non materialis, quantum ad huiusmodi usum sive quantum ad huiusmodi ferire sive percutere gladius extractus, quo Petrus usus est et cum quo feriebat et percuciebat, significat[17] gladium spiritualem; non extractus vero, quo nullus discipulorum usus est et nullus eorum cum eo percussit, significat gladium materialem, quem licet habeat Ecclesia, cum eo tamen ipsamet Ecclesia non debet ferire nec percutere. Habebant quidem discipuli illum gladium non extractum, sed cum eo minime percusserunt. Sic ergo loquendum est de illis duobus gladiis, si consideremus eorum usum et eorum ferire et percutere.

Alio autem modo possunt considerari hii duo gladii: non quantum ad usum, sed quantum ad apparenciam et visionem. Et sic, quia que videntur materialia sunt, que autem non videntur[18] sunt spiritualia, gladius extractus, quia ex ipsa extraccione factus est visibilis, ideo secundum hanc consideracionem figuravit[19] gladium

---

1: nimis] minus FV² 2: debet] debeat CFV² 3: sermo] *om.* F 4: vel] *om.* V² 5: uterque] utrumque V² 6: non] fuit *add.* FV² 7: extractus] et *add.* F 8: volumus] ut quia sunt materialis *add. and del.* C 9: opposita] opinata F 10: materialem et spiritualem] spiritualem et materialem FV² 11: figurare] significare FV² 12: potest] *om.* V² 13: et non extractus] *om.* V² 14: apostoli sunt usi] *om.* F 15: non extracto … usi] *om.* V² 16: usum] unum F 17: significat] figurabat C significabat FV² 18: videntur] sunt *add.* F 19: figuravit] figurat V²

for her to have had only two swords. But since the Lord said neither 'too much' nor 'too little,' but said that it was 'enough,' we are sufficiently given to understand that the Church has two swords and neither more nor fewer. For, in having two swords, the Church does not have too many, for she does not have more than she should; nor does she have too few, for she does not have fewer than she should have. Rather, she has enough, since she has as many as she should have.

Having said all this, let us return to the question from which this discussion first came: that of how the two swords which are in the Church are represented by the two swords mentioned in the Gospel — whether the material is signified by the drawn sword and the spiritual by the undrawn or the converse. It must be known, therefore, that when we discuss the two swords mentioned in the Gospel, we may consider them either literally or figuratively. If we wish to consider them literally, both were material: that which Peter drew and also that which was undrawn and which remained in the sheath. But if we wish to consider them figuratively, it is not inconsistent to say that, viewed under different aspects, one and the same thing may represent opposites, as the lion represents both Christ and Belial or Christ and the devil. The lion indeed represents Christ when it is said, 'The lion of the tribe of Judah has conquered';[1] yet it represents the devil when it is said, 'Your adversary the devil is like a roaring lion.'[2] So also in our proposition: the drawn sword can sometimes be taken to represent the material sword and sometimes the spiritual, and the undrawn sword can sometimes be considered as representing the one sword and sometimes the other.

For the drawn sword and the undrawn can be considered in two ways: either with respect to use, since the apostles made use of the drawn sword and they did not make use of the undrawn; or with respect to appearance, since the drawn sword was visible because it was drawn, and the undrawn sword, as such, was not visible, but was hidden and concealed in a sheath. If we consider the use of the swords, therefore, then, since the Church has the use, or the immediate wielding, not of the material sword, but of the spiritual, or (which comes to the same thing) since the sword which is entrusted to the Church [to wield directly] and with which she herself may strike is spiritual and not material, the drawn sword which Peter used and with which he struck and punished signifies the spiritual sword with respect to such use or such striking or punishing; and the undrawn, which none of the disciples used and with which none of them struck, signifies the material sword with which, although the Church has it, the Church herself may nonetheless neither strike nor punish. And so the disciples had the undrawn sword; but they did not once strike with it. So it is, therefore, when we speak of these two swords and if we consider their use and their striking and punishing.

But there is another way in which the two swords can be considered: not with respect to use, but with respect to appearance and sight. And so, according to this interpretation, since it is material things which are seen and spiritual things which are not seen, the drawn sword, because it was made visible by being drawn, therefore

1. Rev. 5:5.
2. I Pet. 5:8.

materialem, qui est gladius visibilis et facit vulnera visibilia. Alius autem gladius non extractus, qui, secundum quod huiusmodi, erat occultus et invisibilis, significat spiritualem gladium, qui oculis corporeis videri non potest; ad quem gladium spectat ipsam animam ferire et vulnerare, cuius vulnera corporales oculi videre non possunt.

Patet ergo quomodo aliter et aliter uterque gladius in evangelio nominatus significare potest utrumque gladium in Ecclesia existentem. Unde[1] alii et alii sancti per utrumque[2] utrumque[3] figurant.[4]

Sed dices quod, si per gladium extractum potest figurari gladius spiritualis, quare prohibitus fuit Petrus ut non feriret cum illo gladio, cum spiritualis gladius Ecclesie sit creditus et datus ad feriendum et percuciendum cum eo. Sciendum ergo quod ille gladius extractus dupliciter potest considerari: vel secundum rem vel secundum figuram. Si ergo per huiusmodi gladium extractum figuretur gladius spiritualis, prohibitus fuit Petrus ad percuciendum cum tali gladio non[5] racione figure, sed racione rei. Quia, etsi ille gladius sic extractus figurabat gladium spiritualem, ipsa tamen res erat ferrum et erat gladius ferreus[6] et materialis. Sed, si huiusmodi gladius extractus figuret sive significet gladium materialem, tunc utroque modo prohibitus[7] vel increpatus fuit Petrus ut non feriret cum tali gladio: et racione rei, quia res ipsa erat gladius[8] materialis,[9] et racione figure, quia positum est, quod materialem gladium figuraret.

Sciendum insuper quod, cum dixerunt discipuli 'Ecce gladii duo hic' et Dominus respondit 'Satis est,' huiusmodi responsio Domini, secundum varias exposiciones sanctorum, uno modo est ironica et derisiva, alio modo est vera et assertiva. Nam si illi duo gladii considerantur non secundum figuram sed secundum rem, sic responsio Domini erat ironica et derisiva; quia ad defendendum discipulos, si volebant inniti auxilio humano, forte mille gladii non suffecissent eis, cum Iudas proditor adduxisset secum multam turbam cum gladiis et fustibus. Quid ergo erant duo gladii ad defendendum discipulos contra tantam turbam? Secundum ergo hunc modum locutus est Dominus ironice, sicut quis loqueretur ironice contra aliquos[10] qui cum modica pecunia vellent magnalia facere, cum diceretur eis derisive quod satis haberent de pecunia ad talia magnalia faciendum. Sed si hii duo gladii non considerantur secundum rem et secundum id quod erant,[11] sed secundum significacionem[12] et secundum id quod figurabant, tunc responsio Domini est vera et assertiva. Figurabant enim illi duo gladii duos gladios, spiritualem et materialem, quos in Ecclesia esse non est nimis neque parum, sed est satis.

Et hec de hac secunda parte huius operis ad presens sufficiant.

Explicit secunda pars huius operis de ecclesiastica potestate.[13]

1: unde] deum P   2: utrumque] utramque FV² 3: utrumque] utraque FV² utrum P   4: unde alii ... figurant] *om.* V¹   5: non] tali *add.* F   6: gladius ferreus] ferreus gladius C   7: prohibitus] est *add. and del.* C   8: gladius] *om.* V²   9: gladius materialis] materialis gladius F   10: aliquos] alios FPV¹V²   11: et secundum id quod erant] *del.* C   12: significacionem] figuracionem PV¹   13: Explicit secunda ... potestate] *om.* PV¹

represented the material sword, which is a visible sword and which inflicts visible wounds. But the other sword, which was not drawn and which, as such, was hidden and invisible, signifies the spiritual sword which the body's eye cannot see. And it belongs to this sword to strike and to wound the soul, whose wounds the body's eyes cannot see.

It is clear, therefore, how, in different ways, the two swords mentioned in the Gospel can signify the two swords which exist in the Church; and so some of the saints have represented the first by the second and others the second by the first.

But you will ask why, if the spiritual sword can be represented by the drawn sword, Peter was forbidden to strike with that sword when the spiritual sword is entrusted and given to the Church so that she may strike and punish with it. It must be known, therefore, that the drawn sword itself can be considered in two ways: either literally or figuratively. Therefore, if it is the spiritual sword which is represented by the drawn sword, Peter was forbidden to punish with that sword not figuratively, but literally. For although the drawn sword thus represented the spiritual sword [figuratively], it was itself nonetheless a thing of iron, and was [literally] an iron and a material sword. But if this drawn sword represents or signifies the material sword, then Peter was forbidden to strike with that sword, or rebuked [for doing so], in both senses: literally, because it was itself [literally] a material sword, and also figuratively, because it is here assumed that it also represented the material sword.

Furthermore, it must be known that, according to the various interpretations of the saints, when the disciples said, 'Behold, here are two swords' and the Lord replied, 'It is enough,' this reply of the Lord was in one sense ironic and mocking and, in another sense, was true and literal. For if these two swords are considered not figuratively, but literally, then the Lord's reply was ironic and mocking because, if they wished to rely upon human aid, perhaps a thousand swords would not have sufficed for the defence of the disciples. For Judas the betrayer had brought with him a great multitude with swords and staves.[1] What, therefore, would have been the use of two swords for the defence of the disciples against so great a multitude? In this sense, therefore, the Lord was speaking ironically, as one might speak ironically to certain persons who planned to do great things with little money, and say mockingly to them that they had plenty of money with which to do such great things. But if these two swords are not considered literally and in terms of what they were, but as images and in terms of what they represented, then the Lord's reply was true and literal. For these two swords represented the two swords, spiritual and material, which are neither too many nor too few, but enough, in the Church.

And these remarks may suffice for our present purpose in the second part of this work.

Here ends the second part of this work concerning ecclesiastical power.

---

1. Cf. Mark 14:43.

[TERTIA PARS]

Incipiunt capitula tercie partis[1] huius operis, in qua[2] solvuntur obiecciones que contra prehabita fieri possent.

CAPITULUM I: Quod, cum dictum sit quod Ecclesia in temporalia[3] habeat universale dominium, quomodo intelligendum est[4] quod non est de rigore iuris ut a civili iudice appelletur ad papam.

CAPITULUM II: Cum Ecclesia super temporalibus habeat universale dominium, quomodo intelligendum est quod Summus Pontifex non vult iurisdiccionem regum perturbare, et quod non ad Ecclesiam sed ad reges spectat de possessionibus iudicare.

CAPITULUM III: Quod racio persuadet, ista materialia[5] et naturalia manifestant, necnon et tercio divina gubernacio hoc declarat, qualiter Summus Pontifex circa temporalia debeat se habere.

CAPITULUM IV: Quod cum omnia temporalia sint sub dominio Ecclesie, quomodo intelligendum est quod ait Innocencius III: quod 'certis causis inspectis, temporalem iurisdiccionem casualiter exercemus.'

CAPITULUM V: Quod si temporalia fiant spiritualia vel annectantur[6] spiritualibus, vel econverso temporalibus spiritualia sint annexa, sunt spirituales casus per quos Ecclesia temporalem iurisdiccionem[7] debet[8] specialiter exercere.

CAPITULUM VI: Cum pro quolibet criminali peccato possit Ecclesia quemlibet Christianum corripere et ex hoc temporalem iurisdiccionem peragere, qualiter precipue ad Ecclesiam spectat cum litigium temporalium contrariatur paci et cum pacis federa sunt iuramento firmata.

CAPITULUM VII: Quod tam ex parte rerum temporalium, ut superius est narratum, tam[9] ex parte potestatis terrene, ut in hoc capitulo ostendetur, quam eciam ex parte potestatis ecclesiastice, ut in sequenti capitulo declarabitur, possunt[10] sumi speciales[11] casus propter quos Summus Pontifex se de temporalibus intromittet.

CAPITULUM VIII: In quo narrantur speciales[12] casus sumpti ex parte potestatis ecclesiastice in quibus ad Ecclesiam pertinebit iurisdiccionem in temporalibus exercere.

CAPITULUM IX: Quid est plenitudo potestatis, et quod in Summo Pontifice veraciter potestatis residet plenitudo.

CAPITULUM X: Cum in Summo Pontifice sit plenitudo potestatis, non tamen sit

---

1: Incipiunt capitula ... partis] Incipit tercia pars PV[1]   2: qua] parte *add.* FV[2]   3: temporalia] temporalibus C   4: est] sit C   5: ista materialia] *del.* C   6: annectantur] annectentur C   7: temporalem iurisdiccionem] iurisdiccionem temporalem FPV[1]V[2]   8: debet] dicitur *mss*   9: tam] quam C   10: possunt] possint FPV[1]V[2]   11: speciales] spirituales *mss*   12: speciales] spirituales C

[PART THREE]

Thus begin the chapters of the third part of this work, in which the objections which might be brought against what we have so far said are resolved.

CHAPTER I: Since it has been said that the Church has a universal lordship in temporal things, how are we to understand that it is not according to the strictness of the law that appeal may be made from a civil judge to the pope?

CHAPTER II: Since the Church has a universal lordship over temporal things, how are we to understand that the Supreme Pontiff does not wish to disturb the jurisdiction of kings, and that it does not rest with the Church, but with kings, to judge matters involving possessions?

CHAPTER III: That reason demonstrates, material and natural phenomena show, and, third, the divine government most clearly reveals, how the Supreme Pontiff must stand in relation to temporal things.

CHAPTER IV: Since all temporal things are under the lordship of the Church, how are we to understand what Innocent III says: that 'on the examination of certain causes, we exercise a temporal jurisdiction occasionally'?

CHAPTER V: That if temporal things become spiritual, or if they are annexed to spiritual things, or, conversely, if spiritual things are annexed to temporal things, these are special cases by reason of which the Church must exercise a special temporal jurisdiction.

CHAPTER VI: How, since the Church may rebuke every Christian for every criminal sin, and so may exercise a temporal jurisdiction, it especially rests with the Church to do this when a temporal dispute is detrimental to peace and when peace treaties have been confirmed by oath.

CHAPTER VII: That the special cases by reason of which the Supreme Pontiff will intervene in temporal matters can be derived from a consideration of temporal things, as has been discussed above; from a consideration of the earthly power, as will be shown in this chapter; and also from a consideration of the ecclesiastical power, as will be made clear in the next chapter.

CHAPTER VIII: In which are described the special cases derived from a consideration of the ecclesiastical power in which it will pertain to the Church to exercise jurisdiction in temporal matters.

CHAPTER IX: What fullness of power is, and that fullness of power truly resides in the Supreme Pontiff.

CHAPTER X: Since there is fullness of power in the Supreme Pontiff yet no such

in celo huiusmodi plenitudo, quare potestas eius dicatur esse celestis.

CAPITULUM XI: Cum in Summo Pontifice plenitudo resideat potestatis, quomodo intelligendum dictum Hugonis, quod 'pia devocione fidelium temporalia quedam ecclesiis concessa sunt possidenda.'

CAPITULUM ULTIMUM: Quod in Ecclesia est tanta potestatis plenitudo quod eius posse est sine pondere, numero et mensura.[1;2]

———— ✳ ————

CAPITULUM I: *Quod, cum dictum sit quod Ecclesia in temporalia[3] habeat universale dominium, quomodo intelligendum est[4] quod non est de rigore iuris ut a civili iudice appelletur ad papam.*

Ait enim Apostolus secunda ad Corinthios XI: 'Et si imperitus sermone, non tamen sciencia'; que verba referri possunt ad id quod dicitur prima ad Corinthios II: 'Et cum venissem ad vos, fratres, veni non in sublimitate sermonis.' Nam sciencia philosophorum est in sublimitate sermonis et in sapiencia verbi. Ipsi quidem per verba ampulosa suam scienciam protulerunt, ut non minus,[5] immo magis, refulgeret ibi sapiencia verbi et sublimitas sermonis quam sapiencia et profunditas rerum. Theologia vero quodam humili loquendi[6] genere usa est, ut exinde Apostolus diceret quod si sua doctrina videbatur imperita sermone, quia non erat in sublimitate sermonis, non erat tamen secundum scienciam imperita. Que verba non ad nostram commendacionem, ut nos peritos in sciencia asseramus, sed ad nostram excusacionem, ut si in hoc opere non per eadem verba locuti fuimus per que profundiores in hac materia loquerentur, excusatos esse volumus, quia, secundum Augustinum, cum de re constat, nulla debet esse questio de sermone; et Hilarius vult quod non sermoni res, sed rei sermo debet esse subiectus. Que ad ante dicta et ad dicenda possunt congrue adaptari.

Quare, si supra[7] diximus quod decime sunt quasi census possessionum nostrarum et oblaciones sunt quasi tributa que damus Deo et Ecclesie tam pro nobis quam pro[8] rebus nostris in recognicionem[9] proprie servitutis, quia quedam iura videntur dicere quod ipse decime se habent ut tributa, nihil ad propositum. Quia sive decime sint census et[10] oblaciones sint tributa sive econverso, sive utraque sint tributa sive utraque census, non erit litigium rei, sed verborum pocius;[11] quia semper habetur intentum: videlicet, quod si hec[12] tenemur dare Ecclesie, quod ex hoc ipso recognoscamus eam dominam tam nostram[13] quam eciam rerum nostrarum. Et si in aliis[14] iam dictis posset[15] similis[16] verborum controversia exoriri, minime est

1: CAPITULUM VIII ... mensura] *om.* V²   2: CAPITULUM I ... mensura] *om.* PV¹   3: *temporalia*] temporalibus C   4: *est*] sit C   5: minus] *om.* FV²   6: loquendi] legendi PV¹   7: supra] superius F   8: pro] *om.* C   9: recognicionem] recognicione FV²   10: et] *om.* F   11: verborum pocius] pocius verborum CFV²   12: hec] hoc *mss*   13: nostram] animarum F   14: aliis] eciam *add.* FV²   15: posset] possit F   16: similis] simul FV²

fullness resides in the heaven, why is his power said to be heavenly?

CHAPTER XI: Since fullness of power resides in the Supreme Pontiff, how are we to understand what Hugh says: that 'certain temporal possessions have been granted to churches as possessions by the pious devotion of the faithful'?

FINAL CHAPTER: That there is in the Church a fullness of power so great that her power is without limit of weight, number, and measure.

———————— ✳ ————————

CHAPTER I: *Since it has been said that the Church has a universal lordship in temporal things, how are we to understand that it is not according to the strictness of the law that appeal may be made from a civil judge to the pope?*

For the Apostle says in II Corinthians 11: 'Though I be unskilled in speech, yet not in knowledge'; and these words can be referred back to what is said in I Corinthians 2: 'And when I came to you, brothers, I came not in loftiness of speech.' [1] For the wisdom of the philosophers lies in loftiness of speech and in verbal skill. Indeed, they have presented their knowledge through such abundant words that verbal skill and loftiness of speech is no less, but is indeed more, reflected there than wisdom and depth of subject matter. Theology, however, has used a certain humble manner of speaking; so that, accordingly, the Apostle might say that if his teaching seemed unskilled in speech because it did not lie in loftiness of speech, it was nonetheless not unskilled in knowledge. And these words tend not to our praise, so that we may assert that we are skilled in knowledge, but to our excuse. And so if, in this work, we have not spoken by the same words as those by which men more deeply versed in this matter might have spoken, we desire to be excused. For, according to Augustine, when an issue is clear there must be no dispute over mere speech;[2] and Hilary maintains that meaning must not be subordinated to speech, but speech to meaning:[3] and these statements can properly be applied both to what has been said already and to what must still be said.

Thus, although we have said above that tithes are a kind of tax on our possessions and that offerings are a kind of tribute which we give to God and to the Church for ourselves and for our goods alike, in recognition of our own servitude,[4] the fact that certain laws seem to say that tithes are themselves a form of tribute is neither here nor there.[5] For whether tithes be a tax and offerings a tribute or the converse, or whether both be a tribute or both a tax, there will be no room for argument as to meaning, but only as to words; for in every case the meaning is the same: namely, that if we are bound to give these things to the Church, we must for this reason acknowledge her as lord both of ourselves and of our goods also. And if a similar controversy as to words might arise over other statements so far made, this should not

1. II Cor. 11:6; I Cor. 2:1.
2. Augustine, *De catechizandis rudibus* 9 (CCSL 46:135).
3. Hilary of Poitiers, *De Trinitate* 4 (PL 10:107).
4. See Pt. I, Ch. V, pp. 21–23; Pt. II, Ch. X, pp. 177–179.
5. See X. 3:30:22: *Non est*, 26: *Tua nobis*, 33: *Quum non sit* (CIC II:563; 564; 568).

curandum, dum tamen per verba illa possit rerum veritas patefieri. Hec autem que adaptavimus ad iam dicta, adaptari volumus ad dicenda, ut si non per eadem verba proferemus nostras sentencias[1] que proferent qui in hac materia profundiorem industriam habere cernuntur, dum tamen rei veritas per nostra verba aliqualiter possit exquiri, volumus lectorem esse contentum.

Hiis itaque prelibatis, volumus aggredi hanc terciam partem. Nam cum in parte prima ostensum sit quod ipse potestates temporales vel[2] terrene Ecclesie sunt subiecte, in secunda vero declaratum sit quod ipsa temporalia sub dominio Ecclesie collocantur, quia multa[3] possent obici contra predicta, ad perfeccionem et[4] consummacionem huius operis volumus hanc terciam partem componere, in qua que nobis contra prefata obicienda occurrerint secundum nostre sciencie modulum dissolvantur.[5]

Ubi primo[6] nobis dubitandum occurrit, quod cum appellacio nihil esse aliud videatur quam[7] a minori ad maiorem iudicem provocacio, si Ecclesia super omnibus temporalibus primatum habet, ut nos supra diximus[8] et ut magni doctores nostre sciencie notaverunt, videlicet quod quodam iure superiori et primario omnia sub dominio Ecclesie sunt subiecta: hiis itaque sic se habentibus, quomodo verificari potest quod in canonibus ecclesiasticis invenitur, quod non sit de rigore iuris quod a civili iudice appelletur ad papam, ut habetur Extra., *De appellacionibus, Si duobus.* Dicemus igitur quod si Alexander III, vel papa quicumque[9] qui fuerit[10] pro tempore, aliqua protulit contra iurisdiccionem ecclesiasticam vel contra Ecclesie potestatem, in nullo suo preiudicavit vel preiudicare potuit successori. Verum[11] quia non est decens non deferre verbis Summi Pontificis, qui est dominus urbis et orbis, salvare curabimus quomodo illa duo stare possint: quod Summus Pontifex sit in temporalibus universaliter[12] dominus, et tamen non sit de rigore iuris quod a civili iudice appelletur ad ipsum.

Advertendum ergo quod cum ibi dicatur hoc non esse secundum iuris rigorem, oportet quod multipliciter distinguatur de iure. Erit igitur prima distinccio, quod triplex est ius: mite, equum et rigidum; quam distinccionem adaptabimus ad punicionem malorum, ut ex hoc descendamus ad distinccionem potestatum. Nam lex propter transgressores posita est; adversus autem iustos non est lex. 'Ille enim, qui gladium portat, Dei minister est, vindex in iram ei qui malum

---

1: sentencias] per *add.* CV[2]   2: temporales vel] *del.* C   3: multa] nulla V[2]   4: et] *om.* F
5: dissolvantur] dissolventur F   6: primo] primum F   7: quam] ad V[2]   8: diximus] duximus F
9: quicumque] alius CV[2]   10: fuerit] fuit V[2]   11: Verum] verumtamen F   12: universaliter]
om. C verus F

trouble us in the least, so long as the truth of things may nonetheless be made clear through those words. And what we have applied to those remarks already made we wish to be applied to those which remain to be made; so that, if we do not present our arguments through the same words as those through which men reckoned to have a deeper ability in this subject will present them, we wish the reader to be content, so long as some part of the truth of the matter may nonetheless be discovered through our words.

Thus, having first touched upon these considerations, we wish to come to this third part. For since, in the first part, it was shown that the temporal or earthly powers are themselves subject to the Church; and, in the second, it was made clear that even temporal things are placed under the Church's lordship; and because many objections might be brought against the foregoing statements: we wish, in order to bring this work to perfection and completion, to compose this third part, in which those objections which have occurred to us against what we have so far said are resolved according to the small measure of our skill.

This is where it first occurs to us that doubt must arise: that since an appeal would seem to be nothing other than a plea from a lesser judge to a greater, and if the Church has primacy over all temporal things (as we have said above and as the great teachers of our science [i.e. canon law] have noted: that all things are subjected to the Church by a certain superior and primary law),[1] then, all this being so, how can that which is found in the canons of the Church be regarded as true: that, as is established at X. 2:28:7: *Si duobus*, it is 'not according to the strictness of the law' that appeal may be made from a civil judge to the pope?[2] We shall say, then, that if Alexander III, or anyone else who might have been pope at some time, has made any pronouncement detrimental to the jurisdiction of the Church or detrimental to the Church's power, he has in no way prejudiced, nor could he prejudice, his successor.[3] But because it is not fitting not to defer to the words of the Supreme Pontiff, who is lord of the city [of Rome] and of the world, we shall [waive this point for the time being, and here] take care to show how these two statements may stand together: that the Supreme Pontiff is universally lord in temporal things, and that it is nonetheless not according to the strictness of the law that appeal may be made to him from a civil judge.

It must be noted, therefore, that, although it is said here that this is not according to the strictness of the law, it is proper that the law be distinguished in many ways. The first distinction, then, will be that the law is threefold: gentle, moderate and harsh. And we shall consider this distinction with reference to the punishment of the wicked, so that we may pass from this to a distinction between the powers. For the law is established for the sake of transgressors; but the law is not directed against just men.[4] As is said in Romans 13: 'For he who bears the sword is a minister of God, an

1. See e.g. Alanus Anglicus, Commentary on Dist. 96, c. 6, ed. A.M. Stickler, 'Alanus Anglicus als Verteidiger des monarchischen Papsttums,' *Salesianum* 21 (1959), p. 361.
2. CIC II:412; and see Introduction, n. 59.
3. See Ch. IV, p. 315.
4. Cf. Gal. 3:19.

agit. Nam principes non sunt timori boni operis, sed mali,' ut dicitur ad Romanos XIII.

Propter quod sciendum quod non est delictum aliquod quod non habeat suas condiciones et circumstancias, que condiciones[1] et circumstancie referri poterunt vel ad genus delicti, per quod iudicatur reus, vel ad ipsum iudicem, a quo iudicatur reus. Si enim huiusmodi condiciones vel circumstancie comparantur ad genus delicti, aliquando alleviant delictum, aliquando aggravant,[2] quia tali tempore et tali loco et taliter potest fieri delictum, quod levius debet puniri reus, et taliter[3] quod[4] gravius. Ideo dicitur Deuteronomio XXV quod: 'Pro mensura peccati erit et plagarum modus.'[5] Hec autem mensura peccati[6] sumenda est et quantum ad genus delicti et quantum ad circumstancias, quia aliquod genus delicti est gravius alio, et[7] alique circumstancie sunt magis aggravantes quam alie. Comparando ergo circumstancias ad quodcumque genus delicti, distinguemus triplex prefatum ius in[8] mite, equum et rigidum. Nam si huiusmodi genus delicti habet quasi omnes circumstancias alleviantes, debet fieri reo ius mite; debet enim tunc puniri reus cum quadam misericordia[9] et indulgencia. Sed si habeat quasi omnes circumstancias aggravantes, debet fieri reo ius[10] rigidum, quia debet puniri secundum severitatem et rigorem; sed si[11] habeat medio modo, debet ei fieri ius equum, secundum quod requirit genus delicti.[12]

Et quod diximus de circumstanciis relatis ad genus delicti veritatem habet de eis relatis ad iudicem.[13] Quia causa racionabili imminente, iudex aliquando factum aggravat et alleviat et medio modo punit: ut, si expedire videat, potest advertere condiciones aggravantes et punire secundum iuris rigorem; sic eciam potest advertere condiciones alleviantes et facere ius graciosum et mite; vel potest advertere condiciones modo[14] medio[15] se habentes et facere ius equum sive punire secundum equitatem iuris.

Ex hiis ergo que diximus de rigore iuris in peccatis puniendis, patet quid dicendum sit de rigore iuris[16] in foris vel[17] officiis distinguendis.[18] Quia, sicut peccata tunc puniuntur secundum rigorem iuris quando[19] potissime considerantur ut punienda,[20] sic distinccio in foris et in officiis tunc accipitur secundum rigorem quando solum considerantur ut distincta; secundum quem modum quodlibet[21] peragit suum officium et unum ad aliud non reducitur, et per[22] consequens hoc modo ex uno[23] ad aliud minime appellatur.

1: que condiciones] om. F   2: aggravant] gravant V[2]   3: taliter] tali et FV[2]   4: quod] om. FV[2]
5: modus] motus CF   6: erit et … peccati] om. V[2]   7: et] om. FV[2]   8: in] om. CPV[1]V[2]
9: misericordia] miseria F   10: reo ius] ius reo C   11: si] se add. V[2]   12: delicti] non notabiliter factum aggravando nec alleviando per circumstancias annexas add. and del. C   13: iudicem] invicem V[2]   14: modo] om. V[2]   15: modo medio] medio modo CF   16: iuris] iniuris in foris add. V[2]   17: vel] in add. CFV[2]   18: distinguendis] distinguendum FV[2]   19: quando] quoniam F
20: punienda] puniendi V[2]   21: quodlibet] quilibet F   22: per] om. V[2]   23: ex uno] om. V[2]

avenger to execute wrath upon him who does evil. For princes are not a terror to good works, but to evil.'[1]

It must be known, then, that there is no kind of crime which does not have its conditions and circumstances, and that these conditions and circumstances can be considered either in relation to the nature of the crime for which the offender is judged, or to the judge himself by whom the offender is judged. For if such conditions or circumstances are compared to the nature of the crime, they sometimes mitigate the crime and sometimes aggravate it. For a crime may be committed at such a time and place and in such a fashion that the offender should be punished more lightly, and in such a fashion that he should be punished more heavily. And so it is said in Deuteronomy 25 that 'According to the measure of the offence shall the manner of the lashes also be.'[2] But this measure of offence must itself be understood both in the light of the nature of the crime and in the light of circumstances; for one kind of crime is more grievous than another, and some circumstances are more aggravating than others. Therefore, by comparing the circumstances to whatever is the nature of the crime, we shall distinguish the law in the three ways just mentioned: as gentle, moderate, and harsh. For if a crime of a certain kind has circumstances which are almost entirely mitigating, the law must be made gentle to the offender; for the offender must then be punished with a certain mercy and indulgence. But if it has circumstances which are almost entirely aggravating, the law must be made harsh to the offender, for he must be punished according to its severity and strictness. But if it has circumstances of an intermediate kind, the law must be made moderate to him, according to what the nature of the crime requires.

And what we have said of circumstances relative to the nature of the crime holds true of them relative to the judge. For sometimes, for reasonable and pressing cause, the judge takes either a serious or a lenient view of what has been committed, or punishes in a moderate way. And so, if it should seem expedient, he can take account of aggravating conditions and punish according to the strictness of the law; so also, he can take account of mitigating conditions and make the law mild and gentle; or he can take account of conditions having an intermediate character and make the law moderate, or punish according to the moderateness of the law.

Therefore, from what we have said concerning the strictness of the law in relation to the punishment of offences, what we must say concerning the strictness of the law in relation to the distinction between [civil and ecclesiastical] courts or offices is clear. For just as offences are punished according to the strictness of the law only when they are considered especially worthy of punishment, so the distinction between courts and offices is to be taken according to the strictness [of the law] only when they are considered simply as distinct. And, in this sense, each [indeed] performs its own function, and the one is not reduced to the other; and, consequently, there is in this sense no appeal at all from the one to the other. [Where necessary, however, this distinction may be ignored and appeal made from a civil judge to the pope, just as the criminal law can be modified in appropriate cases.]

1. Rom. 13:3–4.
2. Deut. 25:2.

Vel possumus dicere quod non eodem modo gladius terrenus et ecclesiasticus sunt temporales. Immo, sic comparantur hii duo gladii secundum se ad temporalitatem sicut sol et[1] ignis ad caliditatem. Utrumque enim calefacit, et sol et ignis; sed ignis est calidus formaliter, sol vero superexcellenter et virtualiter. Sic gladius terrenus est temporalis formaliter, sed ecclesiasticus, ut ecclesiasticus, est temporalis superexcellenter[2] et virtualiter racione spiritualitatis ad quam temporalia ordinantur.

Sed queres[3] utrum ecclesiasticus gladius possit esse temporalis formaliter. Ad quod dici potest quod ubi Ecclesia pia largicione fidelium vel alio iusto acquisicionis titulo habet iurisdiccionem temporalem, poterit idem[4] dici temporalis formaliter. Et quia rigidum est quod non plicatur, hoc videtur esse rigidum in iure ut secundum eundem ordinem procedatur: ut quod est tale[5] formaliter inferius appellet[6] ad id quod est tale formaliter superius. Et ista videtur esse intencio Alexandri. Non enim ait quod a civili iudice non possit appellari ad papam, sed quod[7] ista rigiditas et uniformitas non servatur nisi ubi papa habet temporalem iurisdiccionem et ubi est temporalis formaliter, sicut et[8] civilis iudex.

Alio autem[9] modo possumus salvare prefata verba, eciam non faciendo vim in hoc quod dicitur 'de rigore', sed distinguendo aliter de iure ipso.[10] Dicemus enim quod est[11] ius distinccionis fori et est ius plenitudinis potestatis. Nam si de uno foro appelletur ad aliud, et si a civili iudice appelletur ad papam, quia gladii sunt distincti et hoc[12] forum est distinctum[13] ab illo, ideo huiusmodi appellacio non erit secundum ius distinccionis fori; erit tamen secundum ius plenitudinis potestatis que in Summo Pontifice reservatur. Non est enim ex impotencia spiritualis gladii quod sibi secundus gladius est adiunctus. Nam et primitus in eadem persona erat utraque potestas, ut in lege nature idem erat sacerdos et rex, ut Melchisedech, ut supra tetigimus et habetur Geneseos XIV,[14] erat rex Salem et erat sacerdos Dei altissimi. Sic et Job, qui Iudeus non fuit, sed vivebat secundum legem nature, rex erat et agebat opera sacerdotis. Immo, quidam magni doctores notaverunt quod in lege nature primogeniti ipsorum magnatum erant reges et sacerdotes. Sic et in lege scripta hee due potestates in eadem persona reservabantur,[15] ut Moyses erat pro populo in hiis que sunt ad Deum, quod est officium sacerdotis, et iudicabat populum, quod est officium materialis gladii; et Samuel, ut ait Magister in *Historiis*,

1: et] *om.* V² 2: superexcellenter] supercellentur F 3: queres] queris F 4: idem] ibi C 5: tale] talis *mss* 6: appellet] appelletur V² 7: quod] ibi *add.* C 8: et] *om.* V² 9: autem] eciam C 10: iure ipso] ipso iure F 11: est] et FV² 12: hoc] hic C 13: distinctum] distinctus C 14: XIV] viii F xiii PV¹V² 15: reservabantur] reservabuntur C

Again, we can say that the earthly and ecclesiastical swords are not related to temporal matters in the same way. Rather, these two swords, as such, stand in the same relation to the temporal sphere as that of the sun and fire to heat. For both make hot, the sun and fire alike; but fire is hot in a secondary way, whereas the sun is preeminently and intrinsically so. So too, the earthly sword is temporal in a secondary way [i.e. it deals with temporal matters only as the Church's delegate], but the ecclesiastical, as such, is temporal preeminently and intrinsically because of the spiritual nature [of the ends] to which temporal things are ordered.

But you will ask whether the ecclesiastical sword may be temporal in the secondary sense [of exercising a day-to-day temporal jurisdiction]. To which it can be said that where the Church has temporal jurisdiction by the pious gift of the faithful or by other just title of acquisition,[1] it will also be able to be called temporal in the secondary sense. And because it is a strict principle that there should be no inconsistency, so it seems to be an inflexible principle of law that procedure should follow a consistent order: that an inferior should appeal to the superior authority appropriate to it. And this seems to be Alexander's intention. For he does not say that appeal may not [ever] be made from a civil judge to the pope, but that this is not done inflexibly and uniformly except where the pope has [direct] temporal jurisdiction and where he is temporal in a secondary sense, as the civil judge is also.[2]

But there is another way in which we can explain the words in question: not by attaching force to the phrase 'according to the strictness,' but by making a further distinction as to the law itself. For we shall say that the law relates to the distinction between [civil and ecclesiastical] courts and that the law also relates to fullness of power. Now if appeal is made from the one court to the other, and if appeal is made from a civil judge to the pope, then, because the swords are distinct and the one court is separate from the other, such appeal will therefore not be according to the law as it relates to the distinction between the courts. It will, however, be according to the law as it relates to the fullness of power which is contained in the Supreme Pontiff. For it is not due to any lack of power on the part of the spiritual sword that a second sword is joined to it. For originally, indeed, both powers were in the same person, so that, under the law of nature, the same man was both priest and king: Melchizedek, for example, who, as we have noted above, and as is established in Genesis 14, was both king of Salem and a priest of the Most High God. So also Job, who was not a Jew, but lived according to the law of nature, was a king and performed the tasks of a priest.[3] Indeed, certain great teachers have noted that, under the law of nature, the firstborn of great men themselves were kings and priests. So also, under the Written Law, these two powers were contained in the same person. For Moses acted for the people in those things which are of God, which is the duty of a priest; and he judged the people, which is the office of the material sword.

1. See Ch. XI, passim.
2. I have translated this and the previous paragraph somewhat freely, largely because there are no satisfactory English equivalents to *formaliter, superexcellenter* and *virtualiter* as Giles is here using them; but the sense is clear enough.
3. Cf. Pt. I, Ch. V, p. 25; Pt. I, Ch. VII, p. 43.

fuit sacerdos, iudex et propheta; et ideo ter vocavit eum Dominus antequam sciret
Samuel quod Dominus vocaret eum, ut habetur primo Regum III: quod ideo factum est ad designandum hoc triplex officium quod[1] sibi committendum erat, ut
Magister in *Historiis* tangit et allegat ad hoc Iosephum. Non est ergo ex impotencia spiritualis gladii quod non possit de temporalibus animadvertere, sed adiunctus
est sibi materialis gladius propter eius excellenciam. Nam quia spiritualis gladius
est tam excellens, et tam excellencia sunt sibi commissa, ut liberius possit eis vacare adiunctus est sibi secundus gladius, ex cuius adiunccione in nullo diminuta
est eius[2] iurisdiccio et plenitudo potestatis ipsius,[3] sed ad quandam[4] decenciam[5]
hoc est factum, ut qui ordinatur ad magna, nisi casus immineat, non se intromittat
per se ipsum et immediate de[6] parvis. Est itaque plenitudo potestatis in spirituali
gladio ut,[7] si expediat, de temporalibus iudicet. Si ergo a civili iudice appelletur ad
papam, et si hoc non sit secundum ius distinccionis fori, erit secundum ius plenitudinis potestatis.

Possumus autem et[8] quarto modo salvare prefata verba.[9] Nam quod hoc sit ius
vel non ius ex ipsa condicione rerum sumit originem, sicut quod hoc sit verum vel
non verum ex ipsa rerum existencia iudicatur. Ideo aliquid est verum uno modo
quod[10] non est verum alio modo, ut quod dulce videatur est verum per accidens
quod non est verum per se. Sic et in proposito, aliquid non est ius uno modo quod
est ius alio modo. Ideo videamus quomodo iudex civilis se habet ad papam et
quomodo[11] unum forum se habet ad aliud, ut ex ipsa rerum existencia concludamus quod si appellare a civili iudice ad ecclesiasticum[12] non est ius uno modo, erit
ius alio modo.

Dicemus enim quod unum forum est distinctum ab alio, est tamen ordinatum ad aliud; quia, etsi[13] gladii sunt distincti, sunt[14] tamen ad invicem ordinati.
Si ergo agitur de iure appellacionis, istud ius oriri non potest ex ipsa distinccione
secundum se, quia distinccio fori secundum se facit quod quodlibet forum agat
suum officium. Orietur[15] tamen istud ius ex ipso ordine fori, quia, si unum forum[16] ordinatur ad aliud, consequens est quod ex uno foro recurratur ad aliud.
Multa enim, ut multa sunt, nisi sint ad invicem ordinata, confusa sunt; ideo
scriptum est: 'Ubi multitudo, ibi confusio.' Ne ergo sit confusio in regimine universi,[17] ad quod regimen eciam ipse hierarchie angelice ordinantur, si sunt duo

---

1: quod] *om.* CPV[1]V[2]   2: eius] *om.* F   3: ipsius] *del.* C *om.* F   4: ad quandam] a quadam F
5: decenciam] decencia F   6: de] in F   7: ut] et *add.* CF   8: et] *om.* F   9: verba] illa C
10: quod] et F   11: quomodo] quorum V[2]   12: ecclesiasticum] si *add.* C   13: etsi] si F
14: sunt] *om.* V[2]   15: Orietur] oritur FV[2]   16: forum] *om.* V[2]   17: universi] *om.* V[2]

And Samuel, as the Master says in the *Historia*, was priest, judge and prophet.[1] And so, as is established in I Samuel 3, the Lord called to him three times before Samuel knew that the Lord was calling him;[2] for, as the Master notes in the *Historia* (citing Josephus to this effect), this was done in order to indicate the threefold office which was to be entrusted to him. Therefore, it is not because of any lack of power that the spiritual sword may not attend to temporal affairs; rather, the material sword has been joined to it by reason of its excellence. For it is because the spiritual sword is of such great excellence, and because such exalted matters are entrusted to it, that a second sword has been joined to it so that it may attend to them more freely. Its jurisdiction and fullness of power are in no way diminished by this joining; rather, this is done for the sake of a certain fitness, so that he who is ordained to great tasks should not personally and immediately concern himself with small ones, save in exceptional circumstances. Thus, there is in the spiritual sword a fullness of power such that it may judge temporal matters if expedient. If, therefore, appeal is made from a civil judge to the pope, and if this is not according to the law as it relates to the distinction between the courts, it will nonetheless be according to the law as it relates to fullness of power.

But there is also a fourth way in which we can explain the words quoted above. For the answer to the question of what is or is not law derives its origin from the actual order of things, just as the question of what is or is not true is decided by reference to the actual nature of things. Thus, something may be true in one way which is not true in another way: for example, it is true accidentally that something may seem sweet, but not true of the thing in itself.[3] So also in our proposition: that which is not law in one way is law in another way. And so let us see how the civil judge stands in relation to the pope, and how the one kind of court stands in relation to the other, so that we may show from the actual order of things that if to appeal from a civil to an ecclesiastical judge is not law in one way, it will be law in another way.

For we shall say that the one court, though distinct from the other, is nonetheless subordinated to the other because, even though the swords are distinct, they are nonetheless mutually ordered. Therefore, if a right of appeal be discussed, that right cannot arise out of the distinction itself, because the distinction between the courts as such means that each court performs its own function. Nonetheless, that right does arise out of the order of the courts, because, if the one court is subordinated to the other, it follows that recourse may be had from the one court to the other [in appropriate circumstances, even if not invariably]. For where there are many things there is confusion if they are not mutually ordered, because they are many. And so it is written: 'Where there is multitude there is confusion.'[4] Therefore, lest there be confusion in the government of the universe, for which government even the angelic

---

1. Peter Comestor, *Historia scholastica*, PL 198:1299.
2. I Sam. 3:4–15
3. What he means, presumably, is that something which is not 'really' sweet may seem so because of accidental circumstances of health, etc.; cf. Pt. I, Ch. II. Perhaps also he is remembering Plato, *Theaetetus* 166D–167B.
4. Cf. *Codex Theodosianus*, ed. T. Mommsen and P. Meyer (Berlin: Weidmann, 1954), 9:45:4:3.

instituti gladii, oportet quod sint ad invicem ordinati et quod de uno[1] recurratur ad aliud: de minori videlicet ad maiorem; quia ius appellacionis hoc postulat, ut non de maiori ad[2] minorem, sed econverso[3] in appellacionibus procedatur.[4] Cum ergo dicitur quod non est de rigore iuris ut a civili iudice appelletur ad papam, dicemus quod et si non est hoc de rigore iuris distinccionis fori, ut patet per habita, est de rigore iuris ordinis fori. Sed quando et quomodo appellari debet inferius[5] dicetur.

Sciendum tamen quod omnis ista controversia quod papa non habeat utrumque gladium et quod[6] de temporali iurisdiccione non debet se intromittere papa, videtur ex hiis radicibus processisse, que[7] notaverunt iuriste aliqui: quod regnum et sacerdocium ab eodem principio processerunt, ut non sit unum institutum per aliud, et quod prius fuit regnum quam sacerdocium. Sed, ut patet per habita, prius fuit sacerdocium quam regnum. Nam antequam fieret mencio aliqua de regno, que mencio facta est Geneseos X de Neroth, qui fuit homo robustus et oppressor aliorum, facta fuit mencio de sacerdocio. Nam legimus Geneseos VIII quod edificavit[8] Noe altare. Domino et obtulit holocausta[9] super altare. Nam cum per diluvium aquarum esset deleta omnis caro exceptis iis que reservabantur in archa, statim cum egressus fuit Noe de archa, edificavit altare Domino et operatus est officium sacerdotis. Fuit ergo prius[10] Noe sacerdocium antequam esset regnum. Sic et ante Noe fuit sacerdocium[11] antequam esset regnum. Nam postquam Adam genuit Caym et Abel, Caym fuit agricola et Abel pastor ovium, et Caym de fructibus terre offerebat[12] Domino, Abel quoque obtulit de primogenitis gregis: quod facere erat officium sacerdotis. Et si Caym et Abel obtulerunt sacrificia Domino, ridiculum esset dicere[13] quod Adam pater[14] eorum non obtulisset huiusmodi sacrificia. In ipso ergo Adam incepit sacerdocium. Fuit ergo sacerdocium[15] antequam esset regnum.

Nam rex est minister Dei, vindex in iram ei qui malum agit. Potestas ergo regia[16] habet pro obiecto homines et potissime homines malos; habet tamen pro causa Deum, quia a Deo tamquam a causa agente est omnis potestas, tam regia quam alia. Sed sacerdotalis potestas[17] et pro causa et pro obiecto habet Deum: pro causa quidem, quia a Deo est huiusmodi potestas; pro obiecto vero, quia in hiis que sunt ad Deum est huiusmodi potestas; unde et eius est offerre sacrificia ipsi Deo. Et quia ordo ad Deum tempore et dignitate est prior quam ordo ad alia, quia ex ordine ad Deum oritur ordo ad alia, consequens est quod potestas sacerdotalis tempore et dignitate sit prior regia potestate. Dicimus autem quod sacerdocium pro causa habet Deum, quia est a Deo; et pro obiecto habet Deum, quia est in hiis que sunt ad Deum

1: uno] domo V²   2: ad] a V²   3: econverso] fiat *add.* C   4: in appellacionibus procedatur] *del.* C
5: inferius] infra CV²   6: quod] que V²   7: que] quia C   quod V²   8: edificavit] hedificatus V²
9: holocausta] oblocausta C   10: prius] post CV²   11: fuit ergo ... sacerdocium] *om.* F
12: offerebat] munera *add.* CV²   13: dicere] *om.* PV¹   14: pater] prior F   15: fuit ergo sacerdocium] *om.* V²   16: regia] *om.* PV¹   17: potestas] *om.* PV¹

hierarchies themselves are ordered, it must be that, if two swords have been instituted, they are mutually ordered and that recourse may be had from one to the other: that is, from the lesser to the greater. For a right of appeal presupposes this: that appeals proceed not from greater to lesser, but conversely. Therefore, when it is said that it is not according to the strictness of the law that appeal may be made from a civil judge to the pope, we shall reply that, though this is not according to the strictness of the law as it relates to the distinction between the courts, it is according to the strictness of the law as it relates to the order of the courts, as is clear from what we have said. But when and how such appeal may be made will be discussed below.

It must be known, however, that all this controversy as to whether the pope does not possess both swords and whether the pope should not concern himself with temporal jurisdiction seems to have sprung from these roots, which a number of jurists have noted: [the belief] that kingship and priesthood proceeded from the same origin, so that the one was not instituted through the other; and that kingship was in being before priesthood.[1] But, as is clear from what has been said, priesthood existed before there was kingship. For before any mention was made of kingship — and such mention was first made in Genesis 10, of Nimrod, who was a mighty man and an oppressor of others — mention was made of priesthood; for we read in Genesis 8 that Noah built an altar to the Lord and offered burnt offerings upon the altar.[2] For when all flesh was destroyed by the waters of the Flood except those who were contained in the Ark, Noah built an altar to the Lord as soon as he left the Ark, and performed the office of a priest. Therefore, the priesthood of Noah was in being before kingship was. For after Adam begat Cain and Abel, Cain was a farmer and Abel a keeper of sheep; and Cain offered to the Lord the fruits of the earth and Abel offered the firstborn of the flock, which was to perform the office of a priest.[3] And if Cain and Abel offered sacrifices to the Lord, it would be ridiculous to say that their father Adam had not offered such sacrifices. Priesthood, therefore, began in Adam himself; therefore, there was priesthood before there was kingship.

For the king is a minister of God, an avenger to execute wrath upon him who does evil.[4] Therefore, royal power has men, and especially wicked men, as its object. It has God as its cause, however; for all power, whether royal or otherwise, is from God as from an active cause. But priestly power has God both as its cause and as its object: as its cause indeed, because such power is from God, and as its object because that power is concerned with those things which are of God, in that it is indeed its duty to offer sacrifices to God. And since the order dedicated to God is prior in time and dignity to the order dedicated to other matters — since the order dedicated to other matters arises from the order dedicated to God — it follows that priestly power is prior in time and dignity to royal power. We say, then, that priesthood has God as its cause, since it is from God; and that it has God as its object, since it is concerned with those things which are of God and

---

1. See Introduction, n. 37.
2. Gen. 10:9; Gen. 8:20; cf. Pt. I, Ch. VI, pp. 31; 35–37.
3. Gen. 4:4.
4. Cf. Rom. 13:4.

et offert sacrificia ipsi Deo.

Attamen huiusmodi sacerdocium[1] est in hiis que sunt ad Deum pro populo, et offert sacrificia Deo pro populo,[2] ut ex hoc super ipsum populum potestatem habeat. Immo, quia sacerdocium est in hiis que sunt ad Deum in hac Ecclesia Militante, consequens est quod ipse in huiusmodi Ecclesia auctoritatem et potestatem habeat in omnibus que ordinantur ad Deum. Et quia ad Deum ordinantur anime nostre, corpora nostra et res nostre sive temporalia nostra,[3] exinde aperte concluditur quod Summus Pontifex super omnibus habeat[4] potestatem, ut et ipse iudicet omnia. Nam ipse est supremus ordo qui potest esse in rebus: ordo videlicet qui est ad Deum. Ille ergo qui est summus in huiusmodi ordine, sicut est Summus Pontifex[5] in Ecclesia Militante, oportet quod sub eo omnia incurventur et iurisdiccioni eius omnia supponantur. Ideo dicitur ad Hebreos V: 'Omnis namque pontifex ex hominibus' assumptus et 'pro hominibus constituitur in hiis que sunt ad Deum.'

Falsum est ergo illud fundamentum quod regnum fuit prius quam sacerdocium, nisi intelligatur de prioritate[6] et excellencia huius[7] non de iure, sed de facto. Quia in primitiva Ecclesia non de iure, sed de facto, quandam prioritatem et quandam excellenciam Deo permittente habebant imperatores et reges, qui erant tunc temporis super sacerdotes et alios fideles, quos capiebant, carceri mancipabant et eciam trucidabant. Quod erat malum ipsorum imperatorum et regum,[8] quia[9] hoc agentes demerebantur et peccabant; et erat bonum ipsorum fidelium, qui per palmam martiri vitam merebantur eternam. Sic ergo erat de facto; sed de iure ipsi imperatores et reges debebant sacerdotali subici potestati. Nam multo perfeccionem principatum dedit Christus sacerdotibus quam regibus: quia numquid iustum videbitur si cedat spiritus carni, si a terrenis celestia superentur?

Sic ergo censendum est de ordine et de perfeccione istarum potestatum, quod una est prior alia et[10] perfeccior alia, et una est sub alia, sicut dicebatur[11] corpus est sub spiritu et terrestria sub celestibus. Sed quod[12] dicebatur, quod tam regnum quam sacerdocium sunt ab[13] uno principio, ut[14] a Deo, et quod unum non est per aliud, dicemus quod hoc est verum et non verum.[15] Nam quod utrumque sit ab uno principio et quod utrumque[16] sit a Deo verum est,[17] quia, ut dicitur ad Romanos XIII, 'Non est potestas nisi a Deo.' Et si volumus descendere ad ipsam sacerdotalem et regiam potestatem, utraque[18] est a Deo. Nam cum congregati essent in unum universi maiores natu Israel et venirent ad Samuelem, ut constitueret super[19] eis[20] regem, dixit Dominus ad Samuelem: 'Audi vocem populi in omnibus que loquuntur,'[21] ut habetur primo Regum VIII. Ergo mandato Domini factum fuit quod constitueretur rex super Israel. Sic[22] eciam Dominus vocavit Samuelem, qui ministrabat

1: sacerdocium] sacrificum FV[2]   2: et offert … populo] om. F   3: nostra] ad deum add. and del. C
4: habeat] habet F   5: super omnibus … Pontifex] om. C   6: prioritate] proprietate V[2]
7: huius] hoc F   8: et regum] om. F   9: quia] quod V[2]   10: et] om. PV[1]   11: dicebatur] om. C
12: quod] quia F   13: ab] sub (corrected to ab in a later hand) V[1]   14: ut] videlicet F   15: et
non verum] om. V[2]   16: sit … utrumque] om. V[2]   17: est] om. V[2]   18: utraque] utrumque FV[2]
19: super] similiter F   20: eis] eos FV[2]   21: loquuntur] tibi add. FV[2]   22: Sic] ut add. PV[1]

offers sacrifices to God Himself.

Yet such priesthood is in those things which are of God for the people; and so, for this reason, it has power over the people themselves. Indeed, since priesthood in this Church Militant is concerned with those things which are of God, it follows that it has authority and power in this Church over all things which are ordered towards God. And since our souls, our bodies and our goods or our temporal possessions are all ordered towards God, it is thus plainly shown that the Supreme Pontiff has power over all things, so that he himself also judges all things. For he himself is [at the summit of] the highest order which can exist in things: namely, the order which is dedicated to God. Therefore, it must be that all things are bowed down beneath him and that all things are placed under the jurisdiction of the one who is highest in that order, as the Supreme Pontiff is in the Church Militant. And so it is said in Hebrews 5: 'For every High Priest is taken from among men and appointed for men in those things which are of God.'[1]

The premise that kingship was in being before priesthood is therefore false, unless it be understood in terms of priority and excellence *de facto* rather than *de iure*. For in the primitive Church, emperors and kings did possess a certain priority and excellence: not *de iure*, but *de facto*, by God's permission. And, at that time, they were above the priests and other members of the faithful, whom they seized, imprisoned and even slew. This brought harm to those emperors and kings; for, by so acting, they deserved ill and sinned. And it brought good to the faithful themselves, who merited eternal life through the palm of martyrdom. So it was *de facto*, therefore; but, *de iure*, those emperors and kings should have been subject to the priestly power. For Christ gave to priests a ruling power far more perfect than that of kings. For would it seem in any way just if spirit were to submit to flesh, if heavenly things were to be overshadowed by earthly?[2]

Therefore, the order and perfection of the powers is to be understood in this way: that the one is prior to the other and is more perfect than the other, and that the one is under the other just as, has been said, body is under spirit and terrestrial things under celestial. But to the statement that both kingship and priesthood are derived from one origin — that is, from God — and that the one does not come into being through the other, we shall reply that this is both true and not true. For it is true that both are from one origin and that both are from God since, as is said in Romans 13, 'there is no power except of God.'[3] And if we wish to consider priesthood itself and royal power, each is from God. [Nonetheless, the one comes into being only through the other.] For, as is established in I Samuel 8, when the whole assembly of the elders of Israel came to Samuel so that he might appoint a king over them, the Lord said to Samuel: 'Hear the voice of the people in all that they say.'[4] Therefore, it came about by the Lord's command that a king was appointed over Israel. So also, as is established in I Samuel 3, the Lord called Samuel, who was ministering

1. Heb. 5:1.
2. Cf. Dist. 10, c. 6: *Suscipitisne* (CIC I:20).
3. Rom. 13:1.
4. I Sam. 8:7.

in templo, ut habetur primo Regum III; propter quod patet quod a Domino constitutus est sacerdos et rex super Israel, ut ex hoc et sacerdocium et regnum intelligatur esse a[1] Deo.[2] Est ergo utrumque a Domino, et unum et aliud; sed unum per
aliud.

Quod ergo dicebatur, quod unum non esset[3] per aliud, si considerentur superius dicta, patet falsum esse. Nam, ut supra dicebamus, potuisset Dominus,[4] sicut
vocavit Samuelem, qui ministrabat in templo et[5] post vocacionem Domini functus
est officio sacerdotis, sic potuisset vocare Saulem, ut fungeretur officio regis.
Noluit tamen hoc facere, sed mandavit Samueli quod constitueret regem super Israel, ut ex hoc cognosceret[6] potestas regia quod esset per sacerdocium constituta.
Et si primus rex in populo fideli fuit de mandato Domini per sacerdocium constitutus, intelligere debent omnes posteriores reges quod vel non regnant ut mandavit
Dominus,[7] vel debent se recognoscere quod sunt[8] in regimine hominum et[9] gubernacione fidelium per Ecclesiam constituti: ut puta, quia sunt per Ecclesiam regenerati. Aliter enim[10] non essent veri reges, cum apud infideles non sunt vera regna,
sed magis, secundum sentenciam Augustini, sunt quedam magna latrocinia. Ipsi
ergo fideles sunt[11] per Ecclesiam constituti reges, quia sunt per eam regenerati et
per eam sunt a peccatis absoluti et per ipsam sunt alia consecuti, que superius[12]
tangebamus, sine quibus veri et digni reges dici minime mererentur.

CAPITULUM II: *Cum Ecclesia super temporalibus habeat universale dominium,
quomodo intelligendum est quod Summus Pontifex non vult iurisdiccionem
regum perturbare, et quod non ad Ecclesiam sed ad reges spectat de possessionibus iudicare.*

Necessitas autem huius capituli secundi[13] oritur ex eo quod dicitur Extra., *De iudiciis*, capitulo *Novit* quod Summus Pontifex iurisdiccionem regum perturbare aut
minuere non intendit. Cum enim perturbacio et diminucio in iniuriam sonent, quia
nulli facit iniuriam qui utitur iure suo, Ecclesia itaque, que est omnium rerum[14] temporalium domina, nec perturbat nec diminuit iurisdiccionem alicuius si, suo iure
utens, de ipsis temporalibus iudicat. Oritur eciam necessitas huius capituli[15] ex eo
quod dicitur Extra., *Qui filii sint legitimi*, capitulo *Causam*, ubi dicitur quod ad regem, scilicet Anglorum, non ad Ecclesiam pertinet de talibus possessionibus iudicare; et capitulo *Lator* dicitur quod[16] seculari domino, sub cuius iudicio de hereditate causa vertitur,[17] intimet esse huiusmodi causam, qui causam super hereditate[18]

1: a] *om.* F *del.* V²   2: Deo] domino FV²   3: esset] *om.* F est V²   4: Dominus] deus C   5: et]
om. V²   6: cognosceret] recognosceret PV²   7: Dominus] deus C   8: sunt] sint F   9: et] in
add. FV²   10: enim] *om.* F   11: sunt] *om.* CFV²   12: superius] sepius V²   13: capituli se-
cundi] secundi capituli C   14: rerum] *om.* CFV²   15: capituli] *om.* C   16: quod] sub *add.* F
17: vertitur] utitur C   18: hereditate] hereditatem F

in the Temple; from which it is clear that both priest and king were appointed over Israel by the Lord, so that, for this reason, both kingship and priesthood may be understood to be from God. Therefore, both are from the Lord: the one and the other, but the one through the other.

Therefore, if consideration be given to the foregoing remarks, the statement that the one did not come into being through the other is clearly shown to be false. For, as we have said above, just as the Lord called Samuel, who was ministering in the Temple and who discharged the office of priest after the Lord's call, so could He have called Saul to discharge the office of king. He did not wish to do this, however. Rather, He commanded Samuel to appoint a king over Israel so that, by this, royal power would understand itself to be appointed through the priesthood. And if the first king of the faithful people was appointed through the priesthood at the Lord's command, all subsequent kings must either understand that they do not reign as the Lord has commanded, or must acknowledge that they themselves are appointed through the Church to the rule of men and the government of the faithful: that is, because they are regenerated through the Church. For, otherwise, they would not be true kings, because there are no true kingships among unbelievers: rather, according to what Augustine says, there are only certain great bands of robbers.[1] Therefore, faithful kings are themselves appointed through the Church: because they are regenerated through her, and are absolved from sin through her, and through her alone attain to the other things upon which we have touched above, without which they would not in the least deserve to be called true and worthy kings.[2]

CHAPTER II: *Since the Church has a universal lordship over temporal things, how are we to understand that the Supreme Pontiff does not wish to disturb the jurisdiction of kings, and that it does not rest with the Church, but with kings, to judge matters involving possessions?*

The need for this second chapter arises out of what is said [by Innocent III] at X. 2:1:13: *Novit*, that the Supreme Pontiff does not intend to disturb or diminish the jurisdiction of kings.[3] For since disturbance and diminution are forms of injustice, and because he who makes use of his own right inflicts injustice on no one,[4] the Church, who is lord of all temporal things, neither disturbs nor diminishes the jurisdiction of anyone if, making use of her own right, she judges even in temporal cases. The need for this chapter also arises out of the statement [of Alexander III] at X. 4:17:7: *Causam*, where it is said that it pertains not to the Church, but to the king — that is, of the English — to judge matters involving possessions. Also, in the chapter *Lator*, it is said that the secular lord under whose jurisdiction a case of disputed inheritance is being argued is to be informed that it is a case of such a kind, and that he is to hear the case and give a decision upon the disputed inheritance.[5]

---

1. *De civitate Dei* 4:4 (CCSL 47:101).
2. Cf. Pt. II, Chaps. VII–XII.
3. See Introduction, n. 21.
4. Cf. Justinian, *Digesta*, ed. T. Mommsen (Berlin, 1877), 50:17:55.
5. See Introduction, n. 61.

audiat et decidat. Si enim Ecclesia super temporalibus habet universale dominium, ad ipsam spectabit de possessionibus iudicare plus[1] quam ad[2] reges, nec debet velle Ecclesia, ut videtur,[3] quod sub seculari domino causa de hereditate iudicetur vel decidatur, cum hoc possit per ecclesiasticum iudicem iudicari.

Sciendum ergo quod hic volumus profundius ingredi et ostendere ex hiis que videmus in naturalibus agentibus quomodo Summus Pontifex debeat se[4] de iudicio temporalium intromittere et quomodo hoc debeat secularibus dominis dimittere et eorum iurisdiccionem minime perturbare. Sic enim videmus in naturalibus quod aliqua fiunt secundum communem legem gubernacionis rerum, aliqua vero secundum divinam dispensacionem et Dei providenciam specialem.[5] Duplici ergo lege gubernatur mundus a Deo, communi et speciali.[6] Secundum quidem communem legem gubernacionis mundi potest Deus assimilari mari vel[7] eciam soli, et[8] potest assimilari cuidam universali agenti. Quod universale agens omnibus rebus suas virtutes tribuit et nullam rem in sua accione impedit, sed omnes res proprios cursus agere[9] sinit. Potest itaque Deus, qui communi lege gubernat mundum, assimilari mari[10] ad quod si diversa vasa portentur, ipsum quidem mare cuilibet vasi se totum exhibebit, sed nullum vas ipsum totum capiet. Accipiet[11] tamen de aqua maris plus unum vas quam aliud,[12] prout unum[13] est maius alio; sed nullum vas poterit de mari conqueri, quia tantum de aqua maris accipiet quantum de ea poterit capere. Igitur, secundum hunc modum loquendi, mare se habebit uniformiter ad omnia, quia cuilibet se totum exhibebit; sed omnia non se habebunt uniformiter ad ipsum, quia aliqua vasa plus, aliqua minus de eius aqua capient. Sic et Deus est quidam fons et quoddam mare virtutis et potencie, a quo mari omnes virtutes et omnes potencie quasi quidam rivuli derivantur. Huiusmodi enim mare vel huiusmodi[14] fons cuilibet rivulo se totum offert et ad omnes rivulos se habet eodem modo. Ipsi tamen rivuli plus et minus suscipiunt[15] de aqua[16] huiusmodi[17] fontis, secundum quod sunt maiores vel minores. Isti autem rivuli maiores vel minores[18] derivati ab hoc fonte sunt virtutes vel potencie ipsarum creaturarum; quarum quedam sunt maiores, quedam minores. Et si vellemus hos rivulos et has virtutes creaturarum secundum diversos gradus distinguere, distingueremus eas sicut distinguimus ipsas creaturas. Quia quedam creature sunt intellectuales, ut angeli et eciam homines;[19] quedam autem[20] sunt sensibiles, ut animalia; quedam autem sunt vegetabiles, ut plante; quedam[21] sunt inanimate, ut lapides et metalla et cetera huiusmodi.

Fantastica ergo erat opinio Platonis, qui secundum diversos gradus rerum posuit diversas ideas, quas vocabat[22] deos; qui dii influebant in res alias, ut erat idea 'lapidis' et idea 'animalium' et sic de ideis aliis. Non sunt enim plures dii, nec sunt plura

1: plus] ergo *add.* FV² 2: ad] a V² 3: videtur] habetur FV² 4: debeat se] *om.* V² 5: specialem] spiritualem F 6: speciali] spirituali F 7: vel] et F 8: et] vel F 9: agere] habere F 10: vel eciam … mari] *om.* V² 11: Accipiet] *om.* V² 12: aliud] alius V² 13: unum] vas *add.* C 14: enim mare vel huiusmodi] *om.* F 15: suscipiunt] suscipi V² 16: aqua] aquis V² 17: huiusmodi] *om.* V² 18: Isti autem … minores] *om.* F 19: homines] accipiendo intellectuales large quia proprie loquendo angeli sunt intellectuales homines vero racionales *add. and del.* C 20: autem] creature *add. and del.* C 21: quedam] *add.* autem FV² 22: vocabat] vocavit C

For if the Church has a universal lordship over temporal things, it will rest with her more than with kings to judge matters involving possessions; nor, as it seems, must the Church be willing to allow a case of disputed inheritance to be judged or decided under a secular lord, since this may be judged by an ecclesiastical judge.

It must be known, therefore, that we wish to enter more deeply into this question and to show from those phenomena which we see among natural agents how the Supreme Pontiff should concern himself in the judgment of temporal disputes, and how he should depute this to secular lords and disturb their jurisdiction as little as possible. For we see among natural phenomena that some are brought about according to the common law of the government of things and that others occur by divine dispensation and the special providence of God. Therefore, the law under which the world is governed by God is twofold: common and special. And, with respect to the common law of the government of the world, God can be likened to a sea, or also to the sun, and He can be likened to a kind of universal agent, which universal agent distributes their powers to all things and impedes none in its action, but allows all things to pursue their own courses. Thus, God, who governs the world by a common law, can be likened to a sea. For if different vessels are brought to it, the sea will indeed offer the whole of itself to each of the vessels, but no vessel will contain the whole of it. Rather, one vessel will take more water from the sea than another, to the extent that the one is larger than the other. But no vessel will be able to conquer the sea, for it will take only as much water from the sea as it can hold. According to this manner of speaking, then, the sea will stand in the same relation to all of them, for it will offer the whole of itself to each of them; but they will not all stand in the same relation to it, for some vessels will hold more of its water and some less. So also, God is a kind of fount and a kind of sea of force and power, from which sea all forces and all powers are derived like streams. For that sea or that fount offers the whole of itself to each stream and stands in the same relation to all streams. The streams themselves, however, receive more or less of the water of that fount, according as they are greater or lesser. And the greater or lesser streams derived from that fount are the forces or powers of the creatures themselves, some of which are greater and some lesser. And if we wished to distinguish those streams and those powers of the creatures according to different grades, we should distinguish them just as we distinguish the creatures themselves. For some creatures are intellectual, such as angels, and also men; and some are sentient, such as animals; and some are non-sentient, such as plants; and some are inanimate, such as stones and metals and other such things.

The opinion of Plato, therefore, was absurd; for he posited different ideas according to the different grades of things and called them gods.[1] And these gods were said to flow into other things, so that there was an idea of 'stone' and an idea of 'animals' and so too other ideas. But there are not many gods, nor are there many

---

1. See, e.g., I.M. Crombie, *An Examination of Plato's Doctrines* (London: Routledge, 1967), vol. 2, ch. 3. The view that the Ideas are 'gods' is more properly to be attributed to the Neoplatonists than to Plato himself.

huiusmodi maria: unus est enim Deus, unum est huiusmodi mare, quod se totum
offert cuilibet creature; sed nulla creatura ipsum totum capit, sed quelibet secundum suum modum capit de influencia eius, quantum potest capere, ut intellectu-
alia[1] capiunt illam influenciam intellectualiter, sensibiia sensibiliter, vegetabilia
vegetabiliter. Ipse ergo Deus ubique totus est, sed nulla res ipsum capit, ut dicit
Augustinus primo *Confessionum*, circa principia.

Non est ergo vera opinio Platonis, qui secundum diversas perfecciones et virtutes
rerum posuit varias ideas, et per consequens posuit plures deos, quia ideas illas vocabat deos.[2] Non est quidem alius Deus a quo est esse vivum,[3] et alius a quo est esse
intellectuale, et alius a quo est esse racionale, et alius a quo est esse sensibile; sed
unus est Deus, a quo sunt omnia ista. Unde Dionysius quinto *De divinis nominibus*,
improbans opinionem Platonicorum,[4] ait quod 'non est aliud esse existens,[5] aliud
esse vitam, aliud sapienciam, neque ponimus[6] multas causas,' scilicet primas; sed
omnia hec[7] sunt 'processus unius Dei, et omnia hec sunt manifestativa unius Dei
prudencie.'[8]

Falsa est ergo opinio Platonicorum, qui secundum diversas perfecciones[9] posu-
erunt[10] plures deos. Falsa est eciam opinio Manicheorum, qui, prout videbant in rebus bonum et malum, duo principia et duos deos inducebantur asserere. Unus est
enim[11] Deus, quem imitantes dicimur boni, a quo deviantes dicimur mali, sicut supra tetigimus. Unum est signum, quod percucientes sagittamus bene, a quo deviantes sagittamus[12] male. Et sic[13] in gubernacione tocius mundi unus est Deus, qui,
prout secundum communem legem mundum gubernat, potest dici quoddam mare,
ex quo omnia vasa replentur, a quo omnia flumina fluunt et in quo[14] omnia[15] flumina[16;17] ordinentur;[18] quod mare, secundum communem legem, se habet uniformiter
ad omnia, quia cuilibet se totum exhibet, sed omnia non se habent uniformiter ad
ipsum.[19] Sic et Deus est quoddam mare perfeccionum, in quo sunt perfecciones omnes, iuxta illud quod habetur in quinto *Metaphysice*, quod est quoddam perfectum in
quo congregantur perfecciones omnium generum:[20] sic est quoddam mare potenciarum[21] et virtutum, quia est in eo omnis potencia[22] et omnis virtus. Unde et omnes[23]
alie virtutes sunt pendentes per virtutem[24] primam et sunt derivate a virtute prima.
Ideo dicitur in decima sexta proposicione *De causis* quod omnes virtutes sunt pendentes per infinitum primum,[25] quod est virtus virtutum. Sunt ergo diversa genera
virtutum et potenciarum, quia alique sunt intellectuales, alique sensibiles, alique

---

1: intellectualia] intelligibilia FV² 2: deos] unus est autem deus a quo sunt omnes iste perfecciones et omnes ista virtutes *add. and del.* C 3: vivum] unum V² 4: Platonicorum] platonicam FV²
5: est aliud esse existens] *om.* V² 6: ponimus] potius C 7: omnia hec] hec omnia V² 8: Dei
prudencie] dominus providencieV² 9: perfecciones] et diversas virtutes quos videbunt in rebus
add. and del. C 10: posuerunt] posuit CPV² 11: enim] *del.* C 12: bene, a quo ... sagittamus]
om. FV² 13: sic] sicut *mss* 14: quo] quem C quod FPV¹V² 15: omnia] *om.* F 16: flumina]
flumine C 17: fluunt et ... flumina] *om.* V² 18: ordinentur] ordinentur *mss* 19: ipsum] quia
aliqua plus aliqua minus de eius influencia capiunt *add. and del.* C 20: generum] et ista est perfeccio primum principium videlicet dei et sicut deus est quoddam mare perfeccionum quia sunt in
eo perfecciones *add. and del.* C 21: potenciarum] personarum V² 22: potencia] potestas F
23: et omnes] *om.* C 24: virtutem] potentia et *add. and del.* C 25: primum] potencialiter F

seas: for there is one God, there is one such sea, which offers the whole of itself to every creature. But no creature contains the whole of it. Rather, each in its own measure contains as much of its influence as it can hold; so that intellectual creatures contain that influence intellectually, sentient creatures sentiently, and non-sentient creatures non-sentiently. Therefore, God Himself is entirely everywhere; but nothing contains Him, as Augustine says near the beginning of *Confessions* 1.[1]

The opinion of Plato is therefore not correct. For he posited various ideas according to the different perfections and powers of things, and, consequently, he posited many gods. But there is not one god from whom comes the essence of life, and another from whom comes the essence of intellectuality, and another from whom comes the essence of rationality, and another from whom comes the essence of sentience. Rather, there is the one God, from Whom all these things come. And so Dionysius, in *De divinis nominibus* 5, rejecting the opinion of the Platonists, says: 'It is not the case that the essence of being is one thing and the essence of life another and that of wisdom another, nor do we posit many causes,' that is, first causes. Rather, all these things have 'gone forth from the one God, and all these are manifestations of the wisdom of the one God.'[2]

The opinion of the Platonists, who posited many gods according to the different perfections, is therefore false. False also is the opinion of the Manichaeans, who, because they saw good and evil in things, were led to assert that there are two first principles and two gods. For there is one God; and if we imitate Him we are called good, whereas, if we turn aside [*deviantes*] from Him, we are called evil, as we have noted above.[3] There is one target: when we hit it, we shoot well; when we miss it [*deviantes*], we shoot badly.[4] And so, in the government of the whole world, there is one God Who, insofar as He governs the world according to a common law, can be called a kind of sea from which all vessels are filled, from which all rivers flow, and in which all rivers will begin; which sea, according to the common law, stands in the same relation to all creatures because it offers the whole of itself to each, but the creatures do not all stand in the same relation to it. And so God Himself is like a sea of perfections in which are all perfections, according to what is established in *Metaphysics* 5: that there is a certain perfection in which the perfections of all the genera come together.[5] Thus, He is like a sea of powers and forces, for every power and every force is in Him. Hence also, all other powers depend upon a primary power and are derived from a primary power; and so it is said in the sixteenth proposition of *De causis* that all powers depend upon a limitless first principle which is the power of powers.[6] Therefore, there are different kinds of forces and powers; for some are intellectual, some are sentient, some are

---

1. *Confessions* 1:3 (CCSL 27:2).
2. *De divinis nominibus* 5 (PG 3:816–817).
3. See e.g. Pt. II, Ch. VIII, p. 145.
4. Cf. Aristotle, *Nicomachean Ethics* 1:2 (1094^{a}25).
5. Perhaps *Metaphysics* Δ:16 (1021^{b}15).
6. Ps.-Aristotle, *Liber de Causis* 16:15, ed. O. Bardenhewer (Freiburg, 1882), p. 177.

celestes, alique terrene.[1] Sed omnia hec non a pluribus fontibus nec a pluribus[2] primis principiis, sed ab uno fonte et ab uno primo principio derivantur.

Hiis itaque prelibatis, adaptemus hoc ad propositum et dicamus quod sicut in gubernacione tocius mundi unus est fons, unus est Deus, in quo est omnis potencia,[3] a quo omnes alie potencie derivantur, et in quo omnes potencie reducuntur, sic et in gubernacione hominum et in tota[4] Ecclesia Militante oportet quod unus sit fons, unum sit caput in quo[5] sit plenitudo potestatis, in quo sit omnis potencia quasi[6] super corpus mysticum sive super ipsam Ecclesiam, apud quem[7] sit uterque gladius, quia aliter non esset in eo omnis potencia.[8] Ab hoc autem fonte omnes alie[9] potencie derivantur; in hunc autem fontem omnes alie potencie reducuntur. Iste autem fons,[10] prout secundum legem communem[11] totam Ecclesiam rigat et inebriat, se habet uniformiter ad omnia, quia modo ordinato, secundum quod requirit gubernacio Ecclesie, cuilibet se totum exhibet; sed nullus ipsum totum capit, quia in nullo est tanta potencia[12] quanta est in ipso.

Sed licet iste fons secundum communem legem se habeat uniformiter ad omnia, quia omnia in suo ordine conservat, omnia in suo statu protegit, ipsa[13] tamen omnia non se habent uniformiter ad ipsum, quia de eius influencia et de[14] eius potencia[15] aliqua plus capiunt, aliqua vero minus. Secundum quod sunt aliqui principatus maiores, aliqui vero minores, sive principatus illi sint ecclesiastici sive terreni, quia principatus omnes tam ecclesiastici quam terreni ab hoc fonte derivantur, per influenciam huius fontis debent suam recognoscere potestatem. Sicut[16] ergo censendum est de Deo, prout secundum legem communem gubernat totum mundum,[17] sic eciam censendum est de vicario Dei, prout secundum communem legem totam Ecclesiam gubernat et[18] inebriat et rigat.[19;20] Quia secundum hoc assimilari potest cuidam mari vel cuidam fonti, a quo sunt omnes alii rivuli et omnes[21] alie potencie, qui se totum cuilibet exhibet, sed nulla res ipsum totum capit. Hoc[22] mare vel hic fons, prout secundum legem communem gubernat Ecclesiam, se habet uniformiter ad omnia, sed omnia non se habent uniformiter ad ipsum.

Sed forte dices quod ab hoc fonte non derivatur omnis potencia,[23] quia non omnes principes vel non omnes reges potenciam quam habent recognoscunt ab ipso. Quia prius fuit regia potestas quam esset Ecclesia, quia Ecclesia[24] formata fuit ex latere Christi pendentis in cruce. Nam ex passione Christi habet Ecclesia plenitudinem sui vigoris, ex cuius latere fluxerunt Ecclesie sacramenta, ut dicit[25] glossa ad Romanos V. Sed antequam Christus pateretur erat potestas regia. Ante enim quam[26] nasceretur Christus, exiit edictum a Cesare Augusto ut describeretur[27] universus

---

1: terrene] terre V²   2: fontibus nec a pluribus] *om.* F   3: potencia] potestas F   4: et in tota] *om.* F   5: quo] *om.* V²   6: omnis potencia quasi] quasi omnis potencia CFV²   7: quem] quod FV² 8: potencia] potestas CF   9: alie] *om.* F autem V²   10: fons] *om.* P   11: legem communem] communem legem FV²   12: potencia] potestas F   13: ipsa] *om.* C   14: de] *om.* V²   15: eius potencia] potencia eius V²   16: Sicut] sic CV²   17: totum mundum] mundum totum C   18: et] *om.* F   19: rigat] *del.* V²   20: inebriat et rigat] rigat et inebriat CF   21: alii rivuli et omnes] *om.* F 22: Hoc] autem *add.* CFV²   23: potencia] potestas F   24: quia Ecclesia] *om.* V²   25: dicit] dixit V²   26: ante enim quam] ante quam enim CFV²   27: describeretur] omnis populus *add. and del.* V²

heavenly and some are earthly. But all of these are derived, not from many founts nor from many first principles, but from one fount and from one first principle.

Thus, having first touched upon these considerations, let us apply this to our proposition and say that, just as there is one fount in the government of the whole world — there is one God, in Whom there is every power, from Whom all other powers are derived, and to Whom all powers are reduced — so also, in the government of men and in the whole Church Militant, it must be that there is one fount, that there is one head in which is fullness of power: in which there is almost every power as over the Mystical Body or over the Church herself, and in which there are both swords, for, otherwise, all power would not be in it. And from this fount all other powers are derived, and to this fount all other powers are reduced. And, insofar as this fount waters and irrigates the whole Church according to a common law, it stands in the same relation to all things; for, in an ordered fashion, according to what the government of the Church requires, it offers the whole of itself to each. But nothing contains the whole of it, for in nothing is there so great a power as there is in it.

But although, according to the common law, this fount stands in the same relation to all things because it preserves them all in their order and protects them all in their condition, things nonetheless do not all stand in the same relation to it; for some contain more of its influence and of its power, and others less. Thus, there are some greater and some lesser ruling powers, whether these ruling powers be ecclesiastical or earthly; for all ruling powers, whether ecclesiastical or earthly, are derived from this fount and must acknowledge that their power comes through the influence of this fount. Therefore, that which must be considered true of God insofar as He governs the whole world according to a common law, must also be considered true of the Vicar of God insofar as he governs and waters and irrigates the whole Church according to a common law. For, according to this argument, he can be likened to a kind of sea or to a kind of fount, from which come all other streams and all other powers, to each of which it offers the whole of itself, but none of which contains the whole of it. This sea or this fount stands in the same relation to all things insofar as it governs the Church according to a common law; but things do not all stand in the same relation to it.

But perhaps you will say that not every power is derived from this fount, because not all princes or not all kings acknowledge that the power which they hold comes from it. For there was royal power before the Church was in being, because the Church was formed from the side of Christ hanging upon the Cross: because the Church receives the fullness of her strength from the Passion of Christ, from Whose side, as a gloss on Romans 5[1] says, there flowed the Church's sacraments.[2] But there was a royal power before Christ suffered; for before Christ was born there went out a decree from Caesar Augustus that all the world should be enrolled,

---

1. *Glossa ordinaria*, on Rom. 5:14 (PL 114:486).
2. Cf. Pt. II, Ch. VII, p. 137.

orbis, et ibant singuli ut profiterentur in[1] suam civitatem. Et cum iret Ioseph cum Maria desponsata sibi uxore pregnante, ut profiteretur in[2] suam civitatem, tunc impleti sunt dies pariendi, et peperit Christum filium suum primogenitum. Prius itaque fuit Cesar Augustus non solum quam[3] Christus pateretur vel eciam priusquam formaretur Ecclesia, sed eciam fuit priusquam Christus nasceretur.[4]

Dicemus ergo quod si loquimur de sacerdocio simpliciter, prius fuit tempore et dignitate sacerdocium quam esset regnum. Sed si per 'sacerdocium'[5;6] Ecclesiam intelligimus et[7] Ecclesiam et[8] sacerdocium non in quocumque tempore vel in quocumque statu, sed[9] sub lege nova vel sub lege gracie, secundum quem modum, quamvis ante sacerdocium simpliciter non esset regnum, fuit tamen ante sacerdocium in lege nova. Sed licet sic sit, adveniente tamen lege nova et ex latere Christi formata Ecclesia, quia ex hoc Ecclesia facta est[10] Catholica, id est universalis domina, nulli fuerunt de cetero reges vel principes qui non fuerint per Ecclesiam reges vel non fuerint[11] per eam digni et veri reges,[12] vel non fuerint[13] per ipsam simpliciter et sine diminucione reges.

Dicuntur autem vel dici possunt reges vel principes fieri vel esse per Ecclesiam tales quando ab ipsa Ecclesia[14] vel auctoritate eius iste deponitur et ille constituitur, sicut ipsum imperium transtulit Ecclesia de oriente[15] in occidente, vel sicut alios[16] principes deponit vel auctoritate sua fuerunt depositi et eadem auctoritate fuerunt alii instituti. Igitur qui sic sunt instituti debent dici esse reges vel esse principes per Ecclesiam, cum antea non essent tales nec deberent[17] esse tales, et postea auctoritate Ecclesie facti sunt tales.[18] Nec refert utrum iste vel eius genitor vel avus vel proavus per Ecclesiam factus sit talis, si ad eum per hereditatem perveniat principatus; quia, si consideratur radix et[19] primus parens qui per Ecclesiam factus est talis, consequens est quod iste qui iure hereditario obtinuit principatum,[20] ipse eciam per Ecclesiam factus sit talis. Multi ergo per Ecclesiam facti sunt principes; sed si non omnes facti sunt per Ecclesiam[21] principes sive reges, omnes tamen per Ecclesiam facti sunt veri et digni tales, quia, ut diximus, apud infideles nec est proprie imperium neque regnum. Quicumque enim est[22] filius ire et non est sub Deo secundum veritatem, nihil est sub eo. Unde et Augustinus, ut supra tetigimus, vult quod nulla sit respublica nec ibi sit vera iusticia cuius non est conditor et rector Christus; sed sine vera iusticia regna et imperia, ut per eundem Augustinum tetigimus,[23] sunt magna latrocinia. Et quia quilibet nascitur natura filius ire, et quilibet per quodlibet peccatum mortale fit filius ire,[24] ideo nullus princeps erit dignus et verus princeps

1: in] om. CFV² del. P   2: in] om. C   3: quam] quod F   4: nasceretur] sacerdotium add. C
5: per sacerdocium] sacerdotium per C   6: sacerdocium] et add. FV²   7: et] om. CFV²   8: et]
om. FV²   9: sed] dicit add. C   10: est] om. C   11: fuerint] fuerunt V²   12: reges] om. FV²
13: fuerint] fuerunt V²   14: ipsa Ecclesia] ecclesia ipsa FV²   15: oriente] origine F   16: alios]
aliquos FV²   17: deberent] dicentur C   18: nec deberent … tales] om. V²   19: et] om. F
20: principatum] quod add. mss   21: facti sunt per Ecclesiam] per ecclesiam facti sunt CFV²
22: enim est] est enim C   23: tetigimus] regna add. mss   24: et quilibet … ire] om. F

and all men went to present themselves in their own city. And when Joseph went to present himself in his own city with Mary his espoused wife, who was with child, the days were fulfilled when she should be delivered, and she brought forth Christ, her firstborn son.[1] Thus, Caesar Augustus was in being not only before Christ suffered, or, indeed, before the Church was formed, but even before Christ was born.

We shall say, therefore, that if we speak of priesthood considered absolutely, priesthood came first in time and dignity before there was kingship. But if by 'priesthood' we understand the Church — both the Church and the priesthood — not in every time or in every condition, but under the New Law or under the Law of Grace, then, in this sense, though kingship did not exist before priesthood considered absolutely, it nonetheless existed before the priesthood of the New Law. But, although this may be so, with the coming of the New Law, and with the formation of the Church from the side of Christ, because the Church was thereby made Catholic, that is, universal lord, there have subsequently been no kings or princes who were not made kings, or who were not made worthy and true kings, through her, or who were not through her made kings absolutely and without diminution.

But kings or princes are said, or can be said, to be made or to be such through the Church when, of herself or by her authority, the Church deposes this one or appoints that: just as the Church has transferred even the empire from the east to the west, or just as she deposes other princes, or has by her authority caused them to be deposed and, by the same authority, caused others to be instituted.[2] Thus, those who have been so instituted must be said to be kings or to be princes through the Church; for they were not such, nor could they be such, before, and have been made such after, the Church's exercise of authority. Nor, if ruling power comes to him by inheritance, does it matter whether it is the king himself or his parent or grandparent or ancestor who has been made such through the Church. For if consideration be given to the fact that his root and first parent was made a king through the Church, then it follows that he who has acquired ruling power by right of inheritance has also himself been made such through the Church. Therefore, many have been made princes through the Church; but if not all of them have been made princes or kings [immediately] through the Church, all have nonetheless been made truly and worthily such through the Church. For, as we have said, there is no proper authority or kingship among unbelievers;[3] for nothing is under one who is a child of wrath and who is not under God in truth.[4] And so, as we have noted above, Augustine himself maintains that there is no commonwealth whose founder and ruler is not Christ, nor is true justice there. Rather, without true justice, as we have noted with reference to the same Augustine, kingdoms and empires are great bands of robbers.[5] And because every man is by nature born a child of wrath, and every man is made a child of wrath by each mortal sin, no prince, therefore, will be a worthy and true prince

---

1. Cf. Luke 2:1–7.
2. See Introduction, n. 41.
3. Pt. II, Ch. XI.
4. Cf. Eph. 2:3.
5. *De civitate Dei* 2:21 (CCSL 47:55); 4:4 (CCSL 47:101).

nisi sit per Ecclesiam regeneratus spiritualiter, et, si incidat in peccatum mortale, nisi sit per Ecclesiam absolutus sacramentaliter.

Tercio, reges et principes dicuntur per Ecclesiam esse simpliciter et sine diminucione tales si sint per Ecclesiam benedicti vel[1] uncti. Quia in regibus et principibus unctis qui iure hereditario succedunt in regnum[2] sive in principatum, hoc facit vel hoc videtur facere in eis ius hereditatis quod facit in prelatis ecclesiasticis ius eleccionis. Et quia electi secundum ecclesiasticam prelaturam non dicuntur simpliciter tales donec sint per superiorem prelatum[3] confirmati, sic et reges et principes qui inunguntur per prelatum ecclesiasticum, ipsa benediccio et ipsa unccio est quasi quedam Ecclesie approbacio, quia per huiusmodi unccionem quasi consecratur Deo, ut ex tunc totus debeat esse divinus, totus se debeat pro Ecclesia exponere, ut ex tunc simpliciter et sine diminucione sit rex et debeat dici rex.

Tripliciter ergo dicuntur aliqui facti reges per Ecclesiam,[4] vel quia sunt per Ecclesiam[5] instituti, vel quia sunt per eam regenerati et absoluti, vel tercio, quia sunt per Ecclesiam uncti et benedicti. Advertendum tamen quod si non omnes reges et principes omnibus hiis tribus modis sunt vel fuerunt tales per Ecclesiam, saltem tamen[6] quantum ad secundum modum, prout per Ecclesiam spiritualiter regeneratus et sacramentaliter absolutus fit quis verus et dignus rex, nullus est qui non debeat suum regnum recognoscere ab Ecclesia, per quam iuste regnat, et sine qua iuste regnare non posset. Bene itaque dictum est quod Deus in regimine tocius mundi, et vicarius Dei sub Deo quantum ad regimen fidelium, est quidam fons et quoddam mare virtutis et potencie, a quo omnes alie potencie derivantur et in quod omnes reducuntur et ordinantur. Qui Dei vicarius, prout secundum communem legem Ecclesiam gubernat et regit, se habet uniformiter ad omnia, quia quoslibet sinit suos cursus peragere et nullum vult in suo officio impedire.

Habito quomodo Deus, prout[7] secundum communem legem gubernat mundum, assimilatur mari et adaptato hoc ad Summum Pontificem, volumus ostendere quomodo secundum huiusmodi gubernandi modum assimilatur soli. Secundum quem modum loquitur Dionysius quarto *De divinis nominibus*, dicens quod 'sicut sol non raciocinans aut preeligens, sed per se ipsum illuminat omnia et facit ea participare lumine ipsius secundum propriam racionem valencia,[8] ita[9] quod est bonum super solem, sicut super obscuram imaginem, per ipsam essenciam[10] suam omnibus existentibus proporcionaliter immittit tocius bonitatis radios.' Dicitur enim sol obscura imago Dei, quia omnia corporalia non ita clare Deum representant sicut spiritualia. Dicitur enim Deus[11] non raciocinando, non preeligendo, immittere in omnia existencia sue bonitatis radios: quod verum est, prout regit universum secundum communem legem. Secundum quem modum uniformiter se habet ad omnia, quia omnia in suo esse conservat, omnia secundum suam virtutem dirigit, nullum in

---

1: vel] et FV²   2: regnum] regimen C   3: prelatum] ecclesiasticum *add.* CV¹V²   4: Ecclesiam] instituti *add.* FV²   5: sunt per Ecclesiam] *om.* F   6: tamen] *del.* C   7: prout] *om.* C   8: valencia] volencia FV²   9: ita] itaque FV²   10: essenciam] ecclesiam F   11: enim Deus] evidens V²

unless he is spiritually regenerated through the Church and, if he falls into mortal sin, unless he is sacramentally absolved through the Church.

Third, kings and princes are said to be such through the Church absolutely and without diminution if they are blessed or anointed by the Church. For, in the case of anointed kings and princes who succeed to a kingdom or to a principality by right of inheritance, the law of inheritance accomplishes in them, or seems to accomplish, what the law of election accomplishes in the case of the prelates of the Church. And because those who are elected as prelates of the Church are said to be not absolutely such until confirmed by a superior prelate, so also, to kings and princes who are anointed by a prelate of the Church, this blessing and this anointing is as it were a kind of ecclesiastical approval. For by such anointing, he is as though consecrated to God, and so, thenceforth, should be entirely given to God and should place himself entirely at the Church's disposal, so that, from then on, he may be a king absolutely and without diminution, and should be called a king.

In three ways, therefore, are kings said to be made through the Church: either because they are instituted through the Church, or because they are regenerated and absolved through her, or, third, because they are anointed and blessed by the Church. It must be noted, however, that if not all kings and princes are or have been made such through the Church in all three of these ways, nonetheless, as regards the second way — that is, inasmuch as a man is made a true and worthy king by regeneration and sacramental absolution through the Church — there is at all events no one who ought not to acknowledge that he receives his kingdom from the Church, through whom he reigns justly and without whom he could not reign justly. Thus, it is well said that God, in ruling the whole world, and the Vicar of God, in ruling the faithful under God, is a kind of fount and a kind of sea of force and power, from which all other powers are derived and to which all are reduced and ordered. For the Vicar of God, insofar as he governs and rules the Church according to a common law, stands in the same relation to all things, because he allows all of them to pursue their own courses and wishes to impede none in its activity.

Having shown how God is like a sea insofar as He governs the world according to a common law, we wish to show how, with respect to this mode of government, He is like a sun. And it is in this way that Dionysius speaks in *De divinis nominibus* 4, saying that: 'Just as the sun, without deliberation or choice, but simply of itself, illuminates all things and causes them to share in its light according to the capacity of each, so that Good which is above the sun as above an obscure image sends forth rays of pure goodness to all beings proportionately, simply by His own Essence.'[1] For the sun is called an obscure image of God because no corporeal substances represent God as clearly as do spiritual substances. For God is said to send forth the rays of His goodness to all beings without deliberation or choice; and this is true insofar as He rules the universe according to a common law. In this way, He stands in the same relation to all creatures because He preserves everything in its existence, directs everything according to its power, and impedes nothing in its activity. And,

---

1. *De divinis nominibus* 4 (PG 3:748).

sua accione impedit. Secundum eciam istum[1] modum, Summus Pontifex est quasi quidam sol, qui prout secundum legem communem[2] gubernat Ecclesiam[3] et[4] ad omnia uniformiter se habet, quia omnia in suo statu conservat, omnia secundum suum statum promovet, nullum in suo officio impedit.

Tercio modo Deus in gubernacione mundi, prout secundum legem communem gubernat ipsum, assimilatur cuidam agenti universali, qui omnibus rebus suas virtutes tribuit, nullam rem in sua accione impedit, sed omnes res suos cursus proprios[5] agere sinit. Et secundum hunc modum loquitur Augustinus de Deo VII *De civitate Dei*, cap. XXX,[6] ubi ait quod 'illum Deum colimus qui naturis a se creatis et subsistendi et movendi inicia finesque constituit, quia rerum causas novit atque disponit, qui vim seminum condidit'; et subdit quod[7] 'sic itaque administrat omnia quo creavit, ut eciam ipsa proprios exercere et agere motus sinat.' Ipse ergo Deus omnium causas disponit et omnibus seminibus[8] vim condidit,[9] quia omnibus creaturis propriam virtutem dedit. Ipse[10] eciam[11] secundum communem legem sic omnia administrat, ut nullas res[12] impediat, sed eas proprios cursus agere permittat.[13]

Et sicut Deus hoc agit in regimine omnium creaturarum, ita Summus Pontifex, Dei vicarius, hoc agit in gubernacione Ecclesie et in regimine fidelium. Quando ergo queritur, cum Ecclesia super temporalibus habeat universale dominium,[14] quomodo intelligendum est quod Summus Pontifex non vult iurisdiccionem regum perturbare, ut habetur Extra.,[15] *De iudiciis*, capitulo *Novit*, et quomodo intelligendum est quod non spectat ad Ecclesiam de possessionibus se intromittere, sed hoc spectat ad reges, ut habetur Extra., *Qui filii sint legitimi*, capitulo *Causam* et eciam capitulo *Lator*, ubi questio de hereditate remittitur ad dominum secularem: dicemus,[16] ut[17] patet per habita, quod sicut Deus secundum duplicem legem gubernat mundum, videlicet, secundum legem communem, secundum quam se habet ut mare, ad quod quodlibet vas accedens plenum redit; se habet eciam ut sol, qui quantum est de se in omnes emittit suos radios bonitatis; se habet et tercio ut universale agens, qui sic dat virtutes rebus et sic administrat omnes res ut eas proprios motus[18] agere sinat. Si ergo hanc communem legem quam tenet Deus[19] in gubernacione tocius mundi ad Summum Pontificem in gubernacione hominum quantum ad temporalia volumus adaptare, ut ipse sit sicut mare, quod[20] se offert ad implenda omnia vasa, quod[21] sit sicut sol, qui immittit in omnia radios sue lucis, quod[22] sit sicut universale agens, quod omnes res[23] et[24] omnes secundas causas suos motus agere sinant, patet quod de temporalibus, quorum cura spectat ad potestates terrenas, Summus Pontifex non se intromittet, quia, hoc faciens, non impleret[25] potestates terrenas, sed magis eas evacuaret,[26] retraheret[27] ab eis radios sue potencie, non

---

1: istum] iustum V[2]   2: legem communem] communem legem FV[2]   3: Ecclesiam] *om.* F
4: et] *om.* P   5: cursus proprios] proprios cursus C   6: XXX] ix° F   7: quod] quia PV[1]
8: seminibus] *om.* F   9: condidit] addidit F   10: Ipse] *om.* FV[2]   11: eciam] enim C   12: nullas res] nulla re V[2]   13: permittat] sinat C   14: universale dominium] dominium universale C
15: Extra] *om.* F   16: dicemus] enim *add. and del.* P enim *add.* FV[2]   17: ut] enim *add.* C
18: motus] cursus FV[2]   19: tenet Deus] deus tenet FV[2]   20: quod] et C   21: quod] *del.* C
22: quod] *del.* C   23: omnes res] *del.* C   24: et] *om.* C   25: impleret] impleres V[2]
26: evacuaret] evacuares V[2]   27: retraheret] traheret V[2]

in this way, the Supreme Pontiff also is like a kind of sun, insofar as he governs the Church according to a common law and stands in the same relation to all things, since he preserves all things in their condition, treats all things according to their condition, and impedes none in its activity.

In a third way, God stands in relation to the government of the world, insofar as He governs it according to a common law, like a kind of universal agent. For He distributes their powers to all things and impedes none in its activity, but allows all things to pursue their own courses. And Augustine speaks of God in this way at *De civitate Dei* 7:30, where he says that: 'We worship that God Who has appointed to the beings created by Him both the beginning and the ends of their existing and moving; for He knows and disposes the causes of things, and He has created the force of seeds.' And he adds: 'Thus, He directs all the things which He has created in such a way that He allows them to execute and act according to their own movements.'[1] Therefore, God Himself disposes all causes and has created the force of all seeds, in that He gives their own powers to all creatures. Also, He directs all things according to a common law in such a way that He impedes none of them, but allows them to pursue their own courses.

And just as God acts thus in the government of all creatures, so does the Supreme Pontiff, the Vicar of God, act thus in the government of the Church and in the rule of the faithful. Therefore, when it is asked how, if the Church has a universal lordship over temporal things, we are to understand the statement that the Supreme Pontiff does not wish to disturb the jurisdiction of princes (as is established at X. 2:1:13: *Novit*), and how we are to understand that it is not the Church's task to intervene in disputes involving possessions, but that this rests with kings (as is established at X. 4:17:7: *Causam*, and also at X. 4:17:5: *Lator*, where a disputed inheritance is remitted to a secular lord): we shall reply that [the pope governs the faithful,] just as God governs the world, according to a twofold law, as is clear from what has been said. That is, He does so according to a common law, with respect to which He is like a sea from which every vessel is filled when it is brought to it; and He is like the sun, in that He sends forth the rays of His goodness from Himself to all men; and, third, He is like a universal agent which gives powers to things and directs all things in such a way that it allows them to pursue their own courses. Therefore, if we wish to apply this [argument concerning the] common law to which God adheres in the government of the whole world to the Supreme Pontiff in the government of the temporal affairs of men — so that he himself is like a sea which offers itself to fill all vessels, and is like the sun, which sends forth the rays of its light to all creatures, and is like a universal agent which allows all things and all secondary causes to act by their own motions: then it is clear that the Supreme Pontiff will not [normally] concern himself with temporal matters, the care of which rests with the earthly powers. For, by doing this, he would not fill up the earthly powers but, rather, would empty them; he would withdraw the rays of his power from them; and he would not

---

1. CCSL 47:211.

sineret eas agere proprios motus et propries cursus. Secundum ergo legem communem non intromittet se papa de temporalibus.

Sed secundum specialem[1] legem,[2] ut quia illa temporalia specialiter[3] sunt data Ecclesie, vel quia in litigio ipsorum temporalium aliquid est annexum quod specialiter ad Ecclesiam pertinet, vel aliis pluribus casibus[4] de quibus in sequenti capitulo volumus plenius pertractare, de temporalibus se Ecclesia intromittet. Non est ergo ex impotencia[5] pape quod non[6] possit de omnibus temporalibus se intromittere, sed quia, nisi[7] aliud[8] speciale in talibus occurrat,[9] decet Summum Pontificem secundum communem legem ad temporalia se habere; secundum quam communem legem[10] permittet reges et principes seculares in temporalibus rebus suos motus peragere: quod non sic est de spiritualibus rebus, ut in sequentibus[11] ostendetur.

Ex hoc autem potest patere solucio eius quod dicebatur in primo capitulo: quod non est de rigore iuris quod a civili iudice appelletur[12] ad papam. Dicemus[13] enim ad hanc questionem quod, preter[14] soluciones in primo capitulo datas, erit hic[15] una solucio: quod non est de rigore iuris quod a civili iudice appelletur ad papam prout in gubernandis temporalibus se gerit Summus Pontifex secundum communem legem. Erit tamen hoc, vel esse poterit[16] de iuris rigore,[17] prout in ipsis temporalibus consideratur aliquid spirituale. Nam sicut Deus habet universale dominium in omnibus rebus naturalibus, secundum quod dominium facere posset quod ignis non combureret[18] et aqua non madefaceret, ipse tamen secundum communem legem mundum gubernat, et, nisi adsit[19] aliquid speciale,[20] permittit res suos cursus peragere, non prohibendo ignem a sua combustione nec aquam a sua madefaccione: sic Summus Pontifex, Dei vicarius, suo modo habet universale dominium super temporalibus,[21] sed, volens se habere in illud secundum communem legem, nisi sit ibi aliquid spirituale, decens est quod permittat terrenas potestates, quibus commissa sunt temporalia, suos cursus peragere et sua iudicia exercere.

CAPITULUM III: *Quod racio persuadet, ista materialia et naturalia manifestant, necnon et tercio divina gubernacio hoc declarat, qualiter Summus Pontifex circa temporalia debet*[22] *se habere.*

Quoniam Summus Pontifex habet utrumque gladium, et quia sibi non a quocumque sed a Christo regni simul terreni et celestis et[23] iura imperii sunt commissa, ut haberi potest XXII Distinccione, capitulo *Omnis*,[24] ideo merito[25] dubitatur, cum ad iura imperii temporalia spectent, quare non indifferenter et passim in temporalibus

---

1: specialem] spiritualem F   2: legem] *om.* C   3: specialiter] spiritualiter F   4: casibus] causis F
5: impotencia] imperio F   6: non] *om.* F   7: nisi] nihil F nichil V[2]   8: aliud] aliquid V[2]
9: occurrat] occurrit FV[2]   10: ad temporalia ... legem] *om.* C   11: sequentibus] sequenti FV[2]
12: appelletur] appellaretur FV[2]   13: Dicemus] ergo *add.* F   14: preter] propter PFV[1]V[2]
15: hic] hec *mss*   16: poterit] potest F   17: iuris rigore] rigore iuris CFV[2]   18: combureret]
comburet CF   19: adsit] absit FV[2]   20: speciale] spirituale *mss*   21: temporalibus] temporali V[2]
22: *debet*] debeat F   23: et] *om.* V[2]   24: *Omnis*] omnes C   25: merito] *om.* V[2]

allow them to act by their own motions and their own courses. According to the common law, therefore [i.e. in the normal course of events], the pope will not concern himself with temporal matters.

The Church will, however, concern herself with temporal matters according to a special law [i.e. in special circumstances]: for example, because temporal possessions have been given to the Church specifically, or because something which lies specifically within the Church's province is involved in a temporal dispute, or in the numerous other cases with which we wish to deal more fully in a subsequent chapter.[1] Therefore, it is not due to any lack of power on the part of the pope that he may not concern himself with all temporal cases, but because, unless some special circumstance arises in connection with such cases, it is fitting for the Supreme Pontiff to stand towards temporal affairs according to the common law; according to which common law he will permit kings and secular princes to act by their own motion in temporal matters. But this is not true of spiritual matters, as will be shown in the following chapters.

And, from this, there can appear an explanation of the statement discussed in the first chapter: that it is not according to the strictness of the law that appeal may be made from a civil judge to the pope. For we shall say that, alongside the answers given to this question in the first chapter, there will be this further solution: that it is not according to the strictness of the law that appeal may be made from a civil judge to the pope because, in governing temporal affairs, the Supreme Pontiff conducts himself according to the common law. Nonetheless, this [appeal] will be made, or will be possible according to the strictness of the law, to the extent that some spiritual element is deemed to be present in such temporal affairs. For just as God has a universal lordship in all natural things, by reason of which lordship He could cause fire not to burn and water not to moisten, yet governs the world according to a common law and, unless some special reason is present, permits things to follow their own courses, not prohibiting fire from its burning or water from its moistening: so, for his part, the Supreme Pontiff, the Vicar of God, has a universal lordship over temporal things, but, wishing to stand towards them according to the common law, should, unless some spiritual consideration be present, permit the earthly powers to which temporal matters have been entrusted to pursue their own courses and to execute their own judgments.

CHAPTER III: *That reason demonstrates, material and natural phenomena show, and, third, the divine government most clearly reveals, how the Supreme Pontiff must stand in relation to temporal things.*

Because the Supreme Pontiff has both swords, and because the earthly and heavenly kingdoms and the laws of the empire have been entrusted to him together by none other than Christ (as can be gathered from the *Decretum,* Dist. 22, c. 1: *Omnis*),[2] it is therefore justly doubted, since temporal things belong to the laws of the empire, why appeal is not made to the pope without distinction and indiscriminately in temporal

1. Presumably he means Ch. V; but see also Chaps. VI–VIII.
2. CIC I:73.

appellatur ad papam. Dubitatur insuper que sunt illa specialia[1] in quibus appellatur ad ipsum et in quibus se de temporalibus intromittit. Dicemus itaque quod hoc racio persuadet, ea que videmus in naturalibus hoc ostendunt, gubernacio divina quantum ad Triumphantem et Militantem Ecclesiam hoc declarat, quod Summus Pontifex in gubernando temporalia secundum communem legem se habere debeat, et, nisi propter spiritualia aliqua,[2] de eis non se intromittat, et eciam quod propter huius-modi spiritualia[3] appelletur[4] ad papam.[5] In hoc tamen capitulo pertractabimus gen-eraliter ista, sed in sequentibus ad spiritualia[6] specialiter[7] descendemus.

Quomodo ergo Summus Pontifex se debeat in temporalibus gerere primo per-suadet hoc racio: quia pluribus intentus minor est ad singula sensus. Summus[8] ergo Pontifex, tamquam spiritualis homo[9] cuius est omnia iudicare, debet de spiritualibus specialiter[10] curam gerere. Nam et ideo adiunctus est sibi secundus gladius, ut possit circa spiritualia liberius vacare, circa que debet specialiter[11] intendere. Exinde est quod quidquid contingit in spiritualibus et in iudicibus ecclesiasticis, potest dici quod sit eius specialis[12] casus, quia specialem[13] curam debet habere de talibus, ut ipse ex hoc sit iudex ordinarius in quolibet tali foro, et ex hoc in talibus indifferenter et pas-sim appellatur ad ipsum. De rebus autem temporalibus, ut possit specialius spirituali-bus intendere, debet quandam curam generalem habere; eapropter, nisi aliqua spe-cialia hoc requirant, non[14] debet de temporalibus secundum legem communem[15] se intromittere, secundum quam, ut diximus, permittuntur[16] res quelibet, id est[17] per-mittuntur quelibet potestates terrene et quilibet civiles iudices, peragere suos cursus.

Viso quomodo hoc radio persuadet, declarare volumus quomodo naturalia hoc ostendunt. Nam[18] materialis gladius habet suam potestatem[19] a Summo Pontifice, cum omnis potestas que est in Ecclesia Militante est a Summo Pontifice derivata; quia nullus potest habere aliquam potestatem iuste nec esse dominus alicuius rei cum iusticia, ut supra diffusius diximus, nisi per Ecclesiam, ut quia est per eam spiritualiter regeneratus et quia[20] sacramentaliter absolutus. Habent ergo seculares principes potestatem ab Ecclesia et sub Ecclesia, et res naturales et corporales po-testatem quam habent a Deo habent. Est enim hic quoddam simile de potestate quam habet gladius materialis ab Ecclesia et de potestate quam habent res natura-les[21] a Deo; etsi non est per omnem modum simile, est tamen suo modo simile,[22] et quantum sufficit ad propositum est simile. Potestatem enim quam habet ignis, quod comburat, a Deo habet;[23] et potestatem quam habet leo, quod sit fortis et fortiter seviat, a Deo habet. Et sicut durum est quod[24] quis tradatur potestati gladii materialis, quia potest iudicium sanguinis exercere, sic durum est quod quis[25]

1: specialia] spiritualia PFV¹V²   2: spiritualia aliqua] specialia aliqua PV¹ aliqua spiritualia C
3: spiritualia] potest *add. and del.* C specialia PV¹   4: appelletur] appellaretur F appellatur CV²
5: papam] ipsum C   6: spiritualia] spiritualiter V² specialia PV¹   7: specialiter] *om.* V²
8: Summus] *om.* C   9: homo] *om.* C   10: specialiter] specialem FV²   11: specialiter] spiritualiter FV²   12: specialis] spiritualis FV²   13: specialem] specialiter FV²   14: non] *om.* CPV¹V²
15: legem communem] communem legem CFV²   16: permittuntur] pretermittuntur PV¹
17: permittuntur res ... est] *om.* V²   18: Nam] sicut *add.* C   19: potestatem] quam habet *add.* C
20: quia] *om.* CFV²   21: naturales] materiales CFV²   22: simile] *om.* C   23: a Deo habet]
habet a deo C   24: quod] *om.* F   25: quis] aliquis FV²

disputes. Moreover, there is also doubt as to what those special circumstances are in which appeal is made to him and by reason of which he intervenes in temporal affairs. Thus, we shall say that reason demonstrates, that what we see in natural phenomena shows, and that the Divine Government considered in relation to the Church both Triumphant and Militant makes clear that, in governing temporal things, the Supreme Pontiff ought to act according to the common law and not concern himself with them except for certain spiritual reasons, and also that, for such spiritual reasons, appeal may be made to the pope. In this chapter, however, we shall deal with these issues in a general way, and we shall devote particular attention to spiritual reasons in subsequent chapters.

First, therefore: reason demonstrates how the Supreme Pontiff should conduct himself in temporal matters. For when the understanding is intent upon many objects, it is less so upon individual things: therefore, the Supreme Pontiff, as the spiritual man whose task it is to judge all things,[1] must bear responsibility especially for spiritual things. And so a second sword has been added to him so that he may attend more freely to the spiritual matters with which he must be especially concerned. And so it is that whatever arises in the spiritual sphere and among ecclesiastical judges can be said to be his special province; for he must have the special care of such matters. Thus, for this reason, he is the ordinary judge in every such [i.e. in every ecclesiastical] court, and, on this ground, appeal is made to him in such matters without distinction and indiscriminately. Over temporal things, however, he must have a kind of general care, so that he may attend more especially to spiritual things. And so, according to the common law under which, as we have said, all things are permitted — that is, all earthly powers and all civil judges are permitted — to pursue their own courses, he should not concern himself with temporal affairs unless some special circumstances require this.

Having seen how reason demonstrates this, we wish to declare how natural phenomena show it. For the material sword receives its power from the Supreme Pontiff, since every power which is in the Church Militant is derived from the Supreme Pontiff. For, as we have said at greater length above, no one can hold any power justly or be lord of anything with justice except through the Church: that is, because he is spiritually regenerated and because he is sacramentally absolved through her.[2] Therefore, secular princes receive power from the Church and under the Church; and natural and corporeal things receive what power they have from God. For there is here a certain similarity between the power which the material sword receives from the Church and the power which natural things receive from God: not, indeed, a similarity in every respect, but a measure of similarity nonetheless; and this similarity is sufficient for our purpose. For fire receives the power which it has to burn from God; and a lion receives the power which it has to be strong and to rage fiercely from God. And just as it is a hard fate for someone to be delivered into the power of the material sword, because it can execute the judgment of blood, so is it a hard fate for someone to be delivered into the power

1. Cf. I Cor. 2:15; Pt. I, Ch. II.
2. Pt. II, Chaps. VII–IX.

tradatur potestati istarum rerum[1] naturalium,[2] ut quod quis tradatur potestati ignis,[3] quod ipsum comburat, vel potestati leonum, quod in eum seviant. Et sicut qui sunt traditi potestati gladii materialis, vel quantum ad res temporales[4] vel quantum ad proprium corpus, multociens appellant ad Ecclesiam, sic qui sunt traditi potestati rerum naturalium: ut potestati ignis vel potestati leonum vel potestati aliorum naturalium[5] agencium, sive hoc sit quantum ad res quas habent, quia ignis forte comburit eorum domos vel leones dilacerant res eorum, sive hoc sit quantum ad proprium corpus, quia ipsum corpus traditum est igni ad comburendum vel expositum est[6] leonibus ad devorandum.

Multociens[7] ergo qui talibus periculis sunt expositi[8] interpellant ad Deum. Sed raro videmus quod Deus interpellaciones et[9] appellaciones quantum ad hec corporalia damna exaudiat et admittat.[10] Aliquando tamen, ex aliqua speciali causa, exaudit[11] et admittit, sicut habetur Danielis III: quod Daniel et socii eius ligatis pedibus missi fuerunt in fornacem ignis ardentis, et fornax succensa erat nimis, et Deus fecit in medio fornacis quasi ventum roris flantem, et non tetigit eos omnino[12] ignis, neque contristavit nec quicquam[13] molestie intulit.

Traditus ergo erat Daniel crudelissimo iudici, quia igni ardenti; a quo iudice appellavit ad Deum qui dederat potestatem[14] igni. Appellavit enim Daniel ad Deum, quia recurrit et reclamavit ad eum. Hoc est enim appellare: a minori iudice ad maiorem recurrere vel reclamare. Admisit enim[15] Deus appellacionem Danielis et eruit eum de potestate crudelis iudicis.[16] Sed hoc est raro, quod talis appellacio admittatur; fuit enim quid speciale in Daniele.

Sic eciam[17] ipse Daniel non solum fuit traditus crudelissimo iudici, quia igni ardenti, ut habetur Danielis III, sed eciam fuit traditus crudelissimis iudicibus, quia leonibus sevientibus, ut habetur Danielis ultimo, a quibus eciam iudicibus et leonibus sevientibus rursus reclamavit ad Dominum, et ex hoc appellavit ad ipsum; cuius appellacionem Deus recipiens, conclusit ora leonum, ut nihil mali ei inferrent. Sed, ut diximus, hoc est[18] raro, et fuit quid speciale in Daniele et in aliquibus aliis sanctis. Communiter enim et ut plurimum Deus gubernat mundum quantum ad ista naturalia[19] que videmus non secundum legem specialem quod non sinat ignem comburere et leones feroces quantumcumque famelicos non sinit eos[20] devorare; sed gubernat mundum secundum legem communem, ut res proprios cursus agere sinat.

Et sicut Deus gubernat mundum quantum ad istas res naturales[21] quas videmus, quia assidue ut plurimum se gerit cum eis secundum communem legem, ut non impediat eas in accionibus suis,[22] raro autem et ex aliquibus specialibus casibus esse contingit quod non sinat hec naturalia[23] agere suos cursus: sic et Summus Pontifex,

1: rerum] *om.* V[2]   2: naturalium] materialium CV[2]   3: istarum rerum ... ignis] *om.* F   4: temporales] materiales F   5: naturalium] materialium C   6: expositum est] exponitur FV[2]   7: Multociens] est *add.* PV[1]   8: expositi] causa duris iudicibus *add. and del.* C et *add. and del.* P et *add.* FV[2]   9: et] vel FV[2]   10: admittat] eorum interpellationes vel eorum appellationes *add. and del.* C   11: exaudit] exaudivit F   12: omnino] eos C *om.* V[1]   13: quicquam] ad quam F ad aliqua V[2]   14: potestatem] illi crudelissimo iudici videlicet *add. and del.* C   15: enim] *del.* P   16: iudicis] iudicii FV[2]   17: eciam] et FV[2]   18: est] *om.* V[2]   19: naturalia] materialia CFV[2]   20: eos] alios C   21: naturales] materiales et quantum ad istas res naturales CFV[2]   22: suis] et *add.* F   23: naturalia] materialia CFV[2]

of these natural things: for someone to be delivered into the power of fire, to burn him, or into the power of a lion, to maul him. And just as those who are delivered into the power of the material sword, whether with respect to their temporal goods or with respect to their own bodies, frequently appeal to the Church, so also with those who are delivered into the power of natural things, as into the power of fire or into the power of a lion or into the power of other natural agents, whether this be with respect to the goods which they have, as when fire burns their houses or lions destroy their property, or whether it be with respect to their own bodies, as when the body itself is delivered to the fire to be burned or exposed to lions to be devoured.

Frequently, therefore, do those who are exposed to such perils petition God; but rarely do we see that God hears and receives their petitions and appeals as to these bodily injuries. Sometimes, however, for certain special reasons, He does hear and receive them: as is established in Daniel 3, where Daniel and his companions were cast into a burning fiery furnace with their feet bound, and the furnace heated exceedingly, and God caused the midst of the furnace to be like the blowing of a wind bringing dew, and the fire did not in the least touch them or distress them or bring them any harm.[1]

Therefore, Daniel was delivered to a most cruel judge in the form of a burning fire; and from this judge he appealed to God, Who gave power to the fire. For Daniel appealed to God in that he turned to Him and called upon Him. For this is what it is to make appeal: to turn to or call upon a greater judge from a lesser. For God received the appeal of Daniel and released him from the cruel judge's power. But it is rare for such an appeal to be received; for, in Daniel's case, a special reason was present.

So too, Daniel himself was not only delivered to a most cruel judge in the form of a burning fire, as is established in Daniel 3; but he was delivered also to most cruel judges in the form of raging lions, as is established in the final chapter of Daniel.[2] And from these judges and raging lions he again called upon the Lord, and thereby appealed to Him. And, receiving his appeal, God closed the mouths of the lions so that they might do him no harm. But, as we have said, this is rare and, in the case of Daniel and certain other saints, a special reason was present. For, as to those natural phenomena which we see, God governs the world generally and in most cases not according to a special law such that He does not allow fire to burn and does not allow even the hungriest of fierce lions to devour their prey: rather, He governs the world according to a common law, so that He may allow things to pursue their own courses.

And just as, so far as those natural things which we see are concerned, God continuously governs the world in such a way that, in most cases, He deals with them according to a common law in order not to impede them in their activities; yet, albeit rarely, when certain special circumstances are present, He does not allow these natural agents to pursue their own courses, so also the Supreme Pontiff

1. Dan. 3:20–26.
2. Dan. 14:30 (Vulgate); a more satisfactory reference would be to Dan. 6:16–24.

quantum ad hec temporalia, et[1] quantum ad[2] ista materialia, debet se gerere secundum communem legem, ut ea[3] proprios cursus agere sinat et ut materiales gladii sua iudicia exequantur,[4] nisi forte aliqua specialia ibi sint advertenda, propter que de temporalibus se intromittat; et in eisdem temporalibus propter huiusmodi specialia eciam a civilibus iudicibus et a terrenis[5] potestatibus poterit appellari ad papam.

In spiritualibus ergo semper cum recurrimus ad Deum et interpellamus ad ipsum dum sumus in vita ista, ubi datum est nobis tempus penitencie, semper Deus exaudit interpellacionem nostram et semper admittit appellacionem nostram. Sic Summus Sacerdos,[6] Dei vicarius, semper[7] circa spiritualia debet habere specialem curam, ut omnes casus in talibus[8] sint ei speciales et ipse sit in talibus ubique[9] ordinarius. Circa temporalia vero, nisi propter aliqua specialia, non debet appellacionem admittere nec de eis se intromittere, sed terrenis potestatibus et civilibus iudicibus sunt talia relinquenda.

Ostenso quod racio persuadet et naturalia manifestant qualiter papa se debeat circa temporalia gerere, volumus ostendere quod gubernacio divina quantum ad Triumphantem et Militantem Ecclesiam hoc declarat. Dicemus quidem quod illa Ecclesia Triumphans tota est spiritualis. Immo, post resurreccionem, quando erimus cum corporibus triumphantes in celis, omnes erimus spirituales. Ipsa enim corpora nostra tunc erunt spiritualia, quia non indigebunt alimento, sicut nec spiritus indigent. Ideo dicitur prima ad Corinthios XV quod 'seminatur corpus animale, surget corpus[10] spirituale.' In illa ergo celesti patria et in illa Ecclesia Triumphante, que tota est spiritualis, indifferenter et passim appellatur ad Deum et habetur recursus ad ipsum, ut in omnibus fiat voluntas sua.

Sunt enim in angelis discordie, sunt in eis litigia,[11] sunt in eis pugne: sine omni tamen peccato et sine omni culpa. Sunt enim in eis[12] discordie, loquendo de discordia large, quando unus vult unum et alius vult aliud. Nam angelus qui loquebatur Danieli volebat liberacionem Iudeorum, quam nolebat angelus qui erat princeps regni Persarum. Sunt autem litigia inter angeles quando non eadem volentes quasi litigantes quilibet pro parte sua racionem assignat: ut forte angelus qui volebat liberacionem Danielis racionem ad hoc assignabat quia Daniel[13] tam sanctus et tam bonus exaudiendus[14] erat; angelus autem princeps[15] Persarum, qui nolebat liberacionem Danielis[16] et aliorum Iudeorum, forte racionem pro se assignabat quia quamdiu Iudei[17] erant inter ipsos Persas exemplo ipsorum Iudeorum gens Persarum retrahebatur[18] a multis malis et inducebatur[19] ad multa bona. Est autem pugna inter angelos quando non solum unus vult quod non vult alius, quod est[20] quasi quoddam discordare, et non solum quilibet ad suam partem racionem assignat, quod est quasi quoddam litigare, sed eciam unus alii resistit, ut

---

1: et] om. F   2: ad] hec add. V²   3: ea] eas F   4: exequantur] exequentur F   5: terrenis] terre V²
6: Sacerdos] pontifex C   7: semper] om. F   8: in talibus] om. V²   9: ubique] ubicumque F
10: corpus] om. C   11: Sunt enim ... litigia] in angelis enim discordie sunt in eis litigia sunt F
12: in eis] om. F   13: Daniel] Danielis F   14: exaudiendus] exaudiens F   15: princeps] regni
add. CFV²   16: Danielis] liberacionem V²   17: Iudei] om. PV¹   18: retrahebatur] retrahebantur F   19: inducebatur] inducebantur F   20: est] om. V²

should conduct himself according to the common law in relation to temporal affairs and in relation to material things, so that he may allow them to pursue their own courses, and so that material swords may execute their own judgments: unless there are perhaps some special circumstances present which must be taken into account, by reason of which he may intervene in temporal disputes. And in the same temporal disputes, by reason of such special circumstances, it will also be possible to appeal from civil judges and earthly powers to the pope.

In spiritual matters, therefore, whenever we turn to God and petition Him while we are in this life, where a time of penance is given to us, God always hears our petition and always receives our appeal. Thus, the Supreme Priest, the Vicar of God, must always have the special care of spiritual things, so that all cases involving such things are specially reserved to him, and he is everywhere the ordinary judge in such cases. But so far as temporal cases are concerned, he should not receive an appeal or intervene in them save in some special circumstances. Rather, such cases should be relinquished to the earthly powers and to the civil judges.

Having shown that reason demonstrates and that natural phenomena reveal how the pope should conduct himself in relation to temporal matters, we wish to show that the Divine Government, considered in relation to the Church both Triumphant and Militant, also makes this clear. For we shall say that the Church Triumphant is wholly spiritual: indeed, after the resurrection, when we shall be triumphant in heaven with our bodies, we shall be wholly spiritual beings. For our bodies will then be spiritual entities, because they will not need food, just as spirits have no such need. And so it is said in I Corinthians 15 that 'It is sown an animal body; it will rise a spiritual body.'[1] In that heavenly realm, therefore, and in that Church Triumphant which is wholly spiritual, appeal is made to God without distinction and indiscriminately, and recourse had to Him, so that His will may be done in all things.

For there are discords among the angels; there are disputes among them; there are contests among them: wholly without sin, however, and wholly without fault. For, speaking of discord in a broad sense, such discords occur among them when one wishes one thing and another wishes another. For the angel who spoke to Daniel wished that the Jews might be set free, which the angel who was the prince of the kingdom of the Persians did not wish.[2] And there are disputes among the angels when, as disputants who do not wish the same thing, each advances an argument for his own side. For example, the angel who wished that Daniel might be set free perhaps assigned as his reason for this that so holy and so good a man as Daniel should be heard. But the angel who was the prince of the Persians, who did not wish that Daniel and the other Jews should be set free, perhaps assigned as his reason that, for as long as the Jews were among the Persians, the Persian nation was restrained from many evil deeds and inspired to many good works by the example of the Jews themselves. But there is a contest between the angels when one not only wishes what another does not wish, which is like a kind of discord, and when each not only advances an argument for his own side, which is like a kind of dispute, but when one actually resists the other

1. I Cor. 15:44.
2. Dan. 10:13; 20.

non faciat quod vult, quod est quasi quoddam pugnare. Ideo angelus ille qui volebat[1] liberacionem Iudeorum dixit quod princeps regni Persarum resistit sibi viginti
et uno diebus, ut dicitur Danielis X.[2]

In hiis ergo litigiis angelorum et in hiis discordiis, Deus facit concordiam[3]
quando docet angelos quid fieri vult de eo quod litigant. Ideo dicitur [4] Job XXV
quod 'potestas et terror apud eum est qui facit concordiam in sublimibus suis,' id
est in angelis suis. Qui sublimes et qui angeli sunt quasi innumerabiles; ideo ibidem sequitur: 'Numquid est numerus militum eius,' id est angelorum eius, ut[5] exponit [glossa] interlinearis. Cum ergo unus angelus resistit alii, statim ille cui re-
sistitur appellat ad Dominum et interpellat ad ipsum, ut fiat inde voluntas sua et ut
ipse sentenciet quid[6] fiendum.[7]

In Ecclesia itaque Triumphante, que tota est spiritualis, indifferenter et passim
appellatur ad Deum,[8] ut ipse sentenciet quid fiendum: in quo docemur quod,
quantum ad spiritualia, indifferenter et passim appellari potest ad Summum Pontificem, ut ipse sentenciet quid fiendum sit et qualiter nos gerere debeamus. Sed in
Ecclesia Militante, que non sic[9] tota spiritualis est,[10] quantum ad dampna corporalia, etsi appellamus et interpellamus ad Deum, nostre appellaciones non communiter admittuntur. Immo, assidue et quasi communiter quantum ad hec temporalia
et corporalia Deus sic administrat res ut eas earum[11] cursus agere sinat, et sic dedit
potestatem rebus ut secundum potestates[12] illas suas acciones eas exercere permittat, nisi forte essent aliqua specialia, propter que Deus preter solitum cursum et
preter communem legem vellet aliqua operari.

Exinde ergo docemur qualiter in temporalibus Summus Pontifex debet[13] se habere. Nam quantumcumque potestas terrena sit per potestatem ecclesiasticam et
sub potestate ecclesiastica constituta, ipsa tamen potestas ecclesiastica, nisi sint
aliqua specialia propter que hoc agat, de ipsis temporalibus non debet se intromittere, nec debet in eis appellaciones admittere, nisi propter aliqua specialia, ut forte
quia illa temporalia specialiter sunt Ecclesie, vel propter aliqua alia que infra dicentur; sed debet iudicia in talibus ad seculares dominos et ad civiles iudices remittere, ut ipsi in eis sua iudicia proferant et sentencient quid agendum.

CAPITULUM IV: *Quod cum omnia temporalia sint sub dominio Ecclesie, quomodo intelligendum est quod ait Innocencius III: quod 'certis*[14] *causis inspectis,
temporalem iurisdiccionem casualiter*[15] *exercemus.'*

Communes quidem sermones circa moralem materiam nos sufficienter non docent
nisi exponantur et declarentur. Dictum est enim quod in spiritualibus indifferenter et
passim appellatur ad papam,[16] et ipse de eis indifferenter et passim[17] se intromittet

1: volebat] nolebat C   2: X] xi F   3: concordiam] contra discordiam F   4: dicitur] *om.* V[2]
5: ut] *om.* PV[1]   6: quid] aliquid F   7: fiendum] sciendum V[2]   8: Deum] dominum F   9: sic]
fit F   10: est] et F   11: earum] eorum FV[2]   12: potestates] potestatem in F   13: debet] debeat F
14: *certis*] cunctis F   15: *casualiter*] *om.* FV[2]   16: appellatur ad papam] *om.* P   17: et ipse ...
passim] et ipse de deus indifferenter et passim *marg.* PV[1]

so that he may not do what he wishes, which is like a kind of contest. And so the angel who desired that the Jews should be set free declared that the prince of the kingdom of the Persians resisted him for twenty-one days, as is said in Daniel 10.[1]

In these disputes of the angels, therefore, and in these discords, God establishes concord when He instructs the angels as to what He wishes them to do in the matter over which they are in dispute. And so it is said in Job 25 that 'Power and terror are with Him, Who establishes concord among His exalted ones,'[2] that is, among His angels. And these exalted ones, these angels, are almost innumerable; and so, in the same place, it goes on: 'Is there any numbering of His soldiers?' that is, of His angels, as the interlinear gloss explains. Therefore, when one angel resists another, he to whom resistance is shown at once appeals to the Lord and petitions Him, so that His will may henceforth be done, and so that He may declare what is to be done.

Thus, in the Church Triumphant, which is wholly spiritual, appeal is made to God without distinction and indiscriminately, so that He may declare what is to be done. And we are taught by this that, in spiritual matters, appeal can be made without distinction and indiscriminately to the Supreme Pontiff, so that he may declare what is to be done and how we should conduct ourselves. But in the Church Militant, which is not wholly spiritual in this way, though we appeal to and petition God with regard to bodily injuries, our appeals are not usually received. On the contrary, in the temporal and corporeal spheres, God continuously and almost invariably directs things in such a way that He allows them to pursue their own courses. And He has given powers to things in such a way that He permits them to exercise their own functions according to such powers — unless, perhaps, there were to be some special circumstances by reason of which God wished to bring about some events beyond the ordinary course of nature and beyond the common law.

Accordingly, therefore, we are taught how the Supreme Pontiff should stand in relation to temporal things. For however much the earthly power may be appointed through the ecclesiastical power and under the ecclesiastical power, the ecclesiastical power itself ought not to intervene in temporal disputes unless it does so in some special circumstances. Nor should it receive appeals except in some special circumstances: for example, because the temporal things in question are the special property of the Church, or by reason of certain other considerations which are discussed below.[3] Rather, it should remit judgment in such cases to the secular lords and to civil judges, so that they themselves may pass judgment on them and declare what is to be done.

CHAPTER IV: *Since all temporal things are under the lordship of the Church, how are we to understand what Innocent III says: that 'on the examination of certain causes, we exercise a temporal jurisdiction occasionally'?*

General discourses on a moral subject do not sufficiently teach us unless they are expounded and made clear. For it has been said that, in spiritual matters, appeal is made to the pope without distinction and indiscriminately, and that he will concern

1. Dan. 10:13.
2. Job 25:2.
3. Chaps. V–VIII.

prout videt bono publico expedire.[1] Declarandum est ergo que sunt illa specialia[2] propter que in litigiis rerum temporalium a civili iudice appelletur[3] ad papam, et in quibus ipse se de temporalibus intromittat; sed de hiis[4] in sequenti capitulo dicetur.

In hoc autem capitulo intendimus declarare quod, cum Ecclesia sit omnium temporalium[5] domina, quomodo veritatem habet et quomodo intelligendum est quod dicit Innocencius III Extra., *Qui filii sint*[6] *legitimi,*[7] capitulo[8] *Per venerabilem*: quod 'certis[9] causis inspectis, temporalem iurisdiccionem casualiter exercemus.' Dicemus ergo quod, ut[10] in secunda[11] parte huius operis dicebamus, temporalia, ut temporalia sunt, Ecclesie sunt subiecta; quod non est intelligendum quod ipsa temporalia per se et primo Ecclesie sunt[12] subiecta, sed intelligendum est quod sunt subiecta Ecclesie per se, sed non primo. Dicitur enim esse aliquid 'per se' quando est hoc per causam existentem in se. Ipsa enim temporalia in se ipsis habent causam ut subiciantur spiritualibus et ut ordinentur ad illa. Non est ergo per accidens, sed est per se et per causam[13] existentem[14] in se, quod temporalia sunt sub spirituali potencia collocata. Sed cum hoc sit 'per se', non 'primo', queres quid est esse 'primo'. Dicemus ergo quod illud est 'primo', ut est in alia sciencia declaratum, quod est alteri per ipsum, non ipsi per alterum: ut habere 'tres' competit triangulo primo quia omnia alia[15] habent tres per ipsum, ipse autem triangulus habet tres per[16] se ipsum, non per aliud. Si ergo temporalia essent subiecta Ecclesie primo, omnia alia essent subiecta Ecclesie[17] per ipsa temporalia: ergo spiritualia essent subiecta Ecclesie per temporalia.[18] Itaque Ecclesia primo haberet potestatem in temporalia et per temporalia in spiritualia; quod est falsum et irracionabile.[19] Secundum hoc ergo, spiritualia sunt subiecta Ecclesie primo, et per spiritualia sunt ei subiecta temporalia. Ipsa itaque temporalia sunt subiecta Ecclesie per se, quia in se[20] habent causam quod subiciantur spiritualibus. Cum ergo dicitur quod temporalia, ut temporalia sunt, Ecclesie sunt subiecta, illud 'ut' non dat intelligere quod hoc sit primo, sed dat intelligere quod non sit per accidens tantum, sed sit per se.

Sed forte adhuc queres utrum aliquo modo primo temporalia sub Ecclesia collocentur. Respondebimus quod temporalia possunt comparari ad spiritualia, quibus sunt subiecta et ad que ordinantur; possunt eciam comparari ad ipsam potestatem terrenam. Si comparentur[21] ad spiritualia, dicemus quod temporalia non sunt

---

1: expedire] experire C   2: specialia] spiritualia F   3: appelletur] appellatur C   4: hiis] eis FV²
5: temporalium] *om.* V²   6: *sint*] sunt F   7: *legitimi*] *om.* F   8: capitulo] *om.* PV¹   9: certis]
cunctis F   10: ut] *om.* V²   11: secunda] prima *mss*   12: sunt] sint FV²   13: sed est ... causam]
om. F   14: existentem] existens F   15: alia] illa PV¹   16: ipse autem ... per] *om.* F   17: primo,
omnia ... Ecclesie] *om.* V²   18: ergo spiritualia ... temporalia] *om.* V²   19: irracionabile] irracionabilem F   20: se] non *add.* C   21: comparentur] compararetur FV²

himself with them without distinction and indiscriminately insofar as he sees this to be expedient to the public good. Therefore, we must also show what those special circumstances are in which appeal may be made from a civil judge to the pope in temporal disputes, and by reason of which he intervenes in temporal affairs. But these questions will be discussed in the following chapter.

In this chapter, however, we intend to show how, since the Church is lord of all temporal things, what Innocent III says at X. 4:17:13: *Per venerabilem* is true and how it must be understood: that 'on the examination of certain causes, we exercise a temporal jurisdiction occasionally.'[1] We shall say, therefore, that, though temporal things are subject to the Church inasmuch as they are temporal, as we have argued in the second part of this work, it must not be supposed that these temporal things are subject to the Church both in themselves and primarily. Rather, it must be understood that they are subject to the Church in themselves, but not primarily. For something is said to be as it is 'in itself' when it is as it is through a cause existing in itself. For temporal things have in themselves the cause whereby they are subjected to spiritual things and subordinated to them; therefore, it is not accidentally, but in themselves and through a cause existing in themselves, that temporal things are placed under the spiritual power.[2] But if this is what 'in itself' means, as distinct from 'primarily', you will ask what 'primarily' means. We shall reply, then, that, as has been shown in another science,[3] an entity is as it is 'primarily' when something else is as it is through it, not when it is as it is through something else. For example, to have 'three' belongs to a triangle primarily because all other things have three through it [i.e. by comparison with it, as a primary or standard case of 'threeness'], but the triangle itself has three in itself [i.e. necessarily or by definition], not through something else. If, therefore, temporal things were subject to the Church primarily, all else would be subject to the Church through temporal things. Spiritual things, therefore, would be subject to the Church through temporal, and so the Church would have power in temporal things primarily, and, through temporal things, in spiritual; which is false and against reason.[4] On this ground, therefore, spiritual things are subject to the Church primarily, and temporal things are subject to her through spiritual things. Thus, temporal things are subject to the Church in themselves, since they have in themselves the cause whereby they are subjected to spiritual things. But when it is said that temporal things are subject to the Church inasmuch as they are temporal, this 'inasmuch as' does not give us to understand that they are primarily so: rather, it gives us to understand that they are so not merely accidentally, but in themselves.

But perhaps you will also ask whether temporal things may in any way be placed under the Church primarily. We shall reply that temporal things can be considered in relation to spiritual things, through which they are subjected and to which they are ordered; and they can be considered also in relation to the earthly power. If they are considered in relation to spiritual things, we shall say that temporal things

1. See Introduction, p. xxvii and n. 60.
2. See Aristotle, *Metaphysics* Δ:18 (1022^{a}25); 30 (1025^{a}15); 7 (1029^{b}13).
3. See Aristotle, *Metaphysics* Z:4 (1030^{a}20).
4. Cf. Aquinas, *Summa theologiae* IIIa 22:6 *obj.* 1.

subiecta Ecclesie primo, quia tunc per temporalia subicerentur[1] Ecclesie spiritualia, quod non est verum: immo, est econverso. Sed si temporalia comparantur ad
potestatem terrenam, distinguemus de hoc quod dicitur 'primo'. Nam 'primo' uno[2]
modo idem est quod 'immediacius'; alio modo idem est quod 'principalius': ut si
faber attingit ferrum per martellum, patet quod 'primo', id est 'immediacius',
martellus attingit ferrum, sed 'primo', id est 'principalius', faber attingit ferrum.[3]
Nam quod martellus attingat ferrum, hoc habet a fabro: itaque 'principalius' attingit faber ferrum quam martellus. Sic et in proposito: potestas quidem terrena est
quasi quoddam organum et quidam martellus potestatis ecclesiastice, et quod potestas terrena habeat[4] dominium super temporalia, hoc habet a potestate ecclesiastica, sicut martellus, quod attingit ferrum, hoc habet[5] a fabro. Nam nullus est princeps super temporalia qui vel non habeat ab Ecclesia quod sit princeps, vel non
habeat ab ea quod sit verus et dignus princeps, ut est per habita manifestum.

Ecclesia itaque super temporalia habet quandam auctoritatem superiorem et
primariam, ut quidam doctores nostre sciencie notaverunt: secundum quam[6] auctoritatem primariam et superiorem instituere habet potestatem terrenam, quod presit temporalibus; secundum quam institucionem ipsa potestas terrena immediate se
de temporalibus intromittit.[7] Temporalia igitur subsunt potestati terrene 'primo',
id est 'immediacius', et subsunt Ecclesie 'primo', id est 'principalius'; secundum
quam principalitatem potest potestas ecclesiastica animadvertere in potestatem
terrenam, ut ex culpa, vel saltem ex causa, possit eam[8] destituere et aliam instituere et eam transferre, sicut supra de imperio tetigimus.

Propter quod patet quod Ecclesia regulariter et generaliter non[9] intromittet[10] se
de temporalibus immediate: tum quia principalius pertinent ad ecclesiasticam potestatem spiritualia quam temporalia, et ex hoc, ut liberius vacet spiritualibus,
regulariter et generaliter non intromittet se immediate de temporalibus; tum[11]
eciam quia potestas terrena immediate se intromittit de temporalibus ne sit confusio in potestatibus, et ut hee potestates, terrena videlicet et ecclesiastica,[12] non sint
confuse, sed[13] sint ad invicem ordinate. Regulariter et generaliter de temporalibus
Ecclesia non se intromittit,[14] sed solum se intromittet[15] immediate et per se ipsam[16]
ex aliquo casu contingente, vel propter aliquid speciale: non quod hoc sit ex Ecclesie[17] impotencia, sed ex eius decencia et excellencia. Nam qui spiritualia iudicat multo magis potest temporalia et secularia iudicare.

Hoc est ergo quod ait Apostolus prima ad Corinthios VI: 'Nescitis, quoniam
angelos iudicabimus, quanto magis secularia?' Potest ergo Ecclesia secularia[18] et
temporalia iudicare, sed non decet quod spirituales iudices, qui sunt maioris meriti,

1: subicerentur] subiicientur F   2: uno] *om.* F   3: ferrum] *om.* V² 4: habeat] habet F   5: ha-
bet] habebat FV²   6: quam] suam F   7: intromittit] et *add.* F   8: eam] eandem F   9: non]
debet *add.* F   10: intromittet] intromittere F   11: tum] cum FV²   12: ecclesiastica] ut *add.* V²
13: sed] ut *add.* FV² ut *add. and del.* P   14: intromittit] intromittet CFV²   15: sed solum se in-
tromittet] *om.* F   16: ipsam] sed *add.* F   17: Ecclesie] exercere V²   18: Ecclesia secularia]
secularia ecclesia F

are not subject to the Church primarily, for spiritual things would then be subject to the Church through temporal; which is not true: indeed, the converse is true. But if temporal things are considered in relation to the earthly power, we shall make a distinction as to the word 'primarily'. For, in one way, 'primarily' is the same as 'more immediately'; and, in another, it is the same as 'more principally'. Thus, if a blacksmith strikes a piece of iron with a hammer, it is clear that 'primarily', that is, 'more immediately', the hammer strikes the iron; but 'primarily', that is, 'more principally', the blacksmith strikes the iron. For the hammer receives the capacity to strike the iron from the blacksmith: thus, the blacksmith strikes the iron 'more principally' than the hammer does. So too in our proposition: the earthly power is indeed a kind of instrument and a kind of hammer of the ecclesiastical power; and, though the earthly power has lordship over temporal affairs, it receives this from the ecclesiastical power just as the hammer receives the capacity to strike the piece of iron from the blacksmith. For no one is a prince over temporal things who either does not have it from the Church that he is a prince, or does not have it from her that he is a true and worthy prince, as is plainly shown from what has been said.

Thus, the Church has a kind of superior and primary authority over temporal things, as certain teachers of our science [i.e. canon law] have noted.[1] And by reason of this primary and superior authority, she must institute the earthly power to rule temporal affairs; according to which institution the earthly power concerns itself immediately with temporal matters. Thus, temporal affairs are under the earthly power 'primarily', that is 'more immediately'; yet they are under the Church 'primarily', that is, 'more principally'. And, by reason of this principality, the ecclesiastical power can act against the earthly power; so that, for fault or for other cause, it might abandon it and institute another, and transfer it, as we have noted above in the case of the empire.[2]

And so it is clear that the Church will not intervene in temporal matters regularly and generally: both because spiritual matters pertain to the ecclesiastical power more principally than do temporal, and, for this reason, so that she may attend more freely to spiritual matters, she will not directly intervene in temporal affairs regularly and generally; and also because the earthly power concerns itself immediately with temporal affairs lest there should be confusion among the powers, and so that these powers — that is, the earthly and ecclesiastical — may not be confused, but may be mutually ordered. Regularly and generally, the Church does not intervene in temporal affairs; rather, she does so, immediately and of herself, only in some unusual case or for some special reason: but this is due not to any lack of power on the part of the Church, but to her worth and excellence. For she who judges spiritual matters is all the more able to judge temporal and secular ones.

This, therefore, is what the Apostle says in I Corinthians 6: 'Do you not know that we shall judge angels? How much more the things of this world?'[3] Therefore, the Church can judge secular and temporal disputes; but it is not fitting that spiritual

1. See n. 1 on p. 273.
2. See Introduction, n. 41.
3. I Cor. 6:3.

se immediate de secularibus sive de temporalibus intromittant: sed debent ad hoc instituere potestates terrenas, qui sunt minoris meriti, ut ipsi de temporalibus et secularibus se intromittant;[1] ut homo spiritualis, militans Deo, non immisceat se negociis secularibus. Unde, cum Apostolus[2] prius dixisset 'quoniam angelos iudicabimus, quanto magis secularia?' postea immediate subiungit:[3] 'Secularia igitur iudicia si habueritis, contemptibiles qui sunt in Ecclesia, illos constituite ad iudicandum'; quod glossa exponens quantum ad unum modum exponendi ait quod 'contemptibiles' debent ad hoc constitui,[4] debent enim[5;6] ad hoc institui[7] aliqui sapientes qui sint[8] minoris meriti, per quos[9] potestates terrenas et seculares principes intelligere possumus. Propter quod glossa ibidem subdit, et sumptum est a Gregorio in *Moralibus*, quod 'hii terrenas causas examinent qui exteriorum rerum sapienciam perceperunt,'[10] et subdit quod 'qui autem spiritualibus donis ditati sunt, terrenis non debent negociis implicari, ut dum non coguntur inferiora bona disponere, valeant bonis superioribus deservire.' Sic enim videmus in ipsis angelis, quod superiores semper assistunt Deo et non mittuntur ad nos, inferiores vero ista temporalia et corporalia disponunt et gubernant. Ipsi ergo superiores angeli ad exteriora non mittuntur. Quia ergo temporalia et secularia sunt negocia exteriora, ideo potestates spirituales, tamquam superiores, ad talia negocia mitti non debent nisi sit aliquid speciale, et nisi casus immineat, quia, ut Beda ait, nonnumquam instante causa quedam de nostri propositi rigore possunt sine culpa intermitti. Rigor ergo potestatis spiritualis[11] est intendere circa spiritualia; sed si casus immineat, si speciale[12] aliquid[13] hoc requirat, potest iste rigor sine culpa intermitti, ut spiritualis potestas se de temporalibus intromittat.

Hiis itaque visis, volumus solvere ad id quod in principio presentis capituli dicebatur:[14] quod 'certis causis inspectis temporalem iurisdiccionem casualiter exercemus.' Quia, si spiritualis potestas principalius debet intendere spiritualibus, et si potestas terrena debet immediate[15] se intromittere de temporalibus, ut supra diximus, duo inconveniencia sequentur[16] si potestas ecclesiastica regulariter et generaliter se immediate intromitteret de temporalibus. Primo quidem, quia non posset ita vacare spiritualibus quibus debet[17] principaliter intendere;[18] secundo vero quia esset confusio; confunderet[19] enim tunc una potestas aliam. Non ergo generaliter, sed circumspectis[20] certis causis et casu imminente intromittet se immediate de temporalibus iudex ecclesiasticus. Hoc est ergo iurisdiccionem temporalem casualiter exercere, quando nonnisi casu imminente et speciali aliqua causa[21] hoc requirente ab ecclesiastica potestate temporalis iurisdiccio exercetur. Que sunt autem illa specialia[22]

1: se intromittant] agant C   2: Apostolus] cum *add.* CPV[1]   3: subiungit] subiunxit FV[2]

4: constitui] institui F id est *add.* FV[2]   5: enim] *om.* F   6: debent enim] enim debent P

7: institui] constitui F   8: sint] sunt FV[2]   9: quos] quas C   10: perceperunt] perceperint F

11: potestas spiritualis] spiritualis potestas F   12: speciale] spirituale FV[2]   13: aliquid] aliquod F

14: dicebatur] videlicet *add.* C   15: debet immediate] immediate debet CFV[2]   16: sequentur] sequerentur CV[2]   17: debet] vacare *add.* C vacare et *add.* FV[2] vacare *add. and del.* P   18: intendere] *om.* C   19: confunderet] confundet F   20: circumspectis] itaque *add.* CFV[2] *add. and del.* P   21: aliqua causa] causa aliqua FV[2]   22: specialia] spiritualia FV[2]

judges, who are greater in merit, should concern themselves with secular or temporal cases. Rather, they must institute earthly powers, who are lesser in merit, to this task, so that these may concern themselves with temporal and secular disputes and so that the spiritual man, being a soldier of God, may not involve himself in secular business.[1] Hence, when the Apostle had first said, 'We shall judge angels; how much more the things of this world?' he then at once added: 'If you have worldly things to decide, then, appoint those who are despised in the Church to give judgment.' And a gloss suggests, as one interpretation of this, that [when it is said that] 'those who are despised' must be appointed for this purpose [what is meant is that] certain wise men who are lesser in merit [than the clergy], by whom we can understand earthly powers and secular princes, should be instituted to this task.[2] And so, in the same place, the gloss adds (and this is taken from Gregory's *Moralia*[3]) that 'those who have acquired knowledge of external things are to examine earthly causes.' And it adds that 'those who are enriched by spiritual gifts must not be involved in earthly concerns, so that, not being obliged to administer inferior goods, they may be able to serve spiritual goods.' For we see this even among the angels: that the superior always stand next to God and are not sent out to us, while the inferior dispose and govern temporal and corporeal things. Therefore, the superior angels are not themselves sent out to the realm of external concerns. Thus, because temporal and secular affairs are external concerns, the spiritual powers, as superior, must therefore not be sent out to such concerns except for some special reason and unless an unusual case should arise. For, as Bede says, the strictness of our duty can sometimes be set aside without fault for some urgent cause.[4] Therefore, it is the strict duty of the spiritual power to attend to spiritual matters; but if a special case arises, and if a special reason so requires, this strictness can be set aside without fault, so that the spiritual power may concern itself with temporal disputes.

Having looked into these questions, then, we wish to explain what was said at the beginning of the present chapter: that 'on the examination of certain causes, we exercise a temporal jurisdiction occasionally.' For if, as we have said above, the spiritual power must attend principally to spiritual matters, and if the earthly power must concern itself immediately with temporal affairs, two undesirable consequences would ensue if the ecclesiastical power were regularly and generally to intervene in temporal cases: first, because it could not then have time for the spiritual matters to which it must principally attend; and, second, because there would be confusion, for the one power would then obstruct the other. Therefore, the ecclesiastical judge will concern himself immediately with temporal cases not generally, but only on the examination of certain causes and when a special case arises. This, therefore, is what it is to exercise a temporal jurisdiction occasionally: when temporal jurisdiction is exercised by the ecclesiastical power only if a special case arises and for some special cause requiring it. But what the special circumstances are

1. Cf. II Tim. 2:4.
2. *Glossa ordinaria*, PL 114:528.
3. Gregory, *Moralia* 19:25 (PL 76:125); Cf. Peter Lombard, *Collectanea*, PL 191:1577.
4. Bede, *In Lucae evangelium expositio* 6 (PL 92:601).

propter que hoc fieri habeat[1] in sequenti capitulo ostendetur.

Ex hiis autem potest clarius apparere solucio eius quod dixit Alexander tercius Extra., *De appellacionibus, Si duobus*: quod 'appellacionem a civili iudice ad Summum Pontificem secundum rigorem iuris credimus non tenere.' Que verba, licet superius multipliciter sint soluta, possumus adhuc prefata verba multipliciter solvere: primo quidem faciendo vim in hoc quod dicitur 'credimus'; quia, ut patet, non dicit hoc asserendo, sed pocius, ut verba sonant, dicit hoc dubitando. Secundo, posset hoc[2] solvi quia ipse modus loquendi, ut prima facie[3] apparet, non arguit quod hoc dicat ut papa et ut volens legem condere, sed pocius quod hoc dicat ut doctor et ut volens suam credulitatem[4] et suam opinionem recitare. Verba[5] itaque prefata ex suo modo loquendi non arguunt quod legem statuant; sed si legem statuunt, hoc[6] non est ex modo loquendi, sed hoc est[7] quia illa verba sunt in decretalibus et in canonibus ecclesiasticis posita.

Tercio quidem modo possent solvi verba prehabita: quod papa predecessor[8] per id quod agit et per legem quam[9] statuit in nullo potest suo successori preiudicare. Quia non est simile de imperatore et papa; quia imperator, et quilibet secularis princeps, per id quod facit potest preiudicare suos successori: quia, quantumcumque imperator vel quicumque secularis princeps sit supremus in ordine potestatum terrenarum, non est tamen superius simpliciter, quia habet superiorem Summum Sacerdotem.[10] Sicut enim nullum corpus potest esse quid supremum simpliciter, licet possit esse supremum inter corpora,[11] quia tota corporalis substancia[12] per spiritualem gubernatur et regitur et est sibi[13] supposita, sic nulla terrena potestas potest esse suprema simpliciter, licet possit esse suprema[14] inter potestates terrenas, eo quod totus materialis gladius ordinatur ad spiritualem et omnes potestates terrene spirituali potencie sunt subiecte. Et quia imperator habet Summum Sacerdotem sibi[15] superiorem, ideo quod facit poterit per huiusmodi sacerdotem confirmari; quod confirmatum successor eius non poterit amovere. Ageret enim potestas ultra suam speciem et ultra suam virtutem si rem confirmatam a superiori posset propria auctoritate dirimere. Sed quia Summus Pontifex a nemine iudicatur et neminem habet superiorem in Ecclesia Militante, quod ipse agit non poterit confirmari per superiorem. Ideo successor eius poterit illud dirimere et[16] in nullo sibi preiudicabit quod predecessor ipsius fecit vel[17] statuit. Quare,[18] si non est de rigore[19] iuris simpliciter, sed est de rigore iuris scripti quod a civili iudice non appelletur ad papam, ut quia credulitas Alexandri tercii circa[20] huiusmodi appellacionem est in decretalibus posita et ipse Alexander istud scripsit et factum est inde ius scriptum, nihilominus tamen hoc ius scriptum et

---

1: habeat] debeat F   2: hoc] hec C   3: facie] *om.* C   4: suam credulitatem] si a crudelitatem V²
5: Verba] ubi C   6: hoc] modo *add.* V²   7: est] *om.* FV²   8: predecessor] decessor V²
9: quam] *om.* V²   10: Sacerdotem] pontificem C   11: corpora] corporalia C   12: substancia]
substancialis V²   13: sibi] ibi F   14: simpliciter, licet ... suprema] *om.* F   15: sibi] *om.* C
16: et] *om.* FV² *marg.* P   17: vel] et FV²   18: Quare] quia V²   19: rigore] ergo *add.* C
20: circa] *om.* V²

in which this may be done will be shown in the next chapter.

Also, from these considerations, a clearer explanation can appear of what Alexander III said at X. 2:28:7: *Si duobus,* that 'we believe that appeal from a civil judge to the pope is not valid according to the strictness of the law.' For although this statement has been explained in several ways above, there are a number of further ways in which we can interpret the words in question: first, indeed, by attaching force to the phrase 'we believe'. For, as is clear, he is not here speaking by way of assertion, but rather, as the words indicate, by way of stating a matter which is open to doubt. And there is a second way in which this statement may be explained; for, as is plain at first sight, his manner of speaking does not of itself suggest that he is speaking as pope and as wishing to establish a law, but, rather, that he is speaking as a doctor [of law] and as wishing to record his belief and opinion.[1] Thus, it is not his manner of speaking which indicates that the words in question constitute a law: rather, if they do constitute a law, this is not because of his manner of speaking, but because the words are embodied in the *Decretales* and in the canons of the Church.

Moreover, there is a third way in which the words quoted above may be explained: by saying that a previous pope can in no way prejudice his successor by what he does and by the laws which he establishes. For the emperor and the pope are not similar in this respect, because the emperor and any secular prince can prejudice his successor by what he does. For no matter how supreme the emperor or any secular prince may be in the order of earthly powers, he is nonetheless not absolutely supreme, because he has a superior in the Supreme Priest. For just as no corporeal object can be supreme in an absolute sense, even though it might be supreme among corporeal objects, since the whole of corporeal substance is governed and ruled through spiritual and is placed under it, so no earthly power can be absolutely supreme, even though it might be supreme among earthly powers: for the material sword is entirely subordinated to the spiritual and all earthly powers are subject to the spiritual power. And since the emperor has the Supreme Priest as his superior, what he does will therefore be subject to the confirmation of that priest; and his successor will not be able to remove this confirmation, because he would exercise a power beyond what is proper to his kind and beyond his capacity if, on his own authority, he could set aside a decision confirmed by a superior. But because the Supreme Pontiff is judged by no one and has no one as his superior in the Church Militant, what he does will not be subject to the confirmation of a superior. Thus, his successor will be able to set it aside, and what his predecessor has done or established will in no way prejudice him. And so, if it is not according to the strictness of the law in an absolute sense, but is only according to the strictness of the written law, that appeal may not be made from a civil judge to the pope — merely because the belief of Alexander III concerning such appeal is recorded in the *Decretales* and Alexander himself wrote it and so made it into a written law — this written law and

---

1. Before his election as Pope Alexander III in 1159, Rolandus Bandinelli was already a canon lawyer of great repute ('Magister Rolandus') and the author of one of the earliest commentaries on the *Decretum.* Giles's remark here possibly owes something to the comments of Huguccio on X. 4:11:3. See W. Ullmann, *Medieval Papalism,* pp. 35 and 60.

hoc[1] dictum Alexandri suis[2] successoribus preiudicare non patuit.

Possunt eciam et quarto modo solvi verba prehabita, dicendo quod iura sunt quedam regule agibilium. Sic autem videmus in regulis materialibus quod tunc regula est dura et rigida quando est dura et[3] inflexibilis et quando est uniformis et implicabilis;[4] secundum quem modum ipsa manens in se rigida se habet regulariter et uniformiter ad omnia, et omnia generaliter et regulariter respicit. Sed, ut diximus, non debet esse generaliter et regulariter quod spiritualis potestas iurisdiccionem temporalem exerceat, sed hoc debet esse[5] casualiter: id est, propter aliquem casum qui tunc immineat,[6] vel propter aliquid[7] speciale quod ibi adest. Ergo non est de iuris rigore[8] quod a civili iudice appelletur ad papam et quod ipse iurisdiccionem temporalem exerceat, quia hoc non est secundum regulam rigidam, que generaliter omnia respicit inflexibiliter et uniformiter; sed[9] hoc est secundum regulam casualem[10] et flexibilem, que aliquo casu contingente et speciali aliquo imminente precipit sic agendum esse. Nam secundum regulam illam[11] communem et generalem, sicut Deus sic administrat istas res corporales[12] ut eas proprios motus[13] agere sinat, sic Dei vicarius sic debet administrare potestates terrenas et temporales ut eas permittat propria officia exercere. Causa tamen racionabili imminente et speciali aliquo[14] existente potest spiritualis potestas preter istam communem legem agere et iurisdiccionem in temporalibus exercere.

Sunt enim actus humani,[15] sicut habetur in morali sciencia, sicut lapides Lesbie. Apud Lesbiam quidem erant lapides indolabiles, qui non poterant dolari secundum aliquam unam uniformem regulam; propter quod illi artifices non edificabant cum linea sive cum regula ferrea, sed cum regula plumbea quam plicabant secundum exigenciam lapidis; per quam regulam sic plicatam advertebant quis lapis cui lapidi conveniret, et hoc modo procedebant in edificio et edificabant. Sic actus humani sunt quasi lapides indolabiles, et non possunt dolari secundum unam aliquam inflexibilem regulam. Ideo, in humanis actibus, quod non est ius secundum regulam rigidam uniformem et generalem est ius secundum regulam specialem plicabilem et reflexam. Que omnia sciencibus naturalia optime placere debent; nam quilibet homo est microcosmus, id est minor mundus. Nam ea que sunt in universali[16] mundo relucent in homine quasi in quodam minori mundo, et illa que videmus in gubernacione omnium hominum in uno et eodem homine conspicere possumus.

Sicut ergo in gubernacione tocius humani generis sunt due potestates per quas regitur vel regi debet totum humanum genus, una corporalis et materialis, ut potestas terrena, alia spiritualis et sacerdotalis, ut potestas ecclesiastica, sic in quolibet homine est duplex[17] genus potencie per quod dirigitur in suis actibus. Unum quidem genus est quasi corporale et materiale, ut sensus; aliud quidem genus est quasi spirituale et abstractum, ut intellectus. Sensus[18] quidem, tamquam potencia corporalis et materialis, directe tendit in hec corporalia; intellectus vero

1: hoc] *om.* V² 2: suis] fuit V² 3: dura et] *del.* C 4: implicabilis] implacabilis F 5: debet esse] habet F 6: immineat] imminet FV² 7: aliquid] aliquod F 8: iuris rigore] rigore iuris CF 9: sed] sunt V² 10: casualem] casualiter V² 11: illam] ipsam C 12: corporales] temporales F 13: motus] cursus FV² 14: aliquo] casu *add.* F 15: humani] morales F 16: universali] universo FV² 17: est duplex] duplex est F 18: Sensus] illius V²

this statement of Alexander nonetheless could not prejudice his successors.

And there is also a fourth way in which the words quoted above can be explained: by saying that the laws are rules of a certain kind governing what can be done. But we see in the case of material rules [i.e. measuring rods] that when a rule is hard and flexible, and when it is uniform and not pliable, then it is hard and rigid. And while, in itself, it remains rigid in this fashion, it stands regularly and uniformly in relation to all objects and applies generally and regularly to them all. As we have said, however, the spiritual power should not exercise temporal jurisdiction generally and regularly. Rather, it must do so occasionally: that is, in some case which may then arise or because of some special reason which is present in the matter. Therefore, it is not according to the strictness of the law that appeal may be made from a civil judge to the pope and that he may exercise temporal jurisdiction [regularly and generally], because this is not according to a strict rule which applies generally, inflexibly, and uniformly to all cases. Rather, it is according to an occasional and flexible rule, which prescribes that it should be done thus in some particular case and if some special circumstance arises. For as a common and general rule, just as God directs corporeal things in such a way that He allows them to act by their own motions, so should the Vicar of God direct the earthly and temporal powers in such a way that he permits them to exercise their own offices. Nonetheless, when reasonable cause arises and some special circumstance is present, the spiritual power can act beyond the common law and exercise jurisdiction in temporal cases.

For, as is established in moral science, human acts are like the stones of Lesbos.[1] For among the people of Lesbos there were certain uncuttable stones which could not be dressed according to any one uniform pattern. And so the craftsmen did not build with a line or with a rule of iron, but with a rule of lead which they bent according to the irregularities of the stones. And, by means of a rule thus bent, they discovered which stone would fit which stone; and, in this way, they proceeded in building, and built. Thus, human acts are like uncuttable stones, and they cannot be dressed according to any one inflexible rule. And so, in human acts, that which is not law according to a strict, uniform and general rule is law according to a special, pliable, and flexible rule; all of which ought excellently to please [i.e. is entirely consistent with] the natural sciences: for each man is a microcosm, that is, a lesser world. For those things which are in the world as a whole are reflected in man as in a kind of lesser world, and those things which we see in the government of all men we can discern in one and the same man.[2]

Therefore, just as in the government of the whole human race there are two powers by which the whole human race is ruled, or ought to be ruled, one bodily and material, the earthly power, and one spiritual and priestly, the ecclesiastical power, so in each man there is a twofold kind of power by which he is governed in his actions. For one kind is as it were corporeal and material: sensation. And the other kind is as it were spiritual and abstract: intellect. And sensation, as a corporeal and material faculty, attends directly to corporeal objects, whereas the intellect attends to

---

1.   Cf. Aristotle, *Nicomachean Ethics* 5:10 (1137^{b}30).
2.   Cf. Aristotle, *Physics* 8:2 (252^{b}25).

non nisi per reflexionem in hec particularia et carnalia et sensibilia tendit. Ideo de potencia intellectiva dicitur in tercio *De anima* quod cum sit reflexa,[1] carnis esse cognoscit. Potestati itaque terrene commissa sunt ista materialia et temporalia quantum ad particularem execucionem et immediatam operacionem directe; sed potestati spirituali quantum ad principale dominium, quantum ad superiorem et primariam potestatem, omnia temporalia et universus orbis de iure, etsi non de facto — quia non omnes obediunt Evangelio — est sibi commissus. Sed quantum ad particularem execucionem et quantum ad immediatam operacionem, generaliter et regulariter non decet Summo Pontifici[2] quod se de temporalibus intromittat, cum ipse specialiter circa spiritualia debeat esse intentus; tamen, ut diximus, casualiter, id est in casu et propter aliquod speciale, debet iurisdiccionem in temporalibus exercere.

Imaginabimur quidem[3] quod spiritualis potencia est quasi quedam virga[4] tendens sursum sive tendens in celestia et in spiritualia. Si ergo debeat huiusmodi virga ad temporalia et ad res terrenas applicari, oportet quod hoc[5] sit per quandam plicacionem et per quandam reflexionem. Sicut dicebamus de intellectu, qui est quedam potencia spiritualis et directe tendit in universalia, si autem tendat in particularia, hoc erit per reflexionem.

Potencia itaque corporalis, cuiusmodi est potencia sensitiva, directe tendit in[6] particularia; potencia autem intellectiva,[7] que est spiritualis, non tendit in particularia directe, sed per reflexionem. Non quod ex hoc aliqua potencia sit in sensu que non sit in intellectu, et quod aliquid possit cognoscere[8] sensus quod non possit intellectus; sed aliqua potencia est in sensu ut[9] non in[10] intellectu. Sic et in proposito. Ad potestatem terrenam spectat regulariter tendere in res temporales et terrenas, ad potestatem autem spiritualem hoc spectabit in casu et propter aliquid[11] speciale, racione cuius regula potest reflecti et plicari. Non quod[12] ex hoc aliqua potencia sit in potestate terrena que[13] non sit in potestate spirituali; sed aliqua potencia est in huiusmodi potestate terrena ut non est in spirituali. Qui[14] autem sunt illi casus et que sunt illa specialia propter que spiritualis potestas se de temporalibus intromittit in sequenti capitulo intendimus declarare.

CAPITULUM V: *Quod si temporalia fiant spiritualia vel annectantur spiritualibus, vel econverso temporalibus spiritualia sint annexa, sunt speciales casus per quos Ecclesia temporalem iurisdiccionem debet[15] specialiter exercere.*

Per habita quidem potest patere[16] quod principatus non est aliud nisi quedam potencia regendi et gubernandi gubernabilia que sunt illi principatui supposita, sicut sciencia non est aliud quam quedam potencia considerandi et speculandi speculabilia sive[17]

1: reflexa] ea *add.* F.   2: Summo Pontifici] summum pontificem CV²   3: quidem] *om.* FV²
4: virgam] iurgam V²   5: hoc] *om.* C   6: in] ad C   7: potencia autem intellectiva] *om.* V²
8: cognoscere] recognoscere F   9: ut] et F   10: in] *om.* V²   11: aliquid] aliquod F   12: Non quod] neque F   13: que] quod F   14: Qui] que F   15: *debet*] dicitur V²   16: potest patere] patere potest CV²   17: speculabilia sive] sive speculabilia C

such particular and carnal and sensible objects only indirectly. And so, in the third book of *De anima*, it is said of the intellective power that it apprehends the essential character of flesh by bending [down to it].[1] Thus, material and earthly things are entrusted to the earthly power as regards execution in particular cases and [as regards] immediate direct action; but, so far as principal lordship is concerned, and as regards superior and primary power, all temporal things and the entire world are entrusted to the spiritual power: *de iure*, even if — since not all men obey the Gospel — not *de facto*. So far as execution in particular cases is concerned, however, and as regards immediate action, it is not fitting that the Supreme Pontiff should concern himself with temporal disputes regularly and generally, since he should be especially intent upon spiritual matters. As we have said, however, he must exercise jurisdiction in temporal cases occasionally: that is, in a particular case and for some special reason.

We shall imagine, indeed, that the spiritual power is like a kind of branch growing upwards, or growing towards heaven and towards spiritual ends. Therefore, if such a branch is to be applied to temporal and earthly concerns, this must come about through a certain pliableness and by a kind of bending, just as we have said of the intellect that it is a kind of spiritual faculty and attends directly to universals, and that, if it attends to particulars, this will be by bending.

Thus, corporeal power, of which kind is the faculty of sensation, attends directly to particulars; but intellective power, which is spiritual, does not attend to particulars directly, but indirectly. It is not the case, however, that there is therefore some power in sensation which is not in intellect, and that sensation may know something which intellect may not. Rather, some power is in sensation in a way that it is not in intellect. So too in our proposition: it is the task of the earthly power to attend regularly to temporal and earthly matters; but this will rest with the spiritual power in a particular case and for some special reason for the sake of which the [general] rule can be bent and modified. It is not the case that there is therefore some capacity in the earthly power which is not in the spiritual power. Rather, some capacity is in that earthly power in a way that it is not in the spiritual. But what these cases are, and what these special circumstances are, by reason of which the spiritual power intervenes in temporal affairs, we intend to show in the following chapter.[2]

CHAPTER V: *That if temporal things become spiritual, or if they are annexed to spiritual things, or, conversely, if spiritual things are annexed to temporal things, these are special cases by reason of which the Church must exercise a special temporal jurisdiction.*

From what has been said, it can indeed be clearly seen that ruling power is nothing but a certain capacity to rule and govern the objects capable of being governed which are placed under that ruling power; just as a science is nothing but a certain capacity to consider and investigate the matters capable of being investigated or

---

1. Cf. Aristotle, *De anima* 3:4 (429^{b}15); though one wonders if, in this and the following paragraph, Giles has quite seen the point of Aristotle's comment.
2. More strictly, in the following chapters: i.e. V–VIII.

scibilia que sunt illi sciencie subiecta. Sic[1] est autem in scienciis, quod cum aliqua sciencia est per se et primo de re aliqua, si autem illa sciencia considerat de rebus aliis, hoc erit prout ille res alie denominacionem suscipiunt illius rei de qua primo considerat huiusmodi sciencia; ut si theologia primo et principaliter est de Deo, si considerat de rebus aliis, hoc erit prout ille res alie suscipiunt denominacionem a Deo, et prout ille res alie[2] dicuntur esse divine:[3] ut si considerat de creaturis, hoc erit prout ipse creature sunt quid divinum, quia sunt quid divinum[4] per participacionem; si autem considerat de sacramentis, hoc erit prout sacramenta sunt quid divinum, ut quia[5] significant aliquid divinum. Nihil enim considerabit theologia nisi de ipso Deo et de hiis[6] que sunt quid divinum.[7]

Sic eciam[8] principatus sacerdotalis per se et primo tendit in spiritualia. Si autem iurisdiccionem exerceat in temporalibus,[9] hoc erit prout temporalia induunt quendam modum spiritualem, ut ipsa temporalia spiritualia dici possunt. Nam quamvis corpus non possit fieri spiritus, res tamen corporalis potest dici spiritualis, et ipsum corpus potest dici esse quid spirituale. Secundum quem modum loquitur Apostolus prima ad Corinthios XV, dicens quod 'seminatur corpus animale, surget corpus spirituale'; ubi glossa ait quod non dicit quod surgat[10] spiritus, quasi corpus convertatur in spiritum, sed quod surget corpus spirituale, quia tunc plene corpus subdetur spiritui et[11] participabit condiciones spirituales, et erit corpus tunc simile spiritui quantum ad condiciones aliquas, quia non indigebit[12] alimentis, sicut nec indiget spiritus, et erit tunc corpus immortale et incorruptibile, non enim corrumpetur nec morietur.[13]

Si ergo ipsum corpus potest dici quid spirituale propter condiciones aliquas spirituales quas participare potest, ipsa temporalia poterunt dici spiritualia propter condiciones aliquas spirituales. Non enim semper denominatur[14] res ab ea quod in ea est, quia potest denominari ab eo a quo est, vel ab[15] eo ad quod est. Quia dicitur opus aliquod esse humanum, non quia aliquid de humanitate sit in opere; propter quod opus illud non denominatur ab eo quod in ea est, sed ab eo a quo est, ut quia est ab homine, ideo dicitur humanum. Sic eciam res que ordinantur ad bonum hominis vel ordinantur ad hominem tamquam ad suum finem, possunt dici res humane quamvis nihil de humanitate sit in eis, quia dignum est omnia denominari a fine, ut dicitur in secundo *De anima.*

Cum ergo queritur que sunt illa specialia[16] et qui sunt illi casus in quibus spiritualis potestas se de temporalibus intromittit, dicemus quod omnibus illis modis quibus temporalia possunt[17] dici spiritualia spiritualis potestas iurisdiccionem suam[18] in temporalibus exercebit.

Advertendum ergo quod ipsa temporalia tripliciter possunt considerari. Primo,

---

1: Sic] sicut V[2]   2: suscipiunt denominacionem ... alie] *om.* C   3: esse divine] divine esse V[2] 4: quia sunt quid divinum] *om.* F   5: ut quia] vel quia F quia ut V[2]   6: hiis] aliis C   7: Nihil enim ... divinum] *om.* V[1]   8: eciam] et si PV[1] et FV[2]   9: temporalibus] tempora V[2]   10: surgat] surgant FV[2]   1·1: et] *om.* P   12: indigebit] indigebis V[2]   13: morietur] movebitur PV[1] 14: denominatur] denominantur FV[2]   15: ab] *om.* FV[2]   16: specialia] spiritualia FV[2]   17: possunt] possint V[2]   18: suam] *om.* V[2]

known which are the subjects of that science. But, in the sciences, it is the case that when, in itself and primarily, a science is concerned with a specific subject, if that science considers other subjects this will be insofar as those other subjects receive their character from that which the science considers primarily. For example, although theology is primarily and principally concerned with God, if it considers other subjects this will be insofar as those other subjects receive their character from God, and insofar as those other subjects are said to be divine. For instance, if it considers creatures, this will be insofar as the creatures are themselves in some measure divine; for they are in some measure divine through participation. And if it considers the sacraments, this will be insofar as the sacraments are in some measure divine because they signify something divine. For theology will consider nothing except God Himself and those things which are in some measure divine.

So also, in itself and primarily, the ruling power of the priest attends to spiritual matters. If he exercises jurisdiction in temporal matters, however, this will be insofar as temporal things assume a certain spiritual aspect such that the temporal matters can themselves be called spiritual. For although it may not be possible for body to become spirit, a corporeal thing can nonetheless be called spiritual, and even the body can be said to be in some measure spiritual. For the Apostle speaks in this way in I Corinthians 15, saying that: 'It is sown an animal body, it shall rise a spiritual body.'[1] And a gloss remarks here that he does not say that it may rise as a spirit, as though body might be transformed into spirit, but that 'it shall rise a spiritual body.'[2] For body will then be fully subdued to spirit, and it will participate in spiritual conditions. And the body will then be like a spirit with respect to certain conditions: for it will not need food, just as spirit has no such need; and the body will then be immortal and incorruptible, for it will neither be corrupted nor will it die.

Therefore, if even the body can be said to be in some measure spiritual by reason of certain spiritual conditions in which it can participate, it will be possible for temporal things themselves to be called spiritual by reason of certain spiritual conditions. For an object is not always defined in terms of what is in it; for it can be defined in terms of what it is from or of what it is for. For a work [i.e. of art or craftsmanship] is said to be human; but not because there is any element of humanity in the work: for that work is not defined in terms of what is in it, but of what it is from. And so, since it is from man, it is therefore called human. So also, the things which are ordained for the good of man, or are appointed with man as their end, can be called human goods, although there is no element of humanity in them; for it is proper that all objects be defined in terms of an end, as is said in *De anima* 2.[3] Therefore, when it is asked what are those special circumstances and what are those cases in which the spiritual power concerns itself with temporal affairs, we shall reply that the spiritual power will exercise its jurisdiction in temporal matters in all the ways in which temporal things can be called spiritual.

It must be noted, therefore, that temporal things can themselves be considered in

1.   I Cor. 15:44.
2.   *Glossa ordinaria*, PL 114:549.
3.   Aristotle, *De anima* 2:4 (416ᵇ20).

quantum ad ipsas res; secundo, quantum ad potestatem[1] temporalem sub qua sunt; tercio, quantum ad potestatem[2] Summi Pontificis. Omnibus autem istis modis temporalia possunt dici spiritualia. Ideo per comparacionem ad omnia ista ipsa temporalia sub iurisdiccione potestatis spiritualis poterunt collocari. Ex ipsis itaque rebus temporalibus et ex potestate terrena et ex spirituali potestate possunt sumi speciales[3] condiciones et speciales casus propter quos iurisdiccio rerum temporalium ad spiritualem potestatem devolvitur. In hoc tamen capitulo dicemus de condicionibus sumptis[4] ex parte ipsarum rerum.

Sciendum ergo quod iurisdiccio potestatis spiritualis se extendet ad temporalia racione ipsarum rerum in omnibus illis casibus in quibus res temporales possunt vocari spirituales, quod, quantum ad presens spectat, tripliciter esse contingit: primo, si sunt a Summo Spiritu imperate; secundo, si sunt spiritualibus annexe; tercio, si sunt spiritualia annexa sibi. Nam sive res spiritualis annectatur[5] rei temporali sive econverso, semper res temporalis poterit vocari spiritualis. Sunt enim spiritualia potenciora quam temporalia,[6] et ideo spiritualia tamquam potenciora denominant[7] temporalia, ut sive annectantur[8] temporalibus sive econverso, ipsa temporalia a spiritualibus denominacionem suscipient, non autem econverso.[9] Et exinde est quod gladius spiritualis potest se extendere ad temporalia, non autem materialis ad spiritualia. Sic enim videmus in nobis ipsis quod corpus denominatur ab anima et a spiritu, non autem econverso. Non[10] enim dicitur spiritus esse corporalis vel anima esse corporalis, sed dicitur corpus esse animale et esse spirituale.[11]

Ipse igitur res temporales possunt dici spirituales si sunt[12] a Summo[13] Spiritu imperate; secundum quem modum decime inter spiritualia computantur, quia non ab homine, sed a Deo, qui est Summus Spiritus, sunt institute. Possunt ergo decime dici esse debita ecclesiis, esse sanctuaria[14] ecclesiarum, et possunt dici esse res spirituales, ad que omnia iura[15] adaptari possunt, ut patet Extra., De [16] decimis.[17] Immo, inhibetur laicis quod iure hereditario non debeant possidere decimas, quia sunt Dei sanctuaria.[18] Inhibetur eciam[19] laicis quod[20] non disponant de decimis.[21] Erit ergo iste unus casus sumptus ex ipsis rebus quod Ecclesia se intromittet de temporalibus: si ipse res temporales fiant spirituales et pertineant ad decimas.

Alius autem casus sumptus ex parte ipsarum rerum est si ipse res temporales sint spirituales quia sunt annexe spiritualibus, ut matrimonio sunt annexe dotes et legitimacioni[22] filiorum est annexa successio hereditatis; quia, ut ait Apostolus ad Romanos VIII, 'Si filii, et heredes.' Intromittet se ergo Ecclesia de rebus temporalibus

---

1: potestatem] terrenam *add.* FV[2]   2: potestatem] spiritualem et potissime quantum ad potestatem *add.* CV[2]   3: speciales] *om.* V[2]   4: condicionibus sumptis] sumptis (*having first written* consumptis) condicionibus P   5: spiritualis annectatur] spirituales annexantur FV[2]   6: temporalia] terrena FV[2]   7: denominant] denominantur FV[2]   8: annectantur] annectentur FV[2]   9: econverso] ipsa temporalia a spiritualibus denominacionem suscipient non autem econverso *add.* F   10: Non] *om.* V[2]   11: esse animale ... spirituale] esse spirituale et animale V[2]   12: sunt] sint CFV[2]   13: Summo] *om.* C   14: sanctuaria] censura F censuaria V[2]   15: iura] nostra FV[2]   16: *De*] *om.* V[2]   17: *decimis*] quia sunt res spirituales *add. and del.* C   18: sanctuaria] censuaria FV[2]   19: eciam] in FV[2]   20: quod] quia F   21: Immo, inhibetur ... decimis] *om.* C   22: legitimacioni] legitimitati FV[2] legitimi PV[1]

three ways: first, with reference to the things themselves; second, in relation to the temporal power under which they are; and, third, in relation to the power of the Supreme Pontiff. But, in all these ways, temporal things can be called spiritual; and so, considered in all these ways, it will be possible for temporal things to be placed under the jurisdiction of the spiritual power. Thus, from temporal things themselves, and from the earthly power, and from the spiritual power, the special conditions and special cases by reason of which jurisdiction over temporal matters devolves upon the spiritual power can be derived. In this chapter, however, we shall speak only of the conditions derived from a consideration of things themselves.

It must be known, therefore, that the jurisdiction of the spiritual power extends itself to temporal matters by reason of things themselves in all those cases in which temporal things can be called spiritual; of which, for our present purpose, there are three: first, if they are commanded by the Supreme Spirit; second, if they are annexed to spiritual things; and, third, if spiritual things are annexed to them. For whether spiritual things are annexed to temporal things or the converse, it will always be possible for temporal things to be called spiritual: for spiritual things are greater than temporal, and so the spiritual things, as greater, define the temporal whether they are annexed to the temporal things or the converse. Temporal things, then, will receive their character from spiritual things, but not the converse; and so it is that the spiritual sword can extend itself to temporal matters, but not the material to spiritual. For we see this in ourselves: that the body is defined by the soul or by the spirit, but not the converse. For spirit is not said to be corporeal, or the soul [*anima*] to be bodily; but the body is said to be animal [*animale*] and to be spiritual.

Thus, even temporal things can be called spiritual if they are commanded by the Supreme Spirit. And, in this sense, tithes are numbered among spiritual things; for they were instituted not by man, but by God, Who is the Supreme Spirit. Therefore, tithes can be said to be debts owed to churches, to be the consecrated property of churches; and [so] they can be called spiritual things, for the sake of which all laws can be modified. And this is clear from the *Decretales* under the title *De decimis* [where the canon law relating to tithes abrogates the civil laws ordinarily applying to the inheritance and transmission of property]: the laity are indeed forbidden to possess tithes by right of inheritance, for they are the consecrated property of God; and the laity are forbidden to distribute tithes.[1] This, therefore, will be one case derived from things themselves: the Church will concern herself with temporal things if temporal possessions become spiritual and pertain to tithes.

But there is another case derived from a consideration of things themselves: if temporal things are spiritual because they are annexed to spiritual things, as dowries are annexed to matrimony and succession to an inheritance is annexed to the legitimation of sons; for, as the Apostle says in Romans 8, 'If sons, heirs also.'[2] The Church will therefore concern herself with temporal things if they are

---

1. X. 3:30:15: *Ad haec donationem*; 17: *Quamvis sit grave*; 31: *Dudum adversus* (CIC II:561; 567).
2. Rom. 8:17.

si sunt annexe spiritualibus, ut intromittet se de dotibus quia sunt annexe matrimonio, ut habetur Extra., *De dotibus*, capitulo *De prudencia*. Sic intromittet se
de possessionibus et de hereditatibus que sunt annexe natis de legitimo thoro.

Sed dices huic dicta esse iura contraria, quia[1] Extra., *Qui filii sint*[2] *legitimi*,
capitulo *Lator*, questionem de hereditate remittit ad dominum secularem, et eodem
titulo, capitulo *Causam*, questionem de possessionibus dicit pertinere ad regem,
non ad Ecclesiam. Sed dicitur ibidem[3] ad Ecclesiam pertinere cognoscere[4] questionem de re principali, videlicet de legitimacione. Sciendum ergo quod qui dicit
unum[5] quodammodo multa dicit, ut dicitur in libro *De physico auditu*, quia dicit
omnia illa que sequuntur ad illud: ut[6] qui dicit Socratem[7] esse hominem, dicit ipsum esse sensibilem,[8] esse animal et esse substanciam, quia omnia ista sequuntur
ad esse hominem. Sic qui unum facit quodammodo multa facit,[9] et qui unum iudicat quodammodo multa iudicat, quia iudicat omnia illa que sequuntur ad illud. Si
ergo ad esse legitimum filium sequitur esse heredem, qui iudicat de legitimitate,
oportet quod iudicet de hereditate. Unde si nulla iura hoc dicerent, vel quicquid
iura dicant,[10] hoc naturalis racio, que iura superat, iudicaret: videlicet, quod qui
iudicat de principali oportet quod iudicet de annexo.

Ad iura tamen in contrarium, dici potest quod soluto hoc principali, an ille qui
de hereditate litigabat esset[11] legitimus, adhuc poterat[12] esse questio an illa hereditas vel ille possessiones essent sue, quia forte pater eum[13] emancipaverat vel
ipse ipsas possessiones vendiderat vel donaverat vel multis aliis modis poterat hoc
contingere, racione cuius poterat huiusmodi questio pertinere ad dominum secularem. Sed si nullum esset aliud dubium an hereditas vel possessio sit huiusmodi
nisi quia dubitatur an sit legitimus, tunc ad illum iudicem ad quem[14] spectaret
iudicare de legitimitate spectaret iudicare de hereditate.

Vel dicere possumus quod, cum loquimur de posse Ecclesie, loquimur de posse
cum decencia; quia si loqueremur de posse[15] simpliciter, est in ea plenitudo potestatis. Sed multa potest Ecclesia eciam cum decencia[16] que liceret ei facere que tamen
non facit quia non expediunt; unde multa indulget que posset facere. Potest ergo
Ecclesia multas questiones remittere ad iudices civiles et dicere quod ille questiones non pertinent ad eam quia non vult ad questiones illas suam potenciam extendere. Secundum quem modum loquebatur Dominus Luce XII, cum quidam de
turba diceret Christo: 'Magister, dic fratri meo,[17] ut dividat mecum hereditatem.' At

---

1: quia] decretali *add*, PV[1]   2: *sint*] sunt F   3: ibidem] *om*. FV[2]   4: cognoscere] recognoscere F
5: dicit unum] unum dicit F   6: ut] quod V[2]   7: Socratem] sortem *mss*   8: sensibilem] risi-
bilem CV[2]   9: facit] *om*. V[2]   10: dicant] dicerent FV[2]   11: esset] ecclesie V[2]   12: poterat]
poterit F   13: eum] enim V[2]   14: quem] *om*. V[2]   15: Ecclesie, loquimur … posse] *marg*. P
om. V[2]   16: eciam cum decencia] *om*. V[2]   17: meo] modo F

annexed to spiritual things. For example, she will concern herself with dowries because they are annexed to matrimony, as is established at X. 4:20:3: *De pruden-tia.*[1] So too, she will concern herself with possessions and inheritances, which are annexed to those born in lawful wedlock.

But you will say that this statement is contrary to the laws; for X. 4:17:5: *Lator* remits a case of disputed inheritance to a secular lord; and X. 4:17:7: *Causam* asserts that a dispute involving possessions pertains to the king, not to the Church.[2] It is, however, said in the same place that it pertains to the Church to take cognizance of the principal question: namely, that of legitimation. Therefore, it must be known that, in a certain sense, he who says one thing says many, as is stated in the *Physics;*[3] for he says all those things which follow from the first. For example, he who says that Socrates is a man says that he is sentient, that he is animate, and that he is a substance, since all these conclusions follow from his being a man. Thus, in a certain sense, he who does one act does many; and, in a certain sense, he who judges one cause judges many, for he judges all the causes which follow from the first. If, therefore, to be an heir follows from being a legitimate son, then he who judges the question of legitimacy may properly judge that of inheritance also. Hence, if no laws said this, or whatever the laws may say, natural reason, which rises above the laws, declares it: namely, that he who judges the principal question may properly judge that which is annexed to it.

As regards the laws [i.e. the decretals *Lator* and *Causam*] to the contrary, however, it can be said that, when this principal question of whether he who is in dispute over an inheritance is legitimate has been decided, there could be further dispute as to whether that inheritance or those possessions were his: perhaps because his father had disinherited him, or he himself had sold those possessions or given them away; or this could arise in many other ways, by reason of which such a dispute could pertain to a secular lord [because it would then involve only relatively trivial matters of fact having no ecclesiastical dimension]. But if there were no other doubt as to whether the inheritance or possessions were his apart from the doubt as to whether he was legitimate, then that judge whose task it was to judge the question of legitimacy would also judge that of inheritance.

Again, we can say that, when we speak of the Church's power, we are speaking of power subject to what is fitting. For if we were to speak of power in an absolute sense, there is fullness of power in her; but there are many things which would be lawful for the Church, and which she might indeed fittingly do, which she nonetheless does not do because they are not expedient.[4] Hence, she passes over many things which she might do. Therefore, the Church can remit many disputes to the civil judges, and say that these disputes do not pertain to her, because she does not wish to extend her power to these questions. And the Lord spoke in this way in Luke 12, when one of the multitude said to Christ: 'Master, tell my brother to divide the

---

1. CIC II:725.
2. See Introduction, p. xxvii and n. 61.
3. Perhaps Aristotle, *Physics* 1:2 (185ª20).
4. Cf. I Cor. 6:12; 10:23.

ille dixit ei: 'Homo, quis me constituit iudicem aut divisorem supra vos?' Constat
autem quod iste[1] constitutus erat iudex vivorum et mortuorum, quia pater omne
iudicium dedit filio. Dicebat tamen se non esse constitutum iudicem ad dividendum
hereditatem, quia nolebat ad hoc faciendum suas[2] interponere[3] partes.

Tercio, res temporalis dicitur esse spiritualis non solum si sit annexa spiritualibus[4]
sed si spiritualia sunt annexa sibi. Et quia omnia crimina et[5] omnia peccata mortalia
possunt dici quid spirituale, quia nostrum spiritum et nostram animam occidunt, consequens est quod spiritualis potestas se poterit intromittere de questionibus quorumcumque temporalium si questiones ille deferantur cum denunciacione criminis, quia
ad spiritualem potestatem spectat iudicare de quocumque peccato mortali et[6] de hoc
corripere quemlibet christianum.[7] Aliter enim non dixisset Deus in evangelio Matthei
XVIII: 'Si autem[8] peccaverit in te frater tuus, vade et corripe eum inter te et ipsum
solum; si autem non te audierit, adhibe tecum unum vel duos; quod si non audierit
eos, dic Ecclesie'; quod non dixisset si ad Ecclesiam non spectaret de quolibet peccato mortali corripere quemlibet christianum. Patet ergo quod ista condicio per quam
potest Ecclesia se intromittere de rebus temporalibus et per quam super temporalibus
potest ad Ecclesiam appellari, est ita[9] lata et ampla ut omnes questiones quorumcumque temporalium comprehendat, quia semper potest denunciari questio cum crimine.[10]
Iudex autem et in notoriis suam dat sentenciam et dubia[11] inquirit, ut possit ibidem
suam sentenciam dare, iuxta illud Job XXIX: 'Causam quam nesciebam, diligentis-
sime investigabam.' Si ergo de peccato vel non peccato debet cognoscere iudex ecclesiasticus, sive sit notorium sive dubium, que pars litigancium habeat iniustam[12]
causam et peccet, propter hoc non subterfugiet[13] iudicium ecclesiastici iudicis.[14]

Concludamus ergo et dicamus quod temporalia, ut temporalia, sunt subdita corporibus et sunt subdita animabus.[15] Sunt subdita corporibus nostris, quia corpora
nostra sine hiis[16] non possent subsistere. Ideo in adminiculum et in[17] sustentacionem corporum nostrorum ista corporalia sunt creata, ut ex hoc dicatur homo quodammodo finis omnium, quia,[18] secundum[19] hoc,[20] corporalia quodammodo creata
sunt[21] propter ipsum. Animabus autem nostris sunt subdita ista temporalia dupliciter. Nam anime nostre sunt spiritus, et sunt spiritus[22] qui presunt corporibus nostris. Utroque autem[23] modo temporalia sunt subiecta[24] eis. Nam si anime nostre
considerantur ut sunt spiritus, subiecta sunt eis ista temporalia quia tota corporalis
creatura est subiecta spirituali substancie. Si vero considerantur anime nostre ut
sunt coniuncte corporibus nostris et ut sunt presidentes eis, tunc ista corporalia que

---

1: iste] ipse CF   2: suas] suos V²   3: interponere] imponere F   4: non solum … spiritualibus]
om. V²   5: et] om. C   6: et] om. F   7: quemlibet christianum] om. V²   8: autem] del. P
9: ita] itaque V²   10: crimine] cum una persona habet litigantium iustam cuius habet alia non
iniustam et si dicas quod potest quis iniustam causam solvere si nesciat eam esse iniustam cum
iudicare an quod aliquid sit iustum vel iniustum sit iudicare an sit peccatum vel non peccatum cum
ad Ecclesiam spectat iudicare de peccato vel non peccato quod est quid spirituale ad eam spectabit
iudicare de iusto et iniusto add. and del. C   11: dubia] dubias P in dubiis V²   12: iniustam]
iustam F   13: subterfugiet] subterfugit F subterfugiit V²   14: Iudex autem … iudicis] del. C
15: animabus] sed add. CFV²   16: hiis] temporalibus add. and del. C   17: in] om. F   18: quia]
quasi F quia si V²   19: secundum] omnia C   20: secundum hoc] non hec FV²   21: sunt] sint F
22: et sunt spiritus] om. P   23: autem] ergo FV²   24: sunt subiecta] subiecta sunt FV²

inheritance with me.' And He said to him: 'Man, who has appointed me judge or arbiter over you?'[1] But it is clear that He was appointed judge of the living and dead, for the Father has given all judgment to the Son.[2] Nonetheless, He said that He was not appointed to judge the division of an inheritance, because He did not wish to use His good offices to do this.

Third, a temporal thing is said to be spiritual not only if it is annexed to spiritual things, but also if spiritual things are annexed to it. And since, in a sense, all crimes and all mortal sins can be called spiritual in that they slay our spirit and our soul, it follows that the spiritual power will be able to intervene in disputes involving any temporal questions whatsoever if those disputes are brought forward together with an allegation of crime; for it rests with the spiritual power to judge every mortal sin and to rebuke every Christian for it.[3] For, otherwise, God would not have said in St Matthew's Gospel, 18: 'And if your brother should sin against you, go and rebuke him between yourself and him; and if he will not hear you, take one or two persons with you; and if he will not hear them, tell the Church.'[4] He would not have said this if it did not rest with the Church to rebuke every Christian for every mortal sin. Therefore, it is clear that this condition by reason of which the Church can concern herself with temporal things, and by reason of which appeal can be made to the Church on temporal questions, is so broad and ample that it may embrace all temporal disputes whatsoever, since such a dispute can always involve an allegation of crime. But the judge both passes sentence in clear cases and makes enquiry into doubtful ones, so that he may deliver his sentence in the same according to what is said in Job 29: 'I enquired most diligently into the cause of which I was ignorant.'[5] Therefore, if the ecclesiastical judge must take cognizance of sin or non-sin, then, for this reason, whether the case be clear or doubtful, that party among the litigants who has an unjust cause and sins will not escape the judgment of the ecclesiastical judge.

Let us conclude, therefore, and say that temporal things, inasmuch as they are temporal, are placed under our bodies and are [therefore also] placed under our souls. They are placed under our bodies because our bodies could not subsist without them. Thus, these corporeal things were created for the aid and support of our bodies, so that, for this reason, man is said to be, in a sense, the end of all things; for, on this account, corporeal things were, in a sense, created for him. But temporal things are placed under our souls in two ways. For our souls are spirits, and they are the spirits which rule our bodies; and temporal things are subject to them in both ways. For if our souls be considered insofar as they are spirits, then these temporal things are subject to them because every corporeal creature is subject to a spiritual substance. But if our souls be considered insofar as they are united with bodies and insofar as they preside over bodies, then those corporeal

1. Luke 12:13–14.
2. Cf. John 5:22.
3. See Introduction, n. 21.
4. Paraphrased from Matt. 18:15–17.
5. Job 29:16.

sunt subdita corporibus nostris, necesse est quod sint subdita istis[1] animabus, quia quod est subditum inferiori oportet quod et[2] superiori subdatur. Hic autem secundus modus subieccionis est magis proprius negocio nostro, quia non est nostrum[3] propositum nos intromittere de animabus[4] separatis et ut sunt secundum se spiritus, sed de animabus coniunctis et ut presunt corporibus. Anime itaque nostre presunt corporibus nostris et mediantibus eis presunt corporalibus[5] aliis. Secundum hunc[6] ergo modum spiritualis potestas habebit super omnibus temporalibus[7] iurisdiccionem superiorem et primariam; potestas quidem terrena et materialis gladius super corporalia[8] habebit iurisdiccionem immediatam et ordinariam.[9]

Verum,[10] quia temporalia non solum sunt in sustentamentum corporis, sed male utentibus eis sunt[11] in malum et dampnacionem animarum, ideo consequens[12] est quod Ecclesia habet super temporalibus duplicem iurisdiccionem: unam superiorem et primariam, prout hec temporalia ordinantur[13] ad corpora nostra, mediantibus quibus ordinantur ad animas; aliam quidem iurisdiccionem habet Ecclesia super[14] temporalia immediatam et executoriam, prout ipsa temporalia male utentibus sunt in malum et in dampnacionem animarum.[15] Ideo, nisi immineat specialis casus, si agatur de temporalibus ut temporalia sunt et ut sunt in sustentamentum corporum nostrorum, spectabit ad iudicem civilem et ad potestatem terrenam de ipsis temporalibus iudicare secundum[16] immediatam execucionem, et ad eam spectabit cognoscere que corpora quibus temporalibus debeant sustentari. Iudicabit enim quod filii huiusmodi debent habere hanc hereditatem et sustentari secundum corpora ex[17] ista hereditate;[18] filii autem illius debent habere hereditatem illam et sustentari secundum corpora ex illa hereditate.[19] Sed si agatur de temporalibus ut sunt in malum et in[20] dampnacionem animarum nostrarum, consequens[21] erit quod Ecclesia habebit super temporalibus iurisdiccionem non solum superiorem et primariam, sed eciam immediatam et executoriam. Et inde est quod immediate se poterit intromittere Ecclesia de questione rerum temporalium si deferatur questio ad iudicem ecclesiasticum cum denunciacione criminis; quia sic defertur questio ut est in malum et in dampnacionem anime, secundum quem modum immediata iurisdiccio ad Ecclesiam spectat.[22]

Apparet itaque quomodo est[23] de rigore iuris et non est de rigore iuris ut a civili iudice appelletur ad papam. Nam si agatur questio de temporalibus que non sunt immediate sub Ecclesia sed sub domino seculari, et agatur de talibus temporalibus[24] non quocumque modo sed ut sunt in sustentamentum corporum nostrorum, modo quo[25] superius exposuimus, poterit dici non esse de rigore iuris quod talis appellacio fiat. Sed si considerantur temporalia ut sunt in malum et in dampnacionem animarum,

1: istis] ipsis FV² 2: et] *om.* FV² 3: nostrum] *om.* C 4: nos intromittere de animabus] de animabus nos intromittere C 5: corporalibus] corporibus FPV¹ 6: Secundum hunc] vel V² 7: potestas habebit ... temporalibus] *om.* V² 8: corporalia] temporalia V² 9: immediatam et ordinariam] *om.* FPV¹V² 10: Verum] verumtamen F 11: sunt] *om.* V² 12: consequens] conveniens V² 13: ordinantur] quomodolibet ordinantur *add.* F 14: super] hec *add.* FV² 15: animarum] nostrarum *add.* FV² 16: secundum] sed per F 17: ex] et V² 18: et sustentari ... hereditate] *om.* C 19: filii autem ... hereditate] *om.* V² 20: in] *om.* FV² 21: consequens] conveniens V² 22: spectat] *om.* V² 23: quomodo est] *om.* V² 24: talibus temporalibus] temporalibus talibus C 25: modo quo] quod F modo quod V²

objects which are placed under our bodies are of necessity also placed under our souls; for that which is placed under an inferior must also be placed under a superior. But this second mode of subjection is more properly our concern. For it is not our purpose to concern ourselves with souls as separate entities and as spirits pure and simple, but with souls as united with bodies and ruling them. Thus, our souls rule our bodies and, by means of them, rule other corporeal things. Therefore, in this way, the spiritual power will have a superior and primary jurisdiction over all temporal things, even though the earthly power and the material sword will have jurisdiction over corporeal things in an immediate and ordinary sense.

Indeed, because temporal possessions not only conduce to the support of bodies but also bring about the harm and damnation of the souls of those who use them ill, it therefore follows that the Church has a temporal jurisdiction of two kinds. Insofar as these temporal possessions are [immediately] ordered to our bodies, through which they are ordered to souls, the one kind is superior and primary [but not immediate, because it is the earthly power which has immediate jurisdiction over bodily things]. But the Church has another, immediate and executory, jurisdiction over temporal things insofar as temporal possessions themselves bring about the harm and damnation of the souls of those who use them ill. Thus, unless a special case arises, if temporal things be considered simply as temporal and as giving support to our bodies, it will rest with the civil judge and with the earthly power to judge temporal disputes with respect to immediate execution; and it will rest with him to take cognizance of which bodies should be supported by which temporal possessions. For he will judge that the sons of this man ought to have this inheritance and receive bodily support from this inheritance, and that the sons of that man ought to have that inheritance and receive bodily support from that inheritance. But if temporal possessions be considered insofar as they bring about the harm and damnation of our souls, it will follow that the Church will have not only a superior and primary, but also an immediate and executory, jurisdiction over temporal cases. And hence it is that the Church will be able to intervene immediately in a temporal dispute if the dispute is brought before an ecclesiastical judge together with an allegation of crime. For a dispute brought in this way is one which bears upon the harm and damnation of the soul; and, in this way, immediate jurisdiction rests with the Church.

It is apparent, then, how it is both according to the strictness of the law and not according to the strictness of the law that appeal may be made from a civil judge to the pope. For if the question at issue be one involving temporal possessions which are not immediately under the Church, but under a secular lord; and if such temporal possessions be considered not in any sense whatsoever, but insofar as they bear upon the support of our bodies in the manner which we have explained above: then it will be possible to say that it is not according to the strictness of the law that such appeal may be made. [For in such a case, because only bodies are involved, jurisdiction will rest entirely with the civil judge.] But if temporal possessions be considered insofar as they bring about the harm and damnation of souls,

vel, quod idem est, si[1] deferatur questio cum denunciacione criminis, quia temporalia hoc modo immediate respiciunt ipsam animam, erit de rigore iuris quod eciam in temporalibus a civili iudice appelletur ad papam. Nam quantumcumque temporalia illa non sint immediate sub Ecclesia, racione tamen annexi, ut racione criminis, quod est malum et dampnacio[2] anime, spectabit ad potestatem sacerdotalem super temporalibus illis[3] immediatam iurisdiccionem habere. Immediata itaque iurisdiccio super temporalibus, quantumcumque temporalia illa non sunt subiecta Ecclesie, poterit ad Ecclesiam pertinere propter malum quod possunt inferre animabus.

Iudex ergo civilis habet huiusmodi iurisdiccionem propter malum quod possunt temporalia inferre corporibus, Ecclesia vero propter malum quod possunt inferre animabus. Sed cum malum anime sit periculosius quam corporis, et cum anima sit superior corpore, immediata iurisdiccio quam habet Ecclesia super temporalia est superior et excellencior quam sit iurisdiccio civilis iudicis vel cuiuscumque domini secularis. Et quia, ut diximus, denunciacio criminis cuilibet questioni quorumcumque temporalium potest esse annexa, ideo Ecclesia super omnibus[4] temporalibus immediatam iurisdiccionem habere potest.

Ex hiis autem[5] patere potest[6] quomodo[7] iurisdiccio temporalium superior et primaria semper competit Ecclesie generaliter et regulariter,[8] ut si modo[9] inciperet Ecclesia et[10] illi qui inciperent credere renunciarent omnibus que haberent et darent pauperibus et nihil haberent de temporalibus secundum immediatam possessionem, nihilominus tamen Ecclesia et illi qui inter credentes essent[11] in hiis que sunt ad Deum haberent iurisdiccionem superiorem et primariam super omnibus temporalibus. Quia nulli possent salvi fieri, et nulli possent temporalia illa[12] iuste possidere nec possent esse digni possessores,[13] nisi recognoscerent Ecclesiam matrem et dominam, et nisi recognoscerent ab ea omnia bona sua, per quam et sub qua omnium bonorum suorum fierent iusti, digni et legitimi possessores.[14]

Sed iurisdiccio temporalium[15] immediata et[16] executoria competit Ecclesie non simpliciter, sed propter denunciacionem criminis vel propter aliquod aliud speciale.[17] Nam in omnibus accionibus, tam naturalibus quam moralibus et iudicialibus sive quibuscumque aliis, est considerare ipsa acta et racionem agendi, ut in accione ipsius visus est considerare visibilia et racionem videndi, et in calefaccione est[18] considerare calefactibilia et racionem calefaciendi, et in iudiciis est considerare iudicabilia et racionem iudicandi. Si ergo consideramus ipsa iudicabilia vel ipsa temporalia de quibus coram aliquo iudice agitur questio, sic iurisdiccio Ecclesie immediata et executoria quantum ad denunciacionem criminis est generalis, quia potest se ad omnia temporalia extendere. Sed si consideramus ipsam[19] racionem iudicandi quantum ad prefatam condicionem, iurisdiccio Ecclesie erit

---

1: si] *om.* F   2: dampnacio] dampnacionem FV[2]   3: illis] illam F   4: omnibus] questionibus F
5: autem] itaque F   6: potest] *om.* V[2]   7: quomodo] quando *mss*   8: regulariter] generaliter F
9: modo] non V[1]   10: et] eciam V[1]   11: essent] erant CFV[2]   12: illa] *om.* CFV[2]   13: possessores] possessione FV[2]   14: possessores] iurisdiccio ergo temporalium in prior et primaria semper competit ecclesie generaliter *add.* C   15: Sed iurisdiccio temporalium] iurisdiccio ergo temporalium sed iurisdiccio temporalium FV[2] sed iurisdiccio temporalium P   16: et] *om.* V[2]   17: speciale] *om.* FV[2]   18: est] ea V[2]   19: ipsam] *om.* F

or (which comes to the same thing) if the dispute is brought forward together with an allegation of crime, then, because, in this sense, temporal things bear immediately upon the soul itself, it will be according to the strictness of the law that appeal may be made from a civil judge to the pope even in temporal cases. For even where temporal things are not immediately under the Church, it will nonetheless rest with the priestly power to have immediate jurisdiction over these temporal things when they involve some reason — for instance, the reason of crime — which brings about the harm and damnation of souls. Thus, even though these temporal things are not immediately subject to the Church, it will be possible for an immediate jurisdiction over temporal cases to pertain to the Church in the event of evils which can injure souls.

Therefore, the civil judge has such jurisdiction because of the evils which temporal things can inflict upon bodies, and the Church because of the evils which they can inflict upon souls. But since harm to the soul is more perilous than that to the body, and since the soul is superior to the body, the immediate jurisdiction which the Church has over temporal cases is superior to and more excellent than the jurisdiction of the civil judge or any secular lord whatsoever. And since, as we have said, an allegation of crime can be related to any dispute involving a temporal matter of any kind, the Church can therefore have an immediate jurisdiction over all temporal cases.

And it can be clearly seen from these arguments how a superior and primary temporal jurisdiction always belongs to the Church generally and regularly; so that even if the Church were now beginning and those who were beginning to believe had renounced all that they had and given to the poor, and held no temporal goods in terms of immediate possession, the Church and those who were among the believers in those things which are of God would nonetheless still have a superior and primary jurisdiction over all temporal goods. For no one could be saved, and none [of the poor?] could possess those temporal goods justly, nor could they be worthy possessors, unless they acknowledged the Church as mother and mistress, and unless they acknowledged that they held all their property of her, through whom and under whom they had been made just, worthy, and lawful possessors of all their goods.

But an immediate and executory temporal jurisdiction belongs to the Church not invariably, but by reason of an allegation of crime or in some other special case. For in all actions, whether natural or moral or judicial or of any other kind, it is necessary to consider both the actions themselves and the reason for acting. For example, in the act of seeing, it is necessary to consider visible objects and the reason for seeing; and, in heating, it is necessary to consider the object capable of being heated and the reason for heating; and, in judging, it is necessary to consider the matters capable of being judged and the reason for judging. Therefore, if we consider the matters capable of being judged, or the temporal matters concerning which a dispute is being argued before a judge, the immediate and executory jurisdiction of the Church is general with respect to an allegation of crime, for it can extend itself to all temporal disputes [in which crime is alleged]. But if we consider the reason for judging in relation to the condition stated above [i.e. that the Church's immediate and executory temporal jurisdiction is exercised only in special cases], the jurisdiction

casualiter et propter aliquid speciale, quia erit in hoc casu cum defertur questio cum denunciacione criminis, et erit propter hoc speciale: videlicet, propter denunciacionem criminis. Ipsa ergo denunciacio criminis erit quedam specialis racio quod Ecclesia de temporalibus iudicet et habeat in temporalibus immediatam et executoriam[1] iurisdiccionem.[2]

In nullo itaque nobis contradicimus dicentes quod Ecclesia in omnibus temporalibus habet dominium superius et primarium non immediatum vel executorium; et dicentes quod dominium habet immediatum et executorium non generaliter sed inspectis certis[3] causis et casualiter; et dicentes quod habet dominium executorium et immediatum generaliter. Nam si considerantur temporalia solum ut ordinantur ad corporalia,[4] quia sunt in sustentamentum vel in adminiculum corporum, sic, nisi sit aliquid aliud speciale, habet Ecclesia de eis dominium superius et primarium. Sed si considerantur temporalia prout ordinantur ad animam, quia possunt esse[5] in malum et in crimen[6] anime, sic habet[7] de temporalibus iudicium immediatum generaliter et casualiter: generaliter[8] quidem quantum ad ipsas res[9] temporales, quia omnes possunt esse in malum et in crimen[10] anime; casuale vero dominium et inspectis certis[11] causis habet, si considerantur non ipsa temporalia, quibus dominatur, sed modus[12] secundum quem dominatur. Quia non dominatur eis immediate et secundum omnem modum et in omni casu; sed habet hoc certis[13] causis inspectis, et potissime in hoc casu: quando fit questio de temporalibus cum denunciacione criminis. Ideo Ecclesia exinde debet[14] temporalem iurisdiccionem casualiter exercere, ut habetur Extra., *Qui filii sint*[15] *legitimi,* capitulo *Per venerabilem.*

Patet ergo qui sunt illi[16] casus propter[17] quos habet Ecclesia iurisdiccionem super temporalibus non solum superiorem et primariam, sed immediatam et executoriam, quia hoc est cum temporalia sunt[18] spiritualia, cum annectuntur spiritualibus et cum eis spiritualia sunt annexa. Utrum autem sint alii casus in sequentibus apparebit.

CAPITULUM VI: *Cum pro quolibet criminali peccato possit Ecclesia quemlibet christianum corripere et ex hoc temporalem iurisdiccionem peragere, qualiter*[19] *precipue ad Ecclesiam spectat*[20] *cum litigium temporalium contrariatur paci et cum pacis federa sunt iuramento*[21] *firmata.*

Utilitas quidem huius capituli ex illa decretali oritur que[22] habetur Extra., *De iudiciis,* capitulo *Novit.* Nam cum inter reges de temporalibus questio oriretur et alter cum denunciacione criminis ad Ecclesiam appellasset, voluit Summus Pontifex se intromittere de huiusmodi questione, pro racione assignans quia[23] 'de quolibet peccato mortali poterat corripere quemlibet christianum,'[24] et precipue hoc poterat cum

---

1: et executoriam] *om.* C   2: iurisdiccionem] inducionem CV²   3: certis] cunctis F   4: corporalia] corpora FV²   5: esse] *om.* V²   6: crimen] crimine F crimine incrimine V²   7: habet] quia *mss*
8: generaliter] *om.* F   9: res] *om.* FV²   10: crimen] crimine F   11: certis] cunctis F   12: modus] modum F   13: certis] cunctis F   14: debet] dicitur V²   15: *sint*] sunt F   16: illi] *om.* V²
17: propter] per FV²   18: sunt] fiunt C   19: qualiter] quare *mss*   20: *spectat*] spectam C
21: *iuramento*] iuramenta CFV²   22: que] qui F   23: quia] quod F   24: quemlibet christianum] christianum quemlibet C

of the Church will be occasional and for some special reason; for it will come into play only in that case where a dispute is brought forward together with an allegation of crime, and it will [therefore] come into play for some special reason: namely, the allegation of crime. Therefore, an allegation of crime will be a kind of special reason on account of which the Church may judge temporal cases and may have an immediate and executory jurisdiction in temporal disputes.

Thus, we do not in any way contradict ourselves when we say that the Church has a superior and primary, but not an immediate and executory, lordship in all temporal matters; and when we say that she has an immediate and executory lordship not generally, but on the examination of certain causes or occasionally; and when we say that she has an executory and immediate lordship generally. For if temporal things be considered simply as ordered towards bodily needs — because they give support or aid to bodies — then, except in some special circumstance, the Church has a superior and primary [but not an immediate] lordship over them. But if temporal things be considered insofar as they are ordered towards the soul — for they can bring about the evil and disgrace of souls — then she has an immediate authority to judge temporal cases both generally and occasionally: generally indeed, as regards temporal things themselves; for they can all bring about the evil and disgrace of souls. But she has lordship occasionally and on the examination of certain causes if we consider not the temporal things themselves over which she has lordship, but the way in which she has lordship. For she does not have lordship over them immediately and in every way and in every case. Rather, she has it on the examination of certain causes, and especially in this case: when a temporal dispute arises in connection with an allegation of crime. Accordingly, then, the Church must exercise a temporal jurisdiction occasionally, as is established at X. 4:17:13: *Per venerabilem*.[1]

It is clear, therefore, what those special cases are in which the Church has not only a superior and primary, but also an immediate and executory, jurisdiction over temporal things. For this is so when temporal things are spiritual, when they are annexed to spiritual things, and when spiritual things are annexed to them. But whether there may be other cases will appear in the following pages.

CHAPTER VI: *How, since the Church may rebuke every Christian for every criminal sin, and so may exercise a temporal jurisdiction, it especially rests with the Church to do this when a temporal dispute is detrimental to peace and when peace treaties have been confirmed by oath.*

The usefulness of this chapter arises from X. 2:1:13: *Novit*.[2] For since a dispute had arisen between kings over temporal matters, and since one of them had made an appeal to the Church together with an allegation of crime, the Supreme Pontiff was willing to intervene in that dispute, assigning as his reason that he could 'rebuke every Christian for every mortal sin' and that he could do this especially when that

1. See Introduction, p. xxvii and n. 60.
2. See Introduction, n. 21.

illud peccatum esset 'contra pacem, que est vinculum caritatis'; et postremo dicit se hoc posse cum 'pacis federa sunt iuramento[1] firmata.' Primo ergo agemus de pace, propter quam[2] precipue debet se intromittere Ecclesia; postea agemus de iuramento quod, ne[3] frangatur, debet Ecclesia suam potenciam exponere.[4]

Advertendum ergo quod gubernacio hominum sub aliquo principante tunc est naturalis et laudabilis quando imitatur gubernacionem tocius mundi sive gubernacionem rerum naturalium sub uno principante, videlicet sub uno Deo. Unde et in alia sciencia probatur, quod est unus principatus et unus princeps, id est unus mundus, cui principatur unus Deus. Sic autem videmus in accione rerum naturalium, et potissime in tractu, prout una res naturalis trahitur ab alia et naturaliter subicitur[5] iurisdiccioni alterius rei que trahit ipsam; quod sapientes philosophi distinxerunt triplicem tractum: a calido, a tota specie et a vacua.

A calido quidem est tractus cum aliquid calefacit alia et ea superius trahit, sicut sol, calefaciens vapores, dat eis quendam[6] calorem incorporatum[7] per quem superius trahuntur sive superius tendunt. Videmus eciam aliquos lapides, qui, si[8] ducantur per pannum et calefiant, aliquam modicam paleam ad se trahunt. A tota quidem specie fit tractus quando non fit ad unam differenciam posicionis tantum, sicut vapores calefacti solum sursum tendunt, sed fit ad omnem differenciam posicionis, et fit a virtute aliqua quam nominate nescimus. Sed quia virtus illa sequitur naturam illius[9] speciei, ideo dicimus hoc esse a tota specie, quia est a virtute aliqua sequente totam speciem, sicut adamas attrahit ferrum; quia in quacumque differencia posicionis sit adamas, ad ipsum trahitur ferrum. Et quia nescimus illam virtutem nominate,[10] ideo dicimus hoc esse a tota specie.[11] Tercio modo fit tractus a vacuo, id est ut non sit vacuum; et iste dicitur esse[12] tractus permaximus; secundum quem modum ventosa trahit carnem. Est enim ille tractus plus a vacuo quam a calido. Nam cum ponitur stupa accensa in ventosa, ita rarefit aer intra[13] ventosam propter calorem stupe accense, tunc[14] modicus aer replet ventosam. Cum ergo[15] ventosa habens aerem sic rarefactum ponitur super carnem, quia tunc stupa accensa extinguitur[16] et aer qui[17] est in ea incipit infrigidari,[18] inspissari[19] et occupare minorem locum, ideo, ne remaneat vacuum in ventosa, trahitur caro ad replendum aliquam vacuitatem ventose. Sic eciam, si cornu habens foramen superius ponatur super carnem et per foramen superius[20] trahatur aer qui est in cornu, ne sit vacuum intra[21] cornu, trahetur caro. Iste itaque tractus dicitur esse a vacuo, quia est ut non sit vacuum. Sed si queratur a qua virtute positiva sit iste tractus, dicemus quod est a

---

1: iuramento] iuramenta FV²   2: quam] quod F   3: ne] quod non C ut non FV²   4: exponere] postremo et [*illegible*] ultimatam *add. and del.* C   5: subicitur] subditur F subdicitur V²
6: quendam] quandam V²   7: incorporatum] incorporeum F   8: si] ubi F *om.* V²   9: illius] *om.* V²   10: nominate] per quam hoc fit scimus tamen quod illa virtus sequitur totam speciem adamantis *add. and del.* C   11: specie] quia est a virtute aliqua *add. and del.* C   12: esse] *om.* F
13: intra] inter F   14: tunc] quod C   15: Cum ergo] et cum F   16: extinguitur] stinguitur F
17: qui] que FV²   18: infrigidari] et *add.* CFV²   19: inspissari] inspissare F   20: per foramen superius] *om.* C   21: intra] inter F

sin was 'detrimental to peace, which is the bond of love'; and, last, he says that he can do this when 'peace treaties have been confirmed by oath.' First, therefore, we shall discuss the question of peace, for the sake of which the Church must particularly concern herself [with temporal affairs]; then we shall discuss that of an oath, [and say] that the Church must deploy her power so that it may not be broken.

It must be noted, therefore, that the government of men under some ruling power is natural and laudable when it imitates the government of the whole world or the government of natural things under the one Ruling Power, that is, under the one God. Hence also, it has been proved in another science that there is one kingdom and one Ruler: that is, one world, whose ruler is the one God.[1] And we see this in the behaviour of natural things, and especially in attraction, inasmuch as one natural object is attracted by another and is naturally subjected to the jurisdiction of the object which attracts it. And those learned in philosophy have distinguished three kinds of attraction: by heat, by the species as such, and by a vacuum.[2]

Now attraction by heat occurs when one object warms others and draws them upwards, as the sun warms vapours and gives them a certain inner heat by which they are drawn upwards or tend upwards. We also see that certain stones, if rubbed with a cloth and warmed, attract small pieces of straw to themselves. Attraction by the species as such occurs when it produces not simply a single difference in position (as with heated vapours, which tend only upwards), but when it effects any difference of position at all, and does so by means of some force of which we do not know the name. But since such a force flows from the nature of that species, we therefore say that the attraction is by the species as such, because it comes about by means of some force which flows from the whole species: as the lodestone attracts iron; for no matter what the position of the lodestone may be, the iron is attracted to it. And because we do not know the name of that force, we therefore say that it comes from the species as such. The third kind of attraction is by a vacuum: that is, in order that there may not be a vacuum; and this is said to be the most powerful kind of attraction. And it is in this way that a cupping-glass attracts the flesh. For this kind of attraction comes more from a vacuum than from heat. For when a lighted taper is put into a cupping-glass, the air in the cupping-glass becomes more rarefied because of the heat of the lighted taper, and a little air then fills the whole cupping-glass. Thus, when the cupping-glass, full of air rarefied in this way, is placed upon the flesh, because the lighted taper is then extinguished and the air which is in it begins to cool, to condense and to occupy less space, the flesh is therefore drawn up to fill part of the empty space within the cupping-glass, so that a vacuum may not remain in the cupping-glass. So also, if a horn with a hole in the end is placed upon the flesh and the air in the horn withdrawn through the hole in the end, the flesh is drawn up so that there may not be a vacuum in the horn. Thus, this kind of attraction is said to be by a vacuum, because it occurs in order that there may not be a vacuum. But if it be asked what positive force may effect this attraction, we shall say

1. Cf. Aristotle, *Metaphysics* Λ 10 (1076ᵃ3); Aquinas, *Summa theologiae* Ia 103:3, *responsio*.
2. Cf. Aristotle, *Physics* 7:2 (243ᵃ5); possibly he also has in mind Aquinas, *In VIII libros physicorum Aristotelis* (Turin: Marietti, 1954) 7, lect. 3.

virtute celi;[1] quia si esset vacuum, influencia celi non posset per vacuum transire. Privaretur ergo celum suo effectu,[2] quia non posset in omnia influere. Ad celum ergo spectat omnia ad invicem continuare, ut possit in omnia[3] influere.

Tractus ergo a calido potest competere elementis, cum caliditas sit qualitas[4] elementalis.[5] Tractus a tota specie potest competere elementatis, cum ipsa elementata[6] possit sequi aliqua virtus que sequitur totam speciem illorum elementorum.[7] Sed tractus a vacuo, sive tractus[8] ut non sit vacuum, vel, quod est[9] idem, tractus ut omnia continuantur[10] et ad invicem coniunguntur,[11] specialissime competit celo, cuius, ut diximus, est omnia coniungere, ut possit in omnia influere. Sic ergo res trahere, ut coniungantur et uniantur, potissime spectat ad virtutem generalem, ne per vacuum discontinuans impediatur[12] influencia eius.

Sicut ergo in naturalibus res trahere, ne discontinuentur, spectat ad virtutem celestem et generalem, sic in gubernacione hominum trahere partes et litigia parcium, ne fiant guerre et ne tollatur pax, que est vinculum caritatis que unit fideles, ut princeps ecclesiasticus possit eos plene gubernare et regere, precipue spectabit ad potestatem celestem et ecclesiasticam, que est Catholica et universalis.

Dicemus enim quod vacuum corporale est quedam discontinuacio corporum, ut ex hoc ipsum celum non possit suam continuare influenciam nec possit in omnia corpora influere. Sic et in proposito: guerra est quasi quoddam vacuum spirituale, quia est quedam discontinuacio animarum. Vult itaque Ecclesia, et potissime ad ipsam pertinet, ab omnibus fidelibus, quantum possibile est, removere hoc spirituale vacuum et huiusmodi guerram tollere et inter omnes fideles pacem facere, ut suam gubernacionem et suum regimen possit in omnibus fidelibus[13] exercere.

Bene ergo dictum est quod dicitur[14] in illa decretali *Novit* quod,[15] etsi Summus Pontifex de quolibet peccato mortali potest corripere quemlibet christianum, propter quod, si deferebatur[16] quecumque questio de quibuscumque[17] temporalibus cum denunciacione criminis, racione peccati criminalis poterit Ecclesia de illa questione se intromittere, precipue tamen hoc debet facere cum illud criminale peccatum militat contra pacem et potest populorum guerram[18] suscitare. Quod patet ex exemplo inducto[19] in naturalibus. Quia, licet celum cooperetur ad produccionem cuiuslibet effectus, specialiter tamen attribuitur virtuti celesti agere ne concordia et unitas et coniunccio istorum inferiorum impediatur. Sic et, si[20] potestas ecclesiastica per denunciacionem cuiuslibet peccati criminalis posset, id est deceret eam, de quacumque questione temporalium se intromittere, precipue tamen[21] decet Ecclesiam hoc facere cum crimen[22] est contra pacem, per quam fideles ad invicem concordant, uniuntur et coniunguntur.

Viso quomodo Ecclesia debet se precipue de temporalibus intromittere ut inter

---

1: celi] dicemus *add.* C   2: effectu] effecto C   3: ad invicem ... omnia] *om.* V[2]   4: qualitas] calidas V[2]   5: elementalis] elementatis F   6: elementata] elementa CF   7: elementorum] elementatorum FV[2]   8: a vacuo sive tractus] *om.* PV[1]   9: est] *om.* CF *marg.* V[2]   10: continuantur] continuentur FV[2]   11: coniunguntur] coniungantur F   12: impediatur] influenciatur V[2]   13: fidelibus] fideliter V[2]   14: dicitur] ibi *add.* F   15: quod] quia CFV[2]   16: deferebatur] deferatur F   17: quibuscumque] quibus F   18: potest populorum guerram] populorum guerram potest FV[2]   19: inducto] adducto CFV[2]   20: si] *om.* F   21: tamen] cum CFV[2]   22: crimen] crimine V[2]

that it comes about by means of the force of heaven. For, if there were a vacuum, the influence of heaven could not cross the vacuum. Therefore, the heaven would be deprived of effect, because it would not be able to influence all things. Therefore, it rests with the heaven to ensure that all things are continuous with one another, so that it may influence all things.

Therefore, attraction by heat can exist in the elements, since heat is an elemental property; attraction by the species as such can exist in compounds, since compounds themselves may have some concomitant force which flows from the whole species of their elements. But attraction by a vacuum, or attraction so that there may not be a vacuum, or (which comes to the same thing) attraction so that all things may be continuous and joined with one another, especially belongs to the heaven, the task of which, as we have said, is to ensure that all things are conjoined so that it may influence all things. Therefore, it especially rests with the general force of heaven to attract things, so that they may all be conjoined and united, lest its influence be impeded by the discontinuity produced by a vacuum.

Therefore, just as, among natural phenomena, it rests with the general heavenly power to attract things in order to prevent discontinuities, so in the government of men will it rest especially with the heavenly and ecclesiastical power, which is Catholic and universal, to draw factions and their disputes together, lest wars arise, and lest peace, which is the bond of love which unites the faithful, be destroyed, so that the ecclesiastical prince may fully govern and rule them.

For we shall say that a corporeal vacuum is a kind of discontinuity of bodies, on account of which the heaven itself may neither continue to exert influence nor influence all bodies. So too in our proposition: war is as it were a kind of spiritual vacuum, for it is a kind of discontinuity of souls. Thus, the Church desires to remove this spiritual vacuum from all the faithful as far as possible, and it pertains especially to her to do so: to remove such war and to make peace among all the faithful so that she may exercise her government and rule over all faithful men.

What is said in the decretal *Novit*, therefore, was well said: that even though the Supreme Pontiff can rebuke every Christian for every mortal sin — so that if any dispute concerning any temporal matter whatsoever is brought forward together with an allegation of crime, the Church will be able to intervene in this dispute by reason of criminal sin — she must nonetheless do this especially when that criminal sin militates against the peace and can stir up wars among the peoples. And this is made clear by an example drawn from natural phenomena: that, although the heaven cooperates in the production of every effect, it is nonetheless given especially to the force of heaven to ensure that the concord and unity and conjunction of inferior things be not impeded. Thus, even though the ecclesiastical power could — that is, could fittingly — intervene in any temporal dispute whatsoever by reason of an allegation of criminal sin, the Church must nonetheless do this especially when the crime is detrimental to the peace by which the faithful are bound to one another and united and conjoined.

Having seen how the Church must concern herself particularly with temporal

suos filios[1] valeat pacis federa reformare, videre restat quomodo[2] postremo debet hoc facere quando talia federa sunt iuramento firmata. Dicemus enim quod fraccio iuramenti dicitur[3] esse crimen ecclesiasticum, quia ad iudicem[4] ecclesiasticum spectat iudicare de periurio sive de fraccione iuramenti. Quod[5] ergo Summus Pontifex volebat se intromittere de[6] litigio quod erat inter regem Francie et regem Anglie occasione cuiusdam feudi, non agebat hoc[7] racione ipsius feudi secundum se, sed propter triplicem aliam[8] causam: ut prima causa esset quia illa questio denunciata erat cum peccata criminali; secunda causa esset quia denunciata erat cum tali peccato criminali quod erat contra pacem, de qua, ut patuit, precipue Ecclesia debet se intromittere; et[9] tercia et postrema causa esset quia pax illa erat iuramenta firmata, et quia fraccio iuramenti est crimen ecclesiasticum, ideo ex hac tercia condicione specialiter pertinebat ad Ecclesiam ut se intromitteret de questione prefata.

Per quod intelligere debemus[10] de omni crimine et potissime de omni crimine ecclesiastico, id est de omni crimine cuius examinacio spectat ad iudicem[11] spiritualem, quia crimen illud specialiter ledit spiritum sive animam. Et ideo usura[12] potest dici crimen[13] ecclesiasticum, quia potest fieri sine lesione rerum temporalium, quia[14] potest quis lucrari plus[15;16] cum pecunia quantum[17] accipit[18] ad usuram[19] quam sit illud quod dat pro usura. Non ergo semper ledit usura ea que sunt corporum, sed semper ledit spiritum sive animam. Sic et periurium, heresis et talia possunt dici crimina ecclesiastica; vel dicuntur crimina ecclesiastica[20] que specialiter sunt contra Ecclesiam et contra res sacras, ut sacrilegium. Quocumque autem modo accipiatur 'crimen ecclesiasticum', patet quod,[21] si de omni crimine se potest vel se debet intromittere Ecclesia, precipue tamen hoc debet facere[22] quando crimen illud est contra pacem; et postremo, id est secundum postremam et ultimatam virtutem, hoc debet facere quando crimen illud est[23] ecclesiasticum, et potissime quando est tale ecclesiasticum quod est immediate contra Deum, sicut heresis, periurium et cetera talia.

Dicemus ergo quod iudex civilis et dominus secularis secundum se non debet suam manum extendere ad aliquid spirituale. Ideo sive res temporales fiant spirituales, ut patet in decimis, sive spiritualia annectantur eis, quod fit quando[24] defertur questio cum denunciacione criminis, sive sit peccatum criminale quodcumque, et precipue si sit[25] contra pacem, et specialiter si sit crimen ecclesiasticum, quia omnia ista sunt quidam morbi spirituales, iudex civilis, qui non debet ad spiritualia suam manum extendere, non habebit de talibus iudicare. Immo, ipse quidem res temporales pertinent ad spiritualem iudicem non solum si fiant spirituales et si spiritualia annectantur eis, sed eciam si ipse sint annexe spiritualibus, ut ponebatur[26] exemplum de dotibus,[27] que sunt annexe matrimonio, et de hereditatibus, que sunt annexe

1: suos filios] filios suos F   2: quomodo] quando PV¹V²   3: dicitur] debet V¹   4: iudicem] invicem V²   5: Quod] quando F   6: de] ut V²   7: hoc] summus pontifex add. and del. C
8: triplicem aliam] aliam triplicem F   9: et] om. F   10: debemus] quod add. CPV¹V²
11: iudicem] invicem V²   12: usura] usuram FV²   13: crimen] crimine F   14: quia] et F
15: plus] om. C   16: lucrari plus] plus lucrari F plus lucra V²   17: quantum] quam FV²
18: accipit] accipiet FV²   19: usuram] usuras FV²   20: vel dicuntur crimina ecclesiastica] om. F
21: quod] et add. F   22: debet facere] facere debet F   23: contra pacem; ... est] om. F
24: quando] cum CF   25: si sit] om. F   26: ponebatur] ponatur FV²   27: dotibus] doctibus V²

affairs in order that she may be able to restore treaties of peace between her sons, it remains, finally, to see how she must do this when such treaties are confirmed by oath. For we shall say that the breaking of an oath is called an ecclesiastical crime because it rests with the ecclesiastical judge to judge cases of perjury or oath-breaking. Therefore, when the Supreme Pontiff was willing to intervene in the dispute between the King of France and the King of England over a certain fief, he did so not because of the fief as such, but for three other causes. The first cause was that the question at issue was alleged to involve a criminal sin. The second cause was that it was alleged to involve a criminal sin which was detrimental to peace, with which, as is now clear, the Church must especially concern herself. And the third and last cause was that the peace was confirmed by oath; and, by reason of this third cause, because oath-breaking is an ecclesiastical crime, it therefore pertained especially to the Church to concern herself with the question at issue.

And we must understand this to apply to every crime, and especially to every ecclesiastical crime: that is, to every crime the examination of which rests with the spiritual judge because such a crime specifically injures the spirit or soul. And so usury can be called an ecclesiastical crime, because it can be committed without injury to temporal goods; for the borrower can make more profit with the money which he borrows at usury than he has to pay for the usurious loan.[1] Therefore, usury does not always injure those things which are bodily; but it always injures the spirit or soul. So too, perjury, heresy and other such offences can be called ecclesiastical crimes; or those acts which are especially directed against the Church or against sacred objects, such as sacrilege, can be called ecclesiastical crimes. But however 'ecclesiastical crimes' be taken, it is clear that, although the Church can or must concern herself with every crime, she must nonetheless do so especially when the crime is detrimental to peace. And ultimately — that is, to the ultimate and utmost of her power — she must do so when the crime is ecclesiastical, and especially when it is ecclesiastical in such a way as to be immediately against God, as in the case of heresy, perjury, and other such offences.

We shall say, therefore, that the civil judge and the secular lord as such must not extend his hand to any spiritual matter. Thus, whether temporal things become spiritual, as is clear in the case of tithes; or whether spiritual things are annexed to them, which occurs when a dispute is brought forward together with an allegation of crime; or in the event of any criminal sin whatsoever, and particularly if it is detrimental to peace, and especially if it is an ecclesiastical crime: the civil judge, who must not extend his hand to spiritual matters, will not have jurisdiction in such cases, for all these things are like spiritual diseases. Indeed, temporal things pertain to the spiritual judge himself not only if they become spiritual and if spiritual things are annexed to them, but also if they themselves are annexed to spiritual things, as in the examples given: of dowries, which are annexed to matrimony, and inheritances, which are annexed to the legitimation of sons.[2]

---

1. Cf. Aquinas, *Summa theologiae* IIa IIae, 78.
2. See Ch. V, pp. 325–327.

legitimacioni filiorum; ut si nulla esset questio super hereditate[1] nisi propter defectum legitimacionis, quantum nobis racio dicat, ad iudicem[2] ecclesiasticum, cuius est iudicare de matrimonio, spectaret iudicare an homo ille cui imponitur huiusmodi defectus esset legitimus et per consequens an eius esset hereditas.

CAPITULUM VII: *Quod tam ex parte rerum temporalium, ut superius est narratum, tam[3] ex parte potestatis terrene, ut in hoc capitulo ostendetur, quam eciam[4] ex parte potestatis ecclesiastice, ut in sequenti capitulo declarabitur, possunt sumi speciales casus propter quos Summus Pontifex se de temporalibus[5] intromittet.*

Enarravimus[6] in precedenti capitulo casus sumptos ex parte ipsarum rerum temporalium, quando huiusmodi res possunt induere quendam[7] spiritualem modum racione cuius earum[8] iurisdiccio pertinet ad spiritualem iudicem. In presenti autem capitulo, et eciam in sequenti,[9] enumerare volumus[10] speciales casus sumptos tam ex parte potestatis terrene quam eciam ecclesiastice propter quos[11] Summum Pontificem deceat[12] iurisdiccionem in temporalibus exercere.

Dicebatur enim supra quod in litigio sive in iurisdiccione rerum temporalium erant tria considerare: prima quidem[13] ipsas res temporales; secundo, ipsum iudicem civilem et ipsum materialem gladium;[14] tercio,[15] ipsam potestatem ecclesiasticam ad quam in certis casibus et certis causis inspectis exercere spectat temporalem iurisdiccionem. Dicimus autem 'in certis casibus', quia ipsa temporalia secundum se et immediate ordinantur ad corpus, quia sunt facta in[16] sustentamentum corporis, et ipsa temporalia secundum se sunt res corporales.[17] Ex mandato tamen Domini, ut patet[18] in decimis; vel ex pia largicione fidelium, ut patet in his que sunt donata ecclesiis; vel[19] insipiencia hominum, ut patet in delinquentibus circa temporalia et circa res creatas, iuxta illud Sapiencie XIV, 'Creature Dei in odium facte sunt et in tentaciones animis[20] hominum et in muscipulas pedibus insipiencium': [ipsa temporalia possunt dici spiritualia.] Ipse quidem creature bone[21] sunt, quia vidit Deus[22] cuncta que fecerat, et erant valde bona; sed propter insipienciam nostram facte sunt in odium, id est in malum nostrum, et facte sunt in tentacionem animarum nostrarum, et hoc[23] modo sunt quedam muscipule sive quedam decipule, non quibuscumque, sed pedibus insipiencium.

In hiis ergo casibus ipsa temporalia possunt dici spiritualia, vel quia sunt a Summo Spiritu imperata, vel quia sunt ecclesiis tamquam rebus spiritualibus exhibita vel donata, vel quia ex insipiencia nostra sunt in malum nostrarum spirituum sive nostrarum animarum condita; propter que iurisdiccio de eis eciam immediata

---

1: hereditate] hereditatem C   2: iudicem] invicem V[2]   3: *tam*] quam C   4: *eciam*] *om.* F   5: *se de temporalibus*] de temporalibus se F   6: Enarravimus] narravimus FV[2]   7: quendam] quomodo V[2]   8: earum] *del.* C   9: et eciam in sequenti] *om.* V[1]   10: enumerare volumus] enunciare volumus F volumus enumerare V[1]   11: quos] quod FV[2]   12: deceat] doceat RV[1]   13: quidem] est ibi considerare *add. and del.* C   14: gladium] quia spiritualis deputatus est ad gubernandum et manutenendum res temporales *add. and del.* C   15: tercio] est ibi considerare *add. and del.* C   16: in] *om.* V[2]   17: corporales] temporales FV[1]   18: ut patet] *om.* C   19: vel] ex *add.* CFV[2]   20: animis] animus V[2]   21: bone] bonum C   22: Deus] *om.* FV[2]   23: hoc] *om.* V[2]

Thus, if there were no question in a case of disputed inheritance apart from a defect of legitimacy, then, as far as reason tells us, it would rest with the judge whose task it is to judge matrimonial causes to judge whether the man to whom such a defect is imputed is legitimate and, consequently, whether the inheritance is his.

CHAPTER VII: *That the special cases by reason of which the Supreme Pontiff will intervene in temporal matters can be derived from a consideration of temporal things, as has been discussed above; from a consideration of the earthly power, as will be shown in this chapter; and also from a consideration of the ecclesiastical power, as will be made clear in the next chapter.*

In a previous chapter,[1] we have discussed cases derived from a consideration of temporal things themselves, when such things can take on a certain spiritual character on account of which jurisdiction over them pertains to the spiritual judge. In the present chapter, however, and also in the following, we wish to enumerate the special cases derived from a consideration of both the earthly and the ecclesiastical power by reason of which it is proper for the Supreme Pontiff to exercise a temporal jurisdiction.

For it was said above[2] that in, or as regards jurisdiction over, a dispute involving temporal things, there were three aspects to consider: first, the temporal things themselves; second, the civil judge and the material sword; and, third, the ecclesiastical power, with which it rests to exercise temporal jurisdiction in certain cases and on the examination of certain causes. And we say 'in certain cases' because, as such and immediately, temporal things are ordered to the body, since they were made for the body's support; and, as such, temporal things are themselves bodily goods [which therefore usually come under the jurisdiction of the material sword]. Nonetheless, even temporal things can be called spiritual by the Lord's command, as is clear in the case of tithes; or because of the pious gift of the faithful, as is clear in the case of those things which are given to churches; or because of the foolishness of men, as is clear in the case of offences involving temporal goods and created things, according to Wisdom 14: 'The creatures of God have become an abomination and a temptation to the souls of men, and a snare to the feet of the foolish.'[3] The creatures themselves are indeed good; for God saw all the things that He had made, and they were very good.[4] But they have become an abomination — that is, harmful to us — because of our foolishness; and they have become a temptation to our souls and, in this way, are a kind of snare or a kind of trap: not to everyone, but to the feet of the foolish.

In such cases, therefore, even temporal things can be called spiritual: either because they are commanded by the Supreme Spirit, or because they are given or granted to churches as spiritual goods, or because, by our foolishness, they have become harmful to our spirits or to our souls. And, in view of these considerations, an

1. Ch. V; and see also Ch. VI.
2. Ch. V.
3. Wisd. 14:11.
4. Cf. Gen. 1:31.

et executoria ad spiritualem[1] iudicem pertinebit.

Fecimus autem mencionem de iurisdiccione immediata et executoria quia iuris-diccionem superiorem et primariam semper et directe super temporalibus habet Ec-clesia; quia si temporalia sunt subiecta gladio materiali secundum iurisdiccionem immediatam et executoriam,[2] cum[3] ipse gladius materialis sit sub spirituali, oportet quod et temporalia, que sunt et ut sunt sub[4] materiali gladio secundum iurisdiccio-nem immediatam et executoriam, sint[5] sub spirituali gladio secundum iurisdiccio-nem superiorem et primariam; ut si ipse gladius materialis[6] delinquat circa[7] tempo-ralia et eciam[8] gubernacula sibi commissa, ex culpa materialis gladii vel eciam ex causa poterit spiritualis gladius animadvertere in ipsum.

A iurisdiccione ergo super temporalibus superiori et primaria numquam potest cadere Ecclesia; sed iurisdiccionem immediatam et executoriam super huiusmodi temporalibus habet[9] certis causis inspectis. Nec tamen propter hoc[10] huiusmodi iurisdiccionem immediatam et executoriam super temporalibus[11] minus habet Ec-clesia quam seculares principes; immo, magis et principalius. Nam si non esset aliud nisi solum id quod nunc[12] diximus, videlicet, quod temporalia possunt dici spiritualia prout ex insipiencia nostra spiritualiter delinquimus circa ea, racione cuius spiritualis delicti iudex spiritualis et ecclesiasticus iurisdiccionem eciam im-mediatam et executoriam habebit super res temporales, sufficienter concludi poterit quod iudex ecclesiasticus sit pocior[13] et principalior[14] in iurisdiccione temporalium quam civilis. Dominus itaque secularis immediatam iurisdiccionem et executoriam habet super[15] temporalia, ne nobis indebite subtracta inferantur.[16] Sed iudex spiritu-alis et ecclesiasticus habebit huiusmodi iurisdiccionem ne ipsa temporalia indebite accepta et iniuste usurpata inferant malum animabus nostris et spiritibus nostris. Et quia principalius et diligencius est cavendum malum animarum quam corpo-rum et malum quod nocet spiritui quam quod nocet carni, iurisdiccionem[17] imme-diatam et executoriam super temporalibus magis et principalius habet iudex eccle-siasticus[18] quam dominus[19] secularis.

Quod ergo dictum est, quod Summus Pontifex casualiter exercet temporalem iurisdiccionem, ut patet ex illo capitulo *Per venerabilem*, istud casuale vel istud[20] quod exercet in certis casibus est longe amplius quam sit istud[21] regulare quod habet dominus secularis. Nam istud[22] casuale quasi[23] universale est,[24] cum omnis questio et omne litigium habeat hoc casuale annexum quod potest deferri cum denunciacione criminis.[25] Propter quod hoc casuale ut respicit animas potest esse eque generale sicut illud regulare quod respicit corpora. Rursus, cum anima sit potencior corpore, istud[26] casuale erit principalius quam illud regulare. Propter

---

1: spiritualem] sive ad ecclesiasticum *add. and del.* C   2: executoriam] sunt sub spirituali gladio *add. and del.* C   3: cum] tamen ut F   4: sub] subter F   5: sint] sicut FV[2]   6: gladius materi-alis] materialis gladius V[2]   7: circa] contra F   8: eciam] circa FV[2]   9: habet] ecclesia *add.* C
10: hoc] *del.* PV[1]   11: temporalibus] rebus *add.* C   12: nunc] non FV[2]   13: pocior] potencior F
14: principalior] et *add.* FV[2]   15: super] *om.* FV[2]   16: inferantur] malum corporibus nostris non reficiendo non a sustenando ipso *add. and del.* C   17: iurisdiccionem] eciam *add.* V[1]V[2]
18: iudex ecclesiasticus] ecclesiasticus iudex FV[2]   19: dominus] deus V[2]   20: istud] illud F
21: istud] illud CF   22: istud] illud F   23: quasi] est *add.* CFV[2] *add. and del.* P   24: est] *om.* C
25: criminis] [*a largely illegible passage of some 13 lines*] *add. and del.* C   26: istud] illud F

immediate and executory jurisdiction over them will indeed pertain to the spiritual judge.

But we have made [specific] mention of immediate and executory jurisdiction because the Church always has a superior and primary jurisdiction directly over temporal things. For if temporal things are subject to the immediate and executory jurisdiction of the material sword, then, because the material sword is itself subject to the spiritual, the temporal things which are, and inasmuch as they are, under the immediate and executory jurisdiction of the material sword must also be under the superior and primary jurisdiction of the spiritual sword. Thus, if the material sword itself offends in relation to temporal things, and even in relation to those matters which are [immediately] entrusted to its government, the spiritual sword will be able to act against the material sword for its fault or for some other good cause.

Therefore, the Church can never lack a superior and primary jurisdiction over temporal matters; but she has an immediate and executory jurisdiction over such temporal matters only on the examination of certain causes. It is not the case, however, that the Church therefore has such immediate and executory temporal jurisdiction in a lesser degree than do secular princes. On the contrary, she has it in a greater and more exalted fashion. For even if there were no other consideration apart from that which we have now stated — namely, that temporal things can be called spiritual to the extent that, by our foolishness, we go spiritually astray with respect to them, by reason of which spiritual straying the spiritual and ecclesiastical judge will indeed have an immediate and executory jurisdiction over temporal things — it would still be possible to show sufficiently that the ecclesiastical judge is mightier and more exalted in temporal jurisdiction than the civil. Thus, [by way of illustration, let us say that] the secular lord has an immediate and executory jurisdiction over temporal matters so that stolen goods may not be wrongfully brought to us. But the spiritual and ecclesiastical judge will have such jurisdiction lest temporal goods, being wrongfully received and unjustly usurped, bring harm to our souls and to our spirits. And because the harm of souls is to be guarded against more primarily and more diligently than that of bodies, and harm which injures the spirit than that which injures the flesh, the immediate and executory jurisdiction over temporal cases which the ecclesiastical judge has is greater than that of the secular lord.

Therefore, as to the statement which appears in the chapter *Per venerabilem*, that the Supreme Pontiff exercises a temporal jurisdiction occasionally: that occasional jurisdiction, or that which he exercises in certain cases, is far more ample than is that regular jurisdiction which the secular lord has. For that occasional jurisdiction is as if universal, since every question and every dispute which can be brought forward together with an allegation of crime may come under this occasional jurisdiction. Thus, this occasional jurisdiction can be just as general in relation to souls as that regular jurisdiction is in relation to bodies. Moreover, since the soul is greater than the body, that occasional jurisdiction will be more exalted than

quod patet quod si questio de temporalibus secundum iurisdiccionem immediatam et executoriam, prout tangit corpora nostra, est sub domino seculari, illa eadem questio eciam hoc modo sumpta erit sub iudice ecclesiastico secundum iurisdiccionem superiorem et primariam. Rursus, quia huiusmodi questio de temporalibus, que tangit corpora prout temporalia sunt ordinata in sustentamentum corporum, ex insipiencia nostra pertinet eciam ad animas,[1] ideo illa eadem questio rerum temporalium, que ut solum tangit corpora est sub iudice ecclesiastico secundum iurisdiccionem superiorem et primariam, poterit esse sub huiusmodi iudice et potissime sub Summo Pontifice ut tangit animas secundum iurisdiccionem immediatam et executoriam,[2] ut ex hoc possit ad Summum Pontificem appellari.

Ad maiorem tamen intelligenciam dictorum et dicendorum, distinguemus duplicem potestatem Summi Pontificis et duplicem eius iurisdiccionem in temporalibus rebus:[3] unam absolutam[4] et aliam regulatam.[5;6] Quia, ut tradiderunt sapientes philosophi, legis positivus debet esse legis observativus. Si ergo Summus Pontifex secundum suum posse absolutum est animal[7] sine freno et sine capistro, ipse tamen debet sibi frenum et capistrum imponere, in se ipso observando leges et iura. Nam licet ipse sit supra iura, loquendo de iuribus positivis, ut tamen det suis iuribus et suis legibus firmitatem, decet eum secundum leges et iura commissam[8] sibi Ecclesiam gubernare. Eapropter sicut distinximus duplex posse Summi Pontificis, sic distinguere possumus[9] duplicem eius iurisdiccionem[10] in temporalibus rebus: unam directam et regularem, et hec est, ut diximus, iurisdiccio superior et primaria quam habet ipse in omnibus, tam super potestates terrenas quam super temporalia, racione cuius ex culpa vel ex causa potest animadvertere in potestates terrenas. Aliam quidem iurisdiccionem habet Summus Pontifex super temporalibus rebus que non est directa[11] et regularis, sed est certis causis inspectis et casualis; et hec iurisdiccio non solum est superior et primaria, sed est immediata et executoria.

Verumtamen huiusmodi iurisdiccio, quod sit sic casualis, non est referenda ad suum posse absolutum, sed ad suum[12] posse ut est quibusdam regulis regulatum. Secundum quem modum dicere possumus quod non est de rigore iuris quod a civili iudice appelletur ad papam, quia secundum regulatum posse ipsius Summi Pontificis non est hoc regulare, sed casuale; quod quidem casuale, quod est in certis casibus et certis causis circumspectis, prevalet et preponderat illi regulari quod habet dominus secularis. Sciendum tamen quod opera nostra, et specialiter opera iudicis ecclesiastici, debent esse conformia rebus, quod non pedetentim et passim de temporalibus subiectis secularibus dominis se intromittat iudex ecclesiasticus, sed casualiter, id est solum in casibus ubi videt Ecclesie et bono publico expedire; spiritualibus[13] autem, pedetentim et passim,[14] regulariter et secundum communem legem,

---

1: animas] prout anime nostre vel spiritus nostri delinquant circa ea *add. and del.* C   2: executoriam] ut in illa eadem questionem ut est cum denunciatione criminis et ut est ibi ius *add. and del.* C   3: rebus] est quidem duplex potestas et duplex posse in summo pontifice *add. and del.* C
4: unam absolutam] unum absolutum CFV² 5: aliam regulatam] aliud regulatum FV²
6: regulatam] absolutum P   7: animal] alias FPV¹V²   8: commissam] commissa PV¹
9: possumus] ut aliqualiter et per huiusmodi manifestum *add. and del.* C   10: duplicem eius iurisdiccionem] iurisdiccionem eius duplicem F   11: directa] directe V²   12: suum] summum FV²   13: spiritualibus] spiritualis F   14: et passim] passim et FV²

the regular. And so it is clear that if a dispute involving temporal goods is under the immediate and executory jurisdiction of the secular lord as touching our bodies, that same dispute will in this way also be brought under the superior and primary jurisdiction of the ecclesiastical judge. But because such a temporal dispute, which touches bodies insofar as temporal goods are appointed for the support of bodies, also pertains to souls because of our foolishness, that same temporal dispute which, simply as touching bodies, is under the primary and superior jurisdiction of the ecclesiastical judge, will, as touching souls, be able to be under such a judge — and especially under the Supreme Pontiff — in terms of immediate and executory jurisdiction also; so that, for this reason, appeal may be made to the Supreme Pontiff.

For the sake of a greater understanding of what has been said and of what must still be said, however, we shall make a twofold distinction as to the power of the Supreme Pontiff and his jurisdiction in temporal matters and say that it is in one sense absolute and, in another, is governed by rules. For as those learned in philosophy have taught, he who establishes the law should observe the law.[1] Therefore, if the Supreme Pontiff is a creature without bridle and without halter by reason of his absolute power, he must nonetheless impose bridle and halter upon himself by observing the statutes and laws in his own actions. For although, speaking of positive laws [as distinct from the natural and divine laws], he himself is above the laws, nonetheless, in order that he may give stability to his laws and statutes, it is fitting that he govern the Church entrusted to him according to statutes and laws. Moreover, just as we have distinguished a twofold power in the Supreme Pontiff, so can we make a twofold distinction as to his jurisdiction in temporal cases. In one sense, it is direct and regular; and this, as we have said, is the superior and primary jurisdiction which he has in all cases, over earthly powers and temporal goods alike, by reason of which he can act against earthly powers for their fault or for some other good cause. But the Supreme Pontiff has another kind of jurisdiction over temporal matters, which is not direct and regular, but which comes into play only on the examination of certain causes and occasionally. And this jurisdiction is not only superior and primary, but is also immediate and executory.

But because such jurisdiction is thus occasional, it is to be attributed not to his power considered as absolute, but to his power insofar as it is governed by certain rules. In this way, we can say that it is not according to the strictness of the law that appeal may be made from a civil judge to the pope because, insofar as the power of the Supreme Pontiff is governed by rules, this is not a regular but an occasional practice. That occasional jurisdiction which applies in certain cases and on the examination of certain causes indeed overrides and outweighs the regular jurisdiction which the secular lord has; but it must nonetheless be known that our works, and especially the works of the ecclesiastical judge, should conform to the nature of things: that the ecclesiastical judge should not concern himself with temporal matters which are subject to secular lords normally and indiscriminately, but only occasionally; that is, only in cases where he sees this to be expedient to the Church and to the public good. Normally and ordinarily, however — regularly and according

1. E.g. Aristotle, *Politics* 3:11 (1282^{b}5).

se debet[1] habere ut permittat in temporalibus[2] terrenas potestates sua officia exercere, accipiens exemplum ab ipso Deo,[3] cuius est vicarius, qui, ut diximus, sic res gubernat ut eas proprios cursus agere sinat.

Diu[4] autem locuti sumus de potestate ecclesiastica tam superiori et primaria quam[5] immediata et executoria. Descendemus ergo ad ea[6] que in rubrica capituli continentur, videlicet, quod tam ex potestate terrena quam eciam ecclesiastica possunt accipi speciales[7] casus in quibus spectabit ad iudicem ecclesiasticum iurisdiccionem agere temporalem. Quos casus speciales, quantum ad presens spectat, dicemus esse septem; quatuor videlicet ex parte potestatis terrene et tres ex parte potestatis[8] ecclesiastice, ut in omnibus sint decem huiusmodi casus: tres ex parte rerum temporalium, de quibus agebatur in precedenti capitulo, et quatuor ex parte potestatis terrene et tres ex parte potestatis ecclesiastice de quibus restat agendum. Aliqui tamen istorum casuum sunt pregnantes, quia casus ille sumptus ex parte rerum temporalium, cum spiritualia sunt annexa rebus temporalibus, videlicet cum questio de temporalibus[9] defertur cum denunciacione criminis, quod est quid spirituale,[10] tripartitus erit.[11] Quia denunciacio illa poterat esse cum quolibet peccato criminali, et precipue cum[12] crimine contra pacem, et potissime cum crimine ecclesiastico, ut cum periurio vel cum[13] quocumque ecclesiastico crimine.[14;15]

Revertamur ergo ad propositum et dicamus quod racione potestatis terrene potest pertinere[16] iurisdiccio super temporalibus immediata et executoria ad iudicem ecclesiasticum in quatuor casibus, ut sit primus casus ex secularis[17] domini carencia, secundus ex eius negligencia, tercius ex eius tollerancia, quartus ex eius[18] donacione.[19]

Primus quidem casus sic patet. Quia, ut habetur[20] Geneseos primo, 'Creavit Deus hominem ad imaginem suam, ad imaginem Dei creavit illum'; et sequitur: 'Benedixitque Deus illis, et ait, Crescite et multiplicamini, et replete terram et subicite eam et dominamini,'[21] etc. Ergo quia Deus creavit hominem ad imaginem suam, ideo dedit ei quod subiceret sibi terram et quod[22] dominaretur omnibus istis corporalibus[23] rebus. Sed, ut ait Augustinus XII *De Trinitate* VII: 'Si spiritu mentis nostre renovamur, et ipse est novus homo qui renovatur in agnicione Dei[24] secundum imaginem eius qui creavit eum, nulli dubium est quod non secundum corpus nec secundum quamlibet partem[25] animi,[26] sed secundum racionalem[27] mentem hominem factum esse[28] ad imaginem Dei.' Non ergo secundum corpus nec secundum quamlibet partem anime, quia non secundum sensum qui est[29] aliquid corporale et organicum, sed secundum spiritualem partem anime

---

1: debet] temporalibus *add.* FV² 2: in temporalibus] *om.* FV² 3: Deo] domino V² 4: Diu] cum F 5: quam] eciam *add.* C 6: ad ea] *om.* V² 7: speciales] substantiales F spirituales V¹ 8: terrene et ... potestatis] *om.* V² 9: videlicet cum ... temporalibus] *om.* V² 10: spirituale] speciale V² 11: erit] erat CFV² 12: cum] ecclesiastico *add.* V² 13: cum] *om.* CF 14: ecclesiastico crimine] crimine ecclesiastico C 15: contra pacem ... crimine] *om.* V² 16: pertinere] participare FV² 17: secularis] secularibus V² 18: negligencia, tercius ... ex eius] *om.* V² 19: donacione] et largitione et pia *add. and del.* C 20: habetur] in *add.* F 21: dominamini] dominabimini F 22: quod] *om.* FV² 23: corporalibus] *om.* FV² 24: Dei] *om.* F 25: partem] mentem PV¹ 26: animi] anime F 27: racionalem] totalem PV¹ 28: esse] est F 29: est] *om.* FV²

to the common law — he must so conduct himself in spiritual matters that he permits the earthly powers to exercise their office in temporal ones, taking his example from God Himself, Whose vicar he is: Who, as we have said, governs things in such a way that He allows them to pursue their own courses.[1]

But we have now said a great deal concerning the [jurisdiction of the] ecclesiastical power both as superior and primary and as immediate and executory. Therefore, let us come to the statements contained in the heading of this chapter: namely, that the special cases in which it will be the ecclesiastical judge's task to exercise temporal jurisdiction can be derived from both the earthly and the ecclesiastical power. And, for our present purpose, we shall say that there are seven such special cases: that is, four derived from a consideration of the earthly power and three from a consideration of the ecclesiastical power. Thus, there are ten such cases in all: the three derived from a consideration of temporal things which were discussed in a previous chapter,[2] and the four derived from a consideration of the earthly power and the three from a consideration of the ecclesiastical power which it remains to discuss. Some of these cases, however, are pregnant [with possibilities; i.e. can take several forms]. For a case derived from a consideration of temporal things when spiritual things are annexed to temporal things — that is, when a temporal dispute is brought forward together with an allegation of crime, which is a spiritual matter — may be threefold in character. For that allegation could be connected with any criminal sin; and particularly with a crime against peace; and especially with an ecclesiastical crime such as perjury, or with any other ecclesiastical crime.

Let us revert to our proposition, therefore, and say that, by reason of [some circumstance having to do with] the earthly power, an immediate and executory jurisdiction over temporal matters can pertain to the ecclesiastical judge in cases of four kinds. The first kind of case arises from the lack of a secular lord; the second from his negligence; the third from his sufferance; the fourth from his gift.

The first kind of case is as follows. As is established in Genesis 1, 'God created man in His own image; in the image of God created He him'; and it continues: 'And God blessed him and said, Increase and multiply, and replenish the earth and subdue it, and have lordship,' and so on.[3] Thus, because God created man in His own image, He has therefore given it to him that he may subdue the earth to himself, and that he may have lordship over all corporeal things. But, as Augustine says in *De Trinitate* 12:7: 'If we are renewed in the spirit of our mind,[4] and if he who is renewed in the knowledge of the God Who created him according to His own image is a new man, then there is no doubt that man was made in the image of God not according to body, and not according to every part of the soul, but according to the rational mind.'[5] Man, therefore, is made in the image of God not according to body, and not according to every part of the soul (because not according to sensation, which is something corporeal and organic) but according to the spiritual part of the

---

1. See esp. Pt. II, Ch. XIV, pp. 249–251, and Ch. II, above.
2. Ch. VI.
3. Gen. 1:27–28.
4. Cf. Eph. 4:23.
5. CCSL 50:366 (commenting on Eph. 4:23–24).

homo factus est ad imaginem Dei. Si igitur homo dominatur corporalibus et temporalibus quia factus est ad imaginem Dei, cum factus sit ad huiusmodi imaginem
non secundum hominem exteriorem sed secundum interiorem et secundum partem
spiritualem, consequens est quod racione spiritualitatis habeat universale dominium. Spiritualis ergo gladius omnibus dominatur. Quod autem sibi adiunctus est
materialis gladius non est propter impotenciam spiritualis gladii, sed hoc est in
adminiculum et in adiutorium eius. Deficiente ergo materiali gladio, consequens
est quod iurisdiccio[1] devolvatur ad spiritualem, cuius est omnibus dominari. Sed[2]
in hoc casu, cum vacat imperium, propter carenciam temporalis gladii et secularis
domini appellatur[3] ad audienciam Summi Pontificis, quia inferiores a superioribus
in sua iusticia oppressi nequeunt ad iudicem[4] recurrere secularem, ut dicitur Extra., *De foro competenti*, capitulo *Licet.*

Secundus casus est[5] negligencia domini secularis. Nam cum materialis gladius
factus sit in adiutorium gladii spiritualis, si huiusmodi materialis gladius sit negli-
gens et negligat iusticiam facere, consequens est quod in illo casu a suo officio[6]
cadat, ut ex hoc ad superiorem gladium recurratur.[7] Ideo notatur in iure quod[8] si
hii qui debent iusticiam facere habeantur suspecti de iusticia facienda,[9] in tali casu
ad audienciam Summi Pontificis recurratur,[10] ut habetur eodem titulo et capitulo
allegato. Et si suspicio probabilis et racionabilis[11] de negligencia iusticie facit
quod a civili iudice appelletur ad papam, multo magis hoc facit ipsa negligencia et
ipse defectus ut cum ipse civilis iudex deficit et negligit facere iusticie complementum.

Tercius casus est secularis domini[12] tollerancia, ut si ipse dominus secularis
pluries tollerat quod in questione rerum temporalium sub eo existencium ad
iudicem ecclesiasticum appellaretur[13] et ex tali tollerancia inducta sit consuetudo, poterit ex tunc ab huiusmodi civili iudice ad ecclesiasticum appellari. Nam
licet Summus Pontifex non possit preiudicare potestati ecclesiastice per ea que
agit, dominus tamen secularis potestati terrene potest preiudicare per ea que facit. Nam Summus Pontifex, ut supra tetigimus, neminem habet superiorem per
quem confirmentur ea que agit. Ideo sicut ipse potuit facere, sic suus successor,
eandem potestatem habens, potest huiusmodi facta non per superiorem confir-
mata dirimere. Est enim hoc naturale ut per eadem, idest per eandem auctoritatem, dirimatur res per quam dignoscitur condita, quia, ut dicitur in secundo *Ethicorum*, 'ex eisdem et per eadem fit omnis virtus et corrumpitur.' Ex eisdem enim
actibus, contrario tamen modo factis, generatur virtus et corrumpitur;[14] sic ex
eadem auctoritate contraria volente potest res fieri et dirimi.[15] Sed licet sic sit
quantum ad spiritualem gladium, qui neminem habet superiorem, non tamen sic est

---

1: iurisdiccio] *del.* C   2: Sed] unde et CFV[2]   3: appellatur] appellaratur FV[2]   4: iudicem] invicem V[2]   5: est] *om.* V[2]   6: officio] *om.* V[2]   7: recurratur] recurrentur F   8: quod] et CF
quod filii V[1]   9: facienda] quod *add.* C et *add.* FPV[1]V[2]   10: recurratur] recurrantur C
11: et racionabilis] *om.* V[2]   12: domini] *om.* V[2]   13: appellaretur] appelletur CF   14: corrum-
pitur] corripitur V[2]   15: dirimi] et fieri *add.* PV[1]

soul. Thus, if man is lord of corporeal and temporal things because he is made in the image of God, then, since he was made in that image not according to the outward man, but according to the inward man and according to the spiritual part, it follows that it is by reason of [the] spirituality [of his nature] that he has such universal lordship. [*A fortiori,*] therefore, the spiritual sword is lord of all things [and of all men], and the material sword has been attached to it not because of any lack of power on the part of the spiritual sword, but as a support and helper. It follows, therefore, that if the material sword is lacking, jurisdiction devolves upon the spiritual, to whom it belongs to be lord of all things. And hence, when the empire is vacant because a temporal sword and a secular lord are lacking, appeal is made for a hearing in this case to the Supreme Pontiff, because inferiors who are oppressed by the judgments of their superiors are unable to have recourse to a secular judge, as is said [by Innocent III] at X. 2:2:10: *Licet.*[1]

The second kind of case arises from the negligence of a secular lord. For since the material sword was made as the helper of the spiritual sword, it follows that, if the material sword is negligent and omits to do justice, it fails in its duty; and so, in this case, recourse may for this reason be had to the superior sword. Thus, it is recorded in the law, under the same title and in the chapter just cited [i.e. in the decretal *Licet*], that if those who must do justice are suspect in the matter of doing justice, recourse may be had for a hearing in such a case to the Supreme Pontiff. And if, on probable and reasonable suspicion that he is neglecting to do justice, appeal may be made from a civil judge to the Supreme Pontiff, this is so much the more true in cases of actual negligence and actual deficiency, as when the civil judge is completely deficient and negligent in doing justice.

The third kind of case arises from the sufferance of a secular lord. For example, if a secular lord frequently suffers appeal to be made to an ecclesiastical judge in disputes involving temporal things which are under him, and if a custom is established by means of such sufferance, then it will be possible thenceforth for appeal to be made from a civil to an ecclesiastical judge [as a matter of course]. For although the Supreme Pontiff cannot prejudice the ecclesiastical power by his actions, a secular lord can nonetheless prejudice the earthly power by what he does. For, as we have noted above, the Supreme Pontiff has no one as a superior by whom his actions might be confirmed.[2] Thus, his successor, having the same power, can set aside whatever he could do, since such acts have not been confirmed by a superior. For it is natural that a provision may be set aside in the same way — that is, by the same authority — as that by which it is acknowledged to have been established. For as is said in Book 2 of the *Ethics,* 'every virtue is made and destroyed by the same causes and by the same means.'[3] For virtue is generated and corrupted by the same acts, although performed in contrary ways. So also, a thing can be done and set aside by the same authority willing in contrary directions. But although this may be true of the spiritual sword, which has none as its superior, it is nonetheless not so of

1. See Introduction, n. 71.
2. Ch. IV, p. 315.
3. *Nicomachean Ethics* 2:1 (1103ᵇ5).

quantum ad materialem, qui superiorem habet. Si ergo iste dominus secularis tolleravit quod in causa rerum temporalium appellaretur ad iudicem ecclesiasticum, et iudex ecclesiasticus facto suo talem tolleranciam approbavit quia huiusmodi appellacionem suscepit, si talis tollerancia consuetudinem induxit,[1] quia consuetudo non est vilis vel levis auctoritas, et maxime si consuetudo illa non sit iniusta, quia si esset iniusta contra ius naturale, quanta diuturnior esset, tanto peior existeret, iuxta illud: 'Tanto graviora sunt crimina, quanto diucius infelicem animam detinent[2] alligatam'; sed si consuetudo non est iniusta et est per superiorem approbata, oportet quod vim legis obtineat. Si ergo iste dominus secularis tolleravit quod in causa rerum temporalium appellaretur ab ipso ad iudicem ecclesiasticum,[3] quia talis consuetudo non est iniusta, cum nemo possit sibi iniustum facere, et est per superiorem approbata saltem de facto, cum spiritualis gladius et iudex ecclesiasticus huiusmodi appellacionem pluries suscipiendo approbaverit,[4] ideo sequens dominus[5] secularis consuetudinem appellandi ad iudicem ecclesiasticum per tolleranciam[6] sui predecessoris inductam dirimere non valebit. Ideo dicitur Extra., *De iudiciis*, capitulo *Novit*: 'Non[7] intendimus iudicare de feudo, cuius iudicium spectat ad regem, nisi forte iuri communi per speciale privilegium vel contrariam consuetudinem aliquid sit detractum.' De ipsis itaque rebus temporalibus subiectis secularibus dominis se intromittet Ecclesia si consuetudo habeat quod in talibus temporalibus[8] a civili[9] iudice ad ecclesiasticum iudicem appelletur.[10]

Quartus quidem casus sumptus ex parte potestatis terrene quod Ecclesia iurisdiccionem immediatam et executoriam in temporalibus exerceat sumitur[11] ex pia donacione[12] et devota largicione ipsorum secularium principum ecclesiis facta; ut si seculares principes speciale privilegium fecerunt alicui ecclesie vel Romane sedi, que ecclesiarum omnium est domina et magistra, de aliquibus temporalibus bonis et dotaverunt eam,[13] et maxime si prefati domini seu principes in huiusmodi donacione vel dotacione nihil sibi speciale retinuerunt, ex tunc illa temporalia bona simpliciter et absolute ad Ecclesiam pertinebunt, et in eis iurisdiccionem immediatam et executoriam habebit, et in huiusmodi temporalibus indifferenter et passim poterit ad Summum Pontificem appellari. In tali ergo donacione hoc facit privilegium secularis principis quod in[14] tollerancia appellandi facit consuetudo appellacionis. Unde sub illo verbo iam allegato,[15] quod Summus Pontifex non se intromittit de feudo, 'cuius iudicium spectat ad regem, nisi forte' etc., notant iuriste quod consuetudo parificatur privilegio. Nam ex huiusmodi donacionis privilegio temporalia subsunt

---

1: induxit] inducit FV² 2: detinent] decet FV² 3: ecclesiasticum] et talis tollerancia tocius iterata quia consuetudo inducit isto consuetudo non potest esse iniusta quia ut sapientes aiunt nemo potest sibi iniustum facere dominus itaque secularis hoc tollerans non fecit sibi iniustum sed sua tollerancia aliqui ecclesie tribuit non quantum ad iurisdiccionem superiorem at primariam quia haec semper habet ecclesia per quam potest animadvertere in potestatem terrenam si delinquant sed quantum ad iurisdiccionem immediatam et executoriam sub quam temporalia subsunt potestati terrene *add. and del.* C 4: approbaverit] hanc consuetudine appellandi *add. and del.* C 5: sequens dominus] dominus sequens F 6: tolleranciam] tollerancia F 7: Non] emin *add.* FV² 8: subiectis secularibus ... temporalibus] *om.* V¹ 9: civili] tali FV¹ 10: appelletur] appellaretur V² 11: sumitur] *om.* V² 12: donacione] devocione PV¹ 13: eam] aliquibus temporalibus rebus *add.* C 14: in] *om.* F 15: allegato] allegando V²

the material, which does have a superior. If, therefore, the secular lord has suffered appeal to be made to an ecclesiastical judge in a temporal case, and if the ecclesiastical judge has approved of his granting such sufferance by receiving the appeal, then, if such sufferance establishes a custom, and especially if that custom is not unjust (for if it were unjust, contrary to the natural law, the longer its duration the worse it would be, according to the saying: 'The longer crimes hold the unhappy soul in bondage the more grievous they are'[1]) — if the custom is not unjust and has been approved by a superior, then, because the authority of custom is neither little nor light, it is fitting that it should acquire the force of law. If, therefore, the secular lord has suffered appeal to be made from him to an ecclesiastical judge in a temporal case, then, because such a custom is not unjust — for no one can do injustice to himself[2] — and, at least *de facto*, has been approved by a superior because the spiritual sword and the ecclesiastical judge has approved of such appeal by frequent acceptance, a subsequent secular lord will not be able to set aside the custom of appealing to the ecclesiastical judge established by the sufferance of his predecessor. And so it is said at X. 2:1:13: *Novit.* 'We do not intend to judge concerning the fief, the judgment of which rests with the king, unless perhaps a special privilege or some custom to the contrary overrides the common law.'[3] Thus, the Church will concern herself with temporal matters [which would otherwise be wholly] subject to secular lords if a custom exists such that, in such temporal cases, appeal may be made from a civil judge to an ecclesiastical judge.

And the fourth kind of case derived from a consideration of the earthly power arises when the Church exercises an immediate and executory jurisdiction in temporal cases because of a pious gift and devout grant made to the Church by secular princes themselves. Thus, if secular princes have conferred a special privilege upon some church or upon the See of Rome, which is lord and governor of all churches, with respect to some temporal goods and have given them to it, and especially if the lords or princes in question have made no specific reservation to themselves out of such a gift or grant, then those temporal goods will thenceforth pertain simply and absolutely to the Church, and she will have an immediate and executory jurisdiction over them, and, in cases involving such temporal goods, it will be possible to appeal without distinction and indiscriminately to the Supreme Pontiff.[4] Therefore, in the event of such a gift, the grant of the secular prince has the same effect upon the practice of making appeal as does the sufferance of appeals. And so, under that statement already cited — that the Supreme Pontiff should not concern himself with a fief, 'the judgment of which rests with the king, unless perhaps,' and so on — the jurists note that the establishing of a custom and the making of a grant have the same effect;[5] for temporal goods are brought under the [immediate and executory] jurisdiction of the Church [both] by the making of such a grant [and by the

1. I have not been able to identify the source of this quotation; but cf. Plato, *Phaedo* 81B–E.
2. Aristotle, *Nicomachean Ethics* 5:6 (1134^b10).
3. See Introduction, n. 21.
4. See Ch. XI.
5. See Bernard of Parma, *Glossa ordinaria ad Decretales Gregoriana* (Paris, 1561), on X. 2:1:13.

iurisdiccioni Ecclesie. Ideo Extra., *De appellacionibus*, *Si duobus*, dicitur quod
tenet appellacio in his que sunt subiecta ecclesiastice iurisdiccioni temporali. Sic
eciam tenet appellacio in temporalibus illis in quibus a civili iudice ad ecclesiasticum consuetum est appellari.

CAPITULUM VIII: *In quo narrantur speciales casus sumpti ex parte potestatis
ecclesiastice in quibus ad Ecclesiam pertinebit* [1] *iurisdiccionem in temporalibus
exercere.*

Narravimus quidem in quinto et in[2] sexto capitulo casus sumptos ex parte rerum
temporalium in quibus se de temporalibus Ecclesia intromittit. In septimo vero[3]
capitulo enarravimus[4] huiusmodi casus sumptos ex parte potestatis terrene. Sed in
hoc octo capitulo volumus tales enumerare casus sumptos ex parte potestatis ecclesiastice. Propter quod sciendum quod Extra., *Qui filii sint legitimi*, in capitulo
Per venerabilem circa hanc materiam, videlicet, quando Ecclesia exerceat iurisdiccionem temporalem,[5] quasi tria tanguntur: primo, quod hoc facit casualiter et
certis causis inspectis; secundo, quod hoc facit in difficilibus; tercio, quod hoc facit in ambiguis. Sed de difficilibus et ambiguis habemus[6] Deuteronomii XVII, ubi
dicitur: 'Si difficile et ambiguum apud [te] iudicium esse prospexeris[7] inter sanguinem et sanguinem, causam et causam, lepram et[8] lepram, et iudicium intra
portas tuas videris variari, surge' etc. Recurrebatur enim tunc ad Summum Sacerdotem,[9] et qui superbiens nolebat obedire imperio sacerdotis moriebatur, idest occidebatur, homo ille. A iudicibus ergo qui sedebant circa[10] portas civitatum[11] in
ambiguis et difficilibus recurrebatur[12] ad Summum Sacerdotem, ut habetur in[13]
Deuteronomio. Unde et Magister in *Historiis* illud capitulum Deuteronomii in quo
de hoc agitur intitulat 'De appellacione fienda ad Summum Sacerdotem.'[14]

Et licet illa tria tacta in capitulo *Per venerabilem*, videlicet quod certis causis
inspectis et in difficilibus et ambiguis iurisdiccionem temporalem exercet Ecclesia, possent[15] ad unum et idem trahi, ut ille 'certe cause' inspiciende essent cause
difficiles, et quia essent difficiles[16] ideo essent ambigue, quia difficultatem sequitur ambiguitas, ut in difficilibus alii alia opinentur.[17] Possumus tamen, si volumus,[18] quemlibet[19] illorum casuum[20] per se adaptare et dicere esse tres casus
sumptos ex parte potestatis ecclesiastice in quibus Ecclesia iurisdiccionem temporalem exercet.

Primo in casibus inopinatis[21] et particularibus, qui quasi possunt dici extra leges, in quibus ex certis causis et casualiter de temporalibus se Ecclesia intromittit;

1: *pertinebit*] pertinentibus F   2: in] *om.* F   3: vero] *om.* C   4: enarravimus] enumeravimus F
5: circa hanc ... temporalem] *om.* F   6: habemus] haberemus FV²   7: prospexeris] perspexeris F
8: et] non *add.* CPV¹V²   9: enim tunc ... Sacerdotem] *om.* V²   10: circa] intra F   11: civita-
tum] civitatis F   12: recurrebatur] recurrebant F   13: in] *om.* FV²   14: Sacerdotem] ut habetur
deuteronomio *add.* F   15: possent] possunt V²   16: et quia essent difficiles] *om.* C
17: opinentur] opinetur V²   18: volumus] nolumus C   19: quemlibet] ad quodlibet CFV²
20: casuum] casum F   21: inopinatis] opinatis F

establishing of a customary right of appeal]. Thus, at X. 2:28:7: *Si duobus*, it is said that an appeal is valid in those matters which are subject to the Church's temporal jurisdiction; so also, [it is said in the same place that] an appeal is valid in those temporal cases in which there is a customary right of appeal from a civil to an ecclesiastical judge.[1]

CHAPTER VIII: *In which are described the special cases derived from a consideration of the ecclesiastical power in which it will pertain to the Church to exercise jurisdiction in temporal matters.*

In chapters V and VI, we have described the cases derived from a consideration of temporal things in which the Church intervenes in temporal disputes; and in chapter VII we have described those cases derived from a consideration of the earthly power. In this eighth chapter, however, we wish to enumerate such cases as are derived from a consideration of the ecclesiastical power. Hence, it must be known that at X. 4:17:13: *Per venerabilem*, some three aspects of this question — that is, of when the Church exercises a temporal jurisdiction — are touched upon. First, it is said that she does this occasionally and on the examination of certain causes; second, that she does this in difficult cases; third, that she does this in doubtful cases.[2] But we have also the testimony of Deuteronomy 17 concerning difficult and doubtful cases, where it is said: 'If you shall perceive there to be a difficult and doubtful matter among you as between blood and blood, cause and cause, leprosy and leprosy, and if you shall see that the judgments within your gates are at variance, arise,' and so on.[3] For recourse was then had to the Supreme Priest, and that man who, being proud, refused to obey the command of the priest, died: that is, was slain. Therefore, as is established in Deuteronomy, recourse was had in difficult and doubtful cases from the judges who sat at the gates of the cities to the Supreme Priest. And so, in the *Historia*, the Master himself gives to that chapter of Deuteronomy in which this is discussed the title, 'Concerning the Appeal which should be made to the Supreme Priest.'[4]

And although these three aspects touched upon in the chapter *Per venerabilem* — namely, that the Church will exercise a temporal jurisdiction on the examination of certain causes and in difficult and doubtful cases — might be brought down to one and the same thing (for the 'certain causes' examined would be difficult cases and, because they were difficult, they would therefore be doubtful; for doubtfulness flows from difficulty, inasmuch as different men give different opinions in difficult cases), nonetheless, if we so wish, we can consider each of these cases in its own right, and say that there are three kinds of case derived from a consideration of the ecclesiastical power in which the Church exercises a temporal jurisdiction.

First, there are the unusual and particular cases which can as it were be said to fall outside the laws, by reason of which the Church intervenes in temporal affairs

1. See Introduction, n. 59.
2. See Introduction, n. 60.
3. Deut. 17:8–12.
4. Peter Comestor, *Historia scholastica*, PL 198:1253 cf. Pt. I, Ch. VIII, p. 53.

secundo, hoc facit in casibus difficilibus; tercio in casibus ambiguis: qui omnes casus sumuntur ex ipsa plenitudine potestatis que in Ecclesia residet. Ex qua plenitudine potestatis ista[1] Ecclesia[2] tripliciter se habet[3] ad leges et ad iura: primo, quia eius est leges condere; secundo, quia ad eam spectat leges conditas populis fidelibus dare; tercio, quia ad eam pertinet leges primo conditas et postea gentibus datas exponere et interpretari. Ideo dicitur in Deuteronomio: 'Cum videris verba iudicum[4] variari, surge, accede ad locum quem elegerit Dominus Deus tuus,'[5] etc. Innuitur[6] enim ibi quod quando variantur verba iudicum, et per consequens quando variatur iudicium,[7] quia unus iudex iudicat unum et alius iudicat aliud, tunc debemus accedere ad locum quem elegit Dominus[8] et debemus[9] habere recursum ad Summum Sacerdotem.

Possumus autem dicere quod propter tria consueverunt variari[10] verba iudicum vel consueverunt variari[11] iudicia iudicancium. Primo, quando contingunt aliqua que sunt quasi extra leges; nam cum leges sunt[12] quedam regule agibilium, secundum quas regulas debemus alia metiri et disponere, cum contingunt aliqua que sunt extra leges vel que non continentur sub legibus, tunc variatur iudicium[13] iudicancium, et diversi[14] diversimode[15] iudicabunt. Variantur ergo iudicia iudicancium cum contingunt aliqua que sunt extra leges.

Secundo, variantur cum contingunt aliqua[16] in quibus difficile est observare leges. Nam possunt aliquando[17] contingere aliqua que, etsi non sunt extra leges sed continentur in legibus, illa forte tangunt magnos reges et magnos principes; et ideo difficile est in eis observare leges[18] quia propter civilem potenciam quam habent reges et principes quilibet timet dicere aliqua contra eos.[19] In talibus ergo, et si non racione ignorancie, racione tamen timoris, ut quia difficile est tunc observare leges, variabuntur iudicia iudicancium, et racione timoris varii varia iudicabunt.

Tercio, consueverunt variari iudicia iudicancium racione ambiguitatis, ut cum contingunt aliqua que, etsi non sunt extra[20] leges, etsi non est difficile in eis observare leges, tamen forte de illis ambigue loquuntur leges.

Primus itaque modus, quod non omnia contineant leges,[21] pertinet ad legum condicionem, quia tales sunt condite leges quod non omnia continentur sub legibus. Secundus autem[22] modus, quando contingunt aliqua in quibus difficile est observare leges, pertinet ad legum dacionem, quia leges non solum sunt date parvis, sed eciam sunt date magnis, iuxta illud: 'Ita magnum iudicabit ut parvum.' Et quia leges aliquando tangunt magnos viros, propter hoc[23] homines formidant et timent; ideo[24] difficile est tunc observare leges. Tercius quidem modus, quando contingunt aliqua

---

1: ista] *del.* C   2: residet. Ex … Ecclesia] *om.* V[2]   3: se habet] habet se FV[2]   4: iudicum] *om.*
FV[2] *marg.* P   5: tuus] *om.* V[2]   6: Innuitur] monetur F   7: et per … iudicium] *om.* V[2]   8: Dominus] deus V[2]   9: accedere ad … debemus] *om.* F   10: variari] viciari FV[2]   11: variari]
viciari FV[2]   12: sunt] sint V[1]V[2]   13: variatur iudicium] variantur iudicia FV[2]   14: diversi] omnes
F   15: diversimode] cum contingunt aliqua *add.* F   16: que sunt … aliqua] *om.* C   17: aliquando] aliunde F   18: leges] et *add.* F   19: eos] *om.* C   20: extra] contra F   21: Primus
itaque … leges] *om.* V[2]   22: autem] *om.* FV[2]   23: propter hoc] *om.* C   24: ideo] propter hoc C

for certain causes and occasionally. Second, she does this in difficult cases; third, in doubtful cases. And all these cases are derived from that fullness of power which resides in the Church, by reason of which fullness of power the Church stands in a threefold relation to statutes and to laws: first, because it is her task to establish laws; second, because it rests with her to promulgate these established laws to the faithful peoples; and, third, because it pertains to her to expound and interpret the laws which she has first established and then promulgated to the nations. And so it is said in Deuteronomy: 'When you shall see the words of the judges to be at variance, arise and go to the place which the Lord your God shall choose,' and so on. For it is there intimated that when the words of the judges are at variance and, consequently, when judgment is divided because one judge judges in one way and another judges in another, we should then go to the place which the Lord has chosen, and we should have recourse to the Supreme Priest.

But we can say that there are three reasons why the words of the judges are wont to vary or why the judgments of the judges are apt to differ. The first is when certain cases arise which are as it were outside the laws. For since laws are certain rules governing what can be done, according to which rules we must measure and dispose other things, when certain cases arise which are outside the laws or which are not contained under the laws, the judgment of the judges may then be divided, and different judges will judge in different ways. The judgments of the judges may be at variance, therefore, when certain cases arise which are outside the laws.

Second, they may be at variance when certain cases arise in which it is difficult to observe the laws. For it is sometimes possible for certain cases to arise which, even though they are not outside the laws, but are contained within the laws, perhaps touch great kings and great princes. And so it is difficult to observe the laws in these cases, for every man is afraid to say anything against the kings and princes because of the civil might which they have. In such cases, therefore — even if not by reason of ignorance, nonetheless by reason of fear, because of which it is then difficult to observe the laws — the judgments of the judges will be at variance and, by reason of fear, different judges will judge differently.

Third, the judgments of the judges are wont to vary by reason of doubtfulness, as when certain cases arise which, although they are not outside the laws, and although it is not difficult to observe the laws in them, are nonetheless perhaps such that the laws speak ambiguously concerning them.

The first reason, then, that the laws do not contain all things, pertains to the establishing of the laws, because the laws are established in such a way that not all things are contained under the laws. And the second reason, when certain cases arise in which it is difficult to observe the laws, pertains to the promulgation of the laws, because the laws are promulgated not only to the small, but they are given also to the great, according to what is written: 'Thus will he judge the great as the small.'[1] And since the laws sometimes touch great persons, men are stricken with terror and fear because of this, so that it is then difficult to observe the laws. And the third reason, when certain cases arise concerning which the laws speak

---

1. Deut. 1:17, but quoted inaccurately.

de quibus ambigue loquuntur leges, pertinet ad legum interpretacionem, quia tunc oportet interpretari leges. Et quia cuius est leges condere[1] eius est leges dare et eius est leges datas interpretari, si iudicia iudicum variantur, sive hoc sit ex condicione legum, quia contingunt aliqua que sunt extra leges, sive sit ex dacione legum, ut quia contingunt aliqua in quibus difficile est observare leges, sive hoc sit ex interpretacione legum, ut quia contingunt aliqua in quibus ambigue loquuntur leges, totum ad Summum Pontificem pertinebit.

Sed dices quod et imperatorum est leges condere et leges conditas[2] dare et leges datas[3] interpretari. Sed,[4] ut supra diximus, gladius est sub gladio et principatus sub principatu; et ideo, si ad principes spectat leges condere, quia 'quod principi placuit legis vigorem habet,' cum principatus principatui famulatur, oportet quod leges legibus famulentur. Ideo Gregorius Nazianzenus, ut[5] habetur Distinccione X, Capitulo *Suscipitis*, loquens imperatoribus Constantinopolitanis,[6] ait: 'Lex Christi sacerdotali vos[7] subicit potestati; dedit enim nobis potestatem, dedit principatum multo[8] perfecciorem principatibus vestris,[9] quod si[10] non recipiatur eius auctoritas, racio[11] tamen non poterit habere repulsam.' Nam racionabile est quod terra subiciatur celo et quod caro spiritui famuletur. Principatus quidem ecclesiasticus est spiritualis et celestis, secularis autem[12] principatus carnalis et terrenus dici[13] potest.[14]

Dicamus[15] ergo quod verba que tanguntur in illa decretali *Per venerabilem*, videlicet quod iurisdiccionem temporalem[16] exercet Ecclesia casualiter et certis causis inspectis, et quod exercet huiusmodi iurisdiccionem in difficilibus et in ambiguis, possunt quasi ad unum et idem trahi, ut dicamus: quod illud casuale et illas[17] certas causas inspicere est cum occurrat[18] aliquid difficile; et si est difficile, erit ambiguum, quia in difficilibus consueverunt homines dubitare. Vel possumus dicere quod non confuse et indistincte sunt illa verba accipienda, sed quodlibet est per se ponderandum, quia aliud est temporalem iurisdiccionem exercere casualiter et certis causis inspectis, quod tangit legum condicionem; et aliud est hoc agere in difficilibus, quod potest pertinere ad legum dacionem;[19] et aliud est hoc agere[20] in ambiguis, quod pertinet[21] ad legum interpretacionem. Et, secundum hoc,[22] omnia prefata verba non trahuntur ad unum et idem, sed sunt tria quedam per se distincta. Immo, si volumus, dicere possumus quod prefata verba non solum sunt tria quedam per se distincta, sed eciam sunt quatuor quedam per se distincta. Dicemus enim quod aliud est temporalem iurisdiccionem exercere casualiter, et aliud certis

---

1: leges condere] condere leges F   2: conditas] datas *add.* V[2]   3: datas] *del.* C   4: Sed] *om.* FP
5: ut] et FPV[1]V[2]   6: Constantinopolitanis] constantinopolis CF   7: vos] nos *mss*   8: multo]
nullo V[2]   9: vestris] nostris FPV[1]V[2]   10: si] *om.* FV[2]   11: racio] racione F   12: autem]
quidem C   13: dici] *del.* F   14: potest] potestate F   15: Dicamus] dicemus F   16: iurisdiccionem temporalem] temporalem iurisdiccionem CF   17: illas] illa V[2]   18: occurrat] occurrit CFV[2]   19: dacionem] donacionem V[1]   20: agere] facere FPV[1]V[2]   21: pertinet] patet V[2]
22: hoc] hec C

ambiguously, pertains to the interpretation of the laws, because the laws must then be interpreted. And because it rests with him whose task it is to establish the laws also to promulgate the laws, and, having promulgated the laws, to interpret them, then, if the judgments of the judges are at variance — whether this is due to the establishing of the laws (because certain cases arise which are outside the laws); or whether this is due to the promulgation of the laws (because certain cases arise in which it is difficult to observe the laws); or whether this is due to the interpretation of the laws (because certain cases arise in which the laws speak ambiguously) — such a case will pertain entirely to the Supreme Pontiff.

But you will say that it belongs also to emperors to establish laws and to promulgate established laws and, having promulgated the laws, to interpret them. As we have said above, however, sword is under sword and one ruling power is under the other.[1] And so, although it rests with princes to establish laws — since 'what has pleased the prince has the force of law'[2] — nonetheless, because the one ruling power is the servant of the other, it must be that the laws of the one are the servants of the laws of the other. Thus, as we read in the *Decretum*, Dist 10, c. *Suscipitisne*, Gregory Nazianzenus, speaking to the Byzantine emperors, says: 'The law of Christ places you under the priestly power; for He has given power to us: He has given us a ruling power far more perfect than your ruling powers.'[3] And even if his authority be not accepted, it will still not be possible to reject the testimony of reason. For reason indicates that earth is placed under heaven and that flesh is the servant of spirit and that the ruling power of the Church is spiritual and heavenly whereas secular ruling power can be called fleshly and earthly.

Let us say, therefore, that the words which occur in the decretal *Per venerabilem* — namely, that the Church exercises a temporal jurisdiction occasionally and on the examination of certain causes, and that she exercises such jurisdiction in difficult and doubtful cases — can as it were be brought down to one and the same thing. Thus, we may say that the exercise of such jurisdiction occasionally and on the examination of certain causes occurs when some difficult matter arises and that, if it is difficult, it will be doubtful, for men are apt to experience doubt in difficult cases. Alternatively, we can say that these words must not be taken in a confused and undifferentiated manner, but that each must be weighed in its own right. For it is one thing to exercise a temporal jurisdiction occasionally and on the examination of certain causes, which touches the establishing of the laws; and another to do so in difficult cases, which can pertain to the promulgation of the laws; and another to do so in doubtful cases, which pertains to the interpretation of the laws. And, on this view, the foregoing words may not all be reduced to one and the same thing, but constitute three statements distinct in their own right. Indeed, if we wish, we can say not merely that the foregoing words constitute three statements distinct in their own right, but even that they constitute four distinct statements. For we shall say that it is one thing to exercise a temporal jurisdiction occasionally, and another to do so on

---

1. E.g. Pt. I, Ch. IV; Pt. II, Ch. VI; Pt. II, Ch. XIII.
2. Justinian, *Institutiones*, ed. P. Krüger (repr. Zurich: Weidmann, 1970), 2:2:6.
3. Dist. 10, c. 6 (CIC I:20).

causis inspectis, et aliud in difficilibus, et aliud in ambiguis. Utrum autem omnia hec intellexerit qui illam decretalem condidit, nihil ad nos. Sufficit autem nobis quod omnia hec vera[1] sint et, si vera sint, quod proficua sint.

Prosequamur ergo nostrum propositum[2] et dicamus quod quia ad Summum Pontificem spectat leges condere, quia etsi alii leges condunt, oportet quod ille leges istis legibus famulentur. Ideo ad eum spectabit exercere temporalem iurisdiccionem casualiter et certis causis inspectis, quod accidit, ut patet per habita, cum aliqua contingunt que sunt[3] extra leges. Esse autem aliqua extra leges dupliciter contingit: vel quia de illis non se intromiserunt leges et non tractaverunt de eis sufficienter[4] leges, vel quia in illis non sunt observande leges.[5] Si ergo Ecclesia volet, sic[6] se habentibus condicionibus, temporalem iurisdiccionem exercebit. Quia inopinatos casus decidere ad principem pertinebit; ergo ad Ecclesiam, de qua potest exponi quod dicitur Danielis VII,[7] 'Omnes reges servient ei.'[8]

Ecclesia igitur[9] temporalem iurisdiccionem casualiter exercebit cum contingunt aliqui casus[10] qui sunt extra leges quia[11] non sunt sufficienter determinati per leges. Secundo,[12] exercebit hoc non solum casualiter, cum contingunt aliqua que non sunt sufficienter determinata per leges,[13] sed eciam certis causis inspectis, cum contingunt aliqua que, etsi sunt determinata per leges,[14] non tamen in illis sunt observande leges. Nam secundum dicta sapientum leges indigent lege,[15] et leges dicunt universaliter quod non est universaliter. Non enim[16] semper et in omni casu et universaliter sunt observande leges, sed possunt contingere aliqua in quibus sunt plicande leges; sed hoc ad solum principem pertinebit, cuius est non solum secundum leges, sed eciam de legibus iudicare. Unde Augustinus in *De vera religione*[17] ait quod in istis temporalibus legibus, cum huiusmodi leges fuerint institute atque firmate, non licebit iudici iudicare de ipsis, sed secundum ipsas. Ad iudices ergo et ad homines communiter non spectat iudicare de legibus, sed secundum leges; sed ad ipsum conditorem legum spectabit non solum iudicare secundum leges, sed eciam iudicare de legibus.

Ergo ipsa condicio legum remittit[18] temporalem iurisdiccionem ad Summum Pontificem vel casualiter, cum contingunt aliqui casus qui non sunt sufficienter determinati per leges; vel legum[19] condicio remittit huiusmodi[20] iurisdiccionem ad Summum Principantem[21] non solum casualiter,[22] sed facit hoc certis causis inspectis, cum[23] contingunt aliqua in quibus propter certas causas non sunt observande

---

1: vera] verba F verba *del.* C   2: propositum] negocium CV[1]   3: cum aliqua ... sunt] *om.* FV[2]
4: de eis sufficienter] sufficienter de eis CFV[2]   5: leges] possunt enim apparere aliqui casus in litigio rerum temporalium de quibus casibus non sunt sufficienter determinati per leges *add. and del.* C
6: sic] si V[2]   7: VII] viii° FV[2]   8: ei] et obedient *add. and del.* C   9: igitur] ergo C   10: aliqui casus] casus aliqui C   11: quia] et C   12: Secundo] ecclesia *add.* C temporalem iurisdiccionem *add. and del.* (*after* ecclesia) C   13: Secundo exercebit ... leges] *om.* F   14: sed eciam ... leges] *om.* V[1]   15: lege] rege F   16: enim] est FV[2]   17: *De vera religione*] de natura religionis F
18: remittit] *om.* V[2]   19: vel casualiter, ... legum] *om.* C   20: huiusmodi] *om.* V[2]   21: Principantem] principem FV[2]   22: condicio remittit ... casualiter] *del.* C   23: cum] tamen F

the examination of certain causes, and another to do so in difficult cases, and another to do so in doubtful cases. But whether he who composed that decretal intended all these distinctions is neither here nor there; for it is sufficient for us that they are all true and that, if they are true, they are profitable.

Let us pursue our proposition, then, and say that, because it rests with the Supreme Pontiff to establish laws — since, even though other men establish laws, it must be that their laws are the servants of his laws — it will therefore rest with him to exercise a temporal jurisdiction occasionally and on the examination of certain causes; which, as is clear from what we have said, occurs when certain cases arise which are outside the laws. But such cases are outside the laws for two reasons: either because the laws have not concerned themselves with them and the laws have not treated of them sufficiently, or because the laws should not be construed strictly in them [by reason of some unusual circumstance]. If the Church so wishes, therefore, she will exercise a temporal jurisdiction when matters are in this condition. For it will pertain to a supreme authority to decide unusual cases, and therefore to the Church, with reference to whom what is said in Daniel 7 can be interpreted: 'All kings shall serve him.'[1]

Thus, [first,] the Church will exercise a temporal jurisdiction occasionally, when certain cases arise which are outside the laws because they are not sufficiently determined by the laws. Second, she will exercise such jurisdiction not only occasionally, when certain cases arise which are not sufficiently determined by the laws, but also on the examination of certain causes, when certain cases arise which, although they are determined by the laws, are nonetheless such that the laws should not be construed strictly in them. For, according to the sayings of the wise, [positive] laws need [the correction of a higher form of] law; for the laws state universally that which does not apply universally.[2] For the laws should not always be construed strictly in every case and universally: rather, some cases can arise in which the laws must be modified [to fit unusual circumstances]. But this will pertain solely to a supreme authority whose task it is to judge not only according to the laws, but also the laws themselves. And so, with regard to temporal laws, Augustine says in *De vera religione* that when such laws have been instituted and confirmed it will not be lawful for the judges to pass judgment on them, but only according to them.[3] Therefore, it does not rest with the judges and with ordinary men to pass judgment on the laws themselves, but only according to the laws. But with the establisher of laws himself it will rest not only to judge according to the laws, but also to pass judgment on the laws themselves.

Therefore, [some difficulty arising from] the establishing of the laws remits temporal jurisdiction to the Supreme Pontiff occasionally, when certain cases arise which are not sufficiently determined by the laws. Again, [some difficulty arising from] the establishing of the laws remits such jurisdiction to the Supreme Pontiff not only occasionally, but on the examination of certain causes: when certain matters arise in which, due to certain causes, the laws should not be strictly construed. Therefore, if

---

1. Dan 7:27.
2. Cf. Aristotle, *Nicomachean Ethics* 5:10 (1137^{b}10).
3. *De vera religione* 31 (PL 34:148).

leges. Ergo si sunt casus extra leges qui[1] non sunt determinati per leges, vel quia certis causis inspectis non sunt in eis observande leges,[2] qui casus pertinent ad legum condicionem; vel si sunt casus in quibus difficile est observare leges quantum ad legum dacionem; vel si sunt casus in quibus ambigue loquuntur leges, quod spectat ad legum interpretacionem: iurisdiccionem exercebit Ecclesia temporalem; que omnia fundantur super plenitudine potestatis quam[3] apud Ecclesiam dicimus residere.

Complete itaque narrati sunt decem casus in quibus Ecclesia iurisdiccionem exercet temporalem, quorum tres sumuntur ex parte rerum temporalium, quatuor ex parte potestatis terrene et tres ex parte potestatis[4] ecclesiastice. Aliqui tamen istarum casuum, ut diximus, sunt pregnantes. Nam qui sunt pregnantes[5] de casibus dictis in aliis capitulis supra tetigimus; in hoc autem capitulo pregnans est casus primus, videlicet, cum dicimus quod Ecclesia temporalem iurisdiccionem exercet casualiter et certis causis inspectis. Nam aliud est, ut diximus, exercere temporalem iurisdiccionem casualiter cum aliqui casus emergunt qui non sunt sufficienter determinati per leges, et aliud cum aliqui casus emergunt in quibus, certis causis inspectis, non sunt observande leges.

Omnes tamen hii casus in quibus dicimus[6] quod Ecclesia potest temporalem iurisdiccionem exercere, undecumque illi casus sumantur, non sunt referendi ad posse Ecclesie simpliciter et absolutum, quia,[7] ut patebit in ultimo capitulo, huiusmodi posse est sine pondere, numero et mensura; sed referendi sunt ad posse Ecclesie ut est quibusdam regulis regulatum. Nam licet Summus Sacerdos sit animal sine capistro et freno et sit homo supra positivas leges, ipse tamen debet sibi imponere capistrum et frenum et vivere secundum conditas leges, et nisi casus emergant et certe cause requirant, debet observare conditas leges. Nam et leges quas ipse condidit observare debet, quia, ut in alia sciencia traditur, legis positivus debet esse[8] legis observativus.[9]

CAPITULUM IX: *Quid est plenitudo potestatis, et quod in Summo Pontifice veraciter potestatis residet plenitudo.*

Quoniam in multis capitulis locuti sumus de plenitudine potestatis, ideo in presenti capitulo volumus declarare quid est plenitudo potestatis. Declarabimus eciam quod[10] huiusmodi plenitudo est in Summo Pontifice, propter quod[11] suum posse est sine numero, pondere et mensura, ut in ultimo capitulo apparebit.

Possent autem multe declaraciones adduci ad ostendendum quid[12] est plenitudo potestatis; sed sufficiat ad presens hoc solum ostendere: quod plenitudo potestatis est in aliquo agente quando illud agens potest sine causa[13] secunda quicquid potest

1: qui] quia V² 2: Ergo si … leges] *om.* C 3: quam] que F 4: terrene et … potestatis] *om.* FV² 5: Nam qui sunt pregnantes] *om.* CFV² 6: dicimus] diximus F 7: quia] quo F 8: debet esse] est FPV² 9: observativus] observandus V² 10: quod] *om.* V² 11: quod] quam C plenitudinem potestatis *add. and del.* C dici potest quod *add.* C 12: quid] aliquid V² 13: causa] *om.* V²

there are cases outside the laws which are not determined by the laws, or if, on the examination of certain causes, they are [seen to be] such that the laws should not be strictly construed in them, which cases pertain to the establishing of the law; or if, because of the promulgation of the laws [to great and small alike], there are cases in which it is difficult to observe the laws [by reason of fear]; or if there are cases in which the laws speak ambiguously, which is a matter having to do with the interpretation of the laws: the Church will exercise a temporal jurisdiction. And all these cases are founded upon the fullness of power which we say resides in the Church.

In conclusion, then: ten cases in which the Church will exercise a temporal jurisdiction have been described. Three of these are derived from a consideration of temporal things, four from a consideration of the earthly power, and three from a consideration of the ecclesiastical power. Nonetheless, some of these cases, as we have said, are pregnant. For we have touched above, in other chapters, upon cases which are said to be pregnant;[1] and, in this chapter, the first kind of case — that is, when we say that the Church will exercise a temporal jurisdiction occasionally and on the examination of certain causes — is pregnant. For, as we have said, it is one thing to exercise a temporal jurisdiction occasionally when certain cases arise which are not sufficiently determined by the laws, and another to do so when certain cases emerge in which, on the examination of certain causes, [it becomes clear that] the laws should not be strictly construed.

Regardless of whence these cases are derived, however, when we say that, in all these cases, the Church can exercise a temporal jurisdiction [only occasionally], this must be understood as referring not to the power of the Church simply and absolutely (for, as will appear in the final chapter, that power [considered absolutely] is without limit of weight, number, and measure): rather, it must be understood as referring to the Church's power insofar as it is governed by certain rules. For although the Supreme Priest is a creature without halter and bridle and is a man above positive laws, he ought nonetheless to impose halter and bridle upon himself, and live according to the established laws; and, unless special cases emerge and certain causes require otherwise, he should observe the established laws. For even he should observe those laws which he has established, since, as is taught in another science, he who establishes the law should observe the law.[2]

CHAPTER IX: *What fullness of power is, and that fullness of power truly resides in the Supreme Pontiff.*

Because we have spoken in many chapters of fullness of power, we therefore wish in the present chapter to show what fullness of power is. Also, we shall show that there is such fullness in the Supreme Pontiff, by reason of which his power is without limit of number, weight, and measure, as will appear in the final chapter.

Many illustrations might be adduced to show what fullness of power is. For our present purpose, however, let it suffice to show only this: that fullness of power resides in some agent when that agent can do without a secondary cause whatever it

1. See esp. Ch. VII; and see p. 347 for what is meant by this expression.
2. See, e.g., Aristotle, *Politics* 3:11 (1282^{b}5).

cum[1] causa secunda. Quod si agens aliquod[2] non habet tale posse, consequens est quod non habeat plenum posse, quia non habet posse[3] in quo reservatur omne posse. Eo itaque modo quo Summus Pontifex habet posse[4] in quo reservatur omne posse,[5] dicimus ipsum[6] habere plenum posse. Et ut per hec naturalia que videmus in gubernacione mundi possimus descendere ad gubernacionem hominum,[7] dicemus quod in celo et in quocumque agente secundo[8] non est plenitudo potestatis, quia non potest celum sine causa secunda quod potest cum causa secunda: ut si celum et leo faciunt ad generacionem leonis, non posset celum sine leone producere leonem, nec posset[9] sine equo producere equum. In ipso autem Deo est plenitudo potestatis, quia quicquid potest cum causa secunda potest sine causa secunda, ita quod posse omnium agencium reservatur in primo agente,[10] scilicet in Deo.[11] Nam in produccione mundi produxit hominem sine homine precedente et equum sine equo precedente. Nunc[12] autem producit equum mediante equo, sed[13] si vellet et quando vellet[14] sine semine;[15] et bovem mediante bove,[16] sed sine bove posset facere bovem.[17] Posset enim facere de trunco vitulum, vel de nihilo facere vitulum, et sicut vellet, sic res ageret. Et quamvis omnia possit, ipse tamen sic administrat res ut eas proprios cursus agere sinat. Facit tamen Deus aliquando[18] miraculum vel eciam miracula,[19] ut agat preter communem cursum[20] nature et non agat secundum communes leges nature inditas.

Sic et Summus Pontifex, quantum ad posse quod est in Ecclesia, habet plenitudinem potestatis et potest sine causa secunda quod potest cum causa secunda:[21] ut si eleccio episcopi dependet ab institucione Summi Pontificis[22] qualiter debeat fieri eleccio prelatorum et quomodo eligentes debeant se habere et quantum[23] ad zelum et quantum ad meritum et quantum ad numerum, ut quantus debeat esse numerus eligencium et quales debent esse eligentes ad hoc, quod electus sit rite assumptus; itaque huiusmodi eleccio dependet a Summo Pontifice statuente et ordinante eleccionis modum sicut produccio rerum naturalium tamquam a causa primaria dependet a Deo, qui indidit rebus naturalibus suas leges, qualiter agant et qualiter suos producant effectus. Dependet eciam eleccio prelati ab assensu canonicorum et ab eleccione eorum[24] tamquam a causa secunda, sicut et produccio rerum naturalium dependet ab ipsis rebus naturalibus que sunt sub uno agente primo, videlicet sub Deo.

Vere ergo in Summo Pontifice, quantum ad posse quod est in Ecclesia, residet potestatis plenitudo, quia potest sine causa secunda quod potest cum causa secunda.[25] Posset enim providere cuicumque[26] ecclesie sine eleccione capituli, quod faciendo ageret non secundum leges communes inditas, sed secundum[27] plenitudinem

---

1: cum] *om.* C   2: aliquod] *om.* F   3: posse] *om.* V²   4: consequens est, ... posse *om.* C
5: Eo itaque ... posse] *om.* V¹   6: ipsum] *om.* V²   7: hominum] aliorum omnium F   8: secundo]
del. F   9: posset] equus *add.* PF   10: in primo agente] in primo agere vel agente P (vel agente *in
marg.*) in ipso agere vel agente V¹   11: scilicet in Deo] *om.* CPV¹   12: Nunc] nec V²   13: sed]
nunc etiam *del.* C   nunc eciam P   eciam V²   14: et quando vellet] *om.* V²   15: semine] posset
facere *add.* V¹   16: et bovem mediante bove] bovis potest facere bovem C   17: sed sine ...
bovem] *om.* CV¹   18: Deus aliquando] aliquando Deus F   19: miracula] mirabilia C
20: cursum] usum PV¹   21: quod potest ... secunda] *om.* V²   22: Pontificis] instituentis et ordinantis *add.* C   23: et quantum] *om.* C   24: et ab eleccione eorum] *om.* F   25: quod potest ...
secunda] *om.* V²   26: cuicumque] cuique V²   27: secundum] suam *add.* FV²

can do with a secondary cause. For if an agent does not have such power, it follows that it does not have a full power because it does not have a power in which all power is contained. Thus, inasmuch as the Supreme Pontiff has a power in which all power is contained, we say that he has a full power. And, so that we may pass to the government of men by way of those natural phenomena which we see in the government of the world, we shall say that fullness of power does not reside in the heaven [i.e. in the natural order] nor in any secondary agent whatsoever; for the heaven cannot do without a secondary cause what it can do with a secondary cause. For example, although the heaven and a lion bring about the generation of a lion, the heaven could not produce a lion without a lion, nor could it produce a horse without a horse. In God Himself, however, there is fullness of power, for whatever He can do with a secondary cause He can do without a secondary cause. And so the power of all agents is contained in the Primary Agent, that is, in God; for, in bringing forth the world, He brought forth a man without a preexisting man and a horse without a preexisting horse. Now, indeed, He brings forth a horse by means of a horse, but, if He wished and when He wished, He could do this without seed; and an ox by means of an ox, but He could make an ox without an ox, for He could make a calf out of a block of wood, or He could make a calf out of nothing, and the result would come about just as He willed.[1] And, although He can do all things, He nonetheless directs things in such a way that He allows them to pursue their own courses. Sometimes, however, God performs a miracle, or even miracles, so that He may act beyond the ordinary course of nature and not according to the established common laws of nature.

So also, to such extent as there is power within the Church, the Supreme Pontiff has fullness of power, and he can do without a secondary cause whatever he can do with a secondary cause. For example, the election of a bishop depends upon the ordinance of the Supreme Pontiff as to how the election of prelates is to be conducted and as to what manner of men the electors should be in respect of zeal and merit and number, so that there should be such a number of electors, and electors of such a kind, as to ensure that he who is elected is properly chosen. Thus, such election depends upon the establishing and ordaining of the mode of election by the Supreme Pontiff [as by a primary cause], just as the production of natural things depends upon God as a primary cause, Who establishes His laws for natural things, which regulate how they act and how they produce their effects. And the election of a prelate depends also upon the assent of the Canons and upon their choice as upon a secondary cause, just as the production of natural things depends upon natural things themselves, which are under one primary agent: that is, under God.

Truly, therefore, to such extent as there is power within the Church, fullness of power resides in the Supreme Pontiff; for he can do without a secondary cause whatever he can do with a secondary cause. For he could make provision [of a bishop] for any church without election by the chapter, and, by so doing, he would not act according to the established common laws, but according to his fullness of power.

---

1. Cf. Pt. I, Ch. VI, p. 33.

potestatis. Fit enim, ut diximus, eleccio prelati tamquam a causa primaria a Summo Pontifice statuente[1] qualiter eleccio fiat, et a causa secunda, videlicet ab eleccione eligencium iuxta formam eis datam.[2] Posset tamen Summus Pontifex sine huiusmodi causa secunda, idest sine eleccione eligencium, providere cuicumque ecclesie de prelato. Et quod dictum est de eleccione prelati veritatem habet de aliis que fiunt in Ecclesia: quod potest Summus Pontifex sine aliis agentibus agere[3] tamquam ille qui[4] habet plenitudinem potestatis, in quo totum posse Ecclesie dignoscitur residere.

Advertere tamen debet Summus Pontifex quod[5] Deus, qui totum habet posse non solum condicionaliter, scilicet[6] respectu huius vel respectu[7] illius, sed simpliciter, tamen, ne sint supervacua opera sapiencie sue, quasi semper agit secundum leges quas indidit rebus et quasi semper observat leges[8] ut agat effectus secundorum agencium mediantibus secundis agentibus. Calefacit enim mediante igne, et[9] infrigidat mediante aqua, quoniam et[10] secundum leges inditas rebus fieri non potest quod existens in igne non calefiat et existens in aqua frigida non infrigidetur, et eciam secundum has leges fieri non potest quod pergens super aquas non madefaciat[11] sibi pedes. Aliquando tamen, sed raro, facit preter has communes leges quod existens in igne non comburitur[12] et quod quis pergat siccis pedibus super aquam.

Sic et Summus Pontifex:[13] suum est statuere leges qualiter debet Ecclesia gubernari, et secundum has leges debet Ecclesiam gubernare et debet permittere quod capitula suas elecciones faciant et prelati suas acciones exerceant et quod alii qui sunt in Ecclesia secundum formam sibi datam sua opera perficiant. Ex causa tamen racionabili potest preter istas communes leges[14] sine aliis agentibus agere, quia posse omnium agencium reservatur in ipso, ut sit in ipso omne posse omnium agencium in Ecclesia,[15] et ut ex hoc dicatur quod in eo potestatis residet plenitudo.

Celum autem, ut tangebamus, in accionibus naturalium non habet plenitudinem potestatis, quia non potest sine secundis agentibus quod potest cum illis agentibus. Quod non solum verum est in produccione rerum perfectarum, ut in produccione[16] animalium perfectorum que generantur a simili in specie, sicut equus generatur ab equo et leo a leone et homo ab homine; non enim posset celum sine equo sive sine semine equi producere equum: sed eciam veritatem habet in animalibus imperfectis, que generantur ex putrefaccione. Nam sicut in produccione equi[17] celum se habet tamquam causa superior et semen[18] equi vel leonis tamquam causa inferior, nec posset celum sine semine producere animal quod habet fieri ex semine, nec[19] posset ex quocumque semine producere quodcumque animal, sed[20] ex determinato semine[21] determinatum animal, ut equum non posset producere[22] nisi ex semine equi et leonem nisi ex semine leonis: sic in produccione animalium imperfectorum,[23] ut in his que generantur ex putrefaccione, celum[24] se habet tamquam causa superior et putrefaccio

---

1: statuente] et ordinante add. C   2: datam] ab ecclesia sua a summo pontifice add. and del. C
3: agere] que sunt agenda add. C   4: qui] om. CV²   5: quod] si add. mss   6: scilicet] om. PV¹V²
7: respectu] om. CFV²   8: leges] illas add. CV¹V²   9: et] ut FV²   10: et] om. FV²   11: madefaciat]
madefiat FV²   12: comburitur] comburetur V²   13: Pontifex] quia add. F   14: leges] om. V²
15: omnium agencium in Ecclesia] om. PV¹V²   16: rerum perfectarum ... produccione] om. F
17: Nam sicut ... equi] om. V²   18: semen] animalis vel add. C   19: nec] om. V¹   20: sed] vel FV²
21: semine] om. V²   22: producere] om. V²   23: imperfectorum] perfectorum FV²   24: celum] om. F

For, as we have said, the election of a prelate is brought about as by a primary cause — by the Supreme Pontiff establishing how the election is to be conducted — and by a secondary cause, namely, by the choice of the electors according to the form given to them. But the Supreme Pontiff could provide a prelate for any church without this secondary cause: that is, without the choice of the electors. And what has been said of the election of a prelate is true of the other things which are done in the Church: that the Supreme Pontiff, as having fullness of power, in whom all the power of the Church is acknowledged to reside, can act without other agents.

The Supreme Pontiff should note, however, that God, Who has all power not only conditionally (that is, with respect to this or with respect to that) but absolutely, nonetheless almost always acts according to the laws which He has established for things, lest the works of His wisdom should be in vain; and He almost always observes the laws [of nature] in order to accomplish the effects of secondary agents by means of secondary agents. For He warms by means of fire, and He cools by means of water; for it cannot come about according to the laws established for things that what is in fire is not warmed and that what is in water is not cooled. And again, it cannot come about according to these laws that he who walks upon water does not wet his feet. Sometimes, however, albeit rarely, He brings about a state of affairs beyond these common laws, such that what is in fire is not burned and that someone may walk upon water with dry feet.[1]

So also, the Supreme Pontiff, because it is his task to establish laws regulating how the Church must be governed, should indeed govern the Church according to these laws, and should permit chapters to conduct their own elections and prelates to exercise their own functions and the other persons who are in the Church to perform their tasks according to the form given to them. For reasonable cause, however, he can act beyond these common laws without other agents; for the power of all other agents is contained in him, in that there is in him all the power of all the agents within the Church. And so, for this reason, it may be said that fullness of power resides in him.

But, as we have noted, the heaven does not have fullness of power in relation to the behaviour of natural agents, for it cannot do without secondary agents what it can do with those agents. And this is true not only of the production of perfect things, as in the production of perfect animals which are generated by others of the same species, as a horse is generated by a horse and a lion by a lion and a man by a man: it holds true also of imperfect animals, which are generated from putrefaction. For just as, in the production of a horse, the heaven operates as a superior cause and the seed of the horse or of a lion as an inferior cause, nor could the heaven produce the animal which is brought into being from the seed without the seed, nor could it produce a particular animal from any kind of seed, but only from a specific seed, so with the production of imperfect animals, as in the case of those generated from putrefaction: the heaven operates as a superior cause and the putrefaction

---

1. Cf. Dan. 3:20–26; Matt. 14:25–31.

tamquam causa inferior. Non ergo posset celum sine putrefaccione generare animal quod habet generari ex putrefaccione, nec ex quacumque putrefaccione posset generare quodcumque tale animal, sed ex determinata putrefaccione determinatum tale animal.

Ideo Commentator super XII [*Metaphysice*] vult quod putrefaccio ex qua generatur animal [imperfectum] est sicut semen in animalibus que generantur ex seminibus. Ideo, sicut ex alio et alio semine generatur aliud et aliud animal perfectum, sic ex alia et alia putrefaccione generatur aliud et aliud animal imperfectum; et quia non eodem modo putrefiunt[1] carnes equine et carnes[2] bovine, dicit[3] Temistius,[4] ut Commentator in XII recitat, quod[5] ex carnibus equinis putrefactis generantur vespe, ex carnibus bovinis apes.

Non ergo in celo est plenitudo potestatis respectu produccionis naturalium, quia nec in produccione rerum perfectarum nec eciam imperfectarum potest sine causa secunda quod potest cum causa secunda. In Deo autem est[6] plenitudo potestatis simpliciter, quia in omnibus potest sine causa secunda quod potest cum causa secunda, nec indiget secundis agentibus ad produccionem cuiuscumque[7] effectus. Quod autem operatur suos effectus mediantibus secundis agentibus, hoc non[8] est ex sua indigencia, sed ex sua[9] bonitate, quia vult dignitatem suam communicare creaturis, et vult quod creature non sint ociose et supervacue, sed vult quod agant suas acciones et sua opera.

In Summo autem Pontifice est plenitudo potestatis non quocumque modo, sed quantum ad posse quod est in Ecclesia, ita quod totum posse quod est in Ecclesia reservatur in Summo Pontifice. Dicimus autem 'totum posse quod est in Ecclesia' quia, si est aliquod posse quod Christus retinuit sibi et non communicavit Ecclesie, non oportet quod tale posse sit in Summo Pontifice: ut puta quia Christus dare poterat effectum sacramenti sine sacramento. Nam puer, quando nascitur, non potest habere baptismum flaminis, quod habeat baptismum in voto, quia non habet racionis usum. Si ergo non haberet baptismum sanguinis, ut si non occidatur pro Christo, et[10] si non haberet baptismum[11] fluminis, ita quod non haberet baptismum nec in voto nec in sanguine nec in flumine, tali puero nato[12] posset Christus conferre effectum baptismi et dare sibi graciam baptismalem sine baptismo, quia non alligavit Christus virtutem suam sacramentis. Potest enim sine sacramento[13] conferre effectum sacramenti. Tale autem posse non communicavit Christus Ecclesie; propter quod non oportet quod tale posse[14] reservetur in Summo Pontifice. Habet itaque Summus Pontifex plenitudinem potestatis, et habet omne posse, non quocumque modo, sed habet omne posse[15] quod communicatum est Ecclesie et quod est in Ecclesia.

1: putrefiunt] putrefaciunt FV²   2: carnes] *om.* C   3: dicit] enim *add.* C   4: Temistius] comistius C semistius V²   5: quod] *in marg.* P *om.* FV²   6: autem est] est autem F   7: cuiuscumque] cuiusque F   8: non] vero F   9: indigencia, sed ex sua] *om.* F   10: et] *om.* V²   11: baptismum] *om.* V¹   12: nato] non habenti baptismum aliquo modo *add.* C   13: sacramento] sacramentis F   14: posse] *om.* V²   15: non quocumque ... posse] *om.* V²

as an inferior cause. Therefore, the heaven could not produce the animal which is generated from putrefaction without putrefaction, nor could it generate every such animal from any kind of putrefaction, but only a particular kind of animal from a particular kind of putrefaction.

Thus, the Commentator on *Metaphysics* 12 maintains that the putrefaction from which an [imperfect] animal is generated is like seed in the animals which are generated from seed. Therefore, just as, from this and that kind of seed, this and that kind of perfect animal is generated, so from this and that kind of putrefaction is this and that kind of imperfect animal generated. And because the flesh of horses and the flesh of cattle do not putrefy in the same way, Themistius, whom the Commentator on Book 12 cites, says that wasps are generated from the putrefied flesh of horses and bees from the flesh of cattle.[1]

In the heaven, therefore, there is not fullness of power with respect to the production of natural phenomena, for neither in the production of perfect things nor even of imperfect can it do without a secondary cause what it can do with a secondary cause. In God, however, there is fullness of power absolutely; for He can do without a secondary cause all that He can do with a secondary cause, nor does He need secondary agents in the production of any effect whatsoever. But the fact that He brings about His effects by means of secondary agents is due not to any need on His part, but to His goodness. For He wishes to share His dignity with His creatures, and He desires that His creatures should not be idle and in vain, and He desires that they should perform their own functions and their own tasks.

But there is fullness of power in the Supreme Pontiff not in every way, but to such extent as there is power within the Church, in that all the power which is in the Church is contained in the Supreme Pontiff. And we say 'all the power which is in the Church' because if there is any power which Christ has retained to Himself and not communicated to the Church, it cannot be that such power is in the Supreme Pontiff. For example, Christ could give the effect of a sacrament without the [actual performance of the] sacrament. For when a child is born, he cannot have the baptism of the Spirit, which baptism one may have by desire, for he does not have the use of reason. If, therefore, he did not have the baptism of blood (as he would not unless he were slain for Christ), and if he did not have the baptism of water, and so had baptism neither by desire nor of blood nor of water,[2] Christ could still confer the effect of baptism upon such a newborn child and give him the grace of baptism without [the fact of] baptism; for Christ has not fettered His own power by the sacraments: for He can confer the effect of a sacrament without the sacrament itself. But Christ has not communicated the power to do this to the Church; and so it cannot be that such power is contained in the Supreme Pontiff. Thus, the Supreme Pontiff has fullness of power, and he has all power: not in every way whatever, but he has all the power which has been communicated to the Church and which is in the Church.

---

1. Averroes, Commentary on *Metaphysics* Λ, 3 (*Aristotelis opera cum Averrois commentariis*, vol. 8, p. 303).
2. Cf. Aquinas, *Summa theologiae* IIIa 66:11 and 12.

Sicut ergo in Deo est plenitudo potestatis simpliciter, quia quicquid possunt quecumque agencia potest Deus et quicquid potest mediantibus quibuscumque agentibus potest sine illis agentibus, sic, quantum ad posse quod est in Ecclesia, habet Summus Pontifex plenitudinem potestatis, quia quicquid possunt quecumque persone ecclesiastice, hoc potest Summus Pontifex; unde ubique esse dicitur ordinarius. Et quicquid potest Summus Pontifex[1] mediantibus quibuscumque personis ecclesiasticis, hoc potest sine illis. Debet tamen esse imitator Dei, sicut eius vicarius carissimus, ut non indifferenter et passim utatur hac plenitudine potestatis, sed certis causis inspectis. Nam iusta et[2] racionabili causa emergente, libere potest hac potestate uti; quia ubi est sancta intencio, ubi est[3] spiritus Domini, ibi est et libertas. In usu quidem huiusmodi potestatis multociens subtrahuntur membris proprie acciones; ut si provideat Summus Pontifex alicui ecclesie[4] inrequisitis[5] canonicis, potest quidem hoc facere de sua plenitudine potestatis,[6] sed hoc agendo subtrahuntur canonicis[7] proprie acciones.

Si ergo Deus, ut supra tetigimus, quia habet omne posse simpliciter, gubernat mundum secundum leges quas indidit rebus et indifferenter et passim non utitur sua plenitudine potestatis ut faciat preter solitum cursum rerum, causa tamen racionabili emergente facit preter has leges inditas et preter hunc solitum cursum: sic et Summus Pontifex, tamquam imitator Dei, si legem indidit quod canonici suum pastorem eligant vel hee persone ecclesiastice hec opera faciant, secundum has leges inditas, secundum[8] hunc solitum cursum, debet Ecclesiam gubernare; causa tamen racionabili emergente, liberam habet potestatem ut faciat preter has leges et preter hunc solitum cursum.

Est autem et alia causa sive alia racio quare spectat ad Summum Pontificem agere secundum leges inditas et secundum cursum solitum, quia quod ait Philosophus in *Politicis* de omni principe potissime verificari habet de[9] Summo Pontifice. Vult enim ipse quod quilibet princeps debet esse homo multorum oculorum, multarum manuum et multorum pedum. Debet quidem esse homo multorum occulorum, quia debet[10] sibi coacervare multos[11] industrios[12] et sapientes per quos possit videre que spectant ad regimen principatus sibi commissi. Debet esse homo multarum manuum, quia debet sibi coacervare[13] viros viriles et virtuosos per quos possit agere que sunt agenda. Debet esse homo multorum pedum, quia debet sibi coacervare[14] multos viros firmos et stabiles, ut suus principatus vacillare non possit. Hoc ergo non est subtrahere suas operaciones ab aliis, sed hoc est[15] magis alios incitare ut agant suas[16] acciones proprias.[17] Hoc enim est[18] incitare oculos, ut videant, idest sapientes, ut considerent; hoc enim est[19] incitare manus, ut agant, idest virtuosos, ut operentur; hoc enim est[20] incitare pedes[21] quorum est alia sustentare,

1: unde ubique ... Pontifex] *om.* V².   2: et] *om.* FV².   3: sancta ... est] *om.* V².   4: ecclesie] ecclesiastico F   5: inrequisitis] requisitis F in requisitis PV¹V²   6: plenitudine potestatis] plenitudinis potestate V²   7: canonicis] canonicus P canonici V²   8: secundum] *om.* FV². 9: de] in FV²   10: esse homo ... debet] *om.* PF   11: multos] viros *add.* CF   12: industrios] industres FV²   13: coacervare] conservare FV²   14: coacervare] conservare FV²   15: est] *om.* V² 16: suas] *om.* CFV²   17: acciones proprias] proprias acciones CFV²   18: enim est] est enim F 19: enim est] enim est F   20: hoc enim est] hos est eciam F   21: pedes] aliorum *add.* F

Therefore, just as, in God, there is fullness of power absolutely, since God can do whatever any agent can do, and whatever He can do by means of any agents He can do without those agents, so the Supreme Pontiff has fullness of power to such extent as there is power in the Church, since whatever any ecclesiastic can do the Supreme Pontiff can do. Hence, he is said to be the ordinary judge everywhere; and whatever the Supreme Pontiff can do by means of any ecclesiastics he can do without them. Nonetheless, as God's most beloved Vicar, he must be His imitator: he must not make use of this fullness of power without distinction and indiscriminately, but only on the examination of certain causes. For where just and reasonable cause has emerged, he can make use of this power freely; for where there is a holy intention, where there is the spirit of the Lord, there is also liberty.[1] And, by the use of this power, their own functions are indeed removed from many members of the Church, so that, if the Supreme Pontiff makes provision [of a bishop] for any church without consulting the Canons, he can indeed do this by reason of his fullness of power, but, when he acts in this way, their own functions are removed from the Canons.

If, therefore, as we have noted above, God, Who has all power absolutely, [nonetheless] governs the world according to the laws which He has established for things, and does not use His fullness of power to act beyond the usual course of things without distinction and indiscriminately, but acts beyond these established laws and beyond this usual course only when reasonable cause emerges, so also the Supreme Pontiff, as God's imitator, if he has established a law under which the Canons may elect their own pastor, or under which certain ecclesiastics may carry out certain tasks, should govern the Church according to these established laws, according to this usual course. When reasonable cause emerges, however, he is free to use his power to act beyond these laws and beyond this usual course.

But there is another cause and another reason why it behoves the Supreme Pontiff to act according to the established laws and according to the normal course. For what Aristotle says in the *Politics* is especially true of the Supreme Pontiff. For he maintains that every prince must be a man of many eyes, of many hands, and of many feet.[2] He must indeed be a man of many eyes, because he must gather to himself many industrious and wise men, through whom he may see those things which pertain to the government of his principality. He must be a man of many hands, for he must gather to himself vigorous and powerful men through whom he may do those things which must be done. And he must be a man of many feet, for he must gather to himself many firm and steadfast men, so that his principality may not stumble. This, therefore, is not to remove their functions from others; rather, it is to encourage them to perform their proper activities. It is to encourage the eyes to see: that is, the wise to deliberate. It is to encourage the hands to grasp: that is, the powerful to act. It is to encourage the feet, whose task it is to support all else, to

---

1. Cf. II Cor, 3:17.
2. Aristotle, *Politics* 3:16 (1287[b]30).

ut firme et stabiliter in bonum pergant.

Redeamus ergo ad propositum et dicamus quod, licet in celo hoc materiali non sit plenitudo potestatis quia non potest[1] hos effectus naturales efficere sine istis causis inferioribus quos potest cum huiusmodi inferioribus causis,[2] in Summo tamen Pontifice non absolute et simpliciter sive non quocumque modo, sed quantum ad posse quod est in Ecclesia, est plenitudo potestatis, ut quecumque potest cum aliis personis ecclesiasticis potest sine illis. Quod si volumus causam huius investigare, dicemus quod ad celum non spectat dare leges naturalibus rebus, sed ad eum spectat agere iuxta leges nature inditas. Ideo in sola virtute celi non possent fieri miracula; quia hoc est miraculum:[3] agere preter leges nature[4] datas. Celum autem, quicquid tacit, agit secundum leges nature concessas. Spectat tamen ad Summum Pontificem condere leges et dare leges omnibus personis ecclesiasticis et toti Ecclesie; propter quod ipse est supra huiusmodi leges, et est in eo potestatis plenitudo, ut possit agere preter leges.

Sunt itaque assignati duo modi plenitudinis potestatis: unus quidem, quando potest sine causa secunda quod potest cum causa secunda,[5] quia Deus sine naturalibus agentibus potest quicquid potest[6] cum ipsis. Sic et Summus Pontifex sine quibuscumque personis ecclesiasticis[7] potest quicquid posset cum[8] illis. Alius vero modus est quod, sicut Deus dat rebus naturalibus leges naturales, ut dat hanc legem igni, quod calefaciat, aque, quod infrigidet, est tamen in eo plenitudo potestatis, quia potest facere preter has leges: sic Summus Pontifex dat gentibus sive hominibus leges positivas morales; est nihilominus in eo plenitudo potestatis, quia potest facere preter huiusmodi[9] leges.

CAPITULUM X: *Cum in Summo Pontifice sit plenitudo potestatis, non tamen sit in celo huiusmodi plenitudo, quare potestas eius[10] dicitur esse celestis.*

Sequendo dicta sanctorum patrum, potestas pontificalis dicitur esse spiritualis, celestis et divina. Sic enim Gregorius Nazianzenus, scribens imperatoribus Constantinopolitanis, ait quod Christus 'dedit' pontificibus 'potestatem,[11] dedit et[12] principatum multo perfecciorem[13] principatibus vestris';[14] et subdit: 'Aut numquid iustum videtur vobis, si cedat spiritus carni, si a terrenis celestia superentur et si divinis preferantur humana?' In hiis ergo[15] verbis principatus sacerdotalis dicitur esse spiritualis, celestis et divinus; potestas autem regalis dicitur esse carnalis, terrena et humana. Et quia in celo, ut diximus, non est plenitudo potestatis, ideo dicebatur in rubrica capituli quomodo potestas pontificalis, cuiusmodi est potestas Summi Pontificis, potest dici celestis, cum in potestate Summi Pontificis sit plenitudo potestatis, in celo autem non habeat esse huiusmodi plenitudo.

Sed dices quod potestas Summi Pontificis dicitur esse celestis quia est divina, per 'celum' enim 'ipsum Deum' intelligere possumus; unde illud Iohannis tercio: 'Qui

---

1: potest] habet FV[2]   2: quos potest ... causis] *del.* C   3: miraculum] iura civilium V[2]
4: nature] *om.* F   5: quod potest ... secunda] *om.* F   6: potest] posset FV[2]   7: ecclesiasticis]
om. PV[1]V[2]   8: ipsis. Sic ... cum] *om.* V[2]   9: huiusmodi] has F   10: *potestas eius*] huiusmodi F   11: 'dedit' pontificibus 'potestatem] *om.* V[2]   12: dedit et] deditque CFV[2]   13: perfecciorem] fortiorem FV[2]   14: vestris] nostris F   15: ergo] *om.* C

walk steadfastly and firmly towards what is good.

Let us return to our proposition, therefore, and say that, although fullness of power does not reside in the material heaven because it cannot bring about those natural effects without inferior causes which it can with such inferior causes, nonetheless, in the Supreme Pontiff, there is fullness of power: not absolutely and as such, nor in every way whatsoever, but to such extent as there is power within the Church. For whatever he can do with other ecclesiastics he can do without them. If we wish to investigate the cause of this, we shall say that it does not rest with the heaven to give laws to natural things; rather, it is its task to act according to the established laws of nature. And so miracles cannot come about simply by the power of heaven, for a miracle is an act beyond the given laws of nature. But it rests with the Supreme Pontiff to lay down laws and to give laws to all ecclesiastics and to the whole Church. And so he is above such laws, and there is in him a fullness of power such that he may act beyond the laws.

Thus, two senses have been assigned to fullness of power. The first is that it can do without a secondary cause all that it can do with a secondary cause; for God can do without natural agents whatever He can do with them. So too, the Supreme Pontiff can do without any persons whatsoever whatever he might do with them. But the other sense is that, just as God gives natural laws to natural things — for example, He gives the law to fire that it may heat and to water that it may cool — and yet there is fullness of power in Him because He can act beyond these laws, so the Supreme Pontiff gives positive moral laws to the nations or to men, yet there is nonetheless fullness of power in him because he can act beyond those laws.

CHAPTER X: *Since there is fullness of power in the Supreme Pontiff yet no such fullness resides in the heaven, why is his power is said to be heavenly?*

According to the sayings of the holy Fathers, pontifical power is called spiritual, heavenly and divine. For Gregory Nazianzenus, writing thus to the Byzantine emperors, says that Christ 'has given power' to the pontiffs, 'He has indeed given a ruling power far more perfect than your ruling powers.' And he adds, 'Or would it seem to you in any way just if spirit were to submit to flesh, if the heavenly were to be overshadowed by the earthly, and if the human were to be preferred to the divine?'[1] In these words, therefore, the ruling power of the priesthood is said to be spiritual, heavenly and divine, but royal power is called fleshly, earthly, and human. And because, as we have argued, there is not fullness of power in the heaven, the question has therefore been raised in the heading of this chapter of how pontifical power, of which kind is the power of the Supreme Pontiff, can be called heavenly when in the power of the Supreme Pontiff there is fullness of power, whereas no such fullness exists in the heaven.

You will reply, however, that the power of the Supreme Pontiff is called heavenly because it is divine; for we can take 'heaven' to mean 'God Himself'. Hence, expounding the words of John 3 — 'He Who comes from heaven is above all'[2] —

1. Dist. 10, c. 6 (CIC I:20).
2. John 3:31.

de celo venit, super omnes est,' exponit Augustinus quod Christus 'venit de celo' quia venit de Deo patre. Sed dicemus quod Deus pater non diceretur[1] 'celum' nisi aliqua esset similitudo celi ad Deum patrem. Sic nec potestas Summi Pontificis dicitur esse celestis nisi posse ipsius celi habeat aliquam similitudinem vel aliquas similitudines[2] cum posse[3] Summi Pontificis.

Sciendum ergo quod nulla est 'similitudo' que sit per omnem modum similis, quia tunc illa non esset similitudo, sed esset identitas,[4] et illud 'simile' non esset simile, sed esset idem. Certum est autem quod Summus Pontifex non est istud[5] celum sensibile quod videmus, et potestas pontificalis non est potestas istius celi sensibilis. Multas tamen conveniencias, multas similitudines, habet potestas pontificalis, et potissime potestas Summi Pontificis, cum potestate istius celi sensibilis;[6] et exinde potestas Summi Pontificis dicitur esse celestis.

Possumus autem tangere quinque[7] que sunt in celo que adaptare poterimus ad Summi Pontificis potestatem. Nam celum quantum ad esse est plenum forma; secundo, quantum ad situm sive quantum ad ordinem est super omnia; tercio, quantum ad magnitudinem sive quantum ad continenciam continet omnia; quarto, quantum ad accionem agit et influit in omnia; quinto, quantum ad compassionem[8] a nullo tangitur et a nullo patitur, cum tangat omnia et agat in omnia.

Primo quidem celum quantum ad esse est plenum forma et plenum perfeccione, ita quod forma celi replet totum appetitum materie, ut non possit materia illa habere ulteriorem perfeccionem nec ulteriorem[9] formam. Talis autem est potestas Summi Pontificis; nam, loquendo de potestate regiminis et gubernacionis que potest competere homini in vita ista, tante perfeccionis est potestas Summi Pontificis ut illi subiecto sive illi supposito non possit competere ulterior potestas regiminis nec gubernacionis. Ideo Extra., *De maioritate et obediencia*, in capitulo *Solite*, potestas sacerdotalis assimilatur luminari maiori, idest soli, potestas autem regalis assimilata est luminari minori, idest lune. Utrumque autem luminare, tam maius, quam minus, tam solare, quam lunare, est in firmamento celi: sic utraque potestas, tam maior, quam minor, tam pontificalis, quam regalis, est in Ecclesia. Sicut ergo luna totum lumen quod habet, habet a sole, et sicut sol est plenus lumine et est fons luminis et non est dare perfeccius lumen quam solare, sic potestas regalis instituta est per sacerdotalem et per potestatem pontificalem, ut supra diffusius declaravimus, et ipse pontifex, et specialiter Summus Pontifex, totus est plenus potestate, et in humanis ipse potest dici fons potestatis, ut nulla sit alia in humanis potestas perfeccior. Ergo si consideramus celum et ea que sunt in celo quantum ad esse, quia ibi est[10] plenitudo quantum ad formam et quantum ad perfeccionem, potestas Summi Pontificis dicitur esse celestis, quia est

---

1: diceretur] esse *add.* F   2: similitudines] similitudinem V[2]   3: posse] ipsius *add.* F   4: identitas] ydemptitas FV[1] ydempnitas P   5: istud] illud C   6: sensibilis] visibilis F   7: quinque] quicumque V[2]   8: compassionem] compassiones C contrapassionem V[2]   9: perfeccionem nec ulteriorem] *om.* V[2]   10: ibi est] est ibi F

Augustine says that Christ 'comes from heaven' because He comes from God the Father.[1] But we shall say that God the Father would not be called 'heaven' unless there were some similarity between the heaven and God the Father. Thus, the power of the Supreme Pontiff power is not [rightly] called heavenly unless the power of heaven itself has some similarity, or certain resemblances, to the power of the Supreme Pontiff.

It must be known, therefore, that nothing which is 'similar' is the same in every respect [as something else]; for then there would not be similarity: rather, there would be identity, and that which was 'similar' [to something else] would not be similar, but would be the same. And it is certain that the Supreme Pontiff is not [identical to] that perceptible heaven which we see, and that pontifical power is not [identical to] the power of that perceptible heaven. Nonetheless, pontifical power, and especially the power of the Supreme Pontiff, has many resemblances, many similarities, to the power of that perceptible heaven; and, accordingly, the power of the Supreme Pontiff is said to be heavenly.

And we can note five things which are in the heaven for which we shall be able to find counterparts in the power of the Supreme Pontiff. For in respect of existence, the heaven is fully formed; second, in respect of location or order, it is above all things; third, in respect of magnitude or content, it contains all things; fourth, in respect of agency, it acts upon and exerts influence in all things; fifth, in respect of its capacity to be acted upon, it is touched by nothing and is acted upon by nothing, but may touch all things and act upon all things.

First, then, in respect of existence, the heaven is fully formed and fully perfected inasmuch as the form of heaven satisfies every impulse of its matter. Hence, that matter may not have any further perfection or any further form. And such is the power of the Supreme Pontiff; for, speaking of that power of ruling and governing which can belong to a man in this life, the power of the Supreme Pontiff is of such perfection that no higher ruling or governing power can belong to those who are subject to him or set under him. Thus, at X. 1:33:6: *Solitae*, priestly power is compared [by Innocent III] to the greater light, that is, to the sun, while royal power is compared to the lesser light, that is, to the moon.[2] But each light, greater and smaller, sun and moon, is in the firmament of heaven, and each power, greater and lesser, pontifical and royal, is in the Church. Therefore, just as the moon receives all the light which it has from the sun, and just as the sun is full of light and is the source of light and there is no need to postulate a light more perfect than that of the sun, so royal power is instituted through the priestly and pontifical power, as we have shown more fully above. And the pontiff himself, and especially the Supreme Pontiff, is entirely full of power and can be said to be the source of power among human beings. Thus, no more perfect power exists among men. Therefore, if we consider the heaven and those things which are in the heaven with respect to existence, then, because there is fullness there in respect of form and perfection, the power of the Supreme Pontiff is said to be heavenly because it is

---

1. *In Ioannis evangelium* 14:7 (CCSL 36:145).
2. CIC II:196.

plena forma et plena perfeccione.

Secundo, si consideramus celum quantum ad situm et quantum ad ordinem, est super omnia. Potestas ergo pontificalis dicitur esse celestis quia est super omnem aliam potestatem. Nam, ut patuit in auctoritate assignata Gregorii Nazianzeni, lex Christi imperialem potestatem sacerdotali subiecit[1] potestati; et in Ieremia dicitur, quod potest exponi de Ecclesia sive de potestate sacerdotali, et potissime de potestate Summi Pontificis, 'Ecce constitui te super gentes et regna.'

Tercio, celum quantum ad magnitudinem et quantum ad continenciam continet omnia. Sic in potestate Summi Pontificis continetur omnis potestas, sacerdotalis et regalis, celestis et terrena, ut possit ipse dicere: 'Data est mihi omnis[2] potestas in celo et in terra.' Ipse enim gladius materialis, per quem significatur terrena potestas, continetur in potestate Summi Pontificis. Est enim huiusmodi gladius in Summi Pontificis potestate, etsi non ad usum, ad nutum. Utrumque ergo gladium habet Ecclesia, spiritualem et materialem: spiritualem ad usum,[3] materialem ad nutum. Spiritualis itaque gladius exercendus est ab Ecclesia, materialis pro Ecclesia. Uterque[4] ergo pertinet ad Ecclesiam, sive exercendus ab ea sive exercendus pro ea. Nam et de gladio materiali dixit Dominus Petro: 'Converte gladium tuum in vaginam.' Petri ergo erat ille gladius, etsi non est[5] exercendus ab eo, propter quod Dominus reprehendit Petrum quia ipsemet volebat uti tali gladio, exercendus tamen erat pro eo, ut hoc modo uterque gladius esset Petri, vel, ut diximus, exercendus ab eo vel pro eo. Que omnia supra tetigimus et Bernardus quarto libro ad Eugenium prosequitur et pertractat. Si ergo celum continet omnia et[6] potestas Summi Pontificis continet quasi omnem potestatem spiritualem et materialem, patere potest quod potestas Summi Pontificis merito dicitur esse celestis.

Quarto, celum quantum ad accionem agit et influit in omnia. Sic potestas ecclesiastica, et[7] potissime potestas[8] Summi Pontificis, agit et influit in omnem aliam[9] potestatem,[10] ut nulla sit vera alia[11] potestas nec verus principatus nisi sit[12] subditus Summo Pontifici. Quia, ut Augustinus ait secundo *De civitate Dei* capitulo XXI: 'Vera autem iusticia non est nisi in ea republica cuius conditor rectorque[13] Christus est.' Sed nulli sunt sub Christo rectore nisi sint sub Summo Pontifice, qui est Christi vicarius generalis. Cum ergo superioris sit agere et influere in inferiora, quia omnes alii principatus, si veri et iusti sunt, subiecti sunt potestati Summi Pontificis, bene dictum est quod potestas Summi Pontificis dicitur esse celestis; quia sicut celi est in omnia influere, sic potestas Summi Pontificis, tamquam in res sibi subiectas, habet agere et habet influere in omnes alios principatus.

Quinto, celum quantum ad compassionem a nullo tangitur, cum tangat omnia.

1: subiecit] subiescit V²   2: omnis] *om.* PV¹   3: ad usum] *om.* V²   4: Uterque] utramque F
5: est] *om.* V¹V²   6: et] *om.* CFV² *in marg.* P   7: et] *om.* V²   8: potestas] *om.* V²   9: aliam]
om. F   10: aliam potestatem] *om.* V²   11: vera alia] alia vera CF   12: sit] *om.* V²   13: rectorque] et rector F

fully formed and fully perfected.

Second, if we consider the heaven with regard to location and order, it is above all things. Therefore, pontifical power is said to be heavenly because it also is above every other power. For, as has become clear from the cited authority of Gregory Nazianzenus, the law of Christ has made the imperial power subject to the priestly power. Also, it is said in Jeremiah, 'Behold, I have placed you above nations and kingdoms';[1] and this can be interpreted as applying to the Church or to the priestly power, and especially to the power of the Supreme Pontiff.

Third, in respect of magnitude and content, the heaven contains all things. So too every power, priestly and royal, heavenly and earthly, is contained in the power of the Supreme Pontiff, so that he can say, 'All power in heaven and on earth is given to me.'[2] For even the material sword, by which earthly power is signified, is contained in the power of the Supreme Pontiff, for that sword is in the power of the Supreme Pontiff to command even if not to use. The Church, therefore, has both swords, the spiritual and the material: the spiritual to use, the material to command. Thus, the spiritual sword should be wielded by the Church, the material on behalf of the Church. Therefore, both belong to the Church, whether wielded by her or wielded on her behalf. For, concerning the material sword, the Lord Himself said to Peter, 'Put up *your* sword into its sheath.'[3] That sword was Peter's, therefore. Even though it was not to be wielded by him (for the Lord rebuked Peter when he wished to make use of such a sword himself) it was nonetheless to be wielded on his behalf, so that, in this way, both swords were Peter's or, as we have said, were to be wielded either by him or on his behalf. But we have noted all these things above, and Bernard, in the fourth Book of his work addressed to Eugenius, pursues and discusses them.[4] Therefore, if the heaven contains all things, and if the power of the Supreme Pontiff contains almost every power, spiritual and material, it can be clearly seen that the power of the Supreme Pontiff is properly to be called heavenly.

Fourth, in respect of agency, the heaven acts upon and influences all things. So also, the ecclesiastical power, and especially the power of the Supreme Pontiff, acts upon and influences every other power, so that there may be no other true power or true principality unless it is placed under the Supreme Pontiff. For as Augustine says at *De civitate Dei* 2:21: 'There is no true justice save in that commonwealth whose founder and ruler is Christ.'[5] But none are under Christ as ruler unless they are under the Supreme Pontiff, who is the Vicar-General of Christ. Therefore, since that which is superior acts upon and influences inferiors, and because all other ruling powers, if they are true and just, are subject to the power of the Supreme Pontiff, it is well said that the power of the Supreme Pontiff is called heavenly. For just as the heaven influences all things, so must the power of the Supreme Pontiff act upon and influence all other ruling powers as things subject to him.

Fifth, in respect of its capacity to be acted upon, the heaven is touched by nothing,

1. Jer. 1:10.
2. Matt. 28:18.
3. Matt. 26:52.
4. See Pt. I, Chaps. VIII–IX; see also Introduction, n. 25.
5. *De civitate Dei* 2:21 (CCSL 47:55).

Distinxerunt ergo[1] sapientes philosophi duplicem tactum: unum superficialem, qui est secundum quantitatem molis, alium profundum, qui est secundum quantitatem virtutis. Tactus autem superficialis, qui est secundum quantitatem molis,[2] est cum superficies aliquorum corporum se contingunt. Est autem hic tactus superficialis quia corpora sic se tangencia solum per superficies se contingunt; est eciam hic tactus secundum quantitatem molis quia, quanto corpora[3] sic se tangencia maiora sunt secundum quantitatem molis, sic maior est[4] huiusmodi tactus. Secundum hunc quidem tangendi modum, quicquid tangit tangitur et econverso, quia si superficies unius corporis attingit superficiem alterius, oportet quod attingatur a superficie illa; et si attingatur a superficie aliqua,[5] oportet quod attingat superficiem illam.

Sed alius est tactus qui est profundus et secundum quantitatem virtutis, secundum quem modum tangendi agens tangit passum, sicut tangit ignis[6] stupam cum comburit stupam. Hic autem tactus dicitur[7] esse profundus et secundum quantitatem virtutis.[8] Profundus quidem est, quia[9] agens potest agere in corpore toto; potest enim accio agentis pertingere usque ad intima passi, et potissime si sit agens naturale. Quia ars videtur agere in extremitatibus corporis. Non enim plus facit ars nisi quod coniungit corpus corpori vel separat corpus a corpore; coniungendo autem corpus corpori superficiem coniungit[10] superficiei, separando[11] autem corpus corpore superficiem a superficie separat.[12] Et si dicas quod potest per artem ignis coniungi ferro vel ligno, qui ignis agit in totum ferrum vel in totum lignum, dicemus quod accio artificialis non plus facit nisi quod superficiem unius corporis applicat superficiei alterius corporis, ut superficiem ignis applicat superficiei[13] ferri vel ex una parte tantum vel ex omni parte: ut puta si per accionem artis undique ferrum circumdetur ab igne. Sed si postea ignis sic[14] coniunctus ferro agat in intima ferri, illa accio non erit artificialis, sed naturalis; ita quod ars agit in extremitatibus corporis, natura autem agit in corpore toto.[15] Est ergo tactus[16] profundus, qui est ab agente naturali; et iste tactus[17] est secundum quantitatem[18] virtutis, quia agens naturale per virtutem activam quam habet tangit passum et agit in ipsum. Secundum hunc tangendi modum non quicquid tangit tangitur, nec quicquid alterat alteratur, nec quicquid agit contrapatitur. Nam, ut declaratur in libro *De generacione*, celum tangit omnia ista inferiora, quia agit in omnia ea, non tamen tangitur ab eis, quia non contrapatitur[19] ab ipsis.

Vere ergo, quantum ad hunc modum, potestas Summi Pontificis potest dici celestis, quia quecumque tangat, in quemcumque[20] agat, non debet tangi ab eis.[21] Iniuriatur ergo iuri et contradicit racioni[22] qui, tactus a Summo Pontifice, nititur contra tangere

1: ergo] enim CFV² 2: alium profundum … molis] *om.* FV² 3: quanto corpora] corpora quanto PV¹ 4: est] *om.* F 5: illa; et … aliqua] *om.* F 6: tangit ignis] ignis tangit CF 7: tactus dicitur] dicitur tactus F 8: et secundum quantitatem virtutis] *om.* F 9: quia] *del.* P ut V¹ 10: superficiem coniungit] *om.* V² 11: coniungit superficiei; separando] superficiei coniungit et separando *marg.* C 12: autem corpus … separat] *om.* C 13: alterius corporis … superficiei] *om.* PV¹ 14: sic] sit FV² 15: corpore toto] toto corpore F 16: tactus] totus V² 17: tactus] actus F 18: quantitatem] qualitatem F 19: contrapatitur] compatitur F 20: quemcumque] quacumque FV² 21: eis] nec contrapati ab ipsis *add.* C ipsis F 22: racioni] racionem CV²

although it touches all things. Therefore, [let us explain this by saying that] those learned in philosophy have distinguished two kinds of touch: the one superficial, which is according to the quantity of magnitude, and the other profound, which is according to the quantity of power.[1] For superficial touch, which is according to the quantity of magnitude, occurs when the surfaces of certain bodies touch each other. But this touch is superficial because the bodies thus touching each other are in contact only on the surface. And this kind of touch is also according to the quantity of magnitude because the greater the objects touching one another are in terms of the quantity of magnitude, the greater is the area of contact. And, according to this kind of touch, whatever touches is itself touched and conversely. For if the surface of one body touches the surface of another, it must be that the former is touched by the surface of the latter; and if it is touched by any surface [of the latter], it must be that it touches that surface in turn.

But there is another kind of touch, which is profound and according to the quantity of power. And, in this kind of touching, an agent touches that upon which it acts as fire touches tinder when it burns the tinder. And this kind of touch is said to be profound and according to the quantity of power. It is indeed profound, because the agent can act upon the whole body; for the action of the agent can penetrate through to the very centre of that upon which it acts. And especially if it is a natural agent. For art can do no more than join body to body or separate body from body; and, when joining body to body, it [merely] joins surface to surface, and, when separating body from body, it separates surface from surface. And if you say that it is possible by art to join fire with iron or wood, which fire acts upon the whole of the iron or the whole of the wood, we shall reply that this action, insofar as it is artificial, does no more than apply the surface of one body to the surface of another body. For example, it applies the surface of fire to the surface of iron: either to one part of it only or to every part, as, for instance, if by the agency of art the iron were to be entirely surrounded by fire. But if the fire thus joined to the iron then acts upon the inmost part of the iron, this action itself will not be artificial, but natural. Thus, art acts only upon the outward parts of a body, but nature acts throughout the whole body. Thus, the touch of a natural agent is profound; and that touch is according to the quantity of power because the natural agent touches that upon which it acts and acts upon it by means of the active power which it has. And, according to this mode of touching, not everything which touches is touched, nor is everything which alters altered, nor is everything which acts acted against. For, as is shown in the book *De generatione*, the heaven touches all inferior beings because it acts upon all of them, but it is not touched by them because it is not acted against by them.[2]

In this way, therefore, the power of the Supreme Pontiff can truly be called heavenly; for, regardless of what it touches and what it acts upon, it must not be touched by them. Therefore, he injures right and contradicts reason who, being touched by the Supreme Pontiff, strives to touch him in turn, and who, being acted

---

1.   Cf. Aristotle, *De generatione et corruptione* 1:6 (322^{b}25); *Physics* 5:3 (226^{b}20).

2.   *De generatione et corruptione* 1:6 (323^{a}15).

ipsum, et qui passus ab eo nititur contra agere in ipsum. Sic enim se habet ipse ad omnia que sunt in Ecclesia sicut se habet celum ad omnia ista inferiora, quod si tangit, non tangitur, si agit,[1] non contrapatitur.[2]

Videmus autem[3] quod celum generat et corrumpit ista inferiora, quia generacio unius est corrupcio alterius et econverso. Si ergo celum generat et corrumpit, oportet quod construat id quod generat et destruat id quod corrumpit. Secundum[4] hunc eciam modum oportet quod statuat et destituat. Immo, quia ad celum spectat varia generare, et celum facit ad generacionem tam gravium quam levium, oportet quod inter hec corpora aliquod faciat ascendere generando in eo formam levis, et aliquod descendere generando in eo formam gravis. Sed quantumcumque celum hoc construat, hoc destruat, hoc statuat, hoc destituat, hoc faciat descendere,[5] hoc autem[6] ascendere,[7] nihil est quod impingat[8] in celum, nihil est quod nitatur contra agere in celum. Et quia est sic de Summo Pontifice, vere potestas eius dici poterit esse celestis.

CAPITULUM XI: *Cum in Summo Pontifice plenitudo resideat potestatis, quomodo intelligendum dictum Hugonis, quod 'pia devocione fidelium temporalia*[9] *quedam ecclesiis concessa sunt possidenda.'*

Est autem per precedencia declaratum quid est plenitudo potestatis et quomodo huiusmodi plenitudo in Summo Pontifice dicitur residere. Declarabatur quidem quod omne posse quod est in Ecclesia reservatur[10] in Summo Pontifice; dicebatur autem[11] quod in Ecclesia est[12] duplex posse, spirituale et temporale. Probabatur[13] enim per textum evangelii quod utrumque gladium habet Ecclesia, spiritualem et temporalem. Nam, cum Christus esset cum discipulis suis, per quos figurabatur Ecclesia, dictum est 'Ecce duo gladii[14] hic'; quod non esset verum nisi duo gladii in Ecclesia esse dicerentur. Et quia Ecclesia habet utrumque gladium, oportet quod Ecclesia habeat utrumque posse, spirituale et temporale.

Ex hoc ergo oritur difficultas tacta[15] in rubrica capituli, quod cum in Ecclesia sive in Summa Pontifice habeat esse potestatis plenitudo,[16] et cum in eo habeat[17] esse utrumque posse, spirituale et temporale, quomodo verificatur dictum Hugonis quod ait [in libro *De sacramentis*] libro II parte II capitulo penultimo: quod 'pia devocione fidelium temporalia quedam ecclesiis concessa sunt possidenda.' Possessio enim temporalium, ut videtur, non competit Ecclesie devocione[18] fidelium sive donacione ipsorum, sed hoc competit Ecclesie ex posse et dominio quod habet

---

1: agit] agat V^2 2: contrapatitur] compatitur F   3: autem] enim P   4: secundum] sed F
5: descendere] ascendere CF   6: autem] *om.* F   7: ascendere] descendere CF   8: impingat]
inpinguat V^2 9: *temporalia*] *om.* C   10: reservatur] reservabatur V^1 11: autem] *om.* V^2
12: est] erat V^2 13: Probabatur] probatur V^2 14: duo gladii] gladii duo F   15: tacta] tracta PV^1
16: potestatis plenitudo] plenitudo potestatis C   17: habeat] habet F   18: devocione] donacione FV^2

upon by him, strives to act against him. For he stands in the same relation to all things which are in the Church as the heaven does to all inferior beings, so that, if he touches them, he is not touched, and if he acts, he is not acted against.

And we see that the heaven brings these inferior things into being and causes them to pass away; for the coming into being of one thing is the passing away of another and conversely.[1] If, therefore, the heaven causes things to come into being and pass away, it must be that it builds up that which it brings into being and overthrows that which it causes to pass away. Also, by the same token, it must be that it establishes and destroys. Indeed, because it rests with the heaven to bring the various things into being, and because the heaven brings both heavy and light things into being, it must be that, among these bodies, it will cause some of them to rise by producing in them the form of lightness and some to fall by producing in them the form of heaviness.[2] But however much the heaven may build up anything, overthrow it, establish it, destroy it, or cause it to fall and rise, there is nothing which may impinge upon the heaven: there is nothing which may strive to act against the heaven. And because this is so of the Supreme Pontiff, his power will truly be able to be called heavenly.

CHAPTER XI: *Since fullness of power resides in the Supreme Pontiff, how are we to understand what Hugh says: that 'certain temporal things have been granted to churches as possessions by the pious devotion of the faithful'?*[3]

It has been shown in the preceding chapters what fullness of power is and how such fullness is said to reside in the Supreme Pontiff. It was indeed shown that all the power which is in the Church is contained in the Supreme Pontiff, and it was said that there is a twofold power in the Church, spiritual and temporal. For we have proved from the text of the Gospel that the Church has both swords, the spiritual and the temporal. For when Christ was with His disciples, by whom the Church was prefigured, it was said: 'Behold, here are two swords';[4] but this would not be true if the two swords were not now said to be in the Church. And, because the Church has both swords, it must be that the Church has both powers, spiritual and temporal.

From this, therefore, arises the difficulty touched upon in the heading of this chapter: that, since fullness of power exists in the Church or in the Supreme Pontiff, and since both powers, spiritual and temporal, have their being in him, how can what Hugh says in the penultimate chapter of *De sacramentis* 2, that 'certain temporal things have been granted to churches as possessions by the pious devotion of the faithful,' be regarded as true? For it seems that the possession of temporal goods does not belong to the Church because of the devotion of the faithful or by their grant, but that this belongs to the Church by reason of the power and lordship which

1. *De generatione et corruptione* 1:7 (324^{a}5).
2. Cf. Aristotle, *De caelo* 4:3 (310^{a}30); cf. 3:2 (301^{b}25); 3:6 (305^{a}25); *De generatione et corruptione* 1:6 (323^{a}10).
3. *De sacramentis* 2:2:7 (PL 176:420).
4. Luke 22:38.

Ecclesia, cum habeat posse et dominium temporale.

Videtur eciam dictum Hugonis fulciri per decretum, quia ut habetur Distinccione LXIII [1] de dono quod fecit primus Lodovicus imperator Romanis pontificibus, ubi dicitur: 'Ego Lodovicus Romanorum Imperator Augustus statuo et concedo domino Paschali Summo Pontifici et successoribus eius in perpetuum, sicut a predecessoribus nostris usque nunc in vestra potestate et dicione tenuistis et disposuistis, civitatem[2] Romanam cum ducatu suo,' etc. Si autem dicatur quod Lodovicus imperator hoc non donavit nec concessit Ecclesie, sed confirmavit quod antea[3] donatum et concessum erat,[4] quia Constantinus imperator hoc fecerat, ut habetur XCVI [5] Distinccione, semper, ut videtur, habetur [6] propositum: videlicet quod [7] ex dono facto ab imperatoribus et ex pia donacione fidelium concessa sunt Ecclesie temporalia possidenda. Possessio itaque temporalium non competit Ecclesie ex suo posse vel ex suo dominio. Non ergo erit in Ecclesia uterque gladius nec habebit Ecclesia[8] utrumque posse, et per consequens non habet Ecclesia plenitudinem potestatis.

Dicemus ergo quod sic reddenda sunt[9] que sunt Dei Deo quod eciam reddantur que sunt Cesaris Cesari, non quod aliquid habeat Cesar quod non sit[10] Dei. Vult tamen Deus quod aliquid habeat Cesar: tamen[11] sub eo. Sic,[12] cum due sint potestates, pontificalis et regalis, spiritualis[13] et terrena, ut habetur in Distinccione XCVI,[14] et in multis aliis locis hec materia tangitur, sic ergo reddenda sunt que sunt Ecclesie[15] ipsi Ecclesie[16] quod tamen potestas terrena suis iuribus non fraudetur; non quod aliqua sint sub potestate terrena que non sunt sub potestate ecclesiastica. Sic tamen voluit Deus suam Ecclesiam ordinare ut potestas terrena[17] sua iura haberet[18] sub potestate ecclesiastica, et gladius materialis suam iurisdiccionem haberet tamen sub gladio ecclesiastico, ut sit potestas sub potestate et gladius sub gladio: sicut et corpus suam proprietatem habet et[19] suam virtutem, tamen sub anima, ut sine anima nec sensum habeat neque motum.

Dicemus enim quod id quod est in corporibus sanitas et vita, hoc est in[20] moribus et in gubernacionibus hominum equitas et iusticia, ut sicut corpus dicitur esse sanum quod habet humores equatos, et si inequalitas humorum prevaleat infirmatur corpus, et tantum prevalere potest quod perdat vitam, sic sine equitate et iusticia nulla est recta gubernacio hominum et nulla est[21] res publica que scilicet[22] sit viva moribus, licet possit esse picta coloribus, prout beatus Augustinus secundo *De civitate Dei* capitulo XXII ait de republica Romanorum ante suscepcionem fidei: quod non erat in vera iusticia et non erat viva moribus, sed erat[23] picta coloribus.

1: LXIII] clxiii F   2: et disposuistis, civitatem] *om.* V²   3: antea] ante eius PV¹   4: erat] fuerat V¹
5: XCVI] nonagesima PV¹   6: ut videtur, habetur] huiusmodi F   7: quod] *om.* C   8: Ecclesia]
om. FV²   9: sunt] cesaris cesari et *add.* FV²   10: sit] *om.* PV¹V²   11: tamen] cum FV²
12: Sic] sit FV²   13: spiritualis] *om.* V²   14: XCVI] nonagesima PV¹   15: Ecclesie] *om.* F
16: Ecclesie] *om.* P   17: ut potestas terrena] *om.* V²   18: haberet] tamen *add.* V¹   19: et]
om. FV²   20: in] *om.* V²   21: recta gubernacio ... est] *om.* C   22: scilicet] sine equitate et
iustitia C   sine ea non F sive sit V²   23: erat] *om.* FV²

the Church has, since she has temporal [as well as spiritual] power and lordship.

But Hugh's statement seems also to be supported by the *Decretum*: by what is recorded in Dist. 63 concerning the gift which the emperor Louis I made to the Roman Pontiffs, where it is said: 'I, Louis, emperor of the Romans, Augustus, grant and concede to the Supreme Pontiff, the Lord Paschal, and to his successors in perpetuity, the city and dukedom of Rome as you have held and disposed it in your power and command from the time of our predecessors until now,'[1] and so on. And if it be said that the emperor Louis did not grant or concede this to the Church, but only confirmed what had already been granted or conceded — because, as is established in Dist. 96,[2] the emperor Constantine did this — it nonetheless seems that the point in each case is the same: namely, that temporal things have been granted to the Church as possessions by a gift made by emperors and by the pious donation of the faithful. Thus, [it seems that] the possession of temporal goods does not belong to the Church by reason of her own power or her own lordship. Therefore, [it seems that] both swords will not be in the Church, nor will the Church have both powers; and it follows that the Church does not have fullness of power.

We shall say, therefore, that those things which are God's must be rendered to God in such a way that those which are Caesar's are also rendered to Caesar, but that Caesar does not have anything which is not also God's. For God wills that Caesar should possess something, but only under Him. Thus, since there are two powers, the pontifical and the royal, the spiritual and the earthly, as is established in Dist. 96[3] (and this matter is touched upon in many other places), so those things which are the Church's must therefore be rendered to the Church in such a way that the earthly power is not defrauded of its rights, but not in such a way that there are some things under the earthly power which are not under the ecclesiastical power. For God has wished to order His Church in such a way that the earthly power should hold its rights under the ecclesiastical power, so that power may be under power and sword under sword: just as the body itself has its own nature and its own power, but under the soul, so that, without the soul, it may have neither sense nor motion.

For we shall say that equity and justice are to morals and the governments of men what health and life are to bodies. Thus, just as the body is said to be healthy when it has an equal balance of humours, and the body is ill if an inequality of humours prevails, and this can prevail to so great an extent that it loses its life, so, without equity and justice, nothing is rightly ordered in the government of men and there is no commonwealth which is a living moral entity, even though it may be a coloured picture, as the blessed Augustine says at *De civitate Dei* 2:22 of the commonwealth of the Romans before the reception of the faith: that there was no true justice in it, and that it was not a living moral entity but a coloured

---

1. Dist. 63, c. 30: *Ego Lodoicus Romanus* (CIC 1:244–245) (= the *Pactum Lodovicianum*: see Introduction, n. 53).
2. Dist 96, cc. 13–14: *Constantinus* (CIC I:342) (= the *Donatio Constantini*).
3. Dist. 96, c. 10: *Duo sunt* (CIC I:340).

Non est enim vera iusticia, ut ipse ibidem dicit et ut est pluries repetitum, ubi non est rector et conditor Christus.

Igitur apud infideles non sunt imperia neque regna, quia, ut dicit Augustinus quarto *De civitate Dei* capitulo IV: 'Remota itaque iusticia, quid sunt regna nisi magna[1] latrocinia?' Immo, apud infideles non solum non sunt regna neque[2] imperia, cum apud eos regna et imperia sunt[3] magna[4] latrocinia; immo, eciam apud eos non sunt aliqua iusta[5] dominia, ut non sit aliquis infidelis iustus dominus sive iustus possessor domus sue vel agri sui vel vinee sue vel cuiuscumque rei sue; quia, ut supra probavimus, qui non vult[6] subesse[7] domino suo, dignum est quod nihil subsit sub dominio suo.

Si ergo non es sub Deo, a quo habes omnia, dignum est quod[8] tibi subtrahantur omnia. Sed qui digne et iuste privandus est qualibet re est indignus et iniustus possessor cuiuscumque rei. Et quia nonnisi per Ecclesiam et sub Ecclesia[9] potest quis placere Deo et esse sub Deo et esse sub Domino suo, non nisi per Ecclesiam et sub Ecclesia habet quisque dominium suum; et quia quod sis[10] iustus dominus cuiuscumque rei, ab Ecclesia et sub Ecclesia[11] habes, consequens est quod tu[12] et omnia tua sint sub dominio Ecclesie collocata. Nullus itaque erit iustus dominus aliquarum rerum nisi sui ipsius et omnium que habet recognoscat[13] Ecclesiam matrem et dominam.[14]

Dicemus[15] ergo quod quecumque temporalia habet iuste potestas terrena,[16] illa sunt sub Ecclesia, non tamen[17] econverso. Potest enim aliqua temporalia[18] habere Ecclesia in quibus nullam iurisdiccionem habet terrena potestas. Hiis tamen sic se habentibus vere dici potest quod Hugo ait et quod iura tangunt: quod pia donacione fidelium vel ex largicione imperatorum et principum temporalia quedam concessa sunt ecclesiis possidenda. Dicemus enim quod licet[19] omnia[20] temporalia que sunt sub potestate terrena sint sub Ecclesia,[21] quia potestas terrena et quisque dominus cuiuscumque[22] rei temporalis non potest aliquid iuste possidere nisi sub Ecclesia et per Ecclesiam, non tamen illa temporalia erunt[23] eodem modo sub Ecclesia et sub domino temporali.

Concedere enim cogimur quod iste dominus temporalis per peccatum originale natus est filius ire, per peccatum actuale factus est filius ire. Natus autem filius ire vel factus filius ire, quia est aversus a Deo et non est sub domino suo, iusticia[24] exigit, ut nihil sit sub dominio suo.[25] Non ergo erit[26] iustus dominus alicuius rei. Regeneratus ergo per Ecclesiam a peccato originali et absolutus per eam a peccato actuali, fit per Ecclesiam iustus dominus rerum suarum; et quia iam est iustus dominus

---

1: nisi magna] *om.* V²   2: neque] et F   3: sunt] sint FPV¹   4: magna] *om.* PV¹   5: iusta] *om.* C
6: vult] sunt F   7: subesse] sunt sub FV²   8: quod] ut C   9: et sub Ecclesia] *om.* F   10: sis]
sit CV²   11: et sub Ecclesia] *om.* C   12: tu] te V²   13: recognoscat] *om.* C   14: dominam]
recognoscat *add.* C   15: Dicemus] dicamus CFV²   16: potestas terrena] terrena potestas C
17: non tamen] sed non F   18: Potest enim aliqua temporalia] aliqua enim temporalia potest C
19: quod licet] quod habet *del.* P quodlibet CF   20: licet omnia] *om.* V¹   21: Ecclesia] ecclesiastica C   22: cuiuscumque] cuiuslibet V²   23: erunt] essent V²   24: iusticia] hoc *add.* V¹V²
25: suo] *om.* V²   26: ergo erit] erit ergo C

picture.[1] For as he himself says in the same passage, and as has been frequently repeated, there is no true justice where Christ is not the ruler and founder.

Among unbelievers, then, there are neither empires nor kingdoms. For, as Augustine says at *De civitate Dei* 4:4: 'Thus, justice removed, what are kingdoms but great bands of robbers?'[2] Indeed, not only are there neither kingdoms nor empires among unbelievers, since, among them, kingdoms and empires are bands of robbers: also, there are not even any just lordships among them. For no unbeliever may be the just lord or the just possessor of his house or of his farm or of his vineyard or of anything else that is his. For, as we have proved above, he who refuses to be under his lord is worthy to have nothing under his own lordship.[3]

Therefore, if you are not under God, from whom you receive all things, it is fitting that all things should be withdrawn from you. But he who, worthily and justly, should be deprived of everything is an unworthy and unjust possessor of anything. And because no one can please God and be under God and under his Lord except through the Church and under the Church, no one has any lordship of his own except through the Church and under the Church. And because you may be the just lord of whatever you possess only from the Church and under the Church, it follows that you and all that is yours are placed under the Church's lordship. Thus, no one will be the just lord of any possessions unless he acknowledges the Church as mother and mistress of himself and of all that he has.

We shall say, therefore, that the earthly power justly holds whatever temporal possessions it has under the Church, but that the converse is not true; for the Church can have certain temporal possessions over which the earthly power has no jurisdiction. This being so, however, it can still be truly said, as Hugh says and as the laws record, that certain temporal things are conceded to churches as possessions by the pious grant of the faithful or by the gift of emperors and princes. For we shall say that although all the temporal possessions which are under the earthly power are under the Church — because the earthly power and whoever is lord of any temporal things cannot possess anything justly except under the Church and through the Church — these temporal possessions nonetheless will not be under the Church and under a temporal lord in the same way.

For we are compelled to grant that the temporal lord is born a child of wrath through original sin and is made a child of wrath through actual sin. And because, born a child of wrath or made a child of wrath, he is turned away from God and is not under his Lord, justice requires that there be nothing under his lordship. Thus, he will not be a just lord of anything [for as long as he remains in a state of sin]. Therefore, because he is regenerated from original sin [only] through the Church and absolved from actual sin through her, he is made the just lord of his possessions through the Church. And because he is now the just lord of his possessions

1. CCSL 47:55.
2. CCSL 47:101.
3. Pt. II, Chaps VII–XII; and see esp. Ch. XI.

rerum suarum et factus est per Ecclesiam,[1] oportet quod res sue sint sub eo tamquam sub iusta domino, et sint sub Ecclesia, a qua habet iustum[2] tale[3] dominium. Sed aliter erunt sub Ecclesia et aliter sub eo erunt,[4] quia sub Ecclesia erunt tamquam sub ea[5] que habet dominium superius et primarium, quod dominium est principale et universale; sed erunt sub dominio temporali tamquam sub domino[6] qui habet dominium inferius et secundarium, quod est immediatum et executorium.[7] Ex hoc autem dominio[8] superiori et primario debentur Ecclesie de omnibus temporalibus decime et oblaciones; ex dominio vero inferiori et secundario debentur potestatibus terrenis et temporalibus dominis de ipsis temporalibus[9] rebus alie utilitates et alia emolumenta que proveniunt ex temporalibus rebus.

Ecclesia igitur, ut Ecclesia est, secundum suum posse et secundum suum dominium habet in temporalibus rebus posse et dominium[10] superius et primarium; secundum quod posse non habet iurisdiccionem et execucionem immediatam, et ideo ex hoc non dicitur temporalia possidere ut hic de possessione loquimur. Cesar autem et dominus temporalis habet huiusmodi[11] iurisdiccionem et execucionem.[12] Ideo videmus potestates distinctas, videmus[13] iura distincta, videmus gladios distinctos. Ista tamen distinccio non facit quod non sit potestas sub potestate, ius sub iure, gladius sub gladio. Immo, facit quod hec sic se habeant, quia ex quo ius et dominium Ecclesie est superius et primarium, ius autem et dominium Cesaris est inferius et secundarium, oportet quod ius sit sub iure et dominium sub dominio.

Aliquod ergo ius, immo[14] magnum ius et plus utile ius, habet Cesar in temporalibus quam habeat Ecclesia, licet non habeat ita dominativum ius sicut habet Ecclesia. Habet tamen Cesar non solum utile ius, sed eciam potestativum et dominativum ius in temporalibus rebus: in civitatibus, castris et terris. Habet enim in eis ius utile et dominium utile, prout ex eis recipit emolumenta et utilitates; habet eciam dominium potestativum, prout in eis exercet iusticiam et iudicium sanguinis. Istud autem dominium quod habet Cesar et dominus temporalis, sive sit dominium utile sive potestativum, non tollit dominium Ecclesie, quod est superius et primarium; ex quo dominio superiori et primario quod habet Ecclesia super temporalibus omnes habentes temporalia sunt tributarii Ecclesie, debentes ei decimas que de suis temporalibus[15] possessionibus[16] colliguntur. Istud autem dominium Ecclesie est dominium magis dominativum et magis altum super ipsis temporalibus rebus quam sit dominium quod habet Cesar vel quod habet quicumque dominus temporalis, quia ex hoc dominio superiori et primario habet Ecclesia a fidelibus et a possessionibus fidelium censum sive tributum. A fidelibus quidem habet oblaciones, a possessionibus autem fidelium habet[17] decimas, ut ex hoc Ecclesia omnibus dominetur et omnium cognoscatur[18] esse domina et magistra.

1: Ecclesiam] sit dominus iustus *add.* C   2: iustum] *om.* FV²   3: a qua … tale] tamquam aliqualiter tale iustum C   4: sub eo erunt] erunt sub eo CF   5: ea] ut superius tangebamus *add. and del.* C   6: domino] deo PV² eo CV¹   7: quod est … executorium] *om.* C   8: dominio] *om.* F 9: dominis de ipsis temporalibus] *om.* V²   10: dominium] et *add.* V²   11: huiusmodi] *om.* V² 12: execucionem] et secondarium *add. and del.* C et *add.* FV²   13: potestates distinctas, videmus] *om.* F   14: immo] *om.* V²   15: temporalibus] et *add.* V¹   16: temporalibus possessionibus] possessionibus temporalibus CF   17: habet] *om.* CFV²   18: cognoscatur] cognoscat FV²

and is made so through the Church, it must be that his possessions are under him as under a just lord, and are therefore under the Church, from whom he receives such just lordship. But they will be under the Church in one way, and they will be under him in another way. For they will be under the Church as under one who has a superior and primary lordship, which lordship is principal and universal; but they will be under temporal lordship as under a lord who has an inferior and secondary lordship, which is immediate and executory. And, by reason of this superior and primary lordship, tithes and offerings are owed to the Church from all temporal goods; and, by reason of the inferior and secondary lordship, the other gains and profits which accrue from temporal things are owed to earthly powers and temporal lords from temporal things themselves.

Thus, by reason of her power and lordship, the Church as such has a superior and primary lordship in temporal things, but she does not have an immediate jurisdiction and [right of] execution by reason of this power. Thus, on this account, she is not said to possess temporal things in the way in which we are here speaking of possession. Caesar and the temporal lord, however, does have such jurisdiction and [right of] execution; and so we see that there are distinct powers, we see that there are distinct rights, we see that there are distinct swords. But this distinction does not mean that the one power is not under the other, the one right under the other, and the one sword under the other. On the contrary, it means that these things are so; for, from the fact that the right and lordship of the Church is superior and primary and the right and lordship of Caesar is inferior and secondary, it must follow that the one right is under the other and that the one lordship is under the other.

Therefore, Caesar has some right — indeed, a great right — in temporal things, and more of a right of use than the Church has, even though he does not have so great a right of lordship as the Church has. Moreover, Caesar has not only a right of use, but also a right of power and lordship in temporal things: in cities, castles and lands. For he has a right and lordship of use in them inasmuch as he receives gains and profits from them; and he has a lordship of power inasmuch as he executes justice and the judgment of blood in them. But that lordship which Caesar and the temporal lord has, whether it be a lordship of use or of power, does not take away the lordship of the Church, which is superior and primary. And because of the superior and primary lordship which the Church has over temporal things, all who possess temporal goods are tributaries of the Church, owing to her the tithes which are gathered from their temporal possessions. And that lordship of the Church is more a lordship of ownership, and is more elevated over temporal things, than is the lordship which Caesar or any temporal lord has. For, by reason of this superior and primary lordship, the Church receives a tax or a tribute from the faithful and from the possessions of the faithful. Indeed, she receives offerings from the faithful, and she receives tithes from the possessions of the faithful, so that, by virtue of this, the Church may be lord of all, and may be acknowledged by all as lord and governor.

Revertamur ergo ad propositum et dicamus quod in[1] temporalibus suum ius habet Ecclesia et suum ius habet Cesar, et utrumque ius est[2] aliquo modo utile et aliquo modo potestativum. Nam ius utile quod habet Ecclesia in omnibus temporalibus sunt decime, oblaciones et ea que de temporalibus debentur ecclesiis. Ius autem utile quod in temporalibus habet Cesar sunt cetera emolumenta que ex[3] temporalibus haberi possunt. Postquam enim Ecclesie de temporalibus date sunt decime tribute sunt oblaciones et[4] exhibita sunt que debentur ecclesiis, tunc reliqua[5] sunt Cesaris, idest domini temporalis. Sic ergo datur Ecclesie quod est Ecclesie[6] et redditur que sunt Cesaris Cesari.[7]

Istud[8] autem ius utile quod habet Ecclesia super omnibus temporalibus est longe excellencius quam illud quod habet Cesar. Sicut enim dominus agri vel vinee recipit aliquid de agro vel de vinea pro censu et pro ostensione[9] dominii, reliqua vero sunt operariorum,[10] sic in signum universalis dominii recipit Ecclesia decimas et oblaciones et ea que debentur ei de bonis fidelium, reliqua vero sunt ipsorum fidelium. Est ergo ius utile Ecclesie quod habet in bonis temporalibus longe excellencius quam sit ius Cesaris vel cuiuscumque domini temporalis.

Sic et ius potestativum quod habet in temporalibus Ecclesia est longe excellencius[11] quam sit ius Cesaris,[12] quia ex culpa vel[13] ex causa potest Ecclesia privare Cesarem sive potestatem terrenam suo dominio et suis temporalibus bonis: quod non esset nisi in ipsis temporalibus bonis haberet Ecclesia excellens dominium non solum utile, sed potestativum. Cesar autem[14] vel potestas terrena, cuius est gladium materialem portare, habet ius potestativum in temporalibus, ut in civitatibus, castris vel[15] agris[16] et vineis et aliis quibuscumque terris, quia forefacientes iudicat et punit. Longe ergo excellencius dominium potestativum habet Ecclesia quam Cesar vel quam potestas terrena, quia potestas terrena solum in laicos potest animadvertere, Ecclesia autem in omnes; quia in ipsam potestatem terrenam quantumcumque altam ex culpa vel ex causa potest animadvertere[17] et privare eam suis temporalibus bonis: quod non esset nisi temporalia et possidentes temporalia[18] essent sub Ecclesia.

Non dicimus ergo quod nullum dominium utile habeat Cesar in temporalibus,[19] sed excellencius est dominium utile quod habet Ecclesia quam illud[20] quod habet Cesar. Immo, ius quod habet Cesar debet[21] ordinari ad ius Ecclesie. Sic eciam, non dicimus quod nullum dominium potestativum et in personis hominum et in rebus temporalibus habeat Cesar; sed dicimus quod dominium potestativum quod habet Ecclesia est longe excellencius quam illud quod habet Cesar, quia potest Ecclesia[22] in personam Cesaris et[23] in bona temporalia ipsius animadvertere. Personam quidem Cesaris potest per censuram ecclesiasticam cohercere,[24]

1: in] om. F   2: ius est] est ius F   3: ex] in FV²   4: et] om. V²   5: reliqua] aliqua F   6: quod est Ecclesie] om. F   7: que sunt Cesaris Cesari] cesari quod est cesaris C   8: istud] illud FV² 9: et pro ostensione] om. C   10: operariorum] operaroriorum FV²   11: excellencius] om. V² 12: vel cuiuscumque ... Cesaris] om. V¹   13: vel] et C   14: autem] eciam C enim FV² 15: vel] om. F   16: vel agris] om. C   17: autem in ... animadvertere] marg., in a later hand C 18: et possidentes temporalia] om. F   19: temporalibus] in quibus dominium utile habet cesar habet et ecclesia add. and del. C   20: quam illud] om. C   21: debet] oportet F   22: Ecclesia] om. FV²   23: et] eciam add. V²   24: cohercere] cohibere F

Let us return to our proposition, therefore, and say that the Church has her right in temporal things and that Caesar has his right, and that, in one way, each is a right of use and, in another way, of power. For the right of use which the Church has in all temporal things consists in tithes, offerings and those things which are owed from temporal possessions to churches. And the right of use which Caesar has in temporal things consists in the various gains which he can receive from temporal possessions. For after tithes have been given to the Church from temporal goods and the offerings and gifts which are due to churches have been made, what then remains is Caesar's: that is, the temporal lord's. In this way, therefore, that which is the Church's is given to the Church, and that which is Caesar's is rendered to Caesar.

But that right of use which the Church has over all temporal things is far more excellent than that which Caesar has. For just as the lord of a farm or a vineyard takes something from the farm or from the vineyard by way of rent and in order to show his lordship, while the remainder belongs to the tenants, so, as a sign of her universal lordship, the Church receives tithes and offerings and those things which are owed to her from the goods of the faithful, while the remainder belongs to the faithful themselves. Therefore, the right of use which the Church has in temporal goods is far more excellent than is the right of Caesar or of any temporal lord [because tithes and similar dues must be paid to the Church before a temporal lord can derive any profit from the goods of the faithful].

So also, the right of power which the Church has in temporal things is far more excellent than is Caesar's right because, for fault or other cause, the Church can deprive Caesar or the earthly power of his lordship and of his temporal goods; and this would not be so if the Church did not have a preeminent lordship in those temporal goods: not only of use, but also of power. But Caesar, or the earthly power, to whom it belongs to bear the material sword, has a right of power in temporal things — for example, in cities, castles or farms and vineyards, and in all other lands — because he judges and punishes offenders. [In doing this, however, he is answerable to the Church.] Therefore, the lordship of power which the Church has is far more excellent than that of Caesar or the earthly power, because the earthly power can act against members of the laity only, and the Church [can act against] all men. For she can act against even the earthly power, however exalted, for fault or other cause, and deprive it of its temporal goods; and this would not be so if temporal goods and the possessors of temporal goods were not under the Church.

Therefore, we say not that Caesar has no lordship of use in temporal goods, but that the lordship of use which the Church has is more excellent than that which Caesar has. Indeed, the right which Caesar has must be subordinated to the right of the Church. So also, we do not say that Caesar has no lordship of power over the persons of men and in temporal things. Rather, we say that the lordship of power which the Church has is far more excellent than that which Caesar has, for the Church can act against Caesar both in his person and in his temporal goods. She can indeed coerce the person of Caesar through ecclesiastical censure,

bona quidem temporalia Cesaris potest[1] in alterius dominium transferre. Immo, dominium potestativum quod habet Cesar, et eciam[2] materialis gladius quo utitur Cesar, est pro Ecclesia[3] et ad nutum Ecclesie exercendus. Licet enim[4] ipsa Ecclesia non utatur per se ipsam gladio materiali, animadvertit tamen in alios secundum materialem gladium, prout huiusmodi gladius,[5] etsi non ab Ecclesia, tamen est pro Ecclesia et[6] ad nutum Ecclesie exercendus.

Aliquod ergo ius, immo magnum ius, habet Cesar sive dominus secularis[7] in rebus temporalibus, quo iure sine culpa et[8] causa minime est privandus. Et quia in temporalibus habet aliquod ius Cesar utile et aliquod ius potestativum, illud ius quod habet potest donare Ecclesie. Potest quidem donare unum ius sine alio vel unum ius cum alio. Potest autem donare unum sine alio quia potest donare ius utile sine iure potestativo, ut potest rex vel princeps donare nemus vel agrum quantum ad ius utile, retento sibi iure potestativo; ita quod Ecclesia illa sic habebit utilitatem et emolumentum de illo nemore vel agro, quid si quis forefaceret in illo nemore vel in illo agro,[9] punicio forefacientis non spectabit ad illam Ecclesiam,[10] sed ad dominum secularem. Potest eciam Cesar sive dominus secularis dare unum ius cum alio, videlicet quod totum spectet ad Ecclesiam, tam ius utile quam potestativum. Sed dato quidem quod Ecclesia habeat ius potestativum, tamen, quantum ad ius potestativum,[11] quod est iudicium sanguinis, numquam exercebit Ecclesia per se ipsam, sed per laicam personam. Rursus, istud ius quod habet Cesar, sive sit utile sive potestativum, potest donare Ecclesie vel simpliciter vel sub condicione, quia quilibet in re sua potest condicionem quam vult apponere.

Propter quod patefactum est quod querebatur in rubrica capituli, quia Ecclesia sic habet plenitudinem potestatis et sic habet super omnibus, eciam super bonis temporalibus ius universale superius et primarium, quod tamen[12] Cesar non destituitur iure suo. Potest ergo Ecclesia habere talem[13] plenitudinem potestatis, et tamen possidebit res temporales pia devocione fidelium et largicione principum, si ipsi fideles dent Ecclesie ius quod habent in[14] temporalibus, et ipsi principes iura[15] temporalium ecclesiis largiantur. Ad hec autem probanda valent dicta Hugonis libro II, parte II, capitulo penultimo.

Ex hoc autem apparere potest quod nulla temporalia sunt sub Cesare que non[16] sint sub Ecclesia, quia a iure superiori et primario quod habet Ecclesia super temporalibus nequaquam cadere potest. Et si aliquis Summus Pontifex[17] aliquod tale ius donaret, successor suus hoc revocare[18] posset, cum hoc non possit per superiorem confirmari, quoniam papa nullum habet superiorem; et posset hoc successor revocare, quia par in parem non habet imperium. Sed Ecclesia potest habere aliqua temporalia in quibus nullum ius habebit Cesar, quia poterit Cesar totum ius quod habet[19] in temporalibus illis dare Ecclesie, et poterit hoc per papam confirmari, ita

---

1: per censuram ... potest] *om.* V[1]	2: eciam] ipse *add.* CFV[2]	3: pro Ecclesia] per ecclesiam F
4: enim] *om.* FV[2]	5: gladius] *om.* V[2]	6: et] *om.* F	7: secularis] temporalis FV[2]	8: culpa
et] *om.* FV[2]	9: vel in illo agro] *om.* FV[2]	10: Ecclesiam] *om.* C	11: tamen quantum ...
potestativum] *om.* V[2]	12: tamen] propterea F cum V[2]	13: talem] totam F	14: in] aliquibus
add. and del. C	15: iura] aliquos *add. and del.* C	16: non] *om.* V[2]	17: aliquis Summus
Pontifex] alicui summo pontifici F	18: revocare] renovare FV[2]	19: habet] *om.* V[2]

and she can indeed transfer the temporal goods of Caesar to the lordship of another. Indeed, the lordship of power which Caesar has, and also the material sword which Caesar uses, must be wielded on behalf of the Church and at the Church's command. For though the Church does not herself use the temporal sword directly, she still acts against others by means of the material sword inasmuch as this sword, though not wielded by the Church, is nonetheless to be wielded on behalf of the Church and at the Church's command.

Therefore, Caesar, or the secular lord, has some right — indeed, a large right — in temporal things; and, without fault or cause, he must not in the least be deprived of this right. And because Caesar has some right of use and some right of power in temporal things, he can give that right which he has to the Church. Indeed, he can give the one right without the other or the one right with the other; for he can give the one without the other in that he can give a right of use without a right of power. For example, a king or prince can give a right of use over a forest or a farm while retaining to himself the right of power, so that, while the Church will receive the gains and profits from that forest or farm, if anyone commits an offence in that forest or on that farm the punishment of the offender will rest not with the Church but with the secular lord. And Caesar or the secular lord can also give the one right with the other, so that the entire right — that is, both of use and of power — will belong to the Church. Given, however, that the Church has a right of power, the Church will nonetheless never exercise such a right of power, insofar as it involves the judgment of blood, herself, but only through a lay agent. Again, that right which Caesar has, whether it be of use or of power, he can give to the Church either absolutely or conditionally, for anyone can impose whatever condition he likes upon his own property.

And so the question asked in the heading of this chapter has been clearly answered. For the Church has fullness of power, and she has over all things, even over temporal goods, a universal, superior, and primary right: not, however, in such a way that Caesar is deprived of his right. Therefore, the Church can have such fullness of power, yet will nonetheless possess temporal things by the pious devotion of the faithful and by the gift of princes if the faithful themselves give to the Church the right which they have in temporal things, and if the princes themselves bestow temporal rights upon churches. And what Hugh says in the penultimate chapter of Book 2, Part 2 goes to prove these things.

But it can become clear from this that there are no temporal things under Caesar which are not also under the Church; for the superior and primary right which the Church has over temporal things can in no circumstances be lost. And if any Supreme Pontiff were to give such right away, his successor could revoke this; for it could not be confirmed by a superior because the Supreme Pontiff has no superior, and his successor could revoke this because an equal has no authority over his equal. But the Church can have certain temporal possessions in which Caesar will have no right; for it will be possible for Caesar to give all the right which he has in these temporal possessions to the Church, and it will be possible for this to be confirmed by the pope, so that Caesar's successor — either

quod succedens Cesar vel succedens imperator vel succedens quicumque dominus
secularis hoc revocare non poterit, quia tunc Cesar vel quicumque dominus secularis ageret ultra suam speciem[1] si rem confirmatam per papam, qui est supremus
dominus, revocaret.

CAPITULUM ULTIMUM: *Quod in Ecclesia est tanta potestatis plenitudo quod
eius posse est sine pondere, numero et mensura.*

Illud autem quod legitur de Deo Sapiencie XI, 'Omnia in mensura et[2] numero et
pondere disposuisti,' potest ad Ecclesiam adaptari. Que verba Augustinus IV *Super Genesim ad litteram* dupliciter exponit: uno modo quidem, quod Deus omnia
disponit[3] in numero, pondere et mensura, idest omnia disposuit ut haberent suum
pondus et[4] suum numerum et suam mensuram; vel omnia disponit[5] in[6] numero,
pondere et mensura, idest omnia disponit[7] in seipso, qui est numerus sine numero,
pondus sine pondere, mensura sine mensura. Hec ergo[8] verba ad Ecclesiam, idest
ad Summum Pontificem, possumus adaptare, ut dicamus quod Summus Pontifex
totam Ecclesiam disponit in numero, pondere et mensura quia omnia que sunt in
Ecclesia disponit ut habeant suum numerum, suum pondus et suam mensuram.
Vel secundum exposicionem aliam, omnia disponit in numero, pondere et mensura[9] quia omnia disponit in seipso, qui est numerus sine numero, pondus sine
pondere et[10] mensura sine mensura, quia suum posse est sine numero, pondere et[11]
mensura. Nam[12] ceteri qui sunt in Ecclesia habent posse in numero, si considerentur illi quibus presunt, in pondere, si consideretur modus secundum quem presunt; est[13] et tercio eorum posse in mensura, si considerentur illi qui presunt.

Omne enim alii a Summo Pontifice habent posse numeratum si considerentur
illi quibus presunt, quia nulli alii prelato commisse sunt omnes oves, sed huic
commisse sunt hee oves, alii alie oves, ita quod quilibet prelatus alius a Summo
Pontifice[14] prelacionem accepit super certas et determinatas oves. Nulli ergo tali
prelato commisse sunt[15] innumerabiles oves, quia nulli commisse sunt omnes
oves. Ergo, si considerentur illi quibus alii prelati presunt, dicitur eorum posse
esse in[16] numero, vel esse numeratum, quia non acceperunt posse nisi super
certas et determinatas oves. Sed si consideretur modus secundum quem presunt,
dicitur eorum posse esse in pondere, vel esse[17] ponderatum; quia posse eorum
non excellit omne pondus. Nulli enim alio prelato committitur quod possit absolvere de omni peccato. Est ergo pondus alicuius peccati[18] quod excedit pondus
potencie eius. Ipsa enim peccata ponderant quia ad[19] inferiora trahunt, iuxta illud

1: speciem] potestatem F   2: et] *om.* FV²   3: disponit] disposuit CFV²   4: et] *om.* CFV²
5: disponit] disposuit FV²   6: in] *om.* PV¹   7: disponit] disposuit CFV²   8: ergo] eciam FV²
9: quia omnia ... mensura] *om.* F   10: et] *om.* C   11: numero, pondere et] *om.* F   12: Nam]
cum *add.* V²   13: est] *om.* F   14: Pontifice] sacerdote PV¹   15: omnes oves ... sunt] *om.* C
16: in] *om.* V²   17: esse] eciam F   18: peccati] potestati F   19: ad] in F

the emperor's successor or the successor of any secular lord — will not be able to revoke this. For if Caesar or any secular lord revoked something confirmed by the pope, who is the supreme lord, he would then be acting beyond what is proper to his kind.

FINAL CHAPTER: *That there is in the Church a fullness of power so great that her power is without limit of weight, number and measure.*

What we read of God in Wisdom 11, 'You have ordered all things in measure and number and weight,'[1] can be applied to the Church; and, in *De Genesi ad Litteram* 4, Augustine interprets these words in two ways. In one way, indeed, [he says that] God orders all things in number, weight, and measure in that He has so disposed all things that they have their own weight and their own number and their own measure. In another way, He orders all things in number, weight, and measure in that He alone, Who is number without number, weight without limit, and measure without measure, disposes all things.[2] Therefore, we can apply these words to the Church, that is, to the Supreme Pontiff; for we may say that the Supreme Pontiff orders the whole Church in number, weight, and measure in that he disposes all things within the Church in such a way that they have their own number, their own weight, and their own measure. Or, according to the other interpretation, he orders all things in number, weight and measure in that he alone, who is number without number, weight without limit, and measure without measure (because his own power is without limit of number, weight and measure), disposes all things. But the rest of those [prelates] who are in the Church have a power limited in number if it is considered in relation to those over whom they rule; in weight if it is considered in relation to the manner of their rule; and, third, if we consider [the degree of power given to] those [other prelates] who rule, their power is limited in measure.

For if we consider [the number of] those over whom they rule, all others apart from the Supreme Pontiff have a power which is countable, for to no other prelate are all the sheep entrusted. Rather, these sheep are entrusted to one, those others to another, so that every prelate apart from the Supreme Priest has received prelacy only over a certain and determinate number of sheep. To no such prelate, therefore, are innumerable sheep entrusted, for to none are all the sheep entrusted. Therefore, if we consider those over whom the other prelates rule, their power is said to be limited in number, or to be countable, because they have received power only over a certain and determinate number of sheep.[3] But if we consider the manner of their rule, their power is said to be limited in weight, or to be weighable, because their power does not exceed all weight. For to no other prelate is the power to absolve from every sin entrusted. Therefore, there is a certain weight of sin which exceeds the weight of his power. For sins themselves are heavy, because they pull downwards, according to the saying of Job: 'They take

1. Wisd. 11:21.
2. *De Genesi ad litteram* 4:3; 5 (CSEL 28(1):98; 101).
3. Cf. Pt. II, Ch. IV, p. 93.

Iob: 'Tenent psalterium et cytharam, gaudent ad sonitum organi, ducunt in bonis dies suos, et in puncto ad inferna descendunt.' Quod ergo rem[1] ponderosam potest sursum trahere, illud preponderat rei ponderose. Illud ergo posse quod potest peccatorem a peccatis absolvere[2] et ipsum ad superiora ordinare preponderat ponderi peccatorum. Quilibet ergo alius prelatus habet posse ponderatum si consideretur modus secundum quem preest, cum hoc modo presit quod non potest absolvere a quocumque peccato. Posse ergo suum non preponderat omni ponderi et per consequens non est sine pondere, sed est ponderatum.[3]

Sed si consideremus alios prelatos qui presunt, erit eorum posse in mensura sive erit[4] eorum posse[5] mensuratum, quia in nullo alio prelato a Summo Pontifice reservatur omne posse quod est in Ecclesia. Ceteri ergo[6] prelati, si considerentur ipsi qui[7] presunt, habent posse mensuratum, quia non habent omne posse quod est in Ecclesia; si consideretur modus secundum quem presunt,[8] habent[9] posse ponderatum. Presunt[10] enim administrando sacramenta Ecclesie, absolvendo alios a suis peccatis; et quia non possunt absolvere ab omni peccato, eorum posse non est sine pondere, quia non preponderat omni ponderi. Tercio, si considerentur illi quibus presunt, habent posse numeratum, quia nulli alii a Summo Pontifice commisse sunt omnes oves, sed sunt ei commisse numerate et determinate oves, et sunt ei commisse solum[11] quedam oves.

Hiis itaque prelibatis, dicamus quod Summus Pontifex omnia que sunt in Ecclesia disponit et ordinat in numero, pondere et mensura;[12] quod dupliciter potest intelligi. Primo quidem, quia omnia disponit ut[13] habeant certum numerum, certum[14] pondus et[15] certam mensuram; quia disponit et ordinat totam Ecclesiam, et omnes prelatos, in numero, pondere et mensura. Quia cuilibet prelato dat posse numeratum quantum ad oves quas sibi committit, quia non committit sibi[16] omnes oves, sed numeratas et determinatas oves; dat sibi posse ponderatum[17] quantum[18] ad modum secundum quem sibi oves committit, quia non dat sibi posse quod absolvat suas oves ab omni pondere peccatorum, sed a determinato pondere peccatorum; tercio, dat ceteris prelatis qui sunt in Ecclesia posse mensuratum quantum ad personas prelatorum quibus oves committit, quia non dat eis posse sine mensura, nec dat in eis omne posse quod est in Ecclesia, sed dat eis determinatum et mensuratum posse.[19]

Erit ergo una exposicio:[20] quod Summus Pontifex totam Ecclesiam disponit et ordinat in numere, pondere et mensura; id est, disponit et ordinat ut omnes prelati qui sunt in Ecclesia habeant certum numerum,[21;22] certum pondus et certam

1: rem] *om.* F   2: a peccatis absolvere] absolvere a peccatis F   3: sed est ponderatum] *om.* V[1]
4: erit] *om.* V[2]   5: in mensura ... posse] *om.* F   6: ergo] autem F   7: qui] quibus V[1]   8: presunt] possunt F   9: habent] hunc FV[2]   10: Presunt] possunt F   11: solum] *om.* C   12: mensura] et *add.* V[2]   13: ut] *om.* V[2]   14: certum] *om.* F   15: et] *om.* V[2]   16: sibi] *om.* CV[2]
17: ponderatum] numeratum F   18: quantum] *om.* F   19: quod est ... posse] *om.* C   20: exposicio] Christo F   21: id est, ... numerum] ut omnes prelati qui sunt in ecclesia C   22: numerum] et *add.* F

psaltery and harp, they rejoice at the sound of the organ, they spend their days in wealth; and in a moment they go down into hell.'[1] Therefore, that which can pull a heavy object upwards [as by a pulley] is heavier than the heavy object. Therefore, that power which can absolve the sinner from his sins and direct him towards higher ends outweighs the weight of the sins. Each of the other prelates, therefore, has a power limited in weight if it is considered in relation to the manner of his rule; for the manner of his rule is not such that he can absolve from every sin whatsoever. His power, therefore, does not outweigh every weight; and it follows that it is not without limit of weight, but is weighable.

But if we consider the [degree of power given to the] other prelates who rule, their power will be limited in measure, or their power will be measurable; for all the power which is in the Church is contained in no other prelate apart from the Supreme Pontiff. The rest of the prelates, therefore, if we consider [the degree of power given to] those who rule, have a measurable power, since they do not have all the power which is in the Church. And if we consider the manner of their rule, they have a weighable power; for they rule by administering the sacraments of the Church, by absolving others from their sins, and, because they cannot absolve from every sin, their power is not without limit of weight because it does not outweigh every weight. Third, if we consider [the number of] those over whom they rule, they have a countable power, because to no other [prelate] apart from the Supreme Pontiff are all the sheep entrusted. Rather, a limited and determinate number of sheep is entrusted to him, and only some sheep are entrusted to him.

Thus, having first touched upon these matters, let us say that the Supreme Pontiff disposes and orders all things which are in the Church in number, weight and measure, and that this can be understood in two ways. First, indeed, because he disposes all things in such a way that they have a certain number, a certain weight and a certain measure; for he disposes and orders the whole Church and all the prelates in number, weight, and measure. For he gives to every prelate a countable power in respect of the sheep which he entrusts to him, because he does not entrust all the sheep to him, but only a limited and determinate number of sheep. And he gives to him a weighable power in respect of the manner in which he entrusts the sheep to him, because he does not give to him a power such that he may absolve his sheep from the whole weight of sins, but only from a determinate weight of sins. Third, he gives to the rest of the prelates who are in the Church a measurable power in respect of [the degree of power vested in] the persons of the prelates to whom the sheep are entrusted. For he does not give them power without measure, nor does he give them all the power which is in the Church: rather, he gives them a determinate and measurable power.

This, therefore, will be one interpretation: that the Supreme Pontiff disposes and orders the whole Church in number, weight, and measure in that he disposes and orders matters in such a way that all the prelates who are in the Church may have a certain number, a certain weight, and a certain measure [of power]. But there is

1. Job 21:12–13.

mensuram. Alia autem modo potest intelligi quod Summus Pontifex disponit et ordinat totam Ecclesiam in numero, pondere et mensura: idest, totam Ecclesiam disponit et in seipso, qui est numerus sine numero, pondus sine pondere et mensura sine mensura. Ipse est enim[1] numerus sine numera quantum ad oves que sunt sibi commisse, quia non sunt sibi commisse hee oves vel ille oves,[2] sed sibi commisse sunt omnes oves. Dixit enim Dominus Petro 'Pasce oves meas,' non distinguens[3] inter has oves[4] vel alias[5] oves;[6] propter quod sibi commisit omnes oves. Non ergo in numero, sed sine numero, idest sine distinccione, commisse sunt sibi universaliter omnes oves.

Secundo, eciam[7] ipse Summus Pontifex est pondus sine pondere si consideretur modus secundum quem commisse sunt sibi oves. Hoc enim modo commisse sunt sibi oves, quod sic administrare possit sacramenta Ecclesie quod possit absolvere ab omni pondere peccatorum. Modus ergo suus presidendi[8] preponderat omni ponderi peccatorum. Est ergo in eo pondus sine pondere, quia si esset pondus ponderatum, non preponderaret omni ponderi. Pondus enim suum est sine pondere. In ceteris autem prelatis, quantum ad absolucionem peccatorum, est pondus ponderatum, et quantum ad culpam et quantum ad penam. Quantum ad culpam[9] quidem, quia non[10] possunt absolvere ab omni culpa; quantum ad penam vero, quia non possunt dare indulgenciam que satisfaciat pro omni pena.[11] Sed in Summo Pontifice quantum ad absolucionem peccatorum est pondus sine pondere et quantum ad culpam et[12] quantum ad penam: quantum ad culpam quidem, quia potest absolvere ab omni culpa; quantum ad penam vero, quia potest tantum communicare de thesauro passionis martyrum et aliorum sanctorum, et potissime de thesauro passionis Christi,[13] qui est thesaurus infinitus, quod potest satisfacere pro omni pena.[14] Ergo, sicut in Summo Pontifice est numerus sine numero quantum ad[15] oves que sibi sunt commisse, sic est in eo pondus sine pondere quantum ad modum secundum quem sibi sunt commisse:[16] idest, quantum ad administracionem sacramentorum seu quantum ad absolucionem peccatorum. Quia hoc modo sunt sibi commisse oves, quod administrando sacramenta absolvat[17] a peccatis; a quibus absolvendo et quantum ad culpam et quantum ad penam est in eo pondus sine pondere, quia est in eo tantum de posse quod preponderat omni ponderi sive sit pondus culpe sive sit[18] pondus pene.[19]

Tercio, Summus Pontifex est mensura sine mensura si consideretur persona eius, cui oves sunt commisse. Quia in persona ipsius habet[20] posse sine mensura et[21] est in eo posse in quo est omne posse quod est in Ecclesia; quia super[22] illo verbo Iohannis tercio, 'Non enim ad mensuram dat Deus spiritum,' dicit Chrysostomus

---

1: est enim] enim est FV[1]   2: oves] *om.* C   3: distinguens] distinguit FV[2]   4: oves] *om.* FV[2]
5: alias] illas FV[2]   6: non distinguens ... oves] *om.* C   7: eciam] *om.* V[1]   8: presidendi] possidendi FV[2]   9: et quantum ... culpam] *om.* FV[2]   10: non] *om.* V[2]   11: pena] culpa FV[2]
12: et] ad *add.* V[2]   13: Christi] *om.* V[2]   14: pena] culpa FV[2]   15: ad] *om.* V[2]   16: sic est ... commisse] *om.* V[1]   17: absolvat] abluat FV[2]   18: sit] *om.* V[2]   19: pondus pene] pene pondus V[2]
20: habet] esse *add.* CF *add. and del.* P   21: et] quia CFV[2]   22: super] sub F

another way in which the statement that the Supreme Pontiff disposes and orders the whole Church in number, weight, and measure can be understood: that is, [by taking it to mean] that he alone, who is number without number, weight without limit, and measure without measure, disposes and orders the whole Church. For he himself is number without number in respect of the sheep which are entrusted to him. For to him have been entrusted not these sheep or those sheep: rather, all the sheep have been entrusted to him. For the Lord said to Peter, 'Feed my sheep,'[1] not distinguishing between these sheep or other sheep; and so He entrusted all the sheep to him. All sheep, therefore, have been entrusted to him universally: not by number, but without number, that is, without distinction.

Second, the Supreme Pontiff himself is also weight without limit if we consider the manner in which those sheep have been entrusted to him. For the sheep have been entrusted to him in such a manner that he may so administer the sacraments as to be able to absolve from the whole weight of sins. Therefore, the manner of his rule outweighs the whole weight of sins. There is in him a weight without limit, therefore, since, if it were a weighable weight, it would not outweigh every weight. For his weight is without limit; but, in the other prelates, there is a weighable weight in respect of the absolution of sins and with regard to both fault and penance. With regard to fault indeed, because they cannot absolve from every fault; and with regard to penance because they cannot grant an indulgence which gives satisfaction for every penance. In the Supreme Pontiff, however, there is weight without limit in respect of the absolution of sins and with regard to both fault and penance. With regard to fault indeed, because he can absolve from every fault; and with regard to penance because he is so able to draw upon the treasury of the passion of the martyrs and other saints, and especially upon the treasury of Christ's Passion, which is an infinite treasury, that he can give satisfaction for every penance. Therefore, just as, in the Supreme Pontiff, there is number without number in respect of the sheep which have been entrusted to him, so there is in him weight without limit in respect of the manner in which they have been entrusted: that is, with regard to the administration of the sacraments or the absolution of sins. For the sheep have been entrusted to him in such a manner that he may absolve them from [every] sin through the administration of the sacraments; and, by virtue of this power of absolution, there is in him a weight without limit with regard to both fault and penance, for there is in him a power so great that it outweighs all weight, be it a weight of fault or a weight of penance.

Third, the Supreme Pontiff is measure without measure if we consider [the degree of power vested in] his person, to which the sheep have been entrusted. For in his person he has power without measure, and in him there is a power within which is contained all the power of the Church. For upon these words of John 3, 'For God does not give the Spirit by measure,'[2] Chrysostom says that

1. John 21:15–17.
2. John 3:34.

quod 'spiritum' hic acciones spiritus nominat.[1] Vult enim ostendere quod omnes quidem[2] nos acciones[3] spiritus suscipimus in mensuram, Christus autem omnem spiritus suscepit accionem. Christus ergo, quia habet omnem accionem spiritus, non ad mensuram accepit spiritum; nos autem, quia[4] non habemus omnem[5] accionem spiritualem, ad mensuram accepimus spiritum. Sic et in proposito. Quia nullus alius habet omne posse quod est in Ecclesia,[6] quilibet alius a Summo Pontifice accepit posse ecclesiasticum ad mensuram.[7] Summus autem Pontifex, quia habet omne posse quod est in Ecclesia, dicitur accepisse omne[8] posse ecclesiasticum non ad mensuram.

Finem ergo loquendi omnes pariter audiamus: Ecclesiam time et mandata eius observa, hoc est[9] enim omnis homo, idest ad hoc ordinatur omnis homo. Ecclesia quidem est timenda et mandata eius sunt observanda; sive[10] Summus[11] Pontifex, qui tenet apicem Ecclesie et qui potest dici Ecclesia, est timendus et sua mandata sunt observanda, quia potestas eius est spiritualis, celestis et divina, et est sine pondere, numero et mensura.

Et hec de potestate ecclesiastica sive de[12] potestate Summi Pontificis dicta sufficiant. Laus sit inde altissimo, qui est benedictus in secula seculorum. Amen.

Explicit liber de ecclesiastica sive de Summi Pontificis potestate.[13;14]

1: spiritus nominat] nominat spiritus C   2: quidem] *del.* C   3: quidem nos acciones] *om.* V[2]
4: quia] qui FV[2]   5: omnem] *om.* V[2]   6: Ecclesia] ecclesiam V[2]   7: mensuram] mensuratam C
8: omne] *om.* CFV[2]   9: est] *om.* F   10: sive] *del.* C   11: Summus] ergo C   12: de] *om.* F
13: potestate] et continet iii partes *marg.* (*in a later hand*) P   14: potestate] Est liber scriptus per
David Galensem deo gracias *add.* (*at foot of final column*) P

'Spirit' here denotes the gifts of the Spirit.[1] For he [i.e. St. John] wishes to show that we all receive the gifts of the Spirit by measure, whereas Christ has received all the gifts of the Spirit. Christ, therefore, because He has all the gifts of the Spirit, has not received the Spirit by measure; but we have received the Spirit by measure because we do not have all the gifts of the Spirit. So also in our proposition. Because no one else has all the power which is in the Church, each apart from the Supreme Pontiff receives ecclesiastical power by measure. But the Supreme Pontiff, because he has all the power which is in the Church, is said to have received the whole of ecclesiastical power without measure.

Let us all attend equally, therefore, to the purpose of this discourse. Fear the Church and keep her commandments, for this is the duty of every man: that is, every man is appointed to this task.[2] The Church is indeed worthy to be feared, and her commandments are worthy to be kept. Again, the Supreme Pontiff, who holds the summit of the Church and who can be called [the embodiment of] the Church, is worthy to be feared, and his commandments are worthy to be kept. For his power is spiritual, heavenly, and divine, and it is without limit of weight, number and measure.

And these remarks concerning ecclesiastical power and the power of the Supreme Pontiff may suffice. Praise be to the Most High, then, Who is blessed for ever and ever. Amen.

Here ends this book concerning ecclesiastical power or the power of the Supreme Pontiff.

1.   *Apud* Aquinas, *Catena aurea* 12:301.
2.   Cf. Eccles. 12:13.

Select Bibliography

(a) Primary Sources

Much of the controversial literature relating to the period 1296–1303 is now available in modern editions and translations. The following may be mentioned.

(i) *Papalist Writings.*

Henry of Cremona, *De potestate papae*, ed. R. Scholz, *Die Publizistik zur Zeit Philipps des Schönen und Bonifaz VIII* (Stuttgart: Enke, 1903), pp. 459–471.

James of Viterbo, *De regimine Christiano*, ed. G.-L. Perugi, *Il De regimine christiano di Giacomo Capocci, Viterbese* (Rome, 1914). This is a printing of one late manuscript only, and not a critical edition; there is a critical edition by H.-X. Arquillière: *Le plus ancien traité de l'Église: Jacques de Viterbe, De regimine christiano* (Paris: G. Beauchesne, 1926). Professor Arquillière's text has many deficiencies, but the Introduction is of value. There is an English translation by R.W. Dyson, *James of Viterbo on Christian Government* (Woodbridge, Suffolk and Dover, New Hampshire: Boydell, 1995).

Anonymous, *Non ponant laici* (possibly by Henry of Cremona), ed. R. Scholz, *Die Publizistik*, pp. 471–486; *Glossa in Unam sanctam*, ed. H. Finke, *Aus den Tagen Bonifaz VIII* (Münster: Aschendorffschen Buchhandlung, 1902), Appendix.

(ii) *Royalist Writings.*

John of Paris, *Tractatus de potestate regia et papali*, ed. J. Leclercq, *Jean de Paris et l'ecclesiologie di xiii ᵉ siècle* (Paris: Vrin, 1942), Appendix; also by F. Bleienstein as *Über königliche und päpstliche Gewalt ... Textkritische Edition mit deutscher Übersetzung* (Stuttgart: E. Klett, 1969). This work has been translated into English twice (both times with the same title, *On Royal and Papal Power*): by J.A. Watt (Toronto: Pontifical Institute of Mediaeval Studies, 1971) and A.P. Monahan (London and New York: Columbia University Press, 1974).

Anonymous, *Antequam essent clerici*, ed. and trans. R.W. Dyson, in *Three Royalist Tracts, 1296–1302* (Bristol: Thoemmes, 1999), pp. 2–11; *Disputatio inter Clericum et Militem*, ed. and trans. N.E. Erickson, 'A Dispute between a Priest and a Knight,' *Proceedings of the American Philosophical Society* 111, 5 (1967), pp. 288–309; also by R.W. Dyson, *Three Royalist Tracts*, pp. 12–45; *Quaestio in utramque partem*, ed. G. Vinay, 'Egidio Romano e la cosidetta "Questio in utramque partem",' *Bulletino dell' Istituto Storico Italiano per il*

medio evo e Archivo Muratoriano 53 (1939), pp. 43–146; also ed. and trans. R.W. Dyson, *Three Royalist Tracts*, pp. 46–111; *Rex Pacificus*, ed. and trans. R.W. Dyson, *Quaestio de Potestate Papae (Rex Pacificus)* (Lewiston, Queenston, Lampeter: Mellen, 1999).

Material not recently edited can be consulted in the older collections, unsatisfactory in varying degrees, upon which historians have for many years relied: P. Dupuy, *Histoire du différend d'entre le pape Boniface VIII et Philippe le Bel Roy de France* (Paris, 1655); A. Baillet, *Histoire des démeslez du Pape Boniface VIII avec Philippe le Bel Roy de France* (Paris, 1718); M. Goldast, *Monarchia S. Romani Imperii* (2 vols, Hanover and Frankfurt, 1611–1614); S. Schard, *De Jurisdictione, Auctoritate, et Praeeminentia Imperiali, ac Potestate Ecclesiastica* (Basle, 1566).

See also:

Les Registres de Boniface VIII, eds. G.A.L. Digard, M. Faucon and A. Thomas (Paris: Bibliothèque des Ecoles Françaises, 1884–1939).

C. H. Hefele and H. Leclerq, *Histoire des Conciles* VI (Paris: Letouzey et Ané, 1914), pp. 408–410 (Letter of the French clergy to Boniface VIII, 10 April 1302); pp. 415–417 (Reply of the cardinals to the nobles of France, June 1302); pp. 417–418 (Letter of Boniface VIII to the French bishops, June 1302); pp. 418–422 (Speech of Cardinal Matthew of Aquasparta and Boniface VIII's injunctions to the French clergy, August 1302).

(b) Secondary Sources

Black, A., *Political Thought in Europe, 1250–1450* (Cambridge: Cambridge University Press, 1992).

Boase, T.S.R., *Boniface VIII* (London: Constable, 1933).

Briggs, C.F., *Giles of Rome's 'De regimine principum': Reading and Writing Politics at Court and University* (Cambridge: Cambridge University Press, 1999).

Burns, J.H. (ed.), *The Cambridge History of Medieval Political Thought* (Cambridge: Cambridge University Press, 1988).

Canning, J., *A History of Medieval Political Thought, 300–1450* (London: Routledge, 1996).

Carlyle, R.W. and A.J., *A History of Medieval Political Theory in the West* (6 vols, Edinburgh and London: Blackwood, 1903–1936).

Del Punta, F., Donati, S. and Luna, C., 'Egidio Romano,' in *Dizionario Biografico degli Italiani*, 42 (Rome: Treccani 1993), pp. 319–341.

Digard, G.A.L., *Philippe le Bel et le Saint Siège de 1285 à 1304* (Paris: Sirey, 1936).

Dyson, R.W., *Normative Theories of Society and Government in Five Medieval Thinkers* (Lewiston, Queenston, Lampeter: Mellen, 2003).

Finke, H., *Aus den Tagen Bonifaz VIII.*

Ladner, G., 'The Concepts of *Ecclesia* and *Christianitas* and their Relation to the Idea of Papal *Plenitudo Potestatis* from Gregory VII to Boniface VIII', *Miscellanea Historicae Pontificiae* 18 (1954), pp. 49–78.

Lagarde, G. de, *La Naissance de l'esprit laïque au declin du moyen age* (Paris: Béatrice Nauwelaerts, 1956–1970), vol 1: *Bilan du XIIIe siècle*.

Lewis, E., *Medieval Political Ideas* (2 vols, London: Routledge, 1954).

Lot, F. and Fawtier, R., *Histoire des institutions françaises au moyen age* (3 vols, Paris : Presses Universitaires de France, 1957-62), vol. 3: *Institutions ecclesiastiques.*

Luscombe, D.E., 'The *Lex divinitatis* in the Bull *Unam Sanctam* of Pope Boniface VIII', in *Church and State in the Middle Ages* (edd. C. N. L. Brooke, D. E. Luscombe, G. H. Martin, and Dorothy Owen) (Cambridge: Cambridge University Press, 1976), pp. 205-221.

McIlwain, C.H., *The Growth of Political Thought in the West* (New York: Macmillan, 1932).

McCready, W.D., 'Papal *Plenitudo Potestatis* and the Source of Temporal Authority in Later Medieval Papal Hierocratic Theory,' *Speculum* 48 (1973), pp. 654–674.

Mundy, J.H., *Europe in the High Middle Ages*, 1150–1309 (London: Longman, 1973).

Packard, S.R., *Europe and the Church under Innocent* III (New York: Russell & Russell, 1968).

Pegues, F.J., *The Lawyers of the Last Capetians* (Princeton, NJ: Princeton University Press, 1962).

Pennington, K., *Popes and Bishops: A Study of the Papal Monarchy in the Twelfth and Thirteenth Centuries* (Pennsylvania: Pennsylvania University Press, 1984).

Picot, G., *Documents relatifs aux États Généraux et assemblées réunis sous Philippe le Bel* (Paris, 1901).

Post, G., 'Two Notes on Nationalism in the Middle Ages,' *Traditio* 9 (1953), pp. 281–320.

Rivière, J., *Le Problème de l'église et de l'état au temps de Philippe le Bel* (Paris: Champion, 1926).

Scholz, R., *Die Publizistik zur Zeit Philipps des Schönen und Bonifaz VIII.*

Strayer, J.R., 'Defence of the Realm and Royal Power in France,' in *Studi in onore di Gino Luzzato* (Milan: Giuffré, 1949).

Strayer, J.R., 'Consent to Taxation under Philip the Fair,' in. J.R. Strayer and C.H. Taylor, *Studies in Early French Taxation* (Westport, Conn.: Greenwood Press, 1972).

Strayer, J.R., *The Reign of Philip the Fair* (Princeton, NJ: Prineton University Press, 1980).

Tierney, B., *The Crisis of Church and State, 1050–1300* (Englewood Cliffs, NJ: Prentice-Hall, 1980).

Ullmann, W., *Medieval Papalism: The Political Theories of the Medieval Canonists* (London: Methuen, 1949).

Ullmann, W., *Principles of Government and Politics in the Middle Ages* (London: Methuen, 1961).

Ullmann, W., *A History of Political Thought in the Middle Ages* (Harmondsworth: Pelican, 1965).

Ullmann, W., *The Growth of Papal Government in the Middle Ages* (London: Methuen, 1970).

Ullmann, W., 'Die Bulle Unam Sanctam: Rückblick und Ausblick,' *Römische Historische Mitteilungen* 16 (1974), pp. 45–58.

Ullmann, W., 'Boniface VIII and his Contemporary Scholarship,' *Journal of Theological Studies* 27 (1976), pp. 58–87.

Watt, J.A., *The Theory of Papal Monarchy in the Thirteenth Century* (London: Burns & Oates, 1965).

Wilks, M.J., *The Problem of Sovereignty in the Later Middle Ages* (Cambridge: Cambridge University Press, 1963).

Wood, C.T., *Philip the Fair and Boniface VIII* (New York: Krieger, 1967).

Index

(All references to the text are to the pages of the English translation)